Over Seas

U. S. Army Maritime Operations
1898 Through the Fall of the Philippines

by Charles Dana Gibson with E. Kay Gibson

The front dust jacket illustrations portray the House Flag of the Quartermaster's Army Transport Service as well as the campaign medals issued for the operations within which the ATS was a participant -- 1898 - 1942. Appendix T contains a description of each medal.

The transport pictured on the back of the dust jacket is the *USAT Meade* which was under Army ownership from July 1898 to June 1917.

Ensign Press; Camden, Maine 04843

Published by Ensign Press; PO Box 638; Camden, ME 04843

Library of Congress Catalog Control Number: 2002102125

ISBN: 0-9608996-6-9

OVER SEAS: U.S. Army Maritime Operations -- 1898 Through the Fall of the Philippines
Gibson, Charles Dana 1928 -
1. Army Transport Service - Merchant Marine - United States. 2. U.S. Wars 1898 - 1942 - Maritime Operations - American and Philippines. 3. Troop Transports. 4. Military logistics.

Printed in the United States of America on acid-free paper that meets the American National Standards Institute Z 39-48 Standard.
Additionally, the paper on which this book is printed meets and exceeds all NASTA specifications.

First edition.

Printed in the United States of America

Dedicated

To Those
-- Both Military and Civilian --
-- American and Filipino --
Who Served In the Defense of the Philippines
December 8, 1941 - June 3, 1942*

*On June 3, the garrison on the Negros Islands under the command of Col. Roger B. Hilsman was the last formal United States force in the Philippines to be surrendered to the Japanese.

Other books by Charles Dana Gibson relative to U. S. Army maritime operations:

The Ordeal of Convoy NY 119 [†]

Marine Transportation in War: The U.S. Army Experience 1775-1860 (out of print)

Assault and Logistics: Union Army Coastal and River Operations, 1861 - 1866. [‡]

Dictionary of Transports and Combatant Vessels, Steam and Sail, Employed by the Union Army, 1861 - 1868. [‡]

Ensign Press
PO Box 638
Camden, ME 04843

www.ensignpress.com

[†] Cited by the U.S. Naval Institute as a "Notable Naval Book", 1973

[‡] *Assault and Logistics* and *The Dictionary* together received the 1995 John Lyman Book Award presented by the North American Society for Oceanic History

TABLE OF CONTENTS

Appendices

Ship Lists and Related Tables

Ship Lists and Related Tables, contd.

Part II

Appendix Section

Maps, Chartlets

We gratefully acknowledge the sources of several of the above listed maps:

Atlas de Filipinas first published in the Philippines, 1899; reproduced in 1900 by the U.S. Coast and Geodetic Service.

Louis Morton's *Fall of the Philippines,* U.S. Army Center of Military History, 1953.

British Admiralty, Naval Intelligence Division, Geographical Handbook Series, *Pacific Islands,* Vol IV, "Western Pacific"

Photographs

Photo sections begin on the following pages: 58, 108, 171, 202, 280, 384

AUTHORS' FOREWORD

Our selection of the period 1898 through to mid 1942 was not an arbitrary decision on our part upon which we have based the chronological scope of this book. Rather, we chose it as being representative of an era in the history of the United States during which the nation reached out beyond its geographic boundaries in an adventure into colonialism. In order to defend and maintain its holdings in both the Caribbean and the Western Pacific, the U.S. Army, under the supervisory control of the Quartermaster General, founded in late 1898 an in-house shipping agency known as the Army Transport Service (ATS) which operated continuously through more than forty years of peace and war. The loss of the Philippines to the Japanese in May of 1942 effectively ended the United States experiment with colonialism in the far western Pacific.[†] It also marked the termination of the Quartermaster's role with ocean shipping and the end of the Army Transport Service as it had been operated from its inception.

It was our initial intent to present this work with primary focus on the ships and the men who manned them. We soon realized, however, that such a narrow approach could not properly relate the impact that the Quartermaster's fleet had on both the military and maritime history of the period covered. What you are about to

---

[†] The United States continued its administration of Puerto Rico; and following its recapture from the Japanese, Guam as well. When the Philippine Islands were retaken from the Japanese in 1945, their indigenous governmental structure was in total disarray. By 1946, the situation had become stabilized, and the islands were granted independence.

read, therefore, is the history of the Army's use of shipping as woven into the broader spectrum of the military, social, economic, and political frameworks within which it functioned.

The termination of the Army Transport Service as a command description did not mark the end of the U.S. Army's direct operation of ships. Far from it. Only the organizational structure and management methods changed. Under the Quartermaster, the ATS had been run much in the manner of a commercial steamship line. When the ships and the civilian crews of the Army Transport Service went under the control of the Service of Supply in early 1942, military exigency became the paramount management concern. With the establishment of the Army Service Forces which replaced the Service of Supply later in March 1943, even the term "Army Transport Service" would be abolished.[‡]

A subject yet to be examined is the operational history of the men and ships which, starting in early 1942, served the Service of Supply and beginning in 1943 the Army Service Forces of which the Transportation Corps was part. Under the Transportation Corps, Water Division, the Army's owned and bareboat chartered fleet increased by gargantuan proportion over what it had been. Given fate's good will, we hope to document that expansion within the near future.

CDG - EKG

[‡] Although not germane to the chronological period covered by this history, we have, nevertheless, incorporated within our Introduction to Part II a brief description of the organizational changes involving the War Department's utilization of ships and small craft following early 1942. The reader is also referred to our Appendix Q which describes the various Army commands which employed ships and small craft during World War II.

ACKNOWLEDGMENTS

In conducting the research for this book, which goes back over fifteen years, we have many people to thank for their considerable and varied assistance. We list them alphabetically.

Frank Braynard, that most prolific of steamboat historians, boxed and sent to us from his collection a considerable amount of helpful material dealing with the shipping business of the 1920s and 1930s. This in turn led us to pertinent congressional investigations of the 1920s and 1930s. Dr. Robert M. Browning, Jr., Senior Historian, U.S. Coast Guard, assisted in untangling the sovereignty of Philippine-registered shipping pre-1946. This is evident in more than one place in this book. We also thank Bob for his painstaking reading of the manuscript. The law firms of Cadwalader, Wickersham, and Taft of New York City and Harmon, Jones, and Sanford of Camden allowed us access to their fine law libraries. A hearty thank you to the library staff at the Camden Public Library, particularly Elizabeth Moran and Dottie Morales, for their interlibrary loan assists. Bernard "Cal" Cavalcante of the Center for Naval History provided us with many vessel status cards which chronicled Army transport and merchant ship movements during World War II. (The Vessel Status Cards have since been transferred to Modern Military Records, National Archives.) John T. "Jack" Crowell, now deceased, was an Air Force major during World War II, assigned as station commander and ship's pilot for the Crystal II project. His verbal remembrances offered to us in 1985 were essential to our understanding of those events. Archie D. Fonte, Air Force Historical Research Agency, Maxwell Air Force Base, alerted us to the Edmonds Collection as well as material dealing with the Crystal Projects. Mrs. Jeannette Ford provided us with valuable ship charter information. Captain Regino "Dodds" Giagonia, prominent maritime and naval historian of the Philippines, pointed out to us the existence of the Philippine Commonwealth Army's Offshore Patrol. Over the years, Alvin H. Grobmeier has shared our interest in Army shipping and provided helpful leads for ship identifications.

Ken Gross for his skill in designing the book's striking and meaningful dust jacket. David Grover, pictorial chronicler of Army shipping, whose fine photograph collection lends this book a special flavor.   Pat Hall kindly provided copies of the *Manila Tribune Shipping Calendar* which helped immeasurably in giving insight into the shipping situation in Manila during December of 1941.   Mary Jane Harvey, Records Custodian at the Maritime Administration, (now retired) who never failed us in requests for War Shipping Administration records. We also thank Donald Post, her successor.   John H. Higgins of Maine Coast Digital Imaging photographically enhanced some of the archival documents contained within the Philippine Archive Collection which otherwise would have been impossible to decipher.   Leslie D. Jensen, former Curator at the U.S. Army Transportation Center, made us aware of many obscure records.   James Johnston alerted us to *The Harmon Memorial Lectures in Military History, 1959 - 1987* which helped us untangle the confusing command arrangement that existed in the Southwest Pacific during 1941-42.   Rear Adm. Thomas A. King, a friend of long standing, master mariner, and former Superintendent of the United States Merchant Marine Academy, read and critiqued our manuscript from the perspective of a seasoned master mariner.   Don Koster, Army historian, led us to many of the Quartermaster Reports which we might otherwise have overlooked. Dr. Harold D. Langley, Curator of Naval History, Emeritus, Smithsonian Institution, took time from his academic commitments to read and critique our manuscript, and his many suggestions have been incorported into the book.   Capt. John M. Le Cato and Marvin Rosenberg, participants in the Crystal Projects, corresponded, relating their personal memories of the endeavor to construct air bases in the Canadian subarctic. Sid Loeb, now deceased, Marine Specialist with the U.S. Army's St. Louis Records Center, gave us much assistance in sorting out Mine Planter Service vessels. Without the untiring contribution of Sid's assistant, Bobbie Sprague Pettys who operated Sid's busy copy machine, the volumes of material Sid located for us would never have reached our research library.   John E. Lundberg, Col. John Robenson's clerk on the 1942 mission to Java, gave us a first hand, *I was there* overview of that mission. This was an invaluable insight into circumstances as they then existed.   Dr. Edward J. Marolda, Senior Historian, Naval Historical Center, took time from his busy schedule to read our manuscript and offer editorial and historical critique.   Frank McGrane, former Curator at the Army Transportation Museum, and now Museum Specialist with the Center for Military History, provided reams of material which he gleaned from Lord only knows where and which we have utilized throughout.   Mary E. McLeod of the Department of State gave us leads on the status under International Law of military transports at the beginning of the twentieth century. She also uncovered for us material regarding the 1912 evacuation of U.S. citizens from Mexico.   Al Millican of the Insurance Section of the Maritime Administration aided us by locating War Risk claims dealing with Army transport personnel.   Captain Arthur R. Moore's knowledge of the *Taiyuan* and the crewmen from the *Collingsworth* enabled him to give us valuable leads into the episodic events concerning those two vessels.   Michael P. Musick of the Navy and Old Army Branch, Military Archives Division, provided helpful research advice. The staff at the Heritage Art Center in Quezon City, Philippines, was extremely helpful in providing several authoritative books on the Philippines 1941-47 which were not available elsewhere. A special thank you to the three young ladies who served us over many years in their capacity as research assistants: Constance Potter and Suzanne Taylor at the National Archives and Sarah Kinsley at Carlisle Barracks. Dr. Jay M. Price, Department of History, Wichita State University, put us in touch with archival researcher William T. Bowers who is well acquainted with the Philippine Archive Collection. From the PAC, Bowers procured those files which we needed for our understanding of that segment of the Philippine merchant marine which served the ATS, 1941-42. John Slonaker of the Military History Institute at Carlisle Barracks went out of his way in guiding us through his library's stacks during our visit to MHI in 1994. Bertrum G. Snow assisted in identifying former trawlers which served the Army Transport Service in the Canadian subarctic during 1942-43. Ann Marie Wells, librarian at the Tampa Campus Library, University of South Tampa, located materials within the Library's stacks describing activities at Port Tampa during the sealift of 1898. Patricia Thomas of the Maritime Administration assisted in a number of ways over the many years this book has been in the making. Mrs. Umbrell of the Military History Institute initially acquainted us with what that fine institution has to offer the historian. Robert L. Underbrink loaned to us what may have been the only copy then extant of the Robenson manuscript. William Joe Webb of the Center for Military History shared valuable material as well as our interest in Army sealift, and he must have often wondered if this book would ever see the light of day. The late Captain Stephen "Coley" Williams, our good friend and Maine neighbor, read and critiqued Part I of the manuscript literally within a few days of his death in 1999. Caroline Wright, Librarian at the Army Transportation Museum, Ft. Eustis, was a great provider of Transportation Corps monographs.

If someone has been overlooked -- and we are sure that will be the case considering the number of years spanned by this project -- we profusely apologize for the oversight and sincerely thank them for their support and assistance.

PART I

1898 THROUGH 1939

INTRODUCTION

After the Civil War ended, the United States Army Quartermaster Department began the dispersal of the Army's fleet which consisted both of those vessels which it owned and those which were still being employed under charter. By late 1866, the Department had divested itself of nearly all of its ownership of the vessels located upon the coasts -- the exception being a few harbor craft and a handful of cargo schooners which it continued to operate within the Gulf of Mexico.* On the western rivers, the Army's waterborne needs became dependent upon commercial steamboat operators, the Quartermaster Department having retained only a few ferryboats and personnel launches which served local garrisons.

During the first decade which followed the Civil War, the Army's primary mission was that of conducting operations against hostile Indian tribes and the supervision of those tribes which were considered *tamed* -- the general interpretation of a tamed Indian being those who resided within the reservation system operated by the Department of the Interior's Bureau of Indian Affairs. During the first half of that decade, the Army maintained a total of thirty garrisons scattered upon the Great Plains and the eastern slope of the Rocky Mountains.[1] Seven of those garrisons depended totally for their resupply on steamers ascending the Missouri River. Field operations against hostile elements on the northern Great Plains were supported in large part by chartered steamers which moved up the Missouri as far upstream as the junction with the Yellowstone River, sometimes even ascending that river when conditions permitted. These field operations were mostly offensive in nature although some were in protective support of civilian exploration -- both governmental and for the private

---

*   For an accounting of the Union Army's role in shipping during the Civil War, see Charles Dana Gibson with E. Kay Gibson, *Assault and Logistics, Union Army Coastal and River Operations, 1861-1866*, (Camden, ME: Ensign Press, 1995) as well as Gibson and Gibson, *Dictionary of Transports and Combatant Vessels, Steam and Sail, 1861 - 1868*, (Ensign Press, 1996).

[1]   Robert M. Utley, *Frontier Regulars, United States Army and the Indians, 1866-1891*, (New York: MacMillan Publishing Co., 1973), p 96.

business sector. An example of the latter was a military escort for a survey party exploring a route for the northern track of the Union Pacific Railroad. During that mission, supply steamers moved up the Yellowstone River as far as the mouth of Glendive Creek.

In June of 1876, following the disaster suffered by George Armstrong Custer's 7th Cavalry at the Battle of the Little Big Horn, the wounded from the surviving companies were evacuated on the steamer *Far West*, its captain having taken his boat up the Big Horn River to the mouth of the Little Big Horn River. This broke the record for the farthest steamboat ascension of the upper Missouri system. To get that far upstream, the *Far West* was dragged through rapids by troops hauling on cables.[2] *Far West's* captain, Grant Marsh, then broke a second record, this one for speed on his run down the Missouri to Fort Lincoln where, upon arrival, the news of Custer's defeat was telegraphed east to an incredulous War Department. Custer's defeat became the catalyst for an all-out effort against the northern tribes which concluded with their permanent confinement to reservations. Steamboats continued to serve the Army's needs in various ways, one typical utilization taking place in 1881 when the Army chartered a number of transports to carry 3,000 Sioux to an assigned reservation.[3]

By the 1890s, the Indian Wars were nearly over, and field expeditions had been largely curtailed. Consequently, the need for hiring vessels within the western territories noticeably decreased. The Quartermaster Department's overall vessel inventory remained relatively static through most of the 1890s. By 1897, the inventory enumerated only one small inter-harbor passenger vessel which was stationed at New York and four tugs. Two of the tugs were stationed at New York and one each at Boston and at San Francisco. There were a handful of small launches still in service, but most of them were of well-worn vintage.

~

With only a few isolated exceptions, those Army posts on the southern Great Plains depended for their logistical support on railroads as well as on horse or mule power. The only steamboats employed directly in support of the post garrisons on the southern Great Plains were those supplying three small forts, one on the Red River and one on the Arkansas River. Supplies and reinforcements for the majority of the Texas garrisons were transported from the eastern seaboard by sail and steamboat to Gulf of Mexico ports from which they were transshipped by wagon to their final destination.

The primary supply of the Arizona and New Mexico departments was handled by steamships routed either from San Francisco or from San Diego. These steamers coasted south along the Southern California Peninsula and then north into the Gulf of California until reaching the mouth of the Colorado River. During the earlier Civil War years, goods going by this route had been unloaded at the mouth of the

---

[2]   James A. Huston, *The Sinews of War: Army Logistics, 1775-1953*, (Washington, DC: Office of the Chief of Military History, 1966), p 266. Other steamers chartered for the campaign against the Sioux in 1876 were the *Peninah, Key West,* and *Josephine.*

[3]   Utley, p 288.

Colorado and then reshipped on small river steamers upriver to Fort Yuma, about 140 miles from the Gulf of California. From there, if river conditions allowed, some further movement continued as far as Fort Mojave which lay almost 300 miles above Fort Yuma. When the Civil War was in progress, a merchant named George A. Johnson had a monopoly of all Colorado River transport; however, his company failed to keep up with the expansion of civilian trade that began during the last year of the war, an expansion which quickly accelerated at the end of hostilities. The result of Johnson's failure to grow with the need was that large amounts of freight were soon left piled up both at the mouth of the Colorado as well as at a freight depot maintained by Johnson near Fort Yuma. Sensing a market for a more efficient and timely traffic, a second company began operations. This competition led to a reduction in rates -- all to the Army's benefit. After the war ended, the Army was paying (during 1867) the rather reasonable sum of $20 per ton for freight transported from the mouth of the Colorado upstream to Fort Yuma, and $37.50 a ton from Fort Yuma to Fort Mojave. The quartermaster who handled these transactions must have been a skilled negotiator since those rates were about one-half less than those normally charged to civilian customers. A third steamship enterprise, the Colorado Steam Navigation Company, was formed for the Colorado trade during 1869. By the following year, this company employed four steamers together with six barges and was the only firm remaining which ran a freight service on the Colorado. In 1871, a west coast ocean shipping company began a scheduled one-ship service from San Francisco to the mouth of the Colorado River. For that voyage, the Army was charged $14 per freight ton. In 1874, that company purchased a second steamer and reduced its shipping rates to $12.50 per ton. In addition to freight, the steamers carried passengers. The rate for officers was $75 one-way and for enlisted men traveling as deck passengers, $40. Through most of the year, the trip from San Francisco was made in insufferable heat once the steamers rounded Cabo San Lucas and started up the Gulf of California. According to one suffering passenger, the cabin rate of $75 was a waste to the Army since most of the officers and their wives ended up sleeping on deck as the cabins proved far too hot.[4]

~

A new responsibility came about for the Army after the United States purchased Alaska from the Russians in 1867. During the following year, the Army established its first military post within the new territory. The sole means of personnel transportation and supply for that post was water transport. Navigation in Alaskan waters proved to be a dangerous enterprise as except for some vague and often misleading charts of Russian origin, little was known of the Alaskan coastline, and that absence of knowledge would lead to many marine casualties. Charting of the Alaskan routes by the United States Coast Survey had begun as early as 1867, even before the actual transfer of Alaska from the Russians, but it would take another eighty years before the entire coastline and its hazards were properly mapped.[5]

---

[4] Darlis A. Miller, *Soldiers and Settlers, Military Supply in the Southwest, 1861-1885*, (Albuquerque, NM: University of New Mexico Press, 1989), pp 293-5.

[5] Ted C. Hinckley, *The Americanization of Alaska, 1867-1897*, (Palo Alto, CA: Pacific Books, 1972), p 33. As late as the Second World War, ships would strike uncharted ledges and pinnacles, one such grounding -- a fatal one -- involving an Army transport supporting the Aleutian Campaign of 1942-43.

By 1877, the Army had withdrawn its garrisons from the Alaskan territory. Any United States military presence remaining after that time was provided by visiting naval vessels and small detachments of United States Marines which were intermittently stationed at Sitka and Juneau. The Army again resumed responsibility in September of 1897 when troops were posted at St. Michael and at several other inland points along the Yukon River.[6] These posts were supplied with enough foodstuffs to last the winter until ice was out in late spring. Troop commitment was never heavy, returns for the Army's fiscal year 1899-1900 showing only two infantry companies plus a small separate detachment and one battery of field artillery as having been stationed within the entire Alaskan territory. There was, however, a sizable civilian contingent consisting of both War Department and Department of the Interior personnel for whom the Quartermaster provided transportation and other support.

An interesting sidelight to the Army's involvement in Alaska, and an episode which required multiple modes of transportation, centered around the relief of civilians working surface gold mines within the Yukon Valley. The year was 1897 during which the miners had been reported to be near starvation, prompting Congress to enact an emergency appropriation of $200,000 for their relief. Of this amount, $142,665 was delegated to the War Department for the purchase of reindeer which were to be shipped from Lapland to a Norwegian port and thence across the Atlantic by steamer. The reindeer were to be landed at New York and then sent across the country by train to Seattle. From Seattle, they were to go by sea to Dyea, Alaska, from where they were to be trailed overland to Dawson City and into the Yukon country. Leaving Trondheim, Norway, under the supervision of Army Lt. D. B. Devore went 539 reindeer along with 250 tons of moss which was the reindeer's principle food in their native environment. The reindeer shipment proceeded without a hitch until the consignment reached Seattle at which point the moss ran out, necessitating the feeding of hay which proved a disaster to the animals' digestive systems. Those reindeer which survived the diet change -- and these were few -- were turned over to the Interior Department. Ironically, the endeavor was for naught as the *desperate needs* of the Yukon miners proved to be widely exaggerated.[7]

~

During 1897, war clouds began gathering in the Caribbean. The focus was the island of Cuba, a remnant portion of what had once been the mighty empire which Spain had maintained within the Western Hemisphere. Historically, American interests in Cuba went back as far as the eighteenth century. By the early nineteenth century, there were extensive American land holdings in Cuba, most of them comprising sugar plantations. As early as 1810, there had been talk in the United States of a possible takeover of Cuba by America's armed forces. Although this thinking had been promoted mainly by the sugar interests, there were other advocates for takeover, including some within the United States Army officer corps. In 1816, Lt. Col. Thomas Sidney Jesup, who years later would become the Army's

---

[6] Annual Reports of the War Department for the Fiscal Year Ended June 30, 1898, *Report of the Secretary of War, Miscellaneous Reports,* (Washington: GPO, 1898), pp 10, 11.

[7] *Report of Introduction of Domestic Reindeer into Alaska,* 55th Congress, Senate, 3rd Session, Document No. 34, 1898, pp 32-47.

Quartermaster General, proposed a joint Army- Navy operation to invade the island.[8] Later, during President Polk's administration, Polk tried to buy Cuba, but Spain rejected the plan.

The American plantations had prospered at first, but by the 1880s, civil unrest began breaking out. Once that happened, the situation of American entrepreneurs became less secure. By 1897, it appeared that the Spanish hold over the island was becoming increasingly precarious which gave encouragement to certain American private interests eager to align themselves with the Cuban insurrectionists through providing them with arms and even some advisory military talent.

Within United States official circles, especially in the Navy, war with Spain began to look not only like a certainty but to some, even a necessity. The campaigns conducted by the Spanish army against insurgent bands in Cuba had badly debilitated the Spanish garrisons, so much so that a military vacuum had begun to develop -- a state of affairs which could be attractive to any ambitious European power wishing to establish a presence in the Caribbean by filling that void. The injection of another European influence, especially in the northern Caribbean, would have been highly detrimental to United States interests, both economically as well as in terms of national security. It was suspected by the McKinley Administration, but not known with certainty, that Germany had a desire to establish a naval foothold somewhere in the Caribbean. On allegedly *excellent authority,* it was reported that the German Kaiser Wilhelm had suggested to his foreign minister that Germany should stand with Spain against what the Kaiser perceived as a conspiracy by, *the 'American-British Society' for international theft at warmongering, to seriously have the intention of snatching Cuba from Spain.*[9] The German foreign minister pledged to the Kaiser his cooperation toward developing plans along such lines but suggested caution against taking too strong a position since the United States had become a viable market for German exports. What seems to have diverted the Kaiser during early 1897 from any direct interference on the side of Spain over Cuba was an unforeseen situation which had developed in China. Germany had long wanted to establish itself in the western Pacific, and the provocation to do so was offered that year through the murder by the Chinese of two German missionaries. This incident gave the Kaiser the excuse he thought he needed. He ordered his Asiatic Squadron to Kaichow Bay, China, there to land and seize the entire province of East Shantung. By that action, Germany gained a naval coaling station on the coast of China. Because of that coaling facility, Germany had the potential ability to exercise a strong influence in the western Pacific.[10]

The Chinese episode was only a temporary diversion to Kaiser Wilhelm's ambitions in the Western Hemisphere, and the Caribbean issue was rekindled -- this time over an incident in Haiti during November of 1897. This involved reported insults made to German citizens by the Haitians at Port-au-Prince. In response, two German warships (which at the time were conveniently visiting Jamaica)

---

[8]   Chester L. Kieffer, *Maligned General, Biography of Thomas S. Jesup,* (San Rafael, CA: Presidio Press, 1979), pp 55-58.

[9]   G. J. A. O'Toole, *The Spanish War, An American Epic, 1898,* (New York and London: W. W. Norton Co., 1984), p 104.

[10]   It was the threat of that German influence in the Pacific which would later play a part in United States policy leading to an annexation of the Philippines.

were ordered to Port-au-Prince. News of this, when received at the White House, caused President William McKinley to order the *USS Marblehead* to Port-au-Prince. Meanwhile, the *USS Maine* was ordered to Key West, her commander to stand by awaiting further instructions. On that same day, a transatlantic cable brought the news that the German cruiser *Geir* had left Kiel, rumored as outbound for the Caribbean. Other reports originating from Havana reached Washington alleging that two German warships were scheduled to make courtesy visits to Havana during January (1898). This last news moved McKinley to request of the Spanish authorities that the *USS Maine* be received on a visit to Havana during that same time frame. McKinley's rationale was that by showing the American flag in a Cuban port, intervention by Germany might be discouraged. The Spanish voiced no objection over the visit of the *USS Maine* which was then scheduled for February.

~

As early as 1894, a few United States naval officers had begun to formulate war plans involving Spain. The first of these plans was prepared by Lt. Cdr. Charles J. Train, then a student at the Naval War College. Train had run a hypothetical study which in part forecast what four years later would take place. He theorized that at the outbreak of war, the majority of the Spanish Navy would be in Spanish ports and that once reacting to a United States threat against Cuba, the fleet would be faced with a transatlantic voyage at the end of which the Spanish ships would be seriously depleted of coal with no guarantee of any coaling opportunity. This situation would limit Spanish options, therefore giving an American fleet a considerable tactical advantage. Later studies made at the Naval War College dealt with the type of land warfare which might have to take place in order to secure Cuba from Spain. The prediction was that a quarter of a million American troops could be required on Cuban soil. Determining that such a commitment would be militarily, if not politically, prohibitive, the Navy's studies largely discounted a land war -- at least one to be fought by American troops. They favored instead a naval action probably to take place off the Cuban coast. Any campaigns that might be required against the Spanish garrisons were to be left up to the native insurgents. During 1897, Train, who by then was on the teaching staff at the Naval War College, proposed three naval campaigns to be carried on simultaneously against the Spanish: the first was to defeat any local Spanish fleet in Cuban waters; the second was to harass the Spanish coast itself, thus tying down Spain's naval resources which otherwise could be sent transatlantic from Europe; the third was to capture and hold Manila Bay in the Philippine Islands. By the end of 1897, the Navy had completed a fairly fixed plan which included all of Train's ideas except that of naval action against the Spanish in European waters. In the event of war, the Navy was to effect a blockade of Cuba and Puerto Rico; in the Far East, the United States Pacific Fleet was to capture Manila. All of this was to be accomplished before the Spanish had time to bring their maximum power into play at either location.[11]

One factor not fully considered, and therefore a major flaw in the planners' thinking, concerned the Philippines. If the United States was to influence the political scene in the Philippines in favor of any future United States interest in Asia, it

---

[11]   O'Toole, pp 97, 98.

would be necessary to establish an American troop presence, at the very least on the capital island of Luzon. A similar presence would also be needed -- at least for a time and for the same reasons -- at Cuba and at Puerto Rico. Train's plans, even when refined, had not addressed the problems of a land campaign, and the Army had not performed even a superficial study of what might be entailed if an American force invaded Cuban soil. Reacting to congressional and presidential fears of Spanish naval attacks against United States ports, the Army's pre-1898 planning, such as it was, centered itself with United States coastal defenses and little else.

~

In February 1898, the battleship *USS Maine* arrived at Havana where the Spanish authorities received her with the normal diplomatic courtesies. There were no outward signs of any anti-American hostility. On 15 February, the *USS Maine* exploded while at anchor, sinking in place and taking many of her crew down with her. The initial belief was that a mine, deliberately set by the Spaniards, was the cause. The Spanish denied this and launched their own investigation into the explosion, an investigation which concluded that the explosion had been internal in origin.[12] Although an internal explosion was also suspected by some American naval engineers, such an explanation would not have been even considered by the American public, or by the American press, or, for that matter, by the United States Congress. Almost universally, a war fever had taken hold of the entire country.

On April 19, the United States Congress, by means of a joint resolution, authorized armed intervention against Spanish forces in Cuba, declaring further that it was in the interest of the United States that Cuba should be free and independent of foreign rule and that Spain must withdraw from the island. The following week, President McKinley ordered a naval blockade of Cuba. In retaliation, Spain cut off diplomatic relations with the United States. On April 25, the Congress formally declared war against Spain. This swift chain of events propelled the United States toward an emergency mobilization. Two days before the formal declaration of war, the President called for 125,000 volunteers for a national army. The day war was declared, he followed this by a call for another 75,000 men, and Congress voted an increase in the Regular Army to 35,000 officers and men, authorizing the formation of sixteen full regiments to represent the infantry, the cavalry, and the engineering arms.[13] It was to be the Quartermaster Department's responsibility to provide the rail transport to move these forces to their initial assembly points, then to their training camps, and then on to ports from which the troops would leave for the enemy's shores. At the ports, ships which were to be arranged for by the Quartermaster Department were to be waiting to carry out overseas deployments. The Congress and the press had called for a fast reaction time, and the War Department was doing all it could to meet that need.

~

Except for a fading remnant of Civil War veterans still on active duty, hardly anyone in the Army's officer corps was personally experienced in the techniques involved in the movement of men and materiel by sea. When the War With Spain

---

[12]   The Spanish were right. Many years later, studies conducted by the U.S. Navy also concluded the explosion to be internal, probably caused by combustion of coal gases within the battleship's own bunkers.
[13]   *Report of the Secretary of War, Miscellaneous Reports,* 1898, p 144.

began, the Quartermaster Department would face a demand which few if any Army officers had even vaguely envisioned. Nevertheless, it would be only five weeks from the time of the initial mobilization order until the Army would send the first echelon of an expeditionary force to the Philippines and only six weeks before a fleet of chartered transports was on its way to invade the island of Cuba.

As James A. Huston describes it in his study, *Sinews of War, Army Logistics, 1775-1953,* the war of 1898 would develop into a miracle of logistics, both in the sense of transportation and in the production of war materiel -- an undertaking which could only have been supported by a nation which in terms of industrial capability had reached world leadership in many of the manufacturing capabilities necessary for a nation to engage in modern warfare.[14] Of equal importance, was that the war came at a time when communications were far improved over what they had been during the Civil War.

Within the War Department itself, there were certain organizational changes which would prove advantageous, particularly within the Quartermaster Department. In that department, a sub-departmental structure had been developed which had its foundations in the trial-and-error experience of the Civil War. By 1898, an organization had been structured which established eight assistants who were placed in charge of the following divisions.

Division	Category
First	Fiscal Affairs
Second	Water and Rail Transportation
Third	Clothing and General Equipage
Fourth	Wagon Transportation, inclusive of animals and forage
Fifth	Construction
Sixth	Physical Support Facilities, for posts and encampments
Seventh	Personnel
Eighth	Operation of National Cemeteries

It was the Second Division which was to procure the vessels which would carry the first American Army to embark for foreign soils since the War with Mexico back in 1846. Despite some rather serious blunders early on, the 1898 sealift would be a significant accomplishment considering the short time frame allowed for the gathering of the ships. A great deal of the credit for that success goes to Brig. Gen. Marshall I. Ludington who was appointed to the post of Quartermaster General on February 3, 1898. With the outbreak of war pending, Ludington's administrative talents would mold Regular Army officers together with volunteer officers who in the main were selected from civilian life on the basis of their expertise in their respective fields of transportation and supply.

---

[14]   Huston, pp 273-275.

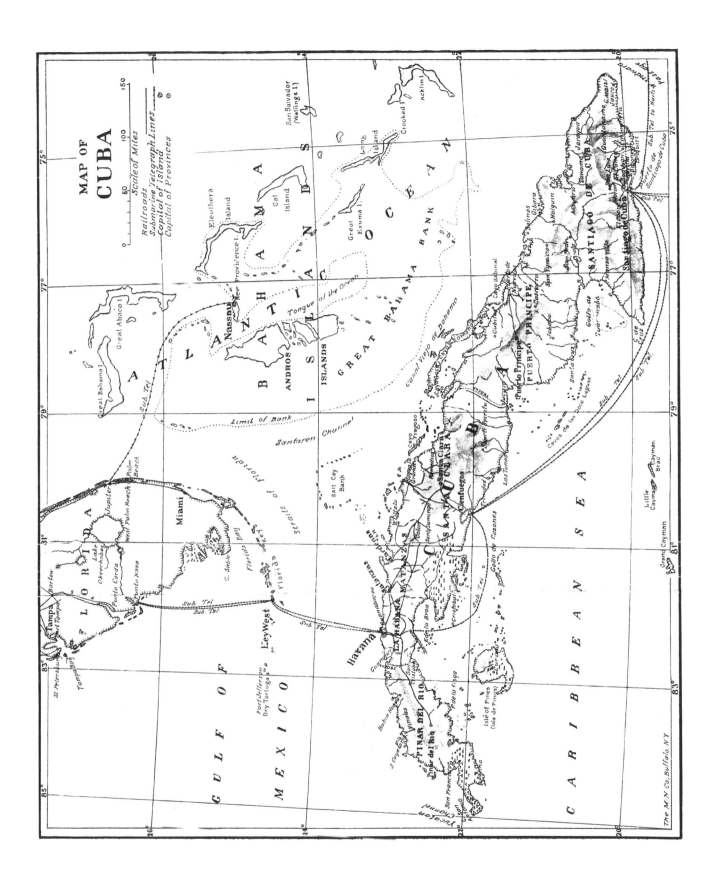

CHAPTER I

THE WAR WITH SPAIN - 1898

Faced with the certainty of United States attacks on Spanish holdings, both in the Atlantic and in the Pacific, the United States began gearing up for those assaults. Operations in the Pacific would first center on establishing an American domination at Manila, a city located on the island of Luzon. The initial phase of that operation was a responsibility which would have to rest with the Navy, specifically with Commodore George Dewey who at the outbreak of the war had his Asiatic Squadron at Mirs Bay on the Chinese coast. What little Dewey knew of the Spanish force that would face him once he arrived at Manila Bay had been derived from the most rudimentary of intelligence: Dewey's Aide-de-camp, Ens. F. B. Upham, who, while posing as a civilian with an alleged interest in maritime trade, had been interviewing merchant ship masters upon their arrival at Chinese ports from the Philippines. The second source was a businessman whose affairs took him on a fairly regular basis to Manila and to other ports within the archipelago. The information derived from the businessman's trips was that at most there were about forty Spanish warships of various types in the Philippines, the majority of them at Manila. These ships were of limited firepower, consisting in large part of gunboats being utilized by the Spanish for interisland patrol work. It appeared that Dewey's only significant opposition would come from half a dozen cruisers, all antiquated, one even being of wooden construction. All told, when compared against the American fleet's one hundred guns of heavy caliber, Spanish strength in ships and armament seemed of negligible concern. The ship masters who had been interviewed by Ensign Upham told of what they believed were mine fields laid in the seaward approaches to Manila Bay. The masters based their beliefs on the fact that their ships had been piloted into the port on a zigzag course. Such an indirect approach made no sense unless its purpose was to avoid mines. Dewey looked upon the mine field stories as a Spanish bluff since, considering the technology of the day, the deep water within Manila Bay and its approaches would have precluded the practicality of mooring mines.[1] Dewey was also of the opinion that even the most state-of-the-art mines would not remain effective for long after being laid in such highly saline tropical waters. More of a worry to him were the Spanish shore batteries about which there was no hard intelligence available.

On April 27, the Asiatic Squadron left the China coast bound for Manila Bay. On arrival there, the American fleet quickly overcame Spanish naval resistance, resulting in the surrender of the entire Spanish fleet. The mine field had proved to be non-existent, just as Dewey had predicted, and the shore batteries a far lesser threat than they might have been. Dewey's victorious squadron commanded the city of Manila and its environs from seaward while a large force of native revolutionaries ringed the city on its land sides. The Asiatic Squadron had not been accompanied by a troop contingent other than a small Marine force attached to its ships. Entering the city of Manila itself would have to wait for the arrival of the Army's troops then being assembled for shipment from the west coast of the United States. Meanwhile, the Marines were landed to take possession of the Spanish naval base at Cavite.

Atlantic Theater: Cuban and Puerto Rican Expeditions

Things in the Atlantic theater were nowhere near as straightforward as the events being experienced in the Pacific. Spring was known to be the beginning of the fever season in Cuba, and the War Department had little enthusiasm for subjecting a large body of troops to what might become a pestilence ridden campaign. A further restraint which would become part of the American rationale cautioning delay was the anticipated arrival of the Spanish home fleet in Caribbean waters. Despite all of this, the McKinley Administration felt that something must be done quickly in order to give encouragement to the Cuban rebels who were then actively engaging the army of the Spanish occupation. In advance of sending any major American expeditionary force to the island, around six thousand troops -- mostly regulars -- were to sail for Cuba under the command of Maj. Gen. William R. Shafter. The original place planned for a landing was near Cape Tunas, about midway on the island's southern coast. Cape Tunas had been picked since it seemed the most advantageous landing spot from which the invaders could move inland to make contact with the main rebel army fighting in the central highlands. The northern coast, albeit much closer in distance from United States ports, had been rejected since that coast, at least at the better landing sites, was thought to be well defended. Sections of the northern coast reported as undefended were rimmed by barrier reefs with only shallow entry passes into the inner lagoons making the approach by transports of even medium draft far too hazardous an undertaking. Having decided on Cape Tunas, the War Department requested convoy protection, but the Navy Department demurred, pleading its case that all available warships should be dedicated toward striking at the Spanish fleet once it arrived from

---

[1]   O'Toole, p 176. Also, *Chart of Philippine Islands Between St. Bernardino Straits and Mindoro Straits with Adjacent Islands,* from Spanish Surveys of 1873 (Washington: Department of the Navy, Bureau of Equipment.)

Spain. When that would happen was very much of a question. Sending six thousand troops to sea without naval protection, particularly in light of the uncertainty as to where and when the Spanish fleet would appear, was considered too great a risk. For the time being, the Cape Tunas expedition would be put on hold.[2]

On March 24, the Quartermaster General, Marshall I. Ludington, ordered a canvas of all shipping companies on the United States east and west coasts in order to determine the availability of ships suitable for use as troop transports. The Quartermaster officers on the east coast who were charged with gathering this information were to discover that some weeks earlier the Navy had placed options for ship procurement with four of the largest steamboat companies. By the decade of the 1890's, few American steam ships remained employed in the transatlantic trade. The American merchant marine operating on the Atlantic had its primary focus on United States coastal and near-foreign trade (Caribbean and trans-Gulf of Mexico). Few steamers in those trades had the size which would lend them to conversion as troop ships for voyages exceeding more than two or three days in duration. From the Navy Department's viewpoint, it was only the larger ships, that is those capable of transatlantic service, which were suitable for conversion into commerce raiders.[3] Those ships placed under option by the Navy were the only U.S.-flagged ships on the east coast considered adequate for use as Army troop transports. It was a *catch 22,* leaving the Army to make good with what was left over after the Navy had taken its pick.

Col. Charles Bird, as commander of the Quartermaster Department's Water and Rail Transportation Division, became the officer directly involved with the chartering of transports on the east coast. A Civil War veteran, he had entered the Regular Army following that war and had served continuously ever since. During his post-war testimony to the Dodge Commission, Bird would indicate his complete lack of cognizance insofar as the Quartermaster Department's past experience in transporting men and materiel by sea.

> *In anticipation of the movement of troops on the oceans -- the Army had never done anything of this kind; we had never transported troops by sea; it was something new to the Army of the United States -- I took the precaution to send an officer -- we had two officers in New York whose duty it was; one whose whole duty it was and another to assist him -- to go to every steamship company and get the*

---

[2] Operating independently of naval protection, the Army, throughout April, May, and into early June 1898, launched a series of one-ship landings along the Cuban coast which had as their purpose the resupply of rebel units. Commercial ships employed for these resupply missions, all of which departed from Port Tampa on Florida's west coast were: *Gussie,* which sailed on May 9 and again on May 27; *Florida,* which sailed on May 18, returning to Tampa on June 2 at which time she collided with the transport *Miami,* putting her temporarily out of service. Following repairs, *Florida* again sailed on June 18. Only one of these missions met with Spanish opposition forcing that mission to be aborted. Graham A. Cosmas, *An Army for Empire...The United States Army in the Spanish-American War,* (Columbia, MO: University of Missouri Press, 1971), pp 103, 104.

[3] *Report of the Commission* [Dodge Commission] *Appointed by the President to Investigate the Conduct of the War Department in the War with Spain,* Vol. I, (Washington: U.S. Senate, 56th Congress, Document 221), p 468.

name of every ship and get the tonnage and everything about that ship and we had that long before we were called upon for a ship. [4]

Colonel Bird had served sixteen years in the Quartermaster Department, and it is surprising that he had not gained some inkling of the Army's past involvement with sealifts. [5] In at least three instances, Civil War troop lifts by sea had involved the numbers of men and materiel closely corresponding to that with which Bird was tasked in 1898. [6]

~

The lack of suitable vessels for long distance voyages made it necessary for the Army to select a port of embarkation that was reasonably close to the Cuban coast. The parameter of limited choice narrowed the selection to a port on the Florida peninsula, preferably one southward of Cape Canaveral. In 1898, with but one exception, none of the east coast Florida ports south of Jacksonville had adequate entrance depths -- that exception being Key West; but that place in the year 1898 had no land connection and therefore no access by rail. This left only Tampa Bay on Florida's central west coast which had adequate depth together with the necessary rail access. [7] There was no deep-water channel to the town of Tampa, its port facility being located to the west of the town on what was then called the Inner Bay Peninsula. (This location is adjacent to the present day MacDill Air Force Base.) That facility, which had been christened Port Tampa by its developers, was reached by ship from the Gulf of Mexico through a channel which had been dredged in 1891. That channel started at Tampa Bay's entrance off Egmont Key and routed eastward up the bay before cutting its way north through a shallow shoal area until it reached the Inner Bay Peninsula's western shoreline. There a feature which was termed a *canal* projected about 1000 feet out into the bay. This was Port Tampa. It had been created by the utilization of dredge material from digging the last 1000 feet of the entry channel. Here, the dredge

---

[4]   Testimony of Col. Charles Bird, December 2, 1898 within *The Dodge Commission Report* Vol. VI, p 2612: When asked for the names of the officers who were directly involved in inventorying the ships, Bird replied, *Colonel Kimball and Major Summerhayes.*

[5]   During the Civil War, Charles Bird had served as an infantry officer, rising to the rank of colonel, U.S. Volunteers. His service was in the eastern theater of operations. Following that war, he was commissioned in the Regular Army, seeing service as an infantry officer, rising to the rank of major. In 1882, he transferred to the Quartermaster Department with which his army service continued up to 1898, the year during which he was promoted to colonel of quartermaster volunteers. He retired in 1902 as a brigadier general, Regular Army. Source: Francis B. Heitman, *Historical Register and Dictionary of the United States Army,* Vol. I, (Washington: Government Printing Office, 1903), p 219.

[6]   See Gibson with Gibson, *Assault and Logistics,* for detailed accounts of troop lifts and shipping employed by the Union Army in the Civil War. The initial expedition which left Tampa in mid-June for Cuba was not governed by regulations for the conduct of troops aboard transports -- this omission being later bemoaned by those involved because of lack of experience or the time to prepare such regulations. Apparently no one had knowledge of the fact that during the Civil War very detailed regulatory procedures had been drawn: *Changes and Laws Affecting Army Regulations and Articles of War to June 25, 1863* (as affecting troops on transports) Article XXXVII; also contents of General Order 276, August 8, 1863. Both are reproduced within Appendix H of *Assault and Logistics.* The War Department would issue a 40-page document titled *Regulations for the Army Transport Service,* dated November 6, 1898.

[7]   A port of sorts (Port Boca Grande) was located on Gasparilla Island in Charlotte Harbor, south of Tampa Bay, but it had no rail access. Rail track from the mainland to Port Boca Grande was not laid until 1907. Charles Dana Gibson, *Boca Grande, A Series of Historical Essays,* (St. Petersburg, FL: Great Outdoors Publishing Co., 1982), p 141.

materials were deposited as parallel spoil banks on each side of the channel. The spoil banks had been connected to the shoreline and bulkheaded on each side, a refinement which had produced the footing for a 1,000' dock face for shipping to come alongside for loading. On the south side of the bulkheaded spoil bank a rail spur had been laid; however, a limiting feature of that arrangement was that the tracks were 50 feet back from the dock face. This meant that cargoes to be loaded or offloaded from docked ships had to be man-handled across the intervening distance upon the backs of stevedores. Up to 1898, only limited use had been made of the Port Tampa facility; however, the troubles over Cuba changed that immediately, bringing about a surge of utilization starting with the landing of survivors from the sunken *USS Maine* who came in on the steamer *Olivette* during late March of 1898. This was soon followed by Americans fleeing from Cuba -- nine hundred of whom arrived on the steamer *Masotte* in April.

The environs surrounding Port Tampa then consisted of a barren flat area of sand overgrown with scattered palmetto scrub. It was a virtual desert. Nine miles to the east of the port at the town of Tampa, there were signs of a growing population; but as a place, the town boasted little in the way of refinements. As the troops began arriving to await their departure to Cuba, they were bivouacked in areas surrounding the town and on the barrens out near Port Tampa. With the troops came a host of newspaper reporters who viewed their surroundings with considerable negativism. When describing the budding *city of Tampa,* one reporter called it *a huddled collection of generally insignificant buildings standing in a desert of sand...* Richard Harding Davis, a reporter for *Scribner's Magazine,* discovered an oasis in this desert, namely, the Tampa Bay Hotel, upon which he and the Army's high brass had descended, seeking refreshment and lodgings. Davis wrote,

> *In the midst of this desolation is the hotel. It is larger than the palace where Ismail Pasha built overnight at Cairo...and so enormous that the walk from the rotunda to the dining room helps one to an appetite.*

Others said the hotel was like a Turkish harem with the occupants left out. One unnamed cavalry general (probably Maj. Gen. Joseph Wheeler) would be quoted as proclaiming, *Only God knows why Plant* [Morton F. Plant, the hotel's developer] *built a hotel here, but thank God he did![8]* The barren flats near the port where most of the arriving regiments ended up being encamped had almost nothing -- no hotel, no business section -- unless one could count a strip of shacks hastily put up to service the more sporting elements among the incoming troops. Nicknamed by parties unknown as *'Last Chance Village,'* it consisted of bordellos and gin mills together with an assortment of shoddy shopping stalls. An occurrence which took place either at the port or at the outskirts of the town of Tampa was written up in the *Tampa Morning Tribune* on June 23. The *Tribune* reporter wrote that a group of Theodore Roosevelt's *Rough Riders* (officially named the 1st U.S. Volunteer Cavalry) became embroiled in an altercation while visiting *Alice May's Whorehouse.* The

---

[8]   Gary R. Mormino, "Tampa's Splendid Little War: A Photo Essay," *Tampa Bay History*, Vol. IV, 2 which cites George Kennan, *Campaigning in Cuba,* (New York: Kennekat, 1899), pp 2-3; and Richard Harding Davis, "The Rocking Chair of the War", *Scribner's Magazine,* (IV, August 1898), p 132.

disagreement resulted in Alice May being shot in the leg as well as having several of her bones broken.

With considerable disorganization and more than an occasional disorder, the American invasion force continued to assemble to await their part in the storming of Spain's Caribbean holdings.

~

The Army's chartering of merchant ships had been handled from the onset by the Quartermaster Department's Second Division (Water and Rail Transportation). None of the chartering transactions were conducted through shipping agents. Despite Bird's testimony later made before the Dodge Commission, some staff members within the Quartermaster Department must have learned a lesson from the Civil War. Unlike the war of 1861-65 when scandals over shipping hire were commonplace, nothing of that sort developed concerning the 1898 sealift. Quartermaster leasing of shipping in 1898 was transacted upon time charter formats under which the owners provided officers and crew plus all operating expenses for the vessels, inclusive of victualing for their civilian crews. (The troops were to carry aboard their own rations.) The Quartermaster officer given responsibility for assembling the ships to be employed for the expedition was Maj. John W. Summerhayes. Summerhayes had begun his Army career in 1861 with a break of only two years service up to 1898. Assigned as an assistant to Summerhayes was a civilian shipwright named Henry T. Kirkham. According to testimony, which would later be made to the Dodge Commission, the procedure before accepting a ship on charter was to first inspect it for general seaworthiness, a task which Summerhayes assigned to Kirkham.[9] Kirkham's inspections included ascertaining a vessel's voyage endurance based on its coal capacity and consumption as taken from information provided by each of the ship's chief engineers. Since none of the ships which were gathered together for embarkation at Port Tampa had sufficient cabin spaces to carry the required number of troops, the cargo holds were measured for the accommodation of bunks in clusters of twelve, stacked 3-high, with a space of two feet on the sides and ends of each 12-bunk cluster. Hypothetically, this would allow adequate air circulation, an assumption which later proved to be incorrect. Commissioned officers were to be accommodated whenever possible in the vessel's regular passenger cabins. The labor for installation of troop bunks, together with any extra through-deck ventilators thought necessary by Kirkham, was performed on a catch-as catch-can basis by those workers who could be collected at a vessel's point of hire. Some of this work was even accomplished while the vessels were in transit to Tampa. Cooking facilities for troop use for the first contingent of transports which would sail for Cuba were almost entirely absent. There was to be an agreed loan of the ships' galleys, but that privilege was only for boiling coffee, and so as not to interfere with the crews' messing schedules, this was restricted to the nighttime hours. The inability to serve hot food to the troops was not at first considered a hardship, as the original thinking for the invasion of Cuba had been developed along the lines of a beachhead somewhere along that island's northern coast. Such a north coast landing site would have meant that the voyage from Port Tampa

---

9   Testimony of Col. John W. Summerhayes within *The Dodge Commission Report,* Vol. VI, pp 2410-2433.

would not exceed much over thirty-six hours. When the invasion plans were later changed to Cuba's southeastern coast, this meant a much longer voyage. As it was to turn out, the stay aboard the transports would be lengthened by yet another six days when false reports of the possible presence of the Spanish fleet along the northern Cuban coast delayed departure from Tampa. By the time Shafter received orders from Washington that he was to delay his expedition's sailing, many of the transports were already loaded. For those packed aboard the ships, conditions quickly became intolerable. The temperature was oppressive as was the humidity, and the woolen clothing with which most of the men were outfitted brought on conditions that were pure torture. (Tropical uniforms were not as yet in sufficient supply to equip most of the regiments.) A water shortage soon developed on some of the transports. This, together with the lack of adequate ventilation in the troop compartments, aggravated an already miserable situation.[10] On many of the ships, the heat forced most of the men topside where they filled every available inch of deck space, some even sleeping precariously on the overhead awnings.

The quartermasters would gain experience from the problems encountered aboard those first transports, and improvements would be made for subsequent troop shipments. First and foremost, the sleeping arrangements would be altered. The slatted boards with which bunks had been originally constructed, had proven to be platforms of virtual agony and were removed. Vertical studs were installed with hooks for hanging hammocks. This arrangement allowed for much better spacing between the sleeping men and less buildup of heat from the packed-in bodies. Distilling machines would also be installed to alleviate shortages of water, and basic troop cooking facilities would be set up. Among the most welcome of the improvements was forced ventilation utilizing electric blowers, but this amenity was generally restricted to the larger transports as many of the ships chartered were too small to allow proper-sized ventilation ducts.

~

At Port Tampa, the actual loading of troops became the task of a civilian, James M. McKay. McKay had been a shipmaster of long standing with the Plant Steamship Company of Tampa, and there was no better man for the job. Not only had he spent eight years as a shipmaster in the Florida- Cuba trade, but for a great deal of that time, he had personally taken his ships in and out of the Port Tampa facility. (McKay would accompany the expedition to Cuba assisting with advice on landing beaches gained from his familiarity of the Cuban coast.) An account of how the troop loading at Tampa was accomplished comes down to us through McKay's own testimony before the post-war Dodge Commission. (McKay was supported by testimony given by his superior, Lt. Col. Charles F. Humphrey.) Contrary to accounts quoting others which appeared at the time in newspapers, neither McKay nor Humphrey spoke of disorders instigated by troop commanders anxious to be certain

---

[10]   The amount of water provided per man on the first echelon of transports leaving Port Tampa was established at one gallon per day minimum on the basis of a 10-day voyage. As it was to turn out, the time spent by some units aboard the transports was thirteen days, inclusive of a 6-day layover at Tampa, a 6-day sea voyage, plus a day waiting off the beach to go ashore at Daiquiri. On some ships, this ration was larger -- that is when space for extra water storage was available. Testimony of Col. John W. Summerhayes within *The Dodge Commission Report,* Vol. VI, p 2412.

that their units would not be left behind. According to both men, the loading went surprisingly well.[11]

During the 1898 mobilization and deployments, the coordination of troop movements, as ordered by the Commanding General of the Army Nelson A. Miles, was conducted through the office of the Adjutant General, headed by Brig. Gen. Henry C. Corbin. Through Corbin, orders were issued to the troop commanders in the field, stipulating times and places for troop assembly. Upon Corbin's memoranda, the Quartermaster's Division of Water and Rail Transportation performed the necessary scheduling for rail and shipping. When Miles later took a field command (invasion of Puerto Rico), Corbin became a sort of de facto chief of staff to Secretary of War Russell A. Alger and subsequently to President McKinley when McKinley took over the general management of the war from Alger.[12]

For the initial troop lift from Port Tampa, thirty-six steamers were assigned for the deployment to the Cuban coast. Six of those were designated for the transport of animals (pack mules and artillery draft horses) in addition to troops. The identification of each transport which left Tampa for Cuba, its owner, and the troop units each carried comes to us from the exhibit which James M. McKay submitted at the time of his testimony before the Dodge Commission.[13] The names of the masters of each ship are derived from the report of the expedition's quartermaster, Lt. Colonel Humphrey. A compilation of that information is given in the following table:

---

[11]   *The Dodge Commission Report,* Vol. 5, pp 2655-2677. In his own testimony on p 2258 of *The Report ...,* Lt. Col. Theodore Roosevelt of the *Rough Riders* refuted McKay's description of the orderly process in the loading. Lt. Col. Charles F. Humphrey (later Brigadier General), in his *Report of The Expedition to Santiago de Cuba,* War Department, October 1898, would state (p 17), *Captain* [James M.] *McKay formed such an important factor in the successful landings of the expedition in Cuba that it does not now seem possible to have overcome many of the numerous difficulties of the situation without him.* Humphrey's report is on file at Military History Institute, Carlisle Barracks.

[12]   In 1905, Congress voted the establishment of the General Staff Corps which replaced the prior functions of the Commanding General of the Army. The responsibility for designation of troop units to be transported was placed with the General Staff in cooperation with the relevant troop commanders in the field.

[13]   *The Dodge Commission Report,* Vol. VI, pp 2678, 2679.

First Expeditionary Force (Maj. General Shafter) -- Tampa Bay to Daiquiri, Cuba - June 1898
Troop Units Carried on Board Each Transports

Vessel name/ Designating No.	Master		Officers	Men	No. small boats
Alamo: 6	Hix	Headquarters band, Cos. C, D, E, and G, 10th U.S. Infantry: Cos. C and E, Engineer Battalion; headquarters, 2nd Brigade; Col. E. P. Pearson, 10th Infantry	33	574	4
Allegheny: 17	Nickerson	Headquarters, Cavalry division, Maj. Gen. Joseph Wheeler; Lt. Col. J. H. Dorst, adjutant general	14	80	3
Aransas: 27	Hopner	Regiment, 3d U.S. Infantry	2	13	5
Berkshire: 9	Dizer	Light artillery battalion: Light Battery A, 2d U.S. Artillery; Light Battery F, 2d U.S. Artillery	14	268	3
Breakwater: 29	Rivero	Regiment, 3d U.S. Infantry	20	467	5
Cherokee: 4	Garvin	Regiment, 12th U.S. Infantry; headquarters and three companies, 17th U.S. Infantry	35	852	6
City of Washington: 16	Stevens	One battalion, 21st U.S. Infantry; regiment, 24th U.S. Infantry	33	751	4
Clinton: 32	Wurtz	Cos. D and B, 2d U.S. Infantry	2	169	4
Comal: 7	Evans	Co. I, 7th U.S. Infantry, and Light Batteries E and K, 1st U.S. Artillery	10	284	4
Concho: 14	Risk	Regiment, 4th U.S. Infantry; regiment, 25th U.S. Infantry; headquarters 2d Brigade	53	1,034	5
Cumberland: 31	Minot	Steam lighter	--	---	
D. H. Miller: 19	Peters	Cos. E, G, and H, 7th U.S. Infantry	8	280	5
Florida: 15	Minor	Horse transport (collision at Tampa; sailed later)	--	---	
Gussie: 3	Burney	Mule transport	--	---	
Iroquois: 25	Kemble	Headquarters, Cos. A, B, C, D, and F, 7th U.S. Infantry; Cos. C, G, H, and K, 17th U.S. Infantry; headquarters, 2d Division, Brig. Gen. H. W. Lawton; Capt. H. C. Carbaugh, adjutant general; headquarters, 3d Brigade, Brig. Gen. A. R. Chaffee; 1st Lt. F. L. Winn, assistant adjutant general	38	722	8
Kanawha: 34	Evans	Water boat	--	---	
Knickerbocker: 13	Butts	Headquarters and two companies, 2d Massachusetts Volunteers	32	588	3
Laura: 33	Spaulding	Steam lighter	--	---	
Leona: 21	Wilder	Regiment, 1st U.S. Volunteer Cavalry (*Rough Riders*); regiment, 10th U.S. Cavalry, headquarters, 1st Brigade, Brig. Gen. S. B. M. Young; Capt. Robert Sewell, adjutant general	51	910	5
Manteo: 36	Brown	Two companies, 17th U.S. Infantry and two companies, 2d Massachusetts Volunteers	10	265	2
Matteawan: 26	Lewis	Regiment, 20th U.S. Infantry; Troops F and D, 2d U.S. Cavalry; Independent Brigade; Brig. Gen. J. C. Bates; Maj. John A. Logan, adjutant general	32	734	4
Miami: 1	McDonald	Regiment, 6th U.S. Infantry; regiment, 9th U.S. Cavalry	55	919	4
Morgan: 30	Staples	Major Rafferty and Troop C, 2d U.S. Cavalry	3	69	5
Olivette: 11	Stevenson	Hospital and water carrier	3	35	8

Vessel name/ Designating No	Master		Officers	Men	No. small boats
Orizaba: 24	Downs	Regiment, 22d U.S. Infantry; Batteries G and H, 4th Artillery (Siege Artillery Battalion)	35	622	6
Rio Grande: 22	C. Staples	Regiment, 3d U.S. Cavalry; regiment, 6th U.S. Cavalry; balloon signal detachment, Maj. J. E. Maxfield	49	882	5
San Marcos: 18	Itzen	Cos. A, E, F, and H, 2d U.S. Infantry; regiment, 16th U.S. Infantry; 1st Brigade, Brig. Gen. H. S. Hawkins; Capt. W. E. Horton, adjutant general	38	1,237	5
Santiago: 2	Leighton	Regiment, 9th U.S. Infantry; one battalion, 10th U.S. Infantry; headquarters, 1st Division, Brig. Gen. J. F. Kent; Maj. A. C. Sharpe, adjutant general	57	739	4
Saratoga: 20	Johnson	Regiment, 13th U.S. Infantry; headquarters band and Cos. C, D, E, and H of 21st U.S. Infantry; headquarters, 3d Brigade, Lt. Colonel Worth, 13th Infantry	38	635	5
Seguranca: 12	Hanson	Regiment, 1st U.S. infantry; balloon signal detachment, Maj. F. Greene; headquarters V Army Corps, Maj. Gen. William R. Shafter; Colonel McClenard, assistant adjutant general	--	477	6
Seneca: 5	Decker	Regiment, 8th U.S. Infantry; two companies 2d Massachusetts Volunteers; headquarters, 1st Brigade; Col. J. J. VanHorn, 8th U.S. Infantry; 1st Lt. Fred Perkins, assistant adjutant general	32	656	7
Stevens: * 35	Vanaman	Water schooner	--	---	
Stillwater: 28	Galt	Troop A, 2d U.S. Cavalry	3	69	4
Vigilancia: 23	McIntosh	Regiment, 71st New York Volunteers	44	954	6
Whitney: 10	G. Staples	Probably with cargo	--	---	
Yucatan: 8	Robertson	Headquarters band and Cos. C, D, G, and B, 2d U.S. Infantry; regiment, 1st U.S. Volunteer Cavalry (*Rough Riders*)	43	773	6
		Totals	**819**	**16,158**	**139**

Note: A tug, the *Captain Sam,* was also with the expedition, but it turned back to Florida, leaving the convoy while en route. There is no record as to any designating number having been assigned to that tug.

* This vessel, designated Convoy No. 35, is the *Anne E. Stevens.*

What would finally clear the way for Shafter's departure from Tampa was the locating of the long threatening Spanish fleet. Short of coal and therefore incapable of further maneuver, the Spanish admiral had entered Santiago, Cuba, undetected. Once the Spanish were discovered there, Rear Adm. William T. Sampson, commander of the pursuing United States naval squadron, set in place a blockade of Santiago which effectively sealed in the Spanish from taking naval action against Shafter's invasion force.[14]

~

On June 14, the Shafter expedition cleared Tampa Bay, outbound for Cuba.[15] Escorted by warships from the North Atlantic Squadron, Shafter's destination was now to be an open roadstead on the southeast coast of Cuba lying some miles to the eastward of Santiago.

Convoy performance proved abominable. According to John J. Pershing, then a major in the 10th U.S. Cavalry, the transport *Leona,* on which Pershing was a passenger, lost the convoy when only three days out of Tampa. Pershing later wrote, *If I had been in command, I should have put him* [the ship's master] *in irons.* Pershing's diary entries for that trip included the suggestions that in order to improve what had been the poor conditions, there should be, *More air* [in the troop compartments] -- *hammocks for the men -- cooking arrangements on board should be provided -- improvement in the Army's travel rations* [the ones they had were unpalatable and stale] -- *more fruit necessary --*[troop] *clothing too hot.*

---

[14] On June 14, Sampson ordered a battalion of Marines landed at Guantánamo with the purpose of establishing a coaling base for the blockading force. Guantánamo, a well protected bay, was located 45 miles to the east of Santiago, close enough so as to provide quick coaling replenishment for Sampson's ships, therefore necessitating that each ship spend only a minimal time off blockade station.

[15] Reports differ as to the exact number of ships which made up the first expeditionary convoy which, in addition to troopships and various auxiliaries also included naval escorts. Maj. General Joseph Wheeler, who commanded the cavalry troops, stated in an account of the expedition to Cuba that in all there were *over fifty-five ships.* See Maj. General Joseph Wheeler, *The Santiago Campaign, 1898,* (Boston, New York, and London: Lamson, Wolffe, and Co., 1898). This does not, however, agree with the report of James M. McKay which listed a total of thirty-six transports, inclusive of cargo vessels. (Gibson note: One of these cargo vessels was left at Tampa.) On page 9 of Wheeler's book, there is a plan portraying the expedition as it left Tampa Bay. On that plan, he shows only thirty transports (troopers and cargo). Additional to that number, he displayed on his plan sixteen naval escorts, naming each. According to the Department of the Navy's *Dictionary of American Naval Fighting Ships,* one of the naval escorts portrayed by Wheeler, *USS Vesuvius,* was off Cuba's south coast at the time of the convoy's sailing; another (*USS Scorpion*) listed by Wheeler was also not in the escort. Listed by Wheeler was the *USS Indiana* which according to the *Dictionary* was off Santiago, Cuba, at the time. *USS Panther,* shown on Wheeler's plan, was also elsewhere, again, according to the *Dictionary...*, being off the coast of Jamaica at the time. If the Navy's *Dictionary* is correct, then there were eleven escorts instead of the sixteen claimed by Maj. General Wheeler. *The Annual Report of the Secretary of War, Miscellaneous Reports, 1898* states that there were thirty-eight Army controlled vessels in the convoy of which thirty-one were troopships or cargo vessels. Two were water boats; three were steam lighters. One was a collier and one a tug. If those figures are accepted, and if the *Dictionary of American Naval Fighting Ships* is correct regarding certain vessels listed contradictorily by Wheeler, then all in all, the convoy departing Tampa would have consisted of a total of forty-nine vessels. Later offlying Key West, an additional five naval escorts would be added to the convoy. The chief quartermaster of the expedition counts thirty-five Army transports and cargo vessels as having been in the expeditionary force of June 14 bound to Santiago de Cuba. He did not, however, count a tug which deserted and a lighter which failed to join.

According to his diary, Pershing anticipated that the landings at Cuba would be *confused,* a prediction that would prove true.[16]

The commandant at the Key West Naval Station, Commodore George C. Remy, had been assigned the responsibility for the convoy's planning. Remy did his best by assigning naval signalmen to each transport and issuing instructions as to routing, ship spacing, and alignment. According to Remy's plan, after leaving Tampa, the transports were to assemble off Rebecca Shoals at the Florida Key's outer limits from where they were to depart in three columns. The fore and aft interval between ships was set at 400 yards; distance between columns was to be 800 yards. Remy's big mistake was that he neglected to assign a naval convoy commodore. Presumably, he must have assumed that the convoy's direct control was to be the responsibility of the naval escort commander; but if so, Shafter was never told of such an arrangement. With no one seemingly in overall charge of the convoy, Maj. General Shafter took over what should have been the Navy's function, doing so despite his total lack of experience with the operation and control of ships and shipping. Had there been an enemy force to contest the convoy's movements, a calamity would surely have resulted. Shafter allowed the transports to burn the normal peacetime lights; and while just north of Cuba, he ordered the rearrangement of some ships, doing this without bothering to inform the naval escort commander. The new arrangement elongated the convoy's formation which seriously weakened what protection had previously been offered by the naval escorts. Shafter's enforcement of anything resembling convoy discipline was totally lacking. William McClellan has pointed out this deficit in his detailed analysis of the Cuban sealift:

> *...failure of Congress to provide for the adequate control of merchant marine captains... by placing them under the* Articles for the Government of the Navy [proved] *to be the greatest weakness of this and other Spanish American War convoys.* [17]

While en route, a barge foundered and was lost; a steam lighter (upon which much depended to ferry troops and equipment to the Cuban beach) had to return to Tampa for repairs; and a tug, *Captain Sam,* turned back, the skipper apparently having a change of heart. While off the northern coast of Cuba, the mule transport *Gussie* messaged that she was running out of water for the animals. She was ordered to Mathew Town on Great Inagua Island in the southern Bahamas. With her went the *Olivette* which was to supply water until a schooner carrying more water could arrive from Florida. Once replenished, *Gussie* and *Olivette* would be ordered to rejoin the other transports off Daiquiri on Cuba's southeastern coast; but that arrangement would take time to effect.

Theodore Roosevelt, the lieutenant colonel of the 1st U.S. Volunteer Cavalry (the *Rough Riders*), was aboard the transport *Yucatan*. Prior to leaving

---

16   Donald Smythe, *Guerrilla Warrior, The Early Life of John J. Pershing,* (New York: Charles Scribner's Sons, 1973), pp 47, 48; quoting from Pershing's diary, its June 18 and 19 entries.
17   William Cave McClellan, *A History of American Military Sea Transportation,* a Ph.D. Thesis, (Washington, DC: The American University, 1953), p 84.

Tampa, Roosevelt had written his friend Henry Cabot Lodge of the conditions he had first encountered on board *Yucatan.*

> *We are in a sewer; a canal* [Port Tampa] *which is festering as if it were Havana harbor. The steamer on which we are contains nearly one thousand men, there being room for about five hundred comfortably.*
> *...Several companies are down in the lower hold, which is unpleasantly suggestive of the Black Hole of Calcutta.*[18]

Once away from Tampa, Roosevelt seemed to have found the sea breezes more invigorating than the fetid atmosphere encountered at Port Tampa. Of June 20, the day when the expedition reached that part of the Cuban coastal area where the landings were to take place, he wrote with seeming enthusiasm, *That day we steamed close to the Cuban coast, high barren-looking mountains rising abruptly from the shore.* The fleet of transports had earlier passed Guantánamo and Roosevelt and the others saw in the distance part of the Navy's squadron which was returning to blockade station off Santiago. On that same day, the expedition's commanding officer, Shafter was ferried ashore to Aserraderos in company with Rear Admiral Sampson, Sampson's naval aide, seven Army staff officers, the British and German attachés, and four newspaper correspondents. Their business was to meet with the Cuban revolutionary leader Calixto Garcia and two of his lieutenants. From this meeting would be decided the best landing beaches and the arrangements for coordination with Garcia. By observation earlier made from offshore, Shafter had tentatively decided that of the entire stretch of beach which ran twenty or more miles to the east of Santiago harbor, only three small areas appeared as possibilities for landing sites. Each of the three sites had ravines cutting through the coastal escarpment which reportedly could provide access into the interior. Guantánamo Bay -- which had been occupied by the Marines -- had earlier been ruled out due to the distance which lay between it and Santiago -- Santiago being the expedition's immediate goal for conquest. The ravine at Aquadores was ruled out because of its proximity (only four miles) to Santiago, a distance which could enable the Spanish commander to quickly move troops to contest a landing. Some distance east of the Aquadores ravine was another ravine at the base of which was the small settlement of Siboney. According to Garcia, there was good access inland from Siboney. To the east of Siboney, seven miles distant, was Daiquiri, another suitable landing place with good inland access. A road running along the seaward base of the coastal escarpment connected Siboney and Daiquiri. Spanish forces at both locations were reported by Garcia to be of minimal strength. According to Garcia, the Daiquiri site was deemed to have the best conditions for landing, and it was there that two days later the American army would first go ashore. Landing of troops would also take place at Siboney. The majority of supplies went in to the beach at Daiquiri and would continue to do so until the port of Santiago was taken and could be cleared of obstacles. Some commissary supplies would also be landed at Siboney

---

[18]   O'Toole, p 244.

after the Army Engineers had constructed a pier at that place.[19]   On June 25, Shafter reported the success of the landings.

> *Adjutant-General, U.S.A., Washington, DC:*
>
> *Daiquiri* [June] *23. Had very fine voyage, lost less than 50 animals, 6 or 8 today...Only deaths 2 men drowned in landing...All points occupied by Spanish troops* [but] *heavily bombarded by Navy to clear them out. Sent troops toward Santiago and occupied Juragua City, a naturally strong place, this morning. Spanish troops retreating as soon as our advance was known. Had no mounted troops or could have captured them. With assistance of Navy, disembarked six thousand men yesterday and as many more today. Will get all troops off tomorrow, including light artillery and greater portion of pack train, probably all of it, with some of the wagons; animals have to be jumped to the water and towed ashore. Had consultations with Generals Garcia, Rader, and Castillo, 1 p.m. of 20th, 20 miles west of Santiago. These officers were unanimously of the opinion that landing should be made east of Santiago. I had* [earlier] *come to the same conclusion. General Garcia promises to join me at Juragua City tomorrow with between 3,000 and 4,000 men who will be brought from west of Santiago by ships of the Navy to Juragua City and there disembarked; this will give me between 4,000 and 5,000 Cubans, and leave 1,000 under General Rabi to threaten Santiago from the west. General Kent's division is being disembarked this afternoon at Juragua City, and will be continued during the night. The assistance of the Navy has been of the greatest benefit, and enthusiastically given. Without them I could not have landed in ten days, and perhaps not at all, as I believe I should have lost so many boats in the surf. At present want nothing. Weather has been good. No rain on land, and prospects for fair weather.*
>
> *Shafter, Maj. General, United States Volunteers Commanding*[20]

Shafter's comment that the landings could not have been accomplished in less than ten days without the Navy was an opinion formed over what he considered the uncooperative attitudes of the masters of the chartered transports. As a body, the masters initially would not close the beach, making protests that doing so would endanger their ships through grounding. Those protests had as their origins the time-charter formats under which the ships were hired. These contracts of charter stipulated that the government did not hold responsibility for damage or losses due to marine casualty.[21] Consequently, the masters felt their primary responsibility was to protect their employer (the ship owner) regardless of the military exigency being faced. The caution of the transport masters in not closing the beach meant small boat trips of two to five miles which resulted in excessive turn around time for the boats. Such delay could have been disastrous had the beachhead been contested by the enemy or had the weather worsened during the offloading operation. This problem was resolved in large

---

[19]   By July 18, following the surrender of the local Spanish forces, transports arriving from the north -- most of which were scheduled to load troops to go back to the United States -- were able to enter the harbor at Santiago.

[20]   *Correspondence Relating to the War with Spain,* Vol. I, Center for Military History, Washington, DC., 1993, pp 53, 54. What Maj. General Shafter had failed to mention was that some injuries occurred when men were transferring from the transports to the boats. One of those injuries which would prove fatal was sustained by a volunteer colonel named James J. Van Horn. Source: Col. William Addleman Ganoe, *The History of the United States Army,* (New York and London: D. Appleton Century Co., 1942), 378.

[21]   Correspondence file, Quartermaster General's Office, Colonel Kimble for Maj. General Ludington, May 11, 1898.

part during the second day of the landings when naval officers carrying instructions from Maj. General Shafter went aboard each transport informing the masters that during the landings any damage from marine casualty would become the responsibility of the Army. Most of the transports were subsequently moved closer in to the beach. Another and more substantive accusation against the transport masters lay with the gross inefficiency of some of their crews in handling their ships' small boats -- endeavors for which most of the crews appeared to have little if any experience.

~

The initial refusal of ship masters to close the beach, coupled with their poor showing of cooperation while in convoy transit became contributory factors in the War Department's and the Dodge Commission's post war recommendations that a permanent Army transportation service be established. Another factor upon which such recommendations would become based was that the chartered ships -- all but one or two of which were designed only for coastal use -- had proven entirely unsuitable as long-haul troop and/or animal transports.

~

Despite Shafter's rosy report sent from Daiquiri to the Adjutant General which stated that the landings would be completed by June 25, considerable troop impedimenta had still not arrived on the beach by evening of that day. In fact, when the transports finally weighed their anchors with orders to return to their assigned ports for reloading, a few still had supplies and troop baggage aboard which by oversight had not been landed.[22] Although most of the initial troop equipment had gone ashore by the 26th, much of what would make up immediate resupply remained unloaded well past that time. The landings of supplies and artillery had been adversely impacted by the shortage of lighters. One towed lighter together with a deck barge departing Tampa with the expedition had been lost to the expedition, having been abandoned with little justification by the chartered tug *Nimrod* while en route. (The lighter was recovered and sent on to Cuba**.**) As already related, the tug *Captain Sam* had turned back, and the self-propelled lighter *Bessie* had developed an engine malfunction, necessitating her return as well. This left only one steam lighter, the *Laura,* for the job of getting supplies and troop equipment onto the beachhead. The absence of tugs to assist the Navy in towing small boats into the beach had become yet another handicap in what can only be evaluated as an operation which had succeeded only because of a lot of luck and a total lack of Spanish resistance at the beaches. The expedition included two shallow draft steamers, the *Cumberland* and the *Manteo,* which, together with the lighter *Laura,* had the ability to come alongside the shallow water pier at Siboney once the engineers made the pier usable.[23] Everything else was to go onto the beach by small boats from the transports or aboard launches loaned for the job by the Navy. (The ships' boats were generally towed to the beach by the Navy's launches.)

---

22   *Correspondence Relating to the War with Spain,* Vol. I, p 157.

23   There is some question as to whether or not the shallow draft *Cumberland* and *Mateo* were ever brought into the industrial pier located at the landing site. Lt. Col. Charles F. Humphrey, chief quartermaster of the expedition, although claiming the adaptability of these two vessels for that use, implies that they may have remained offshore with the other transports. See Humphrey, October 20, 1898.

The slowness in getting supplies ashore resulted in Shafter calling for the emergency departure of tugs and of barges from the United States.[24]

Pvt. Charles J. Post of the 71st New York Volunteers arrived at Cuba aboard the transport *Vigilencia.* The 71st went ashore in front of the hamlet of Siboney. Post would later write of his personal debarkation to one of the transport's small boats which was then towed into the beach by a Navy launch.

> *I got in the boat. Men squatted on the floor boards, packed tight. There was room for a few on the seat that ran around the sides. Sailors at the bow and the stern held the boat to the ship's side. In the stern a coxswain bossed the loading of the soldiers...*
>
> *The four sailors pulled us away from the transport and hooked us into line with the boats already loaded, and in the next moment we were headed for the beach and Siboney. As we neared the shore, the steam launch cast off her line, and the sailors pulled until the deep laden lifeboat grounded a hundred feet off the beach. The surf was light -- it was hardly a surf, merely a heavy ripple from the slow Caribbean swell. A few ragged Cuban rebels and some ragged children -- ragged to the point of mere fluttering nudity -- formed our welcoming committee.*

Private Post's trip into the beach had been far less hazardous than that of the horses and mules which he had observed being discharged out of the transport's side doors -- urged out by whips. Once the horses hit the water, they panicked. Some became disoriented and had to be turned toward the beach by men manning the ship's boats. This proved difficult, and some of the animals kept swimming seaward and drowned.[25]

The day prior to Post's trip to the beach, the correspondent Richard Harding Davis described his own landing at Siboney; the hour was well after sunset of the first day.

> *It was one of the most weird and remarkable scenes of the war, probably of any war. An army was being landed on an enemy's coast at the dead of night, but with somewhat more of cheers and shrieks and laughter than rise from the bathers in the surf at Coney Island on a hot Sunday. It was a pandemonium of noises. The men still to be landed from the 'prison hulks,' as they called the transports, were singing in chorus, the men already on shore were dancing naked around the camp fires on the beach, or shouting with delight as they plunged into the first bath that had [been] offered in seven days, and those in the launches as they were pitched head first at the soil of Cuba, signalized [sic] their arrival by howls of triumph. On either side rose black overhanging ridges, in the lowland between were white tents and burning fires, and from the ocean came the blazing, dazzling eyes of the search lights shaming the quiet moonlight.* [26]

[24]   Quartermaster Consolidated Correspondence File, Williams to Gilmore.   Also, Erna Risch, *Quartermaster Support of the Army,* (Washington, DC: Quartermaster Historian's Office, 1962), pp 548, 549. These tug-barge units departed from Mobile, New Orleans, and Key West. En route, trouble occurred in the nature of heavy weather. Most of the barges were lost while those remaining were turned back with their tugs.

[25]   Charles J. Post, *The Little War of Private Post,* (Boston, Little Brown, 1960), pp 113, 114. Photographic evidence in at least one case shows the occupants of a ship's boat being manned -- not by a ship's crew -- but by soldiers. The boat in the photo was engaged leading horses toward the shore.

[26]   Richard Harding Davis, *The Cuban and Puerto Rican Campaigns,* (New York: Charles Scribner Sons, 1898), pp 137, 138.

The war in Cuba would now become a land contest. Shafter's army would soon take the fight to the outer defensive lines the Spanish had prepared surrounding Santiago. The heroic charge up San Juan Hill took place on July 1, carried on by the 1st U.S. Volunteer Cavalry (the *Rough Riders*) and the 10th U.S. Cavalry (*colored*). The strong point dominating the approach to the Spanish defense line (El Caney) was carried next.

~

On July 3 at 0830 in the morning, Spanish warships began to sortie seaward from Santiago harbor. By noon, the Spanish fleet had been effectively destroyed by Sampson's blockading squadron.

There would follow a static period awaiting a Spanish surrender. It was a wait fraught with danger, in small part from Spanish bullets but in greatest part from tropical disease. Malaria became rampant, but even more frightening, a few cases of yellow fever began to appear. It was apparent to those in the American command that a stay of any duration in front of Santiago was an invitation for the Army's incapacitation from disease. What was delaying the Spanish surrender was Washington's insistence on an unconditional surrender, something which the Spanish commander found repugnant to his honor. Finally, on July 17, following considerable negotiation, it was agreed that the Spanish would be allowed to *capitulate* instead of surrender (a play on words thought by the Spanish to be important). Of more practical significance was that the United States agreed to repatriate the conquered Spanish military to Spain.

~

Following the departure of Shafter's expedition from Tampa in June, additional merchant ships chartered at various Gulf of Mexico and east coast ports had arrived at Tampa. Among the ships arriving at Tampa following June 20 were *Specialist* and *Unionist*. On June 22, *Comanche, Louisiana, Gate City, Hudson*, and *City of Macon* docked there. Under War Department pressure to load and send these vessels outbound in immediate support of Shafter, Col. J. B. Bellinger, the depot quartermaster at Tampa, did his best to assure that despite the urgency, the inadequacies which had been discovered aboard the earlier sailing transports would not be repeated. The *Unionist* and the *Specialist* had been selected for carrying troops; however, since Colonel Bellinger thought that they were also the best of the lot for handling animals, both ships were altered so as to carry horse-drawn light artillery. Of the five other ships, only three were considered to be ready to sail. Meanwhile, transports were returning from off the Cuban beachhead under orders to reload and return to Cuba. A constant stream of telegrams was meanwhile being sent from Shafter's headquarters, calling for the prompt dispatch of everything in the way of loaded ships that the Tampa Depot could sail. To accommodate, Colonel Bellinger worked his shipfitters and stevedore gangs around the clock. On June 27, the *Louisiana* left for the Cuban beachhead with a mixed load of troops, ambulances, pack animals, rations, and ammunition. The *Louisiana* was followed two days later by two other transports carrying troops and some animals. During the last of July and early August, eleven transports arrived back at Tampa after offloading at Cuba. Of these, two returned to the island with hospital personnel and supplies along with a number of civilian Quartermaster employees; two ships returned with troops. Two would sail empty from Tampa following the Spanish surrender of Santiago bringing troop units back to the United States. One transport was sent with troops and supplies to Havana to take part in what would turn out to be an uncontested occupation of that city. On August 3, the last of thirty-three troop and supply transports constituting the follow-up sealift to Cuba had departed Port Tampa.

Problems had become so associated with the use of Port Tampa as a place of embarkation that the War Department decided early-on to switch operations to more suitable ports. The problem with Port Tampa was not so much the port facility itself but rather the inadequacies of the railroad system serving it. Those inadequacies were in large part brought about because of the difficulties in switching cars from one railroad ownership to that of another. The depot quartermaster at Tampa gave one not untypical example which had occurred during late June when a shipment of needed tropical clothing became lost. The special train on which the shipment had been consigned was discovered after ten days of search on a siding eighteen miles from Tampa.[27] Another cause for problems was the competition between the two railroads serving west Florida. The management of each company refused to cooperate with its opposite number toward solving the traffic jam of freight cars which had backed up as far north as the Carolinas. The railroad inefficiencies, when coupled with the lack of general infrastructure at Port Tampa resulted in the Quartermaster Department's decision to shift all further shipping operations to the ports of Charleston, South Carolina, and Newport News, Virginia.

On August 4, orders came from Washington that Shafter's expeditionary force was to evacuate the Santiago area. Fresh troops to serve as an army of occupation would be sent to replace Shafter's men. The last reinforcements which had been scheduled for Shafter arrived following the Spanish surrender of Santiago. Rather than land these troops and expose them to the tropical diseases which by then were devastating Shafter's army, they were kept on board their transports which were shifted to anchorages at the more healthful harbor of Guantánamo, there to await reassignment for the pending invasion of Puerto Rico.

By the time the Santiago campaign had ended, a total of ninety-one separate vessel voyages (not counting those voyages made by loaned naval vessels or vessels taken as prizes) had directly supported that endeavor. Of these voyages, seventy-five were made by transports carrying either troops, horses, or cargo; two steamers served as hospital ships; three of the voyages by schooners loaded with coal for replenishment of transports; and a fourth by a schooner carrying ice. Two others were made by tugs, one by a steam collier, one by a snagboat used in clearing harbor obstructions, two by individual schooners fitted out as water carriers, and four by self-propelled steam lighters.[28] (The part of the 1898 sealift which was earmarked directly for the Shafter expedition had transported a total of 28,195 officers and men.)[29]

---

[27] *Statement 17* as found within the *Report of Tampa Depot, May 18 - August 31, 1898.* On file at Military History Institute, Carlisle Barracks. Call No. UC323.3 - 1898- A4, p 24.

[28] Humphrey, *Expedition to Santiago de Cuba.* This list also contains the names of vessels under Army control which departed Port Tampa following the initial expedition of June 14, including dates of arrival and departure as well as troop units and cargo types.

[29] *Annual Report of the Secretary of War, Miscellaneous Reports*, 1898, p 393.

During late July into August, the cargo of some of the transports which arrived at Santiago was only partially unloaded -- the remainder to be sent on for support of the Puerto Rican operation.

The end of Spanish resistance on Cuba had not relaxed the need for shipping assigned to Cuba. First, there was the requirement of evacuating the sick and wounded. This was followed by Shafter's homeward bound army which started its embarkation during the month of July, continuing into early August. Shafter's army would return to the United States routed not to their original port of embarkation but instead to quarantine at Montauk, New York, on the eastern tip of Long Island. The McKinley Administration was determined that the plagues of malaria and yellow fever would not come home in accompaniment with the troops. While this was taking place, it coincided with preparations to move troops from the United States for participation in the invasion of Puerto Rico. Additional ship bottoms over those which had been kept on hand at Santiago and those which were being used for the evacuation of Shafter's expedition were hard to come by. In fact, it was often refused outright.

> *Your message received. I find no ships except those belonging to the Merchant and Miners Line and Ocean Steamship Line. Both positively decline to charter these and any other vessels. Can vessels be impressed?...*
> *Roy Stone, Brigadier General, U.S. Volunteers* [30]

The political and military situation with Puerto Rico was quite different from that which had existed in Cuba. To begin with, the population of Puerto Rico had not been in rebellion against its Spanish rulers. For the American invaders and what would subsequently become the army of occupation, this posed a two-fold advantage: First -- the governmental infrastructure on Puerto Rico was undamaged by the kind of revolutionary activity which had occurred in Cuba; Second -- the undisturbed agriculture industry on the island provided a source of food for the invader, something which had not been the case in Cuba. A disadvantage was that unlike Cuba, where the presence of American businessmen and plantation owners over the years had helped to provide useful information as to what might be expected, the Spanish military strength on Puerto Rico was an unknown factor. Whether the native population there would or would not support the Spanish was a matter of guesswork. Also, maps descriptive of the island's interior were almost nonexistent. To rectify some of the wide informational gaps, a young Army officer was sent to Ponce, Puerto Rico, during June. Posing as a British subject on a commercial shipping survey, he traveled throughout the island making a rapid reconnaissance. The officer found that Spanish strength was weak and that any prepared defenses were outmoded and therefore of little consequence; however, he could provide little more than a rough idea of the island's interior geography and virtually nothing on the attitudes of the native population.

The general officer detailed by Secretary of War Alger to lead the invasion of Puerto Rico was Maj. Gen. Nelson A. Miles who was assigned at his own request.[31] Miles decided that for his initial landing phase, he would employ only those

---

[30]   *Commission for Conduct of Conduct of the War With Spain*, Vol. II, p 995.

[31]   Nelson A. Miles had begun his military career as a volunteer officer in 1861. By 1864, he was a major general of volunteers and a winner of the Medal of Honor. He remained in the service after Appomattox, entering

troops which were then readily available on the transports waiting at Guantánamo Bay. The remainder of what he would need in the way of troops were to be shipped directly from the United States to a Puerto Rican port which he would later select. The United States purpose once ashore on Puerto Rico had not yet been determined. Was it to be a campaign of conquest with a withdrawal following Spanish removal, as was planned for Cuba, or was Puerto Rico to be held indefinitely by the United States? Miles may have helped settle that question when on July 5 he wrote Secretary of War Alger giving his opinion of Puerto Rico as *the gateway to Spanish possession in the Western Hemisphere,* it being of *the highest importance that we should take and keep that island.* Situated at the northeastern entrance to the Caribbean Sea, Puerto Rico would have tremendous advantage to United States influence within the Caribbean. The McKinley Administration had by now seen the need for a United States presence lest a European power such as Germany or possibly Great Britain decide to fill the power vacuum created by Spain's departure. Looked upon in the long term, Puerto Rico had great potential for a naval coaling station should the Spanish try to reestablish themselves within the Caribbean. This threat was thought to be a realistic one as the Spanish fleet destroyed off Santiago represented but a part of Spanish naval power.[32]

When Miles sailed from Guantánamo, he had slated to make his landing at Fajardo Bay near the northeastern point of Puerto Rico. Whether this destination was merely stated to the Adjutant General at the War Department by Miles on the theory that the news would leak to the newspapers remains a question. In any event, it is clear that the Secretary of War believed Fajardo was the place to which Miles was headed. Described geographically, Fajardo is an open roadstead with offlying reefs through which there were poorly buoyed channels. It would have been a bad choice for the debarkation of troops or for the start of any drive into the island's interior. Miles would later claim to the Secretary of War that in concert with the commander of the expedition's naval escort force, he had changed his mind for a landing place following his departure from Guantánamo. Miles's new choice for the landing became the port of Guánica on the southern coast, a place which allegedly was lightly garrisoned. Guánica lay only a few miles to the west of Ponce which was Puerto Rico's largest city and its major commercial port. From Guánica, a road network led to Mayagüez on the western coast while another good road ran from Mayagüez north and eastward to Arecibo on the northern coast. Along the southern coast from Guánica, a road connected directly to Ponce and from Ponce, another one led to the interior town of Aibonito from where a road connected to the southeastern point of the island and the port town of Arroyo, a location Miles would schedule for a second landing once Guánica had been secured.

Miles's troop transports entered Guánica at first light on July 26, the transports being preceded by J. Pierpont Morgan's former yacht the *Corsair* (now armed as the light cruiser *USS Gloucester).* The Spanish fired off a few defensive shots without injuring anyone and then departed in haste. Miles's entire force was ashore and

---

the Regular Army in 1866 with the rank of colonel. He had a prominent record in the warfare against the western Indian tribes. His record in the west culminated successfully with the capture of the Apache leader Geronimo and the final pacification of the reservation Sioux following the killing of Sitting Bull in the early 1890s.

[32]   O'Toole, p 353. Postwar reports do not indicate that Spain had means to reestablish itself.

well organized by mid-day. Transports which had sailed from the United States, routed toward Fajardo, were intercepted at sea by naval courier vessels and redirected to Guánica. Once reinforced, Miles moved overland to Ponce. By July 29, he was in firm occupation of that city without having so far sustained any casualties. Reporting his progress to the Secretary of War by way of telegram transmitted via Haiti, Miles announced his plan to make a multi-column advance with one column heading to Mayagüez and two more northward through the island's interior with San Juan as their eventual destination. Up to this point, the operation had gone extremely well, the one troublesome exception coming about when two transports arriving from the United States grounded on the reefs offlying Ponce. Miles described the circumstances of those groundings to the War Department.

> *Ponce, August 5, 1898*
> *No excuse whatever for either ship going ashore.* Roumania *was off yesterday and gone to Arroyo to disembark. It is expected the* Massachusetts *will be off today. Her captain totally incompetent. I have asked Captain Sands to place Navy officer in command. Troops are disembarking at Guánica, Ponce, and Arroyo; balance of siege train can be held until I ascertain what resistance will be made at San Juan. Cavalry much needed, and I request authority to send either* Mohawk *or* Mobile *directly to Tampa for 5th Cavalry. No more hay required; abundance of grass in country. Commissary and quartermaster funds most needed.[33]*

Meanwhile on Cuba, the sick list was increasing every day that Shafter's men were forced to remain. Made fully aware through a round-robin letter of protest signed by most of the field commanders of the need for early evacuation from Cuban soil, Washington put pressure on Miles to expedite the unloading of all the transports which had so far arrived in Puerto Rico. Instead of sending those ships back to the United States for supplies and reinforcements for the Puerto Rico campaign, Miles was to route them directly to Santiago, there to take on Shafter's troops for return to the United States. Miles messaged the War Department, assuring his compliance:

> *Owing to serious condition of* [Maj.] *General Shafter's command, I would not delay a single ship, notwithstanding our need of cavalry, and will order* Mohawk *and* Mobile *and every other vessel that can be spared to go with all speed to Santiago.[34]*

Some of the reinforcements being sent to Miles from the United States were units originally slated for Shafter's command. There were still remaining at Tampa some artillery units whose guns were to serve as the *siege train* which Miles had referenced in his cable of August 5; however, Spanish defenses proved so weak that the need for siege artillery was canceled. The artillery units at Tampa, now not needed at Puerto Rico, were moved back to their home stations by rail. Tampa was discontinued as a port of embarkation during late August when the last of the

---

[33] *Correspondence Relating to the War with Spain*, p 362, Vol. I, Ponce, August 5, 1898. The *Massachusetts* had been recently purchased by the Army, therefore its "incompetent" master would have been an Army employee. *Roumania* [also *Romania* in some reports] was a recent Army purchase; she was renamed *Crook*.

[34] *Correspondence Relating to the War with Spain*, Vol. I, p 366, Ponce August 6, 1898.

remaining supplies was shipped from there. For the invasion of Puerto Rico encompassing the period 20-28 July, 3,571 officers and men left from Charleston; 5,317 from Newport News; and a leftover 2,896 from the phasing-down Port Tampa.

When Miles's men left Ponce and Guánica for the advance toward Mayagüez and the island's interior, his forces totaled around 14,000 officers and men. Prior to leaving Ponce, Miles informed the War Department that he now had sufficient troops to accomplish the conquest of the island.[35] The Spanish had counted heavily on locally recruited militia to augment their few regular army units; but in large part that militia either retreated or deserted outright, in many cases even before the Americans came into sight. Some of the militia even went so far as to offer their services to the Americans. The two separate columns being marched into the interior toward the north coast were to rendezvous at Arecibo and from there follow the rail line connecting to San Juan. They met with virtually no resistance. The column which had marched to Mayagüez occupied that place on August 11. By the following day, all the Spanish commands had surrendered. Puerto Rico had been a victory earned with little bloodshed. Only four Americans had been killed during the 18-day campaign, and less than four dozen had been wounded.

~

In accordance with surrender terms, Spanish troops at both Cuba and at Puerto Rico would soon begin boarding Spanish merchant ships chartered by the United States to transport the surrendered back to Spain.

~

There was to be an army of occupation established in Cuba, but the American presence there was planned as only a temporary expedient until the native population could take over the reins of government. As it would turn out, that would take time. The island's economy was in disarray, as was the local political apparatus, leaving the time frame for the occupation no where near certain. As it turned out, the Americans were to stay until 1902.[36] The occupation of Puerto Rico would be a different matter. Puerto Rico was to become a permanent United States possession. Although tropical disease was a factor at both places, on Puerto Rico, it was never the menace that had been the case in Cuba. The Army's initial solution for protecting the health of the army of occupation, at least in the high risk fever regions of Cuba, was to assign to the occupation only those troops which had been recruited in the deep south of the United States where the scourge of malaria, and to a limited extent yellow fever, were at the time thought to have provided partial immunity to the populations. At the beginning, most of that immune category was interpreted as meaning Negro regiments (referred to informally as *immunes*.) Later, the term *immunes* would also refer to units

---

[35]   *Correspondence Relating to the War with Spain,* Vol. I, p 368, Miles to Secretary of War, Ponce, August 8, 1898.

[36]   United States occupation of Cuba by American troops ended in 1902. In 1906, civil unrest on the island created a need for intervention by United States troops. A provisional government appointed by the United States remained until 1909 at which time control was again passed to the Cubans. Cuba remained under the protectorate of the United States until 1922.

composed of officers and men who had recovered from yellow fever and who thereafter possessed immunity to that disease.[37]

~

Supplying the forces garrisoning Cuba and Puerto Rico required support by sea. The management of much of that support would fall to the Quartermaster Department and to the newly created Army Transport Service (ATS) which came under that department's organizational jurisdiction.[38]

---

[37] There was, however, no immunity for malaria except for those persons whose long-term racial genetics offered that protection. That of course could only translate as applying to Negroes whose origins were Africa. Brig. Gen. James Parker, *The Old Army...Memories, 1872 - 1918*, (Philadelphia: Durance and Co., 1929). While a lieutenant colonel in 1898, Parker served in Cuba; he later served in the Philippines.

[38] The Quartermaster Department would remain as such until 1912, when on August 24, the Congress created the Quartermaster Corps which absorbed the Quartermaster Department, the Subsistence Department, and the Pay Department.

Vessels Purchased by the Quartermaster Department, 1898

The reader is urged to check all notes at the end of this list as the use and tonnage was often changed throughout a vessel's Army career.

Sources: *Report of the Secretary of War, Fiscal Year Ending June 1898; Report of the Quartermaster General, 1898; Correspondence Relating to the War with Spain; Merchant Vessels of the United States; Report of Tampa Depot, May 18-Aug 31, 1898; Report by Humphrey, Expedition to Santiago de Cuba.*

Original Name of vessel	Renamed under ATS in 1898	Type	Flag	From Whom Purchased[1]	Date of purchase	Amount paid plus refit cost	Gross Tons	Carrying Capacity[2]
Adonis	*Williams*	Lighter, steam	American	W. C. Cahill	Nov 26	$26,000	177	–
Arizona	*Hancock*[8]	Transport	British	Northern Pacific Rwy Co.	July 16	$600,000	5,000	–
Bay State[3]	*Wright*[8]	Hospital ship	American	Massachusetts Relief Assn.	Nov 15	$100,000	777	–
Ben	--	Lighter	American	Mobile Coal Co.	June 27	$1,500	180	–
Britannia	--	Tug	American	Baker-Whiteley Coal Co.	July 14	$40,000	135	–
City of Berlin[9]	*Meade*[8]	Transport	unknown	International Navigation Co.	July 13	$400,000	5,641	75 o; 2000 m; -- a
City of Chester	*Sedgwick*	Transport	British	International Navigation Co.	July 27	$200,000	4,770	–
Edward L. Ward	*Baker*	Lighter	American	E. L. Ward	Nov 7	$25,000	200	–
Eugene Graselli	*Poe*	Lighter	American	Gustav A. Schwarz	Nov 25	$39,500	157	–
Gypsum King	*Slocum*	Tug, ocean	American	J. G. King Transportation Co.	July 25	$150,000	581	–
Harry	--	Tug	American	G. H. Hill	Nov 26	$6,000	–	–
J. C. Watson	*Reynolds*	Tug	American	J. D. Dailey	Nov 28	$14,000	58	–
John Englis	*Relief*[8]	Hospital	American	Maine SS Co.	May 20	+ $450,000 $136,851	3,095	–
L. E. Rinehardt	--	Lighter	American	Bernard Campbell	July 13	$5,500	–	--
Major McKinley, USQMD	*Sumner*	Tug	American	Frederick A. Verdon	Nov 7	$13,000	60	–
Manitoba[9]	*Logan*[8]	Combination[3]	British	Atlantic Transport Co. thru Bernard N. Baker	July 20	$660,000	5,673	80 o; 1000 m; 1000 a

Ship	Former name	Type	Nationality	Owner/Seller	Date	Price	Tonnage	Carrying Capacity
Massachusetts [9]	Sheridan [8]	Combination [3]	British	Atlantic Transport Co. [1]	July 14	$660,000	5,673	80 o; 1000 m; 1000 a
Michigan [9]	Kilpatrick [8]	Combination [3]	British	Atlantic Transport Co. [1]	July 14	+$350,000 $85,854	3,722	40 o; 800 m; 800 a
Minnewaska [9]	Thomas [8]	Combination [3]	British	Atlantic Transport Co. [1]	July 26	$660,000	5,796	100 o; 1200 m; 1000 a
Mississippi [9]	Buford	Combination [3]	British	Atlantic Transport Co. [1]	July 14	$350,000	3,732	40 o; 800 m; 800 a
Missouri, USQMD	Egbert	Hospital	British	Atlantic Transport Co. [1]	–	$200,000	2,903	–
Mobile [9]	Sherman [8]	Combination [3]	British	Atlantic Transport Co. [1]	July 14	$660,000	5,780	80 o; 1000 m; 1000 a
Mohawk [9]	Grant [8]	Combination [3]	British	Atlantic Transport Co. [1]	July 14	$660,000	5,658	80 o; 1000 m; 1000 a
Obdam	McPherson	Transport	British	Samuel D. Coykendall	July 1	$250,000	3,656	50 o; 1300 m; 100 a
Olympic	Weitzel	Tug	American	Frederick A. Verdon	Nov 19	$12,000	59	–
Panama	Hooker [8]	Freight and cable ship	Spanish	Captured [4]	June 2	[5]	2,085	10 o; 400 m; -- a
Port Victor [9]	McClellan [8]	Freight	British	Irwin, McBride, Catherwood and Co.	July 8	$175,000	2,792	25 o; 400 m; -- a
Rita	Burnside [8]	Freight	Spanish	Captured [4]	July 8	[6]	2,194	15 o; 700 m; -- a
Roumania [9]	Crook [8]	Combination [3]	British	Austin, Baldwin and Co.	July 12	$240,000	4,126	45 o; 1100 m; 50 a
Sarah	Ord	Tug	American	Long Island Machine and Marine Construction Co.	July 14	$6,300	21	–
Scandia	Warren [8]	Transport	German	Hamburg-American Line	July 5	$200,000	4,243	–
Touart [7]		Lighter	American	W. C. Taylor	June 25	$2,000.	200	–

1. The ships Army purchased from Atlantic Transport Co. came about through Bernard N. Baker of Atlantic Transport Line. They were transferred by ATL to Baker, an American citizen, who then sold them to the War Department. By this means, the War Department was able to purchase them as U.S. vessels, thus satisfying congressional concerns and U.S. law.
2. Carrying Capacity: officers (o); men (m); animals (a); civilians (civ)
3. Combination type vessels had refrigeration capability in addition to carrying passengers and animals.
4. Captured from Spanish by the U.S. Navy; after condemnation by prize court was purchased by the Quartermaster Department.
5. Later paid $41,000.
6. Later paid $125,000.
7. TOUART was part of the first expedition, Tampa to Cuba. Was cut loose from the chartered tug NIMROD while en route but apparently was later recovered as she was reported to be part of the second echelon of shipping which left Tampa for Cuba.
8. Philippine Insurrection service and/or China Relief Expedition in the years 1899 through 1901.
9. Following the war, converted to combination passenger and troop w/ hospital accommodations and cargo capacity. At conversation, tonnage was changed on many of these vessels.

VESSELS UTILIZED BY THE QUARTERMASTER DEPARTMENT WHICH WERE TIME CHARTERED OR OTHERWISE HIRED, Atlantic and Gulf Coasts - 1898

All told, the Army expended for fiscal year ending June 30, 1898, a total of $1,007,952 in ship charter fees on the Atlantic and Gulf coasts.

Sources: *Report of the Secretary of War, Fiscal Year Ending June 1898*; *Report of the Quartermaster General, 1898*; *Correspondence Relating to the War with Spain*; *Merchant Vessels of the United States*; *Blue Book of American Shipping*; *Report of Tampa Depot, May 18–Aug 31, 1898*; *Report by Humphrey, Expedition to Santiago de Cuba.*

Name of vessel [1]	Type	By Whom Owned [1]	Chartered	Canceled	Rate p/ day [2]	Gr Tons	Carrying Capacity [3]
Adria (Signal Service)	Unknown	Western Union Telegraph Co.	Apr 21	Aug 15	$200	519	35 o; 700 m; 10 a
Alamo	Transport	New York and Texas SS Co.	Apr 29	Sept 23	a)$600;b)$550	2,943	25 o; 300 m; 200 a
Allegheny	Transport	Merchants and Miners' Trans Co.	Apr 29	Sept 12	a)$600;b) $550	2,014	25 o; 300 m; 200 a
Anne E. Stevens, schooner	Water boat	W. S. Vanaman	May 13	Nov 1	$50	–	100,000 gallons
Aransas	Transport	Southern Pacific Co. (Morgan Line)	May 12	Sept 3	$400	1,156	10 o; 200 m; 200 a
Arcadia (also *Arkadia*)	Transport	New York and Porto Rico SS Co.	June 15	Sept 2	$250	2,317	15 o; 250 m; 300 a
Bergen, schooner	Coal		Aug		–	–	
Berkshire	Transport	Merchants and Miners' Trans Co.	Apr 29	Sept 12	a)$600;b) $550	2,014	25 o; 250 m; 200 a
Bessie	Lighter	Galveston SS and Lightering Co.	May 24	–	$50	185	–
Bratten	Lighter	W D. Munson	Nov. 11		a)$105;b) $130	705	–
Breakwater	Transport	New Orleans Belize Royal Mail	May 12	Sept 10	$340	500	25 o; 500 m; -- a
Captain Sam	Tug	W Chase Spotswood	June --	July 9	$75	93	–
Catania	Transport	Tweedie Trading Co.	June 13	Sept 13	$600	3,700	40 o; 800 m; -- a
Charles E. Balch, schooner	Ice	Use donated by McKay of New York	July	Aug	–	843	–
Cherokee	Transport	William P. Clyde and Co.	May 11	Aug 22	$500	3,557	40 o; 950 m; -- a
City of Macon	Transport	Ocean SS Co.	June 6	Aug 26	$500	2,098	25 o; 600 m; -- a
City of Washington	Transport	New York and Cuba Mail SS Co.	May 10	Sept 15	$450	2,648	20 o; 200 m; 200 a
Clinton	Transport	Southern Pacific Co. (Morgan Line)	June 8	Sept 11	$400	1,187	
Columbia	Transport		–	–	–	2,976	–
Comal	Transport	New York and Texas SS Co.; transferred to Army Subsistence Dept	Apr 29	Oct 25	a)$625;b)$575	2,934	40 o; 400 m; 400 a
Comanche	Transport	William P. Clyde and Co.	June 3	Sept 2	$640	3,202	50 o; 500 m; 50 a
Concho	Transport	New York and Texas SS Co.	May 10	Sept 23	$550	3,704	35 o; 700m; 10 a
Cumberland	Steamer	Cumberland SS Co.	June 1	–	$50	119	–
D. H. Miller	Transport	Merchants and Miners' Trans Co.	Apr 29	Sept 3	a)$600;b)$550	2,296	25 o; 450 m; 300 a
Fanita	Transport	James McKay (utilized by Secret Service)	–	Sept 8	$150	432	–
Florida	Transport	Plant Investment Co.	May 2	Sept 9	$600	1,786	25 o; 500 m; 175 a
Gate City	Transport	Ocean SS Co.	June 6	Aug 18	$500	1,997	25 o; 600 m; -- a
Gladisfen	Tug	William E. Myers	July 11	–	$90	110	–

Name	Type	Owner/Operator	Date	Date	Rate	No.	Capacity
Goldsworthy	Tug		—	—	—	124	
Gretchen	Inspection					40	
Gussie	Transport	Southern Pacific Co. (Morgan Line)	Apr 30	Sept 11	$350	998	20 o; 100 m; 300 a
Harrisburg	Collier		—	—	—	1,283	
Hudson	Transport	Cromwell SS Co.	June 9	Sept 6	$400	1,800	35 o; 600 m; -- a
Iroquois	Transport	William P. Clyde and Co.	May 11	Aug 18	$600	2,944	40 o; 700 m; -- a
Kanawha	Water boat	John A. Donald	June 3	Oct 3	$175	—	180,000 gallons
Knickerbocker	Transport	Cromwell SS Co.	June 3	Sept 21	$400	1,642	45 o; 900 m; -- a
La Grande Duchesse	Transport	Plant Investment Co.	July 5	Sept 2	$1,200	5,018	
Lampasas	Transport	New York and Texas SS Co.	June 13	Aug 13	$650	2,237	35 o; 200 m; 400 a
Laura	Lighter	Galveston SS and Lightering Co.	May 24	Oct 6	$50	185	
Leona	Transport	New York and Texas SS Co.	May 10	Aug 29	$500	3,329	45 o; 700 m; 10 a
Louisiana	Transport	Cromwell SS Co.	June 3	Aug 12	$500	2,849	30 o; 325 m; 300 a
Manteo	Steamer	New York and Cuba Mail SS Co.	May 28	Oct 7	$300	583	10 o; 250 m; 100 a
Matteawan	Transport	Miami SS Co.	May 11	Aug 24	$600	3,300	35 o; 720 m; 368 a
Maverick	Water boat	Standard Oil Co.	May 16	Sept 2	$500	—	440,000 gallons
Miami	Transport	Miami SS Co.	May 13	Aug 24	$550	3,050	27 o; 900 m; -- a
Minnewaska [5]	Transport					5,796	100 o; 1200 m; 1000 a
Missouri [4]	Hospital	Atlantic Transport Co. (B. Baker)	Dec		—	2,903	
Mohawk [4]	Transport	Southern Pacific Co. (Morgan Line)	May 12	Aug 31	$400	5,596	80 o; 1000 m; 1000 a
Morgan	Transport	New York and Texas SS Co.	June 13	Sept 16	$650	994	20 o; 250 m; 230 a
Neuces	Transport	H. T. Hartwell	June 25	July 15	$80	3,367	25 o; 800 m; 300 a
Nimrod	Tug	Plant Investment Co.	Apr 3	—	a)$500;b)$450	110	
Olivette	Transport	W. C. Taylor	June 25	July 2	$10	1,611	25 o; 600 m; 40 a
Ora	Lighter	New York and Cuba Mail SS Co.	May 10	Sept 17	$500	60	
Orizaba	Transport	Under hire of Aken Co. w/Army contract				3,497	30 o; 640 m; 125 a
Panama	Transport	New York and Texas SS Co.	May 10	Aug 26	$500	—	
Rio Grande	Transport	Standard Oil Co.	May 14	Aug 7	$100	2,566	50 o; 500 m; 10 a
S. O., No. 77	Water boat	New York and Texas SS Co.	May 10	Sept 8	$500	—	100,000 gallons
San Marcos	Transport	New York and Cuba Mail SS Co.	May 10	Sept 3	$450	2,837	45 o; 800 m; 350 a
Santiago	Transport	New York and Cuba Mail SS Co.	May 10	Sept 21	$450	2,359	40 o; 600 m; 250 a
Saratoga	Transport	New York and Cuba Mail SS Co.	May 10	Sept 30	$600	2,820	40 o; 800 m; 250 a
Seguranca	Transport	New York and Cuba Mail SS Co.	May 10	Sept 29	$450	4,115	35 o; 600 m; 500 a
Seneca	Transport	Henry Hanaw (Angier Line)	June 3	Sept 23	a)$425;b) $375	2,729	27 o; 600 m; 250 a
Specialist	Transport	New Orleans Belize Royal Mail	May 16	Nov 2	$325	2,802	10 o; -- m; -- a
Stillwater	Transport					1,019	8 o; 60 m; 168 a
Suwanee [6]	Snag boat				—	—	

	Type	Owner/Operator	Date	Date	Rate	Tonnage	Capacity
Swan, schooner	Coal	—	Aug	—	—	—	
Tarpon	Water boat	Plant Investment Co.	July 10	Oct 2	$250	450	
Tofa, schooner	Coal	—	Aug	—	—	631	
Triton	Tug	Morse and Co., New York	Aug 6	Oct 1	$212.50	—	
Underwriter	Tug	La Branch Pilots' Assn, New Orleans	July 8	Oct 2	$160	171	10 o; -- m; -- a
Unionist	Transport	Henry Hanaw (Angier Line)	June 10	Sept 23	a)$375;b) $325	2,158	
Ute	Transport	H. P. Kirkham	July 20	Sept 14	$165	899	45 o; 800 m; -- a
Vigilancia	Transport	New York and Cuba Mail SS Co.	May 10	Sept 18	$600	4,115	
Viona	Transport	—	July	—	—	—	
Wanderer	Transport	New Orleans Belize Royal Mail	July 5	Sept 10	$220	531	20 o; 250 m; 250 a
Whitney	Transport	Southern Pacific Co. (Morgan Line)	Apr 30	Sept 2	$350	1,337	45 o; 1000 m; 250 a
Yucatan	Transport	New York and Cuba Mail SS Co.	May 10	Sept 30	$500	3,525	

1. Primary Quartermaster correspondence indicates that certain ships on the east coast were chartered from the New York and Texas SS Co. and others from the New York and Porto Rico SS Co.; however other Quartermaster correspondence of May 1898 indicates that respective charters were from Mallory SS Co. and Ward SS Line.

2. Rate per day: a) Rate for first thirty days of charter; b) Rate after thirty days on charter

3. Carrying Capacity: officers (o); men (m); animals (a); civilians (civ)

4. Sent to PI from New York via the Mediterranean. In War Department correspondence of December 1898, there is mention of *Mohawk* as being chartered at New York for shipment of troops to the Philippines. A *Mohawk* was purchased through Bernard M. Baker in July 1898. Whether the charter reference of that December is an error, referring instead to the Army owned vessel or whether it referred to an entirely separate vessel cannot be reconciled.

5. *Missouri* served gratis for duration of war.

6. *Suwanee* was not self-propelled.

Vessels Originally Identified For Use as Naval Auxiliary Cruisers; Sub-chartered and/or Loaned to Army During 1898 for use as Troop Transports

These ships remained crewed by Navy during the time they were on loan to the Army. At least one, *Harvard*, had a largely civilian crew under a naval commander. Later in the war, her crew was militarized into the naval service. All but *City of Peking* were in the Atlantic.

Sources: *Report of the Secretary of War, Fiscal Year Ending June 1898*; *Report of the Quartermaster General, 1898*; *Correspondence Relating to the War with Spain*; *Merchant Vessels of the United States*; *Blue Book of American Shipping*; *Dictionary of American Naval Fighting Ships*.

Name of vessel	Type	Status	Used by Army	Canceled	Disp tons (from Navy)	Gross tons (from MVUS)
Badger, USS		Commissioned naval vessel; aux cruiser	Aug 18	Aug 24	4,784	2,332
City of Peking		Under charter to Navy				5,079
Columbia, USS		Commissioned USN vessel	July	Aug 14	7,375	2,026
Harvard, ex New York, ex City of New York		bb chartered by Navy from American Line. As *City of New York* was British.	July 15	Aug 27		10.799
Panther, USS		Commissioned naval vessel; aux cruiser	Aug	Aug	6,620	–
Prairie, USS		Commissioned naval vessel; aux cruiser	Aug	Aug	4,260	–
Resolute, USS		Commissioned naval vessel; aux cruiser	Oct	Nov	4,175	2,126
St. Louis		bb chartered by Navy from International Navigation Co.	July 11	Aug 24		11,629
St. Paul		bb chartered by Navy from International Navigation Co.	July 1	Aug 16		11,629
Yale, ex Paris		bb chartered by Navy from International Navigation Co.	June 27	Sept 2		10,668

Statement of Time Chartered Vessels of the Quartermaster's Department For Use at Montauk Point Quartermaster Post

Sources: *Report of the Secretary of War, Fiscal Year Ending June 1898; Report of the Quartermaster General, 1898; Correspondence Relating to the War with Spain*

Name of vessel	By Whom Owned	Type	Chartered	Canceled	Rate per day	Gr Tons	Carrying Capacity
Alfred W. Booth	Michael Moran	Tug	Aug 15	Sept 24	$75.	118	–
Columbia	James P. McAllister	Lighter	Aug 15	Oct 3	$60.	175	–
James A. Lawrence, ex C. E. Evarts	Alfred Dutch	Tug	Aug 10	Oct 9	$75.	86	–
Lewis Pulver	John Nichols	Tug	Aug 11	Oct 4	$50.	71	–
Shinnecock	Montauk Steamboat Co.	Steamer	Aug 30	Sept 22	$1,000.	1,205	–
Vigilant	John Delany	Steamer	Aug 11	Oct 1	$100.	150	–

Vessel Providing Service Without Cost to Army: Puerto Rican Campaign

Name of vessel	By Whom Owned	Type	Chartered	Canceled	Rate per day	Gr Tons	Carrying Capacity
May	Messrs VanRensselair, Van Uxem, G-off, Potter, for National Relief Assn	Yacht	August				Supplies

Spanish Vessels Captured at Santiago Harbor and Used by U. S. Army 1898

Sources *Report of the Secretary of War, Fiscal Year Ending June 1898;*
Correspondence relating to the War with Spain; Report by Humphrey, Expedition to Santiago de Cuba.

Name of vessel	Type	Passenger Capacity [1]
Mexico	Transport	approximately 100 persons
Mortera	Transport	approximately 300 persons
Reina de Los Angeles	Hospital ship	??
San Juan	Small cargo/passenger	??
Thomas Brooks	Small cargo/passenger	??

[1] **Carrying Capacity**: officers (o) men (m) animals (a) civilians (civ)

Vessels Time Chartered by the Quartermaster Department
For Transport of Spanish Prisoners of War to Spain From Cuba and Puerto Rico

Report of the Tampa Depot Quartermaster regarding the passenger list of those vessels repatriating Spanish prisoners differs somewhat from the passenger numbers given on this list. This list's figures were derived from the Report of the War Department. All ships listed here were of Spanish registry.
Sources: *Report of the Quartermaster General, 1898; Correspondence Relating to the War with Spain;* Report by Humphrey. *Expedition to Santiago de Cuba.*

Name of vessel	Type	Passenger Capacity [1]
Alicante [2]	Steamship	38 o; 1069 m; 17 civ
Cheribon [2]	Steamship	18 o; 905 m; 37 civ
Ciudad de Cadiz	Steamship	53 o; -- m; 33 civ
Colon	Steamship	100 o; 1316 m; 59 civ
Colon	Steamship	23 o; 726 m; 5 civ
Covadonga	Steamship	109 o; 2148 m; 79 civ
Isla de Luzon	Steamship	137 o; 2056 m; 44 civ
Isla de Panay	Steamship	99 o; 1599 m; 31 civ
Leon XIII	Steamship	113 o; 2209 m; 108 civ
Leonora	Steamship	15 o; 1118 m; -- civ
Montevideo	Steamship	136 o; 2108 m; 124 civ
P. de Satrustegui	Steamship	128 o; 2359 m; 68 civ
San Augustin	Steamship	65 o; 800 m; 45 civ
San Francisco	Steamship	18 o; 588 m; 11 civ
San Ignacio [2]	Steamship	59 o; 1408 m; 20 civ
Villaverde	Steamship	52 o; 565 m; 34 civ

[1] **Carrying Capacity:** officers (o); men (m); civilians (civ)
[2] Was fitted out as a hospital ship.

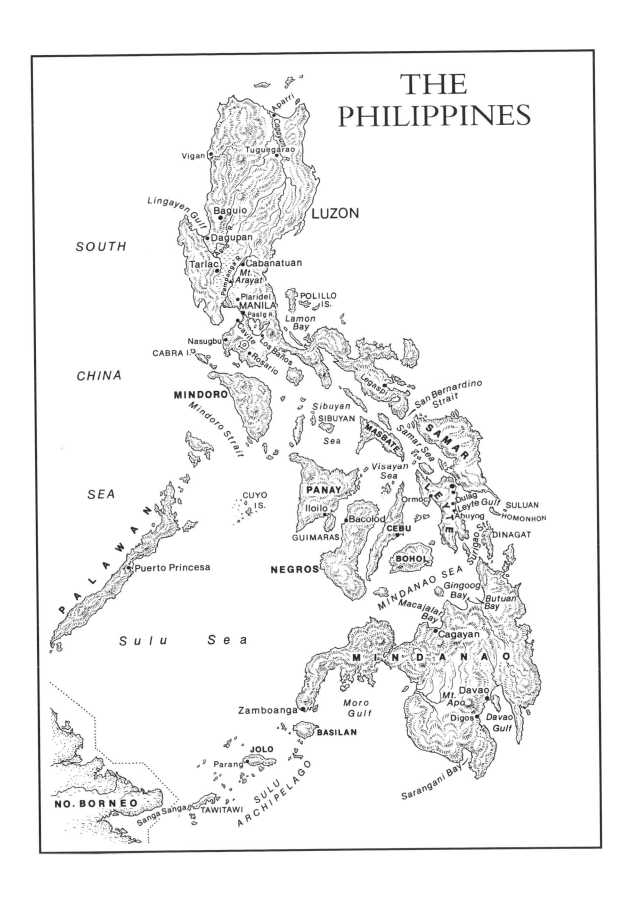

THE
PHILIPPINES

Aparri

Cagayan R.

Vigan

Tuguegarao

LUZON

Lingayen Gulf

Baguio

SOUTH

Dagupan

Agno R.

Tarlac

Pampanga R.

Cabanatuan

Mt. Arayat

Plaridel

POLILLO IS.

MANILA

Pasig R.

CHINA

Lamon Bay

Nasugbu

Cavite Los Baños

CABRA I.

Rosario

Legaspi

San Bernardino Strait

MINDORO

Sibuyan

Mindoro Strait

SIBUYAN

MASBATE

Samar Sea

SAMAR

Sea

SEA

Visayan Sea

CUYO IS.

PANAY

LEYTE

Ormoc

Dulag

Iloilo

Leyte Gulf

SULUAN

HOMONHON

Bacolod

Abuyog

CEBU

DINAGAT

GUIMARAS

Surigao Str.

PALAWAN

BOHOL

Puerto Princesa

NEGROS

MINDANAO SEA

Gingoog Bay

Butuan Bay

Macajalar Bay

Sulu   Sea

Cagayan

M I N D A N A O

Moro Gulf

Mt. Apo

Davao

Zamboanga

Digos

Davao Gulf

BASILAN

JOLO

Parang

SULU

Sarangani Bay

NO. BORNEO

Sanga Sanga

TAWITAWI

ARCHIPELAGO

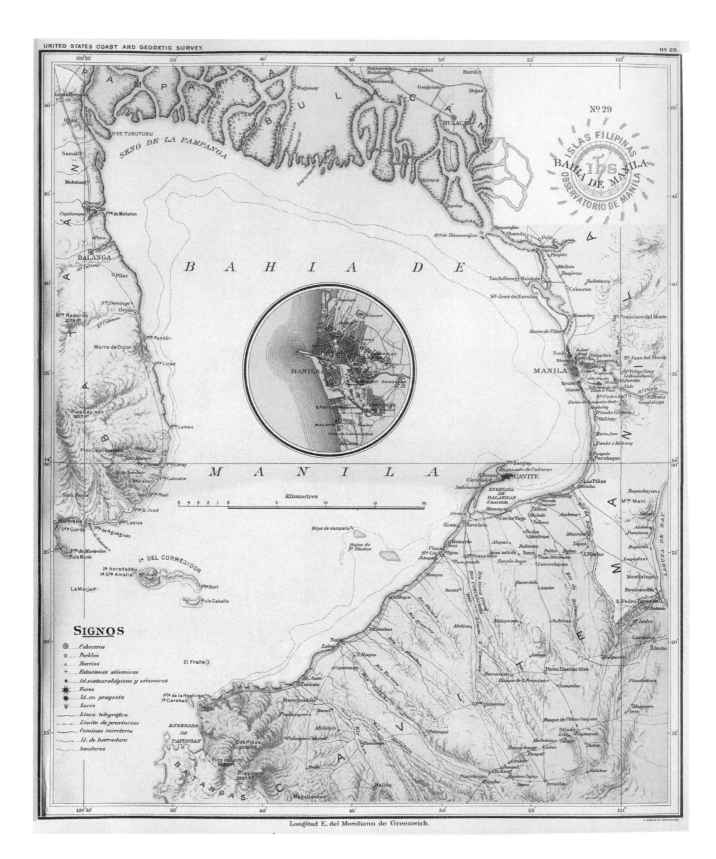

Nº 29

ISLAS FILIPINAS
BAHIA DE MANILA
OBSERVATORIO DE MANILA

BAHIA DE

MANILA

Kilometres

SIGNOS

◎ Cabeceras
○ Pueblos
○ Barrios
+ Estaciones seismicas
● Id.meteorológicas y seismicas
✳ Faros
✴ Id.en proyecto
⌄ Luces
— Linea telegráfica
— Limite de provincias
— Caminos carreteros
— Id.de herradura
— Senderos

The Philippines

Following his victory over the Spanish fleet at Manila Bay during early May of 1898, Commodore George Dewey found himself cut off from any direct communication with Washington. News of his victory over the Spanish fleet would not reach President McKinley for days. The Spanish had refused to give Dewey access to their shoreside cable facilities and in an attempt to tap into that cable, Dewey had ordered that it be grappled up from the bottom of the bay. While trying to recover the cable, it was severed, rendering it useless both for the Americans and for the Spanish. The only communications link with Washington was through cable from Hong Kong, access to which required a steamer trip of almost six hundred miles from Manila. It was by such a courier vessel sent off to Hong Kong that Dewey reported his victory. A cable of congratulations along with the authorization for Dewey to hoist the pennant of a rear admiral was returned to Manila by the same courier vessel.

On May 6, the German warship *Irene* arrived at Manila Bay. Three days later, the German cruiser *Cormoran* arrived. Both German ships had tried entering the bay in defiance of the American's blockade line. Although *Irene* had been allowed to pass in without challenge, *Cormoran* had been stopped by a shot across her bow forcing her commander to formally request entry. Of the Germans' intention at Manila, Dewey was uncertain. He decided that the best policy would be an unbending firmness starting with a warning to the Germans against any and all interference with American activities. The Germans would be allowed to remain, but only as observers.[39]

A second worry for Dewey began taking form when on May 12 information reached him via Hong Kong that the Spanish were preparing a strong expeditionary force for the relief of the Philippines. Allegedly, it consisted of a squadron of modern warships in escort to troop transports with forty thousand Spanish troops aboard being routed eastward via Suez. That threat never materialized, but this was something which remained as another unknown for some time.[40]

The Spanish garrison then in occupation of Manila was nearly isolated. The remnant lines of contact the Spanish still retained with those outside the city's limits were diminishing daily. Dewey's fleet had sealed off approaches by sea, and the Filipino rebels were tightening a ring around the city on its landward side. The rebels were becoming bolder each day, some of their entrenchments reportedly encroaching into the city's outer suburban limits. Some weeks before Dewey's arrival, Oscar F. Williams, the U.S. Consul at Manila, had cabled Washington describing the situation which at that time was being faced by the Spanish. Not only was the rebel armed force growing stronger by the day, but mutiny was beginning to break out within some of the native regiments attached to the Spanish army. When the enlisted men of the regiment refused to participate in an attack against the rebels, the Spanish reacted by executing all of the unit's non-commissioned native officers. The remaining enlisted men

---

[39] One of the best accounts of Dewey's relationship with the German naval commander is to be found within Ivan Musicant, *Empire By Default,* (New York: Henry Holt and Co., 1998).

[40] The report which reached Dewey via the Hong Kong wireless station had as its origins the American Consul's Office at Lisbon which had cabled Washington: *Spanish Reserve Fleet sail 18th instant. Five auxiliary cruisers accompanying it with 40,000 troops. Every newspaper rumor believes for China Sea.* Although it would not be known to Dewey for some time, before the Spanish fleet cleared Suez, it was re-called to Spain because of the Spanish government's fear that an American fleet might attack the Spanish coast.

continued their refusal in defiance of Spanish orders. After being ordered into barracks, the men deserted en massé, taking their weapons with them. It had been the Consul's estimate that during the last week in March, some eight thousand armed rebels were at the outskirts of Manila. Within the entire archipelago, he believed that the Spanish troops had become outnumbered by a ratio of 20:1. The Spanish reaction to insurgency had developed itself into a rule by terror, a grisly example of which was the incarceration of rebel prisoners within cells fronting Manila Bay. These flooded at high tide effectively drowning their occupants. From his personal observations, the native population of the Philippines normally outdid itself in its friendliness toward Americans, but what remained a question was whether the revolutionary forces, or even the unaligned non-Spanish population would welcome a military occupation by the Americans. Only time and the taking of Manila could give the answer to that.

~

If the United States Army was to become an occupying force either at Manila or anywhere else in the Philippines, that was not to take place anytime soon judging from the delays which were being encountered at San Francisco. To get an army to the Philippines required ships, but the assemblage of ships at west coast ports was proving to be a difficult proposition for the Quartermaster. At the onset, it was realized that it would be impossible to send out an expedition in one integrated convoy. Also, a transpacific sealift was not of the short voyage tenure experienced by the force which invaded Cuba. The distance to the Philippines was immense -- almost 7,000 miles -- and it would be a voyage allowing for only one stop in the Hawaiian Islands to take on necessary coal. Not only were American ships of such long-haul endurance in short supply, but most of those which did exist were being currently employed on commercial routes. This meant that the Army would have to await the arrival back in port of those ships it wished to charter. Of necessity, this would occur over widely staggered intervals. To make matters more difficult, most of them were cargo/passenger types not easily adapted for mass troop use. Once the ships did become available, considerable work would be needed in order to make them usable. Taken altogether, the time delays to be faced added up to the fact that the expeditionary force could not be sailed to Manila for quite some time.

In a wire dated 18 May from San Francisco sent to the Adjutant General by Maj. Gen. Elwell S. Otis, there is an explanation of the limited arrangements which had been put into place up to that time. Otis had been given the hands-on responsibility of ordering the assembling and readying of those transports which could be gathered up for charter. He related to Washington that only three vessels considered suitable had so far been chartered: *City of Sydney*, *Australia*, and *City of Peking,* the last a Navy hire but which had available space to take on a few troops. Prior to being considered as adequate, each of these ships required fitting out with bunks, improvements to their ventilation systems, and new sanitation facilities, plus a number of assorted galley alterations. Even then, the estimated aggregate capacity for the three vessels was not over 175 officers and 2,500 enlisted men. Still then at sea, but reported to be arriving soon at San Francisco, were seven more steamers which, as claimed by their agents, were suitable for conversion into troopers. However, of that seven, only the owners of two of the seven ships reported due to arrive (*China* and *Colon*) had declared a willingness to charter. The owners of four others had protested that their ships would not be available at the time to the Army, meaning that they would probably require seizure if they were going to be used at all. (Authorization for seizure was later granted by the War Department in cases where a need arose.) The situation with the seventh ship was not referenced by Otis. Conferences held between the ships' owners, shipyard officials, and those Army officers who would be directly involved were of the collective opinion that once chartered, the two (whose owners expressed willingness to charter) would each require up to four weeks to be put into the required condition for the voyage.[41] What had started out as Otis's pessimistic appraisal of availability improved somewhat when it turned out that three other ships -- *Zealandia, Centennial,* and *Senator* -- would be in port within the next couple of weeks. Their owners were willing to charter; but like the *China* and *Colon,* the three ships would need extensive conversion work before going into troop service.

The only naval vessel on the west coast available to act as escort for the troopships was the cruiser *USS Charleston.* She was to wait at Honolulu for the first group of Army transports to sail from San Francisco. After the transports had coaled at Honolulu, they were to depart for Manila under *USS Charleston's* protection. Making up the first contingent would be *City of Peking,* 5,079 tons; *City of Sydney,* 3,000 tons; and *Australia,* 2,755 tons which in company sailed from San Francisco on May 25. Given command of that vanguard force was Brig. Gen. Thomas M. Anderson. After leaving Honolulu, the Anderson group was to touch at Guam where the commander of *USS Charleston* was to demand the surrender of that island's small Spanish garrison.[42] The next stop would be Manila. Anderson's command consisted of the 1st California Infantry; the 2nd Oregon Infantry; five companies of the 14th U.S. Infantry; a detachment of the California Heavy Artillery; and a small hospital detachment -- in all, 2,499 officers and men. A full month would pass before additional transports could be made ready. Lacking the availability, there would be no naval escort; however, the assessment by this time was that chances of encountering Spanish warships en route would be slight.

The general officer who had been assigned to lead the Manila expedition was Maj. Gen. Wesley Merritt, a West Pointer and a Civil War veteran who like most officers who stayed in the Army following the Civil War had seen extensive service campaigning against Indians in the west. The expedition's second in command, Maj. General Otis, had been a volunteer officer during the Civil War. He had entered the Regular Army following 1865, and like Merritt, he had campaign experience against the Indians. Merritt and Otis both possessed considerable staff and administrative experience in addition to that of field command. Merritt had been Superintendent at West Point, and Otis had been the founder of the School of Application for Infantry and Cavalry at Fort Leavenworth, Kansas.

Not only did the making ready of the transports present difficulties to the hard pressed team of Merritt and Otis, but so did the gathering together of regiments adequately equipped and trained. Unlike the Cuban campaign, the work

---

41   *The Dodge Commission Report,* Adjutant General from Otis, May 18, 1898.

42   Unaware that a state of war existed, the small Spanish garrison at Guam, taken by surprise, would surrender without a shot being fired.

which lay ahead in the Philippines was expected to last for a lengthy period, and a long-term overseas deployment was not a circumstance designed for short-term volunteers. The job required Regular Army troops, but what regiments there were, and which had not already been scheduled for the Cuban expedition, were performing essential duty in the western states. The Sioux Indians of the northern Great Plains, although by 1898 confined to reservations, still remained a focus for trouble which could erupt at any time. The Apaches in the Southwest had recently begun to argue among themselves, so they too required close surveillance. The War Department was trying its best to solicit interest for the relief of regular regiments by volunteer regiments from the various western states, but enthusiasm for guarding Indians was not a popular idea to volunteers anticipating a grand martial adventure overseas. Accordingly, pressure was being exerted by the various state governors in order that their state troops would be slated for the overseas expeditions.[43] As it would turn out, the bulk of troops initially sent to the Philippines came from state volunteer regiments -- their members being enlisted only for the duration of the war. Few of the volunteer regiments were adequately equipped, and none were properly trained.

On June 15, *Zealandia,* 2,730 tons; *China,* 5,000 tons; *Colon,* 2,700 tons; and *Senator,* 2,409 tons, sailed for the Philippines via a coaling stop at Honolulu. The designated senior officer for that second group was Brig. Gen. Francis V. Greene. With Greene were the 10th Pennsylvania Infantry; the 1st Colorado Infantry; the 1st Nebraska Infantry; a battalion of the 8th U.S. Infantry; a battalion from the 23rd U.S. Infantry; Batteries A and B from the Utah Artillery; and small detachments of U.S. Engineers and Medical Department personnel. There were also some civilian employees from the Post Office Department charged with organizing mail service for the Army once in the Philippines. The total number for this second contingent came to 3,540 officers and men. After their stop at Honolulu for coal, the ships touched at uninhabited Wake Island where a small landing party planted the United States flag, thus taking formal possession of that atoll.

The third contingent sailed for Manila on June 27 under the command of Brig. Gen. Arthur MacArthur on the transports *Morgan City* of 2,300 tons, *Ohio* of 3,488 tons, *Indiana* of 3,158 tons, *Valencia* of 1,598 tons, and *City of Para* of 3,532 tons.[44] This contingent left San Francisco in company on June 27, bound first for Honolulu to coal before proceeding toward their final destination. Aboard were four companies of the 23rd U.S. Infantry and that regiment's band; four companies of the 8th U.S. Infantry and its band; four batteries of the 3rd U.S. Artillery; a company of Army Engineers; the 13th Minnesota Infantry; two battalions of the 1st Idaho Infantry; two battalions of the 1st North Dakota Infantry; one battalion of the 1st Wyoming Infantry; detachments from the 1st Nebraska Infantry; a company of the Regular Army Signal Corps; the *Astor Battery* (a volunteer outfit); and a detachment of Hospital Corps personnel. The transport *Newport* of 2,735 tons sailed the following day with

---

[43]   *Correspondence Relating to the War with Spain,* Vol. II, p 689, Assistant Adjutant General Carter to Maj. General Merritt, Washington, June 4, 1898.

[44]   Arthur MacArthur was a winner of the Medal of Honor, earned for valorous for conduct at the Civil War Battle of Murfreesboro. Of the four generals who would initially be under Merritt, MacArthur was to have the longest term of influence on the islands. His son, the then 9-year-old Douglas, would carry on the MacArthur family impact well into the mid-twentieth century.

Maj. General Merritt and his staff aboard. This third contingent, inclusive of those aboard *Newport,* numbered 4,847 Army personnel and 35 civilian employees.

The total of Merritt's expedition consisting of the three contingents was organized as the VIII Army Corps. In all, it mustered 10,916 officers and men. Considering the uncertainty of the Spanish strength which was to be expected in the islands, this was far from being an overpowering force. The lack of troop strength provided to Merritt could probably have resulted in a defeat had Spanish reinforcements arrived from Spain as a challenge to Dewey's presence. Fortunately, the Spanish squadron had turned back before transiting the Suez Canal leaving some badly demoralized countrymen in occupation at Manila. When Merritt left San Francisco, he had no way of knowing what the enemy situation was. The VIII Army Corps sailed westward toward a decidedly uncertain future.

It was not until the month prior to his own departure for the Philippines that Merritt was made privy to the policy under which he would be charged to operate once the Spanish were defeated and an American occupation of the islands began. Developed personally by President McKinley, the rules for occupation were forwarded to Merritt in San Francisco by the Secretary of War. Their essentials read as follows:

> *The first effect of the military occupation of the enemy's territory is the severance of the former political relations of the inhabitants and the establishment of a new political power...*
>
> *It will therefore be the duty of the commander of the expedition, immediately upon his arrival in the islands, to publish a proclamation declaring that we come, not to make war upon the people of the Philippines nor upon any party or faction among them, but to protect them in their homes, in their employment, and in their personal and religious rights...*
>
> *Our occupation should be as free from severity as possible...*
>
> *Though the powers of the military occupant are absolute and supreme and immediately operate upon the political condition of the inhabitants, the municipal laws of the conquered territory, such as effects private rights of persons and property and provide for the punishment of crime, are considered as continuing in force, so far as they are compatible with the new order of things, until they are suspended or superseded by the occupying belligerent; and in practice they are not abrogated, but are allowed to remain in force and to be administered by the ordinary tribunals substantially as they were before the occupation...*
>
> *The freedom of the people to pursue their accustomed occupations will be abridged only when it may be necessary to do so...*
>
> *While the rule of conduct of the American commander in chief will be such as has just been defined, it will be his duty to adopt measures of a different kind if, unfortunately, the course of the people should render such measures indispensable to the maintenance of law and order. He will then possess the power to replace or expel the native officials in part or altogether, to substitute new courts of his own constitution for those that now exist, or to create such or supplementary tribunals as may be necessary...*
>
> *The real property of the state he may hold and administer, at the same time enjoying the revenues thereof, but he is not to destroy it save in the case of military necessity. All public means of transportation such as telegraph lines, cables, railways, and boats belonging to the state, may be appropriated to his own use...*
>
> *Means of transportation such as telegraph lines and cables, railways and boats, may, although they belong to private individuals, or corporations, be seized by the military occupant but unless destroyed are not to be retained...*

> *As the result of military occupation the taxes and duties payable by the inhabitants of the former government become payable to the military occupier unless he sees fit to substitute for them other rates or modes of contribution to the expenses of the government. The moneys so collected are to be used for the purposes of paying the expenses of government under the military occupation; such as the salaries of the judges and the police, and for the expenses of the army.* [45]

Nowhere in McKinley's instructions was there to be found a hint of how long the American occupation of the Philippines was to last, or of any intent on the part of the United States toward creating a framework of self rule for the native population. Whether the American occupation was to constitute an expansion of America's power into the western Pacific through annexation of the Philippines remained at that juncture an undecided issue. The decision as to how the United States was to handle itself in the western Pacific Basin would depend in large part upon the future posturing of those European powers with interests there. Those nations included Great Britain, France, and Germany -- they being the principle players -- although a concern would soon arise as to Japanese intentions as well.

In the spring of 1898, the McKinley Administration had yet to question the economic potential of the Philippines. Could it become an asset, or would it be a liability to an occupying power? To a great extent, this of course would have to depend on native acceptance when the actual occupation began taking place. An unwilling population could necessitate the maintenance of a large military presence in the islands, and that could become uncomfortably costly. Within the American Congress, sentiments for annexation had begun to take root well prior to Merritt's departure from San Francisco. A leading senator, Henry Cabot Lodge, had imperialistically proclaimed, *Where the flag once goes up it must never come down.* [46] But the final answer for the Philippines -- at least for the short term -- was to rest with President McKinley. The historian Ephraim K. Smith, writing in *Crucible of Empire*, has exhaustively examined the *historiographic debate* which over the years has developed among historians dealing with McKinley's decision-making over what to do with the islands once the Spanish were evicted. Smith's own conclusion is that McKinley remained indecisive even up to the time of Merritt's actual arrival at Manila. By way of reinforcing that belief, Smith points to a news story that was published in the *Christian Advocate* during January of 1899 in which the writer quoted McKinley:

> *The truth is I didn't want the Philippines, and when they came to us, as a gift from the gods, I did not know what to do with them ...One late night it came to me...It would be cowardly and dishonorable to return the Philippines to Spain and it would be bad business and discreditable to turn them over to our commercial rivals...and that the Filipinos were unfit for self government.* [47]

---

[45]   *Correspondence Relating to the War with Spain*, Vol. II, p 676, President McKinley to Secretary of War, dated The White House, May 19, 1898.

[46]   O'Toole, p 383.

[47]   Ephraim K. Smith, "William McKinley's Enduring Legacy," essay within *Crucible of Empire, The Spanish-American War and Its Aftermath,* edited by James C. Bradford, (Annapolis, MD: Naval Institute Press, 1993).

Religion may have also played a part in what some Americans believed was the white man's obligation to civilize the Philippine people through the promotion of Christianity. The leader who commanded the revolutionaries on Luzon who were then threatening the Spanish at Manila was considered by those who had studied him to be anti-Christian. Whether that was accurate remains an unknown. Actually, Catholicism had been a strong factor for years on Luzon as well as in some parts of the other islands; but as a church structure, it was heavily dominated by the Spanish Jesuits, a circumstance which the natives resented. The indigenous populations in some sections of Luzon and also throughout parts of the other islands of the archipelago were clearly antagonistic in their relationships with the Jesuits. On Luzon, a recent note of urgency had developed over the safety of the Spanish monks residing in Cavite Province, a political jurisdiction which bordered the Manila area. The Adjutant General's Office in Washington notified Merritt shortly after his arrival in Manila Bay that the monks as well as Spanish civil prisoners being held by the rebels were in immediate danger of being put to death.[48] This news was widely disseminated by the American press, resulting in wide support for annexation. Walter Millis, the author of *The Martial Spirit,* makes the argument that despite some pre-1898 beliefs over the potential importance of southwest Asian markets, annexation of the Philippines had never been given consideration in that regard before the summer of 1898.[49] What seems to have been ignored by the majority of historians, including Millis, who have debated United States decision-making over the pros and cons of annexation of the Philippines has been the long-standing relationship of American commercial interests with those islands. For some years prior to 1860, the only international banking houses operating in the Philippines were American firms.[50]

~

The troops which constituted the three elements of Maj. General Merritt's command, all of which had sailed from San Francisco before the end of June 1898, were the only units which would arrive in the Philippines in time to participate in the taking of Manila. Troops which arrived in the Philippines following the surrender of that city and up to the beginning of September were designated as part of Merritt's VIII Army Corps. Those units left San Francisco between July 16 and July 29. Each of the transports which carried those last contingents would be independently routed. Transports involved were the chartered ships *City of Puebla* of 2,623 tons, *Peru* of 3,500 tons, *Pennsylvania* of 3,166 tons, *Rio de Janeiro* of 3,548 tons, and *St. Paul* of 2,440 tons. *Scandia* and the *Arizona* -- having been purchased by the Army and respectively renamed, *Warren* and *Hancock* -- sailed for Manila with troops and military supplies during early August.[51]

---

[48] *Correspondence Relating to the War with Spain*, Vol. II, p 743, Adjutant General to Maj. General Merritt, August 1, 1898.

[49] Walter Millis, *The Martial Spirit, A Study of Our War with Spain*, (Chicago: Ivan R. Dee, 1989), p 339.

[50] Max L. Tornow, "The Economic Condition of the Philippines," *National Geographic Magazine,* (Vol. X, No. 2, February 1899), p 51.

[51] Hawaii was annexed by the United States during July of 1898. The original garrison assigned to Hawaiian duty during July of 1898 was booked aboard regularly scheduled ships serving those islands. Three such ships were *Mariposa, Lakme,* and the *Charles Nelson.*

~

By the time of Brig. General Anderson's appearance on the scene and well before Merritt's arrival, the situation at Manila had become badly confused. The major problem facing the American command came not from the Spanish then in possession of the city, nor from the presence of the German warships, but rather, it lay with how to deal with the local revolutionary leader Emilio Aguinaldo. On July 24, Aguinaldo had protested to Anderson that American troops were not to set foot in areas then under the control of Aguinaldo's troops unless he or one of his generals granted permission. Anderson ignored this by not replying, deciding to await Merritt's decision on how to handle Aguinaldo.

Following Rear Admiral Dewey's victory at Manila Bay but before Merritt or Anderson's arrival, Dewey had ordered part of his fleet's Marine force to occupy the Spanish naval base at Cavite. The base there was ideally situated for defense, being built on an appendix-like land feature jutting out into Manila Bay from the coast of Luzon. When Anderson's vanguard contingent reached Manila and following his immediate briefing of the situation by Dewey, Anderson made it his first order of business to relieve the Marines at Cavite. The Army troops were offloaded from the transports on to the ships' lifeboats which were then taken under tow by the Navy's steam launches. Once ashore at Cavite, Anderson's men were billeted in the former Spanish naval barracks. The barracks proved hot and terribly crowded but certainly were more livable than had been the accommodations on the transports. Or so it seemed at first. Within a few hours after being settled in, a wind shift off the bay brought with it a putrefying odor which, when traced to its source, proved to be from bubbles rising to the surface from the hulks of the Spanish warships sunk by Dewey in the naval battle of early May. The gaseous odors brought up by the bubbles were from the decaying bodies of the over one hundred dead Spaniards who had gone down with their ships. It must have been a bad initiation for troops expecting momentarily to go into battle.

When Merritt later arrived and was briefed by Anderson, the senior general decided that discussions would not be conducted with Aguinaldo until after the American army had taken possession of the city. In the interest of keeping the rebel leader at arm's length, Merritt decided that VIII Army Corps would take Manila without assistance and that he would follow a policy of rejecting any offer made by the rebels, including that of military cooperation with the Americans. This last, as will be seen, would not be completely adhered to.

Prior to Merritt's arrival, Anderson had sent a reconnaissance patrol from Cavite to examine the approaches to Manila. On its return, it reported that the distance to the Spanish lines was about seventeen miles by a road no better than a carabao track. It also reported that Aguinaldo's troops were well dug in just short of the Spanish entrenchments. The difficulties of the route, coupled with the nauseating odors coming off the bay, caused Anderson to decide to move most of the American force closer to the Spanish lines. Selected was the beach village of Tambo which was about two miles from a section of the rebel trenches which directly faced the Spanish defensive perimeter. These rebel positions would have to be passed over before any assault against the city could be contemplated. This was a problem for Merritt to deal with when the time arrived for a decision.

The move from Cavite to Tambo was made by water utilizing cargo barges called *cascos* which were chartered from their native owners. Although the offings of the Tambo beach were reef free, the shallows off the beach reached out a considerable distance. Rear Admiral Dewey, continuing the Navy's spirit of cooperation, provided his ships' launches to tow the cascos to the beach. Information gained from the locals was that the surf was a constant one and although only of moderate amplitude, it was usually bad enough to make dry landings on the strand a difficult proposition. It was found that in order to bring the cascos in close enough to unload, they had to be cast loose from the towing launches offshore of the surf line, at which point the anchors were dropped, the crews paying out their anchor lines so as to gradually let the surge of the surf push the cascos close to the beach but just short of grounding out. The troops could then wade onto the dry sand -- the wading method was also employed to bring supplies ashore. Once offloaded, the cascos were man-hauled by their anchor rodes out past the surf line at which point the launches would again take them under tow for the return trip to Cavite and another load of troops, or to the transports for supplies. Many of the cascos broached broadsides in the surf, with everything and everyone aboard becoming soaked. At those times when surf and tidal conditions made it impossible to bring the cascos in close, small row boats had to be used to shuttle people and materiel onto the beach. It was anything but a perfect set-up.

With his men on the beach, Anderson established an encampment on the outskirts of Tambo which was christened Camp Dewey. Soon to be added to the buildup there were the troops of Maj. General Greene's command whose transports arrived on July 17. The landings over the beach had now become a near continuous operation carried on as long as a glimmer of light remained in the sky. To speed things up, two steam launches were chartered from local owners. Dewey continued to provide two launches, but he restricted that to stated periods of time. This at times conflicted with the Navy's own needs, producing friction between the involved parties. One such instance occurred when Lt. Colonel Pope, who was the quartermaster in charge of getting men and supplies into the beach at Tambo, hailed a Navy launch operator and asked him to transport some sick soldiers from Camp Dewey to a temporary Army hospital which had been set up at Cavite. The sailor operating the launch shouted back, *Who the devil are you anyway?* Pope answered, *I'm Colonel Pope, the Chief Quartermaster.* To that the launch operator yelled back, *To Hell with the Pope; I take my orders from Admiral Dewey. Get out of the way or I'll swamp you.* [52] When the *Newport* came into the bay on July 25 and Merritt made his personal landing the next day, he suffered the indignity of being carried piggy-back onto the

---

[52]   William T. Sexton, *Soldiers in the Sun, An American Adventure in Imperialism* (Published by author at Fort Leavenworth, KS, 1939; reprint, Freeport, NY: Books for Libraries Press), p 33. The Lt. Colonel Pope mentioned was not fully identified by Sexton, but we believe him to have been James Worden Pope, West Point, Class of 1864, who was appointed lieutenant colonel of volunteers in 1898 being named "*a chief expeditionary quartermaster.*" Heitman, Vol. I, p 798. Details of the landing methods used at Tambo have largely been taken from *Annual Report of the Major General Commanding the Army,* Part 2 of 3, 1899, Government Printing Office, 1899.

beach by a native worker. Pope, anticipating having to face a disgruntled Merritt, began looking for a better landing site. He found one about three miles south of Tambo near the outlet of a small river. The river's discharge flowed into the bay over an entrance bar which when sounded was found to be adequate in depth to bring the launches and the cascos into the river but only at those times near high tide. Close inside the entrance was a small pier which was large enough to accommodate two cascos for unloading. Awaiting the time of high tide to cross the bar was an inconvenience, but it proved no more time consuming than offloading through the surf at Tambo beach. Shortages of cascos had at first been a handicap; but when word spread of the high charter rates being paid by the Americans, more than enough natives were willing to rent them. Best of all, the quartermasters were able to charter the sidewheel steamer *Kwong Hoi* which had a shallow enough draft to cross the entrance bar at anything except the lowest tide conditions.

~

A command decision was now reached over the most serious problem: How to deal with Aguinaldo without making him an active partner. The rebel leader had his troops well organized, and by now they were established in trenches which entirely ringed Manila. To cross those trenches without triggering a confrontation with the rebels would, it seemed, require Aguinaldo's permission -- something which Merritt deplored. Nevertheless, it began to appear imperative that some form of communication had to be established between Aguinaldo and the American command. It was decided that the wisest way to handle the matter would be for Merritt to personally remain aloof, leaving any direct contact with Aguinaldo in the hands of subordinates. In any event, before an assault against the Spanish lines could take place, Merritt would have to await the arrival of regiments from the third contingent of transports under Brig. Gen. Arthur MacArthur --those transports being still in transit. Merritt knew he would be badly outnumbered by the Spanish even with the addition of MacArthur's troops. If forced into an armed confrontation with Aguinaldo prior to the surrender of the Spanish, the situation could become militarily impossible.

On August 4, the transports of MacArthur's contingent pulled into Manila Bay. Considerable discussion then took place between the American commanders as to what might happen if Aguinaldo's men should enter the city on the heels of the conquering American forces. Almost certainly, widespread looting would occur, and there might even be a blood bath directed by the rebels against the hated Spanish. If that should happen, then the United States would share much of the blame in the eyes of world opinion. Taken into consideration were talks which Dewey had opened with the Spanish commander prior to the Army's arrival. These had been conducted through the medium of the British Consul who, because of his neutral status, had free movement in and out of the city. During May, the British Consul became incapacitated by illness and turned his role as intermediary over to the Belgian Consul. Through that liaison, it had become clear that the Spanish commander recognized the inevitability of an American victory, a realization which grew stronger once he realized that a relief expedition was not coming to his aid. Like the Americans, he feared what might happen if Aguinaldo and his men ever got into Manila. The problem remaining was how to cross through the rebel lines. Delegated to the job of resolving that conundrum, Anderson worked at developing a friendly communication with Aguinaldo's subordinate general whose section of line lay between Anderson's own and the Spanish defensive perimeter. Out of that effort came that officer's willingness -- with Aguinaldo's concurrence -- to allow American troops to take over a part of the rebel trenches from which the Americans would launch their attack against the city. Within an hour after Anderson shifted his division into those vacated entrenchments, Spanish rifle fire erupted. The firing continued intermittently over the span of the three days. Meanwhile, through the Belgian Consul, terms were explored under which the Spanish commander would agree to surrender. He stated his willingness to run up the white flag but only after making a brief resistance in order to salve Spain's (and his own) honor. It was tacitly agreed by Merritt's staff officer who was handling these arrangements that the Americans would actively prevent the entry of Aguinaldo's troops into the city.

On August 14, the American attack against Manila began. Spanish resistance, as agreed upon, was light. In less than five hours resistance had totally stopped, following which some fast footwork on the part of both the Spanish and the Americans was employed toward keeping out the rebel forces -- all of it accomplished without triggering any serious incidents between the rebels and the Americans. By the end of the day, a draft of interim surrender terms was on paper. In that draft, the Spanish commander ceded to the Americans the city of Manila along with all military outposts located on Manila Bay and all public property in the region. In all, twelve thousand Spanish military personnel and their weaponry were to be surrendered. The Spanish soldiers were to be paroled under the control of their own officers to wait upon the terms of a formal surrender as agreed to by the government in Spain.[53] As Merritt was to later discover, his conquest of Manila had taken place four days after peace negotiations had been initiated between the United States and Spain. Since Manila had been taken with a minimum of casualties on either side, no one involved could have suffered any remorse over the timing.

Once the telegraph cable which Dewey's men had earlier severed was repaired by Army Signal Corps troops, cable communication became available directly with Hong Kong which in turn had a cable connection with the United States. This meant a communication's savings of many days, affording both Merritt and Dewey the luxury of passing along for the approval of their respective Washington superiors an assortment of vexing political questions which would develop following the American takeover.

~

All told, the operations in the Pacific had come off much better than had originally been expected. Unlike many of the deficiencies which had surrounded the sealifts to Cuba and to Puerto Rico, the shipments of men and materiel from San Francisco to Manila had been relatively problem free. There had been inadequacies, of course, but these had all been relatively minor, surprisingly so in light of the huge distances that had been involved with the Pacific operation. Of the difficulties which did occur, most were not directly attributable to those charged with ship acquisition or

---

[53]   The formal surrender terms would include the repatriation of the Spanish to Spain at American expense. A similar surrender condition had been granted to the Spaniards in Cuba as well as in Puerto Rico.

the preparation of the ships for sea. One discomforting episode during transit had involved infestations from lice brought aboard with the troops. When the lice problem became severe following departure from the coaling stopover at Honolulu, eradication involved the application of high pressure steam to the men's underclothing. The treatment killed the lice, but in the process the underclothing disintegrated.[54] Since many of the units had only been issued one set of underclothes per man, it takes little imagination to appreciate the discomfort of those having no chaffing protection between their skin and their coarse britches. Another shipboard problem -- this one directly charged against equipment integral to many of the chartered ships -- concerned their built-in cold storage facilities. In general, these systems had not been designed to handle the hot conditions of the Southwest Pacific; consequently, the temperatures within the storage rooms rose once tropical waters were reached, resulting in high rates of meat spoilage. Those ships without mechanical refrigeration systems had similar problems with spoilage of meats which had been packed in layers of ice, the ice melting well before arrival in the Philippines. There were also complaints of inadequate ventilation in the troop compartments despite the widespread use of canvas wind scoops rigged to direct air below. On *Zealandia*, the quality of the water was reported as being very poor. Despite these problems, the health of the troops had generally been satisfactory. There were a handful of typhoid cases, but only one death took place en route, that being due to appendicitis. As might have been expected, there were a few instances of friction between ships' officers and the passenger Army officers. Most of these were traced to misunderstandings as to where one group's authority took over and the other's left off. A few of the senior troop commanders complained about over-crowded troop accommodations, a condition which should have been anticipated and well understood prior to departure but was probably unavoidable due to the exigency of the sealift. The performance of the transport masters in Anderson's group of transports which left in the vanguard under the convoy protection of *USS Charleston* resulted in complaints from the Navy over poor station-keeping and improper signal procedures. Out of that complaint as well as similar ones which followed Shafter's expedition to Cuba came the recommendation that regulations be promulgated through agreements between the services for the proper procedures to be followed by transport masters while in naval convoy.

~

From the experience gained during the Atlantic and Pacific sealifts as conducted from May through August of 1898, the War Department determined that the Army needed its own fleet of ships if American forces overseas were to be adequately served. A formal declaration of that need was included within the *Report of the Secretary of War for 1898* wherein it was stated to the Congress that a permanent transportation system should be organized for movement of troops by sea.

It soon became clear, following the occupation of Manila, that an American presence in the islands would be of considerable duration and that it would require the support of a sizable sealift. Experience had shown that once ships were purchased for use as transports, they almost always needed a great deal of alteration

---

[54] *Correspondence Relating to the War with Spain,* Vol. II, p 777, Report of Brig. General Anderson to the Adjutant General, Washington, July 9, 1898. Received August 29, 1898.

before going into troop service. This would mean a time lag which in the interim required the charter of commercial bottoms. After hostilities ended with the Spanish, chartering opportunities for the Army widened over what they had been. This was because the law which had prohibited the War Department from utilizing ships of foreign registry was applicable only during times when the United States was in open contention with a foreign power. Once the Spanish had surrendered, such prohibition no longer applied, and foreign bottoms under charter were utilized extensively by the Army until 1902. After that time, the Army's shipping needs in the Pacific lessened to a marked degree, and most sealift needs were handled by the Army's own ships.

SS *Seneca.* Chartered by the Army for the 1898 expedition to Cuba. *Seneca's* capacity was approximately 686 officers and men. National Archives Collection.

SS *Yucatan*. Chartered transport showing troops being rowed ashore in ship's boat during 1898 landings at Siboney, Cuba. *Yucatan* carried Lt. Col. Theodore Roosevelt and his *Rough Riders*. *Yucatan's* troop capacity was a little over 800 officers and men. National Archives Collection.

Deck scene aboard time chartered *SS Rio Grande* en route to 1898 invasion of Cuba. Troops here are Regular Army cavalrymen. National Archives Collection.

Unloading horses. The number of anchored ships in the background makes the scene probably offlying Siboney during the 1898 invasion of Cuba. National Archives Collection.

SS *Peru*. Time chartered for the 1898 expedition to Manila. *Peru* had a rated capacity of 1050 officers and men; crowded as the photograph shows. National Archives Collection.

CHAPTER II

INITIATING CONTROL AND SUPPLY OF
THE PHILIPPINES, 1898 - 1899

The warlike events which involved the American military with the native populations of the Philippines started shortly after the Spanish surrender and did not completely come to an end until 1913, if counting in operations against the Moro sultans located on Mindanao. Operations up to 1903 have been termed *the Philippine Insurrection.* After that, the Army would refer to its Philippine operations as *the Pacification period.*

~

Since the sixteenth century, Spain had held power in the Philippines. It had first made its presence felt in 1565, when it began an occupation that lasted over 300 years.[1] Control throughout the three centuries of Spanish rule had been less than complete. On many of the islands, Spanish domination had never extended much beyond the coastal fringes. Beyond such enclaves, the only direct contact that the Spanish had with the native populations was through the Jesuits, and even that contact was more often than not less than authoritative. During the mid-nineteenth century an educated native elite had begun to emerge and from that group arose leaders desirous of throwing off the Spanish yoke. Starting in 1896, a rebellion broke out, headed by

---

[1]   The Philippine Islands were discovered by Magellan in 1521. A Spanish colony was established on the island of Cebu in 1565. Luzon was occupied in 1570 when Spain established a colony at what was to become the city of Manila. The Spanish began a trade route inaugurated in the last quarter of the sixteenth century that ran between Manila and Acapulco, Mexico. (The British had attacked and occupied Manila in the 1760s but only held it for a short period before returning it to the Spanish.)

Emilio Aguinaldo; the same leader who was now bedeviling Merritt.[2] The events which followed the taking of Manila by the American army in 1898 -- at least in the eyes of the majority of the islands' indigenous populations -- became nothing less than a continuity of the former Spanish occupation.

By way of retrospect, it is probably accurate to state that the American struggle against the followers of Aguinaldo (the Insurgents) could have been avoided had the United States offered them the independence of the islands in exchange for the grant of a naval base somewhere on Luzon. The obvious choice for such a base would have been either at Cavite, annexed together with those land features guarding Manila's approaches, or at Subic Bay on the west coast of Luzon. Rear Adm. George Dewey thought Subic Bay was more easily defensible than Manila Bay, and Dewey was the leading advocate for that choice. A recognition of Philippine sovereignty in return for naval base rights would have almost certainly appealed at the time to Aguinaldo, particularly if the offer had included a treaty with the United States guaranteeing military protection for the entirety of the Philippines. The practicality of that idea was marred by the fact -- certainly obvious to the American command on the scene -- that Aguinaldo's movement had a limited allegiance which was largely restricted to the population of the island of Luzon and to a limited extent on Mindoro. There were a number of reasons for this, not the least of which was that the southern islands had little political or cultural identification with Aguinaldo's followers. To have expected that Aguinaldo could have exerted his sovereignty over the entirety of the Philippine archipelago would have been a forlorn hope -- one which the McKinley Administration had been made aware by Merritt. If the Philippine Islands were to ever become a stabilized political grouping it would require a steady and powerful hand well into the future. It was also obvious that if the United States did not annex the entirety of the Philippines but instead settled for only a naval base on Luzon (as Dewey had advocated), another power, most likely Germany or, given time, Japan, would have laid claim to the other islands of the archipelago. The justification for their doing that would have been the accurate argument that the islands to the south of Luzon possessed only fragmented and very localized tribal rule. From the viewpoint of the United States, considerable logic rested with an argument that should Germany or Japan become an occupant on any part of the archipelago, then the value to the United States of a naval base either at Manila or at Subic Bay would become strategically compromised.[3] A foreign presence would have been especially serious if the occupying force was Japan. Japanese interest in the Philippines was a long-standing one. Even before the discovery of the islands by Magellan in 1521, the Japanese had founded temporary colonies on northern Luzon. In the mid-1800s they had begun large scale development of hemp plantations on the island of Mindanao where, by the decade of the 1890s, they were firmly established as part of the local business community.

~

---

[2] Within the military correspondence of that era, Aguinaldo's troops as well as other indigenous groups actively opposing the American occupation would no longer be called "rebels," but rather were named "Insurgents."

[3] R. E. Welch, *Response to Materialism,* (Chapel Hill: University of North Carolina Press, 1979), p 9.

While the Americans at Manila were wondering how to handle the Aguinaldo problem, peace talks between Spain and the United States were being conducted in Paris. The United States envoys opened those talks by offering $20 million dollars for Puerto Rico and the Philippines. After some wrangling, Spain agreed on that price which was to be incorporated into the peace Accords which were signed that December. The Accords were subsequently ratified by the United States Senate on February 3, 1899. With their ratification, the United States became the owner of what would soon prove to be a contentious chunk of real estate -- difficult and expensive to manage as its logistical support would have to stretch all the way to the continental United States.

~

Prior to their surrender, the Spanish at Manila had been surrounded by Aguinaldo's army. Now, it became the American's turn to be surrounded. Confrontation with the Insurgents began to take an open militant form following a series of incidents aimed at the American occupation of the city. Wars or uprisings usually develop out of small incidents, and the volatile situation at Manila was to be no exception. The most serious aspect of the encirclement was that Aguinaldo controlled Manila's water supply, and he could shut it off at will.

Maj. Gen. Wesley Merritt soon departed the scene, having been ordered to Paris to take part in the peace negotiations. The Philippine command then fell upon Maj. Gen. Elwell S. Otis. On September 8, 1898, Otis issued an ultimatum which ordered Aguinaldo to remove his troops from the city's outskirts or face retaliation if this was not done immediately. Aguinaldo in turn counter-threatened, stating that he would meet force with force. He later softened this a bit by writing Otis that if the American order was changed to a *request,* this might help mollify the *patriotic feelings of my men* and thus avoid an open confrontation. Otis agreed and subsequently toned down the September 8 order. The Insurgents then pulled back except for one of Aguinaldo's generals, Pio del Pilar, who refused to budge. Aguinaldo would claim that he personally ordered del Pilar to withdraw, but that del Pilar had ignored the order. True or false? Probably the former. In any event, del Pilar was looking for trouble as over the next few days, his patrols repeatedly crossed over into the American sector to commit acts of robbery as well as to perpetrate a series of kidnappings of Manila's citizens against whom del Pilar, had complaints. The final straw came in early October when Brig. Gen. Thomas M. Anderson and three of his officers, allegedly on a sightseeing excursion on the Pasig River, were detained by del Pilar's pickets. Anderson reported to Otis what had happened:

> *I have the honor to report that yesterday, while proceeding up the Pasig River in the steam launch* Canacao *with three officers of my staff, the American flag flying over the boat, I was stopped by an armed Filipino guard and informed that we could go no farther. Explaining that we were an unarmed party of American officers out upon an excursion, we were informed that by orders given two days*

before, no Americans, armed or unarmed, were allowed to pass up the Pasig River without a special permit from President Aguinaldo. [4]

Upon inquiring of the Insurgent guard officer as to the authority under which he was being halted, Anderson was told that it was on the direct orders of Aguinaldo. A copy of the order was handed to Anderson, and indeed, its origins read as coming from Aguinaldo. Whether or not Aguinaldo was truly behind that prohibition could not be ascertained, but that uncertainty was only temporary as events soon made it clear that Aguinaldo had no intention of knuckling under to the American army.

Besides trying to guess what was going on in the Insurgent leader's mind, Otis had other worries as well. With the War With Spain at an end, the officers and men of the state volunteer regiments who but a few months before had so eagerly volunteered for martial glory against Spain were now clamoring to go home. As some of them coarsely put it, they had signed up to fight the Spanish, not a bunch of *goo-goos*. Otis realized that if the presence of the United States was ever to reach beyond the environs of Manila, he would need an army dedicated for that task. The War Department agreed, but it would not be until July of the following year (1899) that Congress would act to authorize new regiments specifically enlisted for service in the Philippine Islands.[5] It would of course take time to recruit, train, and ship out these new regiments, a process which would not be entirely accomplished until late in the fall of 1899. For the time being, any difficulty involving the Aguinaldo forces would have to be handled by those Regular Army regiments together with any state volunteer outfits that Otis had at hand.

Outbreak of Hostilities at Manila

In early February of 1899, open warfare broke out between Aguinaldo's men and American troops. In the suburbs of Manila, an American sentry fired on a native who attempted to pass a picket post without stopping on challenge. During that night, scattered firing took place between the pickets of both sides. The next day, Insurgents attacked in strength along part of the American perimeter. They were repulsed after suffering heavy casualties. Otis ordered a counter attack which resulted in more losses to the Insurgents but with close to three hundred killed and wounded on the American side. Believing that he could not hold his positions, Aguinaldo withdrew his entire force moving it well beyond the city's suburbs and out into the countryside.

---

[4]   *Annual Reports of the War Department for the Fiscal year Ended June 30, 1899,* Vol 5. Testimony, 56th Congress, 1st Session as quoted by Sexton, pp 67,68. The title of "President" had been bestowed on Aguinaldo by the Insurgent Congress.

[5]   The regiments which would be organized for special duty limited to the Philippines were not considered by Congress to be additions to the Regular Army. Instead, they were given temporary status for the duration of hostilities against the Insurgents. Assigned numerical identity, the regimental designations ran from the 26th through the 49th. Of these units, the 36th and the 37th Infantry, together with the 11th Cavalry were recruited from Spanish War veterans of the state regiments then in the Philippine Islands during the time frame when those units were awaiting repatriation. The rest of the new regiments were to be enlisted in the United States. The 48th and 49th Infantry were to be "colored;" the remainder were to be white. The temporary regiments would be officered by Regular Army officers as well as by those commissioned personnel from the Spanish War's state regiments who wished to stay in the Army, provided that their past performance warranted that retention. A number of such officers would later successfully apply for retention as Regular Army officers.

Otis did not follow. He feared an uprising at Manila in the belief that sending an adequate force after Aguinaldo would weaken his position in the city. That worry proved without foundation. As soon as Aguinaldo's departure became known, the city's population wanted no part in resisting the American occupation. In fact, they seemed relieved that Aguinaldo had vacated the scene, thus removing any uncertainty in the population's collective mind that the United States would remain. For Manila's residents, the presence of Americans meant stability. No longer did they have to split their allegiance for fear of a possible American defeat. The major hope for Manila's residents was for improved economic conditions, something which had clearly not existed during the last years of Spanish rule and which most of them did not think an Aguinaldo regime could provide either.

In the early fall of 1898, transports carrying some Regular Army units and the remaining state volunteer regiments that had originally been slated as part of Merritt's VIII Army Corps had arrived at Manila. The tenure of the state regiments in the Philippines would be short-lived as they had been enlisted only until the War With Spain ended. They did, however, give Otis enough troop strength to conduct limited field operations. It was his hope that he could first pacify Luzon before tackling the more southern islands. Fortunately at the time, the Spanish commanders on the other islands had expressed a willingness to remain in place until properly relieved by American troops, but all of a sudden, those helpful promises began evaporating. The reneging started with the Spanish commander at the port town of Iloilo on Panay who announced through an officer messenger that he planned to evacuate Iloilo and bring his command by ship to Manila, there to await repatriation to Spain. No sooner had word gotten around Iloilo that the Spanish troops were leaving than a panic started among the local population which feared that if the Spanish left before the Americans could take over, anarchy would result. To try and encourage an early American occupation, the city fathers put together a delegation which appeared before Otis at Manila to plead their case. Having no choice, if he was to be taken seriously by the Philippine people, Otis responded by ordering that three transports with a brigade of infantry be made ready to sail for Iloilo. Because of the problems on Luzon, the equation there became much more complex. Not only would any operations on Luzon be deprived of a full brigade of sorely needed troops, but Luzon was itself on the threshold of total disorder, a situation separate and apart from the Aguinaldo insurgency. Spanish units from locations scattered throughout Luzon had begun coming into Manila to surrender. Their departures from what had been orderly Spanish garrison towns left behind power vacuums which were quickly filled by gangs of brigands which began preying on the peasantry. (Brigands were referred to in the Philippines as *landrones*.) If the majority of the populace was to look upon American power as a welcome presence, the kind of lawlessness which was now taking place had to be brought under control; but Otis simply did not have the troop resources to bring that about. There was, though, a positive side to the dilemma as reports began coming in that the landrones were falsely representing themselves as being allied with Aguinaldo. This began to sour a good part of the peasantry against the Aguinaldo forces.

Desperately trying to arrange field deployments where they were most needed, Otis received a further shock. Friendly traders returning from some of the islands to the south brought word to him that certain Spanish merchants believed to be cooperating with the Americans were now telling the natives that when the Americans took over, they could expect a much harsher rule than that which had been imposed under the old Spanish regime. For whatever reason, the Spanish had apparently decided against any further cooperation with American forces. Perhaps they viewed what seemed to be a developing rebellion against the Americans as sweet revenge for Spain's defeat by the United States. On the last day of 1898, Otis's adjutant transmitted a report to Washington informing that all the Spanish garrisons in the Philippines, except for the post at Zamboanga on Mindanao, had been closed down and that the Spanish garrisons had either arrived at Manila or were in transit to that city.

New Years Day got off to an especially bad start when Brig. Gen. Marcus P. Miller, who had been given command of the expeditionary force which Otis had sent to Iloilo, messaged Manila that a hostile force of around three thousand were in occupation of that city. Miller's troops had remained on the transports while Miller and his staff went ashore to negotiate with the native leader who, purporting to be one of Aguinaldo's generals, refused permission for Miller to land, saying that if an American occupation of the city was attempted, they would be fired upon. Despite that threat, Miller told Otis that he could take Iloilo with ease once authorized. Otis wired the War Department for that permission but was told that a confrontation with any native force was to be avoided if at all possible. Miller was then told that his command was to remain in Iloilo harbor, staying on the transports for the time being. That wait would turn out to be a hot and miserable one. Finally, after three long months, Otis gave Miller the go-ahead to take possession of Iloilo which was accomplished without any great difficulty.

For the present, the American plan for the Philippines would be to keep the lid on until enough troop strength became available to begin offensive operations. To the extent that any action at all would be taken against an Insurgent force would have to be decided on a case by case basis.

The arrival in the Philippines of reinforcements would be contingent on the amount of shipping made available at San Francisco, a situation which translated in part on how fast the ships then being detained in the Philippines could be turned around.[6]

~

There was an assortment of complexities to be faced over the occupation and subsequent pacification of the Philippines that initially was not appreciated by the policy makers in Washington or even by those senior military officers on the scene who had been directly charged with carrying out the task. A good part of those complexities had to do with the multitude of groups which composed the population. There appears to have been only one American, and a civilian at that, who had enough experience within the islands and depth of judgment to be able to provide any real analysis on the potpourri of peoples with which the military would have to

---

[6] *Correspondence Relating to the War with Spain*, Vol. II, p 871, Adjutant General's Office, Washington, to Brooke, Quartermaster at Manila, January 7, 1899.

deal. That man's name was Dean C. Worcester. Worcester first came to the Philippines as a member of the Steere Scientific Expedition (1887-1890). As indicated by his later writings, Worcester, a zoologist by profession, also possessed the bent of an anthropologist. While with the Steere expedition and later as a participant in another expedition (1892-1895), Worcester traveled extensively throughout the islands, observing and recording his impressions with skill.[7] In his published studies on the Philippine people, Worcester described the population by dividing it into four general categories: The first comprised those who were commonly referenced as *Filipinos,* a term which included only those persons who had become *civilized* through assimilation while under Spanish rule and who were widely differentiated from the remainder of the population. Many of these so-called civilized Filipinos possessed an infusion of Spanish, Japanese, or Chinese blood -- the mix-bloods being referred to as *Mestizos.* The professional and moneyed classes of the islands largely consisted of the Mestizo type, Aguinaldo being one such individual. The second distinct grouping consisted of the Moro tribes which resided in the southern islands. The Moros were a maritime oriented people with piracy their special forte. The Moros were Muslims of the more militant variety, the more fanatic going so far as to believe that their elevation to heaven was only attainable by the killing of a Christian. Feared by all, the Moros had never been brought into line by the Spanish who by the early 1800s had virtually written them off as being impossible to subjugate. Thereafter, the Spanish had practiced a policy of containment with the aim of limiting Moro depredations against those geographic areas of special interest to the Spanish. Worcester's third category was what he called the *Wild Men* or *Wild Tribes.* This was a term that he applied to encompass numerous tribal groupings found upon all of the islands. There were literally scores of such tribes, most lacking co-identification from island to island or even from tribe to tribe on the same island. Worcester's fourth categorization were the Negritos, a pygmy-like black people, having kinky woolen hair and flat noses, who closely resembled the Aborigines of Australia. The Spanish had considered the Negritos impossible to civilize, an impression that came to be shared by Worcester and later by the American army.

> An appreciation of the population groups as they existed at the beginning of the twentieth century is vital to an understanding of the early-on difficulties faced by the United States in its pacification of the islands. Appendix A of this volume discusses in some detail Worcester's description of those groups.

---

[7]   Dean C. Worcester was appointed to the Investigative Commission on the Philippines in 1900. With the appointment of a United States civil administration for the Islands in 1901, he was appointed Secretary of Interior for the Philippines, retaining that position until 1913.

CHAPTER III

MANAGING THE ARMY FLEET
EARLY PHASE, 1898 - 1901

The War Department had made a provident decision when in 1898 it had recommended the creation of an Army-operated shipping agency to be designated the Army Transport Service (ATS).[1] A board of senior officers under the chair of Maj. Gen. William Ludlow was given the charge of promulgating regulations for the organizational structure of the new ATS and for its management. These regulations were approved by Secretary of War Alger that November and were published at the beginning of 1899. The regulations designated two separate home ports, San Francisco and New York. Each port was to have full control of all Army shipping routed to and from it. Each would have as its General Superintendent an Army officer who was to be autonomous from the control of any other Army command in that respective Military District. All activity involving the port would be coordinated by the General Superintendent directly with the Quartermaster General in Washington. Reporting to each of the General Superintendents was an Assistant Superintendent and a Port Medical Officer, these positions being filled by commissioned officers. The rest of the General Superintendent's staff consisted of civilian employees -- the most senior at each port carrying the title of Marine Superintendent. Further down the civilian chain was an Assistant Marine Superintendent; a Superintending Marine Engineer; an Assistant Superintending Marine Engineer; a Port Steward; and a Chief Stevedore.

The assembling at San Francisco of the transport fleet that had carried Merritt's VIII Army Corps to the Philippines during the early summer and fall of 1898 had in large part been created by the hands-on effort of Maj. Oscar F. Long who had held the pre-war post of Depot Quartermaster at San Francisco. In the spring of 1899,

---

[1] Officially, the ATS was created August 18, 1898. under War Department General Order 122.

Long was appointed to the post of General Superintendent of the ATS for that port. Long's counterpart at the port of New York became Col. A. S. Kimball who held the job as a temporary assignment until August of 1900 when he was relieved by Maj. Carroll A. Devol.

At both San Francisco and New York, the posts of civilian marine superintendent were given to men whose careers had ideally suited them for the job. John Barneston, who held that post at San Francisco, in addition to having been a master of ships for many years, had the experience of nine years ashore in an executive position with a San Francisco shipping company. The War Department's dictate was that the ATS was to be run like a commercial shipping company, contingent, of course, upon the exigencies of extraordinary military requirements. Experience of the sort provided by Barneston was of course vital if the ATS was to function along lines similar to those followed by the shipping industry.

Operating personnel aboard Army owned ATS transports were to remain civilian, to be recruited from the merchant marine.[2] To be assigned aboard each of the owned ATS transports was a commissioned Army officer carrying the title Transport Quartermaster, his function to act as the ship's business manager and as liaison between the civilian master and the senior officer of the troop passengers who carried the designation Transport Commander. The responsibility of the Transport Commander under these new rules was the control and discipline of all troops as well as any civilian passengers. The civilian master was charged with the navigation of the ship and the discipline of its civilian crew.

Obviously, in the minds of those who had formulated the regulations, the master was not to be interfered with in his navigational duties; however, it did not always work out that way. The regulations, as they were written that first year, were ambiguous, allowing a potential for friction to develop between the three shipboard central command figures, i.e., the master, the Transport Quartermaster, and the Transport Commander. The problem stemmed from one paragraph of the regulations which stated that the Transport Commander was to be in charge of all on board. One suspects by this contradiction that the regulation drafters -- all of them Army officers -- may have held reservations over the wisdom of delegating too much authority to a civilian. If that is true, the inherent ambiguities of those initial regulations may have been of deliberate design However, as time would soon tell, the lack of judgment exercised by a few Transport Commanders as well as by a few Transport Quartermasters would impugn upon the traditional authority of the masters, a circumstance not at all contributory to a happy or efficient ship. To resolve that problem, the regulations were partially rewritten, one improvement being to redefine and change the title of Transport Commander to that of Troop Commander. Later, the functions of the Transport Quartermaster would be transferred to civilian status with that person serving under the master and reporting directly to him.

---

[2]   Although classed as federal employees of the Army Quartermaster Department, the civilian officers (licensed personnel) and the other crewmembers (unlicensed) were not at first classified under civil service. This decision had probably been made because of the uncertainty at the time of how long the ATS fleet might remain an active entity. Civil service classification would come later, but not until 1912.

Regarding those ships which were time chartered by the Army (as against those in Army ownership or on bareboat charter) the crews were not Army employees, being instead employees of the owners. In such cases, the ATS regulations as just described did not apply. On many of the time chartered ships an Army officer was temporarily assigned aboard to represent the government's interest as it might involve troop passengers and cargoes.

Crew management aboard transports under Army ownership (or bareboat charter) was vexing from the start. Under the original 1899 regulations, the ships' officers as well as the unlicensed personnel were to be governed by those federal statutes which applied to crews in the merchant marine. There were, however, a number of contradictions from the practices of the merchant marine. When reporting for shipboard assignment on an Army transport, each man was required to sign the same type of shipping articles as those used in the merchant marine, except that there was an addition of what was termed the *Army Supplement.* [3] Further, he had to take an oath of allegiance to the government and pledge his fidelity to all his superiors. Under the Army Supplement, employment remained continuous between voyages. On the other hand, merchant marine crews by law automatically went off articles whenever a voyage was terminated. There was an advantage with the ATS system since its seamen, by remaining on articles, continued on pay between voyages. The negative side was that Army ship turn-arounds were rapid, and crewmembers received only short leaves of absence between voyages -- so short on some ships that shore leaves consisted of no more than twelve hours. (Under unusual circumstances, long leaves could be granted to an individual, but only upon his application to the General Superintendent at the port.) Those short leaves became a source of dissatisfaction among the ATS crews. To circumvent the lack of free time, many unlicensed personnel as well as some ships' officers left Army employment (by resignation) after the completion of a voyage. Although crewmembers doing this could reapply for employment, the system resulted in a high turnover rate that would otherwise not have been the case had the Army's shore leave policy been more liberal. [4] Another difference from the merchant marine was that in the ATS, uniforms were required for all members of the crew. Uniforms for unlicensed personnel were issued by the Army but were paid for by the employee through salary deductions. [5] The officers procured their uniforms from commercial tailors.

---

[3]   As recognized under the U.S. Navigation Laws for the merchant marine, shipping articles are a contract between a ship's master and the seamen stating rate of pay and other conditions of employment. Under U.S. practice, shipping articles are not entered into until the start of a voyage from a vessel's point of departure from a U.S. port. The term of employment ends upon the termination of the voyage on return to a U.S. port.

[4]   New regulations for the ATS would be promulgated in 1908. These would help solve many of the shipboard problems inherent to prior years. Foolishly, however, the leave policy was not liberalized at that time to bring it more in line with the industry norm. Later, under the civil service, a system of annual leave would be put in place.

[5]   The ATS regulations of 1899 prescribed uniform standards in considerable detail. The subject of uniforms became a focal point for criticism by the International Seamen's Union of America on the Pacific Coast which also protested against the ATS's alleged practice of hiring Chinese seamen for some jobs in preference to whites. According to seamen labor groups, whites were said to be more amenable to discipline. This was a position which the Army would agree with to a degree before the decade was over. Source: *Coast Seamen's Journal,* (Vol. XI, No. 45, August 10, 1898), p 7. It should be noted here that union activity was forbidden on the transports. The union was accordingly hostile to the Army's involvement with shipping. For more on uniform

Disciplinary problems involving ATS crews took on a cyclical nature, being largely affected by the employment situation within the overall shipping industry. When shipping was tight, the attractiveness of government employment led to placid crews; but when jobs in the commercial sector were plentiful, there was discontent. During the Civil War, the practice of maintaining control over the Army's Quartermaster employees (including vessel crews) had been enforced by the exercise of military law.[6] However, following 1865, military law imposed against civilians during peacetime was not deemed appropriate, and the practice was dropped.[7] This lack of direct military legal jurisdiction would plague the orderly administration of the ATS during most of its existence.[8]

The ATS regulations of 1899 had an unfortunate effect of creating a social scenario which tended to denigrate the status of junior ship's officers serving on the transports. Under the messing arrangements which were established by the 1899 regulations -- and carried through into the 1908 regulations -- ships' officers of the junior grades dined in company with the Army's noncommissioned officers who were aboard as passengers. Only the masters, first officers, chief engineers, first assistant engineers, and chief stewards messed in the salon in company with the Army's commissioned personnel. Taking into account the fact that the ATS deck officers of the junior grades (and many of the engineering officers as well) were filling job slots on the transports equivalent to those normally assigned commissioned or warrant officers aboard ships of the Navy, the resentment created by these messing arrangements was considerable. Although the average merchant marine officer in the early years of the twentieth century did not usually come from as high a social or educational background as did the commissioned officers of the military, the regulation's drafters had taken an unwitting step backward from attaining the War Department's goals of attracting a better grade of merchant marine officer into the government's service.

---

regulations within the ATS, circa 1898 - 1942 and its successor Transportation Corps - Water Division, Civilian Branch, circa 1942 - 1950, see: William K. Emerson, *Chevrons...Catalog of U.S. Army Insignia,* (Washington: Smithsonian Institution Press, 1983), pp 228-230. Dave Collar, *The Trading Post...Journal of the American Society of Military Insignia Collectors,* Fall (Oct - Dec issue), 1954, pp 29-43. Dave Collar, *Military Collector and Historian...*Journal of the Co. of Military Historians, Vol. XLV, No. 4, Winter 1993, pp 186-188. Emerson's work covers the period 1898 through to the 1930s. Collar's works concentrate on the era of World War II.

[6] For a detailed discussion of military law imposed against Quartermaster Department employees during the Civil War, see Gibson with Gibson, *Assault and Logistics*, Appendix E.

[7] Neither the Philippine Insurrection nor the China Relief Expedition was considered a state of war, at least in reference to the imposition of military law for civilian transport crews. It would not be until World War I that military discipline was again attempted toward the management of the Army's civilian crews. Even then, this could only be brought to bear while at sea or within a military jurisdiction. Once the voyage terminated in the United States, so did the Army's control over the crews. Military discipline applied against Army civilian crews was exercised to a limited extent during World War II. During the early 1950s, a series of court cases, some reaching the U.S. Supreme Court, negated the imposition of military law against the military's civilian employees during periods of peace. The courts determined that such authority was limited only to periods of active hostilities against a foreign power and then only while civilians *were serving with the Armed Forces in the field.*

[8] Up to and including the beginning of the Second World War, there were frequent suggestions that Army transport crews should be militarized, but nothing came of it except in the case of the Army Mine Planter Service, an organization which was militarized shortly prior to World War II. See Appendix S for further discussion of the Army Mine Planter Service.

The Overseas Support Fleet

The transpacific sealift for the VIII Army Corps which had been organized on the west coast to transport Merritt and his men to Manila within the period May to December 1898 had required a total of 19 ships procured through time charters. In addition there were 2 Army-owned transports. Of the 19 originally chartered, 9 would have their charters extended into 1899, with some ships having them extended into 1900. (See separate ship lists for 1898 and for 1899-1901 which follow Chapter IV.) An additional 62 ships would be time chartered for the support of those operations conducted against the Insurgents following the Spanish surrender and which encompassed the period 1899-1901 as well as for the China Relief Expedition of 1900-1901. During the 1900-1901 time frame, the Army employed, exclusively for transpacific service, 24 of its own transports. Thus, the owned and chartered Army transpacific fleet for that particular period totaled 95 oceangoing ships. Additional to that number of owned and chartered ships were 9 commercial ships upon which the Army would send cargoes to or from the Far East on an affreightment basis.[9] The Army also chartered during this time frame another 31 steamships and 6 sailing vessels for interisland Philippine service.[10]

To handle the offloading of ships coming into Manila and for the reloading of cargo on to interisland freighters, the ATS at Manila constructed a total of fifty-five non-self propelled cargo lighters which became identified within the Army's inventory as QMD #1 through QMD #55.

Some of the time chartered ships which went into the Army's Pacific fleet were initially engaged on the United States west coast, but others were chartered on the east coast. All except two of the Army owned fleet or bareboat-chartered fleet as well as those ships under time charter, made the trip from the east coast by way of the Mediterranean, the Suez Canal, and the Indian Ocean.[11]

The volume of troops sent out to the Philippines dramatically increased when the new volunteer regiments became ready to leave for the islands. Their numbers were augmented by Regular Army units, many garrisons having been closed in the western states as the need for policing the Indians was phased out. During the fiscal year ending June 1899, a total of 34,661 officers and men left the United States for the Philippines. During the following fiscal year, that number was approximately equaled. Returning to the United States from the Philippines were the complements of those state regiments which had enlisted for the duration of the war against Spain.

The ATS had its first loss in 1899 when the cable ship USAT Hooker, recently transferred from the Atlantic fleet and bound out of Manila for Hong Kong, struck a reef offlying the island of Corregidor. She became a total loss. Since the

---

[9]   Under a contract of affreightment, (or gross freight), money is paid to the ship's owner without any allowance for navigation charges or dues, cost of fuel, etc., the payment being solely made for the carriage of the cargo. [International Maritime Dictionary]

[10]   Report of the Quartermaster General, Fiscal year 1901, p 13.

[11]   Two ships purchased by the Army went from the east to the Pacific coast around the southern tip of South America. (The Panama Canal would not open until 1914.) One was the seagoing tug USAT Slocum. The other was a sail collier called the St. Mark, purchased at Philadelphia, which went to Manila for use as a coaling hulk. USAT Slocum was based at San Francisco. She was the only Army Transport Service vessel to see service during the Spanish-American War as well as World War I and World War II.

Philippine Department badly needed a cable ship, *USAT Burnside* was taken out of trooper service and ordered into shipyard for refitting with a cable reel of 550-mile capacity. A second ship loss occurred that same year when a vessel of the chartered fleet, the *Morgan City,* struck a reef off Nagasaki, Japan, it, too, becoming a total loss.

As early as 1899, Nagasaki had become a major coaling stop on the Army's transpacific run. Some coaling of transports was done at Manila, but this service was largely restricted to vessels engaged in interisland service. For replenishment of the interisland fleet, the ATS purchased two large sailing ships (one at Philadelphia and the other at San Francisco) together with a vintage steam vessel (purchased either at Hong Kong or Manila). These three vessels were fitted with derricks and were placed on permanent moorings in Manila Bay. Coal for these moored hulks was supplied by the Mitsui Bussan Kiska Company of Japan under contract to the Chief Quartermaster in the Philippines.[12] During the fiscal year 1901-1902, the Quartermaster at Manila, received 60,293 tons of coal from that Japanese firm, all of it being delivered to the hulks by the Japanese firm.[13]

~

No one during 1898 could have forecast the extent of the campaigns which were to develop against the Insurgents. One of the biggest surprises which developed during the conduct of those campaigns was the huge need for horses and mules. Originally, it had been thought that the native horse and the water buffalo (*carabao*) would be sufficient to handle the Army's requirements. But no one had foreseen the heavy demands for the cavalry and the field artillery, nor had it been foreseen that supplies would have to be hauled by wagon and pack animal over the great distances which would develop. The native horses, although small in size, were tough enough for the haulage of guns and, to a limited extent, for use as cavalry mounts, and they did well on the kind of rank forage grasses which grew on the islands. However, they had no immunity to a debilitating and sometimes fatal disease called glanders which in late 1898 put in an appearance on the islands and spread widely.[14] By the time the disease struck, nine hundred of the native horses had been purchased, most of which either died or were rendered useless by the disease. Replacement animals were shipped in from Australia as well as a few from China, but most of them proved worthless, and even the better of the lots had difficulty in acclimating to Philippine conditions. Carabao were experimented with for pulling artillery and supply wagons, but they were awkwardly slow, unable to stand the rigors of forced marches, and difficult to handle by troops inexperienced with their use. If all this was not enough to deal with, a second animal disease appeared -- this one also imported, probably coming in with the horses shipped from Australia. This newest disease called rinderpest infected both horses and carabao. Under its onslaught, the carabao, having no natural immunity, dropped like flies.[15] The only option remaining to the

---

12   According to Max L. Tornow, there were extensive coal seams of excellent quality throughout the Philippines but up to that time, they had not been commercially exploited. See Tornow, p 41.
13   *Annual Report of the Quartermaster for the fiscal year ending June 30, 1902.*
14   *Annual Report of Major General Commanding the Army for the fiscal year ending June 30, 1899,* p 221.
15   *Annual Report of the Quartermaster General for the fiscal year ending June 30, 1900,* p 35.

Quartermaster was to import horses and mules from the United States and to hope that glanders and rinderpest would not devastate them as well.[16]

During the fiscal year ending June 1900, the Army shipped to the Philippines 10,315 horses and mules from United States west coast ports. During the following fiscal year, another 17,943 were sent out. Three of the early shipments met with disaster during transit. The first heavy loss was on the chartered ship *Siam*. Of *Siam's* cargo of 47 horses and 326 mules, only 15 mules but none of the horses were still alive upon arrival at Manila. The losses resulted from the animals being battered to death in their stalls during typhoon weather. The chartered ship *Leelanaw* lost her entire cargo of 236 mules, all heavy weather casualties. A third chartered ship, the *Victoria,* lost 83 animals with many more injured. To prevent such losses in the future, special slings were designed and installed so that during heavy weather, the animals could be hoisted clear of the deck. The sling arrangements acting as gimbals prevented the animals from losing their footing which had been the cause for most of the past injuries and deaths. Thanks to the slings, no further losses of any consequence occurred in shipments of horses or mules for the rest of the year.

Safe arrival of the horses and mules was not the end of the quartermaster's worries. Feeding them once they arrived on the islands became another challenge. American horses -- mules as well -- did poorly when placed on the tough grasses of the Philippines -- the hay made from it being even less acceptable. Australia was at first tried as a source for hay, but the first shipment was of terrible quality -- so bad in fact that the young quartermaster officer who inspected it before it was unloaded was reproved for not refusing it outright.[17] The only remaining hay source was the United States. Despite the distance involved, the American hay, inclusive of shipping, proved less costly than the poor quality hay which had come from Australia. During fiscal year 1899-1900, 12,362 tons of hay; 11,211 tons of oats; 307 tons of bran; and 15 tons of barley -- all in the form of animal feed -- was shipped out from the west coast of the United States on the Army's chartered ships. From west coast ports, another 2,878 tons of hay; 1,357 tons of oats; and 39 tons of bran was received at Manila from commercial ships hired by the Army at affreightment rates. Other cargo sent from the United States to the Philippines during that same fiscal year amounted to 161,160 tons of general Army supplies; 1,093,812 individual packaged goods; 336,247 pounds of mail; and $5,844,500 worth of currencies. From Australia came refrigerated meats. Tropical uniforms were procured from Chinese tailoring firms at Hong Kong. Only rice, fruits, and vegetables were purchased locally from Philippine farmers. The support of the Philippines had become a sealift of considerable tonnage dimension carried out over an impressive distance.

~

While the occupations of Cuba and of Puerto Rico still required a certain amount of transportation commitment, by mid summer of 1899, shipping

---

[16]   During 1903, a serum was developed to prevent rinderpest.
[17]   *Correspondence Relating to the War with Spain,* Vol. II, p 902, Otis to Adjutant General's Office, Washington, February 12, 1899.

activity to those islands had slackened considerably.[18]   In May of 1900, civil government went into effect on Puerto Rico thus further curtailing the Army's shipping needs to that island. In June of 1901, ATS scheduled service between Cuba and Puerto Rico was canceled, and all Army cargo as well as personnel being shipped to either place was henceforth handled by commercial carriers. In 1902, the Army's occupation had ended on Cuba, leaving only Puerto Rico as a shipping destination for the Army's personnel and materiel.

Alaska had begun to take on a new importance to the War Department. The ATS had been given the task of providing the shipping needs for the Department of the Interior which would administer the territory. Beginning in 1900, scheduled service by the ATS was inaugurated. One Army ship, *USAT Seward,* was specifically fitted out for service under ice conditions and assigned to the Alaska run. In addition, three commercial freight/passenger ships began carrying cargo northward throughout most of the year on an affreightment basis. In 1901, the *USAT Seward* was withdrawn. She then entered a shipyard at Seattle and was fitted out as a refrigerated carrier for Philippine service.

~

During 1898 and the early months of 1899, all Army shipping to the Philippines made its entry at Manila. Cargo and personnel destined for the other islands were transshipped from that place. To handle this interchange of men and materiel, and as stated earlier, the ATS set up a special interisland transport service. Beginning in late 1899, interisland shipment would begin increasing to a marked degree; and to meet the increased need, a number of vessels were chartered from Philippine ship owners. These were augmented by the *USAT Hancock* and *USAT Warren,* two medium-sized steamers which the Army had purchased on the west coast. The majority of those vessels chartered locally were found to be of questionable condition and so from a safety standpoint, they were limited to only cargo carriage unless, of course, an emergency situation dictated otherwise.   Troop lift would paramountly remain the task of the Army's own transports, or of ships which had been chartered in the United States. During 1900-1901, which was the fiscal year during which the heaviest hiring of local vessels would take place, chartering expense for the islands came to $746,596. That same fiscal year saw the Quartermaster Department purchase at Hong Kong the 1,072 ton freighter, *Kong See,* (renamed *USAT Liscum*).[19] During the fiscal years 1899-1901, eight gunboats were obtained by the Quartermaster and manned with Army crews. Three of these were decked-over launches of from 75 to 90 feet in length which the Quartermaster armored and equipped with cannon and rapid fire weaponry. Four of the gunboats had served in that same capacity under the Spanish, two having been earlier captured by the Americans from the rebel forces who in turn had captured them from the Spanish. These four were rearmed, one being mounted with four Gatling guns. During this period, five launches were taken by

---

[18]   By mid-summer of 1899, everything sent to Cuba or Puerto Rico was being dispatched out of New York.

[19]   National Archive records of the Office of the Quartermaster General, Microfilm Series (see No. 1808) contains crew lists for 1900 for the Army transports *Burnside, Kilpatrick, Buford, McClellan, Crook, Rawlins, Sedgwick, Reno, Reynolds, Viking, McPherson.* There are also assorted crew lists for the years 1901 and 1902.

capture and one by purchase; all averaged between 45 and 50 feet in length. These were equipped with light weaponry as they were employed in forward areas which brought them into gunfire range of hostile forces.[20] The Quartermaster Department, although responsible for fitting out these craft, usually did not retain tactical control over their use as more often than not the control of the vessels, as well as their crews, was provided by the field commands involved with the particular operation.

GUNBOATS AND ARMED LAUNCHES EMPLOYED BY THE ARMY ON LUZON DURING THE PHILIPPINE INSURRECTION

GUNBOATS	**LAUNCHES**
Laguna de Bay	*Albert*
Manileno †	*Covadonga*
Mareveles	*Florida ‡*
Mindoro †	*Oceania*
Napidan	*Oeste*
Pampanga †	*Wright*
*Panay * †*	
Pittsburg	

*	Another vessel named *Panay* was lost in China by Japanese attack during 1937.
†	Transferred to the Navy during 1899.
‡	Purchased at Hong Kong and converted into a gunboat at Manila.

---

[20]   One Army report of the time listed all of the launches as "gunboats," but considering their light firepower, they hardly deserved such a classification.

CHAPTER IV

THE CHINA EXPEDITION: 1900 - 1901

During 1900, a number of European and American missionaries in China were attacked and killed by members of a fanatical group called Boxers. These atrocities were followed up by a siege conducted against the foreign compounds at Peking and Tientsin. This brought about the need for American troops to reinforce an international relief force that was organized for the rescue of European, Japanese, and American citizens who were in the compounds. At the onset, American units were sent from the Philippines to Taku, China; later more troops would be sent to Taku directly from the United States. For the United States Army, there would now be a 2-front war in the Far East.

In 1800 an edict of the Chinese Imperial government had forbidden the importation of opium into China. The British-owned East India Company had been in the forefront of that trade. The East India Company, apparently with Crown concurrence, defied the Chinese edict and continued to import the drug which was usually offloaded at the Portuguese-held port of Macao from where it was smuggled to illegal dealers on the Chinese mainland. Other western powers with interests in China also participated in the opium traffic, but as far as the record tells us, American ships did not take part, and the United States did not condone the trade in any recognizable way.

For years, the Chinese government took a rather laissez faire attitude about enforcement of its opium ban -- that is until 1839 when it began cracking down. Seeing its trade being adversely affected, the British reacted militantly in what came to be known as the Opium Wars of 1839-1841. The British won these contests with the terms of their victory being the paying of indemnities by China for the prior destruction of any British-owned opium as well as for Britain's costs of the war. Also as part of the terms, Hong Kong was to be ceded over to the British, and all the major Chinese ports were to be declared open to foreign trade. Not satisfied, the British additionally demanded the right to establish European enclaves within some Chinese cities with the caveat that the foreign residents residing therein were to have immunity from Chinese law. In 1842, a show of naval strength by a U.S. navy squadron brought similar trading rights to American commercial interests -- a welcome development since commerce with China had become a significant factor in the foreign commerce of the United States. In the past, trade with China had been a tenuous arrangement. With the new agreement, much of the prior risk was eliminated, and American trade interests in the far Pacific had become a secure reality. The commercial advantages brought about would indirectly provide one of the rationales which had led the United States toward the annexation of the Philippines in 1898.

The weakened condition of the Imperial government encouraged a series of rebellious outbreaks against it by factions of the Chinese peasantry. To an extent, part of that peasant unrest can be laid against a quasi-Christianity movement which had its unwitting origins with European missionaries who, following the granting of the treaty rights of 1841, had opened missions throughout much of eastern China. Some missions had existed prior to that time, but the treaty rights accelerated the establishment of more of them. In addition to the teaching of religious doctrine, some of the missionaries preached social reform, instructing their converts that many Chinese political and cultural practices were pagan in nature. The first of the peasant rebellions occurred in 1850, led by a Christian convert named Jung Xinchuan. Xinchuan had founded an order which was independent of missionary influence. He preached a doctrine under which God was *the father,* Jesus *the elder brother,* and Xinchuan himself *the devine younger brother.* At first, Xinchuan called for many of the same reforms which the missionaries had advocated; but as he gained followers, his preaching took on a fanaticism which incorporated a type of nationalism that began to cause concern to both the European embassies and to the Imperial Chinese government. For some reason, Xinchuan eventually lost support from what had been a growing congregation, and he disappeared as a threatening factor on the Chinese scene. Nevertheless, the seeds of dissension that he had sown left their legacy. Some historians who have delved deeply into Chinese history of that period have written their belief that the roots of what would become the *Boxer movement* can be traced back to Xinchuan.

Beginning in 1856 and continuing into 1858, further military operations were conducted by the British and French against the Chinese Imperial government. These resulted in the Chinese giving up to the British as well as the French even more territorial and trade rights. Shortly thereafter, many of those same privileges were granted to the Russians and to the United States.[1] The war with the *foreign devils,*

---

[1] The British and French war against the Chinese government that was waged in the years 1856-58 was termed the "Arrow War," so named because a ship, the *Arrow,* of British registry, had been accused by the Chinese of harboring pirates. The Chinese boarded the ship, took off part of its crew as prisoners, and hauled down the British flag. The Chinese, although finally releasing the crewmen, had refused to apologize.

which was what the Chinese collectively called outsiders, had again lessened the power of the Imperial government's rule over China's population.

The term *Boxers,* was a westernized synonym for a Chinese secret society called the *Righteous and Harmonious Fist.* Initially, this society gave its quiet assistance to another peasant rebellion which occurred during 1890 and which was directed against Imperial Chinese rule. That rebellion fizzled out under severe oppression by the Imperial army. The secretiveness of the Boxers had made it a difficult organization to target; consequently, its members emerged relatively unscathed from the government's crackdown with only a handful of its leaders suffering prosecution. The Boxers next began agitating for the removal of foreign influence from China, a sentiment which they soon found was equally shared by the Imperial government then headed by the Dowager Empress. Feeling themselves to be on safe ground, the Boxers raised their sights toward advocating the destruction of all foreigners. The Boxers were of the belief that while following such a cause, they were invulnerable to bullets and that at certain times of crisis they even possessed the ability to fly. This belief had the effect of attracting a large following for whom combat against the weaponry of the *foreign devils* held no great fear. As the movement grew, there was a scattering of murders first directed at missionaries located in the more rural areas. As the killing spread to the suburbs of the cities, this became such cause for alarm within the international embassies, that home governments were called upon for additional legation guards.

The spring of 1900 issued in the first major Boxer outbreak resulting in their cutting off the railroad which ran between Tientsin and Peking. With that, the international groups both at Tientsin and at Peking found themselves isolated. On June 21, the Boxers instituted a tight siege against the international compounds at Peking. To lift that siege and another one which was being conducted against Tientsin, an international relief force was quickly assembled at the port of Taku on the China coast. As initially organized, the force was made up of British, French, Russian, Japanese, and American troops.[2] The American troop contingent for that initial force was sent directly from the Philippines. The hastily established international force was not of a strength large enough to assure an easy victory; but time was of the essence if the besieged compounds were to be reached in time to avert a massacre of those trapped there. Providentially, by sending regiments that were already in the Far East, the United States was able to make its early contribution of over five thousand officers and men.[3] The problem facing the international force -- assuming of course that Tientsin and Peking could be relieved -- was that if an allied force was to remain at Peking to assert domination over the Chinese, the railroad running between there and Tientsin would require rebuilding and its subsequent guarding so as to assure that a line of communication could remain open from the coast at Taku. A river, the Pei Ho,

---

2   Some contributory support for the international relief force was provided by the Austrians and Italians. Germany had volunteered to supply a large troop contingent, but most of it would have to come from Europe, and by that time, those in the compounds might be out of provisions and forced to give themselves up to the murderous mercy of the Boxers.

3   Later, the United States would contribute another 10,000 troops, mostly infantry to be sent from the west coast. Huston, pp 302, 303.

closely paralleled the railroad, but the use of that river for long term resupply, especially in winter, was clearly not in the cards. The railroad was the key.

No sooner had what became known as the International Relief Force (IRF) departed Taku than it found itself seriously hampered by Chinese of nondescript identification who harassed every patrol sent out to reconnoiter what lay ahead. The situation quickly became rife with uncertainty, the largest question being the position that the Imperial government was taking in its relationship with the Boxers. Some of the IRF's officers believed that the troops then presently harassing their patrols were Imperial troops. Also perplexing was how well the Dowager Empress could control her army. During early June, a detachment of the Imperial Army became engaged against a Boxer force outside of Tientsin; but then shortly after that, another Imperial Army unit, clearly identified as such, opened fire against a forward element of the IRF. There is probably little question that the Dowager Empress and her advisors distrusted the Boxers; but at the same time, they probably viewed the Boxer movement as a convenient way to rid China of the *foreign devils.* The situation was probably uncertain if not totally confusing to those Chinese close to the Empress Dowager. It was certainly so for the allied commanders of the IRF who had no real inkling of the identity of the forces opposing them on the way to Peking.

On July 13, Tientsin was occupied by Japanese troops supported by American and British units. At Tientsin, a messenger arrived from the Imperial government offering to escort all of the allied nationals out of Peking and to deliver them into the allied lines. Totally distrustful of all Chinese, official or otherwise, the IRF commanders refused. In counter, they called for the Imperial government to assist the IRF in getting to Peking. That counter offer was ignored. Smuggled reports were now coming out of Peking that a unit of Imperial troops was firing into the legation compounds.[4] It was not known as to whether the court of the Dowager Empress was supporting this.

Patrol reports were consistent in that beyond Tientsin, armed Chinese were massing.[5] Imperial Army units were reported to be entrenched at Peitsang which was seven miles up the Pei Ho River beyond Tientsin. This news brought with it the ominous conclusion that the Boxers were now openly supported by the Imperial government. The opposition at Peitsang did not prove to be significant, and the IRF's march resumed, the approach toward Peking still paralleling the Pei Ho River. (Supplies and reserve ammunition were being sent up the Pei Ho aboard river junks *powered* by tow ropes in the hands of coolies moving upstream along the river's bank.)

The American units that had so far arrived in China were from the Philippines, consisting of the 6th Cavalry, the 9th Infantry, and the 14th Infantry. The 9th Infantry and a troop of the 6th Cavalry now made up part of the lead element of the IRF advance. The remainder of the American force was given the assignment of

---

[4]   *Correspondence Relating to the War with Spain,* Vol. I, p 442, Colonel Coolidge, 9th Infantry, to Adjutant General, Washington, July 31, 1900.

[5]   The state of crisis was brought into sharp focus for American officials in Washington when the news arrived by cable that Col. Emerson H. Liscum, regimental commander of the 9th Infantry, had been among those killed at Tientsin. *Correspondence Relating to the War with Spain,* Vol. I, p 426, Adjutant General's Office to MacArthur, July 16, 1900. Of the total allied force in front of Tientsin, 775 officers and men were killed or wounded.

assisting in the guarding of the line of communication which ran along the banks of the Pei Ho River, the course of which, as earlier stated, reached back to the supply port of Taku.

On August 12, the Imperial government requested of the international command that peace negotiations be started which it claimed could lead to a cessation of the attacks against the legations. Apparently, the success of the IRF's advance was worrying the Chinese, and well it might have, as on that day, the forward element had occupied Peking's suburb of Tungchow. Three days later, with only light opposition, the IRF marched into Peking. To everyone's relief, those besieged had made it through their ordeal. The civilians had suffered minimal casualties. The legation guards, including a contingent of U.S. Marines, had taken the brunt of enemy fire, and a number of them had been killed in the defense.

It was soon discovered that the Chinese royal family, including the Dowager Empress, had escaped from the city -- the Empress, so the story went, having disguised herself as a peasant. The Imperial palace grounds were entered on September 6. The only Chinese left there were a few servants, the entire court having fled. The international occupation of Peking soon began to turn into a rampage of looting along with some cases of rape -- witnesses reporting that the Russian troops were the worst of the lot. By the strictest imposition of discipline, the American troops were to remain relatively blameless during most of that early phase of the allied occupation.

On the 16th of August, a thousand Boxers attempting to breach the line of communication running back to Taku were routed by British and Russian troops. Following that point, Peking was in full communication with the coast and would remain so.

Once the siege of Peking was relieved, the task assigned by Washington to the American contingent was to protect American citizens both at Tientsin and at Peking and to contribute toward keeping open the lines of communication from Taku to those places. Once those conditions could be assured, it was thought possible that American troops could be withdrawn entirely; but considering the unsettled situation in China, that would not come about. It had become evident that the remaining Chinese government would not lean toward the perpetuation of foreign interests in China. The presence of troops belonging to those nations with trade interests would therefore be necessary. The American commander and legation personnel on hand, together with representatives of the other foreign powers, worked toward arranging peaceful accommodations with the Imperial government; but in so doing, care was exercised in order that previously held trade rights were not compromised.

By the end of the first week in September (1900), Brig. Gen. Adna R. Chafee, the officer who had led the American force, was able to report to the War Department that hostilities had practically ceased with only occasional shots being fired at small parties repairing telegraph lines and occasionally at those patrols which had been sent out foraging. Were those shots coming from regular Chinese troops or were they from Boxers? The hope was that the Imperial government, in order to insure its self-preservation, would soon firmly re-establish itself and by so doing give the situation a measure of stability. Gradually, the Dowager Empress as well as Chinese officials drifted back to Peking, their motivation seemingly being for China to recover a measure of its political identity. To accomplish that end and to satisfy the allies, the Empress would declare the Boxers persona non grata. The indemnities laid by the allied powers against the Imperial government had included a provision for the trial of those Chinese officials who had assisted the Boxers. The trials of those selected were to be conducted by the Chinese themselves -- subsequent executions to be witnessed by representatives of the allied powers. With that done, a measure of calm that was satisfactory to allied interests was restored.

Peking was garrisoned throughout the winter of 1900-1901. The United States contribution to the garrison during that first winter was a reinforced regiment of infantry. In the spring, the Peking garrison was cut back -- a United States force remaining as a part of it but reduced to company strength.

~

The fast response that was made by the United States toward its contribution to the IRF was a matter of *Borrowing from Peter to pay Paul.* Regular Army regiments then in the Philippines and badly needed for service there had to be sent to China. One of the units from the Philippines which was committed to China had been stationed at the old Spanish naval base. That unit was immediately replaced by a contingent of Marines sent ashore from the fleet.[6] Replacements for other units sent north was not to be that easy nor could they be replaced for some time. Movement of units from the Philippines resulted in not only putting a hold on operations against the Insurgents, but it had allowed Aguinaldo a much needed breathing space in which to reorganize and consolidate his control in the rural provinces.

In protest over what was happening within his area of responsibility, Maj. Gen. Arthur MacArthur (who in May had replaced Maj. Gen. Elwell S. Otis as Military Governor of the Philippines) wired his concerns to the Adjutant General's office on June 16.

> *Force in Philippines has been disseminated to limitation of safety; concentration slow to avoid evacuation of territory now occupied which would be extremely unfortunate. Have not cared to emphasize this feature of situation. Loss of a regiment at this time would be serious matter, but if critical emergency arises in China can send regiment two days notice.*[7]

With the eyes of the world on what was happening in China, the denuding of MacArthur's command had become of secondary concern to those in Washington. By return cablegram, MacArthur was ordered to send another full regiment, *as soon as possible;* however, on-the-spot needs of the Philippine command were not entirely ignored. Washington informed MacArthur that it had been decided

---

[6]   *Correspondence Relating to the War with Spain,* Vol. I, pp 409-506 covering the period May 30, 1900, to June 1, 1901.

[7]   *Correspondence Relating to the War with Spain,* Vol. I, p 412, MacArthur to Adjutant General's Office, June 16, 1900.

that eight troops of cavalry badly needed in China would not be taken from the Philippine force but instead would be sent directly to China from the United States. The regiment which MacArthur had been ordered to ship to China was the 9th Infantry, then based on Samar. Its departure was delayed by a typhoon which tore through that island destroying the docking area from which the troops were to embark. Repairs were completed within a few days, and the 39 officers and 1,271 men of the regiment left for China aboard *USAT Logan* and the chartered steamer *Port Albert.*

In early July, MacArthur was informed that in addition to the troops he had already sent to China, he was to immediately dispatch yet another infantry regiment together with a full battery of artillery. Ten days later, he was told that replacement troops would be sent to the Philippines from San Francisco. This was not to happen. Unfortunately for the Philippine commander's peace of mind, the loss of Colonel Liscum and other Americans in the battle for Tientsin had so alarmed the War Department that the promise given MacArthur was rescinded. The Philippines had been placed even farther down on the priority list.

~

The transports that were being routed that summer for China made stops either at Nagasaki or at Kobe for coaling. From those ports, they were directed to Taku for discharge of their troops and cargoes. Instead of returning to ports on the United States west coast, eight of those ships were diverted for shuttle service between Manila and Taku with coaling stops at Nagasaki. Those retained for that shuttle service were: *Pennsylvania, Flintshire, Wyefield, Westminster, Port Stephens, Port Albert, Indiana,* and *USAT Sumner.*[8] Once Peking had been relieved by the IRF in mid-August and the communications between there and Taku made secure, shipping volume directed for the China expedition gradually eased. The reduction in requirements for China enabled the use of those ships for the transport of the new volunteer regiments scheduled for the Philippines. With that accomplished, MacArthur was no longer deprived of the men and materiel he needed.

The first troops to leave China were mounted units, having been selected in order to relieve the demand for animal forage which had to be shipped in. The 9th Infantry left Peking on May 23, 1901. By the end of 1901, the majority of American units which had helped make up the IRF had been returned either to the Philippines or to the United States. Although the relief of Peking had ended the sense of crisis which had earlier surrounded the events in China, threats of trouble there which could target American interests did not abate. Accordingly, the United States

---

[8] Things went fairly smoothly insofar as the juggling of shipping was concerned although the Quartermaster officer stationed at the Nagasaki shipping terminal was admonished by the Adjutant General's office for changing the routing of *USAT Thomas* without higher authorization. The Quartermaster criticized for re-routing *USAT Thomas* is believed to have been Maj. John M. McEwen.

A bi-product of the affair of 1900-1901 in China was the international recognition of the Army's transports as "public vessels," a classification which gave the transports the same immunities and privileges accorded to vessels of war. A detailed discussion of how that came about is contained within Appendix B of this volume.

would continue its military presence up to the eve of World War II. The 15th Infantry regiment was permanently assigned to the China station, its garrison at Tientsin. This regiment was maintained at full strength until 1938. From 1900 into the pre- World War II period, a company of Marines served as legation guards at Peking, and a full strength regiment of Marines was posted at Shanghai.[9] The U.S. Navy maintained a sizable fleet in Chinese waters up to the beginning of World War II.[10]

---

[9]   Dennis L. Noble, *The Eagle and the Dragon: The United States Military in China, 1901-1937,* (New York: Greenwood Press, 1990), p 32.

[10]   For a description of American naval activity in Chinese waters, see Kemp Tolley, *Yangtze Patrol,* (Annapolis, Naval Institute Press, 2000).

Vessels of the Larger Class Purchased During 1899 and 1900 by Quartermaster Department Specifically for Pacific Service *
(Philippine Insurrection Effort and China Relief Expedition)

Renamed by ATS in 1898	Original Name of vessel	Tonnage	Year Purchased	Amount paid	Remarks
Collier No. 1	St. Mark		1900	$50,000	Sail vessel purchased at Philadelphia, PA. Sailed to Manila via Cape Horn. Stationed as a coaling ship at Manila.
Collier No. 2	Cyrus Wakefield		1900	$45,000	Blt Thomaston, ME. Sail vessel purchased at San Francisco, CA. Used in Manila as a coaling ship.
Collier No. 3			1900	?	Steamship purchased at Manila for use as coaling ship.
Dix	Samoa (British)	7,212	1900	$425,000	Blt 1892 at Sunderland, England. Purchased at Hong Kong. Utilized in transpacific service. Assigned to PI interisland fleet for a time.
Egbert	Missouri (British); USQMD Missouri	2,903	1899	$200,000	Blt 1889, Hartlepool, England. Purchased from Atlantic Transport Co. through Bernard N. Baker during 1898. Pacific fleet, 1899. China Relief Expedition, 1901. Out of service 1902.
Ingalls	Clearwater (British)	1,147	1899	$150,000	Blt 1894, Newcastle, England. Purchased New Orleans. Operated in Caribbean as troopship and later as freight vessel. Converted at New York to hospital ship for PI service. Transferred to Pacific; used for PI interisland service.
Lawton	USS Badger	3,497	1900	Transferred	Blt Chester, PA. Pacific fleet. Transpacific to PI; interisland service, 1901-02.
Liscum	Kong See (British)	1,072	1901		Blt Newcastle on Tyne, England. Purchased in Philippines for PI service.
Rosecrans	Columbia	2,976	1899		Blt 1883. Grounded in Alaska in May 1899. Lost deck cargo, but vessel was successfully salved by tug. China Relief Expedition 1900. Transferred to Pacific fleet in 1901. Out of service in 1902. Sold for $50,000 to Matson Navigation Co.
Seward	G. W. Dickenson	2,100 (1,275)	1900		Blt 1900 in Seattle, WA. On Alaskan service during most of 1901; then fitted out for refrigeration service with PI interisland fleet.

Colliers 1, 2, 3 were to be anchored in Manila Bay for receiving and dispensing coal to arriving transports. Source: Report of QM General, 1900

Crew lists for transports, 1899-1901, are noted as available within RG- 92 Military Reference Branch, Military Archives Division, under Part I, Inventory, Office of the Quartermaster General, NM 81.

* Note: During this time frame, the Army also purchased two ships for Atlantic service, the *Terry* of 1338 tons and the yacht *Viking*.

Vessels Time Chartered (or Otherwise Hired) by the Quartermaster Department: War With Spain, Pacific Area; and for Philippine Insurrection Effort As Well As China Relief Expedition and Alaskan Supply Service

1898 - 1901

Sources: *Reports of the Secretary of War*, Fiscal Years Ending June 1898 and 1899; *Reports of the Quartermaster General, 1899, 1900, 1901*; *Correspondence Relating to the War with Spain*; *Merchant Vessels of the United States*; Microfilm Records, Office of the Quartermaster General (Film Series: 1794, 1808, 1829, 1870, 1874, 1882, 1886). These microfilms contain the itineraries of transports hired or chartered, 1898 through 1906.

Name of vessel	Type	By Whom Owned	Chartered	Canceled	Rate of pay[1a]	Tonnage	Remarks[2a]
Almond Branch [1,11]	Transport		July '00	?	?	?	Freight
Arab [1,4]	Transport		Aug '00	April '00	?	?	,
Argl [1,4]	Transport		Sept '00	Jan '01	?	?	Freight
Athenian [23]	Transport	Canadian Pacific Railroad Co.	July '99	May '00	$800	3,882	Troops and animals
Athenian [1] (rechartered) ⊗	Transport	Canadian Pacific Railroad Co.	Sept '00	Jan '01	$600	3,882	Freight
Australia ⊗	Transport	Oceanic SS Co.	May '98	Aug '98	m) $20,000	2,755	50 o; 1000 m
Australia ⊗ (rechartered)	Transport	Oceanic SS Co.	1899	?		2,755	50 o; 1000 m
Aztec ⊗ [7]	Transport	Pacific Mail SS Co.	Aug '99	May '00	$800	3,508	Animals
Aztec ⊗ (rechartered)	Transport	Pacific Mail SS Co.	Aug '00	Oct '00	?	3,508	Animals
Aztec ⊗ (rechartered)	Transport	Pacific Mail SS Co.	Dec '00	June '01	?	3,508	Troops and animals
Belgian King	Transport	M. J. Brandenstein and Co.	Sept '99	Nov '99	$700	3,379	Trooper
Belgian King (rechartered)	Transport	M. J. Brandenstein and Co.	Aug '00	Dec '00	?	3,379	Trooper and freight
Benmohr	Transport	Macondray and Co.	Oct '99	Feb '00	$700	3,000	Trooper
Benmohr (rechartered)	Transport	Macondray and Co.	Apr '01	?	$9/ton	3,000	Hired, freight tonnage basis
Bidston Hill	Sail		Apr '99	?	$19,967/trip to Manila	?	Contract freight carrier for Philippines
Buckingham [1]	Transport		Nov '00	Feb '01	?	?	Freight
Californian [1,10]	Transport		July '00	June '01	?	?	Freight.
Cavanaugh [1]	Transport		Nov '99	Jan '01	?	?	Animals
Centennial ⊗	Transport	Charles Nelson Co.	Jan '99	July '99	$275	2,975	Trooper and animals
Centennial ⊗ (rechartered)	Transport	Charles Nelson Co.	July '99	Jan '00	$275	2,975	Animals
Charles Nelson ⊗	Transport	Charles Nelson Co.	Mar '99	June '99	$300	1,057	Trooper

Vessel	Type	Operator			Rate	Tonnage	Notes
Charles Nelson ⊗ (rechartered)	Transport	Charles Nelson Co.	Sept '99	Dec '99	$300	1,057	Trooper
China ⊗	Transport	Pacific Mail SS Co.	May '98	Sept '98	$1,500	5,000	75 o; 1500 m
City of Para ⊗	Transport	Pacific Mail SS Co.	June '98	Nov '98	$1,000	3,532	50 o; 1000 m
City of Para 5⊗ (rechartered)	Transport	Pacific Mail SS Co.	July '99	Apr '00	$800	3,532	Trooper
City of Peking ⊗	Transport	Pacific Mail SS Co.	Oct '99	Jan '00	$1000	5,079	Trooper
City of Puebla ⊗	Transport	Pacific Coast SS Co.	June '98	June '99	$900	2,623	59 o; 930 m
City of Puebla 5⊗	Transport	Pacific Coast SS Co.	Aug '99	Feb '00	$600	2,623	Trooper
City of Rio de Janeiro ⊗	Transport	Pacific Mail SS Co.	July '98	Oct '98	$1,000	3,548	–
City of Rio de Janeiro 5⊗ (rechartered)	Transport	Pacific Mail SS Co.	Sept '99	Dec '99	$875	3,548	Trooper
City of Sydney ⊗	Transport	Pacific Mail SS Co.	May '98	Aug '98	$1,000	3,000	50 o; 1000 m
City of Sydney 5⊗ (rechartered)	Transport	Pacific Mail SS Co.	Aug '99	Jan '00	$750	3,000	Trooper
Cleveland ⊗	Transport	Charles Nelson Co.	Mar '99	June '99	$200	1,161	Freight
Colon ⊗	Transport	Pacific Mail SS Co.	May '98	Sept '99	$750	2,700	58 o; 950 m
Conemaugh ⊗	Transport	Empire Transportation Co.	Feb '99	?	$650	2,328	Animals
Conemaugh 1⊗ (rechartered)	Transport	Empire Transportation Co.	June '00	?	$450	2,328	Animals
Dainy Vostock	Transport	John Rosenfeld's Sons	Nov '99	Feb '00	$600	3,688	Troopship
Duke of Fife	Transport	John Rosenfeld's Sons	Nov '99	Mar '00	$900	3,821	Trooper
Duke of Fife (rechartered)	Transport	John Rosenfeld's Sons	June '00	?	?	3,821	Freight
Flintshire 1	Transport	G. W. McNear	Nov '99	Oct '00	$700 to $500	3,815	Animals
Frederica 1	Transport	?	Aug '00	Jan '01	?	?	Animals
Garonne 1⊗	Transport	E. L. Waterhouse	July '99	Apr '00	$700	3,901	Animals, trooper
Garonne 1⊗ (rechartered)	Transport	E. L. Waterhouse	July '00	Apr '01	?	3,901	Animals, trooper
Gelnogle	Transport	Fred Dodwell	Sept '99	Dec '99	$300	3,750	Trooper
Gelnogle (rechartered)	Transport	Fred Dodwell	Sept '01	?	?	3,750	Freight
George W. Elder ⊗	Transport	Goodall, Perkins and Co.	Sept '99	Nov '99	$550	1,709	Trooper
Gulf Pachile 1, 12	Transport	?	June '00	?	?	?	Troops and freight

Hyates [23] ⊗	Transport		June '01	Aug '01	?	?	–
Indiana ⊗	Transport	Empire Transportation Co.	June '98	[3a]	m) $25,000	3,158	58 o; 950 m
Indiana [1, 14] (rechartered)	Transport	Empire Transportation Co.	Sept '00	July '01	?	3,158	Troops and freight
Kintuck [1, 15]	Transport		Aug '00	July '01	?	?	Animals
Kvarven	Transport	PI ownership	July '00	Aug '00	?	?	Freight
Kwong Hoi [5a] ⊗	Transport	Saginaw Steel SS Co.	July '98	?	?	?	1000 o and m
Leelanaw [1, 16] ⊗	Transport	North Pacific SS Co.	Apr '99	Jan '01	$600; $475	1,924	Trooper; Animals
Lennox [1]	Transport	North Pacific SS Co.	Sept '99	Sept '00	$700-$575	3,677	Animals
Lennox [1, 17] (Rechartered)	Transport	Harry J. Hart	Sept '00	Aug '01	?	3,677	Freight
Manauense	Transport		Sept '99	Feb '00	$500	1,672	??
Marion Chilcott ⊗	Transport	Johnson-Locke Mercantile Co.	Apr '99	?	$21,531/trip to Manila	?	Freight
Morgan City ⊗	Transport		June '98	[4a]	$660	2,300	32 o; 700 m
Newport ⊗	Transport	Pacific Mail SS Co.	June '98	June '00	$1,000	2,735	30 o; 800 m
Nipon Maru	Transport	Japanese	Apr '99	?	?	?	Contract carrier-transpacific
Ohio ⊗	Transport	Empire Transportation Co.	May '98	Feb '00	m) $25,000	3,488	26 o; 916 m
Ohio ⊗ (rechartered)	Transport	Empire Transportation Co.	Apr '01	June '01	?	3,488	Trooper
Olympia ⊗	Transport	North American Mail SS Co.	Oct '99	Jan '00	$800	2,608	Trooper
Oopac [13]	Transport	?	Oct '00	May '01	?	?	Animals
Pakling [7]	Transport		July '00	July '01	?	?	Freight; animals
Pathan	Transport	Macondray and Co.	Oct '99	Feb '00	$700	2,709	Trooper
Pennsylvania ⊗	Transport	Empire Transportation Co.	July '98	[3a]	m) $25,000	3,166	–
Pennsylvania ⊗ (rechartered)	Transport	Empire Transportation Co.	?	June '01	?	3,166	Trooper
Peru ⊗	Transport	Pacific Mail SS Co.	June '98	Nov '98	$1,000	3,500	50 o; 1000 m
Port Albert [8, 18]	Transport	Frank Waterhouse	July '99	Mar '01	$600	3,514	Freight; animals
Port Stephens [1]	Transport	Frank Waterhouse	Oct '99	Feb '01	$750 to $600	3,554	Freight; animals
Portland ⊗	Transport	Alaska Commercial Co.	Feb '99	May '99	$300	1,420	Freight
Roanoke ⊗	Transport	North American Transportation and Trading Co.	Feb '99	May '00	$500	2,354	Trooper
Senator ⊗	Transport	Pacific Coast SS Co.	June '98	Aug '99	$1,000	2,409	43 o; 957 m
Senator [5] ⊗ (rechartered)	Transport	Pacific Coast SS Co.	Aug '99	Feb '00	$750	2,409	Trooper
Siam [19]	Transport	Macondray and Co.	Aug '99	June '00	$600 to $500	3,160	Animals
Siam (rechartered)	Transport	Macondray and Co.	Aug '00	Nov '00	?	3,160	Freight

Vessel	Type	Owner			Rate	Tonnage	Use
Sikh	Transport	John Rosenfeld's Sons	Aug '99	Dec '99	$600	3,606	Trooper
St. Paul [3] ⊗	Transport	Alaska Commercial Co.	July '98	Jan '00	$1,000	2,440	–
St. Paul [3] ⊗ (rechartered)	Transport	Alaska Commercial Co.	Aug '99	Feb '00	$700	2,440	Trooper
Strathgyle [20]	Transport	?	Aug '00	Dec '00	?	?	Troops; animals
Tacoma ⊗	Transport (sail rig)	Alaska Packers' Association	July '98	Unknown	$200	1,738	Animals
Tacoma [6] ⊗	Transport	Fred Dodwell	Sept '99	Dec '99	$650	2,811	Trooper
Tartar [22]	Transport	Harry J. Hart	July '99	Apr '00	$1,000	4,425	Troops; freight
Thyra [1]	Transport		Sept '00	July '01	?	?	Animals
Universe [1] ⊗	Transport		Aug '00	Nov '00	?	?	Freight [25]
Valencia ⊗	Transport	Pacific Steam Whaling Co.	June '98	Unknown	$650	1,598	29 o; 606 m
Valencia ⊗ (rechartered)	Transport	Pacific Steam Whaling Co.	June '99	Dec '99	$400	1,598	29 o; 606 m
Victoria [24] ⊗	Transport	North American Mail SS Co.	Aug '99	Mar '00	$800	3,502	Animals
Victoria [9]	Transport	J. -. Moore and Co.	Oct '99	May '00	$500	2,574	Freight
Westminster [1] [21]	Transport	Harry J. Hart	Oct '99	Jan '01	$650 to $450	3,859	Animals
Wilhelmina [1]	Transport		Oct '00	Feb '01	?	?	Freight
Wyefield [1]	Transport	Harry J. Hart	June '99	Jan '01	$650	5,200	Freight; animals
Zealandia ⊗	Transport	Oceanic SS Co.	May '98	Feb '99	m) $20,000	2,730	20 o; 750 m
Zealandia ⊗ (rechartered)	Transport	Oceanic SS Co.	June '99	Feb '00	m) $18,000	2,730	20 o; 750 m

Note 1: Upon the arrival of the expeditionary force at Manila, the expedition's quartermaster chartered a number of native lighters (caicos); later in the year and during 1899, other Filipino craft were also chartered. Vessels chartered in the Philippines will be enumerated on a separate list.

Note 2: Unless stated otherwise, all charters seem to have been of the time charter form.

⊗ American flag

1 Utilized in China Relief Expedition, 1900

1a All rates are daily except those prefixed with m) which are monthly

2 Still in service as of June 1900

2a Principle service of vessel is indicated; where information was available for troopers, capacity is given for carriage of officers (o); men (m)

3 Not to be confused with the naval auxiliary *St. Paul* on the east coast.

3a Still in service as of June 1900

4 Damaged by typhoon, en route to China.

4a Sank off Japan, September 1899

5 This vessel was chartered earlier during 1898, going off that first charter at some point (usually noted).

5a Chartered at Manila. Shallow draft enabled unloading of troops at Cavite pier which larger transports could not approach.

6 Not to be confused with the sail vessel *Tacoma* of 1,738 tons which was chartered during 1898.

7 Selected for China Relief Expedition, 1900, but rerouted to Manila.

8 Took troops from Philippine Islands thence China Relief Expedition during 1900.

9 Not to be confused with the *Victoria* of 3,502 tons, this apparently being a different vessel.

10 Brought U.S. dead back from China

11 Made trip to Kobe with horses and mules for China. All 771 animals arrived safely.

12 Chartered or hired to carry troops and freight from Nagasaki to Taku, China

13 Carried 750 horses and mules to Philippine Islands

14 Reported aground en route but floated off after unloading cargo and troops

15 Apparently was on bareboat charter to ATS

16 On one trip in 1900, she lost in a typhoon her entire cargo of 236 mules. Vessel was not damaged

17 Shaft broke while off of San Francisco; was towed to port

18 Routed to Alaska thence Manila and China

19 Lost 357 animals in typhoon, September 1899

20 She took aboard 100 personnel and a total of 723 horses on her one trip to Philippine Islands

21 Lost 47 horses and mules en route to Manila, probably from disease

22 Made three trips to Manila. In total carried 1,644 horses with no reported losses

23 Alaska run

24 Lost 83 animals en route Manila

25 Carried oats and hay as well as 50 barges for China Relief Expedition

Vessels Named in Army Operational Reports, Testimony, Correspondence, Memoirs, etc., As Being Army Utilized (apparently by charter or seizure) During the First Months of the Philippine Insurrection (1898-1901) But Which Are Not Listed in Charter Records or in Army Quartermaster Reports to War Department

Army sources: Parker, *The Old Army*; House of Representatives Document No. 2, Vol. 5, 56th Congress, 1st session

Name of vessel	Type of Usage
Francisco Reyes	Transport, interisland
Montanes	Transport, interisland
Vertus	Transport, interisland

Note: It is clear that some field commanders, other than Quartermaster officers, at times chartered or seized native vessels; however, the identifications of these vessels did not find their way into Quartermaster reports.

Foreign Vessels Time Chartered For Repatriation of Spanish Prisoners of War From Manila

Most, if not all of the vessels on this list are believed to have been of Spanish registry.

Sources: *Report of the Quartermaster General, 1899; Correspondence Relating to the War with Spain*

Name of vessel	Date of sailing	Passenger Capacity [1]
Alicante	Mar 13, 1899	72 o
Buenos Aires	Nov 8, 1898	97 o; 814 m
Buenos Aires	Mar 10, 1899	83 o; 984 m
Caebenore	Dec 12, 1898	30 o; 1,067 m
Catalona	May 6, 1899	71 o; 30 m
Ciudad de Cadiz	Apr 8, 1899	159 o; 93 m
Isla de Luzon	Dec 20, 1898	74 o; 600 m
Isla de Luzon	Mar 17, 1899	93 o; 35 m
Isla de Luzon	July 1, 1899	13 o; 16 m
Leon XIII	Jan 11, 1899	71 o; 625 m
Leon XIII	May 30, 1899	4 o; 6 m
P. Satrustegui [2]	Mar 6, 1899	140 o; 1,094 m
R. M. Christina	Feb 12, 1899	100 o; 807 m
Rio Negro	Feb 25, 1899	75 o; 991 m
Satrastegui [3]	June 3, 1899	11 o; 79 m
Sontserrat	Jan 16, 1899	46 o; 479 m
Uruguay	Feb 13, 1899	79 o; 989 m

[1] Carrying capacity: officers (o); men (m)

[2] Probably *P. de Satrustegui* on first charter.

[3] Probably *P. de Satrustegui* on a second charter.

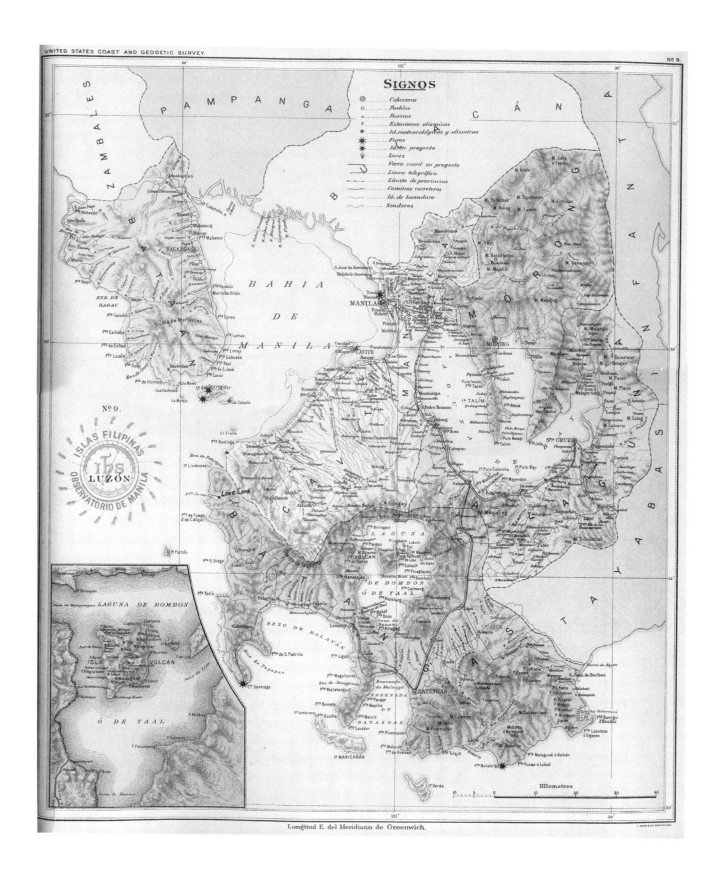

CHAPTER V

THE PHILIPPINE INSURGENCY AND THE LATER PACIFICATION CAMPAIGNS, 1899 - 1913

Late February of 1899 had marked the beginning of a determined offensive against the Insurgents. At that point, the Boxer problem in China was still well into the future. Although it would be over six months before the new volunteer regiments would begin to arrive in the Philippines, Maj. Gen. Elwell S. Otis, the then commander in the Philippines, decided that the troop strength he had on hand was sufficient to begin moving small exploratory columns beyond the perimeter of Manila. These operations began with an amphibious strike into the region lying to the west of the city.

Using the Pasig River as the avenue of approach, troop-carrying launches supported by a bevy of river gunboats moved a force of brigade strength into the great lake called Laguna de Bay. The operation turned out successfully and for the time being neutralized Insurgent strength in that region. However, it would not be until January of the following year that Laguna de Bay and its environs could be declared safe for commercial traffic.[1] Following that operation, Maj. Gen. Arthur MacArthur's command was sent north from Manila on a campaign which resulted in the capture of the town of Malolos in late March 1899. The taking of Malolos was highly significant as that place had been named the capital of Aguinaldo's declared republic. While the taking of the town dealt a telling blow to Insurgent morale, it also influenced many Filipinos to remain neutral who otherwise might have joined the Insurgent movement.

---

[1] *Correspondence Relating to the War with Spain,* Vol. II, p 1138, Report of MacArthur's headquarters received by Adjutant General, Washington, January 24, 1900.

Although Otis's immediate concern was Luzon, the archipelago's southern islands were also not to be neglected. Port Cebu, later to be named Cebu City and located on the eastern coast of the island of Cebu, was occupied by a naval force of Marines and *blue jackets* which was soon relieved by one of Otis's regiments which settled in for what looked to be a peaceful occupation. But it was not peaceful for long. Almost immediately trouble started from what at first appeared to be bandit groups (landrones) with a thirst for mayhem which they directed to all within reach, including American forces. As later discovered, it was Aguinaldo's agents who had stirred things up.

Negros, an island lying across a narrow strait to the west of Cebu, was a somewhat different story. The Filipino part of the population was restricted to towns on the coastal fringes where the people showed a strong desire for peace. Their leaders were active in seeking American protection against wild tribal elements from the island's interior who had been encouraged in their depredations by the removal of the Spanish garrisons. To meet the request for protection, Otis shipped in an infantry battalion from Manila. Although clearly an inadequate force considering the territory to be policed, it was all that could be spared. The choice of that battalion was a good one as its commander was a volunteer officer with a civil background in administration. He organized a native government and police force which, operating under his direct supervision, quickly brought stability to the coastal region, thus allowing the Americans to strike into the interior. Everything went very well until Aguinaldo's agents arrived on the scene. The situation soon became even worse than it had been prior to the American arrival.

Meanwhile on Luzon, and following the taking of the town of Malolos, columns of MacArthur's troops penetrated deeper into Insurgent-held territory. In almost all instances, they bested against the enemy; however, little was actually accomplished as once the columns out-marched their supply, they were forced to withdraw, allowing the Insurgents to return and again take up their old positions. Clearly, if anything constructive was to happen, all the rural provinces would have to be occupied, but that would take manpower not yet available.

By the early fall of 1899, the new volunteer regiments together with fresh units of the Regular Army began arriving in the islands. Confident that he finally had enough troops to bring about a lasting defeat of Aguinaldo's army, Otis ordered MacArthur to conduct a sustained campaign consisting of a 2-pronged offensive, one thrust moving northward from Malolos through central Luzon and the other taking the form of an amphibious landing on the Lingayen Gulf which was intended to block off Aguinaldo's army from returning into the mountainous section of Luzon's most northern provinces. That campaign lasted a little over two months, culminating in the collapse of anything Aguinaldo could claim as an organized force. From that point on, the Philippine Insurrection would take on the appearance of scattered guerrilla warfare. The belief commonly held by the American commanders, when prognosticating over what would be Aguinaldo's new strategy, was that he would attempt to tie up Otis's troops with their attendant expense to the United States until the American presidential elections. For the second time, William McKinley's opponent was William Jennings

Bryan; and as Aguinaldo was surely aware, Bryan stood solidly against the annexation of the Philippines.

On the premise that Aguinaldo was no longer able to field any force in large strength, Otis decided on a policy of occupation throughout the archipelago. The major population centers would be garrisoned with troop strengths that were based on the best available estimates of guerrilla or landrone forces operating in the respective areas. In most cases, this policy would work out, although in some provinces where intelligence estimates proved wrong, the Americans found themselves to be dangerously contested. In conjunction with the occupying troops, Otis established military governorships tasked with infusing a doctrine of Americanization which relied heavily on school systems and free market economics.

~

The very dictates of Philippine geography with its lack of roads made transport of the Army's strike forces by sea and river a necessity.[2] Most of those operations utilized the Army's own craft although a few landings were with the assist of the Navy. If ports were available, the troops were usually carried to the site by the Army's interisland transports; but during the majority of operations, port facilities were not conveniently located, therefore mandating over-the-beach approaches. These landings employed smaller craft which the Army classified as launches.

By the summer of 1902, military garrisons had been located on every island of the archipelago. The need for their logistical support meant a marked increase in the numbers of small ships and lessor craft. The Chief Quartermaster, Division of the Philippines, on June 30, 1902, informed the Quartermaster General of the numbers of vessels then being employed by the Division of the Philippines for interisland service. Excluding minor craft such as row boats, the total came to 265.[3] Broken down into categories there were:

10   Coastal class vessels classified as U.S. Army transports (USATs).

2   Oceangoing USATs temporarily assigned to ATS command, Philippines.

12   Coastal freighters, classified as U.S. Chartered Transports (USCTs) on bareboat charter from their Filipino owners.[4]

15   Coastal freighters hired on time charter formats.

3   Coal hulks moored for replenishment purposes, Manila harbor.

6   Heavy launches, armed and armored, dedicated to gunboat service.

54   Launches varying from 100-ton class down to a 20-80 ton class. A 1902 report listed these as gunboats, but in reality they seem to have been transportation launches which at times were armed.

10   Tugs. Unknown as to whether these were bareboat or time chartered.

6   Schooners. Unknown as to whether these were bareboat or time chartered; probably the latter.

9   Steam lighters.

55   Wooden, towed lighters, some built by the QM Department in the Philippines and some by private contractors for the QM.

83   Cascos (small towed harbor cargo craft) *leased* by QM.

---

[2]   The origin of modern amphibious warfare doctrine has been credited to the United States Marine Corps. A review of United States Army deployments within the Philippines, circa 1899-1902, tells a somewhat different tale and seems to provide a fertile field for inquiry.

[3]   From letter dated June 30, 1902, Chief QM, Division of the Philippines, to Quartermaster General. Microfilm Records, National Archives, Series 1794, 1808, 1829, 1870, 1874, 1882, 1886. See year group for 1901-1902. The June 30 letter attachments have the names of the vessels; however, we found some name duplications as well as some omissions, one omission being that of the launch *Oceania* mentioned in a report of Maj. General Lawton describing an operation at San Isidro when that particular launch was under the command of "Sergeant Harris on the Rio Chico River."

[4]   The QM, Philippines, reported that there were eleven coastal transports classed as USCTs; however, another report issued by that same officer lists twelve USCTs, each by name, that list being reproduced at the end of this chapter.

To handle the flow of troops and materiel, the infrastructure at Manila required extensive improvement and reorganization over that which had been hastily put in place during 1898. From 1898 into early 1901, the operations at the port at Manila were administered under a sub-branch of the Chief Quartermaster's Office for the Philippines. This sub-branch was placed under the direct command of Manila's Depot Quartermaster. On April 1, 1901, depot functions were absorbed by the newly constituted Philippine Office of the Army Transport Service which was assigned a staffing organization similar to that which had been put into place at the ports of San Francisco and New York. The responsibility of ATS, Philippines, would now cover the shipment of all troops and Army cargoes routed from the Philippines to the United States, whether upon Pacific or Atlantic based transports, and for all interisland shipments of troops and cargoes. Four commissioned officers were assigned to ATS headquarters at Manila with a number of others being assigned to the sub-ports on the other islands. By June of 1902, 234 civilians had become entered into federal employment as part of the management team. The majority worked in supervisory capacities; or as Quartermaster agents assigned aboard interisland transports; or as masters, mates, and engineers on those transports. A roster within the records of the Quartermaster General for that year indicates that the large majority of these people were of Anglo-Saxon origin, only four having Hispanic names. On the strength of that, it can be reasonably concluded that a large part of these individuals had been hired in the United States for duty in the Philippines.

According to the Officer in Charge, Water Transportation, ATS, Philippines, for the fiscal year 1901-1902, the ATS had transported the following number of personnel to and from the Philippines as well as upon interisland routes:

U.S. to Manila	731 commissioned officers
	2,375 civilian passengers **
	14,661 enlisted men
Manila to U.S.	1,051 commissioned officers
	2,660 civilian passengers **
	27,540 enlisted men
Manila to interisland ports	802 commissioned officers
	2,732 civilian passengers **
	15,326 enlisted men
Interisland ports to Manila	710 commissioned officers
	2,030 civilian passengers **
	16,842 enlisted men
Manila to China	10 commissioned officers
	42 civilian passengers **
China to Manila	3 commissioned officers
	107 civilian passengers **

** dependents and civil government employees

The number of individual ships which were named as having made entry or departure from Manila harbor and which were directly in ATS service for the fiscal year totaled: 155 steamer listings of transpacific routings and 652 steamer listings for vessels engaged on interisland routings.[5]

---

[5] Report of the ATS Office, Philippines, Officer in Charge, Water Transportation, as addressed to Chief Quartermaster, Division of the Philippines, dated June 30, 1902, taken from Records, Office of the QM General - AN4. The figures given in this particular report relating to passengers, "U.S. to Manila," 1901-1902, differ to a small degree from those reported by the Quartermaster General as incorporated within the *Report of the War Department*.

~

Gradually the occupations of many of the various islands were expanded from the coastal towns and villages into the interior. The native populations, sensing that full American control was but a matter of time, began losing whatever enthusiasm or fear they held regarding the Insurgents or the landrones, whichever the local case might have been. The more opportunistic Filipinos soon began providing the Americans with intelligence.

The formal fighting force which had made up the Aguinaldo independence movement ended in March of 1901 with Aguinaldo's capture following which he took an oath of allegiance to the United States. Aguinaldo at that time also wrote a manifesto calling on the population of the Philippines to accept the rule of the United States. Throughout that summer, most of Aguinaldo's subordinate generals gave up with only three of them continuing to proclaim the goal of independence. One holdout general was located in the Province of Batangas in southern Luzon; the two others were located on the islands of Samar and Leyte. The American military effort against these holdouts would last well into 1902 and would mark the most bitter part of the entire struggle.

For those American Army personnel who participated in the campaigns against the Insurgents and landrones between 1899 and 1902, it was a costly affair: For the period February 4, 1899, through July 4, 1902, 1,004 officers and men were killed in combat; 2,911 were wounded; and 4,165 died from disease and accidents.[6]

With the independence movement at an end, there were still the landrone problems as well as the Moro of the southern islands left to deal with. It would be eleven years into the future before true peace was realized.

The Process of Americanization

As earlier stated, Maj. Gen. Arthur MacArthur relieved Maj. Gen. Elwell S. Otis as Military Governor of the Philippines in the spring of 1900. MacArthur was a strong personality, and from the start an umbrageous relationship had developed between him and the president of the Philippine Commission, the equally strong-headed William Howard Taft. Taft, a jurist of some reputation, had been appointed to the Philippine Commission by President McKinley to succeed Jacob Gould Schurman. Established in January of 1899, the Commission had been originally charged *to investigate affairs in the Philippine Islands.* With that charge fulfilled, the Commission submitted its report to President McKinley on January 31, 1900.[7]

In an earlier interim report dated April 4, 1899, the Commission had laid out a suggested policy which had been developed after consultation with the McKinley Administration. In summary, that policy declared to the people of the Philippines:

---

[6]   Brian McAllister Linn, *Guardians of Empire: The U.S. Army and the Pacific, 1902 - 1940,* (Chapel Hill and London: University of North Carolina Press, 1997), p 16.

[7]   Although civilian in authority and structure, the Philippine Commission was initially made up of both military and civilian members as represented by Rear Adm. George Dewey, Maj. Gen. Elwell S. Otis, Dean C. Worcester, and Charles Denby.

- Overall sovereignty of the United States over the islands of the Philippines, but with considerable liberties to be granted to the peoples of the islands, inclusive of a mechanism for self-government, provided that local actions were reconcilable and compatible with the interests of the United States.

- The forbidding of outside interests to exploit the Philippines in a manner harmful to the native population.

- A guarantee that the Philippines were to have a civil service integral to the Philippine's indigenous population, provided that the people of the Philippines showed the capability for undertaking that responsibility.

- All taxes collected were to be for the benefit of the Philippine Islands and their population.

- The inauguration of a speedy and just system of criminal and civil justice.

- The establishment of a transportation network and other vital public utilities.

- The encouragement of domestic and foreign trade for the benefit of the Philippine people.

- A program for education through elementary schools as well as higher grade institutions.

- Reforms made throughout the extant system, both within local government and within the islands' internal and external commerce.

The Commission would work closely with Filipino civic leaders in an attempt to effect a compromise with the United States toward the goal of implementing these policies. In general, the immediate goal was to develop a constitution giving a modified self-rule through the creation of a legislature overseen by a civil governor general aided by an administrative staff appointed by the United States. The eventual goal was to nurture the Philippines into becoming a protectorate of the United States with total self rule to be granted once the islands' populations had gained sufficient experience with democratic processes to be able to govern themselves with stability. It had become evident to those Americans who had been closely involved that it would be some years before the islands could even reach the point where law and order, not to mention internal compatibility of its diverse populations, would allow all of this to happen.[8] Prior to and for some months following the issuance of the Commissioner's final report in January 1900, the role of governor general remained vested in the military commander, and it was the military during that period which provided administration for the various provinces.

At first MacArthur was opposed to a civilian takeover of what he considered to be the unsettled situation throughout the archipelago. He believed that in the situation which existed, the task of governing belonged with the military. Taft's influence with the administration in Washington along with his skillful manipulation of the difficult MacArthur brought about an arrangement which, if not exactly pleasing to the general, was acceptable to both the War Department and to the White House. Under that arrangement, the Commission would be continued and would consist, as it had in the past, of both a military and a civil membership. Detailed to the Commission's

---

[8] *Report of the Philippine Commission to the President,* Vol. I, (Washington, DC: Government Printing Officer, 1900), pp 216-228, Exhibit VI.

day-to-day administration were to be personnel assigned by the Army together with civilians sent out from the United States, the latter having backgrounds specific to creating and training a civil service as well as supervising a teaching corps. There was to be a gradual Americanization, both in political terms as well as in the islands' social and commercial structuring.

During July of 1901, William Howard Taft was inaugurated as Governor General of the Philippines, thus beginning a civilian-dominated administration. Convenient to a smooth transition of power, the War Department replaced Maj. General MacArthur with Maj. Gen. Adna R. Chaffee as troop commander for the islands. Since it appeared that complete pacification of all of the islands would take some time, the plan was to leave under the jurisdiction of the military those provinces which were not yet considered pacified. However, once a province was brought under control, its administration was to be handed over to civil jurisdiction. During what would be the transition phase from military to civil, troops would remain on hand until a civil structure established by Commission personnel had taken firm root. Then a provincial governor would be appointed by the Commission as chief administrator for the particular province. Appointments as provincial governors were initially given to officers detached by the Army for that duty. Military officers given such assignments (all of whom became subordinate to the Commission) were detailed to the more remote or potentially troublesome areas where close liaison with Army units was still considered necessary. By 1904, much progress had taken place and most provincial governorships were being held by civilians. In a few areas which were deemed by the Commission as being especially secure, elections had been held, turning over the provincial governor slots to local choice.

To police the provinces, the Commission at its onset had established a Philippine Constabulary. It was organized and officered by the Army but was in effect a form of state police subordinated to the governor of the respective province in which the Constabulary units were stationed. By early 1902, the Constabulary force consisted of two thousand men, most of whom had been recruited within the immediate district where they were stationed. With an eye toward the reduction of the American Army's presence in the Philippines, the Army would establish the Philippine Scouts, an organization integrated with the U.S. Army, and officered by detached commissioned and non-commissioned American officers. On many operations which were conducted against landrone bands, Philippine Scout detachments worked in conjunction with the Constabulary. Whenever on such missions, the Constabulary became tactically subordinate to the senior officer of the respective Scout unit.[9]

Reporting directly to the Governor General of the Philippines were a variety of departments and bureaus, one of which was the Bureau of Coast Guard and Transportation to which was assigned a number of vessels employed for general transportation as well as support of Constabulary missions. The vessels were officered

---

[9]   *Annual Report of the War Department,* Vol. XI, Part 1, "Report of the Philippine Commission for the Fiscal Year Ended June 30, 1904",. (Washington, DC: Government Printing Office, 1905), pp 14-16.

by Americans with indigenous crews.[10] On a few occasions, the Philippine Coast Guard was called upon to assist with Army field expeditions; however, in general, it was held apart from military missions.

The road construction program which had originally been instituted by the Army was later taken up by the Philippine Commission, continuing an impressive effort which brought mobility, commerce, and civilization to the provinces -- especially to those areas which before boasted of little more than foot paths.

The system of secondary schools and the public health improvements which the United States established throughout the islands have never been equaled by any other colonial power before or since. The American occupation of the Philippines would become, without much question, a benevolent assimilation. The civilian administrators, technicians, and teachers who brought all this about and who would gradually replace American military personnel were mostly recruited in the United States and transported to the Philippines (and later returned) by the Army Transport Service.

~

President William McKinley, victim of an assassin's bullet, died on September 14, 1901. He was succeeded by his vice president, Theodore Roosevelt. On July 4, 1902, Roosevelt proclaimed -- somewhat inaccurately -- that peace had at last arrived in the Philippines. That proclamation stated that provincial governments had been established in all *the territory of the archipelago excepting those areas inhabited by Moro tribes.* [11] Such a pronouncement was premature by more than a decade. Long an advocate of the United States taking a leading role in world affairs, Roosevelt was being confronted at the time with segments of the body politic which believed that the cost of retaining the Philippines had already become inordinately high for what it might be worth in eventual pay-back. Accordingly, many historians of those years hold that Roosevelt's 1902 pronouncement of hostilities having come to an end was made to mollify those in Congress and within the press who were then advocating a pullout from the islands. The reality was that pacification was still a long way off. Much, but not all of the problem remaining was with landrone bands operating against Filipino settlements as well as neighboring tribal groups. A major outbreak had occurred on southern Luzon at the very time that Roosevelt had made his claim of peaceful coexistence. Concurrently on the islands of Samar and Leyte, terrorists who appeared to have some sort of mystic quasi-Christian motivation behind their violence,

---

[10]   The Bureau of Coast Guard and Transportation was initially created as of October 17, 1901, to assist in the general task of pacification and of guarding against smuggling operations and of providing a Lighthouse Service. The Lighthouse Service had the opening task of rebuilding and adding to the lighthouse network of the archipelago which had fallen into a state of abandonment and disrepair under the Spanish. To that effort the Bureau appointed Cdr. J. M. Helm, USN, as Superintendent of Construction. Between October of 1901 and September of 1902, the United States appropriated $52,709.00 for construction and general purposes for the Lighthouse Service and for steam launches the sum of $96,855.00. For the Coast Guard, during the same time frame, appropriations were $435,599.00 for vessels and cutters. Source: Regino Dodds Giagonia, *The Philippine Navy, 1898-1996,* (Manila: Publication of the Philippine Navy, 1997), pp 111-115. For an account of one American's service in the Philippine Coast Guard, see Capt. Carl Rydell, *On Pacific Frontiers,* (Chicago: World Book Co., 1926). Also, see David Grover, "America's First Coast Guard," *Sea Classics,* (Canoga Park, CA: Vol. 26, July - August, 1993), an informative article on the Philippine Coast Guard.

[11]   *Correspondence Relating to the War with Spain,* Vol. II, p 1350, transmittal of wireless message to General Chaffee from Elihu Root, Secretary of War, Washington, July 2, 1902.

had come close to rendering the interior of those two islands untenable to all but their own followers. In one policing foray launched against them, two companies of Constabulary were nearly wiped out. In 1902 and again in 1903, under the urging of the Governor General, policies were legislated which established that hostile elements -- regardless of their purpose -- who operated against the peace would be viewed as outlaws to be dealt with as such. A claim of ideology, whether political or religious in orientation, would no longer provide amnesty or prisoner-of-war protection to such persons.[12]

Starting with the summer of 1902, field operations were carried out by the Constabulary backed up by local garrisons of the Regular Army and by the Philippine Scouts. To help make the Constabulary into an effective force, its numbers would eventually be increased to seventy-five hundred men. The one major exception to the employment of the Constabulary against hostiles was within those provinces peopled by the Moro. The fighting qualities of the Moro and their excellent internal discipline was such that it was felt that the Constabulary would be outfought. Consequently, that job was to be left to the Army and to the American-officered Philippine Scouts.[13]

The story of the U.S. Army's effort toward attaining peace in the Philippines was not without blemish. Charges of atrocities by the occupation army would prove all too accurate. One case resulted from an attack against an Army garrison on Samar carried out by guerrillas and aided by local townspeople. Taken by total surprise, the garrison lost forty-eight out of its strength of seventy-four men. In retaliation, the Army commander on Samar, Brig. Gen. Jacob H. Smith, ordered that the island be turned into *a howling wilderness,* and that every male over the age of ten be shot. Fortunately for the islanders, most of Smith's subordinates, cognizant of the lack of rationality within such an order, interpreted it in a more moderate fashion than Smith had intended. Because of that order, Smith was relieved and shipped back to Washington to await formal court martial charges.[14] On Luzon, the American brigade commander in charge of the southern provinces instituted a program which concentrated the rural population into small areas, doing so with the intent of isolating guerrilla units from the support formerly provided to them by the farmers of the countryside. Some of the concentration areas were actually fenced camps into which people were herded. Lacking any plans in advance for these population concentrations, food supplies were soon down to starvation levels, and sanitary facilities were almost non-existent. The result was severe outbreaks of disease and subsequent deaths. The War Department had never advocated methods of this severity, rightly believing that they could only bring about negative results. There were also a number of well-proven instances of the *water torture* having been practiced by Army intelligence officers attempting to pry information from captured guerrillas. In retrospect, though, the

---

[12]   The legislation changing the ground rules for dealing with hostile groups was the Brigandage Act of 1902 and the Reconstruction Act of 1903.

[13]   By the 1920s, the Philippine Scouts would have largely replaced the Regular Army on most of the islands. The 1923 *Report of the Secretary of War* listed that organization as comprising 7,007 Filipino enlisted men.

[14]   *Correspondence Relating to the War with Spain,* Volumes I and II, pp 335-337, 1344, 1347, 1348, 1354.

occasional episodes of barbaric treatment of the Philippine people by the U.S. Army were blown out of all proportion by those newspaper editors in the United States with anti-imperialistic leanings. They latched on to such instances as grist for the mill as to why the United States should not have occupied the Philippines.

After all was said and done, and when taken under close examination, the U.S. Army did an outstanding job of bringing order out of chaos, achieving that accomplishment within areas which throughout the centuries had known only violence.[15] Put into perspective, instances of atrocities by Americans were far surpassed by those cruelties carried out by the Insurgents and other assorted hostiles against the Americans as well as against those of the indigenous populations who sided with or otherwise assisted the occupation.

The Moro

Within the sub-archipelago of the Sulu area and on the big island of Mindanao, the slave-holding Moro were to remain a serious problem well into the second decade of the twentieth century. Historically, Moro aggression had been directed against neighboring tribal groups as well as any Spanish administrators bold enough to venture into Moro territory. Any and all outsiders remained unsafe in such territories, including sizable patrols of the American military. Even the sea adjacent to the southern islands was no refuge since much of the Moro economy was dependent upon revenues made from piracy.

The year following his 1902 pronouncement that peace had at last come to the Philippines, President Theodore Roosevelt suffered the personal embarrassment of having to order an all-out military effort against the Moro of Mindanao. Roosevelt was motivated in this by the realization that the Stars and Stripes must fly without challenge throughout all of the islands of the Philippines. The chessboard of the western Pacific was then being actively played by a number of European powers, and intervention by any of them in the southern islands of the archipelago would be clearly against the strategic position of the United States. For some time, the Army had garrisoned three of the major towns on Mindanao's coastline, but it was a tenuous holding at best. Now, complying with the President's instructions, three battalions of infantry penetrated in from the north coast of Mindanao toward Lake Lanao where, short of the lake by some miles, they went into permanent encampment. Observing the American strength, the local Moro sultans promised peace but warned that the Americans should not move farther inland. Refusing to bow to a threat of that sort, the Army followed up with a major effort, this time in brigade strength against the Moro forts located along the banks of Lake Lanao. By November (1904) all but one of the Moro sultans had either surrendered or fled to the mountains. The hold-out, one Datto Ali, continued armed opposition until 1905 when he was killed following an assault on his ranchero. His followers immediately gave themselves up, and it was thought at the time that this marked the end of the Moro trouble. But this was not to be. Spasmodic defiance against American occupation carried out by Moro groups continued for the next decade. Their eventual pacification -- especially in the Lanao Lake District -- was

---

[15]   Brian McAllister Linn, *The U.S. Army and Counterinsurgency in the Philippine War, 1899-1902*, (Chapel Hill, NC and London: University of North Carolina Press, 1989), pp 26, 27.

in large part due to improvement in the mobility of American forces. This was brought about by the Army's salvage of four gunboats which the Spanish had scuttled in Lake Lanao in 1898. These four gunboats, together with one of American manufacture which the Army transported overland to the lake in pieces, provided the necessary firepower and speed of movement which had not been available prior to their employment.

The effort against the Moro had been long and costly. Casualties were heavy, especially on the Moro side. New American weaponry, the most telling of which had been the Gatling gun, played havoc. When Maj. John J. Pershing attacked a Moro fort at Bud Basak in January of 1913, the Moro who fought there appeared to welcome death, a wish -- if indeed it was a wish -- that resulted in five hundred of them being killed as against the better-armed Americans who suffered only fifteen dead and twenty-five wounded. The action at Bud Basak marked the end of the war against the Moro.[16]

Acts of brigandage would continue on most of the islands right up to the eve of the Second World War; but they were scattered in occurrences, and where and when they did occur, the outlaws involved were small in number and were easily handled by the Constabulary. After the defeat of the Moro, the U.S. Army's role in the Philippines reverted to that of guarding against foreign interlopers -- a task which except for the Japanese scare of 1907 remained passive in nature until that fateful date of December 8, 1941 (Philippine time).

The War Scare of 1907

During 1904, Japan won a resounding victory over the Russian Navy in the Far East. Japan subsequently occupied Port Arthur (now Lüshun) on the Yellow Sea. To the alarm of the west, it was a victory which placed Japan into the position of a world power. In an effort to bring stability into what could develop into a volatile scene for European and American presence in the western Pacific, the United States offered to mediate the peace negotiations between Russia and Japan. President Theodore Roosevelt met with the parties at Portsmouth, New Hampshire, where the arrogant attitude of the Japanese delegates boded an uncertain future for western presence in Asia.

Trouble erupted during 1906 between Japan and the United States, brought about, it is strange to say, by a local school board in San Francisco. The Californians had long practiced discrimination against Orientals, but it was generally minor when compared to the 1906 episode. The San Francisco School Board had voted to not only segregate Oriental children to special *Oriental public schools,* but it also assigned to those same schools, *children of filthy or vicious habits, or children suffering from contagious or infectious diseases.* The reaction from the Japanese diplomatic and business community in San Francisco was immediate. Their indignation was transmitted to Tokyo where the issue became of such magnitude that by 1907 Japan stood at the brink of war with the United States.

---

[16]   Or so it was for the period of American occupation. However, as late as the year 2001, this same ethnic group was engaged in terrorist activity against the Philippine Government.

The obvious target for the Japanese in such a war would be the Philippines, and that is where the United States was most vulnerable. The remnants of the old Spanish forts were so outmoded as to be entirely useless. Little had been done to establish permanent fortifications. The U.S. Navy held the idea of constructing a base on the west coast of Luzon at Subic Bay, a recommendation put forth in 1901 but from which nothing had since materialized. In 1907, on the initiatives of the War and Navy Departments, President Theodore Roosevelt called a conference of the top officers and the Secretaries of both departments resulting with the establish of a joint Army-Navy survey to decide where and how the Philippines were to be fortified. The survey concluded that it would be best to concentrate a defense on the island of Luzon rather than dilute the effort among the outer islands.[17] Another of the decisive factors was that a loss of Manila (which was the political capital of the islands) would be catastrophic to United States relations with the Filipinos, not to mention the loss of prestige that the United States would suffer from the world-at-large.

The keystone for Manila Bay defenses was to be the rocky island of Corregidor which could be easily supported by interlocking fire zones from heavy guns mounted on the southern shore of the Bataan Peninsula as well as from neighboring islands to the south. The board stressed the importance of the United States maintaining control of the sea approaches to the Philippines, warning that without it, an enemy force could land as it wished anywhere on northern Luzon and at its leisure move in and encircle Manila from the land side. The capitulation of the city and of the Army's defenses on the outer bay would then be but a matter of time.[18]

Fortunately, the crisis of 1907 passed, but the seeds of racial divisiveness remained to fester and permeate relations between the United States and Japan. In time, the plans to fortify the approaches to Manila and establish a naval base near the city of Cavite on Manila Bay became a reality. The survey board's warnings over the importance of controlling the sea approaches to the islands would prove prophetic when an inadequacy of naval strength in the Western Pacific from December of 1941 to May of 1942 resulted in the loss of the Philippines to the Japanese.

---

[17] The decisions arrived at were not without controversy: the Navy held a preference for Subic Bay while the Army argued for Manila. The Army officers assigned to the survey held that to concentrate on Subic Bay (on Luzon's western coast) would be a poor choice since it precluded an adequate defense against an attack coming either from the sea or overland.

[18] The events of 1906 and 1907 are taken from: Louis Morton, "Military and Naval Preparations for the Defense of the Philippines During the War Scare of 1907," *Military Affairs,* (Journal of the American Military Institute, Summer, 1949), pp 95-104.

Steam Vessels Being Utilized By The Army Transport Service As Interisland Transports In The Philippines, Circa 1902

Source: *Report of the ATS, Philippines, to the Quartermaster General for Fiscal Year Ending June 1902*
contained within Record Group 92
These vessels were chartered under a form of bareboat, their names were prefaced at that time by the
Philippine Quartermaster Department as USCTs (United States Chartered Transports)

USCT Brutus	*USCT Ibandan*
USCT Buen Diaje	*USCT Isla de Negros*
USCT Castellano	*USCT Lal Loc*
USCT Columbia	*USCT Pronto*
USCT Formosa	*USCT Salamanca*
USCT Hai Mun	*USCT Sam Shui*

Coastal Class Vessels Employed Under Hire By The Army Transport Service In The Philippines, 1902

Taken from the *Reports of the ATS, Philippines, to the Quartermaster General for Fiscal Year Ending June 30, 1902*
contained within Record Group 92; and in the case of *PEERLESS*, from the memoirs of Carl Rydell.
Vessels listed are believed to have been employed on time charter format.
Within the Army's reports, they were not designated as USCTs.

STEAMERS	TUGS	SCHOONERS
Butuan	*Aeolus*	*Carmen*
Cerrantes	*Bacolod*	*Franz*
Francisco Reyes	*Bisayas*	*Lorenzo*
Hai Loong	*Churrica*	*Loyalo*
Venus	*Fanny*	*Mayo*
	Isabel	*Neuva Caceres*
	Legazpi	*Peerless*
	N.S. Del Carmen	
	N.S. Del Gracia	
	Pleuhue-Chuelo	

Naval Gunboats Used In Joint Army-Navy Operations, Philippines, 1898-1911

Sources: Smythe, *Guerrilla Warrior; Dictionary of American Naval Fighting Ships*;
Linn, *The U.S. Army and Counterinsurgency in the Philippine War, 1899-1902*

Name of vessel	Sources
Callao, USS	Dictionary
Don Juan de Austria, USS	Dictionary; Linn
Quiros, USS	Dictionary
Samar, USS	Smythe; Dictionary

Army Gunboats Known To Have Been Put Into Active Service Between 1904 and 1907 On Mindanao, Philippine Islands

Sources: Feuer, *Combat Diary; Annual Reports of the War Department*

Name of vessel	Comments
Corcuera	Scuttled by Spanish, 1898; salved by Army 1907 for service against the Moro
Flake	Constructed for Army, 1904 for service against the Moro
General Almonte	Scuttled by Spanish, 1898; salved by Army 1904 for service against the Moro
General Blanco	Scuttled by Spanish, 1898; salved by Army 1907 for service against the Moro
Lanao	Scuttled by Spanish, 1898; salved by Army 1905 for service against the Moro

Note: The gunboats employed on Mindanao circa 1904-18 do not appear to have been under the charge of the Quartermaster Department as none of the five above listed, nor a number of salvaged barges, are found within the Army Transport Service vessel rosters.

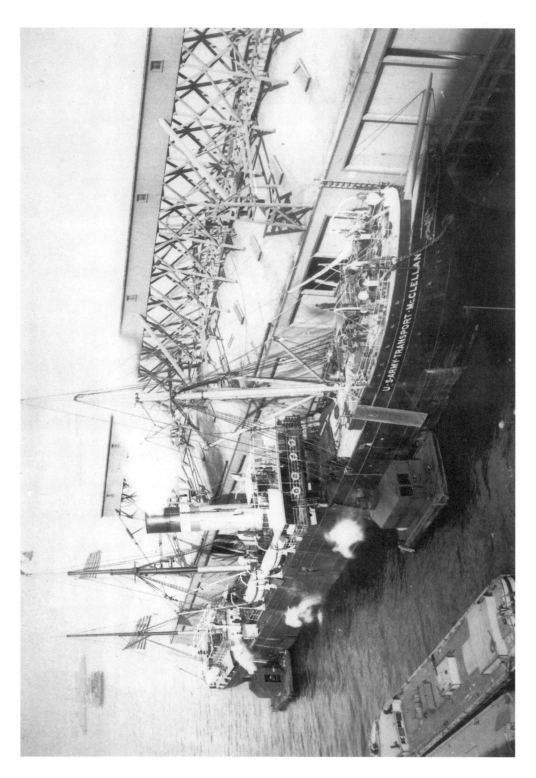

USAT McClellan, ex *Port Victor.* Veteran transport. Purchased by the Army in 1898 for service during the *War with Spain.* Used for interisland service during the Philippine Insurrection and for Vera Cruz operation of 1914. During WWI, made one round trip between New York and France before returning to France where she was moored for use as a stationary refrigeration warehouse. Went out of Army service in 1920. National Archives Collection.

*USAT **Burnside**, ex Rita.* Captured from Spanish in 1898. Served in Army Transport Service (Atlantic fleet) through 1899; then transferred to the Pacific Fleet. Converted to a cable ship in 1914. Went out of Army service in 1920. National Archives Collection.

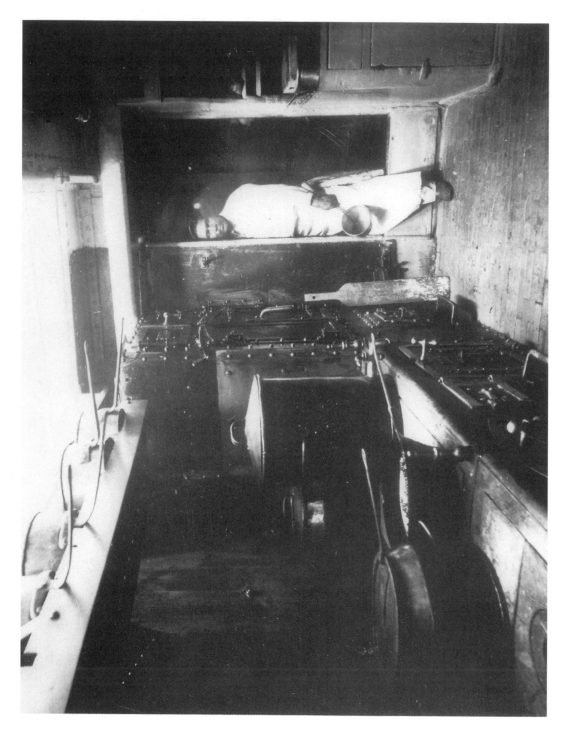

Galley scene aboard the time chartered *SS Australia,* circa 1898–1899. National Archives Collection.

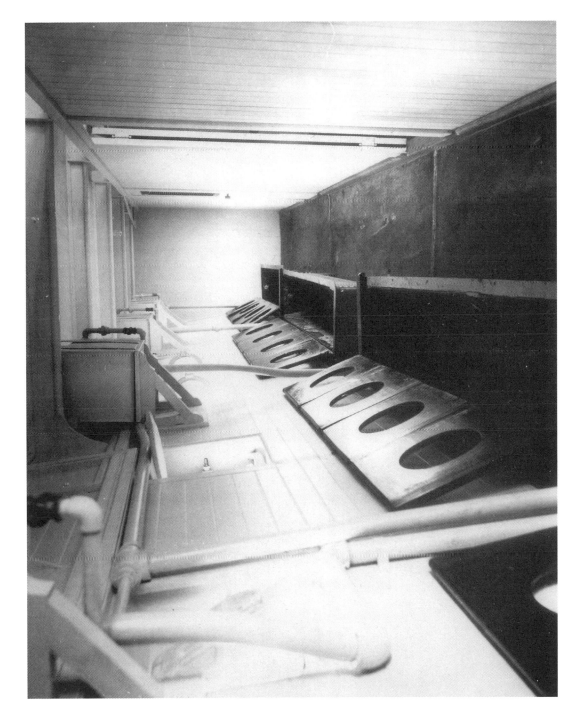

Enlisted men's head on *SS Australia*. Ship was time chartered by the Army for transpacific service during 1898 and 1899. National Archives Collection.

Officer's head, USAT Thomas. Purchased from Atlantic Transport through Bernard N. Baker on July 26, 1898, for $660,000. Photo was probably taken soon after purchase; see company name on towel. National Archives Collection.

Enlisted men's quarters aboard the **USAT Grant**, ex *Mohawk*, circa 1901. This was a different ship than the *USAT U.S. Grant*; ex *USAT Madawaska*; ex *USS Madawaska*; ex *Konig Wilhelm II*, which did not go into Army service until September 1919. National Archives Collection.

Loading horses for the Philippines aboard the time chartered **SS Aztec,** 1901. In the background is the **USAT Rosecrans,** ex *Columbia.*
National Archives Collection.

CHAPTER VI

ARMY SHIPPING IN THE ATLANTIC
1901 - 1916

Preliminary to the 1898 invasion of Cuba, a congressional resolution authorizing United States intervention had as its Article 4 the stipulation that the United States *hereby disclaims any disposition of intention to exercise sovereignty, jurisdiction, or control over said island except for pacification thereof, and asserts its determination when that is accomplished to leave the government and control of the island to its people.* [1]

Following the Spanish surrenders, nothing in the McKinley Administration's policy gave a promise or even an expectation of when independence was to be granted to the Cuban people. Underlying the lack of any set timetable was the Administration's concern that things in Cuba needed first to be put into political and social order lest internal dissension on the part of the Cubans again give rise to European ambitions in the Caribbean such as those which had led to the American intervention of 1898. There was also the need to safeguard American business interests which had been displaced by the turmoil which had led to the War With Spain, but which had reestablished themselves on the island.

Following the departure of the Spanish, observation on the part of the American leadership was that the Cuban people, taken as a collective entity, were incapable of self-government. The American press added its voice to that opinion, one reporter from the *New York Times* putting it this way: *We must hold* [Cuba]. *If we leave it to the Cubans, we give it over to a reign of terror -- to the machete and the*

---

[1]   Louis A. Perez, Jr., *Cuba Under the Platt Amendment, 1902-1934,* (Pittsburgh, PA: University of Pittsburgh Press, 1986), p 30.

torch. [2] Among the Cubans themselves, there was considerable division as to whether independence from or annexation by the United States was preferable. The Spanish colonists who had remained on the island following departure of the Spanish military and who were joined in their sentiment by many of the better educated mixed bloods, favored annexation. At the other end of the spectrum, the lower classes, particularly the Negroes who represented nearly one-third of the population, wanted independence. It was the Negro segment of the population which caused the most concern to the upper classes as they feared that a takeover by the Negroes would occur once the occupying American Army departed. One example of the apprehension held by the upper classes is given by the historian Louis A. Perez, Jr., who writes of a situation at Santiago where a delegation of the city's businessmen (mostly Spanish nationals) met with Maj. Gen. William R. Shafter to obtain his assurance that the American Army planned to remain. If not, *the merchants indicated, they would liquidate their assets and return to Spain.* [3] Several weeks later at Havana, a petition signed by several hundred planters appealed to President McKinley asking for annexation by the United States. The McKinley Administration did not favor annexation yet it was clear both to it and to the United States Congress that an American pullout was not advisable until a stabile government run by the Cubans was in place and operating. By 1900, the American occupying authorities had the situation enough in hand to inaugurate a suffrage of sorts extending local rule. The suffrage was of a privileged format limited to males of 21 years of age with at least $250 in assets and/or to those who had seen service in the pre-1898 Cuban Liberation Army.

During 1901, the island's leadership had developed a constitution that seemed to be well received at least by most literate Cubans. Under the suggestion of United States Senator Orville H. Platt, a caveat was added which called for the United States to remove its occupation forces, conditional on a return of American military force in the event a foreign power threatened the independence of Cuba or if the island's constitutional government should be overturned from within. As written, this left that judgment not to the Cubans but to the United States. Reluctantly, the Cuban Commissioners agreed with the terms, and the United States's occupation of Cuba formally ended on May 20, 1902. Contingent upon the limitations which had been put in place the year before, Cuba had at last become an independent and sovereign state.

~

During the summer of 1906, the situation in Cuba had reverted to a point of political disarray, a condition compounded in large part by the meddling of an assortment of foreign business interests, all jockeying for their own advantage. On September 29, the War Department received orders to reoccupy the island. A prompt response proved difficult in that only one active transport, *USAT Sumner,* was then available on the Atlantic coast. As it had done in 1898, the Quartermaster Department was forced to turn to the commercial steamship lines from which a total of twenty-one steamers were time chartered. Five were American-owned although flying the Cuban

---

2 *New York Times,* July 29, 1898.
3 Perez, p 34.

flag; two were British, one German, one Norwegian and one Danish. The rest were of American registry.[4]

By October 7, the first of the chartered ships left for Cuba in the wake of the *USAT Sumner* (ex *USS Cassius*) which had departed New York on October 2. Three more of the chartered ships sailed on October 8, two more the next day, and the rest within the week. Of those chartered, only one ship made more than one trip. Two, the merchant ships *Kanawha* and *Cabana* experienced problems en route, running headlong into a hurricane with their cargoes of horses and mules suffering heavy losses. Before the end of that fiscal year, *USAT Sumner* had made twelve round trips to Cuba carrying a total of 216 officers; 4,005 enlisted men; 1,046 civilians; and 42,883 tons of baggage and general cargo. Other Army transports which eventually were assigned to the Cuban run prior to July 1907 made eighteen sailings and were credited with lifting from New York as well as Newport News 5,312 officers and men together with their impedimenta. Credited to the twenty-one short-term chartered ships (which made in toto twenty-three one-way trips to Cuba) was a total of 265 officers; 4,097 enlisted men; and 381 civilians with cargoes consisting of 3,700 horses and mules and 11,818 tons of freight.[5]

This second military occupation of Cuba, which was carried out peacefully, ended in 1909. Beginning in mid 1907 and lasting until the termination of the occupation in 1909, the Army Transport Service maintained a scheduled bi-monthly liner service between New York and various ports in Cuba.

The Congressional Inquiry of 1902 and Subsequent Attempts to Disband the ATS

Despite the War Department's intention to maintain its own shipping service for as long as American troops were committed overseas, there were those who challenged the need in light of the claimed availability of commercial bottoms. Consequently, in March of 1902, a congressional inquiry was instituted through resolution by the House of Representatives. The resolution resulted from pressures brought to bear by the U.S. Export Association, a consortium of steamship companies, shipping agents, and others with vested interests.[6] The War Department initially responded to Congress with a strong argument for continuance of the Army Transport Service while at the same time admitting that there were inherent problems which would require legislative remedy.

> *To the Speaker of the House of Representatives:*
> *In the absence of* [enabling] *legislation, the vessels are manned by crews employed under the laws governing the merchant marine, which are not adapted to a service semi-military in its character. The proper and economical operation of the transports requires trained and experienced officers and crews. Under the merchant marine laws, these men cannot be held to their engagement or contract beyond the limit of the voyage or return to a home port, and experience has*

---

[4] Letter from D. S. Stanley to Marguerite Biery dated February 7, 1910, QMG file 260469 (as cited within McClellan's doctoral thesis, p 93, fn 147.

[5] The total cost for the charters came to $642,943. or an average per charter of $1,162 per day. *Report of the Quartermaster General for fiscal year 1907*, pp 28, 29.

[6] Risch, p 568.

demonstrated that without exception, the greater part, and at times all of the crew of a transport demand their discharge immediately upon reaching the home port while under the merchant marine laws, must be given... Because of this handicap, it is necessary to offer both officers and crews the highest rate of wages paid as in the merchant service on first class passenger steamers.

  If the Army Transport Service is to be permanent or even maintained for some years to come, better organization and service and greater economy could be secured by having an enlisted force to man the transports. [7]

   The War Department, under the prodding of Secretary of War Elihu Root, had already instituted an inquiry as to performance, positive or negative, of the ATS in carrying out its transpacific sealift. The responsibility for that investigation had been assigned to a board of officers under the presidency of Brig. Gen. A. E. Bates. The findings of that board would comprise the full content of the submission which the War Department would later forward to the House of Representatives. According to the Bates board, there was an assortment of flaws that needed correction, not the least of which was the lack of authority the Army possessed in its ability to maintain well trained and disciplined crews. This was the first of many strongly worded Quartermaster Department requests for militarization. Strangely enough, opposition over the 1902 recommendation and one of a similar vein which followed shortly came from the Army's General Staff. There had been no objection by most officers over enlisting unlicensed crewmembers. The criticism rested on the issuance of commissions to the ship's officers, a development which the General Staff felt would denigrate the status of the Army's commissioned ranks. This opposition helped put the damper on whatever enthusiasm the idea to militarize ATS personnel might have generated within Congress. Failing militarization, the crew problems seemed insurmountable unless some other mechanism could be brought to bear. In 1908, civil service status was given the crews, but still the Army suffered from the lack of a definitive legal boundary by which its civilian maritime personnel could be held apart from the laws and practices governing merchant seamen.

   The ATS was to again find itself challenged over the fiscal benefits of its operations. This occurred both in 1905 and again in 1908. The Army's success in surmounting that challenge appears to have been the result of the War Department's internal accounting procedures which on an almost annual basis compared the costs of shipping men and materiel with the Army Transport Service as against what the costs would have been had commercial steamship lines been employed. In all cases illustrated, the savings from the use of the Army's ships were substantial. During the 1905 and 1908 challenges, the Army was assisted in its defense by testimony before Congress of Clara Barton as well as officials from the American Red Cross who had collective praise for the high standards encountered on Army transports. Both Barton and the American Red Cross representatives cited the comfort and health conditions which they had personally witnessed.[8] Another strong argument for continuance of the

---

[7]   House of Representatives, Document 537, *The Inquiry of the House of Representatives in Relation to the Transport Service Between San Francisco and the Philippine Islands,* (Washington, DC: Government Printing Office, 1902).

[8]   According to the reports the Quartermaster General submitted to Congress, only one serious episode of disease had occurred during this entire 4-year period -- that being an outbreak of small pox on *USAT Burnside*

ATS, and one which was received well by a cost conscious Congress was that U.S. mail consigned to the Philippines as well as to Hawaii was carried free of charge aboard Army transports.[9]

U.S. Intervention in Mexico, 1913-16

Bordering the United States on the Rio Grande, the Mexican nation had suffered a turbulent past since its conquest by the Spanish conquistadors. Following numerous insurrections during the early years of the nineteenth century, remnant control by the Spanish crown ended in 1822 when Antonio Lopez de Santa Anna proclaimed a republic. Following that, divisive and competing factions created a chaotic society. In 1846, the United States invaded and occupied the country. It withdrew two years later after Mexico had formally ceded much of its territory to the United States. Mexico then suffered under a number of internal power grabs topped off by another foreign occupation -- this time during 1862 by France which, in collusion with a junta of Mexico's land-holding interests, installed the Austrian Archduke Maximilian as the Mexican regent. Maximilian remained in power until 1867 when he was overthrown by Benito Juarez who established a republic lasting six years. He in turn was deposed by Porfirio Diaz who ruled as a dictator until 1911. From that point on, it was again all down hill on the Mexican political scene. Americans doing business and residing in the country began to find themselves in uncomfortable and often dangerous circumstances. The United States had been held in low regard by Mexicans in general ever since the war of 1846-47, and that lingering resentment would now burst forth in the destruction and takeover of American-owned properties as well as threatening actions against the lives of American residents. Alarmed by this and concerned by what seemed to be political anarchy within the borders of its immediate neighbor to the south, American President Woodrow Wilson attempted to arbitrate in Mexico's internal affairs. Wilson's envoys, having little knowledge concerning the various factions which were dividing Mexico, only made matters worse. As early as the spring of 1912, Americans living on Mexico's west coast took the advice of the U.S. State Department and requested evacuation. The administration ordered the War Department to send one of its transports south to meet that need. The *USAT Buford* was broken out of the Army Transport Service's west coast reserve and routed from San Francisco. Aboard in addition to her crew were 40 cavalrymen to act as a guard should protection for the ship and the refugees be required. On May 5, *USAT Buford* arrived at Mazatlan to take on passengers; by the 16th, she was at Salina Cruz where she took on 224 more Americans together with 9 Europeans. Her next stop was Manzanillo where she took aboard another 127 refugees before heading north to San Diego.

In September of 1913, *USAT Buford* was again sent south in response to dangers affecting Americans. On the 27th of that month, she was at Qusnapaniji where

---

while in the Alaskan service. A panic ensued at Juneau when the local population took up arms to prevent the sick persons from being landed. *USAT Burnside* was subsequently diverted to Honolulu quarantine where only one further case developed.

[9]   Risch, p 569.

she boarded 37 Americans, the next day moving to Acapulco she took on a few more. On the 29th of the month, she touched at San Blas where she boarded 110 Americans. Later at Mazatlan, her master received instructions to stay at that port until relieved by a naval vessel. While at Mazatlan, *USAT Buford*'s master was to represent American interests by providing wireless communication to the United States. The U.S. Consul earlier had requested such assistance, stating,

> *Revolutionary troops in vicinity of Mazatlan, and have cut line leading out of city.*
> *No means of communication with outside world except for wireless. My belief that*
> *Navy vessel is desired in order to facilitate communication by wireless.*

Once relieved by the requested naval vessel, *USAT Buford* continued her quest for refugees stopping at the outports of Morro de Petatlan, Zehuatenejo, Altata, Topolobampo and finally LaPaz. From there she steamed back north landing her passengers at San Diego and at San Francisco where her voyage terminated on October 28. The trip had lasted forty-four days, being accomplished under challenging conditions both as to navigational hazards as well as the sensitive role her master played in the many difficulties presented by Mexican port authorities. All told, this second voyage for *USAT Buford* had brought out 248 refugees.[10]

Although the United States Navy had shown the flag on the Mexican coasts during 1912 and again in 1913, this had only been done through the appearance of single ships of war. By the fall of 1913, President Wilson decided that no other choice remained but to show the Mexicans that the United States was ready to use force to protect American holdings and the lives of its citizens. To effect that result, during October of 1913, Rear Adm. Frank Fletcher with a division of the U.S. Atlantic Fleet took up station off Vera Cruz.

By the spring of 1914, Mexican factions had begun fighting over control of Tampico, and part of that city had been set ablaze. Rear Adm. Henry T. Mayo, with another division of the U.S. Atlantic Fleet, had been assigned to station off that port under the direction of Fletcher. It had become an extremely tense situation for Americans and Europeans residing at Tampico, most of whom had sought refuge on American, British, and German naval vessels which were offlying the city.[11] An incident directly effecting the American force developed when a landing party from the *USS Dolphin* was sent ashore to purchase gasoline for Mayo's launch. They were promptly arrested by Mexican authorities but were soon released with expressions of regret addressed to Mayo. On his personal volition, Mayo demanded more than regrets, stating so in a note which was sent to Tampico's federalist commander. The

---

[10] Information on the refugee sealifts carried out by *USAT Buford* and as related here has been taken from the following sources: *Records of the QM General,* Microfilm Series 1794, 1808, 1829, 1870, 1874, 1882, 1886, specifically referencing "*Buford*, 1912." Also, State Department files, 212.11/293a/288a/304/306d/446 containing: Letter, Secretary of State to the Secretary of War, Washington, April 25, 1912. Also, Charles Jenkinson, "Bringing 60,000 Americans Out of Mexico," *The World's Work*, (February 1914). Jenkinson was a special representative of the Department of State.

[11] Unwilling to encumber the efficiency of his naval vessels, Rear Admiral Fletcher was authorized the charter of the merchant ship *Esperanza* to serve as offshore lodging for the refugees at Tampico. The merchant ship *Mexico* was authorized for impressment for the same use. See Jack Sweetman, *The Landings at Veracruz*, (Annapolis: U.S. Naval Institute Press, 1968), p 44.

American's conditions called for a formal apology from the highest authority in Mexico City. Additionally, the American flag was to be hoisted over the city of Tampico -- that act to be accompanied by a 21-gun salute. Mayo was refused at first on the basis that to comply might be taken as an act of servitude to a foreign power and damaging to Mexican prestige. As the crisis deepened, the federalist government at Mexico City entered directly into the negotiations, and compliance with Mayo's demands was agreed to but only upon condition that the United States fleet would return a 21-gun salute to the Mexican colors. This was unacceptable both to Mayo and to President Wilson who was by now monitoring by wireless what was taking place on the Mexican coast. Wilson decided to hold off further talks while going before Congress for that body's concurrence as to how he was to handle the situation. A hawkish atmosphere had taken root within Congress, and a resolution was drafted which called for direct military intervention on Mexican soil. When informed of this while on station off Tampico, Mayo became increasingly nervous that the place was unsuitable for an amphibious landing if such was to be made against anything resembling a serious defense. In consultation with Fletcher, both admirals believed that Vera Cruz was both strategically and geographically the better place to land.[12] Besides, U.S. State Department information had come to Fletcher that on April 21, a German merchant ship was due at Vera Cruz with a load of guns and ammunition destined for the Mexican federalist forces. Soon to be reinforced by other ships of the Atlantic Fleet, Fletcher received the order to effect a landing at Vera Cruz, seize the Customs House, and prevent any landings of arms and munitions consigned to any Mexican force, whether federalist or revolutionary.

On the morning of April 21, detachments of sailors and Marines went ashore. Although they were first greeted by desultory firing, resistance became heavier as they moved into the town. The situation soon turned into a house-by-house, block-by-block fire fight, made especially difficult when the Mexican authorities released and armed convicts previously held in the municipal prison. By the time Vera Cruz was secured four days later, the Americans had suffered 17 killed and 63 wounded. By best estimates made at the time, the Mexican loss was 126 killed and 195 wounded, although later evaluations would put the Mexican figures substantially higher.[13] Once the fighting stopped, the Navy set martial law into place while attempting at the same time to gain the cooperation of the local civil officials. There was not much success in that regard as the Mexicans who were approached feared retaliation as collaborators once the Americans withdrew from the city.

It was not feasible for the Navy to carry on any long-term occupation of Vera Cruz or any other place on the Mexican coast as to do so would seriously hamper the efficiency of the vessels from which the landing parties had been detached. Accordingly, the Navy had earlier requested that it be relieved of occupation duties and replaced in that task by the Army. That request had been anticipated, and the War Department had already instructed Brig. Gen. Frederick Funston to stand ready to send

---

[12] During the early years of the twentieth century, Vera Cruz was the correct spelling for this Mexican city. This is the spelling that is found in the War Department's reports and correspondence dealing with the 1914 operations there.

[13] Sweetman, p 123.

the 5th Infantry Brigade which was composed of the 4th, 7th, 19th, and 28th Regiments together with support units, all of which were then on hand at Galveston, Texas. A long stint in the Philippines had given Funston considerable experience with military government; and of all general officers on active duty at the time, he was perhaps the most suited for the assignment. He was also a fighting general, an ability which could serve him well as there was still the possibility that an invasion into the interior would have to be launched to rescue American nationals reportedly held under close arrest at Mexico City. That possibility was put aside just prior to Funston's arrival when a trainload of Americans and Europeans pulled into Vera Cruz. They had come from Mexico City under the protection of the British Consul General. On April 28th, a second train carrying 206 Americans arrived from the towns of Soledad and Cordoba.

On April 27, the transports *USAT Meade, USAT Kilpatrick, USAT Sumner,* and *USAT McClellan* dropped anchor off Vera Cruz. On May 1, Rear Admiral Fletcher formally turned over the city's occupation to Funston. The naval elements then withdrew except for the majority of the Marines who were temporarily placed under Funston's command. With the Marines, Funston had close to 5,000 troops, and their needs required more of a resupply effort than the Army's transports were able to provide. To meet this requirement, the Quartermaster Department chartered 11 commercial steamers. Until the termination of the occupation which would last seven months, the chartered ships would make a total of thirty-four trips into Vera Cruz.[14]

On the international scene, the occupation was having the deleterious effect of making enemies for the United States throughout the Spanish speaking southern hemisphere. Wilson soon came to realize that to continue an armed force in place on Mexican soil was proving to be a pointless exercise. To all outward appearances, Victoriano Huerta, the then head of the federalist Mexican government, remained firmly in office while the various revolutionary factions opposing him were, it seemed, undiminished in their efforts to displace him. The Mexicans were together in one respect, though, this being a mutual hostility toward their *gringo* neighbor from the north. The U.S. State Department was attempting some diplomatic damage control throughout South America, and it appeared that those efforts were bearing fruit when Argentina, Brazil, and Chile (referred to at the time as *the ABC*) volunteered to mediate between all parties, an offer which was more or less forced on the Huerta government by the British Consul at Mexico City. The ABC delegation strove to first arrive at a pacification arrangement between the country's political parties; but the differences between them were so great that this got nowhere. The ABC delegates eventually gave up on that approach as they soon would in their attempts to develop an atmosphere amenable to the protection of American and European residents and their interests.

Meanwhile, Funston, entrenched at Vera Cruz, was carrying out a revolution of his own which involved cleaning up that city which many had judged in the past to be one of the filthiest places in the entirety of the Spanish-speaking hemisphere. Funston's worst fear was that epidemics similar to what had occurred in Cuba during 1898 and 1899 would strike to the detriment of the American occupiers.

---

[14]   *Annual Reports of the Quartermaster General for the fiscal year 1914* (p 47) *and 1915* (p 45).

But Funston's sanitation drive was so successful that the health record for his command was better than that experienced at many garrisons within the United States.

It was Mexican politics-as-usual which finally broke the impasse over the United States Army's presence. Huerta was deposed and the federalist reins in Mexico City were taken over by one Venustiamo Corranza. Corranza proved almost as difficult to deal with as Huerta, but at least he seemed open to negotiation. It was finally agreed that the United States would pull its army out of Vera Cruz conditional on Corranza first appointing a competent official to take over the city's government. Funston cautioned President Wilson to allow him enough time prior to evacuation of the city as it still was not adequately functioning; and most importantly, Corranza should be made to promise that his government would protect from harm and job loss those Mexican officials who under the Americans had at last begun to function as efficient administrators. After considerable parlay, Corranza agreed to those terms, probably, it was thought by most officers on Funston's staff, because the Mexican federalist government urgently needed the customs revenues which the port of Vera Cruz had provided before the occupation.[15] On November 23, 1914, Funston's command boarded transports for the United States, thus ending the American presence. The Navy's blockade of the Mexican east coast ports was lifted at the same time. However, the trouble with Mexico did not end there.

During January of 1916, the revolutionist followers of Pancho Villa halted a train serving an American-owned mine at Santa Isabel in the province of Chihuahua in northern Mexico. Villa's men killed sixteen Americans. Two months later, Pancho Villa crossed over the United States border to raid Columbus, New Mexico. President Wilson immediately retaliated by ordering Brig. Gen. John J. Pershing to cross the Rio Grande after Villa. Pershing's command consisted of 6,600 Regular Army troops which would penetrate almost 500 miles south into Mexico, but Pershing never made contact with Villa's main body. Anticipating war with Mexico, Wilson ordered a call-up of the National Guard units of Texas, New Mexico, and Arizona which were sent to the border to await the reaction to Pershing's invasion.[16] On February 5, 1917, after an arduous and frustrating campaign, Pershing's men reforded the Rio Grande back into United States territory. The American invaders had been south of the border for almost eleven months.

This second invasion of Mexican territory within a span of two years had sparked panic among those American nationals who had remained in Mexico through the crisis of 1912-14 and with those who had reentered the country following Funston's departure from Vera Cruz. Meeting the need to evacuate these individuals, and upon the request of the U.S. State Department, the War Department during early 1916 had sent the *USAT Sumner* to Vera Cruz where she took aboard a total of 606 American refugees. She made another voyage that summer for the same purpose and one more at the end of the year.

---

[15]   Corranza's promise proved worthless and the Mexican officials who had been put into office by Funston were summarily removed shortly after the Corranza government's takeover of Vera Cruz.

[16]   On June 16, 1916, Wilson mobilized the entirety of the nation's National Guard.

Vessels Chartered for Support of the Vera Cruz Operation, April and May 1914.
-- All U.S. Flag Vessels --

(These vessels were time chartered; in some cases they entered shipyards to be refitted as troop or animal transports.)

Name	Gr Tonnage	Rate per day	Owner Company
City of Macon	5311	$1,000	Ocean SS Co.
City of Memphis [†]	5252	$1,000	Ocean SS Co.
Colorado	2764	$442	Mallory SS Co.
Cristobal [‡]	9606	---	U.S. Government (Panama Railroad Co.), assigned temporarily to ATS as troopship
Denver	4549	$910	Mallory SS Co.
Kansan	7913	$1200	American-Hawaiian SS Co.
Minnesotan	6665	$900	American-Hawaiian SS Co.
Ossabaw	2667	$425	Texas City Line
Panaman	6649	$900	American-Hawaiian SS Co.
San Marcos	2839	$600	Mallory SS Co.
Satilla	2667	$450	Texas City Line

[†] The last vessel to remain on charter; it was released on December 14, 1914.

[‡] *Cristobal* remained in ATS service into 1915.

Outside of the punitive effect which the 1916-17 expedition against Pancho Villa had in warning Mexican banditry away from the U.S. border, that invasion as well as the preceding one at Vera Cruz in 1914 had done little to advance American business security, either in Mexico or for that matter anywhere else in Latin America. And those interventions certainly never helped toward improving the internal Mexican political system. Woodrow Wilson's hope aimed at the United States assisting in the creation of a stabile and democratic Mexican nation had proved a failure.

The United States would soon be involved in a conflict across the Atlantic, a conflict which would push the Mexican problem to the back burner where the Wilson Administration and the Army hoped it would remain.

CHAPTER VII

WORLD WAR I

The First World War began in August of 1914 through what was a chain of miscalculations on the part of the Central Powers.[1] Before it was over, it would envelope most of Europe, the Steppes of Russia, the Middle East, Africa, and would even reach into Asia. Its most horrific consequences developed on the eastern and western fronts of Europe. It was four long years later on the Western Front that the war would reach a decisive conclusion, the result in large part of American intervention.

At first the conflict on the Western Front was a war of movement, the Germans striking at France through Belgium. The French, aided by a British expeditionary force, finally halted the German's opening offensive -- the French doing so on the line of the Marne and the British, a month after, at Ypres. The French suffered upwards of 300,000 casualties along the Marne; the British, the virtual destruction of its original expeditionary force. By 1915 open maneuver of the armies had virtually ceased, the opposing forces becoming restricted to a line of deep entrenchments stretching from the North Sea to the Swiss border. For the remaining duration of the war in the west, most success would be measured not in miles but in yards of territory gained. It would evolve into a contest of attrition measured by men's lives. At Verdun in 1916, French casualties would approach 350,000 -- for the Germans about the same, with only part of the dead of either side ever being recovered for burial. The mud of that awful field had simply swallowed them up. At the Somme

---

[1]   The Central Powers was a coalition of Germany, Austria-Hungary and Bulgaria; to be joined by the Ottoman Empire. The Allied forces, against which the Central Powers were engaged were: the British Empire, France, Belgium, Portugal, Russia, Italy, Japan, and later the United States.

during 1916, the British and French casualties were 500,000, and the German's close to 450,000 -- those in a series of brutal attacks and counter-attacks which ended up as proving nothing. By 1917, following many other battles of the trenches, all of them taking a colossal toll, the contestants on both sides of the wire had arrived at a state of near total exhaustion.

After the battle off Jutland in May of 1916, the German high seas fleet was to remain bottled up in port by the British blockade. By 1917, the sea war had evolved into a German undersea offensive against the allies' supply lines while on the Allied side it had become one of countermeasure, the convoy system being preeminent in that respect.

The year 1917 had been a year of near crisis for the allies. Mutinies breaking out in April and May of 1917 had involved sixty-eight of France's front-line divisions. The cause was the refusal of the French poilu to take further part in what to the minds of the men in the ranks had been the never-ending assaults on the German trenches -- suicidal and doomed to failure from the start. In the British sectors, morale was at a low ebb for the same reason, but the British *Tommy* held his discipline. From all indications, that steadfastness could become short-lived as at a British training camp in the rear, a protest had turned into a riot which took three days for military police to quell. On the southern front, the Italian line had been breached, leaving the Italians in disarray with 300,000 of them surrendering and many more deserting to the rear. If that was not enough, a revolution had broken out in Petrograd, Russia, against the Imperial Czarist government. The red banner of the Bolsheviks quickly spread to dominate the Czar's conscript armies on the Eastern Front. Although the Bolsheviks remained in the Allied camp -- at least for the time being -- the northern part of the Eastern Front soon became static consequently freeing up a number of German divisions to fight in the west.[2] The southern sectors of the Eastern Front were manned by Cossacks and other White Russian troops who were loyal to the Czar, and they remained actively engaged. Even there, though, weaknesses would develop as the White Russian forces soon became preoccupied with a contest for power against the Bolsheviks. The timing had been fortunate for the allies as Germany was not then in the position to exploit the situation to full advantage. Meanwhile on the Western Front, the French command was able to restore order within its army, doing so through a combination of internal reforms and execution of the mutinies' ring leaders.

For the British and French, the entry of the United States into the war could well spell the difference between total stalemate or total victory. By 1916, the voices of America's isolationists had become far less vocal than they had been. American bankers would loan the British and the French $500 million. In probable retaliation, German saboteurs blew up a munitions loading dock on the outskirts of Newark, New Jersey, causing millions of dollars in damage as well as considerable loss of life. That and German attacks against shipping on the high seas which resulted in the deaths of American citizens began to turn American public opinion against the Central Powers. As early as January of 1915, a German surface raider had captured and then

---

[2]   The Bolshevik leaders Vladimir Lenin and Leon Trotsky were suspected -- probably correctly -- as having been funded in their revolutionary movement by the Germans, in return having made a deal to take Russia out of the war. On March 13, 1918, the Bolsheviks entered into an armistice agreement with the Germans.

sunk the American schooner *William P. Frye.* Between May 1, 1915, and January 4, 1917, eight American steamships had gone down, the result of submarine attacks.[3] In what he thought would remain secret, German Foreign Minister Arthur Zimmermann by telegram dated January 19, 1917, informed the German Ambassador to Mexico that unrestricted submarine warfare would begin during the following month. Upon what almost certainly was the assumption that the United States would enter the war in protest, Zimmermann invited Mexico to take up arms in alliance with Germany and against the United States. That message read:

> *On the first of February, we intend to begin unrestricted submarine warfare, notwithstanding that it is our intention to endeavor to keep neutral the United States of America. If this attempt is not successful, we propose an alliance on the following basis with Mexico. That we shall make war together and together make peace. We shall give general financial support, and it is understood that Mexico is to reconquer the lost territory in New Mexico, Texas, and Arizona. The details are left to you for settlement. You are instructed to inform the President of Mexico of the above in the greatest confidence as soon as it is certain that there will be an outbreak of war with the United States, and suggest that the President of Mexico, on his own initiative, should communicate with Japan suggesting adherence to this plan. At the same time, offer to mediate between Germany and Japan. [At this point in time Japan had joined the Allied Powers against Germany and had recently engaged in action against German forces in the Orient. Ed.] Please call to the attention of the President of Mexico that the employment of ruthless submarine warfare now promises to compel England to make peace in a few months.* [4]

The Zimmermann message was intercepted by British signal intelligence and passed along to Washington. Once it had been authenticated as genuine, the Wilson Administration released the text to the American press. The effect it had on public opinion in the United States was explosive, setting the stage for Congress's enactment of a state of armed neutrality for American merchant shipping. On March 12, a formal notice to that effect was issued by the U.S. State Department and hand delivered to the Swiss Ambassador for transmittal to the German government.

> *In view of the announcement of the Imperial German Government on January 31, 1917, that all ships, those of neutrals included, met within certain zones of the high seas, would be sunk without any precaution taken for the safety of the persons on board, and without the exercise of visit and search, the Government of the United States has determined to place upon all American merchant vessels sailing through the barred areas an armed guard for the protection of the vessels and the lives of the persons on board.* [5]

---

3 *American Ship Casualties of the World War,* compiled by the Historical Section, Navy Department, corrected to April 1, 1923, (Washington, DC: Government Printing Office, 1923).

4 Francis W. Halsey, *History of the World War,* Vol. IV, (New York and London: Funk and Wagnalls Co., 1919), pp 14, 15. Although in 1917 the fear that Mexico might take advantage of the opportunity and invade the southwestern United States was very real, this never progressed beyond a state of concern, nor is there any evidence that Japan was approached to change sides.

5 Green Haywood Hackworth, *Digest of International Law,* Vol. VI, (Washington: Department of State, 1961), pp 500, 501.

As had been the case in 1898, the United States was ill-prepared for war, especially in its ability to deploy an army across the wide divide of the Atlantic. Regardless, war would follow in less than a month from the date of the U.S. State Department's notification to the German government.

As War Clouds Gathered

The war in Europe was having its effect on those countries which held neutral status. For one thing, it had put a substantial strain on world shipping. By 1916, a huge amount of tonnage belonging to the warring powers had either been sunk or interned in neutral ports. Tonnage belonging to Germany and the other Central Powers and which so far had escaped destruction or internment was bottled up by the British blockade of the German coast. The Allied merchant fleets, having suffered tremendous losses, had become seriously overtaxed in the effort to fulfill their countries' needs in terms of troop lift, the carriage of materiels of war and vital foodstuffs. Neutral countries were suffering economically due to the difficulties posed by the lack of available shipping for exporting their products. This had raised shipping rates to astronomical levels. To help alleviate the effect this was having on the Philippines in 1916, Washington authorized that Army transports returning to the United States in ballast were to carry commercial cargoes. Under the arrangement, the Commonwealth government was to reimburse the War Department for all incidental expense borne by the Army Transport Service (ATS), and freight rates collected were to be deposited to the general credit of the U.S. government.[6] Elsewhere, Army transports were employed to carry raw materials considered to be of a strategic nature. One example of that carriage involved the *USAT Buford* which in the summer of 1916 took on a cargo of coal at Nagasaki, Japan, for delivery to the Army's Honolulu coal reserve depot. Once the coal had been unloaded, the ship was ordered to proceed light to the Canal Zone where she took on 2,500 tons of scrap iron consigned to Philadelphia. She was then ordered to take on bulk nitrate at Iquiqui, Chile, and proceed to Communipaw, New Jersey, for discharge. *USAT Buford* would make a second trip for nitrate during February-March of 1917. Another transport, *USAT Sumner,* while on a cargo mission, Panama to New York, grounded off the coast of New Jersey and was declared a total loss.[7]

---

[6] *Annual Report of the Quartermaster General for Fiscal Year 1916,* p 40.

[7] *USAT Sumner* was carrying a cargo of scrap iron at the time she grounded on December 11, 1916. The following day, she was declared a total loss.

On the eve of war, the Quartermaster Corps had under the management of the ATS a total oceangoing fleet of fourteen ships in commission -- eight of these being assigned to the Pacific fleet.[8] These were:

USAT Burnside	Engaged in repairing undersea cable
USAT Crook	On loan to Department of the Interior for Alaska service
USAT Dix	Animal and freight ship in support of Pacific garrisons
USAT Logan	Troopship in support of Pacific garrisons
USAT Sheridan	Troopship in support of Pacific garrisons
USAT Sherman	Troopship in support of Pacific garrisons
USAT Slocum	Seagoing tug based at San Francisco for ship handling
USAT Thomas	Troopship in support of Pacific garrisons

In the Philippines three ships were actively utilized in interisland troop and/or cargo service:

USAT Liscum   *USAT Merritt*   *USAT Warren*

Following the loss of *USAT Sumner,* the ATS Atlantic fleet consisted of three ships:

USAT Buford	Troopship in Canal Zone/Puerto Rican cargo-passenger service
USAT Kilpatrick	Troopship in Canal Zone/Puerto Rican cargo-passenger service
USAT McClellan	Refrigerator ship in support of garrisons at the Canal Zone and at Puerto Rico

The Army also had a total of sixty-five harbor class vessels in active operation which fell into the category of exceeding 50 gross tons:

6	First class steel mineplanters
2	Cable steamers
2	Ferry Steamers
24	Freight and passenger steamers
28	Tugs and artillery steamers
3	Self-propelled lighters

In 1904, a Harbor Boat Service was created as a separate branch distinct from the Army Transport Service; but like the ATS, it was part of the organization of the Quartermaster General. Mine Planters and tug/artillery steamers were under the operational control of the Coast Artillery; however the custody (ownership) of those vessels remained under the Harbor Boat Service (HBS). When a vessel was temporarily laid up or otherwise put in a non-operational mode by the Coast Artillery, those vessels then reverted to the jurisdiction of the HBS. See the Appendix S of this volume for a discussion of the Army's Mine Planter Service.

Harbor craft in active service and falling under 50 gross tons included such vessel types as steam and gasoline launches, miscellaneous work boats as well as Coast Artillery distribution box boats and mine yawls. They numbered in all 202 units, stationed at various locations on the Atlantic, Pacific, and Gulf coasts with a few serving Army installations on the western rivers and at the Panama Canal Zone.

---

[8]   The listing of ships and harbor craft in service in April 1917 is from *Annual Report of the Quartermaster General for 1917, p*p 55, 62.

~

   The War Department's central administration in Washington, particularly that part of it inherent to the Quartermaster Corps, had been reorganized during the early years of the century in recognition of lessons learned from the 1898 War with Spain. Other changes had been made in 1912 when the Quartermaster Department was redesignated as the Quartermaster Corps. The Quartermaster Corps shoreside establishment concerned with the administration of the Army Transport Service and the Harbor Boat Service was of a composition adequate for a peacetime role, but it was certainly not equipped to handle a shipping expansion of even minor magnitude. Since the changes, economy drives had resulted in personnel cutbacks with a major impact on the numbers of staff officers. This in turn had resulted in a reduction of those divisions within the Quartermaster General's office that would have to deal with any War Department employment of marine transportation. With a state of war imminent, the Army was to soon find itself faced with inducting, equipping, training, and transporting overseas an army of a size totally unimagined up to that time. In the first months of the war, only select regiments and a few service units would be sent to France. Arranging for those first troop contingents was to prove rife with administrative difficulties. Crewing of the transports was to become a special problem.

   Back in December 1915, as a result of numerous instances of insubordination, frequent unauthorized absences from duty, and outright refusals to work on the part of its civilian crews, the Quartermaster General had recommended that Congress authorize an auxiliary corps consisting of civilian personnel to man the vessels of the War Department. Under the proposal, the crews would become subject to military law. This was put into the form of a bill introduced January 6, 1916. The following month, the Chief of the Coast Artillery made a somewhat different appeal, arguing that since the nation's defenses revolved around the mining of major harbors, it had become imperative that the crews of the Army's mineplanters be made part of the armed forces and that special legislation was needed to that effect. After a number of go-rounds between the Quartermaster General's office and the Coast Artillery people as to the pros and cons of separating the status of mine planter crews from that of the transports and harbor craft, it was finally agreed that all of the Army's ships should be militarized. Adding emphasis to the fact that the civilian system of crewing was not working, a series of labor crises arose during early 1917. The first occurred on March 30 and concerned the transport *USAT Sherman* which was about to sail from San Francisco with lumber for construction at Schofield Barracks in the Hawaiian Islands. The crew refused to sail unless an increase of wages was not just promised but was actually paid before the ship departed. Then on April 3, a walkout was staged by most of the crew of the *USAT Thomas*. In that same week -- in fact on the very day (April 6, 1917) that the Congress of the United States declared war on Germany -- harbor craft employees at Newport, Rhode Island, threatened immediate resignation unless they received an increase in pay.[9] On top of that, a wireless message came in from the commanding general of the Panama Canal Zone stating that he was having difficulty in

---

[9] In fairness to the patriotism of the harbor craft employees at Newport, it should be mentioned that a few of them had threatened enlistment into the Naval Reserve Force where they stated pay was higher than that of the Army.

keeping a crew aboard the Zone's one mineplanter. The Quartermaster General, as part of his office's request for remedial legislation to resolve these labor problems, explained to the Congressional Committee on Military Affairs that in large part, labor incidents such as the ones which had occurred in the past were temporary aberrations, but now that the country was in a state of war, the situation had become critical, so much so that it could easily prevent the War Department from fulfilling its mission. The Committee chairman promised to push a bill forward to militarize the crews, but he would first ask the Army's Judge Advocate General to render an opinion as to the legality of drafting the present crews into the military, thereby freezing them on the vessels. (A Selective Service act was then in the process of final work-up by the Congress with the initial call-up of men planned for June.) In his May 18th reply to the Congressional Committee, the Judge Advocate wrote that no specific authority had been given within the Selective Service Act allowing government crews to be drafted into the positions they presently held. Further, he believed that under existing law, the crews could not be drafted. That last was seemingly predicated upon language contained within the Militia Act of June 3, 1916, which exempted certain occupational groups from draft for militia duty, one exempted class being *mariners actually employed in the sea service of any citizen or merchant within the United States.* [10] If the 1916 Militia Act was indeed the rationale upon which the Judge Advocate had based his opinion, it would seem he had come to a questionable conclusion. The 1916 Act, as it referenced commercially employed seamen, had addressed itself to a group that was entirely civil in makeup and certainly not to be applied to those already on the federal government's payroll as was the case with the crews of the Army's transports, harbor boats, and mineplanters. Despite that, the Militia Act of 1916 was perhaps viewed by the Army lawyers as touching on a gray area best left undisturbed. There was, however, another federal law then on the books, having been passed in 1896, which could have been invoked and which exempted licensed mariners from draft in time of war, except for duties to be performed under their professional licenses. It allowed the drafting of licensed mariners into the government's service but continued them in a civilian status while in that service. [11] The problem with the 1896 law, assuming that it had even been considered by the Judge Advocate, was that it effected only licensed ships' officers. The majority of the labor problems being encountered by the Army on the eve of entry into the war had been with unlicensed (non-officer) personnel. It seems that any hope for legislation to bring about militarization was at a questionable impasse.

The Army's militarization of the crews of Army transports and the Harbor Boat Service did not take place. However, during 1918, following further

---

[10]   32 U.S.C., 59, 39 Stat. 197.

[11]   Laws of 1896, 255, 29 Stat. 188. There is no legislative history concerning the Act of 1896 having ever been utilized by the government, either during the War with Spain, WW I, or WW II. In order to establish any practical applicability to contemporary merchant marine personnel during the 1980s, a Congressional Research Service study was conducted by Marie B. Morris. That study concluded that the Act of 1896, which has been recodified over time and is now found as 46 U.S.C., § 7113, is unclear and rather ambiguous in its interpretation. Morris was of the opinion that the intent at the time of passage in 1896 was to establish a form of civilian reserve during time of war for manning four ships belonging to a company called the American Line. The four ships which had been constructed under naval subsidy were: *St. Louis, Paris, St. Paul,* and *New York.*

requests by the Chief of the Coast Artillery, some of the crews of mineplanters were militarized, that activity thereafter becoming known as the Army Mine Planter Service. (Complete militarization of the mineplanters did not take place until 1922.)

During the fall of 1917, Col. Chauncy B. Baker submitted to the Quartermaster General the draft of a study bill which would establish six *Transport Regiments* for service as crews. The proposal was to be an amendment to the act of May 18, 1917, which had authorized the temporary expansion of the Regular Army. Baker's proposal was at first disapproved by the Quartermaster General; however, after some minor revisions, it was endorsed for transmittal to the General Staff where it was approved and then submitted to the Congress, but it failed enactment into law.[12]

In a hopeful effort to resolve the problem on the transports and the harbor boats, President Wilson, under the authority of the war power acts granted to him by Congress, issued an order during 1917 which was designed in part to place civilian seamen employed by the military within a more controllable framework. The order stated that requisitioned merchant ships (meaning ships requisitioned by the United States Shipping Board)

> *...shall not have the status of a public ship and shall be subject to all laws and regulations governing merchant vessels. When, however, the requisitioned vessel is engaged in the service of the War or Navy Department, the vessel shall have the status of a public ship and the masters, officers, and crew should become the immediate employees and agents of the United States with all the rights and duties of such, the vessel passing completely into the possession of the masters, officers, and crew absolutely under the control of the United States.* [13]

This clear-cut separation which Wilson's order made between vessels of the civil branches of the government and those of the military branches must have been of some assist toward altering the behavior of the Army's civilian mariners since they could no longer logically hold the attitude that they were merchant mariners. Therefore, the President's order was no doubt a move in the right direction. But it still had not provided the Army with a means for holding its seamen aboard the transports once a voyage terminated, nor would it materially reduce disciplinary infractions despite the fact that in a few cases during World War I, military coercion was imposed against crewmembers guilty of desertions once shipping articles had been signed.

It was only at times when jobs were scarce in the shipping industry that the Army enjoyed the ability to hold its crews, but the year 1917 was not such a time. As early as May 12, which was only a month following the entry of the United States into the war, a naval officer charged with the work of arming merchant ships commented,

> *Every ship that has* [so far] *been armed has been delayed from four to ten days because of lack of merchant crews. Most that come in on ships leave them just before sailing.*

---

[12] Henry Granville Sharpe, Maj. General, *The Quartermaster Corps in the Year 1917 in the World War,* (New York: The Century Co., 1921).

[13] *International Law Situations,* (Newport, RI: The Naval War College, 1930), p 49.

Even ships' officers were scarce.

> *One company asked if the Navy could furnish first and second deck officers and engineer officers as they couldn't get them. Sailings are becoming more serious everyday, and the delays become longer.* [14]

It was this depleted labor pool from which the ATS would have to draw its own crews, not an enviable prospect since the extra stringency imposed against the crews of Army transports was no doubt considered a detraction by seamen having the alternative of other employment.

Transportation Reorganizations, Zone of the Interior

Once the United States entered the war, the Army's General Staff concluded that the old system which had been in place for the movement of men and materiel was no longer workable. Under that old system, the Superintendents of the ATS headquartered at New York and at San Francisco had reported directly to the Depot Quartermaster at each port. The Depot Quartermaster had in turn reported to the head of the Water Transport Branch of the Transportation Division which operated as part of the staff of the Quartermaster General. A reorganization which would take place on August 4, 1917, inaugurated an entirely new mechanism for the management of that Army shipping which operated out of east coast ports in support of the American Expeditionary Force to France. This took the form of a new bureau designated the Embarkation Service which was established within the General Staff. Its commander was to hold overall responsibility for operations at the ports of New York and at Newport News as well as at any respective subports which might be subsequently developed.[15] The control of port operations on the west coast and all Army shipping in the Pacific was to continue under the Army Transport Service, integrated as before to the Quartermaster Corps.

The primary mission of the Embarkation Service was to support the American Expeditionary Force (AEF) from within the Zone of the Interior.[16] The Port of New York was selected as the main shipping point for troops en route to France -- Newport News being slated as the place from where most of the general cargo and munitions would leave.[17] The former role of the ATS Superintendents' offices at New

---

[14] Written comments from J. L. Kaufman, Lt., USN, as contained within the draft portfolio of a monograph (never published) on the Naval Armed Guard of WW I. Naval Records Collection of Office of Naval Records and Library, File "ZSA", 11W4-Box 984.

[15] The creation of the Embarkation Service was preceded on July 3, 1917, by the formation of two separate commands titled Ports of Embarkation, the commander of each given the responsibility for its management. These two commands were the Port of New York and the Port of Newport News. Under that arrangement, the Superintendent of the ATS at each port operated under the respective Port of Embarkation commander. The port commanders reported directly to the Army's Chief of Staff. This structure was quickly determined to be lacking a workable liaison with other transportation elements, i.e., incoming rail and road. The Embarkation Service was then given wide control over all transportation routing to the ports as well as port management, inclusive of shipping for the AEF operating from the U.S. east coast. Source: Chester C. Wardlow, *The Administration of Transportation in the United States Army, April 1917 - March 1942,* a monograph, (Washington, DC: Office, Chief of Transportation, Army Service Forces, July 1944).

[16] The United States, along with all ports of embarkation within the country, i.e., the U.S. east coast, Gulf of Mexico, and west coast, were considered as the Zone of the Interior.

[17] Newport News would later become a shipping point for troops although in that function, it never reached the volume of the Port of New York.

York and at Newport News was joined to the Embarkation Service as a sort of suboffice which carried on under a changing series of subdepartment titles before finally being settled into the table of organization as the Water Transportation Branch. The Embarkation Service had been organized as an entity separate and apart from the Quartermaster Corps, yet its Water Transportation Branch, replete with the prewar personnel from the old ATS structure, continued reporting as before to the Quartermaster General.[18]

A further reorganization took place in February of 1918 with the establishment of the Shipping Control Committee chaired by a civilian agency, the U.S. Shipping Board (USSB). The responsibility of this committee was inclusive of the military's concerns with troop and cargo movement -- military personnel representing those concerns sitting as part of the committee. The Shipping Control Committee absorbed a number of the functions which had previously been carried out by the Embarkation Service. The transportation historian Chester C. Wardlow wrote that part of that absorption included the carry-over of the original organizational structure of the Office of the Superintendent, ATS, both at New York and at Newport News.[19] In retrospect, the new arrangement had accomplished nothing, more or less, than the continuance of some unwieldy practices, including a split in responsibility for ship operations under which the Quartermaster General retained partial control over the Army's tonnage. The result of this division of authority caused not only confusion but considerable inefficiency which was not rectified until April of 1918 at which time the Quartermaster General was removed from all control involving the Army's transports and its harbor craft, that responsibility being turned over to the Vessel Operations Branch under the Chief of the Embarkation Service. How all this impacted the interwoven relationship with the Shipping Control Committee is vague, to say the least. What does seem clear is that the personnel who had originated from the prewar offices of the Superintendents of the ATS still continued working with a certain autonomy, something which the higher command came to consider intolerable. A sort of final solution came about through an order of September 17, 1918, which officially abolished the Office of the Superintendent of the Army Transport Service, both at New York and at Newport News.[20]

If the assorted reorganizations which took place between August of 1917 and September of 1918 leave the reader in a state of total bewilderment, imagine what it was like for those working within such an ever-changing scenario. And there were more changes to come.

Following the end of the war in Europe -- at which point the AEF was being returned to the United States -- yet another reorganization took place involving the Embarkation Service. (At that point, the record stands mute as to the subsequent role of the Shipping Control Committee insofar as its relationship to Army shipping.) An Office of Superintendent of Water Transportation was created in January of 1919 with responsibility for the operation, maintenance, and repair of all water

---

[18] *Order of Battle of the United States Land Forces in the World War,* "Zone of the Interior," Vol. III, Part 1. (Washington, DC: Center of Military History), p 499.

[19] Wardlow, p 4.

[20] *Order of Battle...,* "Zone of the Interior", Vol. 3, Part I, p 502.

transportation, inclusive of both oceangoing ships and harbor craft. Unlike the organization which had been in place before the war under the Offices of the Superintendents, ATS, where crew hiring and payroll were handled internal to those offices, under this newest arrangement, those functions were placed under the Army's finance officers stationed at the ports from which each vessel operated, at that time being either New York or Newport News. The January 1919 restructuring had apparently taken place in preparation for the forthcoming abolishment of the Embarkation Service. The responsibilities of that service were soon to be transferred to a new command known as the Transportation Service which would be charged with all War Department movements of troops and materiel on the east coast -- both by sea and by land. Activities concerning oceangoing vessels and harbor craft would remain under this newest command for just over a year. On June 4, 1920, the National Defense Act eliminated the Transportation Service and in a sort of flip-flop, restored the functions of marine transportation, as well as the Army's vessel construction, back to the Quartermaster Corps.

   With all east coast Army shipping again under the Quartermaster Corps, the Army Transport Service of prewar days regained its former identity. (As the reader will recall, the Army's west coast shipping activity had remained throughout the war with the Army Transport Service as part of the Quartermaster Corps.)

Beginning of the Troop Lift

   Although General John J. Pershing is usually thought of as being in the vanguard of the American Expeditionary Force, he was in fact preceded by a medical contingent which sailed from New York during the first week of May 1917. That group had been hastily organized at Cincinnati with orders to set up a hospital in France prior to the landing of American troops. Their mobilization had been so hasty that the unit arrived in New York with its enlisted men still in civilian clothing. This unit sailed on the British Cunard liner *Orduna.* The Depot Quartermaster for the New York area, Col. J. M. Carson, who had only recently been given the additional role of Commander, Army Transport Service, New York, was ordered to immediately make arrangements for the soon-to-follow departure of Pershing, together with his headquarters staff and a guard company detailed from the 2nd Cavalry Regiment. (At that juncture, the organizational identity of the Army Transport Service had not been preempted by the reorganizations which were to follow.) For security reasons, the Pershing group was given the code name *The McCarthy Party,* and was scheduled for sailing aboard the Cunard liner *Baltic* on May 29.

   From the start, the commitment of American troops on the Western Front was based upon the policy that the AEF was to be a distinct and separate component of the Allied force. It had been decided prior to Pershing's departure from the United States that the AEF was not to be committed to action until it was sufficiently trained and of enough strength to warrant operation as an independent command. Almost immediately upon his setting foot on French soil, Pershing was pressured by the French, and to an extent by the British, to parcel out his regiments for the reinforcement of British and French sectors on the line where they would serve under other than American commanders. It became painfully obvious that the British and the French wanted American soldiers but not an American army. Only Pershing's forcefulness would prevent that from happening; and Wilson, to his credit, would back Pershing all the way.

~

Immediately upon receiving notification of the declaration of war, the U.S. Bureau of Customs, accompanied by military escorts, had seized all German and Austrian ships which lay under internment at U.S. ports. On the east coast, these ships in largest part had been on transatlantic runs, a number of them having been in the passenger trade making them suited for troop transports with but little conversion. After the seizures, it was discovered that all but one of those ships had been sabotaged by their crews. The one spared was the *Printz Eitel Friedrich.* (She was immediately taken over by the Navy, hastily converted into an auxiliary cruiser, and renamed *USS DeKalb.*) Repairs on the others would take time. Upon survey by naval architects, it was estimated that none of them could be ready for sea before mid-fall. If troops were to be sent across the Atlantic before that time, they would have to sail either on Allied ships or aboard American ships then engaged on scheduled trade routes. The first contingents would go on American ships, and the job of assembling them would rest with ATS at New York. Colonel Carson and an assistant, Col. Chauncy B. Baker, had earlier prepared a list of those ships which they considered as probably acceptable for the transatlantic passage despite the fact that only one of them had actually been designed for the transatlantic trade.[21] Appreciative of his and Baker's own lack of experience with shipping, Carson would reach out to the industry for advice. It was found that unlike the self-interest which some in the shipping business had displayed during the Army's attempts to gather together shipping in 1898, this time around cooperation was freely given. Foremost in that regard were Philip A. S. Franklin, president of International Mercantile Marine Company and Harry H. Raymond of the Clyde Line.[22] These two men picked from the Carson list 25 ships which were of a class and capacity sufficient for safe crossing of the Atlantic and which were known to be available on short notice. In the meantime, the Navy was readying the escorts which would safeguard the troop transports while en route. As the Navy strongly emphasized, a convoy's makeup was in large part predicated upon the speed of the

---

[21]   Col. Chauncy B. Baker had been selected to join the Army Transport Service at New York based on his past experience when he had been assigned as depot quartermaster during the occupation of Vera Cruz in 1914.

[22]   By 1917, the Clyde Line as well as the Mallory Line were operated as subsidiaries of their parent company Atlantic, Gulf and West Indies Steamship Lines. Harry H. Raymond was the president of both companies. Philip A. S. Franklin, the president of International Mercantile Marine Co. had his business start as an office boy working for Bernard M. Baker. Baker was the ship owner earlier mentioned by us who in 1898 had transferred the registry of a number of foreign flag vessels under his personal financial control to the American flag, thus allowing their employment for the sealift to Cuba since in 1898 the law forbid the utilization of foreign flag ships for military service during time of war. Philip A. S. Franklin had risen rapidly in the shipping business and by 1917 was considered by many as the dean of that industry. During WW I, Franklin was appointed by President Woodrow Wilson to be Chairman of the United States Shipping Board. He was the father of John M. Franklin who would become the President of United States Lines. During World War II, John M. Franklin served with the Army Transportation Corps and rose to the rank of major general. The threesome of Baker - Franklin - Franklin were key players in the history of Army marine transportation, their individual involvement extending throughout three major conflicts. Source: Rene de la Pedraja, *An Historical Dictionary of the U. S. Merchant Marine and Shipping Industry*, (Westport, CT and London: Greenwood Press, 1994).

slowest ship within the convoy. Since speed varied considerably for those ships Franklin and Raymond had selected, they next subdivided them into four groups of roughly equal capability. Each group was to be made up into a separate convoy formation with its own escorts. The plan was that the assemblages would depart New York at roughly the same time, each group routing independently. Of the 25 selected ships, a few were then at berths at New York with others due to arrive within a matter of a few days. Bareboat charters were executed between the owners and the ATS, and as each ship was brought under charter, work was begun toward fitting it out with standee bunks and sufficient cooking and sanitary facilities to accommodate the numbers of troops each would be scheduled to carry.[23] Four ships had temporary stalls built into their cargo holds for the handling of horses and mules. Due to the short time available, together with the absence of prior experience on the part of many who were involved, not everything worked smoothly or on schedule. When the time came to board the troops, some of the men found their assigned berthing spaces in disarray with workers struggling to finish the work in time for sailing. Besides the necessary conversions, defensive guns had to be installed, and in most cases, the decks beneath the gun mountings had to be strengthened and shored up. The Navy supplied the guns from storage at its yards at New York, Boston, and Philadelphia. The gunners were borrowed from the complements of the Navy's battle cruisers based at New York.[24] Meanwhile, the ATS staff was busy hiring crews for the chartered ships, that effort stressing recruitment from within the chartered ships' prior crews. The hiring process placed emphasis toward those who were believed to be *loyal,* a condition interpreted at the time as meaning seamen who would not create disciplinary problems -- a factor which remained of primary concern.

The naval escorts consisted of five cruisers, twelve destroyers, and two armed yachts to be evenly divided to protect each of the four convoyed groups. Since the destroyers -- all oil burners -- did not possess sufficient fuel capacity for the trip, they were to be refueled at a mid-ocean point. To accomplish that, the naval tanker *USS Maumee* departed Boston and proceeded to the preassigned mid-ocean refueling

---

[23]   Standee bunks are 3-, sometimes 4-tiered canvas/pipe connected bunk beds, the bottom bunk connected to the deck and the top bunk secured to the overhead thus giving rigidity to the tier.

[24]   The first ship to be armed in accordance with the Armed Neutrality Act had been the merchant ship *Manchuria* on March 16, 1917. Prior to the decision to supply armed guards for the first convoys from the Navy's battle cruisers, there had been thought given to the shipping companies hiring gunners as part of the civilian crewing makeup. According to the *New York Times* of March 3, 1917, the International Mercantile Marine Co. had started hiring trained gunners (presumably Navy veterans) as early as March 1917 in anticipation of its ships being armed. In May, J. L. Kaufman, Lt., USN, submitted an evaluation report on the feasibility of training merchant mariners as ships' gunners. His conclusion was a negative one based on his personal observations that the unlicensed seamen were mainly foreigners *of non-descript character not amenable to incorporation to naval gun crews.* It had also been considered that eventually, once trained, merchant seamen could take over from the naval gun crew, finally replacing them entirely. This idea was soon abandoned as impractical due to the *low quality and transient nature of the average merchant crew.* Source: Naval Armed Guard files: Letter from Chief of Naval Operations to shipping company executives, April 10, 1917.

In June of 1917, a Naval Armed Guard command was established, its personnel at first being taken from the fleet. Later (except for senior petty officers) the gunners consisted mainly of wartime enlistees. By December 1917, the supply of stored guns had been entirely depleted at which point guns up to 5" caliber were removed from the Navy's heavy cruisers and installed on merchant ships.

position.[25]   A Navy collier, the *USNS Cyclops* was added to one of the groups to provide a rebunkering service for the coal-burning transports after their arrival in France, the French having warned that coal was not available at the port of destination, St. Nazaire.

The troop transports were to carry the infantry element of what was being organized as the 1st Division. Attached to the 1st Division and to accompany the infantry was a motor car company as well as hospital and quartermaster detachments. (The artillery element of the 1st Division would sail to France on a later date.) Two regiments of Marines were included to sail aboard the naval transports *USS Hancock* and *USS Henderson.*   In all, the troops to be shipped, inclusive of the Marines, numbered around 12,000 officers and men. The transports would carry 500 civilian stevedores.[26]

The actual loading of the troops and their equipage became a hard-taught learning experience since almost nothing went off as planned. Due to train delays and mix-ups at assembly areas, units arrived on the piers at widely staggered intervals. A good part of the unit baggage appeared at the piers out of context with the ship upon which the particular unit was to sail. When it was realized that mistakes had been made, cargo holds were unloaded, the baggage was sorted out, and it was again loaded -- this time on the correct transport. For the Army, the one saving grace to all of this was that the Navy escorts were themselves delayed. Despite the many problems, departure was only a day late which, everything considered, was a triumph unto itself. The first convoy group cleared New York harbor on June 14, the second and third groups carrying troops followed closely. The fourth group, which consisted of cargo and animal ships, followed two days later. Outside of a few minor mishaps and a submarine scare en route, all the ships arrived safely at St. Nazaire, the last ship docking there on July 2.

---

[25]   Assigned to the *USS Maumee* in 1916-17 was Lt. (jg) Chester Nimitz (later in World War II a Fleet Admiral). Nimitz has been credited with being instrumental in the technique of replenishment while underway as it was first developed aboard *USS Maumee.* The *USS Maumee* would also serve throughout World War II. Among her many duties, she was the replenishment oiler during 1944 for Convoy NY-119. See Charles Dana Gibson, *The Ordeal of Convoy NY 119,* (Camden, ME: Ensign Press, 1992).

[26]   See Appendix C which relates the circumstances surrounding the shipment of civilian stevedores to France.

THE FIRST TROOP LIFT TO FRANCE
June/July 1917

Convoy Group #1

Owner	Army Transports	Naval Contingent	
NY & Cuba Mail SS Co	*Havana:* 6 Cos and Hq Co	*USS Corsair*	Converted yacht
United Fruit Co.	*Pastores:* 5 Cos, 28th Inf and QM troops	*USS DeKalb*	Auxiliary cruiser
NY & Cuba Mail SS Co	*Saratoga:* 7 Cos, 16th Inf	*USS Roe*	Destroyer
United Fruit Co.	*Tenadores:* 4 Cos, 28th Inf	*USS Seattle*	Armored cruiser
		USS Wilkes	Destroyer

Convoy Group #2

Owner	Army Transports	Naval Contingent	
Southern Pacific Co	*Antilles:* 4 Cos, 28th Inf and Hq Co	*USS Aphrodite*	Converted yacht
Clyde Line	*Lenape:* 5 Cos, 26th Inf, and 1st Div Hq	*USS Birmingham*	Scout Cruiser
Southern Pacific Co	*Momus:* 4 Cos, 26th Inf	*USS Burrows*	Destroyer
		USS Fanning	Destroyer
		USS Henderson	Naval transport (carried Marines)
		USS Lamson	Destroyer

Convoy Group #3

Owner	Army Transports	Naval Contingent	
Int'l Mercantile Marine	*Finland:* 6 Cos, 18th Inf and Motor Co	*USS Allen*	Destroyer
Mallory SS Co	*Henry R. Mallory:* 6 Cos, 18th Inf	*USS Charleston*	Cruiser
Mallory SS Co	*San Jacinto:* 4 Cos, 26th Inf and Hq Co and Field Hospital	*USNS Cyclops*	Collier
		USS McCall	Destroyer
		USS Preston	Destroyer

Convoy Group #4

Owner	Army Transports	Naval Contingent	
American-Hawaiian SS Co	*Dakotan* ‡	*USS Ammen*	Destroyer
Luckenbach SS Co	*Edward Luckenbach* ‡	*USS Flusser*	Destroyer
Southern Pacific Co	*El Occidente* ‡	*USS Hancock*	Naval transport (carried Marines)
American-Hawaiian SS Co	*Montanan* ‡	*USS Shaw*	Destroyer
		USS St. Louis	Cruiser
		USS Terry	Destroyer

‡ These four ships carried unit impedimenta, general cargo, and/or animals. They also carried some personnel -- probably the civilian stevedores.

The second shipment of troops which would arrive in France left New York at the end of July. Having returned from France after delivering the first expedition, the *USAT Pastores, USAT Tenadores, USAT Henry R. Mallory, USAT Saratoga, USAT Finland, USAT Antilles, USAT San Jacinto* and the Navy's transport *USS Henderson* were included in the second expedition to sail. A new addition would be the Navy tanker *USS Arethusa,* along to refuel the naval escorts while en route. The troop makeup of the second expedition consisted of the field artillery to be integrated to the 1st Division as well as a number of additional support units-- the second expedition, in all, totaling 274 officers and 7,337 enlisted men. Among the cargo consignments were the artillery's field pieces and a total of 797 vehicles ranging from motor cars to horse-drawn wagons. The transports were divided into two convoyed groups, the first leaving New York on July 31 and the second on August 5.

Troop shipments sent to France so far had been mainly composed of Regular Army personnel -- all that could be spared while still leaving enough in the United States to form training cadres around which the nation's rapidly expanding National Army would be formed. It would not be until well into September that additional regiments could be sent overseas.

The Navy Takes Over the Troop Lift

Following the departure of the second expedition, it was decided jointly between the services that the Navy's Cruiser and Transport Force (CTF) would take over and man the interned enemy passenger liners once they had been repaired and made ready for service. At the same time, the decision was made by the War Department that the civilian crews of the Army's chartered transports should also be replaced by naval personnel; however, the Navy found it had all it could do at that time to crew the interned liners. Only the Army crew of the *USAT Havana* was replaced by naval personnel before the spring of 1918. In the spring, five of the nine other ships used as troop carriers in the first two sealifts were taken over by the Navy. Of the remaining four: *Antilles* had been lost to enemy action in October of 1917; *Saratoga* had gone under USSB manning during the winter; *San Jacinto* would remain under Army crewing throughout the war although it is not known whether she continued to carry troops or was shifted to the carriage of freight; and *Momus* had been released from Army control, apparently returning to commercial service.

Staff Structure in France Relative to Water Transportation

The U.S. Army organization for supply and transportation in Europe differed widely from the organization which existed within the Zone of the Interior. Within the Zone of the Interior, functions relating to supply and its transportation all ultimately reported back to the Office of the Army's Chief of Staff in Washington. General John J. Pershing, prior to his leaving the United States to take up the command of the American Expeditionary Force (AEF) in France, had asked for and had been given an almost autonomous authority for setting up his own organization for the AEF's lines of communication which stretched from the French ports to the forward lines of battle.[27] Pershing would initially follow the organizational procedures as generally promulgated by the Army's Field Service Regulations; however, numerous operational difficulties encountered during the first few months of operation resulted in changes to what had been designated as the AEF's Service of Supply (SOS). Some of those changes were minor, but others were radical in departure from any practice of the past.[28] After a period of experimentation, the AEF's Transportation Corps was established and structured into six divisions, one of which was titled the Army

---

[27] The AEF's line of communication also included shipping to the account of the Army which operated between the ports of the United Kingdom and the French ports.

[28] *Order of Battle of the United States Land Forces in the World War, American Expeditionary Forces,* Vol. I. (Washington, DC: Center of Military History), pp 34-36.

Transport Service Division.[29] That division was given the responsibility for port operations in France and in the United Kingdom as well as for that portion of cross-channel shipping which dealt with AEF support.[30] The Transportation Corps and its various divisions which had been molded into being by Pershing's staff performed remarkably well within the overall Allied supply matrix, especially considering the overtaxed transportation environment within which it was forced to operate. In his final *Report to the Secretary of War* following the Armistice, Pershing wrote:

> *The Transportation Corps [AEF] as a separate organization was new to the Army. Its exact relation to the supply departments was conceived to be that of a system acting as a common carrier operating its own ship and rail terminals. The equipment and operation of port terminals stands out as a most remarkable achievement.* [31]

Twenty-seven years later during the Second World War and following the Allied landings in northern France, the American Army would take over control of virtually all of France's internal transportation system. Such was not the case during the First World War. During 1917 - 1918, logistical movements in France were carried out under the handicap of a port and connecting rail network which had to mesh with well-established French and British requirements. By 1917, the French were under considerable strain toward providing their own military needs, not to mention its war manufactory and the handling of essential foodstuffs for the civilian sector. What Pershing's staff had been faced with was the need to create a transportation network of its own, but they had to accomplish this within the overriding framework of the host country's systems.

Cross-channel shipping under the Army Transport Service's Division of the AEF's Transportation Corps was operated as a shuttle service. At the point of maximum activity, the AEF's Army Transport Service Division was utilizing 116 ships of which 73 were American-flag. Our research indicates that twenty-one of the American bottoms were manned by the Army's civilian employees; one by a USSB crew; and five by U.S. private operators under time charters with the Army.[32] Forty-six others were commissioned naval vessels operated by the Naval Overseas Transportation Service (NOTS) for the Army's account. The remainder -- or forty-three -- were Swedish under U.S. Army time charters and manned by their owners. The cross-channel shuttle was charged with carrying out a myriad of tasks, some of it involved troop lifts, others with the carriage of munitions and freight. But well over half of the employed tonnage was engaged in what was referred to as the *Army's coal trade*. That trade fueled the AEF's Transportation Corps rail system, bunkered

---

[29]   This Transportation Corps created by Pershing was in no way correlated to the later Transportation Corps which would be created in 1942 and which would become a permanent command.

[30]   *Order of Battle, AEF,* Vol. I, pp 37-50. Also see: McClellan, p 277, fn 18, which cites: U.S. War Department "Pertinent Paragraphs About the Transportation Corps," AEF Records, National Archives, Box 174.

[31]   "Final Report of General John J. Pershing" contained within the *Annual Report of the Secretary of War, 1919*, p 618.

[32]   See ship list at the end of this chapter titled "Army Manned Transports in Support of the American Expeditionary Force (AEF), 1917-19."

transatlantic troop and cargo transports prior to their return to the Zone of the Interior, and kept the AEF warm.[33]

The Overseas Ports

The ports of debarkation which the AEF used for the reception of incoming troops were Liverpool, England, and the French ports of St. Nazaire, Brest and Bordeaux. During June and July of 1917, 1,308 American personnel arrived from the United States. The numbers sent over after that increased substantially but would not exceed thirty thousand monthly until November and December of 1917 when for those two months an aggregate of 91,631 were sent over. The monthly volume remained at around that level until the next spring when in April, 105,076 were sent. The following month, the figure exceeded 200,000 and by July, the peak transport month, it had reached over 300,000 and continued at a high volume until the Armistice. All told, for the years 1917 and 1918, 2,083,865 U.S. armed forces personnel were sent to Europe. Of those, approximately 40% were landed at Liverpool and the rest at French ports.[34]

---

[33]   Sources for the makeup of the AEF Service of Supply as well as the AEF's Transportation Corps subordinate agency, the Army Transport Service:

- General Johnson Hagood, Chief of Staff, SOS, *The Services of Supply*, (New York and Boston: Houghton Mifflin Co., 1927.)
- Huston, pp 356-387.
- Lt. Col. O. D. Miller, Executive Officer, ATS, *History of the Army Transport Service, AEF.* This is an unpublished monograph submitted by Miller in compliance with instructions from Chief of Staff, AEF. For those with specific interest in cross-channel vessel identification and any of its related details, Miller's monograph is disappointing for its inadequacy. However, on his p 136, Miller does state that the Army in France as of December of 1918 had 116 vessels employed in its inter-theater service, 20 being ocean-class transports and 53 lake-class steamers. Miller does not differentiate which of these were manned by Army crews, USSB crews, or naval personnel of the NOTS command. He states that at that time, the AEF's Army Transport Service Division had under time charter forty-three Swedish vessels operating in the cross-channel service.

For a partial listing of the names of vessels employed on the cross-channel shuttle: Benedict Crowell and Capt. Robert F. Wilson, *How America Went to War, The Road to France*, (New Haven, CT: Yale University Press, 1921), pp 598-602. The reader is advised that the manning information therein references only one time frame, that being near the end of the war. By that time, the Naval Overseas Transportation Service had already taken over sixteen of the twenty-two vessels that had originally been under the Army's manning.

[34]   *United States Army in the World War, 1917 - 1919, Reports of the Commander in Chief, AEF, Staff Sections and Services,* (Washington, DC: Department of the Army, 1948), pp 23, 37-40. The reason Liverpool was used was that neither St. Nazaire or Bordeaux met the draft limitations of the largest troop ships. Troop units landed in England were held over in rest camps before being forwarded across the English Channel. In general, the troopships under British entry made their arrivals at Liverpool.

FRENCH PORTS ASSIGNED FOR USE OF THE AEF (1917 - 1918)

On the Bay of Biscay

Port	Location	Usage	Incoming Ships	Incoming Cargo*
St. Nazaire	Coast	Troops and general cargo	397	1,600,000
Nantes	Loire River	General cargo	248	639,000
Bordeaux	Gironde River	Troops and general cargo	381	1,749,700
LaPallice	Coast	General cargo	141	788,809
Rochefort	Coast	General cargo and coal	166	517,995

On English Channel

Port	Location	Usage	Incoming Ships	Incoming Cargo*
Brest	Entrance to Eng Channel	Troops and cargo	394	533,000
Cherbourg	Cherbourg Peninsula	General cargo	**	7,125
Granville	W of Cherbourg Penin.	Coal	**	26,000
Dieppe	E of Cherbourg Penin.	Hospital trains	**	**
LeHavre	Mid-channel point, east of Cherbourg Penin.	Troops and general cargo	185	**
Rouen	Outport of LeHavre	General cargo	**	186,433
Calais	Eastern Entrance, English Channel	General cargo	**	**

In Mediterranean

Port	Location	Usage	Incoming Ships	Incoming Cargo*
Marseilles	Southern France	Cargo	62	431,598

* In tons

** Not locatable from the records we searched.

Note: Following the war and with the establishment of an American army of occupation in the Rhineland in 1919, the port of Antwerp on the Scheldt River and the Dutch port of Rotterdam were used for supply and incoming and outgoing shipments of troops.

PORTS IN THE BRITISH ISLES UTILIZED BY THE
ARMY TRANSPORT SERVICE, AEF, SERVICE OF SUPPLY (1917 - 1919)

Port	Location	Major Usage
Cardiff	Bristol Channel - West Coast	Coal dispatch
Penarty (subport)	Bristol Channel - West Coast	Coal dispatch
Newport (subport)	Bristol Channel - West Coast	Coal and cargo dispatch
Barry (subport)		Coal and cargo dispatch
Swansea	Bristol Channel - West Coast	Cargo dispatch
Liverpool		Troop debarkation from United States
Batavia Docks	Thames River	Cargo and ordnance dispatch
Royal Albert Dock	London Basin	Cargo dispatch
Southampton	English Channel	Embarkation of troops for France; general cargo; munitions; dispatch and reception of hospital trains from Dieppe, France
Portsmouth	English Channel	Motor trucks and field artillery dispatch
Hartlepool	East Coast	Lumber dispatch
New Castle	East Coast	Coal dispatch
Hull	East Coast	General cargo dispatch
Glasgow	Scotland	Substitute port for debarkation of troops from United States
Belfast	Northern Ireland	Foodstuffs dispatch

Sources for the above lists:

- *United States Army in the World War, 1917 - 1919.*
- *History of the Army Transport Service, AEF.*
- *Order of Battle..., AEF,* Vol. I.

The Makeup of the AEF Sealift

According to the 1919 *Report of the Chief of Transportation Service,* the direct logistical support for the movement of the AEF to France was carried out by 616 troopships and cargo ships engaged both on transatlantic and cross-channel routings. That number refers to the total ships -- both under military and civilian management -- which were operated for what was referred to as *the Army account.* The total number encompasses those bottoms managed and manned by the Army as well as those managed and manned by the Navy's Cruiser and Transport Force (CTF) and the Navy's Naval Overseas Transportation Service (NOTS). It also includes merchant ships managed and crewed by the USSB as well as by private operators. A number of the employed merchant ships flew the flags of Sweden, Japan, Norway, Denmark, and Great Britain. Arriving at the number of ships that were managed and crewed by each entity is a difficult task since in most cases, the records only give a vessel's status for some undefined point in time within the twenty months' span of the war. Our research, summarized within the AEF ship list at the end of this chapter, shows that at some point over the span of the war, eighty-five bottoms (of 1000 gross tons or over) were under direct Army management and manning; however, as we indicate, during the war a number of those vessels went out from under Army management, coming under either the control of the CTF or NOTS. By the spring of 1918, the CTF was operating and manning with Navy crews approximately forty-five troop transports for the Army's account. By the Armistice in November, the Army was manning only twenty-six ships; NOTS had under naval manning 287 of its cargo ships, animal carriers, and tankers in service for the Army's account. Had the war continued into 1919, the remainder of the AEF support fleet, or around 250 merchant ships flying the American flag were scheduled to phase over to NOTS and its manning.[35]

Although the American cargo lift -- both U.S. flag and foreign flag -- was largely an American-managed affair, that was not the case with the troop lift: 45% of American troops went to France on American troopships; 50% on British troopships; and 5% on French and Italian troopships.[36]

Throughout the war, the troop lift was highly successful. Of the American share of that lift, only three troopships were lost; and those losses occurred when the ships were returning empty to the United States. Of the British troopers carrying Americans, three were lost -- two of them while returning empty.[37] A great part of that good fortune can be attributed to the high speed of the selected ships and to the excellent protection given them by the naval escort groups of the British and American navies.

---

[35] Lewis P. Clephane, *History of the Naval Overseas Transport Service in World War I,* (Washington, DC: Naval History Division, 1969), pp 213-251. Vice Adm. Albert Gleaves, *History of the Transport Service,* (New York: George H. Doran Co., 1921), pp 246-250. Crowell and Wilson, pp 577-602. Lt. Col. O. D. Miller, p 136.

[36] Crowell and Wilson, pp 330.

[37] The British troopship that was lost while eastbound with troops was the *RMS Tuscania,* with the deaths of 147 Americans. Halsey, IX, pp 367, 368.

The AEF U.S. flagged cargo fleet was not so lucky. Forty-one ships were lost: twenty-four through enemy action; two from mines; five from collisions at sea; eight from groundings, and two from fire. Of that number, thirteen were being manned at the time of their loss by NOTS, sixteen by the Army, and twelve by either the USSB or private operators.[38]

One of the early difficulties encountered by Pershing's Service of Supply in France was a lack of available locomotives for the rail system which it was operating. Box cars and flat beds were sent broken down to Europe where they were reassembled on arrival, a practice which continued throughout the war without any significant difficulties. Locomotives were another matter. At first, they were shipped over in pieces to be assembled in France, but that was a time-consuming process resulting in serious backlogs as supplies jammed the limited port facilities. The solution was to ship the locomotives over intact. This was not a new approach since over the past two years, the British had sent a number of locomotives across the English Channel by ferry; and for a number of years, the Florida East Coast Railroad had operated a ferry which transported rail cars and some fully assembled locomotives to Cuba from Florida. The Army at first considered taking that railroad's ferry into its service, but after a survey, it was obvious that the vessel was not of a design fit for North Atlantic weather. The answer was to request that the USSB assign to the Army the ore carriers *Cubora* and the *Feltore* which were owned and operated by the Bethlehem Steel Company. Each had oversized hatches which would allow for the horizontal loading of objects as long as locomotives; and being ore carriers, the flooring in their cargo holds was more than heavy enough to take the concentrated burden of locomotives. They subsequently went under requisition by the USSB and were immediately bareboat chartered to the Army. *USAT Feltore* made a number of trips to France with assorted rolling stock and survived the war, but *USAT Cubora* was not so lucky. While en route back to the United States from France following her delivery of the first load of assembled locomotives, *USAT Cubora* was torpedoed and lost.

There were other innovations to meet the assorted cargo needs of the AEF. It soon became the practice to dedicate some ships for specific carriage, horses and mules being one such specialization. Although the first sealifts had included ships in which animal stalls had been hastily installed, these were but temporary expedients. Later, a number of ships were selected to go through permanent modifications for that carriage. Munitions ships required special dunnage arrangements, and a number of bottoms became dedicated to that risky employment. A special need at the French ports developed for tugs and barges, few being available locally. To meet the shortage, barges and a number of small tow boats for use in the French canals were shipped over as deck cargo. Large tugs suitable for ship handling presented more difficulty because of their size and weight which precluded their carriage aboard ships. The only option was to send them across under their own power, not a simple challenge as tugs of the type required usually had insufficient freeboard to handle the kind of crossing conditions which could be expected. To overcome their inadequacies, each of them --

---

[38] Compiled from tables in Clephane. For Army-manned ship losses, see the AEF ship list at the end of this chapter.

twelve in number -- were fitted out with wooden *turtle backs* extending over their bows and carried back to the sterns. They all made the transatlantic passage safely.[39]

The Army Crews

Although the efficiency of those ships manned by the Army certainly varied, little is available, either from the official record or from the few popular accounts written after the war, to document that experience. From what records there are, there appears to have been a tendency to stereotype the Army's crews with the broad brush strokes of labor militancy, ill-discipline, and irresponsibility. How universally true those stereotypes were remains uncertain because of the paucity of case history.

Problems certainly involved the *USAT Finland* when she became a victim of enemy action on October 28, 1917. Following her third transit with troops to France, *USAT Finland* was returning from Brest to New York in convoy when she was struck by a torpedo. Thinking the ship was sinking, most of the crew and a number of passengers rushed the boats, doing so in a state of panic and without orders to abandon ship. Vice Adm. Albert Gleaves, in his history of the CTF, writes that the panicked abandonment of *USAT Finland* by part of its crew was a strong factor in the decision to integrate all troopships within the Navy's CTF.[40] In contradiction, there is the Army's 1919 *Report of Chief of Transport Service* which remarks (pp 176, 177) on the event: That report states that at the time of the torpedoing, the crew was Navy and that they behaved *in an heroic manner,* clearly implying that there was a willingness of the crew to stand by the ship and subsequently reboard it, *in keeping with the highest traditions of the American Navy.* The facts, as documented by the report of an on-the-spot naval officer, are entirely different. The Navy record is clear that *USAT Finland* was not manned by a naval crew until she had arrived back in the United States some weeks

---

[39]   *The Report of the Chief, Transport Service, 1919* relates the deployment to France of twelve Army-manned tugs, eight of which were named, but he does not discuss coaling which would have been necessary. Obviously a stop would have been required en route (possibly the Azores) since it is doubtful that replenishment at sea would have been practical. A few of the selected tugs were formerly Coast Artillery. Others were commercial tugs purchased by the Army. Our research has disclosed the identity of one other, the *USAT Slocum.* These are named within the ship list at the end of this chapter. During this period, the Army had other tugs, but we could not confirm their identities.

[40]   Gleaves, pp 108-110. Actually, Gleaves had stated earlier in his book that the decision to man troop transports with Navy crews had been made some six weeks prior to the affair of the *USAT Finland.*

The title of Gleaves's book is somewhat misleading. The command of which he writes, the Navy's "Cruiser and Transport Force," should not be confused with any Army commands which held the name "Transport Service." The misuse of command names was not confined to Gleaves's book title, the practice being widespread in much of the literature describing the sealift of World War I. Much of that misuse can be traced to the numerous reorganizations which took place over a relatively short period of time. In one attempt toward the correction of such mislabeling, Adm. W. S. Benson, Chief of Naval Operations, on September 27, 1918, wrote to George Creel who was then the chairman of the government's Committee on Public Information, stating to Creel that since most of the troop transports were by then Navy manned, they should not be referenced as Army transports which had been the practice up to that time. Instead, they should be referred to as "U.S. Troop Transports," since albeit originally chartered by the Army, *they were now commissioned naval vessels with Navy crews.* Source: Armed Guard, File "ZSA," 11 W4, Box 984, Naval Records Collection, Office of Naval Records and Library. Whenever the Cruiser and Transport Force took over a ship for Navy manning, the ship was first commissioned. With only a few exceptions, the same applied to ships taken over by the Naval Overseas Transportation Service.

following.[41] It is also clear that the crew -- civilian in makeup -- acted in a less-than-heroic manner.

To appreciate the circumstances of what actually occurred on *USAT Finland,* it is helpful to understand the rather strange command arrangement which prevailed on the Army's transports during the first months of the war. Those Naval Armed Guards first assigned to Army transports were commanded by commissioned naval officers who functioned through direction of *Presidential Order Relating to Army Troop Transports.* Paragraph 9A of that order stated,

> *The senior naval officer attached to the transport shall at all times, both in port and*
> *at sea, have complete command of the transport in all matters relating to speed,*
> *course, maneuvering, anchorage, and defense of the vessel.* [42]

As should have been expected such instructions played havoc with the authority of the ships' civilian masters. It did not take long to discover how unworkable this was, and paragraph 9A was canceled during the late fall of 1917. After that, naval officers would continue to be assigned as gun crew commanders aboard transports carrying troops; but they were restricted in their authority to the defense of the ship, and under no circumstances were they to supersede the authority of the master.[43] The torpedoing of the *USAT Finland* had, however, taken place at a time when Paragraph 9A was still in force.

The panic which occurred on the part of the *USAT Finland* crew created the kind of situation under which the Naval Armed Guard commander felt he should exercise the authority given under Paragraph 9A, and he had taken over command. He, together with the ship's officers, brought order out of what for a time had been chaos, but not before most of the lifeboats had reached the water and at least one of them had capsized, spilling its frightened occupants into the sea. The engine and fireroom gangs, had meanwhile deserted their posts contrary to the direct orders of the ship's engineers, and they had to be driven back to their stations, *with the aid of a revolver and a heavy wooden mallet.* With order restored but the ship still considered as being in danger of sinking, the remainder of the boats were lowered, this time with the acquiescence of the Naval Armed Guard officer and under the direct supervision of the ship's officers. Despite the fact that the torpedo had torn a hole 35' long by 23' high, completely flooding No. 4 hold, the adjoining watertight bulkheads had held. What saved the ship was that No. 4 hold contained the reserve bunkers. The coal spilled out through the gap caused by the torpedo, lightening the ship, and giving it added buoyancy. Once it had been determined that the ship was not going to sink, the occupants of the lifeboats were ordered back aboard, and the ship then proceeded back to France. Because of the danger of lurking submarines, the departure was understandably made in haste, and not all the boats were recovered -- those overlooked being picked up by the escort vessels.

---

[41]   Cdr. S. V. Graham's report on *USAT Finland* as quoted by Gleaves, pp 109, 110. Also see *Dictionary of American Naval Fighting Ships* for date of Navy takeover of *USAT Finland.* The *Dictionary* verifies the statement made by Graham.

[42]   This arrangement is related within the World War I Naval Armed Guard historical file under a letter dated January 15, 1919 on file at the Naval History Center, Washington, DC.

[43]   Commissioned officers were always assigned as commanders of the Naval Armed Guard detachments on troopships. On cargo ships, the Naval Armed Guard commanders were petty officers.

USAT Finland made it safely into Brest and from there went to Margate in England where she entered a shipyard. Once repaired, she was returned to the United States during the spring of 1918. It was only then that *Finland* was given a naval crew.

Gleaves gave as his rationale for why the panic had taken place the fact that the transport was carrying as passengers the crewmen survivors of an earlier sinking (*USAT Antilles*). He claimed that those men, apprehensive of a further brush with death, had infected *USAT Finland's* crewmembers with the same fear.[44] The Naval Armed Guard commander wrote that both crews were made up largely of foreigners and were the *sweepings of the docks* from which they had been hired.

An entirely different impression of the behavior of a civilian crew under Army hire is related within the action report of the Naval Armed Guard officer aboard *USAT Dwnski*.[45] Owned by Russian nationals, the *Dwnski* had gone under bareboat charter to the Army directly from her owners. She was then manned by the Army with its civilian employees. During the spring of 1918, this ship, in company with thirteen other transports, was headed back to the United States in ballast, having unloaded troops in France. Once clear of what was believed to be the area of greatest danger from enemy submarines, the convoy was dispersed and each ship proceeded independently. Upon independently reaching latitude 38° 30' North, longitude 60° 58' West, or around seven hundred miles eastward of Delaware Bay, *USAT Dwnski* was torpedoed, all indications being that the hit was a mortal one. (The ship was at the time under the indisputable command of its civilian master since Paragraph 9A of the presidential order had been rescinded in the late fall of 1917.) The master ordered engines stopped and all boats lowered. Fortunately, there were no casualties either from the attack or in the process of abandoning ship which was reportedly done in a directed and orderly fashion. No sooner had the lifeboats pulled clear of the ship than the submarine surfaced and began firing on the still-floating *USAT Dwnski*. The German marksmanship was poor, no one in the lifeboats spotting a hit. The submarine then approached the lifeboats with the probable intention of making the ship's officers prisoners, but that was frustrated since they had taken off and hidden their jackets and hats which otherwise would have distinguished them. Moving away and resuming their firing on the ship, the sub's gunners finally scored, exploding the powder magazine; but it would take altogether eighteen more rounds before the ship finally sank. The submarine then submerged.

What followed was a tale of survival described by the Naval Armed Guard officer, a Lieutenant Whitemarsh, who commanded No. 6 lifeboat. On the first afternoon, rescue seemed imminent when a destroyer appeared, heading for them at flank speed. The submarine which had been lying undetected at periscope depth, using one of the other lifeboats as a decoy, fired at the destroyer with a torpedo. Its lookouts fortunately spotted the torpedo in time to avoid. That was the last anyone in No. 6

---

[44] According to the report of Lt. Cdr. D. T. Ghent, the Naval Armed Guard officer on the *USAT Antilles*, that ship was abandoned in good order with no show of panic. In his words, *the ship was abandoned in excellent order and without undo excitement. The savings of 71% of those on board in the rough sea that was running while the ship went down in the unusually short time of 6 ½ minutes was a creditable performance.* Source: Gleaves, p 106.

[45] The account of the *USAT Dwnski* sinking and subsequent lifeboat voyage has been taken from Gleaves, pp 207-215.

lifeboat saw of the destroyer which quickly departed the scene. For Whitemarsh and the others in No. 6 lifeboat, what followed would be eleven days of severe deprivation. All there was for emergency rations were a few moldy biscuits and twenty-four gallons of stale water. Before being finally rescued, they would go through gale conditions during which one man was swept overboard and lost.

What makes Whitemarsh's account of the lifeboat voyage of specific interest is his impression of the civilian seamen who shared the experience with him. There were twenty in the boat besides the lieutenant. This number included two additional Americans as well as a *Frenchman* and a *Maltese*. From the roster of names which Whitemarsh included in his report, the others appear to have been Anglo-Saxon in origin. At least one, a cadet, was the son of *a famous English sportsman and a banker*. Where the other men were recruited, i.e., in England or in the United States, Whitemarsh did not say. The responses of the men to the naval officer's orders were prompt and without argument, and all readily adjusted to the harsh conditions they encountered. Whitemarsh praised the spirit of unselfishness which prevailed among all in the lifeboat. In contrast to the claims made by the Naval Armed Guard officer regarding the crew of the *USAT Finland*, the crewmen off the *USAT Dwnski* certainly could not have come from the *sweepings of the docks*.

The Takeover Plan of June 1918

During June of 1918, a joint conference relating to the manning of noncombatant ships took place at which representatives from the Navy, the Army, and the U.S. Shipping Board were in attendance. The following month, the chairman of that meeting wrote Josephus Daniels, Secretary of the Navy, laying out the agreed-upon plan for his final consideration. The plan spelled out a manning program which was to take effect starting that July.[46]

> *I. All troop ships and hospital ships are to be manned by the Navy.*
>
> *II. Armed transports and vessels engaged exclusively in the service of the War and/or Navy Departments are to be manned as directed by the interested department, which we understand will, in a great majority of cases, require that they be manned by Naval personnel.*
>
> *III. Commercial vessels engaged exclusively in the trade to ports within the war zone are to be manned by Naval personnel.*
>
> *IV. Commercial vessels engaged occasionally in trade as above, but which are likely to be sent to other ports in strictly commercial trade, are to be manned, as far as possible, by merchant seamen.*
>
> *V. Commercial vessels engaged exclusively in safe trade, such as for instance, to West Indies, South America, Orient, Australia, and coastwise are to be manned by merchant seamen.*

By the time the war ended that November, the NOTS takeover plan had not reached its full momentum, either regarding the Army's tonnage as referenced in Paragraph II or for those ships manned by the USSB as described by Paragraph III of the plan. As of the end of 1918, the Army was still manning twenty ships on

---

[46]   Clephane, pp 69, 70.

transatlantic service and another six in cross-channel service. Whether the War Department had intended to divest itself entirely of its manned fleet or whether its intentions were to retain a nucleus of bottoms and a cadre of its better crews for post-war employment remains as one of many unanswered questions in the history of the sealift of the First World War.

Victory in November

On March 12, 1918, an unprecedented volume of artillery fire erupted against the British trenches in northern France. The first shells contained gas, followed by explosives, and then by a creeping barrage moving ahead of seventy German divisions on the attack. The British put up a stubborn defense but were forced back to their third line of trenches some forty miles to the rear. Before the Germans could be stopped, the British would suffer 280,000 casualties and the loss of 1200 artillery pieces. French divisions would move north to plug the gaps in the lines, with Pershing immediately agreeing to commit the AEF in division-sized strengths when and wherever they were ordered by the French high command. The German advance would bring it within fifty miles of Paris before it could be halted. What finally checked the Germans was the ability of the French to quickly move their own and the American divisions into the gaps.[47]

The German Army had given its all in a desperate last attempt to win the war, but for them, time was running out. On the German home front, defeatism was taking over, and the last of the country's manpower reserves had been called to the colors. Mutiny broke out in the German High Seas Fleet and soon blossomed into revolution.

During May and into early June at Château-Thierry and Belleau Wood, the French, supported by the American 2nd and 3rd Infantry Divisions, launched successive punishing counter-attacks against the German lines. By mid June in most sectors, the Germans were driven back to their pre-March positions. In late July, Pershing issued a general order establishing the United States First Army which brought under one American command those divisions which he had earlier sent into battle under the French. The United States First Army took over the Saint-Mihiel salient. There, the Americans, to a strength of 550,000, reinforced by 110,000 poilu and supported by 1,400 American and 600 French aircraft, 3,000 French artillery pieces and 267 tanks, began a push that would soon end the war. By mid-October, Pershing had enough additional divisions on hand to consolidate them as the United States Second Army which he moved to the front to take position on the line south of the United States First Army. By then, American strength, actively engaged, counted forty-one divisions, each American division possessing almost twice the number of troops as the other Allied divisions or of the enemy divisions. The American presence had become a rejuvenation beyond measure for the Allied side, and the defeat of Germany had become a certainty.

---

[47] The French had developed -- as had Pershing -- a large motor corps. The Germans, conversely, were handicapped in their mobility because of a lack of vehicles, their advances being made mainly on foot which brought the German troops to a state of near physical exhaustion by the time their offensive was checked.

The guns fell silent on November 11, 1918. It was over at last. Although the active participation of the United States on the Western Front had encompassed only a few short months, it had been an intensive and bloody involvement. The toll of U.S. Army and U.S. Marine Corps personnel killed in action numbered 52,921; the number of non-mortal wounded, 203,183.[48]

The Expedition to Russia in 1918

During early 1917, President Woodrow Wilson had made it the declared policy of the United States that America's role in the European war would be restricted to the Western Front. However, the unexpected Bolshevik overthrow of Russia's Czarist government brought with it a deviation from that policy which arose out of the need to safeguard military supplies which had earlier been shipped to Russia. At the ports of Murmansk and Archangel in northern Russia and at Vladivostok in eastern Siberia, the distribution of those supplies was held up when intelligence was received by the allies that the Bolsheviks were considering an independent armistice with the Germans.

The British and the French had reacted to the Bolshevik takeover with considerable alarm not only over the issue of a separate Russian armistice but because they feared that the seeds of revolution might spread to their own countries and to their armies. Accordingly, the British and the French decided to send expeditionary forces to Russia. Once on Russian soil, if the situation appeared provident, they would join the Czarist supporters in action against the Bolsheviks and then organize a new Russian army to fight the Germans.

In July 1918, Wilson authorized the departure of two small American expeditionary forces to the northern Russian ports for the express purpose of protecting the stockpiled supplies with orders to prevent their distribution until such time that the uncertainty surrounding the events in Russia could be clarified. A third American expeditionary force to be known as the Expedition to Siberia and consisting of 8,632 officers and men was sent to Vladivostok. Approximately two-thirds of that force, consisting of the 8th Infantry Division, sailed from San Francisco aboard *USAT Thomas, USAT Sheridan,* and *USAT Logan.* The rest went from the garrison in the Philippines aboard *USAT Crook, USAT Merritt, USAT Sherman,* and *USAT Warren* and a later contingent on *USAT Thomas.* The diversion of the Army's shipping for the Siberian troop movement caused a cancellation of scheduled ATS liner service to the Philippines for the remainder of 1918 and part of 1919.[49]

---

[48] Despite the short time engaged, total battle deaths of the U.S. Army and U.S. Marine Corps during the First World War exceeded by almost 9,000 the number of battle deaths suffered by the U.S. Army and U.S. Marine Corps during the 1960s and 1970s in Southeast Asia over the more lengthy period of that involvement.

[49] Record Group-165, Entry 310. *History of the American Expedition to Siberia.* War College and War Plans Division; Records of Historical Section, 1900-1941, Box 145, Folder, History of American Expedition to Siberia (7-46.1), pp 7-9, 33, 34. Also, American Expeditionary Forces, Siberia Office of Chief Quartermaster, Vladivostok, January 30, 1919, Record Group-395, M917, Roll #11, Z1-46. In addition to the troops, there were at least five hundred civilians, inclusive of those assigned to the Russian Railway Corps. See fn 50 for more on this corps.

Wilson had publicly declared that the United States would not take an active role in Russia's internal strife, so the presence of United States troops in Siberia was to follow a somewhat different goal than that set by the British and the French. Wilson optimistically hoped that the appearance of U.S. troops might result in stability. How that was to come about was in large part left to the American commander, based on his evaluation of the situation.[50] What appears to have been of mutual concern to all the allies was the uncertain fate of an estimated 50,000-man Czech-Slovak army.

The Czech-Slovaks were the survivors of military units which, at the outbreak of the war in Europe, had broken away from the Austro-Hungarian forces to join with Imperial Russia to fight the Central Powers on the Austro-Hungarian sector of the Eastern Front. In 1918, that part of the front was being held by Cossack divisions which, following the Bolshevik revolution, remained steadfast in their loyalty to the Czarist government. (Russian troops loyal to the Czar were termed *White Russians*.) Because of the Czech-Slovak's concern over what might develop over the White Russians' willingness to continue the war against the Central Powers, the Czech-Slovaks informed the French in the spring of 1918 that they wished to join their compatriots then fighting with the French on the Western Front, and that they would cross eastward through Siberia to Vladivostok on the Pacific via the Trans-Siberian Railroad, there to await sea transport to France. Leon Trotsky, the Bolshevik minister of war, had guaranteed them safe passage through Bolshevik territory in exchange for handing in their heavy weapons. Having done so, the Czech-Slovaks entrained on the Trans-Siberian Railroad in a series of echeloned departures. Despite Trotsky's promise, all of the groups experienced delays and finally armed harassment by the Bolsheviks who even demanded their small arms in exchange for safe passage. Realizing that they had no alternative but to stand and fight, the Czech-Slovaks consolidated, fortunately in time, as they came under attack by a Bolshevik force consisting of former German and Austro-Hungarian prisoners of war. The Czech-Slovaks won that engagement and a number of others which followed. Joining forces with White Russian units in June 1918, they established an eastern barrier which for a time thwarted Bolshevik control of Siberia along the line of the Ural Mountains.

The Czech-Slovak command received a message in late June from the French Ambassador to Russia informing that the Czech-Slovaks should now consider themselves a formal part of the Allied army fighting against the Central Powers. On July 22, the Czech-Slovak commander received wireless instructions from the American Consul General (assumed then to have been at Moscow) that the Czech-Slovaks should seize full control of the Trans-Siberian Railroad system. The message stated that the French Consul General joined in those instructions.[51] Following soon after came another communication originating from the American Consul General by then located at Irkutsk, addressed to the American vice consul at Omsk, and copied to the Czech-Slovak command.

---

[50] The situation in Russia during the summer of 1918 held the likely promise that the factions loyal to the Czar would eventually overcome the Bolsheviks (the Reds) and restore, if not a renewal of a Czarist regime, at least a semblance of the old Imperial government. As we now know, that hope did not materialize.

[51] Those instructions were seemingly issued in reinforcement to a United States sponsored program then just going into effect which had established for Siberia a quasi-military organization known as the Russian Railway Corps made up of American civilian railway engineers and railway executives. When that organization arrived in Russia, it had discovered its mission frustrated by an assortment of Russian factions, both White and Red, each claiming jurisdiction over the Trans-Siberian Railroad. It is possible that the July 22 instructions to the Czech-Slovak commander from the American Consul General may have had the purpose of bringing the Trans-Siberian under American control while avoiding too close a physical proximity of the Americans with the Bolsheviks.

> *I consider this* [the seizure of the Trans-Siberian Railroad] *wise in view of the fact that the allies wish the Czechs to be the main backbone and support of Allied action in Siberia and Russia against Germany.*
>   *Harris* [52]

From most Allied viewpoints, it had by then been recognized that Bolshevik control in Russia would be to the advantage of Germany, thus it followed that a struggle against the Bolsheviks was to be considered the same as a struggle against Germany. As a result, the French and the British promised the Czech-Slovaks that they would reinforce them but without a set timetable. The Americans did not, however, join in that promise.

The situation became even more complicated when cohesiveness between the Czech-Slovaks and White Russian units began to disintegrate. Having been promised Allied reinforcement from Vladivostok, but having received none, Czech-Slovak morale plummeted. Next followed a series of disagreements between various White Russian commanders as to who had seniority of command. This, of course, quickly worked to the advantage of the Bolsheviks, and they moved to fill the power vacuum which resulted. The Czech-Slovak troops, refusing to fight a lost battle, fell back toward Vladivostok.

By early 1919, the Allied presence in eastern Siberia would include not only the French, British, and Americans, but Canadian, Japanese, and Italian units, and of course the tragic Czech-Slovaks to which the allies had become joined through obligation if nothing else. From all appearances, staying in Siberia had become a losing proposition for all. Thus did the Bolsheviks triumph.

Of the 50,000 Czech-Slovaks who started from the Eastern Front, by late 1918 they had lost almost half of their ranks either from battle causes, desertions, or disease. When finally evacuated from Vladivostok aboard U.S. Army transports in the summer of 1920, only 26,928 of them would be left to be taken out. [53]

---

[52]   Carl W. Ackerman, *Trailing the Bolsheviki, Twelve Thousand Miles With the Allies in Siberia,* (New York: Charles Scribner's Sons, 1919), pp 135, 136. Ackerman was a special correspondent of the *New York Times.* The actions of the American Consul General appear to either have been made on his own cognizance, or else the State Department was to later decide that Washington's complicity in Russian internal matters was best stricken from the record. In any event, the U.S. State Department would deny its authorization for Harris's instructions having been sent to the Czech-Slovaks.

[53]   Service in the Czech-Slovak Army for those who later became American citizens would be recognized by the U.S. Congress through unprecedented legislation which granted to them the same benefits entitled to veterans of the United States armed forces, provided that such foreign nationals had been residents of the United States for a minimum of ten years at the time of their application for such benefits. The same veterans benefits were made to apply (under the same restrictions) to former Poles who had served in the Polish Army as that army was founded at Paris under Allied sponsorship in 1918. The legislation covered U.S. citizens of Polish extraction who during World War I either traveled to France from the United States, or being then in France, joined the Polish Army when it was created at Paris. 38 U.S.C. § 109(c), (1). A description of the Polish-American troops and their evacuation to the United States is given within Appendix D of this volume.

ARMY MANNED TRANSPORTS IN SUPPORT OF THE AMERICAN EXPEDITIONARY FORCE TO FRANCE (AEF) 1917 - 1919
(Owned and/or Chartered)

Major sources for list:

American Ship Casualties of the World War.
Clephane. *History of the Naval Overseas Transportation Service in WW I.*
Crowell and Wilson. *How America Went to War, The Road to France*
Dictionary of American Naval Fighting Ships
Gleaves. *History of the Transport Service.*
Hurley. *The Bridge to France.*
Merchant Vessels of the United States for the years 1916-21.
Miller. *History of the Army Transport Service, American Expeditionary Force.*
Order of Battle, AEF, Volume 3, Part I.
Report of Chief of Transportation Service for the fiscal years ended June 30, 1919 and June 30, 1920..
Report of the Quartermaster General for 1917.

Note regarding all vessels listed here as: "going over to Navy," or "acquired by Navy" or "went under Navy control". This indicates that they became commissioned naval vessels attached either to the Cruiser and Transport Force or to the Naval Overseas Transportation Service.

Note: *American Ship Casualties of the World War* does not list the vessels *USAT Crimdon* or the *USAT Dwnski.* These two vessels were chartered to the Army by foreign owners and were not U.S. flag vessels.

Note: The title of Gleaves' book is somewhat misleading as his work covers the history of the Navy's Cruiser and Transport Force which was not a part of any Army organization carrying the title "Transport Service." Gleaves does, however, touch on some episodes which involved transports under Army crewing and operations.

Note: Miller's work was unpublished and undated but by all indications it was submitted during early 1919. This report discusses in small part the operation of cross-channel shipping and inland shipping in France, 1917-1919, but it does not include transatlantic operations which were under the initial purview of the Army Transport Service at New York -- later the Embarkation Service.

Note: According to *Report of Chief of Transportation Service,* 12 tugs were sent to France. In this list, we were only able to identify 9 of them by name.

UNDER ARMY MANNING	USAT VESSEL NAME	FRMR NAME/ FLAG	TYPE OR CLASS	TONNAGE	YR.BLT	REMARKS
1917	A. A. Raven		Freighter	2458	1912	Blt Ecorse, MI. BB chartered to Army from American Transportation Co., Nov 1917. Sunk by submarine off Lands End, England, Mar 14, 1918. Seven lives lost.
1917-19	Amphion	Koln, Ger	Animal Transport	7409	1899	Blt Geestemunde, Germany. Seized at Boston, 1917. Served as Army transport throughout war operating on runs, U.S. to France. During spring 1919 was transferred to Navy. In Sept 1919, turned over to USSB.
1917	Antilles		Transport	6878	1907	Blt Philadelphia, PA. On BB charter to Army May 1917. Part of first troop convoy to France; convoy attacked on return voyage to U.S. but without casualties. Sunk by submarine U-62 in Bay of Biscay, Oct 17, 1917. Sixty-seven lives lost; fifty-one of those were crewmembers.
1918	Ausable	Laura, Dutch	Collier	3153	1901	Blt Holland. On BB charter to Army from USSB in Feb 1918. On 19 July 1918 went to Navy at Cardiff, Wales.
1917-18	Berwind	Boston City, Br	Transport	2589	1893	Blt Sunderland, England. BB chartered to Army from New York and Porto Rico SS Co. during Sept 1917. Sunk by submarine off Benmarsh, England, on Aug 3, 1918. Six lives lost.
1917-19	Black Arrow	Rhaetia, Ger	Freighter	6599	1904	Blt Vegesack, Germany. Seized by Army for support AEF in 1917; transferred to Navy Jan 27, 1919.
1918-20	Boswell		Tug/formerly artil steamer	311	1890	Blt Camden, NJ. Sent to France during 1918.
1918	Bremerton		Freighter	7530 dw	1918	Blt Seattle, WA. Assigned to Army on BB charter by USSB. Routes of her war service unknown.
1917-18	Buena Ventura	Buena Ventura, Br	Transport; freight	4881	1913	Blt Howden-on-Tyne, England. Requisitioned for Army use by USSB from U.S. Steel Products Co. in Oct 1917. Transferred to Navy 1918; sunk by submarine Sept 1918 while under Navy crewing.
1898-1922	Buford	Mississippi, Br	Transport	5040 (3732) (4805) 6000 dw	1890	Blt Belfast, Ireland. Purchased from Atlantic Transport Co. through Bernard N. Baker July 14, 1898, for $350,000. Atlantic Fleet, 1899. Two runs, New York to Manila, before official transfer to Pacific fleet in 1902. During 1906, rescued crew and passengers of the merchant ship Mongolia stranded on Midway. Placed into decommissioned status in 1911. Recommissioned in 1912 to evacuate U.S. citizens from ports on the west coast of Mexico. Performed the same function during 1913. Was then placed on Alaskan shuttle service. During 1916, carried bulk cargoes to the War Dept's account from Japan and later carried nitrate from Chile consigned to the Ordnance Dept. Used in support of AEF, 1917-18, being the only prewar ATS trooper in that support.
1917-18	Calameres	Calameres, Br	Transport	7782	1913	Blt Belfast, Ireland. BB chartered by Army in 1917 from United Fruit Co. for support AEF. Transferred to Navy, April 1918.

UNDER ARMY MANNING	USAT VESSEL NAME	FRMR NAME/FLAG	TYPE OR CLASS	TONNAGE	YR.BLT	REMARKS
1917-18	Chattahoochee	Sachsen, Ger	Freighter	8232	1911	Blt Belfast, Ireland. BB chartered to Army in Feb 1918; sunk by submarine U-55 Mar 23, 1918, off Penzance, England. No casualties
1917-18	City of Atlanta		Transport; freighter	5433	1904	Blt Chester, PA. BB chartered to Army from Ocean SS Co. Operated during 1917. Redelivered to owner at end of war.
1917-18	City of Savannah		Transport; freighter	5654	1907	Blt Chester, PA. BB chartered to Army from Ocean SS Co. Operated during 1917. Redelivered to owner at end of war.
1918	Crimdon		Collier			Chartered to Army by Swedish owner, apparently on BB basis. Sunk by submarine July 29, 1918 in English Channel.
1918	Cuba		Tug			Sent to France during 1918.
1918	Cubora		Freight; locomotive carrier	7117	1917	Blt Sparrows Point, MD, for Bethlehem Steel Co. Taken over by USSB; was BB chartered to Army on June 10, 1918. Sunk by submarine U-107 on Aug 15, 1918, in Bay of Biscay while en route France to US
1917-18	Dakotan		Freight, converted to troop transport	6660	1912	Blt Sparrows Point, MD. Incorrectly spelled Dackotan in some records. Commandeered and subsequently BB chartered to Army June 1917. Was in first troop convoy to France in June 1917.
1918	Dora	Dora, Austrian	Transport; freighter	7037	1913	Blt Triesteno, Austria. Seized. BB chartered to Army by USSB during May 1918. Sunk by submarine U-57 while 400 miles off French coast on Sept 4, 1918. No casualties
1918	Dwnski		Transport			BB chartered to Army by Russian owners. Sunk while en route to U.S. on June 18, 1918
1917-18	Edward Luckenbach		Freighter	7900	1916	Blt Quincy, MA. BB chartered to Army from Luckenbach SS Co., as of June 1917. Part of first troop convoy to France in June 1917; on return trip to U.S. was narrowly missed by a torpedo. Turned over later to USSB which chartered her to Navy in 1918.
1917	El Occidente		Freighter	6008	1910	Blt Newport News, VA. As of June 1917 was on BB charter from Southern Pacific Co. to Army. Was part of first troop convoy to France, June 1917. Turned over to USSB at some point following that time.
1918	El Oriente		Freighter	6008	1910	Blt Newport News, VA. Apparently under BB charter to Army prior to her commissioning in the Navy in July 1918.
1917-18	El Sol		Freighter	6008	1910	Blt Newport News. BB chartered to Army during 1917 in support AEF. Transferred to Navy in commissioned status 3 August 1918. Redelivered to owners Sept 1919.
1917-18	F. J. Luckenbach		Freighter	7821	1917	Blt Quincy, MA. BB chartered to Army circa 1917-18.
1917-18	Feltore		Freighter and locomotive carrier	11300 dw	1917	Blt Sparrow Point, MD, for Bethlehem Steel Co. Taken over by USSB; was BB chartered to Army in 1918.

UNDER ARMY MANNING 1917-18	USAT VESSEL NAME	FRMR NAME, FLAG	TYPE OR CLASS	TONNAGE	YR.BLT	REMARKS
	Finland		Transport	12222	1902	Blt Philadelphia, PA. BB chartered by Army from International Mercantile Marine Co., June 1917 and was part of first troop convoy to France that month. Torpedoed on Oct 28, 1917, while en route France to U.S. She was able to return to Brest and then Margate, England, where repairs were made before leaving again for U.S. Nine lives lost. Transferred to Navy 24 April 1918. Redelivered to Army 15 Nov 1919 and shortly thereafter redelivered to owners.
1917	*Florence Luckenbach*	*Damara*, Br, *Damara*	Transport; freighter	5505	1910	Blt Glasgow, Scotland. BB chartered from Luckenbach SS Co. in 1917. Redelivered to owner at end of war.
1918-22	*Gwalia*	*Gwalia*	Tug/formerly artil steamer	415	1907	Blt Philadelphia, PA. Sent to France during 1918.
1918-22	*Gypsum Prince*		Tug/formerly artil steamer	299	1917	Blt Baltimore, MD. Sent to France during 1918.
1917-18	*Harry Luckenbach*	*Surry*, Br, *Michigan*, Br, *Michigan*, Norweg; *Michigan*, Am	Freighter	2798	1881	Blt West Hartlepool, England. BB charter to Army by Luckenbach SS Co. during Nov 1917. Attacked by submarine *U-84*, Jan 6, 1918, and sunk off Penmarch Point, France. Eight lives lost.
1917	*Havana*		Transport	6391		Under BB charter to Army from New York and Cuba Mail SS Co. as of June of 1917. Was part of first troop convoy to France. Acquired by Navy in Sept 1917 and converted into a transport then converted to a hospital ship, becoming the *USNHS Comfort*.
1917-21	*Henry R. Mallory*		Transport	6063		BB chartered to Army by Mallory SS Co. in June 1917. Was in first convoy to France June 1917. During April 1918 was transferred to Navy. Transferred to Army October 1919.
1918	*Hercules*	*Bulgaria*, Ger	Animal transport	11440	1898	Blt Hamburg, Germany. Seized 1917. During February of 1918 under BB charter to Army from USSB. Encountered heavy weather en route to France. Lost her steering necessitating the closing of air ducts. 250 mules died of suffocation. Taken over by Navy in May 1919.
1917-18	*Herman Frasch*		Freighter	3803	1910	Blt Quincy, MA. ATS 1917 under BB charter. Taken over by Navy Sept 19, 1918; lost the following month in collision off Nova Scotia.
1917-18	*Hewitt*	*Pacific*	Transport	5398	1914	Blt Quincy, MA. BB chartered to Army from Union Sulphur Co. Was redelivered to owner after war.
1917-18	*Hilton*		Collier	3102	1911	Blt Newport News, VA. BB chartered to Army from A. H. Bull and Co. in Sept 1917. Acquired by U.S. Navy at Cardiff, Wales, Nov 6, 1918.
1918	*Iowan*		Tug	5640	1894	Sent to France during 1918.
1917-19	*Iroquois*	*Wittekind*, Ger	Transport			Blt Germany. Seized from her German owners in 1917. BB chartered to Army for use as troop transport; renamed *Freedom* in 1918. Acquired by Navy January 1919.

UNDER ARMY MANNING	USAT VESSEL NAME	FRMR NAME/FLAG	TYPE OR CLASS	TONNAGE	YR.BLT	REMARKS
1917-18	John G. McCullough	S. C. Reynolds	Transport	1985	1890	Blt Buffalo, NY. Was BB chartered to Army from J. F. Whitney and Co. or United States SS Co. (records disagree) during April 1918. While in Army employ, was sunk by German submarine off French coast on May 18, 1918. One life lost.
1917-18	Joseph Cudahy		Tanker	3302	1917	Blt Baltimore, MD. BB chartered to Army from Frank J. Egan in Oct 1917. Sunk by German submarine U-90 en route France to U.S. One life lost. Dates of sinking vary according to source; either Aug 8, 1918 or Aug 17, 1918. Claim made for her sinking and that of John G. McCullough and A. A. Raven under war reparations became case examples of the Mixed Claims Commission in the early 1920s. See Appendix B, this volume, for discussion of that issue.
1917-18	Kerkenna	Borneo	Freighter	3621	1900	Blt Scotland. BB chartered to Army Nov 1917; taken over by Navy at Brest, France, Sept 1918.
1917-18	Kerlew	Virginia, Austrian	Collier	3563	1906	Blt Stockton-on-Tees, England. BB chartered to Army from Kerr Navigation Co. of New York, Oct 1917; taken over by Navy in Nov 1918 at Cardiff, Wales.
1918	Kermoor	Morawitz, Austrian	Collier	4795	1907	Blt Sunderland, England. BB chartered to Army by Kerr Navigation Co., March 1918; taken over by Navy Nov 1, 1918, at Cardiff, Wales.
1918	Kroonland		Freighter	12241	1902	Blt Philadelphia. BB charter to Army in Feb 1918. Navy took her over upon her return from France that April and converted her to carry troops.
1918	Lake Capens		Freighter	2026	1918	Blt Superior, WI. BB chartered to Army June 15, 1918, and sailed to France where she was taken over by Navy in Oct 1918.
1918	Lake Charlotte		Collier	2239	1918	Blt Ashtabula, OH. BB chartered to Army by USSB, Aug 1918. Went under Navy manning but still remained a U.S. AT under charter to Army following arrival at Cardiff, Wales, Oct 1918. Was never commissioned into Navy.
1918	Lake Clear		Freighter	2054	1918	Blt Chicago. Following launching in Feb 1918 was BB chartered to Army by USSB. Transferred to Navy, Nov 1918.
1918	Lake Crescent		Collier	2051	1918	Blt Chicago. BB chartered to Army by USSB in Feb 1918. Transferred to Navy, Oct 1918 at Cardiff, Wales.
1917-18	Lake Edon		Collier	2371	1918	Blt Cleveland, OH. Under BB charter to Army from USSB in May 1918. Employed in cross-channel coal shuttle run. Sunk by German submarine in English Channel on Aug 21, 1918. Sixteen lives lost.
1917-19	Lake George	Farragaux	Collier	2486	1917	Blt Ashtabula, OH. Under BB charter to Army, circa 1917-18. (Probably a charter arrangement with USSB). Employed in cross-channel coal shuttle. Redelivered to USSB after the war.
1917-19	Lake Linden		Collier	2150	1918	Blt Manitowoc, WI. Under BB charter to Army, circa 1917-18. (Probably a charter arrangement with USSB). Employed in cross-channel coal shuttle. Redelivered to USSB after the war.

UNDER ARMY MANNING	USAT VESSEL NAME	FRMR NAME/FLAG	TYPE OR CLASS	TONNAGE	YR.BLT	REMARKS
1917-18	Lake Otisco		Collier	2015	1917	Blt Cleveland, OH. Under Army BB charter from USSB. At Cardiff, Wales, went under time charter to Navy in Oct 1918. Army civilian master remained in command under the Navy's orders. She was never commissioned into Navy, continuing her wartime service with a civilian crew.
1917-18	Lake Owens		Collier	2308	1918	Blt Ecorse, MI. Under BB charter to Army from USSB in May 1918. Employed in cross-channel coal shuttle. Sunk by submarine off English coast on Sept 3, 1918. Five lives lost.
1918	Lake Pewaukee		Freighter	3500 dw	1918	Blt Manitowoc, WI. Assigned to Army on BB charter from USSB. Taken over by Navy in Sept 1918.
1917-18	Lake St. Clair		Collier	2308	1917	Blt Ecorse, MI. Placed under BB charter to Army by USSB. Operated in cross-channel coal shuttle run. Went under Navy control in Oct 1918.
1917-18	Lake St. Regis		Collier	2238	1917	Blt Ashtabula, OH. Placed under BB charter to Army by USSB. Operated in the cross-channel coal shuttle run. Acquired by Navy in Oct 1918.
1917-18	Lake Sunapee		Collier	2009	1917	Blt Toledo, OH. Placed under BB charter to Army by USSB. Operated in cross-channel coal shuttle run from Cardiff, Wales. Taken over by Navy in Nov 1918.
1917	Lake Traverse		Collier	1192	1917	Blt Duluth, MN, for USSB. Placed under BB charter to Army. Acquired by Navy in Oct 1918 at Cardiff, Wales.
1917-18	Lake Tulare		Collier	2005	1917	Blt Superior, WI. Placed under BB charter to Army by USSB. Operated in cross-channel coal shuttle run. Taken over by Navy in Oct 1918.
1918	Lake Western		Freighter	2875 dw	1918	Blt Detroit, MI. Assigned to Army on BB charter by USSB.
1918	Lake Weston		Collier	1948	1918	Blt Detroit. Placed under BB charter to Army by USSB. Operated in cross-channel coal shuttle run. Acquired by Navy in Nov 1918. Lost to grounding while in Navy service.
1918	Lake Yahara		Collier	2338	1918	Blt Jacksonville, FL. Placed on BB charter to Army by USSB. Operated on cross-channel coal shuttle run. Taken over by Navy in Dec 1918.
1917-18	Lenape		Transport	5179	1912	Blt Newport News, VA. BB chartered by Army in 1917. Was part of first troop convoy to France in June 1917. Convoy attacked on return trip to U.S. but escaped casualties. Taken over by Navy in April 1918. Returned to Army, Oct 1918.
1917-18	Lucia	Lucia, Austrian	Freighter	6744	1912	Blt Monfalcone, Austria. Seized by U.S. during 1917. Went under BB charter to Army from USSB. Scheduled for Navy takeover but was still under Army manning when she was torpedoed by German submarine U-155 in the Western Atlantic on Oct 17, 1918. Four lives lost.

UNDER ARMY MANNING	USAT VESSEL NAME	FRMR NAME/ FLAG	TYPE OR CLASS	TONNAGE	YR BLT	REMARKS
1917-22	Martha Washington	Martha Washington, Austrian	Transport	7412	1908	Blt Port Glasgow, Scotland. Seized from Austrian owners April 1917 and taken over by Army which never put her into service. Acquired by Navy, Nov 1917. Returned to Army Nov 1919. Sold to original owners in 1922.
1898-1920	McClellan	Port Victor, Br	Transport; refrigeration ship	2792 (3060)	1885	Blt Newcastle, England. Purchased from Irwin, McBride, Catherwood and Co. July 8, 1898, for $175,000. Atlantic fleet, 1899. During 1901 made two trips NY to Manila. In 1902 was placed on PI interisland service. In April 1914, transported Army troops for occupation of Vera Cruz, Mexico. According to Crowell and Wilson, in How America Went to War, The Road to France, she went to France during summer of 1917 to determine her suitability as a troop carrier but was found to be unsuitable. Was retained in France as a floating refrigeration warehouse. Sold to French private interests in 1920.
1917-18	Medina		Transport; freighter	5426	1914	Blt Newport News, VA. BB chartered from Mallory SS Co. After utilization in support of AEF was redelivered to owner.
1917-18	Minnesotan		Animal trans	6676	1912	Blt Sparrows Pt, MD. BB chartered by Army Sept 1917 from American-Hawaiian SS Co. Taken over by Navy Aug 1918.
1917	Momus		Transport	6879	1906	BB chartered to Army by Southern Pacific Co. as of June 1917. Was in first troop convoy to France June 1917. Further service not known.
1917-18	Montanan		Freighter	6659 dsp	1913	BB chartered to Army in June 1917 by American-Hawaiian SS Co. Was in first troop convoy to France in June of 1917. On Aug 15, 1918, was torpedoed off Portugal coast by U-90. Abandoned. Five lives lost. Part of crew boarded her the next day but despite best efforts, she sank.
1917-18	Montoso		Transport	3063	1911	Blt Newport News, VA. BB chartered by Army from USSB, during 1917. Turned over to Navy, Dec 1918.
1917-19	Nansemond	Pennsylvania, German	Transport	13332	1896	Seized from owners by Treasury Dept. and turned over to Army. Transferred to Navy, 1919.
1917-18	Neches		Transport; freighter	5426	1914	Blt Newport News, VA. BB chartered to Army from Mallory SS Co. Sunk in a collision with British patrol vessel off Plymouth, England, on May 14, 1918.
1917	Pastores		Transport; freighter	7781	1913	Blt Belfast, Ireland. BB chartered to Army from United Fruit Co. Was in first troop convoy to France, June 1917; on return to US, convoy was attacked but without ship losses. Transferred to Navy May 1918.
1918	Pennsylvania		Transport			Under charter to Army circa 1918, but evidence is unclear as to whether charter was of BB or time format.
1917	Princess Matoika	Princess Alice, Ger	Transport	10492	1900	Blt Stettin, Germany. Seized from owners in 1917 at Cebu; transported troops from PI to France. Apparently went under Naval Overseas Transportation Service in 1918, but no record of commissioning in Navy. Officially came under ownership of Army in Sept 1919.

UNDER ARMY MANNING	USAT VESSEL NAME	FRMR NAME/FLAG	TYPE OR CLASS	TONNAGE	YR.BLT	REMARKS
1918-21	*Printer*	*Printer*	Tug/formerly artil steamer	110	1889	Blt Hoquiam WA. Sent to France during 1918.
1918	Richmond		Tug			Sent to France during 1918.
1917-18	Sagua	*Van der Duyn*, Dutch	Transport; freighter	3298	1914	Blt Newcastle, England. BB chartered to Army from Atlantic Fruit Co. Redelivered to owner following the war.
1917	San Jacinto		Transport	6069	1903	Blt Chester, PA. BB chartered to Army from Mallory SS Co. Was part of first troop convoy to France in June 1917. Redelivered to owner after the war.
1917	Saratoga		Transport	6391		On BB charter to Army June 1917. Was part of first convoy to France in June 1917. Was rammed while at anchor off Stapleton, Staten Island, in July after return to New York. Beached and then repaired before reported as going to Navy in Sept 1917. However, she appears not to have been commissioned as she is not listed in the *Dictionary of American Naval Fighting Ships*. She probably went back into commercial service.
1918	Seattle		Freighter	8571 dw	1918	Blt Seattle, WA. Assigned to Army on BB charter by USSB. Routes of her war service unknown.
1898-1943	Slocum	*Gypsum King*	Tug/artil stmr	581	1898	Blt Philadelphia, PA. Purchased from J. G. King Transportation Co. July 25, 1898, for $150,000. Only known Army vessel to have been in service for the Sp-American War; WW I; and WW II. MVUS 1927-41 incorrectly gives ex name as *Britannia*. *Britannia* became *Reno*. Following Sp-American War, transferred from east coast to west coast via southern tip of South America during 1899. In WW I, *Slocum* was the only vessel from the ATS Pacific fleet to be sent to France. Following the war, returned to the west coast. Was extensively rebuilt during 1935. Lost by grounding in Alaskan waters, Feb 1943. Crew of 22 men was saved.
1918-21	Tascony		Tug/formerly artil steamer	353	1899	Blt Philadelphia, PA. Sent to France during 1918.
1917-18	Tenadores		Transport	7782	1913	Blt Belfast, Ireland. On BB charter list of June 1917. Was in first troop convoy to France in June 1917. Transferred to Navy April 1918 and while in that service was lost to grounding off St. Nazaire.
1918	Texamo					On charter to Army. Evidence is unclear as to charter format – probably BB.
1917-18	Tiger		Transport; freighter	6273	1917	Blt San Francisco. BB chartered to Army Nov 1917. Turned over to Navy in Dec 1918.
1917-18	Western Front		Freighter	8800 dw	1917	Blt Seattle, WA. Assigned to Army on BB charter by USSB. Routes of her war service not known.
1918	Westgrove		Freighter	8800 dw	1918	Blt Portland, OR. Assigned to Army on BB charter by USSB. Routes of her war service unknown.

UNDER ARMY MANNING	USAT VESSEL NAME	FRMR NAME/ FLAG	TYPE OR CLASS	TONNAGE	YR.BLT	REMARKS
1917-18	*Westland*		Freighter	8800 dw	1917	Blt Portland, OR. Assigned to Army on BB charter by USSB. Routes of her war service unknown.
1917-18	*William O'Brien*		Collier	5211	1915	Blt Camden, NJ. BB chartered to Army from Huron Navigation Co. Operated on cross-channel coal shuttle run. Redelivered to owner.
1917-18	*Woonsocket*		Freighter	9530 dw	1917	Blt Bath, ME. Assigned to Army on BB charter by USSB. Routes of war service unknown.
1918	*Yosemite*		Freighter	9400 dw	1918	Blt Oakland, CA. Assigned to Army on BB charter by USSB. Routes of her war service unknown.

CHAPTER VIII

INTERVAL BETWEEN THE WARS
1919 - 1939

The repatriation of the American Expeditionary Force from France began within a month after the fighting ended. The return of the troops required a heavier utilization of ships within a more concentrated time frame than had been the case when the AEF went to France. The overseas buildup of 1917-18 had been accomplished in stages, each embarkation for the far shore dependent on the readiness of the divisions to be sent over and on the ability to receive them when they arrived. With the war now over, there was a clamor to bring the boys home. In order to meet that demand, every bottom capable of carrying human cargo was pressed into service. The Navy put twenty-four of its battleships and cruisers into troop carriage, and it supplied the crews for ten liners that had been taken over in German ports after the Armistice by the Inter-allied Maritime Transport Council.[1] With the submarine menace gone, Naval Overseas Transportation Service (NOTS) cargo ships which had been considered too slow during the war to safely carry troops were now put into that service. The NOTS ships, together with the troop transports of the Cruiser and Transport Force (CTF), when joined by the battleships and cruisers and by the former German liners, all told would develop a per-trip capacity of almost a quarter of a million men. This would be augmented even further by converted cargo ships of the U.S. Shipping Board. Between December of 1918 and the end of the following June, 1,531,810 officers and men debarked at the Port of New York and at Newport News. By October, another 508,444 had come home.[2] Unlike the west-to-east sealift of 1917

---

[1]   Crowell and Wilson, pp 323, 573.

[2]   The figures of arrivals in the United States include both War Department and Navy Department personnel as well as some French nationals. *Report of the Chief of Transportation Service to the Secretary of War, Fiscal Year 1920*, p 19.

and 1918 when more than half of the men of the AEF had sailed aboard foreign ships, 83% made their homecoming on ships under the American flag.

During January and February of 1920, those American troops which had been sent from the Philippines as part of the American Expedition to Siberia were evacuated. The remainder of that expedition would leave for the United States before the end of the coming summer.[3]

~

During the war a large amount of tonnage had gone over to Navy management. This had taken place with War Department concurrence. Now the reverse would happen. In early 1919, the CTF and NOTS started transferring ships over to War Department manning. By July of 1919, the War Department's Vessel Operations Branch reported 168 of its ships in trans-ocean operation -- most of those having come under the Army's control since the Armistice. As the effort to return the AEF wound down, that ship inventory would shrink. Under the reorganizations of 1920, the Army Transport Service (ATS) was placed back in charge of all War Department shipping. By July, it would report only 23 of its passenger/cargo class ships still in service.

During the early post-war period, transports were not restricted just to the carriage of United States troops and federal employees. In 1920, five Army transports were diverted from their regular run (New York to Antwerp) and routed to Danzig (now Gdansk), Poland, via the Kiel Canal. At Danzig, they took aboard American citizens of Polish descent who had entered Poland's armed forces during the war.[4] Between January and June of 1920, eleven Army transports arrived at Vladivostok for the evacuation of the stranded Czech-Slovaks, to return them to their homeland via the port of Trieste at the head of the Adriatic Sea.[5]

The Labor Upheavals of 1919

The end of the war and the return of the AEF took place during a period of economic and social crisis in the United States. American businesses which had rapidly expanded for purposes of war production were now back to their peacetime pursuits. This created severe upheavals in the nation's industrial structure leading to widespread unrest and a rash of strikes to a number previously unheard of within the history of labor in the United States. This provided a platform for radical elements which over recent years had infiltrated the ranks of organized labor. Indications were that Bolshevism, so obviously becoming a part of the European political scene, was making inroads in the United States as well. From the perspective of eighty-odd years

---

[3]   *History of the American Expedition to Siberia.* Record Group-165, Entry 310. War College and War Plans Division; Records of Historical Section, 1900-1941, Box 145. Folder, "History of American Expedition to Siberia," (7-46.1), p 51.

[4]   Appendix D relates the story of how these American citizens had entered the Polish armed forces and the importance of their role to the history of the World War I and the peace that followed.

[5]   For at least one of those transports, it became an epic voyage: Chartered at New York, *USAT Heffron* traveled via the Panama Canal across the Pacific to Vladivostok. From Vladivostok, it sailed to Trieste by way of Singapore and Suez; thence westward for the return to the United States via Gibraltar, having circumnavigated the world. A photographic section of this volume pictures a silk needlework souvenir commissioned by one of *USAT Heffron's* officers when that ship stopped in Japan for coaling.

we now view the events of 1919 as having been overblown insofar as the threat they posed to American democracy. However, at the time, the possibility of a social upheaval in the United States seemed very real. In Russia, *The Third International* had been organized by the Bolsheviks for the express purpose of exporting revolution. One American publication, *The Literary Digest,* went so far as to warn that outside of Russia the United States had become the storm center of Bolshevism, pointing out that in the United States, two Bolshevik-inspired political parties had taken form -- the Communist Party and the Communist Labor Party.

The Communists were only a part of the threat. There were also the *Wobblies,* a cognomen for the Industrial Workers of the World, a mixed ideological bag, some of whose members were outright anarchists. This was the group suspected of mailing twenty-two bomb packages to prominent government and industrial leaders during May of 1919. The first of those packages had gone to a United States senator -- the hand of the senator's maid being ripped off when she opened it. An alerted Post Office employee discovered the other twenty-one bombs which were safely disarmed. One of those disarmed packages had been addressed to the Attorney General of the United States, A. Mitchell Palmer. A month later, seven bombs exploded -- all targeted at either public buildings or at groups considered anti-labor -- and a second assassination attempt was made against Attorney General Palmer. Fortunately the only person injured in that attempt was the bomber himself who apparently stumbled while attempting to gain access to Palmer's home in Washington, DC. The bomb he was carrying went off, blowing the would-be assassin to bits -- his body parts ending up on the front lawn of Assistant Secretary of the Navy Franklin D. Roosevelt who lived across the street.[6]

During 1919, the *USAT Buford* was assigned to handle the deportation of 249 aliens of Russian nationality who were considered by the Justice Department to have been involved in the revolutionary activity which threatened the nation. Shackled and under guard of a company of soldiers, the Russians were marched up the ship's gangway to begin a voyage which would terminate twenty-five days later at Hango, Finland. Under a flag of truce (Finland was then at war with Russia) the deportees were marched to the border and delivered over to Russian authorities. These deportations -- although later criticized for being carried out without due process -- had the effect of calming down the more volatile elements of labor and driving many of the more visible Communists and Wobblies from their positions of prominence within the ranks of the labor movement.[7]

On July 15, a seamen's strike began on the east coast paralyzing all commercial shipping in transatlantic service. Although the crews of Army transports, being federal employees, could not strike, the turmoil on the labor scene had its impact on the Army's crews:

---

[6]   Allan L. Damon, "The Great Red Scare," *American Heritage,* (XIX, February 1968), p 22.

[7]   The Communists continued their presence in most of the maritime unions -- especially on the west coast -- for years to come. It would not be until the end of World War II and the advent of the Cold War that they would be driven out of the unions, partly by internal reforms within the unions themselves, and partly by government measures which required security clearance for those having access to ships and waterfront areas. Source: Joseph P. Goldberg, *The Maritime Story: A Study in Labor Management Relations,* (Cambridge: Harvard University Press, 1958), p 89.

> *On several occasions, pilfering of Government stores was discovered while in other instances outright mutiny was rumored to have existed on transport voyages. While a thorough investigation of the latter incidents failed to reveal actual mutiny, there was found to exist considerable dissatisfaction which may be attributed to the generally unsatisfactory personnel situation prevalent in all steamship circles at the time.* [8]

In the hope of assuring an adequate supply of reliable seamen for any future conflict, *The Report of Transportation Service for 1919* under the subtitle *Reserve Personnel,* recommended the creation of a civilian reserve for crews of those merchant ships scheduled for mobilization into the government's use during times of war or national emergency. The concept was that upon mobilization a ship would have at least part of its crew already in place, ready to sail. The fallacy of the plan, and what killed it, was that it was predicated upon *the cooperation of the Seamen's Organization,* meaning the unions. To the unions, any government-run shipping service manned by government-employed crews was a threat. [9]

Because of the severe unemployment conditions within the maritime industry during the early 1920s, as well as a revulsion on the part of some men against the extremism then being encountered within the maritime unions, civil service employment with the ATS became an attractive alternative. An equal if not a larger reason why men became attracted to the Army's ships can be credited to enlightened labor relations on the part of the Army. The ATS had finally come to the realization that seamen required reasonable time off if shipboard morale was to be maintained. This it accomplished through a system of arranged tours to points of interest while the transports were in overseas ports. Additionally, the crews were accorded the privileges of the Army's overseas recreational facilities, something which up to that time had been denied. There had also been improvements in the civil service system, first in retirement pay, and later in paid annual leave -- benefits not then generally available in the merchant marine. When measured against the uncertainty of a career in commercial shipping, employment on Army ships was now offering much more by way of job security. This was especially so for those holding licenses as deck and engineering officers. [10]

---

[8]   *Report of Chief of Transportation Service, 1920,* p 15.

[9]   Plans for a civilian maritime reserve as was suggested within the *Report of Chief of Transportation Service to the Secretary of War for the Fiscal Year 1919,* p 188, were first proposed by the War Department for Army transports in 1915. The idea has since then been proposed in one form or another by various federal agencies dealing with shipping. The latest of such ideas was put forth during the 1990s, being sponsored by the Administrator of the Maritime Administration Vice Adm. Albert Herberger, USN, Retd. Like all earlier proposals, Herberger's idea went no further than initial discussions, largely a result of a lack of enthusiasm by the maritime unions whose political muscle has grown over the years, having been gained through campaign contributions made to members of the Merchant Marine and Fisheries Committee of the Congress.

[10]   One person who chose the ATS as a career in the early 1930s was William A. Parta who wrote his memoirs following his retirement in 1955. A summary of those memoirs, "The Story of One ATS Master," is to be found in Appendix E.

Early Post-War Acquisitions

Fiscal year 1919-20 found eleven oceangoing transports under construction by the USSB at Hog Island, Pennsylvania. Once completed, they were scheduled for operation by the ATS.[11]

During 1919, a number of harbor-class vessels were delivered to the War Department and assigned to the Harbor Boat Service (HBS). During fiscal year 1919-20, HBS reported delivery of more small craft: ten diesel tugs, five 100' water boats; one coastal tanker; six 130' concrete-hulled river boats; and six concrete car floats. For assignment to the Mine Planter Service, HBS received three 172' mineplanters to replace existing mineplanters considered outmoded because of technological changes in the handling of defensive mines. That same year, new contracts were let for seven 150' concrete river steamers; three 310' concrete oil tankers (one self-propelled and two for towage); three 72' double-bottom boats; twelve 24' motor mine yawls; and nine barges. During 1921, construction was completed for six additional 172' mineplanters; four 130' steel river steamers; and three 130' concrete river steamers.[12]

The Congressional Hearing of 1921

In 1921, HR-5348, went before the Merchant Marine and Fisheries Committee. Hearings were held on May 25. The bill was initiated at the request of the steamship companies to abolish the ATS and in its place substitute commercial ships to handle the overseas transportation of the Army's personnel and its general cargo. The bill was intended to amend §17 of *The Merchant Marine Act of 1920* so as to allow the government to issue contracts of 10-year duration for the establishment of liner service for the carriage of military and other government traffic between stated points. Under the concept, the companies involved would have the opportunity to build up a commercial trade route while simultaneously serving the Army's carriage. The routes under consideration were the ATS's transpacific, transatlantic, and Caribbean runs.

At the invitation of the Merchant Marine and Fisheries Committee, Brig. Gen. W. D. Conner, the Chief of the Transport Service (of which ATS was then

---

[11]   In a side discussion which developed from a Congressional Hearing on HR-5348, 1st Session, 67th Congress (May 1921) the Army testified that the eleven ships which had been under construction at Hog Island during fiscal year 1919-20 had proved inordinately expensive to operate and that considerable alteration had been necessary once the ATS took delivery of them. Examples of the problems: Latrines reached temperatures of 120° due to exposed steam pipes; in the galleys, temperatures reached to 137°, a condition preventing the cooks from working more than 15-minute shifts. By the spring of 1921, eight of those ships had been placed in the ATS reserve fleet. The other three had gone into service, but only after changes were made. The War Department requested that the USSB take back the eight then in the ATS reserve fleet and replace them with twin-screw vessels suitable for the ATS's transpacific run. (Hearing Record, pp 11-13.)

[12]   *Report of Chief of Transportation Service, 1920*, pp 32, 33. According to this report, the use of concrete in vessel construction was still considered a sound practice, at least to the extent that its use was being carried over to the postwar period. However, before the end of the decade, the service life for such construction would prove to be unsatisfactory. Henceforth, steel would be the preferred construction material although wood was used for barges and many of the smaller harbor craft. During World War II, in an effort to conserve steel, concrete was again put to use. But again, it would be found wanting. Although some concrete ships made transpacific voyages (1943-44), the trips were one-way for most of them. Following their arrival in the Southwest Pacific, they were moored and used as stationary warehouses.

subsidiary), gave lengthy testimony in which he described the ATS as the federal shipping agency authorized by the Congress to carry:

> ...members of the Army, Navy, Marine Corps; the Coast Guard; members of the Congress; employees of the Philippine Government and of the territorial governments of Hawaii and Puerto Rico as well as employees of all civil branches of the federal government under reimbursement made on the basis of each passenger's cost of subsistence.

Conner made a strong argument for the continuance of the ATS, using as his basis three major points: First, that Army transports carried troops at less expense and in a better manner than would be the case on commercial ships; secondly, that the small peacetime fleet of ATS vessels and their crews served as a nucleus around which a military sealift could be built in time of war. (Those same arguments had been offered successfully to the Congress in the past.) Conner's third point stressed that the direction of Army shipping properly required at its head an Army officer experienced in the military's requirements. His opinion was that such expertise was not extant within the management of commercial steamship companies.

Also testifying before the Committee was Capt. A. W. Marshall of the Office of Naval Operations. Marshall's office had charge of the Navy's ship movements, including the operation of the post-war Naval Transport Service (NTS), the successor to the wartime NOTS.[13] Although the gist of Marshall's testimony centered around the necessity for the Navy Department to hang on to the limited number of transports then being operated by NTS, he apparently intended to assure their continuance at the expense of the Army while at the same time laying the foundation for some future empire building. This came as a surprise to all since this was the first time that the Navy Department had shown any desire to have the ATS replaced with a shipping agency of its own.

Starting with the sealift for the Seminole Wars in Florida and later during the war against Mexico in 1846-47, the Navy had welcomed the War Department's taking responsibility for the shipment of its own men and materiel by sea. During the early months of the Civil War, Flag Officer Silas H. Stringham, USN, had written to the Assistant Secretary of the Navy stating that the Navy wished to divest itself of all responsibility for handling the Army's sea transport, *lest the task become accepted as a normal Navy function.*[14] During the War with Spain in 1898, the Navy had shown a total lack of interest toward transporting the Army, either to Cuba or to the Philippines. In the recent war of 1917-18, the Navy's takeover of the majority of Army shipping had been at the Army's own initiative.

Marshall's testimony would reverse the Navy's prior attitudes by stating to the Committee:

---

[13] Unlike the wartime Naval Overseas Transportation Service, the Naval Transport Service of post 1919 dealt solely with the Navy Department's own shipments.

[14] Gibson with Gibson, *Assault and Logistics,* p 12.

> *In our opinion, there should not be any other transport service; the Navy should operate all transports. It did it in the late war, and undoubtedly will in any future war.*

One of the Committee members then asked,
> *You mean not only for the Navy, but to meet the Army's needs?*

Marshall replied:
> *To meet the Army's needs. The Navy would control everything afloat in the next war as it did in the last.*

A reading of the hearing transcript makes it evident that Marshall's proposal was not given consideration by the Committee.[15] [16]

The ATS Fleet - 1923 through 1939

Between 1923 and 1930, the ATS oceangoing fleet remained relatively static, averaging between eight and ten ships in service.

The Atlantic fleet operated from the Brooklyn Army Base, a facility which had been developed during World War I and which in the post-war period was now servicing Puerto Rico and the Canal Zone.

The Pacific fleet operating from the port of San Francisco serviced the Hawaiian Islands, Guam, the Philippines, and the supply and transportation needs of the Army and Marine Corps garrisons in China. In 1928, a Central American stop was added in order to give logistical support for the Marine Corps's expeditionary force which had been deployed to Nicaragua.[17]

The Harbor Boat Service's inventory remained fairly stabilized during the period 1925-30. Changes which did occur came through modernization programs during which a number of older small craft were sold to be replaced by new ones. The biggest changes that occurred involved the Mine Planter Service in which there was a wholesale shift from coal to diesel propulsion. In 1930, the HBS reported in its active service 194 river and harbor craft and 120 of various types on assignment with the Mine Planter Service.

---

[15]   As this volume will later relate, discussions entered into during 1940-41 between the War Department and the Navy Department had as their aim a total Navy takeover of the military's transportation by sea. To this, the Army was initially agreeable. However, the rapid expansion of the Navy during that time resulted in its inability to supply crews. To meet the needs of 1941 - 45, the Army put together its own fleet of transports.

Following World War II, the Navy made another bid for control of all military transports, an attempt which succeeded in 1950 with the reorganization of the Armed Forces and which among other things resulted in the creation of the Military Sea Transport Service (MSTS), an agency of the Department of the Navy. In that takeover, the Navy absorbed into its employment all of the Army's oceangoing vessels and civil service crews. The MSTS has since evolved into the Military Sealift Command.

[16]   Another attempt directed to the Congress by the steamship companies to have the ATS abolished was made during 1932. That one also failed, largely due to a self-orchestrated campaign by employees of the ATS who solicited the lobby support of supply firms doing business with the Army's ships and with the Army's ports of embarkation. See Appendix E, "The Story of One ATS Master."

[17]   The port used in Nicaragua was Corinto, the entrance proving nearly disastrous for *USAT Cambrai*. On one trip in, the ship struck an uncharted reef suffering damage requiring a return to San Francisco for dry-docking. The Marines were withdrawn from Nicaragua in 1932; thereafter, the Corinto stop was canceled.

During 1931, the ATS turned back the *USAT Somme* and the *USAT Cambrai* to the USSB. In exchange, the Army received the *Republic*. With the *USAT Republic* added, the ATS Atlantic fleet now had two ships in passenger service, the other being *USAT Chateau Thierry*. Cargo needs were handled by *USAT Ludington* and *USAT Kenowis*. In addition to interisland transports operating within the Philippines, the Pacific passenger fleet consisted of *USAT U. S. Grant* and *USAT St. Mihiel,* with *USAT Meigs* and the time chartered merchant ship *James Otis* handling cargo requirements.

On occasion during the 1930s, the ATS was called upon for emergency service such as bringing foodstuffs and construction materials to scenes of civil disaster in Puerto Rico following a hurricane there in 1928. In 1934, at San Francisco, an Army transport boarded a shipload of farmers and their families, victims of the midwest drought years. These families were taken to Seward, Alaska, for resettlement in the Matanuska Valley as part of a federally funded relief program.

The year 1932 marked the beginning of joint amphibious exercises in which Army transports participated. The first of these took place off the Hawaiian Islands where the *USAT Chateau Thierry* (transferred that year to the Pacific) rendezvoused with ships of a naval task group. Moving in toward the main island, a simulated beach assault was made by troops offloaded from the *USAT Chateau Thierry*. Later in 1940, the Pacific ATS fleet would assemble in Puget Sound, Washington, to load Army infantry units before proceeding to Port Angeles where the transports were taken under naval escort before sailing south to California. Laying-to off Monterey Beach, landing craft were put over the side for the troops to disembark. While the over-the-beach landings at Monterey went well, considerable difficulty was experienced in getting the landing craft on and off the transports proving the need for specialized ships if over-the-beach operations were to become a significant factor in future wars. The Army transports of the 1930s were clearly not adaptable for such service. When joined with the general nervousness of the military establishment over utilizing civilian crews in close combat situations, that inadequacy would result in the development of the Navy's attack transports of the AKA and APA class which were provided with improved landing craft as standard equipage.[18]

~

By 1939, planners within the higher echelons of the military were preparing for a war which by all indications the United States would not be able to avoid.

---

[18] The Navy's Amphibious Forces, Atlantic and Pacific, which landed troops of the Army and the Marine Corps on enemy-held beaches during the course of World War II, and which operated attack transports together with independently operated landing craft such as LSTs and LCIs, were not alone in conducting amphibious operations. Beginning in 1942, the Army Ground Forces command established Amphibious Engineer Brigades. Although not possessing ships or the larger classes of landing craft, the Amphibious Engineer Brigades did have as part of their integrated equipment landing craft types such as LCMs, LCVPs, and "Buffaloes". The Amphibious Engineer Brigades became operational in the Pacific theater in 1943. There is some indication that late in the Pacific war, they may have operated a few LCIs and even some LSTs.

*USAT **Ludington**, ex James Otis.* Used for Army freight service on transpacific service between 1931 and 1941. Shown here in San Francisco Bay. Tug in foreground is *USAT **Slocum**,* the only vessel of the Army fleet to see service in the War with Spain; World War I; and in World War II. Following the War with Spain, *USAT Slocum* was sent to San Francisco via the southern tip of South America. During World War I, she was sent back to the east coast (this time via Panama) and from there went to France. Sometime prior to World War II, she returned to the west coast and while serving on the Alaskan run in 1943 was lost by grounding. Grover Collection (National Maritime Museum).

USAT U.S. Grant; ex *USS Madawaska*; ex *USAT Madawaska*; ex *Konig Wilhelm II*. Photo was probably taken when the ship was being operated by the Navy during World War I. Entered Army service 1919 and was retired in 1941. Grover Collection.

USAT Meigs, ex *West Lewark*. Entered Army Transport Service in 1922; retired in 1941. Grover Collection.

USAT Chateau Thierry. Served the Army Transport Service 1920–1941.
Grover Collection (U.S. Army Military History Institute).

USAT Republic, ex *President Buchanan,* ex *President Grant.* Served with Army Transport Service
1818–1921 and 1931–1941. Transferred to Navy in 1941. As *USS Republic* was part of Pensacola Convoy.
Grover Collection (U.S. Army Military History Institute).

USAT General John McE. Hyde. Entered service with the Army Transport Service in 1924. Went transpacific to the Philippines where she was employed as an interisland transport. Lost through enemy action, April 1942. Grover Collection (National Archives).

Silk embroidered souvenir commissioned in Japan by D. J. Farrell as a memorial of *"My Cruise Around the World."* Farrell had been a ship's officer aboard the bareboat chartered **USAT Heffron.** This ship evacuated Czech/Slovak troops from western Siberia to Trieste in 1920. Memorial is part of Authors' Collection.

PART II

1940 THROUGH TO THE FALL OF THE PHILIPPINES

INTRODUCTION

Shipping challenges which were to be faced by the Army beginning in 1940 were many and varied, some of them rather radical departures from the norm. One of those came about as the result of the German invasion of Denmark on April 9, 1940. This was followed the same day by the invasion of Norway. Those events stranded a number of American citizens. To bring these people out of harm's way, President Franklin Roosevelt ordered the *USAT American Legion* (recently assigned to the Army from the U.S. Maritime Commission reserve fleet), to the port of Petsamo in the Baltic Sea.[1] Arriving at Petsamo in August, *USAT American Legion* boarded a total of 898 passengers, most of whom were Americans. Non-American refugees who made up part of the passenger list included members of the Norwegian Royal Family. Coming aboard as cargo was an unmarked crate obtained through the secret cooperation of the Swedish and Finnish governments. Inside was a twin-mounted 40 mm Bofors antiaircraft gun together with spare parts and ammunition. Following the gun's testing in the United States, it went under manufacture to later become the U.S. Navy's most effective antiaircraft weapon for fighting off Japanese Kamikaze air attacks during 1944 and 1945 in the western Pacific.[2]

September of 1940 brought the United States openly over to the side of Great Britain. It was then that the U.S. Navy began to operate in open cooperation with the Royal Navy in the North Atlantic and that President Roosevelt authorized the transfer of fifty of the Navy's *4-stacker* destroyers to Britain. In return, the United States was given 99-year leases for base sites at Newfoundland, Bermuda, British Guyana, and on the British islands in the Caribbean and Bahamas.

~

---

[1]   Petsamo is in the territory of Petsamo, now Pechenga. It was in 1940 part of Finland, having been ceded by the USSR to Finland in 1920.

[2]   Harold Larson, *Water Transportation for the United States Army, 1939 - 1942* (Washington, DC: Office, Chief of Transportation, Army Service Forces, August 1944), pp 41, 42. One of the passengers evacuated by *USAT American Legion* was the young Danish pianist and comedian Victor Borge who would later reach entertainment stardom in the United States.

During 1940, the Army Transport Service (ATS) found itself stretched to the limit. Army facilities in the Philippines and in the Hawaiian Islands required extensive reinforcement, both in terms of new construction and added personnel. From estimates made at the time, the Caribbean bases would need garrisons totaling upwards of 60,000 officers and men -- all of whom would require transportation by sea. At the very least, twelve additional Army transports would be required for that purpose alone, and this did not count the ongoing cargo lift needed to keep the bases supplied.[3] By December, the ATS fleet had grown in number to fifteen transports, but this was only a fraction of what the Army would need over the months to follow.

During August of 1941, joint Army-Navy amphibious exercises took place on the East Coast. Both Army and Marine units participated. The Army unit involved was the 1st Infantry Division which embarked aboard Army transports at the Brooklyn Port of Embarkation. The maneuvers were a disaster, pointing out to both the Army and the Navy everything that could go wrong during over-the-beach assaults. It was found that the transport had been improperly loaded and that their cargo gear was totally inadequate for what it was tasked to accomplish. Men went off the landing craft encumbered by full field equipment, including packs, and some men were totally submerged as were a number of tanks. Beach masters had little if any idea of how they were to handle or distribute the arriving cargoes. The cardboard cartons containing rations disintegrated, wiping out all identification of what the food cans held. The exercises took place over a 5-week period. One Army observer commented critically in his report, ... *an effective landing is impossible unless all resistance is previously neutralized.* [4]

The exercises which had been along the North Carolina coast had not taken place any too soon as in May a directive from President Roosevelt called on both the Army and the Navy to plan for an expeditionary force of 25,000 troops to occupy the Azore Islands (Portuguese territories). The troops to be employed were to consist of the Army 1st Infantry Division and the Marine Corps 1st Marine Division. The Navy, apparently not wanting to trust the Army with the transportation of its Marines, requested the transfer of six of the Army's transports which the Navy needed for conversion into combat loaders.[5] Although the invasion of the Azores never materialized, the preparations for such an invasion were not officially canceled until late that fall.[6]

---

[3]   Larson, p 43. Following Chapter IX, see list of transports (over 1000 gross tons) in service during 1941.

[4]   Richard M. Leighton and Robert W. Coakley, *Global Logistics and Strategy, 1940 - 1943,* (Washington: Office, Chief of Military History, 1955), pp 66-68.

[5]   The Navy received four of its requested six. Two transports, the *Frederick Funston* and the *James O'Hara*, were then under construction, having been scheduled for ATS operation. At first the Quartermaster General agreed to the Navy taking them once completed, but he later changed his mind. Both ships were delivered to the ATS and operated as Army transports through 1942. In the spring of 1943, they went over to the Navy as commissioned attack transports. They were returned to the Army at the end of the war.

[6]   Memorandum: Joint Army / Navy Board, No. 320, Serial 715, as quoted by Larson, pp 78,79.

Reorganizations -- Military, Affecting the Army's Shipping

Prior to 1940, the Water Transport Branch (an integral part of the Transportation Division within the Office of the Quartermaster General) consisted of only five officers and eight civilians. The Water Transport Branch had charge of overseeing ATS Superintendents at the Army's two peacetime ports of embarkation, New York and San Francisco. ATS operations in the Philippines were conducted in loose cooperation with the Philippines Department's commander, with reports being directed to the Water Transport Branch for review and transmission to the Quartermaster General.

Col. Clarence H. Kells, who became Chief of the Quartermaster Corps's Water Transport Branch in 1941, oversaw functions carried out through four sections: Transport and Freight; Harbor Boat; Passenger Traffic; and Office and Mail. It was the Transport and Freight Section which oversaw, directed, and planned the operations of the ATS, besides arranging for whatever was needed in the way of extra tonnage to get the shipping task accomplished.[7] When the need for shipping increased, brought on by base construction in Greenland and Iceland, as well as for those bases obtained through lend lease at British Guiana and in the Caribbean, the Bahamas, and in the Canadian Maritime Provinces, the Water Transport Branch's staff grew to 19 officers and 167 civilians.

A radical reorganization of the entire Army took place shortly after Pearl Harbor. Effective as of March 9, 1942, transportation activity was removed from the Quartermaster General's jurisdiction and integrated within a newly constituted parent command that was charged with dealing with the entire range of the Army's logistics. This parent command was named Service of Supply (SOS).[8] On April 9, the former Transportation Division of the Quartermaster General's Office -- renamed the Transportation Service, SOS -- was handed responsibility for all of the transportation functions within SOS. The old Water Transport Branch, now redesignated as the Water Division under the SOS's Transportation Service, was given responsibility for that part of the Army's transportation conducted by sea, by river, or within harbors. The Water Division's sections, formerly four in number when its predecessor organization was under the Quartermaster Corps, was now enlarged to eight sections, one titled the Army Transport Service Section and another the Harbor Boat Section. Under the reorganizations, the Offices of the Superintendents, ATS, were continued at the two Ports of Embarkation with each Superintendent reporting his activity to the relevant staff section depending on whether the report involved harbor craft or transport activity.[9]

---

[7]   Larson, pp 27-29.

[8]   The Service of Supply (SOS) was organized under authority of the War Powers Act of December 18, 1941. Established by Executive Order 9082 dated February 28, 1942, the SOS was to soon absorb from other Army service commands all supply and related services (including transportation). See *Annual Report, Service of Supply, for the Fiscal year Ending June 30, 1942,* for complete discussion on this command. This change, which in effect removed transportation responsibility from the jurisdiction of the Quartermaster General, did not apply to the Philippines where the Army Transport Service continued as a Quartermaster function through to the surrender of the Philippines to the Japanese in May of 1942.

[9]   By the late spring of 1942, the fleet of ships being utilized by the Army had expanded to 486 oceangoing bottoms, most of them freighters -- the greatest part having been acquired through time charters. By July of 1942, the Harbor Boat Service would report 1211 craft of all types, all of which were owned outright by

Reorganizations -- Civilian, Affecting the Army's Shipping

In 1936, the U.S. Maritime Commission (USMC) was established as the federal agency charged with apportioning merchant ship tonnage belonging to or controlled by the government.[10] An enlargement of the authority of USMC came about on February 4, 1941, through a Presidential order addressing a serious shortage in shipping needed for military and civilian purposes. Through that order, both the War Department and the Navy Department were instructed to request only the minimum number of ships needed from USMC's reserve fleet, and once those ships were acquired, to assure that they were not held idle. If idled, they were to be loaned back to USMC for crewing by merchant seamen and for allocation to other purpose. This put an abrupt end to the War Department's attempt to enlarge its fleet from the USMC reserve fleet.

The Presidential Order of February 4, 1941, was followed two weeks later by the establishment of a Division of Emergency Shipping within USMC. This Division was given the function of maintaining liaison with both the Army and the Navy

---

the Army. Larson, p 38. In July 1942, the Transportation Service of the SOS would be reconstituted as the Transportation Corps. By the fall of 1942, the Transportation Corps would absorb from its parent command (the SOS) all transportation aspects dealing with the broad realm of military logistics. Transportation equipment and personnel which were integral to the Army's combat arms remained under those combat arms, e.g., unit trucks, armored personnel carriers, tanks, etc.

Army Regulation 55-305, paragraph 5, dated October 10, 1942, descriptively divides Transportation Corps vessel activity into two categories:

> b. *Army Transport Service -- includes all vessels under the control of the War Department utilized in overseas transportation of troops and supplies for the military establishment, including coastwise oceangoing vessels.*

> c. *The Harbor Boat Service -- includes harbor craft at the various ports, Army posts, camps, and stations, and inland waterways required for the movement of troops and supplies, target practice, dispatch service, rescue work, etc.*

AR 55-305 also spoke to those who manned the ships and small craft:

> *The allocation and assignment of personnel for the operation and maintenance of Water Transportation activities including vessels, floating equipment, and shore installation [exceptions being engaged in river, harbor and fortification work under the Chief of Engineers, and those assigned to mine laying and mine tending within defense commands] which utilize military personnel will be made by the Chief of Transportation, and the employment of all civilian personnel required for such activities will be under his direction.*

The Army Transport Service and the Harbor Boat Service would retain their historic functions and titles through 1942. During 1943, those titles were abolished, the ATS and the HBS then going collectively under the management of sub-branches of the Transportation Corps's Water Division.

In March 1943, the SOS was renamed the Army Service Forces (ASF), the Chief, Transportation Corps, thereafter being directly subordinate to the Chief, Army Service Forces. § 385, *Military Agencies - Federal Record of WW II*, (Washington, DC: General Services Administration, National Archives, 1951). Republished Detroit, MI: Gale Research Co., 1982

The term "ATS," as it related to the civilian manned shipping of the Transportation Corps, remained in common usage throughout the war, the term appearing in some official correspondence as late as 1944 -- that despite an order issued from the Chief of Transportation during 1943 which imperiously stated that the term was obsolete and was not to be used again, either in orders or in official correspondence.

[10] The U.S. Shipping Board (USSB) as established by the Shipping Act of 1916 was abolished in 1936 to be succeeded by the U.S. Maritime Commission (USMC), a federal agency owing its creation to the *Merchant Marine Act of 1936*. The USMC was given the functions previously held by the USSB. Merchant ships owned by the United States for which title was held by USSB were automatically transferred to USMC when that agency came into being. However, by a succession of careless errors, the government's annual publication *Merchant Vessels of the United States* continued to inventory ship ownership as USSB rather than as the correct USMC for some years following 1936.

as well as with any other federal agencies concerned with shipping needs. *Liaison* was perhaps too weak a term since under this latest authority USMC held the reins over approvals for all noncombatant ship construction, sales, charters, and even route reallocations for ships to which USMC either held title or otherwise controlled. From then onward, all purchases and charters for shipping undertaken by the War Department could only take place with the approval of the Maritime Commission's Division of Emergency Shipping.

Upon the entry of the United States into the war in December of 1941, USMC's then chairman, Rear Adm. Emory S. Land, suggested to President Roosevelt the advisability of creating a new agency separate and apart from USMC, arguing to the President that the structure of the existing USMC was not such that it could comfortably handle the extra responsibilities which it had recently been given. The President agreed. In April of 1942 the War Shipping Administration (WSA) was created and charged with the administration, operation, and training of what was scheduled to grow into a merchant marine of huge dimension.[11] The Directive, which established the WSA and which named Rear Admiral Land as Administrator, gave the new agency power to acquire and subsequently employ all merchant tonnage flying the flag of the United States as well as such foreign tonnage which might be taken under U.S. control, c.g., enemy and Danish ships seized by United States authorities as well as any friendly foreign shipping obtained under charter to the United States. In early 1942, that Philippine-registered shipping which was cut off from its home islands also went under the control of WSA. Exceptions to Land's authority were the combatant ships of the Navy, the Army, and the Coast Guard and of any auxiliaries belonging by title to the Navy or to the Army. Also excepted were vessels which the Army or Navy had obtained through bareboat charters prior to the creation of the WSA. In summary, Land had been handed the task of balancing the use of the nation's shipping by allocating tonnage where it would best serve the war effort, whether in direct support of the military's supply needs, or for the carriage of war production materials, or for the needs of the civilian sector.[12]

WSA also became part of the government's arbitration mechanism which dealt with labor relations in the maritime industry. This included the adjustment of merchant seamen's wages and bonuses which was conducted through an entity known as the Maritime War Emergency Board. Originally, membership on that board consisted of representatives from USMC and the Department of Labor. With the

---

[11] When the WSA was established, thereby relieving USMC of the additional responsibilities which had been thrust upon it under Executive Order, USMC retained its primary function of overseeing the construction of ships being built under government contract. Rear Adm. Emory S. Land, the appointed Administrator of WSA, also retained his chairmanship of USMC which he had held prior to the Executive Order of February 7, 1942. When the WSA was liquidated as of September 1, 1946, the extant functions of that agency were absorbed by USMC. Under the federal reorganizations which took place in 1950, USMC's functions were absorbed jointly by the Federal Maritime Board and the Maritime Administration.

[12] Once the WSA came into being in April 1942, the delegation of tonnage requested by the Army was handled as follows: Those ships for which the Army required total control as USATs with the Army's own crews were sub-bareboat chartered to the Army by the WSA. Those ships over which WSA retained control but which were assigned to the Army for its exclusive use, say for a period of time or for a particular voyage, initially went to the Army under voyage or time charters; however, starting around June of 1942, the voyage or time charter arrangement was replaced by a system of allocation.

creation of WSA, the USMC's membership was replaced by WSA. President Roosevelt, ever concerned with the cooperation of organized labor in its support of the national war effort, had instructed Land that whenever practical, WSA was to cooperate with the maritime unions. Toward that goal, but keeping within reasonable parameters, the Maritime War Emergency Board worked closely with the unions. In its policies over manning in the merchant marine, the WSA was respectful of union contracts; nevertheless, WSA maintained its own manning and recruiting service. Relationships with the maritime unions were oft times complex. For instance, WSA operated a modified open shop policy toward manning its ships, doing so despite the fact that many of the ships which it operated, either directly through their owners or through shipping agents, were under union agreements. In cases where the unions could not supply a ship with a full crew, the WSA manning service signed aboard non-union seamen, agreeing, however, that the seamen involved were later to join the respective union if they intended to remain on the ship beyond the original voyage for which they had been hired by WSA.

As the U.S. Shipping Board had done during World War I, the WSA in World War II would establish a number of facilities for basic training as well as for the upgrade training of ships' officers and experienced seamen. Although most of the graduates of those programs would serve on merchant ships, many ended up being hired by the Army.

The Army's procurement of ships officers differed in many respects from that of the merchant marine. To a marked degree, this was because the Army was not bound by the sea service requirement for officer eligibility which was required under that part of the United States Code which governed the merchant marine. Later in the war, the Army contracted with WSA for establishment of two civilian maritime officer cadet training schools, entry to which required the students' contractual obligations to serve on the Army's vessels after graduation. One of the schools was located at St. Petersburg, Florida, and the other at New Orleans, Louisiana. During their existence, these schools graduated a total of 2,588 men for assignments as deck and engineer officers in the Army's fleet.

Interagency agreements were developed from time to time between the War Department and WSA. One of these involved War Risk Insurance, a program which WSA had instituted for merchant marine personnel and which allowed a payment of $5,000 to the heirs of a ship's officer or seaman in case of his death and for proportionate payments in cases of disability. Under interagency agreement, the WSA administered the same program for the Army's seamen, such payments chargeable against the Army's account. Another of the agreements which were to be developed between the WSA and the Army concerned the on-again, off-again policy of the War Department not to award military campaign ribbons to its civilian employees. However, since merchant seamen were being presented war zone ribbons and other awards by the WSA, the Army felt that the civilians serving on its ships were deserving of similar recognition. With that in mind, the Chief of Transportation entered into another interagency arrangement whereby the WSA administered the issuance of merchant marine war zone ribbons and certain meritorious service awards to Army seamen upon the Army's attest of eligibility.[13]

The Army and Organized Labor

Following June 1940, the Army had a distinct advantage over the WSA in the area of labor relations. On June 28, the Congress enacted *The Alien and Sedition Act*. Section I of Title I of that act gave the Army the handle it would need to restrain labor agitation aboard its transports and small craft.[14]

> *(a) It shall be unlawful for any person, with intent to interfere with, or impair, or influence the loyalty, morale, or discipline of the military or naval forces of the United States --*
>
> > *(1) to advise, counsel, urge, or in any manner cause insubordination, disloyalty, mutiny, or refusal of duty by any member of the military or naval forces of the United States; or*
> >
> > *(2) to distribute any written or printed matter which advises, counsels, or urges insubordination, disloyalty, mutiny, or refusal of duty by any member of the military or naval forces of the United States.*
>
> *(b) For the purposes of this section, the term 'military or naval forces of the United States' includes the Army of the United States, the Navy, Marine Corps, Coast Guard, Naval Reserve and Marine Corps Reserve of the United States and, <u>when any merchant vessel is commissioned in the Navy or is in the service of the Army or Navy, includes the master, officers, and crew of such vessel</u>.* [emphasis added] [15] [16]

The existence of *The Alien and Sedition Act* of 1940 was the tool through which the War Department was at last able to resist organized activity on the part of troublesome employees or by the maritime unions. The Army made every effort during the war to maintain good relationships with its seamen labor force. However, it consistently resisted interference by the unions and held to a strict policy of maintaining an open shop and forbid activities such as grievance committees among its crews.[17]

---

[13]   The award of campaign medals and other military awards to the Army's civilian employees was not carried on with any consistency. For instance, from the beginning of the war, the Army did not normally bestow the Purple Heart to civilian employees; yet in June 1948, Purple Hearts were awarded to the Quartermaster Agent and the Chief Engineer of the *USAT Meigs* for wounds they had received at Darwin, Australia, in February of 1942. For a further discussion on this subject, see Appendix K of this volume.

[14]   The *Congressional Record* (Volume 86, Part 8) concerning Congressional discussion on *The Alien and Sedition Act* of 1940 does not inform as to whether the War Department played an active part in that bill's development where it concerned the civilian crews of auxiliaries operated by the Army. Nevertheless, a safe assumption can be made that considering the importance of the matter at that time, the War Department would have instigated such inclusion.

[15]   54 Statutes-at-Large 670. Section 1(b). The Act's absence of specifically naming Army Reserves, while it names *Navy and Marine Corps Reserves*, was because the term *Army of the United States*, as defined within Title 10 § 2 U.S.C., then included all of the Army's Reserve components. The penalty for violation of the terms of *The Alien and Sedition Act* was set at not more than ten years' imprisonment or more than $10,000, or both.

[16]   Case history is not available to indicate whether paragraph (b) of the Act of June 28, 1940, was deemed to be descriptive only of transports owned by or bareboat chartered to the Army or Navy, or whether it was also meant to include merchant ships on time charter to the military.

[17]   As of the attack on Pearl Harbor, the Secretary of War transmitted his wishes to the Quartermaster General stating that the theory underlying the granting of danger zone pay -- as it was then practiced for the merchant marine -- was essentially wrong. The Secretary believed that it was *unjustifiable to assert that seamen*

Problems early-on with the maritime unions had come to a head at New Orleans in 1942 where the Army was in the process of taking over the freighters *Yarmouth, Evangeline,* and *Florida* through sub-bareboat arrangement with WSA. Local officials of the unions, which up to that time had represented the former merchant marine crews, persuaded the men to walk off the ships unless the Army met the unions' wage conditions. Although the matter was finally reconciled when most of the men agreed to sail under the War Department's established wage scale, the episode brought the matter of union interference to full boil. In a conference over the affair called in Washington by the labor relations consultant to the Secretary of War, and which was attended by union representatives, the Chief of Transportation Maj. Gen. Charles P. Gross stated flatly that the War Department would employ those sources of labor it normally utilized, meaning its own recruiting facilities and not those of the unions; nor would it adhere to any wage scale not of the Army's own design. In referencing the matter of shipboard disruptions, Gross further stated that suspension of undesirable employees for *subversive or other inimical activities would be executed summarily* and that mass meetings and the formation of committees on board ship were prohibited.[18] Gross's message seems to have gotten through to the union leaders, and except for some minor annoyances in the future, nothing anywhere near approaching the seriousness of the New Orleans affair would be repeated. Apparently *The Alien and Sedition Act* was not something to be ignored either by the Army's crews or by would-be union agitators.[19]

Discipline

Minor infractions such as not showing up on time for duty, intoxication, or unauthorized absences of short duration (AWOL) were offenses handled by ships' masters through minor fines, restrictions, or short-term confinement in the ship's brig. By War Department policy, the masters were instructed in the imposition of that discipline to generally pattern themselves after practices prevalent in the merchant marine. For more serious offenses, the Articles of War, as they pertained to civilians

---

are lacking in patriotism to such an extent as to insist upon extra pay for taking risks which their fellow citizens in the Army are taking cheerfully without thought of additional gain. The Secretary's reliance on the patriotism of the seamen would prove wrong. The Army was to find it impossible to crew its ships without conforming with extra danger zone pay. Source: From the files of the Chief of Transportation. As early as late December of 1941, the War Department agreed to conform in general with the wage and bonus decisions of the Maritime War Emergency Board. This, as earlier explained, was a joint agency of the Maritime Commission (later WSA) and the Labor Department. However, despite its general adhesion to the wage and bonus standards set by the Maritime War Emergency Board for the merchant marine, the War Department never committed itself to compliance with the Board's decisions. Up to 1943, the law did not allow the payment of overtime to the crews of Army transports. An act passed by the Congress during 1943 authorized such payments. After that, overtime was allowed for the crews of the larger transports and for the crews of harbor craft in the United States, but the Army continued to deny overtime for crews engaged in small ship operations conducted within overseas theaters of operations.

[18] Chester Wardlow, *The Transportation Corps: Responsibilities, Organization, and Operations,* (Washington, DC: Office of the Chief of Military History, 1951), pp 230, 231.

[19] Converse to the unions' disruptions early in the war, most unions would later become quite cooperative, often referring their members to Transportation Corps hiring offices in circumstances where a shortage of crews would otherwise have held up transports ready to sail -- that courtesy, of course, being offered only under conditions when the unions' own seamen pools were in plentiful supply.

serving with the armed forces in the field, was to be invoked. If the offense was committed aboard ship, the master was to prefer charges whereupon the miscreant was taken ashore for trial by military court-martial. If found guilty, sentences included terms in either a military prison or stockade.

During 1942, a revised edition to a publication issued by the Judge Advocate General had given the Army's prosecutors in the field full legal justification as it had been established under case law during the latter months of World War I.

> *In time of war, all persons in any manner employed on or serving with chartered transports or transports otherwise in the service or under the control of the Quartermaster's Department of the United States Army are persons 'serving with the armies of the United States in the field,' and are amenable to military law. When seamen enter into contracts to render service on such transports for a specified period, the Government has the right to rely upon them for the performance of their obligation, and if they leave their place of duty with intent to escape service for which they have engaged, they may be arrested as deserters, tried by general court-martial, and punished as prescribed by the Articles of War. (251, Feb 5, 1918.)*
>
> *Crews of Army transports and Army tugs signed on under shipping articles containing 'Army clauses' may be arrested and confined by the provost marshal upon the authority of the master of such vessels. The nature of the duties actually performed by these men, and which under these 'Army clauses' they undertook to perform, brings them within the scope of the Articles of War and subjects them to the control of the Army both as to discipline and punishment and as to the means and methods of enforcing the same. The master is warranted in causing the arrest and confinement by the Articles of War and the Army Transport Service Regulations, Spec. Reg. No. 71, 1917, to which the crew have voluntarily submitted themselves; and it is his duty, in a proper case, to cause such arrest and confinement....The words 'in the field' do not refer to land only but to any place, or fortifications, where military operations are being conducted.*
>
> *Under former section 1473 of this title, a civilian employed in time of war by the Quartermaster's Department and assigned as cook on a vessel transporting Army supplies was 'serving with the armies in the field,' and court-martial had jurisdiction to try him for his attempt to desert the ship just before sailing.* [20]

During World War II, the authority of court-martial was invoked against Army crewmembers on numerous occasions, both in the European and in the Pacific Theaters of Operation. On occasion, the Army brought the authority of the Articles of War to bear against members of the WSA-controlled merchant marine. However, such instances were relatively rare and applied only in those cases where a ship had been allocated to the Army and where the Army had charge of such vessel's unloading or reloading for turnaround at an overseas destination. In general, the discipline of the merchant marine relied upon *Title 46, U.S.C.*; and on the mechanisms of the WSA and the U.S. Consular Service whenever those authorities were available. On the other hand, the discipline of Army seamen -- at sea or while overseas -- rested solely with the Army as neither the mechanisms of the WSA nor the U.S. Consular

---

[20]   The *Opinions of the Judge Advocate General 1942*, cites a case that went before the Federal Courts in 1918 which encompassed the Army's attempts during that earlier war to bring its civilian crews under military discipline. The Court upheld the Army's authority in that regard. See ex parte Gerlach, 247 Fed 616, 250.4, May 31, 1918. Also see ex parte Falls, D.C.N.J. 1918, 251 F.415.

Service nor that spelled out within *Title 46, U.S.C.,* were authoritative toward civil service crews directly employed by the Armed Forces.[21]

Method of Hiring

All categories of the Army's seamen wartime force were hired under temporary civil service. The Army's method for hiring crews for the larger class of troop transports, hospital ships, and cargo ships differed from that of the small craft crews serving within overseas theaters of operations. In the case of the large ships which in general operated from U.S. ports, crewmembers were signed onto ships through shipping articles (Army clause). Such articles were binding for the duration of a voyage. At the end of the voyage, a crewmember could, if he wished, leave the ship by signing off the articles. In the case of crews employed on small craft overseas, such personnel signed one-year contracts under which they could, at the Army's pleasure, be transferred from one vessel to another or to related shore duties.[22] Another contractual arrangement applied to men who attended the Transportation Corps's civilian cadet training schools. Some portion of those trainees did so on the contractual agreement that they would serve upon graduation in the capacities of civilian maritime officers for the duration of the war.

Foreign Tonnage and Foreign Seamen Employed by the Army

The Army's shipping needs would be met through a variety of means. This included Danish and Norwegian ships and their crews which had been cut off from their homelands by the German occupations.

The capitulation of Denmark in April of 1940 had included, in exchange for the continuance of Danish self-rule, a pledge of cooperation by the Danish government to Germany which included the stipulation that resistance would not be offered to German forces. Not all Danes agreed with Copenhagen's position, and among that defiant number was Henrik Kaufman, Danish Consul at New York. Kaufman declared himself independent of the Copenhagen government and established himself as representative of all Danish interests outside of Germany's control. In that capacity during 1941, he entered into a treaty with the United States giving over wartime control of Greenland to the United States. At the time of the German occupation of Denmark, 230 Danish merchant ships were either on the high seas or at neutral or allied ports. Those Danish ships in American and British controlled ports were seized. Of those seized within American jurisdiction, a number ended up as part of the Army fleet. Many of the 6,000 Danish seamen who were cut off with the ships

---

[21] For a complete discussion of the disciplinary mechanisms relative to civil service crews employed on Army transports during World War II and relative citations thereto, see Charles D. Gibson, *Merchantman or Ship of War,* (Camden, ME: Ensign Press, 1986.)

[22] Some seamen contracts -- seemingly those applying to harbor craft at North Atlantic and Caribbean bases -- were for 6-months' duration; however, contracts for the European and Pacific theaters of war were for one year.

from their homeland volunteered to serve on allied merchant ships. [23] The Army -- not being restricted in its hiring by those laws governing the U.S. merchant marine which prohibited the licensing of foreign citizens -- would employ a number of these Danes as ships' officers, some of them as masters. [24]

The situation with Norway and its merchant marine was somewhat different. Unlike the Danes, Norway's government did not surrender. The heads of the Norwegian government had escaped, going into exile in England. Large numbers of Norway's naval and military forces also escaped, and they would fight on under British command. The Norwegian merchant marine in largest part had been absent from home waters at the time of the invasion and was therefore kept out of German hands. Over one thousand Norwegian ships and their crews served as part of the allied effort at sea, most sailing under their own national colors. [25] During the war, the administration of Norwegian ships and their crews was conducted by the Norwegian organization Nortaship. Through charter formats entered into with Nortaship, starting in 1940, a number of Norwegian ships became an important part of the U.S. Army's shipping effort. A substantial number of Norwegian seamen were recruited directly into the Army Transport Service, in that process becoming civil service employees. [26]

A number of ships which had previously flown the flags of Central American nations (Nicaragua, Honduras and Panama) went under Army control, some through purchase and others either under direct bareboat charter or through sub-bareboat arrangements with the WSA.

Strategic Cargoes

During the first part of 1941, voyages by Army transports returning from the Philippines were being made in ballast. This was objected to by the USMC since it was taking place at a time when imports of strategic materials such as rubber were critical to the defense buildup. The question had arisen from an inquiry to the USMC made by the Reconstruction Finance Corporation, a federal agency charged with the purchase and transport of critical materials as well as other functions. [27] Upon being queried over the legality of Army transports carrying non-military cargo, the Judge Advocate General of the Army held forth no objection. Thereafter, on return

---

[23]   Of the 230 ships of the Danish merchant marine which served under allied flags during World War II, 60% of them were lost as were 1500 Danish seamen. Source: I.C.B. Dear and M. R . D. Foot, Editors, *The Oxford Companion to World War II,* (New York and Oxford: Oxford University Press, 1995), p 294.

[24]   *Statutory restrictions pertaining to employment of civilian crews on vessels pertain only to merchant vessels and not public vessels, Army vessels being public vessels therefore not subject to Navigation Laws.* From letter dated March 13, 1941, File NO. QM 231.8. That letter cites Public Law No. 808 and 835; 46 U.S.C.A. 672 and 672 (a).

[25]   During the war, 570 Norwegian ships were lost as were 4,000 Norwegian seamen. The figures given here are taken from a memorial plaque located at Battery Park, New York City, dedicated to those Norwegian seamen of World War II who served the allied effort.

[26]   In the postwar period, as a result of that wartime service, Norwegians, as well as the Danes who shared a similar experience, became eligible for U.S. citizenship.

[27]   The Reconstruction Finance Corporation was first established in 1932 (47 Stat. 5) as a Roosevelt Administration measure to assist the country's banking institutions during the Great Depression. On June 25, 1940, the agency's authority was statutorily increased allowing it to produce, to acquire, and to carry strategic goods and material. (54 Stat. 573)

runs to the United States, transports owned or otherwise under the control of the Army were first routed to Penang on the Malay Peninsula or to Java to take aboard cargoes of rubber. Transports outbound from San Francisco or New York with cargo consigned to the Canal Zone were sent from there to Chile for a load of copper before returning to the United States. These detours were first put into force as temporary measures, but later they became formalized through an executive directive issued June 28, 1941, which extended such carriage beyond that of consignments for the account of the Reconstruction Finance Corporation. Thereafter, such carriage could include the cargoes of any federal agency, the relevant Army instructions stipulating that expenses incurred through the deviation of transports to load such cargoes were to be reimbursed by the federal agency to which the cargo was consigned. With the Japanese attacks of December 1941, the haulage of rubber from Penang and Java of course came to an end. However, the carriage aboard Army transports of strategic cargoes such as copper from Chile as well as coffee from Colombian ports and sugar from the Caribbean islands continued throughout the war.[28]

A Question of Navy Takeover and Developing Relationships with the WSA[29]

Based upon the Navy's operation of the Naval Overseas Transportation Service during World War I, the Supply Section, G-4, of the Quartermaster General's staff discussed during late 1940 the advisability of a repeat of such a program once the United States entered the war. The Assistant Chief of Staff, G-4, formalized those discussions by stating *that it might be appropriate during this transition period to make the same arrangements.*[30] The Quartermaster General noted in reply that most mobilization plans which had been drafted over the years following World War I had in fact called for a Navy takeover. He went on to state that consideration should be given to the fact that the ATS had been diligent toward meeting its schedules and that the Navy might find it difficult to meet the Army's demands which were of critical importance at that time. By that last, the Quartermaster General undoubtedly meant the buildup of U.S. forces in the Philippines which was then being slated for further acceleration. Although not negating the advisability of a full Navy takeover as of the time of mobilization, he advised that even if it should become necessary to man the transports beforehand with Navy crews, the Army should retain operational control over them. The Assistant Chief of Staff, G-4, stuck to his guns, stressing that the basic concern rested with a need for militarization of the crews. Nothing concrete seems to have taken place from those discussions although as the transportation historian Harold Larson relates, a close liaison over the matter was maintained with the Navy over the

---

[28]   Army Regulation AR 55-455, November 18, 1942, Paragraph 10, adjusted the procedures under which non-military cargoes were authorized for carriage aboard Army transports. Under that Regulation, application for carriage aboard transports made by any agency, other than by the Army itself, was to be jointly arranged between the agency applicant and the Army's Chief of Transportation, accompanied by WSA concurrence.

[29]   The question of Navy takeover as covered here by the authors has been derived in largest part from the following sources: Larson's *Water Transportation for the United States Army, 1939 - 1942*; Wardlow's *The Transportation Corps*; and from John D. Millett, *The Army Service Forces: The Organization and Role of the Army Service Forces,* (Washington, DC: Office of the Chief of Military History, 1954).

[30]   Larson, p 64.

following few weeks during which joint conferences took place. As it would turn out, the Chief of Naval Operations finally determined that the Navy was not then, nor would it be within the near future, in a position to take over the ships. The idea for remanning with naval crews was shelved -- at least for the time being. On further reflection that the Navy manning program needed to be at least concretely planned for, the Chief of Naval Operations sent the following memorandum on April 5, 1941, to the Chief of Staff of the Army:

> *In a national emergency, according to plan* [meaning the former inter-war mobilization plans, Ed.], *the Navy operates all Army vessels and provides transportation required by the Army.*
> *It is recommended that officers be designated by the Chief of Staff to discuss with representatives of the Chief of Naval Operations and the Bureau of Navigation the advisability of manning at the present time Army transports and cargo vessels with Navy crews.* [31]

By that juncture in time, the Quartermaster General and G-4, Army General Staff, had come to agree that in light of the increasing probability of war, Navy crews would be the way to go. As it was expressed by Lt. Col. Charles P. Gross, then head of the Transportation Section, G-4, of the General Staff, handing over manning of the transports to the Navy, *was a good solution from the national viewpoint.* He noted further the possibility of *mutinous conduct* by the civilian crews and concluded by stating, *If our job is to get ready for war, why not anticipate all we can and get accustomed to Navy crews on our transports rather than postpone the confusion to more critical times?* [32] [33] However, Gross would continue to hold fast to his conviction that control of the transports, as that control applied to all facets of the ships (except their actual navigation and crewing), should remain with the War Department.[34]

With that settled, Navy manning went into gear; but it was a low gear, and progress was anything but immediate. One of the problems encountered, which

---

[31]   Larson, p 66.

[32]   The Gross quotation given here is from Larson, pp 66, 67. Within a year, Charles P. Gross, a lieutenant colonel in 1941, became the Chief of Transportation when the Transportation Corps was created on July 31, 1942. The month following, he was promoted to the rank of major general. Gross had graduated from the U.S. Military Academy in 1914. During World War I, he served with the AEF in France. Between the wars, among other duties (all with the Corps of Engineers), he was assigned to Nicaragua as part of the Canal Survey. Upon assignment during 1940 to the Army General Staff, Gross adopted the doctrine that military transportation in all its facets should be controlled through a single headquarters as to do otherwise could only bring weakness to the system. As quoted from Chester Wardlow's study *The Transportation Corps,* p 75. From the very beginning, Gross proclaimed, *shipping is the key to the war effort.*

[33]   During the time of these discussions (Spring of 1941), the nation was not yet at war; therefore, the imposition of military law against the crews of the Army's transports could not be brought to bear, such imposition being applicable only *in time of war.*

[34]   Gross's conviction that control of all passenger and cargo shipments relating to the Army should remain with the War Department would be adopted and would be carried over into the system of merchant vessel allocation which in 1942 came to be administered by the War Shipping Administration. Under such allocations, merchant ships delegated by WSA for the carriage of Army personnel or supplies and which were crewed by merchant marine personnel were to be exclusively devoted for that delegated purpose, leaving the loading of the ships, their dispatch, and the reception of personnel and cargoes exclusively to the Army. Only the actual operation of the ships and their manning remained with WSA under such allocations.

none of the concerned parties seemed to have taken into account during the planning phase, was that under the Navy's system of manning, far larger crews would be required than on ships being operated by the Army.[35] The Navy was already having difficulties in providing full crews for its combatant ships then undergoing commissioning. Another problem was the consumption of time the Navy was taking to convert an assigned ship to Naval Bureau of Ships standards. Two good examples of the last were the cases of the merchant ship *Manhattan* and *USAT Washington*. While undertaking shipyard conversion for the Army as a troopship, *Manhattan* was transferred to the Navy. The *USAT Washington,* earlier taken under bareboat charter by the Army from United States Lines, was being actively utilized by the Army as a troopship at the time of its takeover by the Navy. As it would turn out, both ships would take inordinately long periods before being made ready for the Navy's use; and once ready, they were diverted to missions not consistent with the Army's best interests. That situation had led to a reversal in thinking within the War Department, heightened by the Navy's own admission on June 7, 1941, that events now made it impractical to further pursue the manning program, and that it would be best if it were *deferred until such time as Navy personnel can be assembled.* [36] A memorandum Gross issued shortly after this reported that the ATS was not then having difficulty in getting crews. Gross was also pleased that the problem of crew discipline had not been as bad as he had first anticipated.

Despite the above, the idea for Navy manning remained alive through that summer. However, by November 19, out of the twenty-nine Army transports which were in service under the ATS and which had earlier been scheduled for Navy crewing, only seven had actually been transferred. Gross's assistant, Col. Stephen J. Chamberlin, would declare:

> This has been due to lack of men, friction within the Navy Department and to subordination of the task to other matters considered more vital to the Navy's interests.

Chamberlin recommended that no further action should be taken to transfer the Army Transport Service (meaning the ships) to the Navy. On December 8, the day after the Pearl Harbor attack, what remained of the program was killed, both services coming to the understanding that the Navy did not have the organizational mechanism or the manpower to take over any more ships. However, that apparently did not end the matter as a little over two months later, the Chief of Naval Operations proposed to not only place all Army transports under Navy operation but in addition, to make the Navy responsible for arranging with WSA for the allocation of all ships dealing with the logistical needs of both the Army and the Navy. To that bombshell the

---

[35] This was because watch-standing complements were much larger on naval ships; and on those destined as combat loaders, the crew served as stevedores during unloading operations, necessitating extra personnel. When a ship was taken under Navy crewing in the 1940s, the crew was generally three times larger than under Army crewing. Expenses increased accordingly.

[36] Memorandum, July 7, 1941, Chief of Naval Operations, sent to Commandants of Naval Districts. From Larson, p 75.

Army Chief of Staff, Gen. George C. Marshall, made strong and immediate objection, citing the executive order which had set in place the authority of the WSA and which had included a provision that the Army was to retain the control of its own transports as well as any ships that became allocated for Army carriage by the WSA. A quietude was placed over the matter by both the Army and the Navy throughout most of 1942; but the pot was restirred that November when Gross proposed a plan of his own, suggesting that the supply of overseas bases, whether Army or Navy, become the responsibility of the Army. According to this idea, the ships to be used were to be directed and controlled by the Army, but they were to be manned with Navy or Coast Guard crews. Gross soon developed second thoughts which he addressed to his boss, Lt. Gen. Brehon B. Somervell, the head of the Service of Supply, cautioning that if the Army should consent toward handing over all of its troopships and cargo ships to manning by the Navy, it would be losing *much of the power of independent action.* Judging, probably with accuracy, that the Navy would object to the Army controlling the supply of naval bases, Gross would now suggest that just the actual transportation be left with the Army, leaving the management of the Navy's cargo with that agency. What was not being considered by Gross was the Executive Order of April 1942 which had established the prerogatives held by WSA. If the Gross proposal had gone any further, WSA would almost assuredly have objected, and that would have probably ended it then and there.

      Gross's overlooking of the authority which had been vested with WSA may have been intentional. Somervell had been unhappy from the beginning with the power over shipping that the President had granted to WSA. Although Emory Land nominally headed the WSA, the man who had charge of its control over shipping was Lewis Douglas, a former Congressman. Up to the time that Douglas was appointed, Somervell had enjoyed a direct relationship both with President Roosevelt and with Roosevelt's right-hand man, Harry Hopkins. Douglas was a long time friend of Roosevelt, and Douglas's sudden appearance on the scene had greatly diminished Somervell's influence with the White House. Friction between the two men developed almost immediately, centering around what Douglas felt was a tendency on the Army's part to waste tonnage space by dispatching ships before they were fully loaded and by sometimes keeping ships tied up too long between trips. Douglas believed that ships should be allocated to applicant agencies, whether civil or military, on a per-trip basis rather than reserving a ship's continuous use through bareboat or long-term time allocation. Such thinking was, of course, at odds with the War Department's doctrine of wanting to have its own dedicated tonnage. Other issues also arose between the two men, and the interagency antagonism which developed permeated through the chain of command where it especially seems to have impacted Gross. While Somervell and Douglas would finally come to terms, antagonism toward the WSA appears to have remained with the Chief of Transportation. At one point Somervell would hint that the source of the Army's remaining friction with WSA could be traced to Gross who seemed *predisposed to reject anything ensuing from WSA simply because it came from WSA.* [37]

Controversy between Somervell and Douglas would again erupt over the allocations of cargo space for aid to Britain. Gross and Somervell argued that it had become excessive in comparison to the essential needs of the American military. It would not be until late 1943 that the disagreement became reconciled. For the remainder of the war, working relationships between the Army and WSA can be said to have been generally good.

As 1943 grew to a close, the nation's manpower resources began to shrink, and it became increasingly difficult to find crews for the Army's fleet. Because of this, the Navy was approached by Gross to take over a number of new transports then under construction even though doing so would mean a partial loss of shipping readily available to the Army. Gross would again call on the Navy Department in early 1944 to supply Coast Guard crews for a large number of the Army's coastal class tankers and freighters as well as seagoing tugs then operating within the Southwest Pacific or being readied for assignment there. The takeover was targeted to cover 272 Army vessels of the small tonnage classes: LT tugs; Y tankers; FS cargo vessels; and various small freight-passenger types. Six larger vessels of a class used as marine repair ships would also be involved. As part of that arrangement, the vessels were to remain under the operational control of the Transportation Corps and were not to be commissioned into either the Coast Guard or the Navy. The Coast Guard crews were to be concerned only with the vessels' actual navigation. The reason that Gross had specifically asked for Coast Guard crews was that he had been made aware that a large number of Coast Guardsmen, previously utilized as beach patrolmen and for harbor security in the United States and for small craft patrol duties along the American coast, would soon become available for other assignments. Since the Navy Department was no longer experiencing the personnel crunch under which it had suffered during the war's early months, it had agreed to honor Gross's request. The manning by the Coast Guard was formally authorized by the Joint Chiefs of Staff, March 14, 1944. Under Coast Guard manning which was in line with the Navy system, much larger crews would be required than those normally manning Army vessels. However, since the vessels were to remain under the Army, it was agreed that the Coast Guard would pattern crew sizes in line with the Army's system. Originally, 4,823 Coast Guard officers and men were assigned, but that number was later increased by 1,100, bringing total Coast Guard manning to 5,923 officers and men. Under the usual Army system, following 1943, most gun crews had become Navy although in the Southwest Pacific, they in part remained Army. Radio operators were almost always Army enlisted men, usually in the grade of sergeant. The Coast Guard, however, did not want mixed-service crews, so on vessels scheduled to be crewed by the Coast Guard, the gunners and radio operators were replaced by Coast Guardsmen.

---

[37]   John Kennedy Ohl, *Supplying the Troops -- General Somervell and American Logistics in World War II,* (DeKalb, IL: Northern Illinois University Press, 1994), p 103.

This was the reason for the additional 1100 in Coast Guard manning.[38] Between 1944 and 1946, Coast Guard crews manned 288 of the Army's vessels, mostly within the Southwest Pacific, although some Coast Guardsmen took over Army small craft operating within the Caribbean. There is no record of Coast Guard crewing of any Army vessels operating within the European Theater of Operations.[39]

---

[38] *Manning Report* signed by Nathan Pool, 30 June 1944; obtained from U.S. Coast Guard, Office of the Historian.

[39] In addition to the crewing of vessels owned and/or bareboat chartered by the Transportation Corps, the War Department operated other vessels under the management of other Army branches. The manning of those as well as the various classes of vessels under Transportation Corps management was covered in a report issued in 1943 by the Office of the Chief of Transportation during 1943. That report has been duplicated within Appendix Q of this volume.

CHAPTER IX

WESTERN HEMISPHERIC DEFENSES AND THE CONSTRUCTION OF THE TRANSATLANTIC AIR ROUTES

Policy had evolved during the late 1930s which set the defense boundaries of the United States. Encapsulated within that parameter in the Atlantic were the land masses of North, Central, and South America and that part of the outer rim of the western hemisphere consisting of Greenland, Bermuda, and the Falkland Islands. (Iceland and the Azores were added to the concept during 1941.) In the Pacific, the outer defensive rim included the entirety of the Aleutian chain and all oceanic islands lying to the east of the 180th Meridian.[1]

During May 1940, following the British evacuation from Dunkirk and the subsequent surrender of France during the following month, the U.S. Army General Staff, joined by the Office of the Chief of Naval Operations, believed that Britain was doomed to go down in defeat even if given immediate American aid in the form of war materiel. It was a gloomy but realistic prognosis, and it gave impetus for the United States's establishment of a ring of bases reaching eastward into the Atlantic. Obtaining the land areas needed for the establishment of those defenses led in substantial part to the destroyers-for-bases agreement entered into that September between the United States and Great Britain.

The specter of an aggressive Germany possessing unfettered control of the Atlantic seaway diminished somewhat when the Royal Air Force defeated the

---

[1] Stetson Conn, Rose C. Engelman, and Byron Fairchild, *Guarding the United States and Its Outposts,* (Washington, DC: Center of Military History, 1989), p 3. Although not considered part of the hemispheric defense area, the Pacific islands of Guam and Wake were to be defended. However, Guam was never placed into an acceptable defensive posture and Wake Island would remain without fortification well into 1941. According to plan, the Philippines were to be strongly held, although the point for reaching a full stage of preparedness there was not expected until well into 1943.

Luftwaffe in the air war over Britain, a victory closely followed by the dispersal during mid-September of the fleet of landing barges which the Germans had staged at the Channel ports preliminary to their planned invasion of southern England. With Britain safe from immediate disaster, an incursion of the western hemisphere by Germany was not quite the concern it had been, although a lodgment by German forces somewhere on the outer perimeter of the western hemispheric defense zone was a clear possibility; and it would remain so until the point was reached where control of the Atlantic went decisively into the hands of allied naval power. Until that happened -- and that would be a long into the future -- the American base sites leased from Great Britain and which were located in Bermuda, British Guyana, and on the Caribbean Islands would be vital bulwarks. The United States would also construct naval and air bases in Iceland, Greenland, and in northern Canada.

Occupation of Iceland[2]

Up to the mid-nineteenth century, Iceland had been part of the Danish kingdom, directly administered from Copenhagen. In 1845, the Icelandic people established a separate parliament which gave them partial independence. In 1918, Iceland's autonomy became almost complete through the signing of the *Treaty of Union* with Denmark which provided for the same regent as Denmark but left that regent with little executive power over Iceland. When Germany invaded Denmark in the spring of 1940, the Icelandic parliament decided to replace the Danish king with an elected regency of its own selection, thus cutting off ties completely from what had once been the mother country. In May of 1940, the British, after promising to respect the Icelandic government, landed an occupation force, a step taken primarily to prevent what might otherwise have been a German occupation. From the standpoint of Britain, a German presence there would have given the enemy a platform from which to deny the North Atlantic trade routes to all but German-controlled shipping.

During 1941, Iceland and the United States entered into a treaty arrangement by which the United States agreed to defend Iceland through the establishment there of an American garrison. On July 7, 1941, United States Marines landed to join the British troops in what for a time became an Anglo-American occupation.[3] The Marines were reinforced by Army troops which arrived on September 5 aboard four Navy transports: *USS President Grant* (the former Army transport *Republic* transferred to the Navy and renamed); *USS Heywood; USS Harry Lee* and *USS William P. Biddle.* The original Marine contingent was relieved shortly after Pearl Harbor, being replaced by Army units.

Airfields would be constructed in Iceland by the United States to accommodate not only bomber aircraft being ferried to the British Isles but also attack bombers stationed there as part of the mid-Atlantic anti-submarine effort.

---

[2]   The source material utilized for our discussion on the American occupation of Iceland has been derived from E. H. Dunham, *Transportation of the U.S. Forces in the Occupation of Iceland, 1941 - 1944,* a monograph prepared in 1945 by the Office of the Chief of Transportation.

[3]   The British troops in occupation of Iceland would soon be relieved by Canadian troops. The Canadians remained until 1942, their departure placing the garrisoning of Iceland solely in the hands of American forces.

During the buildup phase of the American presence in Iceland, the transport of troops and construction supplies would be largely a Navy affair. For the first months of the occupation, around twenty troop and cargo ships were involved. Only one of them -- *USAT American Legion* -- was part of the Army's fleet, the others being either naval transports or merchant ships under time charter to the Navy. From July 1941 through to October of 1943, upwards of 90,000 passengers (troops and civilian construction workers) were transported from the United States to Iceland. Although the initial occupation of the island was the result of the fear of German invasion, that concern was largely put aside after 1942 and combat troops departed for other duties. Service troops remained into 1945 as Iceland continued to serve as a military air base, both for the transmission of aircraft to the British Isles and for anti-submarine patrol.

The Initial North Atlantic Air Route

As the involvement of the United States in the European war grew more likely, the necessity to be able to transport aircraft to Britain took on added importance. Shipments of aircraft by ship were not practical at the time unless the planes were broken down into component sections and crated. And even then, shipment was restricted to smaller aircraft such as light bombers and fighters. The labor to reassemble crated shipments of aircraft at their destination was prohibitively costly both in time and in the employment of skilled personnel.

During 1940, the Canadians and the British had begun to ferry bomber aircraft from Gander, Newfoundland, to Prestwick, Scotland. It was a long and dangerous flight of 2119 miles, made especially difficult because of conditions at Gander where fog rolling in from the Atlantic frequently made the airfield there unusable.

The first improvement to the air route to Scotland was undertaken at Goose Bay, Labrador, by the Canadians. Meteorological conditions along the Labrador coast were far better than at Gander -- less fog in the warmer months as well as less snow the rest of the year. The construction of the Goose Bay airfield began in September of 1941 with one runway becoming serviceable by early that December.[4] Utilizing an extant airfield at Presque Isle, Maine, as the jump-off point to Goose Bay, the resultant new route crossed over southern Greenland in a direct line to Reykjavik, Iceland, a distance of 1550 miles. From Iceland, the next hop was to Scotland, a distance of 846 miles. This was 277 miles longer than the straight route across the Atlantic from Gander, yet it offered considerable advantage. In addition to less fog and snow, the stopover at Iceland provided a refueling opportunity if head winds or other factors had lengthened flight time bringing fuel to critical levels. It also gave an opportunity for repairs to the aircraft if mechanical difficulties had developed, and it allowed needed rest for the air crews.

---

[4]   The airfield at Goose Bay would later be improved by additional runways constructed by the United States.

The Greenland Bases

Beginning in 1940, there was considerable concern that the Germans would establish a presence in Greenland. In fact this did occur on three separate occasions when enemy weather parties were landed on Greenland's east coast. To counter these incursions, the Coast Guard operated patrol vessels along both coasts, and the United States maintained defensive garrisons well into 1943.[5] The fact that Greenland now lay on the North Atlantic flight path opened the advisability of developing an airfield in the vicinity of Narsarssuak where there was enough level terrain to accommodate the necessary runways. Once completed, a field at Narsarssuak could substantially shorten the distance between stopovers and would even allow the transit of light bombers and even fighters -- something which had previously been impossible.[6]

In 1941, work began on the Narsarssuak airfield (code name Bluie West 1) as well as at a second location farther up Greenland's west coast at the head of Sandre Stromfiord (code name Bluie West 8).[7] The idea for the Greenland airfields had been initiated by the Canadians; however, the construction was by the United States as was the subsequent support -- most of which came by sea.[8]

The cost to the Army for the construction and subsequent garrisoning of the Greenland bases was a high one, not only in treasure but in the loss of men and

---

[5] During 1943 into 1944, the Germans established weather stations on Greenland's east coast. During the summers of 1943 and 1944, U.S. forces destroyed three German bases, two support trawlers, captured one trawler, and took sixty-two enemy prisoners. Source: Conn, Engelman, Fairchild, pp 552-554.

[6] According to Wardlow, *The Transportation Corps,* Table 29, p 365, there were never any of the Army Air Corps's heavy or medium bombers transported by ship, all of them having been flown to their overseas destinations. (Army Air Corps was not changed to Army Air Force until later in the war.) Of the Air Corps light bombers, around 150 were sent overseas in 1942, half as deck cargo aboard ships and half flown over. It would not be until 1943 that a method would be devised for transporting light bombers and fighter planes in an assembled state aboard tankers. This was accomplished through the erection of loading platforms mounted above the ships' tank tops. With such platforms in place, planes of the smaller sizes could be cradled and lashed fast -- they and the platform upon which they rested being well clear of the decks so as to allow the tankers' crews to work the petroleum cargo without obstruction. During the years 1943 through 1944, 1502 light bombers were sent from the U.S. -- 897 flown across, the rest going by ship. The statistics Wardlow gives for fighter planes show that in the year 1942, 433 were flown over while 12,607 were transported by ship. During the span 1943 through 1944, 20,627 fighters went overseas, 457 of them flown across. Wardlow does not break down his numbers to tell us which theaters of war were involved, but the spans of the Pacific Ocean would have made flights of low endurance aircraft such as fighters or light bombers nearly impossible. Therefore, a safe assumption can be made that the light bombers and fighters Wardlow indicates as being flown overseas generally applied to those which went to Europe. Another source for the numbers of aircraft flown across the North Atlantic is Craven and Cate (see below) who state that in the 6-month period between June 1942 and January 1943, 366 heavy bombers, 150 medium bombers, 183 P-38 fighter planes and the same number (183) of transport type aircraft were delivered to Europe, all flown across by their regular crews. Of those numbers, 38 were wrecked or otherwise lost while en route. Wesley F. Craven and James L. Cate, *The Army Air Forces in World War II: Services Around the World,* Volume VII, (Chicago: University of Chicago Press, 1950), p 92.

[7] The second Greenland airfield site at Sandre Stromfiord was to prove a superior location since the weather between there and Iceland was usually much better than on the more southern flight route that utilized Narsarssuak. Craven and Cate, p 344.

[8] Although the northern air ferry route from Gander to Greenland and Iceland, thence to the United Kingdom, would be used into 1945, an alternate transatlantic route for bombers would take shape in late 1943, which promised more dependable flying conditions. This route was from the United States direct to the Azore Islands and then to either American airfields in North Africa, Italy, or Great Britain. The use of the Azores became possible on October 12, 1943, when Great Britain and Portugal signed an agreement. At first, U.S. planes were denied access, but this was soon resolved by disguising American planes as British.

ships. The cargo ship *USAT Nevada* with twenty-four of its crew was lost in a gale southwest of Cape Farewell. Another cargo ship, *USAT Halma,* was lost when it struck a mine laid by a German U-boat. Merchant ships and those aboard also suffered. During August of 1942, the U.S. flag merchant ship *Chatham,* while en route from the United States with supplies and 428 passengers for the construction site at Narsarssuak, was attacked and sunk by the *U-517.* Fortunately only seven crewmen and seven passengers were lost. The results were not so fortunate for the U.S. flag merchant ship *Dorchester* when during February of 1943 while also en route to Narsarssuak with 705 troops and civilian workers, she was sunk by a torpedo launched from *U-223.* In that sinking, 117 of *Dorchester's* crew and naval armed guard were lost along with 558 of the passengers, making it one of the worst troopship disasters of the entire war. In February 1942, the *Lake Osweya* was torpedoed while loaded with cargo for Iceland; 30 of her crew were lost.[9]

The Crimson and Crystal Projects

The North Atlantic air route system was to include yet another route which would cross over the top of Canada and provide a flight path for fighter aircraft routed from airfields in the state of Montana, thence north to Paz, Manitoba, followed by a stopover for fuel at Port Churchill located on the western shore of Hudson Bay. From there, the route would carry on to Southampton Island located at the north end of Hudson Bay. (The airstrips at Churchill and Southampton Island were to be code-named *Crimson.*) From Southampton Island, the flights would continue to a selected site (or sites) located either in northern Quebec or on Baffin Island in Canada's Northwest Territory. (That part of the route to be code named *Crystal.*) From the Crystal airstrips, planes would fly on to Greenland with a stop either at Sandre Stromfiord (Bluie West 8) or at Narsarssuak (Bluie West 1), and thence on to Iceland and then to Scotland. A secondary purpose planned for Crystal was the establishment of weather stations equipped with powerful radio equipment for the transmittal of meteorological data to England forecasting eastward-moving weather fronts. This information was deemed essential for the success of bomber operations planned against Germany. Construction of the project was to be an American endeavor. Materials and labor contracting were to become the responsibility of the U.S. Army Corps of Engineers with sea-borne transportation (as applicable to all locations except the base at Port Churchill) falling under the aegis of the Army Transport Service.

The Crimson segment of this northern Canadian air route offered no substantial challenges. The Port of Churchill which was to be the first stopover after planes left Montana, already had an infrastructure. A rail service connected it directly with the eastern and western provinces of Canada. As a port, it was a long-going

---

[9] Other Army transports lost during 1942 within the Atlantic/ Caribbean Theater were *USAT Jack,* torpedoed off Haiti in May, and *USAT Lt. Col. Charles W. McClure (*ex *Merrimack*), torpedoed off Cozumel Island, Mexico, in June. Both ships suffered heavy losses in crew and gunners -- *USAT Jack* losing thirty-nine men and *USAT Lt. Col. Charles W. McClure* losing forty-three. Another loss was the *USAT Major Gen. Henry Gibbins.* Source: WSA Insurance Claims file for U.S. Army Transport personnel losses as paid by WSA for the account of the War Department. Records are now held by Division of Insurance, Maritime Administration, Washington, DC.

concern during the ice free months of July through October with shipping reaching Churchill from the Atlantic by way of the Hudson Straits. Since the turn of the century, Churchill had become a valuable transshipment point for Canada's grain and cattle going to the European markets. Building an airfield there would be relatively easy as men and equipment could conveniently reach it either by rail or by sea, and there were extensive level areas immediately adjacent to the port which were ideal for airfield construction. An airstrip at Southampton Island, Crimson's third stopover, would present some difficulty, but its approaches by sea were relatively well charted, and the place did have a harbor of sorts for the landing of equipment.

Crystal was quite a different matter. It would require three separate sites. No one knew at the onset even with the slightest degree of certainty whether areas could be found that would be suitable for airfield construction and whether, if and when found, they would be accessible from the sea -- that being a prerequisite for bringing in workers and construction equipment. A tentative air reconnaissance made of the northern Labrador coast during 1940 indicated possibilities; but in 1941, a more detailed over-flight showed the Labrador coast to be totally unsuitable. A follow-up aerial reconnaissance of the Ungava Bay region in northern Quebec resulted in the discovery of a favorable site for what was to become Crystal I. The selections for Crystal II and Crystal III was by necessity carried out by sea using fishing trawlers chartered by the Army Transport Service which landed over-wintering base camp parties at Frobisher Bay on Baffin Island and on Padloping Island at the edge of the Arctic Circle.

Construction for the Crystal bases continued through 1942 and into 1943. It was a Herculean effort employing hundreds of men and costing the loss of three ships and the lives of many in their crews. Yet once completed, few if any fighters or light bombers in transit to Europe ever utilized the air strips. By 1943, the submarine menace in the Atlantic had largely abated, and the development of practical methods for shipping fully assembled light aircraft on tankers had made the concept for Crimson and Crystal obsolete. Although they had been conceived and constructed out of vital necessity, the northern Canadian air route would come to be looked upon as a military white elephant. Some use did result from Crystal II and III, both locations serving as weather stations until the conclusion of the war in Europe. Crystal I mainly functioned as a support base for planes of the Coast Guard's North Atlantic ice patrol.

> The ships and men involved in the construction effort that went into the development of the Crystal project have been virtually ignored by chroniclers of World War II. We believe it deserves much more, and in that spirit, we have included the story of that project within this volume as our Appendix F, titled *The Crystal Project, 1941 - 43*. Appendix F includes a map of the Arctic and subarctic regions on which we have located the sites of the Greenland Air Bases as well as the three Crystal Project facilities.

USAT Jack. Torpedoed in Caribbean during May of 1942. Grover Collection (U.S. Army Military History Institute).

USAT Cynthia Olson. The first America ship to be lost at sea in the war against Japan. Sunk by Japanese submarine attack, en route from the west coast to Hawaii on December, 1941. There were no survivors. Grover Collection.

U. S. Army Transports (Over 1000 Gross Tons)
Owned and/or Bareboat or Sub-bareboat Chartered
During the Calendar Year 1941

In most cases this list does not describe Army service beyond mid 1942. Many of these ships continued under Army employment throughout World War II; however, since that period is not pertinent to the chronological scope of this volume, we have only included later service in a few isolated instances -- and then only for clarity.

Cautionary Note: It was often the Army's practice, when purchasing a commercial ship, to change its name at that time or at some interval thereafter. With the exigencies of the 1941 shipping crisis, there was often not time to affix the new name upon the hull. This would later take place during a repainting of the hull. Another scenario involves ships first bareboat chartered by the Army in which event they would carry their commercial name prefixed by USAT. If later purchased, the Army would then most commonly change the name.

To give two examples: The *Irwin* was first bareboat chartered to be later purchased becoming the *USAT John L. Clem*. The *Deltargentino* was purchased becoming the *USAT J. W. McAndrew* and for a time went to sea with its commercial name prefixed by USAT.

These situations have the potential of creating confusion on the part of those who either sailed the ships or who have accessed the Army's photographic ship records for the period in question.

Sources utilized for this list

ABS Record of American Shipping for the years 1938 through 1943. It was the practice of the Army to have its ships classed by ABS regardless of whether they were owned or on bareboat charter.

Authors' Casualty List is a listing of vessels sunk or damaged by marine peril or enemy attack, or attacked with damage. It was compiled by the authors from the following sources:
- *British and Foreign Merchant Vessel Losses, World War II*: "BR 1337".
- *Lloyd's War Losses, The Second World War*, Volumes I and II
- Summary of Statements of Survivors. Files of the Chief of Naval Operations.
- Ward, Frederick A. "Report of Army Transport Service Activities in the Philippine Islands from 8 December 1941 to 6 May 1942."

Charles, *Troopships of World War II.*

Dictionary of American Naval Fighting Ships

Larson, *Army Cargo Fleet in World War II*

Larson, *Water Transportation for the U.S. Army, 1939 - 1942*

Lloyd's Register of Shipping, 1941-42.

Merchant Ship Movement Report Cards. Modern Military Records Center, Archive II, National Archives, College Park, MD

Merchant Vessels of the United States for the years 1919 through 1943.

Not on Navy List: A list maintained by the Navy for large tonnage ships under the authority of the Army. Obtained from Division of Naval History, Department of the Navy. According to Dr. Dean Allard, former Director of the Center for Naval History, this list was only maintained by the Navy for April through August of 1942. It lists vessels purchased by and bareboat chartered to the Army. We found the list to be incomplete as vessels contained within Army files and which are known to have been owned or bareboat chartered are not listed.

Record Group 336, Files of the Chief of Transportation, which also contains records of the Water Transport Branch of the Quartermaster General's Office.

Status of Transports, Report on Procurement Activities (Senate Resolution No. 71) Water Transport Branch, Transportation Division; Office of the Quartermaster General, May 5, 1941.

Technical Manual No. 10-380, Water Transportation, War Department, February 14, 1941.

WSA Report No. 190-92; based on information received through January 15, 1946, by Charters and Agreements Section, Operating Contracts Division, WSA. Many names are either incorrectly stated or incomplete. Some listed vessels were allocated and not on bareboat charter. (The report does not differentiate between bareboat and sub-bareboat charters.)

ARMY'S VESSEL NAME	FORMER NAME	TONS	YR.BLT	REMARKS
American Legion	*American Legion*	13736	1921	Blt Camden, NJ. Brought out of the USSB Reserve Fleet in November 1939 and assigned to Army. Evacuated American citizens from Finland in August 1940; thereafter assigned to Caribbean runs until April 1941, and on Bermuda-Trinidad shuttle from New York until July 1941. *ABS Record 1941* indicates vessel was then owned by Army. Took part in transporting first contingent of U.S. troops sent to Iceland. On 22 August 1941, she was transferred to the Navy, becoming *USS American Legion.*
American Star		5354	1919	Blt Arlington, New York. Acquired by Army on bareboat charter 30 September 1941; used on Alaska run.
Arthur Murray	*Munargo*	6336	1921	Blt Camden, NJ. Purchased by Army 27 March 1941. Used in establishment of Greenland Base Command before being transferred to Navy. (She was later turned back to Army and renamed *USAHS Thistle.)*
Aun		1908	1930	Blt Middlesbro, England. Operated under Army bareboat charter as early as 1941.
Azra		1700	1936	Blt Helsinger, Denmark. Danish vessel seized from its owners 16 June 1941. Was taken over by the Maritime Commission and according to *ABS Record 1942* was on charter (bareboat) to Army.
Barbara Olson	*Corrales*	2146	1918	Blt Manitowac, WI. Vessel was under bareboat charter to Army as early as December 1941.
Chateau Thierry	*Chateau Thierry*	7555	1920	Blt Hog Island, PA. Transferred by USSB to Army in 1920. Purchased by Army on 21 February 1921. During June of 1941, transported an Army construction force to build an air base in southern Greenland.. Operated as a troopship until August 1941. Shortly after was delivered to the Navy.
Chirikoff	*Lurline*	6509	1908	Blt Newport News, VA. Bareboat chartered to Army from August 1940 into April 1941. Rechartered to Army September 1941 for a short period.
Clevedon	*Feltre*	7314	1927	Blt Trieste, Italy. Bareboat chartered to the Army 25 September 1941. On 11 January 1942, while at Yakytat, Alaska, caught on fire. Was towed clear of the dock and beached; shortly thereafter exploded. Total loss. No personnel casualties.
Colabee	*Pagasset*	5617	1920	Blt Portsmouth, NH. Acquired by Army following 1 January 1941, presumably continuing under Army status (probably on bareboat) to the end of that year. Routes during that period not known.
Columbia	*Lovcen*	2390	1911	Bareboat chartered to Army as early as June 1941; used as interisland transport within Caribbean area.
Cynthia Olson	*Coquina*	2140	1918	Blt Manitowac, WI. Went under bareboat charter to Army in November 1941. On 7 December 1941, she was attacked by the Japanese submarine, *I-26.* At the time, she was 1000 miles northeast of Hawaii (33° 42' N 145° 29' W). The attack took place in the same time frame during which Japanese aircraft were attacking Pearl Harbor. (Honolulu was on local zone time.) The 33-man crew and 2 Army radio operators were never heard from again.

David W. Branch	Santa Olivia; ex Ecuador	5544	1915	Bareboat chartered by owner to Army in December of 1941 at Kodiak, Alaska. On 12 January 1942, was "wrecked at Seward and subsequently abandoned." Refloated 9 February and towed to Seattle for survey.
Don Esteban		1616	1936	Blt Kiel, Germany. Owned by De la Rama Steamship Company. Bareboat chartered by ATS Manila on Oct 30, 1941. Unlike those Philippine registered vessels which the ATS chartered following the outbreak of hostilities, *Don Esteban* was organized along the same staff lines as stateside Army transports with a full Army staff. On Feb 22, 1942, departed Corregidor with "special party" for Iloilo on Island of Panay where they were disembarked to *Princess of Negros*. Thence to Antique where she took on foodstuffs for Corregidor. After leaving Paluan Bay, Mindoro, on March 1, Japanese planes bombed and strafed the ship, setting her afire. Total loss. Crew escaped with only one man wounded.
Edmund B. Alexander	America; ex Amerika	21329	1905	Blt Belfast, Ireland. U.S. troopship of WW I. According to Maritime Commission report, vessel was bareboat chartered on 17 October 1940 to Army by Maritime Commission; however Army records indicate she was purchased by Army on that date. *ABS Record 1941* states vessel was owned by Army.
Eli D. Hoyle	Redwood	1793	1917	Blt Bellingham, WA. Purchased by Army on 17 February 1941. Used on Alaska run as a freight vessel but occasionally utilized for the carriage of a limited number of troops.
Ernest J. Hinds	Kent; ex Santa Teresa	5341	1918	Blt Philadelphia, PA. Purchased by Army 13 April 1941. As of July 1941 was being operated by Navy. Returned to Army in March 1942.
Etolin	Matsonia	9476	1913	Blt Newport News, VA. Time chartered by Army during 1940 for two voyages. Army records state vessel was bareboat chartered as of 20 August 1941.
Fluorspar		5055	1919	Blt Hog Island, PA. This vessel is named within Army Ship Files as having been acquired under bareboat charter by the Army for the period between 1 January 1941 and 23 December 1941. She served on Atlantic, Caribbean, and Indian Ocean routes.
George F. Downey	Lake Miraflores	2702	1921	Blt Saginaw, MI. Purchased on 12 September 1941. In early January 1942, made first run for the Army from Seattle to Alaska, apparently continuing this duty until 15 August 1942 when she was involved in a serious collision with a civilian-manned Navy salvage vessel, the *Discoverer*. George F. Downey was towed back to Seattle for repairs.
Haleakala		3679	1923	Blt Chester, PA. Sub-bareboat chartered to Army by Maritime Commission during October 1941. Utilized as an interisland transport involved with transportation of men and supplies for the construction of mid-Pacific air bases. Initially, charter was for period of one year with renewable option clause.
Halma	Nora	2937	1940	Blt Aalborg, Denmark. Seized and placed with the Maritime Commission under Public Law 101; then sub-bareboat chartered to Army shortly after October 1941. Was assigned to Greenland service. She had an eventful career of near and then complete disasters. First, she grounded in a Greenland fjord on 6 January 1942, her crew abandoning ship. Was later salved. On 17 December 1942, a fire did considerable damage. Finally, was sunk 3 June 1943, eight miles from Sambro Light, Nova Scotia, by mines laid two days earlier by the German submarine *U-119*. No casualties.

Henry T. Allen	*President Jefferson*	14174	1921	Blt Camden, NJ. Maritime Commission owned vessel. Transferred to the Army for conversion into a troopship in 1940 but was never actually placed into Army operation. Before completion, she was transferred to the Navy to become the APA-15.
Hugh L. Scott	*President Pierce; ex Hawkeye State*	12579	1921	Blt Sparrows Point, MD. First taken under bareboat charter, then purchased by the Army 31 July 1941. That summer took reinforcements to the Philippines. While in Manila, she underwent a technical transfer by sub-bareboat charter from the Army to the American President Lines. This was done at the request of the State Department for a special mission to evacuate American civilians and military to Manila from Hong Kong and Shanghai -- an assignment which might have proven diplomatically embarrassing if performed while under the house flag of the U.S. Army. Following that short detour from military status, she was redelivered back to the Army.
Hunter Liggett	*Pan America*	13713	1922	Blt Sparrows Point, MD. Delivered to the Army in February 1939. *ABS Record 1940* lists vessel as owned by Army. Used in both intercoastal and Caribbean service. In June 1941, was delivered to the Navy which operated her throughout the war years.
Irvin L. Hunt	*Edenton*	6958	1918	Blt Seattle, WA, for USSB. Army files indicate she was in Army service as early as November 1940, apparently having been placed under bareboat charter. Sold to Army by Maritime Commission 5 February 1941. Afterward was assigned to Alaskan runs until August when she embarked on a transpacific voyage to Manila, returning with a strategic cargo (probably rubber) taken on at Sumatra for delivery to the United States. While off northeast Borneo, she grounded but was pulled off. Returned to San Francisco in January 1942.
J. Franklin Bell	*President McKinley*	14127	1921	Blt Camden, NJ. Acquired by Army from Maritime Commission 9 January 1941. During conversion into troopship was transferred to Navy to be operated as an attack transport. Under naval operation, she carried the number AP-34.
J. W. McAndrew	*Deltargentino*	7997	1940	Blt at Sparrows Point, MD. Purchased by Army 28 June 1941. Initially utilized on Caribbean service.
Jack	*Lake Fresco*	2622	1919	Blt Lorain, OH. Purchased by Army 27 October 1941. Based out of New Orleans with runs to Panama and Caribbean island bases. The typical practice then carried on by the Army in cooperation with the U.S. War Production Board was that available cargo space on military transports was to be filled with strategic commodities. The *Jack* was operating in conformity with this practice when on 27 May 1942, at a position south of Haiti and bound to New Orleans with sugar consigned to the account of the War Production Board, she was torpedoed and sunk. Out of a full complement of 60 which included her crew, Armed Guard, and military casuals, 39 died. Most of the survivors were rescued within three days; however, seven men spent 32 days on a raft before being picked up.
James Parker	*USAT Panama*	10021	1939	Blt Quincy, MA. Originally this ship was operated by the U.S. Government's Panama Railroad Company. Transferred 13 June 1941 to the Army as a troopship. Some confusion arises within the records as to this ship's name. She was *Panama* when first transferred to Army, but later, in August 1941, and following some alterations, she became the *James Parker*. Initially served upon Caribbean runs, New Orleans to Panama.

John L. Clem	*Irwin; ex Santa Cecilia; ex Guatemala; ex Santa Ana*	5211	1918	Blt Philadelphia, PA. First bareboat chartered to Army as the *Irwin*. Purchased on 6 March 1941 and renamed the *John L. Clem*. First used in Caribbean service, sailing from New York, Charleston, and New Orleans.
John R. R. Hannay	*Waukegan*	6209	1919	Blt Kearny, NJ. As *Waukegan*, came under Army control in 1939 by bareboat charter from the Maritime Commission. According to Army files was transferred to Army ownership 5 February 1941. Following transfer was renamed *John R. R. Hannay*. Ran between Newfoundland and east coast ports during 1941.
Jonna		1517	1933	Blt Nakskov, Denmark. A note on an Army memo signed by Kells 20 September 1941 states that as of 12 August 1941, vessel was to be used in the Army's West Indian interisland traffic. According to *ABS Record 1942*, vessel was chartered to Army from the U. S. Maritime Commission Whether the arrangement was in the form of a sub-bareboat charter is not entirely certain. At some later point vessel was named *Pillory*.
Joseph T. Dickman	*President Roosevelt; ex Peninsula State*	13869	1922	Blt Camden, NJ. Purchased by Army October 1940 as the *President Roosevelt* and placed into ATS reserve. Conversion to troopship by Army began in February 1941 and was completed by June 1941. During that time was renamed *Joseph T. Dickman*. Was shortly after transferred to Navy becoming USS *Joseph T. Dickman*.
King	*Lake Faristell*	2624	1918	Blt Cleveland, OH. Purchased by the Army as *Lake Faristell* on 24 October 1941 and renamed *King*. Converted into a refrigeration ship. She was engaged in servicing bases within the Caribbean.
Kvichak		1063	1900	Blt Portland, OR. Bareboat chartered to Army for use on the Alaska run. On 27 January 1941, she grounded on the coast of British Columbia. Was towed off and immediately sank. Two civilian seamen and one military passenger were lost. Later, was salvaged through the use of pontoon floats. The standard terms of Army bareboat charters were that if a ship was lost, the Army took title -- as was done in this case -- paying the owner the prior agreed-on value established at time of charter. The ship was repaired following her salvage, and the Army renamed her *James B. Houston*.
Leonard Wood	*Western World; ex Nutmeg State*	13713	1922	Blt Sparrows Point, MD. Purchased by Army in 1939. Used between New York and Panama and then put into intercoastal service until transferred to Navy June 1941.
Liberty		6211	1918	Blt Kearny, NJ. On bareboat charter to Army from Maritime Commission as of December 1939. Service included a transpacific voyage from San Francisco. After loading rubber at Panang, Malay, returned to San Francisco. Then routed to Manila with Army supplies and equipment, arriving Manila 11 November 1941. From there to New Guinea and Java, picking up rubber for the homebound voyage. Outbound from Java, she was torpedoed by a Japanese submarine in Badung Straits. Was taken under tow by an American and a Dutch destroyer and beached on Bali where she was judged a total loss. No crewmember losses. According to Lloyd's, she was beached at 8°54'S, 115°28'E.
Ludington	*James Otis*	8292	1920	Blt Gloucester, NJ. Came under Army ownership from USSB in October 1931. Used as a freight vessel with special accommodations for animals. She was one of only two freight vessels owned by the Army in 1939, the other being the *Meigs*. *Ludington* was utilized in Honolulu/Manila service. Was en route to the Philippines on 7 December 1941 but was turned back to the west coast on orders because of uncertainty of enemy ship dispositions.

M. G. Zalinski	*Ace*	2626	1919	Blt at Lorain, OH. A lake type vessel purchased by Army on 22 September 1941. Initially used as a reefer vessel in Atlantic service then transferred to Seattle for Alaskan runs.
Major General Henry Gibbins	*West Elcasco*	5766	1918	Blt at Seattle, WA. (Not to be confused with *Henry Gibbins, ex Biloxi* of 12097 GT.) First Army owned vessel to be specially fitted out as a munitions carrier. Employed during the spring of 1941 on runs to Panama and other Caribbean bases; on return voyages carried strategic cargoes. Torpedoed in the Gulf of Mexico by *U-158* on 23 June 1942. At the time of her sinking, she had aboard 41 crewmen and an Army armed guard of 21; there were no casualties.
Maui		9940	1917	Blt at San Francisco, CA. Purchased by Army 3 December 1941. Made first trip on 27 December 1941, San Francisco to Honolulu, with troops which had originally been scheduled for the Philippines.
Meigs	*West Lewark*	7358	1921	Blt Los Angeles, CA. (Not to be confused with *USS General M. C. Meigs.*) Purchased by Army January 1922, from USSB. Converted for carriage of reefer cargo; also had stalls for 268 animals. Initial voyage planning in 1941 was that she was to carry military supplies from the U.S. West Coast to the Hawaiian Islands, and then to the Philippines, returning with strategic cargoes (rubber) from the East Indies for the space charter account of the United States Reconstruction Finance Corporation. In December of 1941, she was selected as one of the seven ships to be sent to the Philippines in the "Pensacola Convoy." Following the Japanese attack on 7 December 1941, that convoy was rerouted, being ordered to Australia. Upon arrival, *Meigs* was held over. On 15 February 1942, while under naval convoy to Timor, Dutch East Indies, convoy was taken under heavy air attack. *Meigs* was damaged and ordered into Darwin. During bombing of Port Darwin the next day, *Meigs* was sunk. Casualties: one crewmember killed; eight wounded.
Monterey	*Puerto Rico; ex Haiti*	5236	1932	Blt Newport News, VA. (Not to be confused with larger Matson liner of same name.) Under direct bareboat charter from her owners to Army prior to 7 December 1941. Was converted during 1942 into a troopship by Army, entering shipyard for that work in March 1942.
Nevada		1685	1915	Blt Manitowoc, WI. Purchased by Army 9 December 1941; used in Newfoundland and Greenland service. Became a marine casualty later in the war.
North Coast	*Carabobo*	2916	1923	Blt Camden, NJ. Army records state that on 18 December 1941 was bareboat chartered to Army by Maritime Commission. MARAD files indicate charter changed to bareboat from WSA on 26 June 1942. Assigned to Seattle-Alaskan routes throughout the war.
North Pacific	*Doylestown*	2632	1919	In September 1941, ship was bareboat chartered to Army either by owner or by the Maritime Commission. On 15 June 1942, after USMC records were transferred to WSA, she was sub-bareboat chartered to Army. Used throughout war on Seattle-Alaska run operating as far westward as Adak and Attu.
Orizaba		6937	1918	Blt Philadelphia, PA. Was in naval service 1918-19. Decommissioned by Navy Sept 1919; turned over to Army which utilized her for about two years as a transport before returning her to owner. Acquired again by Army in early 1941; but was commissioned as a naval transport on 15 June 1941.

Perida	*Marchen Maersk; ex Caldera*	6579	1937	Blt Vegesack, Germany. Her Danish owners delivered her to the Army in Manila during June of 1941. Was in Army service until going under WSA control in mid 1943.
Raritan	*Lake Fairton*	2649	1919	Blt Wyandotte, MI. Under bareboat charter to Army during 1941. Still under charter as of 25 February 1942 when she stranded on Frying Pan Shoals, North Carolina. Constructive total loss; no personnel casualties.
Republic	*President Buchanan; ex President Grant*	17886	1907	Blt Belfast, Ireland. Former German flag *President Grant*. Was used by U.S. Navy starting in July 1917. In 1919 was assigned by USSB to Army for use as a troopship. In 1920, evacuated Czech-Slovaks from Vladivostok to Trieste. Was laid up in USSB reserve fleet in 1921. Assigned to U.S. Lines in 1924 and renamed *President Buchanan*. Later renamed *Republic*. Sold to Army in 1931 and carried by Army as *Republic*. In 1941 transferred to Navy as the *USS Republic*, AP 33.
Saint Mihiel		7555	1920	Blt Hog Island, PA. (Not to be confused with *USS Saint Mihiel*, 10296 GT, built in 1945.) Delivered to Army in 1920. Her peacetime Army career included such varied service as transporting drought impoverished dust bowl farmers from San Francisco to Alaska for resettlement. Laid up temporarily in 1939, she went back into Army service in 1940, operating initially from the west coast to both Alaska and Hawaii. Later in the war she underwent conversion into a hospital ship.
Scotia	*Lake Galewood*	2649	1919	Blt Manitowac, MI. Initially bareboat chartered by owners to Army for Alaskan service in 1941; on 14 July 1942 was placed on sub-bareboat status to Army by WSA.
Siboney		6937	1918	Blt Philadelphia, PA. Former troopship during World War I. Army bareboat chartered her in June 1941 directly from owner. Her initial service was on runs to St. Johns, Newfoundland and later the Caribbean and Bermuda while homeported out of New York. In December 1941, left New York to begin a series of five transatlantic voyages including one eastward to India.
Sicilien		1654	1938	Blt Elsinore, Denmark. Seized under Executive Order, then transferred by Maritime Commission on bareboat charter to Army on 23 July 1941. In the fall of 1941, she took the forward elements (surveyors and hydrographers) of the Crystal Project to the Canadian Arctic. Was lost later in the war from enemy action.
Siletz		5757	1919	Blt Portland, OR. The *Siletz* was pulled out of the Maritime Commission's Reserve Fleet and loaned to Army (apparently on a bareboat basis) for a voyage in the fall of 1940 to move Army cargo from New York to Puerto Rico. It is not known how long she was operated by the Army or if her service extended past the one round trip to Puerto Rico. It is known that on 6 March 1942 she began operating under a general agency agreement with Grace Line, Inc. until transferred to the USSR under Lend Lease and renamed *Vtoraia Piatilitka*.
Silverado		2249	1918	Long Beach, CA. Under charter (apparently bareboat) from her owners to the Army for Alaskan service during 1941. She was put under sub-bareboat charter by WSA to Army on 14 June 1942. Used as a cable laying ship.
Stanley A. Griffiths	*Chinca; ex Nosa Ing; ex Capital of Nebraska*	3237	1920	Blt Mobile, AL. Prior to takeover by Maritime Commission in December 1941, she had been under bareboat charter to Army. That December, she carried poison gas canisters to Wellington, Australia, for the Army's account. The gas had been previously consigned to Manila.

T. W. Drennen		1737	1941	Blt Camden, NJ. Bareboat chartered by the Army during part of 1941 until purchased 11 December 1941.
Taku	*Ormes*	1364	1930	Blt Brooklyn, NY. Bareboat chartered by owner to Army in 1941 for unknown period. Grounded "off San Juan Island" October 1941, but was towed off without damage.
Tasker M. Bliss	*President Cleveland; ex Golden State*	12568	1921	Blt Newport News, VA. Bareboat chartered to Army 1941. Used initially as a trooper on Alaska run; then made a transpacific voyage during October 1941, returning to the west coast that November; thence to Australia.
Thomas H. Barry	*Oriente*	11250	1930	Blt Newport News, VA. Purchased by Army 14 June 1941. Service started with voyages to Bermuda and to the Caribbean.
U.S. Grant	*USAT Madawaska; USS Madawaska; ex Konig Wilhelm II*	9410	1907	Blt Stettin, Germany. Seized in 1917 and operated by Navy until Sept 1919 when she was transferred to Army. Army renamed her *U.S. Grant.* (Some Army records incorrectly refer to this vessel as *GRANT II.*) Evacuated Czech-Slovaks from Vladivostok to Fiume, Croatia, in 1920. Was involved in a collision at sea in 1921. In 1939 ran aground on a reef off Guam but was pulled off with relatively minor damage. In June of 1941 was transferred to Navy and commissioned *USS U.S. Grant* (AP-29).
Washington		24289	1933	Blt Camden, NJ. Bareboat chartered to Army 1 March 1941. Under Army operation she made one trip, New York to Manila via Panama and Honolulu -- returning to Philadelphia. Returned to owners. Delivered by owners to the Maritime Commission on 14 June 1941 which subsequently transferred her to the Navy. Navy renamed her *USS Mount Vernon.*
West Cressey		5596	1918	Blt Seattle, WA. Owned by U. S. Maritime Commission and bareboat chartered to Army in 1941 for transpacific service.
Will H. Point	*West Corum*	5795	1919	Blt Portland, OR. Went under Army ownership on 5 February 1941. One Army record lists her as being "obtained" by the Army in 1940 and as being "formally obtained" (presumably meaning transfer of title) during February 1941. Assigned to Alaska run throughout 1941.
Willard A. Holbrook	*President Taft; ex Buckeye State*	14812	1921	Blt Sparrows Point, MD. Purchased by Army 17 June 1941. Made two trips from San Francisco to Manila before the outbreak of the war. On 30 November 1941, as part of the "Pensacola Convoy," she left for the Philippines but was rerouted to Australia. Later the vessel was individually scheduled to run fighter planes into the Philippines, but the Japanese blockade was so tight that the mission was aborted.
William R. Gibson	*West Segovia*	5701	1919	Blt Portland, OR. Carried in MARAD records as *Brig. Gen. William R. Gibson*, but that appears to be incorrect. Obtained by Army in 1940 through bareboat charter from the Maritime Commission. Went under direct Army ownership 5 February 1941. Grounded in Dutch Harbor, Alaska, in September 1941 but was refloated.

CHAPTER X

DEFENSE STATUS IN THE WESTERN PACIFIC
UP TO DECEMBER 1941

In October of 1932, Douglas MacArthur, then Chief of Staff of the United States Army, predicted that there was little likelihood of any belligerent outbreak which might involve the United States in the Pacific.[1] In 1935, he was assigned to the Philippines to organize and train a native defense force during which tour of duty MacArthur altered his earlier prediction based upon the fresh realization that Japan posed an immediate threat to the Philippines as well as to the rest of Southeast Asia. Appreciating the importance of a strong Philippine Army toward discouraging Japanese aggression, and since he was facing assignment to other duty, MacArthur retired from the U.S. Army in order to complete the job of training the Filipinos.

The general consensus during the mid-1930s, as shared by most senior American officers, was that a Japanese movement against the Philippines -- if such should take place -- would not occur before 1943. By that time, it was hoped that the Philippine Army would have reached a state of combat readiness sufficient to thwart a Japanese invasion provided that the Filipinos were buttressed by American troops. The Philippines were slated to become an independent nation by 1946 at which point, according to plan, the new nation would have an army of 300,000 officers and men -- all with at least basic training behind them and organized into thirty combat divisions.

In the early fall of 1940, Japan's timetable for aggression took a new turn when she entered into a tripartite agreement with Germany and Italy which

---

[1]   During his tenure as Chief of Staff, Douglas MacArthur held the rank of full general (temporary). At the end of that assignment, he was given the rank of major general (permanent).

acknowledged a new order in Europe headed by Japan's new European partners. According to the agreement, Japan was to hold sway in the Far East as the leader of *a New Order in Greater East Asia.* What was particularly disturbing was that part of the agreement called for each of the parties to go to the aid of the other *if attacked by a power at present not involved in the European War or in the Sino-Japanese conflict.* [2] This last could only be interpreted as referencing the United States. Although the Lend Lease program between the United States and Great Britain (including the destroyers-for-bases deal) had not been an overt act of war, it left little doubt that United States sympathies lay with the British. In April of 1941, America's coalition with Great Britain became more warlike in tone when President Franklin D. Roosevelt ordered the U.S. Navy to begin patrols of the Atlantic sea lanes eastward to a mid-ocean line delineated at 26° west longitude. The Navy's orders were that it was to locate and then broadcast the movement of hostile (German) ships and aircraft. That September, the American destroyer *USS Greer* located a *U*-boat southwest of Iceland and began hounding it through sonar contact, keeping the *U*-boat on the bow until a British plane arrived and dropped depth charges. Even the most impartial observer would have considered such an act by *USS Greer* as hostile; however, neither Germany nor Japan made an issue of it -- both nations at the time hoping to keep the United States from entering the war.

For Japan, the provocation which would excite her into aggression against the United States would be of a more telling nature. In July of 1940, Roosevelt, acting under powers granted to him by Congress, issued an order stopping the United States export to Japan of both aviation fuel and lubricating oils. A year later, Roosevelt enlarged that embargo to include all petroleum products as well as strategic metals. He also ordered the freeze of Japanese financial assets in the United States.

If Japan continued its present campaign against China, she would require substantial imports of petroleum. Those imports amounted to 88% of what Japan had been consuming; and of that amount, around 80% came from the United States. As postwar records have disclosed, by the end of March 1941, Japan had a stockpiled inventory of 22,850,000 barrels of crude oil and 15,110,000 barrels of refined petroleum products.[3] Although American intelligence in 1941 had only a rough estimation of what the Japanese had stockpiled, the information at hand was sufficient to conclude that Japan would come dangerously close to petroleum deprivation within a year following the time that the embargo had gone into effect. Before she depleted that stockpile, she would be forced to strike southward to gain control of the oil fields of the Dutch East Indies. The exact timing of when the Japanese attack would take place was an impossible assessment for Washington to make; but given the clear and hard circumstances of Japan's situation, it almost certainly would take place before the middle of 1942. The question might then be posed as to why the Roosevelt Administration instituted the embargoes against Japan at a time when the United States had not itself reached an adequate point of military preparedness. The obvious answer

[2]   Samuel Eliot Morison, *The Rising Sun in the Pacific, History of United States Naval Operations in World War II,* Vol. III, (Boston: Atlantic Little Brown, 1968), p 45.

[3]   Morison, *Rising Sun in the Pacific, p* 63.

is that had the embargoes not been put in place, the United States would have been viewed as supporting Japan's aggression against China -- a position which Roosevelt felt would have been morally indefensible as well as politically damaging to his administration -- both at home and abroad.

~

The military situation as it existed in 1940 in the Philippines was such that it pointed to the probability of the loss of those islands should Japan attack before 1943. Primarily, United States military priority in 1940 was being directed to western hemispheric defense. Secondarily, was the critical importance of aiding Great Britain with arms and other war materiel. The priority given to western hemispheric defense was clearly spelled out under the United States *War Plan Rainbow 4*. Under that plan, the threat of Japanese aggression in the Pacific was to be countered by the U.S. Navy but only within the eastern Pacific basin, meaning no farther westward of the U.S. mainland than the Hawaiian chain which ended at Midway. Even this had its caveat in that should Britain fall, the Navy was to shift its major strength into the Atlantic. The war planners warned that the United States was not then, and would not be for several years, prepared to conduct a major operation in the Far East.[4] What could have been the timely arming of the Philippine Army was handicapped in June of 1940 by the transfer to Britain of 500,000 Enfield rifles with 130 million rounds of ammunition; 80,583 machine guns; 316 mortars; 25,000 Browning automatic rifles; and 895 75-mm cannon with a million artillery shells. Yet another factor stalling the buildup for an adequate response to Japanese aggression in the Southwest Pacific was the inability of the United States to fulfill $83 million in armament contracts with the Netherlands Government for the defense of its holdings in the East Indies.

> *...the possibility of early deliveries for the Dutch East Indies are hopeless under present law and priority conditions...they are competing with the United States and Great Britain in a market with limited immediate supplies and must wait a long time for sizable deliveries.*
>
> *Lt. Col. Edward E. MacMoreland*
> *Secretary, Clearance Committee, U.S. Army-Navy Munitions Board.[5]*

The one bright spot regarding a defense against a Japanese move in Southeast Asia was Britain's declared resolve to thwart a Japanese grab of the Dutch East Indies which in turn would threaten Australia. Prime Minister Winston Churchill had affirmed this during August of 1940 in a message he sent to the governments of New Zealand and Australia:

> *...we should then cut our losses in the Mediterranean and sacrifice every interest, except only the defense and feeding of this island, on which all depends, and would proceed in good time to your aid with a fleet able to give battle to any*

---

[4]   Leighton and Coakley, p 42, as quoted from "Memo A, C of S, WPD for C of S, 25 September 1940, sub: Problem of Production of Munitions in Relationship to the Ability of the U.S. to Cope With Its Defense Problems in the Present World Situation, WPD 4321-9".

[5]   Leighton and Coakley, p 41.

Japanese force which could be placed in Australian waters and able to parry any invading force, or certainly cut its communication with Japan. [6]

Churchill's message did not of course correlate toward British defense of the Philippines; nevertheless, a British fleet arriving in strength in the Southwest Pacific would materially serve American interests. British intent to defend the Southwest Pacific was reinforced as late as February of 1941 by a British officer who, during a United States - British staff conference in Washington, stated that the loss of the Far East would mean ...*disintegration of the British Commonwealth and a crippling reduction in our war effort.* [7] There was also a belief on the part of some western planners -- both British and American -- that the naval base at Singapore was almost impregnable, a belief which would be disproved before the year was out.

In March (1941), an agreement was worked out between the United States and Britain which laid the groundwork for the U.S. Army - Navy *War Plan Rainbow 5* which was to be implemented as soon as the United States entered the war. Under that plan, the priority goal would be, as before, the defense of the western hemisphere with American military power concentrated in the Atlantic and only *navally* in the Mediterranean. An effort was to be made toward keeping Japan from entering the conflict; but if that could not be accomplished, the defeat of Germany and Italy would remain paramount. The British had wanted the United States Pacific Fleet to aid in repulsing any Japanese naval strike into the Southwest Pacific, but the American naval planners balked at the idea, agreeing only that the United States Asiatic Fleet, a relatively weak force then based at Manila, would leave the Philippines and join with the British in defending the approaches to Singapore (the Malay Barrier). The Pacific Fleet was to remain based from Hawaii.

The *War Plan Rainbow 5* established the maximum number of United States troops which would be sent overseas during the first six months following an outbreak of hostilities. In the Pacific, the Army was to reinforce Hawaii, but no troops were to be scheduled for the Philippines. *War Plan Rainbow 5* was out of synchronization with the Army's *War Plan Orange 3* which called for relief of the Philippines to take place within a stipulated six months. As this account will soon relate, the strategy followed by Douglas MacArthur in the Philippines after December 23, 1941, was executed in conformity with the earlier *War Plan Orange 3*. [8] Following agreements with Britain, United States naval responsibility in the Pacific would extend westward to Japan; but it would not include Formosa, the Philippines, or any of the islands to the south of the Philippines. In essence, by the spring of 1941, the Philippines seems to have been written off by Washington as being impractical to hold against a determined Japanese invasion.

---

[6]   Winston S. Churchill, *Their Finest Hour,* (Boston: Houghton Mifflin Co., 1949), p 436.

[7]   Leighton and Coakley, p 48.

[8]   For a full overview of the *War Plan Orange* plans as they were developed in stages during the 1930s, see Edward S. Miller, *War Plan Orange, the U.S. Strategy to Defeat Japan 1897 - 1945,* (Annapolis: Naval Institute Press, 1991). Also see Louis Morton, *The Fall of the Philippines,* (Washington: Office of the Chief of Military History, 1953), pp 61-64, which gives an excellent summarization of *War Plan Orange 3.*

The Philippines in that event would be a beleaguered citadel far beyond the limits to which American power, for many months after the outbreak of a war in the Far East, could hope to expand. [9]

The morality of leaving the people of the Philippines and the American soldiery to their fate in those islands came under critical scrutiny shortly after *War Plan Rainbow 5* was drafted. What brought this on was the Japanese occupation in July 1941 of military and naval installations belonging to the Vichy-French in Indochina -- a move that seriously threatened the Philippines, in fact virtually surrounding the Philippine Islands since the Japanese already held the Caroline Islands to the southeast and the Mariana Islands (except Guam) to the east. Added to these circumstances was the realization that Japan had just ordered its merchant shipping in the Atlantic to leave for the Pacific. War seemed very close at hand.

As his first move toward an acceleration of preparedness for the Philippines, Roosevelt recalled Douglas MacArthur to active duty and placed him in command of the U.S. Army's Philippine Department with the rank of lieutenant general. The Philippine Defense Forces were brought directly under U.S. Army command, and the previous goal for a 300,000-man Filipino force was shelved and substituted with call-up by September of 75,000 men who were to be trained and equipped within a 3- to 9-month period. Those Filipino units already trained and in a reserve status were to be mobilized in September. American troop presence was to be increased as soon as shipping became available.

MacArthur's level of authority was enhanced at the end of July by his appointment as Commander of U.S. Army Forces, Far East (USAFFE). This new command arrangement was to activate as of January 1, 1942. Without counting in the Philippine Defense Forces, United States Army strength in the Philippines as of July 31 stood at 22,532 enlisted men, inclusive of the Philippine Scouts, an organization long part of the U.S. Army. Of American officers available for all purposes, MacArthur had 1,340 -- a little over half of them reservists called to active duty. (That number was to be enhanced by 425 additional reserve officers who were to be sent to the islands from the United States to train the soon-to-be mobilized Filipinos.) By the fall of 1941, all but around 400 of the American troops were stationed on Luzon and at the off-lying defenses for Manila Bay, the main part of those defenses being centered on the fortress of Corregidor. [10]

A revised War Department policy for the defense of the Philippines took form on August 1, 1941, when Gen. George C. Marshall, the Army's Chief of Staff, announced to his staff that it had now become United States policy to defend the Philippines through a heavy infusion of troops and equipment. Louis Morton, an historian in the Office of the Chief of Military History, in his definitive history on the loss of the Philippines, states that in large part this new determination had come about because Secretary of War Henry L. Stimson was of the opinion that the U.S. Army's newest bomber, the B-17, would act as a strong deterrent to Japanese expansion. [11]

---

[9] Leighton and Coakley, p 52-56.

[10] Morton, p 21. Corregidor's satellite defense installations were: Fort Drum on El Fraile Island; Fort Hughes on Caballo Island; and Fort Frank on Carabao Island.

[11] Morton, p 31.

Stimson's reliance on the B-17 was predicated upon the ability to deliver enough of them to the Philippines in a timely manner. On October 6, Stimson told Secretary of State Cordell Hull that this would require a delay in a Japanese attack for another three months by which time the Philippine Department would have secured its position -- not only in terms of plane arrivals but in troop strength then scheduled for shipment from the United States.[12]

By August 16, a regiment of Coast Artillery (anti- aircraft) and a tank battalion were being readied for departure to the islands. MacArthur was asked at the time if he needed additional infantry regiments. He answered in the negative, stating that the then Filipino regiments in training would soon be able to fill the manpower gap. It would not be long, though, before he would reverse this assessment and ask for an infantry regiment and at least two more field artillery battalions. The War Department was more than willing to oblige, but a severe shortage of shipping was to delay much of the reinforcement that otherwise would have been sent. Up to November of 1941, shipment priority in the Pacific had been given to the support of the Hawaiian Islands. This priority was now to be shifted to the Philippines, nine ships being slated for departure to Manila during the month of December. As of the time of the Japanese attack on Pearl Harbor, the Philippine garrison had only been reinforced by 8,563 American officers and men. Over 11,000 more were en route, but as events will relate, they were not to arrive. For the Philippines, it was to be a matter of too little, too late.

---

[12]   Morison, *The Rising Sun in the Pacific*, pp 153,154. Morison's relating of Secretary of War Stimson's conversation with the Secretary of State was derived from Stimson's biographer MacGeorge Bundy. Considering the logistical difficulties which were to be incurred during the defense of Bataan and from the Japanese decimation of MacArthur's air power during the early phase of the attack, it appears doubtful that the eventual outcome would have been different even had the Japanese not struck until after the three month period that Stimson said would be required for the buildup of American air power.

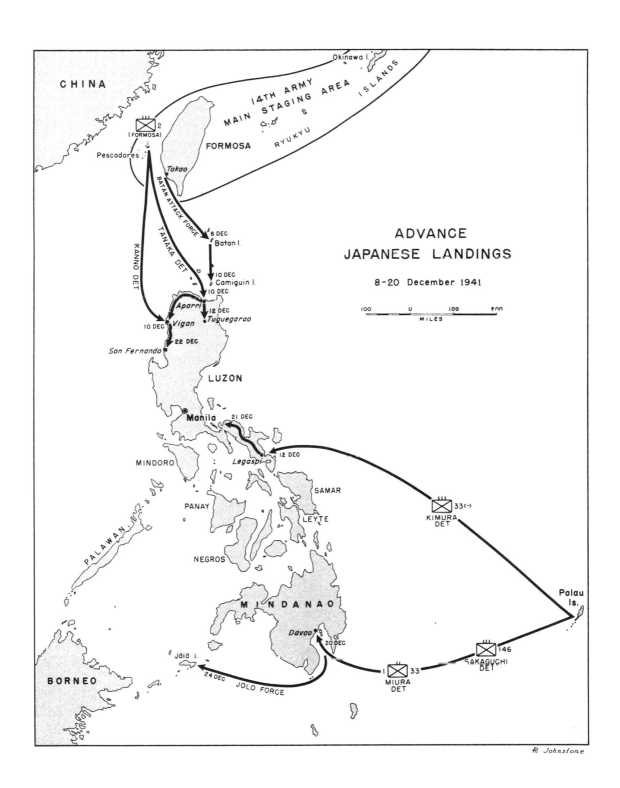

CHINA

Okinawa I.

14TH ARMY
MAIN STAGING AREA

RYUKYU ISLANDS

FORMOSA

2 (FORMOSA)

Pescadores

Takao

BATAN ATTACK FORCE

ADVANCE
JAPANESE LANDINGS

8-20 December 1941

100   0   100   200
MILES

KANNO DET

TANAKA DET

8 DEC
Batan I.

10 DEC
Camiguin I.

10 DEC

Aparri

12 DEC
Tuguegarao

10 DEC   Vigan

22 DEC

San Fernando

LUZON

Manila

21 DEC

MINDORO

Legaspi

12 DEC

SAMAR

PANAY

LEYTE

33(-)
KIMURA DET

Palau Is.

NEGROS

PALAWAN

MINDANAO

Davao

20 DEC

Jolo I.

24 DEC   JOLO FORCE

1   33
MIURA DET

146
SAKAGUCHI DET

BORNEO

R. Johnstone

CHAPTER XI

JAPAN ATTACKS THE PHILIPPINES:
EARLY DEFENSE PHASE, DECEMBER 1941

December 7, 1941, was a beautiful Sunday morning in the Hawaiian Islands -- at least it started out that way. Then at 0755 local time, an attack was launched against Pearl Harbor by carrier-based Japanese aircraft. By 1000 hours, the raid was over. In its wake was the near decimation of the U.S. Navy's battle fleet in the Pacific. The only thing which had saved American naval power from irreversible harm was the fact that the fleet's aircraft carriers were at sea and thus out of harm's way. Had that not been the case, the United States at worst might have lost the war with Japan on the very day it started; at best, the conflict would have been extensively prolonged.

At the same moment that the Japanese were first sighted over Pearl Harbor, the *USAT Cynthia Olson* was 1000 miles to the northeast with a cargo of construction material consigned to the Army on Oahu. Thirteen minutes after the attack began at Pearl Harbor, the transport's radio operator sent off an *SOS - SSS - SSS,* followed by the ship's position and a message stating that they were under attack by a submarine. That was the last ever heard from the ship. A search of the area was later made by a destroyer, but no trace of the ship, crew, or cargo was found.[1] The United States was now at war, and an Army transport's crew had been among the first to feel its bite.

Far to the west of Hawaii on the opposite side of the International Date Line, it was December 8. At 0230 in the morning (Philippine local time) a radio operator at U.S. Navy Headquarters, Manila, received the message, *Air raid on Pearl Harbor. This is no drill.* Within hours, the Japanese began landing operations at Kota Bharu on the northeastern coast of then British Malaya. Heavy air and naval strikes were taking place at Singapore and Hong

---

[1]   A U.S. Navy evaluation report would later determine that the attacking Japanese submarine was *I-26.*

Kong, and Japanese surface naval attacks were being initiated against the American possessions of Wake and Guam.

For the commander of the Japanese aircraft squadrons stationed on Formosa, the news of the attack on Pearl Harbor came as a shock. He had not been informed that a raid on Pearl Harbor was to take place, being under the impression that his planes would arrive over the Philippines unannounced. With the surprise element now missing, the Japanese commander feared that the American B-17s would either have been evacuated to the south out of range of attack, or worse yet, might be on the way to Formosa to strike their own blow.

An American raid on the Japanese airfields on Formosa did not materialize, and by dawn, the Japanese bombers were on their way to Luzon where American military and naval power was largely based. At 0900 the Japanese planes were reported to have been seen crossing over the Lingayen Gulf, heading south. American B-17s stationed at Clark Field, north of Manila, were ordered into the air as soon as the report was received, a step which would prove unnecessary when it developed that after crossing over the coastline, the Japanese planes had turned eastward toward other target areas. The B-17s, upon receiving the *all-clear* returned to Clark Field where landings were completed by 1130. The planes then began taking on bomb loads for a raid against the enemy's airfields on Formosa. At that point, another early alert was received that a second group of Japanese bombers had crossed over the northern Luzon coastline heading south. For some reason -- even today unexplained -- that early alert was never updated, so it came as a complete surprise to those at Clark Field when Japanese planes appeared overhead. Not only were the B-17s along with their fighter escorts caught on the ground, but Clark Field's anti-aircraft defenses failed abysmally -- the fault of outdated ammunition, much of which failed to detonate. In the midst of the attack, a group of American fighter planes returned from patrol, only to be pounced on by Japanese fighters. The Army Air Corps pilots were to discover that their fighters were no match for the Japanese *Zero;* American losses in the air over Clark Field were heavy. Equally heavy were the losses at nearby Ebba Field where fighters, although left free to take off, could do little once airborne to impede the Japanese attack. Eighteen B-17s out of a total Luzon-based force of thirty-five B-17s were destroyed. Fifty-six fighters and about two dozen other aircraft were also destroyed. Japanese losses were slight. If there was anything positive to reflect on after that first day of war in the Philippines, it was that some days earlier, two squadrons of B-17s had been sent south to Mindanao where they were safe from these initial attacks.

Responsibility for the crushing blow to MacArthur's air power on December 8 has become a point of argument over the ensuing years. Some critics have blamed MacArthur and some his Chief of Staff, Maj. Gen. Richard K. Sutherland. Other fingers point to Maj. Gen. Lewis H. Brereton, MacArthur's air commander. Finger pointing aside, the result of the losses spelled any and all hope of being able to seriously hamper the Japanese amphibious landings which were soon to follow. The first of those landings took place on December 10 at Aparri in northern Luzon and was followed by a second on Luzon's northwestern coast. In both of these cases, the enemy's landing force was relatively small. American resistance was light although the potential for air power to contest amphibious operations was demonstrated when a remnant of MacArthur's air force appeared over the Aparri landing sight and sank a Japanese minesweeper. A third Japanese landing was attempted at Pandan, a bit to the west of Aparri. There the attackers were repulsed by a combination of heavy surf conditions and American B-17s and fighters which succeeded in sinking another minesweeper and damaging two troop transports so severely that the ships had to be beached to prevent their sinking. That repulse was short-lived. The next day the same Japanese force moved farther south along the coast and this time put troops ashore without opposition. Three other beachheads were subsequently secured by the Japanese on northern Luzon. The Japanese purpose with these early landings had been to secure airfield sites for support of the main invasion which was to follow.

The Attack on Cavite and Manila Shipping

The Japanese goal for the air strikes of December 8 had been to neutralize MacArthur's air power. Their attention would next be directed at the naval base at Cavite and at merchant shipping lying off Manila.

Following the air raids on Clark Field, Adm. Thomas C. Hart, Commander, Asiatic Fleet, had immediately ordered Manila Bay closed to merchant ship departures. At that time, there were thirty-nine ships in the bay. Hart's order to hold those ships in port was issued primarily because of the uncertainty of the location of Japanese naval forces within the South China Sea; but it was also to prevent them from leaving port before the discharge of their cargoes which the military might consider necessary for the forthcoming defense. Following the closure of Manila Bay, a number of merchant ships came in seeking safety -- their masters judging Manila to be preferable to the uncertainty of what might face them at sea. By midday of December 10, Manila Bay held a total of at least sixty large merchant ships.[2] That morning -- given ample warning of the approach of enemy planes -- American fighters intercepted eighty enemy bombers escorted by fifty-two fighters at a position north of Clark Field. Far outnumbered and outclassed in maneuverability by the Japanese Zeros, the American fighters were soon rendered hors de combat, allowing the Japanese to fly unencumbered to their selected target areas. Part of the enemy force struck at Nichols and other airfields -- targets only lightly damaged during the raid of two days prior; but the largest part of the raid was reserved for the naval base at Cavite. Approaching Cavite at an altitude beyond the range of anti-aircraft fire, the bombers turned the naval base into an inferno. En route, the Japanese pilots attacked targets of opportunity -- namely, the shipping in Manila Bay, but because the enemy's primary target was Cavite, the shipping at Manila got off lightly with only three ships hit -- two seriously, the third suffering only light damage from shrapnel.[3] A more fruitful target would have been the city's docks; but for the time being, they had been spared.

---

[2]   *Manila Pilots Association Record of Incoming and Outgoing Shipping for November and December 1941.* See RG-407, PAC, Box 1566, Folder - Marine Statistics Branch.
[3]   One ship seriously hit was the Philippine-registered freighter *Sagoland.* Set ablaze, she had to be abandoned, foundering and sinking the next day. One slightly damaged ship was the American-owned tanker *Gertrude Kellogg.* Source: RG-407, PAC, Box 1565, Folder - Maritime Matters. Also, affidavit of Alfredo de Leon, RG-407, PAC, Box 1566, Folder - Marine Statistics Branch. The owners of the British, Hong Kong-

By the second week of December, American air power had been reduced to fourteen B-17s, and there were not enough fighter planes left to provide the B-17s with even a modicum of protection. In full realization of that inadequacy, and with MacArthur's approval, his air commander Maj. General Brereton, ordered the B-17s south to Darwin, Australia. Naval defenses had also been whittled drastically by the casualties suffered on December 10. In compliance with *War Plan Rainbow 5,* most of the Navy's remaining ships departed Manila to assist the British and the Dutch in defending the Malay Barrier. Left at Manila were only two destroyers (which were to be ordered to Java on December 26); three submarines; three river gunboats; three minesweepers; a squadron of PT boats; and a handful of service craft.[4] The supplies and munitions that escaped destruction at Cavite were ferried either to Corregidor or Manila aboard a variety of craft hired by the Naval Port Director at Manila.[5]

The Withdrawal Phase

Given the prospect that the Japanese landings would remain low in troop strength, MacArthur believed that the enemy could be repulsed at the beachheads. However, that hope had been quickly shattered when between December 22 and 24 large numbers of enemy troops had come ashore at Lingayen Gulf in northwestern Luzon and at Lamon Bay south of Manila on Luzon's east coast. The locations that had been chosen by the Japanese for their landings had been predicted well in advance by MacArthur's staff as choices that could best serve an enemy's tactical envelopment of Manila. The danger in this lay with a Japanese offensive coming simultaneously from the north and from the south. If developed swiftly, that could cut

---

registered *Taiyuan* state that its ship was also hit. Taking on water, *Taiyuan* was beached, and cement boxes were poured to close off damage to the hull. After being pulled off the beach, she allegedly left for Soerabaja, Java. However, within the reports of the Manila Pilots Association for December of 1941, there is no record of the *Taiyuan's* entry or departure from Manila. None of the Army or Navy accounts mention her there nor do they mention her being hit in the attacks. In Chapter XV, we will take up the story of *Taiyuan* following her appearance at Soerabaja.

[4]   Also under naval command was the 4th Marine Regiment which had recently been evacuated from China. With the withdrawal onto Bataan, the Marines would be placed under MacArthur's overall USAFFE command. An excellent first hand account of the U. S. naval situation in the Philippines at the time of the attack is to be found in Adm. Kemp Tolley, *Cruise of the* Lanikai, (Annapolis: Naval Institute Press, 1973). Tolley, a lieutenant at the time of the attack, witnessed the air attack at Cavite.

[5]   The policy for the utilization of merchant vessels and small craft by both the Navy and the Army during the first two weeks of the war in the Philippines was to hire them from local shipping firms at a daily rate or on termed time charter. Most of the Filipino vessels hired by the Navy prior to the withdrawal to Bataan were later turned over by the Navy to ATS control. Before December 24, commercial vessels do not appear to have been bareboat chartered by either the Army or the Navy, and only a few were seized, most of the latter being cases where their owners could not be located. Source: *Interview Conducted by Office of the General Counsel, Department of the Navy, Washington, DC, 26 February 1946, with former Commander Charles Parson, USNR, Office of the Port Director, USN, Manila (1941).* This interview is to be found within RG-407, PAC, Box 1565, Folder - ATS. Also see statement by Col. Richard G. Rogers, QMC, taken following his repatriation as a POW of the Japanese in 1945. Rogers claimed that prior to December 24, 1941, the owners paid the crews and furnished all supplies. Following that date, *...it became the policy of the Army to pay the crews and furnish all necessary supplies for the vessel.* Source: RG-407, PAC, Box 1568, Folder - Status of ATS Employees. Our in-depth perusal of other archival records substantiates Rogers's statement. Following December 24, the ATS began instituting bareboat charters. See our Appendix G for a sample of the standard charter form which was employed following December 24.

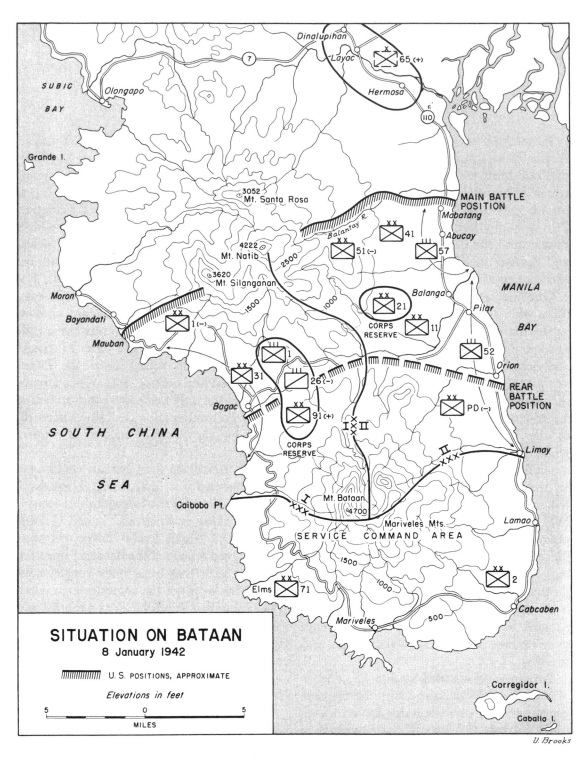

SITUATION ON BATAAN
8 January 1942

|||||||||| U. S. POSITIONS, APPROXIMATE

Elevations in feet

5   0   5

MILES

U. Brooks

This chartlet depicts the Main Line of Resistance (MLR) as well as the secondary position
as of January 8, 1942. By January 26, troops had withdrawn to the secondary position
which then became the MLR.

off MacArthur's North and the South Luzon Defense Forces from each other and prevent one or both of those forces from making their way safely onto the Bataan peninsula, that being the withdrawal strategy envisioned under *War Plan Orange 3*. To keep that from happening, on December 23, MacArthur ordered that *War Plan Orange 3* be put into full effect. Under that plan, MacArthur's North Luzon Defense Force under Maj. Gen. Jonathan M. Wainwright was to begin staged withdrawals to Bataan, allowing as much time as could be safely factored for movement of supplies onto Bataan and for the preparations of defensive positions there. Maj. Gen. George M. Parker, commanding the South Luzon Defense Force, was to move northward; and in conjunction with Wainwright's force, it was also to move onto Bataan. That same day (December 23), Parker was replaced by Maj. Gen. Alfred M. Jones, Parker having been ordered to proceed without delay to Bataan to supervise the preparation of defensive positions there.

By December 30th, the bulk of the South Luzon Defense Force had passed along the southern shore of the Laguna de Bay preparatory to moving northward toward Manila when Jones received orders to stop his withdrawal and hold position so as to allow more time for Parker to get supplies onto Bataan.[6] That order was rescinded within the hour by MacArthur's headquarters with the explanation that the Japanese were closely pressing Wainwright and that the enemy might soon be in position to cut Jones off from reaching Bataan. The South Luzon Defense Force still had over 90 miles to go before gaining the defensive positions being established by Parker. Despite the distance and the rugged terrain over which Jones was moving his force, the southern command joined Wainwright's at the road junction at San Fernando on the first of January. From San Fernando, both forces deployed onto the Bataan peninsula.

On January 7, the Bataan Defense Force was consolidated, having been created out of Jones's and Wainwright's forces. The initial defensive line was divided into two sectors, the west sector placed under Wainwright and the east sector under Parker. The sectors locked together on a high mountain ridge running along the spine of the upper Bataan peninsula. Behind the primary defense line, the rear echelon area was 22 miles in depth before reaching the shoreline of Manila Bay. Three miles distant over water from there lay the island fortress of Corregidor.

Elsewhere in the Philippines

The Japanese plan for its initial conquest of the Philippines was at first concentrated on the island of Luzon. A small enemy force had been landed on Mindanao on December 20, an effort launched in the optimistic belief that victory there would be easy. That was a premise that proved more difficult than they envisioned. Part of that enemy landing force, after failing to penetrate inland, was withdrawn and ordered to occupy Jolo, a small island between southern Mindanao and northern Borneo. Offensive movements south of Luzon would consist of naval patrols and small unit actions up to April 1942 when an overall movement was begun against the rest of the archipelago.

---

[6]   Morton, pp 199, 200.

The American defense of the islands south of Luzon was initially vested with the Visayan- Mindanao Force under the command of Brig. Gen. William F. Sharp. The Visayan- Mindanao Force consisted almost entirely of Filipino infantry units with garrisons on Mindanao, Cebu, Panay, Negros Oriental, Negros Occidental, Leyte, and Samar.

Manila Evacuated

Following the elimination of American air power, there was virtually nothing in the way of defenses to protect shipping in Manila Bay.[7] With the exception of two or three naval vessels present in the Manila anchorage area, none of the ships carried armaments. The only anti-aircraft defenses were those guns located on distant Corregidor; and as events were to prove, even they were far from sufficient. The situation appeared hopeless, a fact accurately appreciated by Admiral Hart and his staff. On December 12, a meeting was called at the Naval Port Director's Office on the harbor front.[8] Invited to attend were ship owners and agents as well as any ship masters who could be reached. Those present were handed copies of a memorandum from Admiral Hart stating that the Navy could not give effective protection to shipping either at Manila or anywhere else in the South China Sea. Advised that Manila Bay was to be reopened to ship departures, those who wished to send their ships out would be given guided passage through the minefields beginning at 1800 hours that evening. Among the owners, agents, and ship masters, the reception to this was mixed. Many elected to leave immediately; however, others decided to first discharge their cargoes, and a few elected to stay -- a decision based on the belief that the Japanese would not take Manila and that the place provided a safer alternative than the risks awaiting ships at sea. Those who chose to leave were instructed that if capture appeared imminent, they were to scuttle their ships.[9]

The pier area at Manila had become a scene of frantic activity aimed at getting those ships at the piers unloaded so others could come in to discharge. One of the more valuable cargoes was aboard the *Don Jose*. Under charter to a Canadian firm, she carried motorized gun carriages and trucks that had been consigned to the British at Hong Kong. At the news of the Japanese attack, her master had diverted into Manila where MacArthur's headquarters, apprised by port authorities of the cargo, wired Washington for permission to seize it. After consulting with the Canadian government, Washington gave its permission. The vehicles were unloaded, assembled, and made serviceable with the aid of civilian mechanics from automotive firms in the city, after which the assembled vehicles were rushed to units in the field. Other cargoes taken

---

[7]   Both the naval anchorage and the commercial anchorage at Manila were devoid of anti-aircraft protection. For the situation at Manila Bay prior to the Japanese attack, see "Minutes of the Joint Board," discussion of 3 November 1941 by the Joint Army-Navy Board in Washington which culminated with the viewpoint to put off *the war with Japan for as long as possible,* a conclusion formulated because of a general lack of preparedness on the part of the United States, particularly in the Philippines.

[8]   Most of the accounts found within RG-407, PAC, claim the date of this meeting as being December 12; however two affidavits taken after the war claim it was December 14.

[9]   1st Lt. John O. Zimmerman, *My Report of the History of the War.* Zimmerman was Assistant Operations Officer, ATS, Corregidor, 1941 - 42. From RG-407, PAC, Box 12.

ashore were moved out of the pier area as fast as possible so visibly stacked materiel would not be an attraction to Japanese bombers over-flying the pier area.

In what little has been published regarding port activity in Manila between December 10 and December 31, 1941, the impression has been given that the control of the piers and the operation of harbor craft was orchestrated by the U.S. Navy's Port Director. However, as the archival records bear out, this was only true until December 15; thereafter, control of the piers passed to Col. Frederick A. Ward, Superintendent of the Army Transport Service (ATS). The Navy, lacking crews, took over only one tug (*Henry Keswick)* and a few launches.[10] All other harbor craft as well as larger shipping came under the direction of the ATS.

On December 14, air raids against the harbor's outer anchorage area resumed with increasing frequency; but as before, the inner harbor was spared.[11]

On December 24, owners and/or agents of Filipino companies operating interisland freighters and tankers as well as those owning local towing and barge companies were summoned to the office of Manila Harbor Traffic Control. Addressed there by Lt. Col. Richard G. Rogers, the attendees were requested to turn over to the ATS control of all interisland freight and tank vessels then at Manila while the owners of towing and barge companies were asked to have their craft made available for call-up.[12] [13]

On December 26, General MacArthur declared Manila an *open city.* The civilian population as well as the American military was immediately made aware of this either through direct communication or through the local media.[14] Tokyo Radio acknowledged receipt of the announcement that night; however, the Japanese Army's Imperial General Headquarters in Tokyo did not formally forward the information to its

---

[10]   At the end of December, the *Henry Keswick* earlier under naval direction but having been deserted by her British merchant crew, lay unattended behind the Manila breakwater. On January 2, an ATS volunteer crew took her under tow. Undetected by the Japanese, she was taken to Corregidor.

[11]   The documentation within the Philippine Archive Collection (PAC) differs widely as to when the inner harbor was first bombed, some reports and affidavits claiming it was December 24 and others December 27. The best evidence points to attacks on the inner harbor beginning on the 24th and against the docks on the Pasig River on the 27th.

[12]   As most of the relevant affidavits found in RG-407 attest, the *request* of December 24 was more of a requisition. The exigency of that moment was such that the owners and agents were told that receipts for the vessels would be immediately issued, to be followed up as soon as circumstances allowed by formal charter parties protecting the owners against losses. Most accounts indicate that the crews were to be paid the standard Filipino seamen's wages plus 100% to cover war risk.

[13]   Archival documentation covering the requisitioning of Filipino vessels at Manila is within the following: RG-407, PAC, Box 1565, Folder "Maritime Matters" (Affidavits of Fernando Guerrero, Purser for Aboitiz and Co., Inc.); *History of ATS Activities in Manila and Cebu,* Archive file 500-21 to be found in RG-407, PAC, Box 1568. *History of ATS Activities in Manila and Cebu* is a lengthy but largely illegible document which appears to have been microfilmed from either an onion skin copy or from a 2-sided mimeographed copy since on some of its pages *bleeding* of type occurred from the back side onto the front. In August of 2000, we had that document digitally enhanced enabling a transcription of 95% of the first part of the report and 45%-50% of the remainder. The probability is that it was prepared by ATS participates who composed it from notes preserved during their captivity as POWs of the Japanese.

[14]   According to Morison in *Rising Sun in the Pacific, p* 195, Admiral Hart was not earlier notified of the declaration of Manila's open city status and its subsequent abandonment. The result, as Hart would later state, was that the Navy was unable to remove supplies and other materials which could have aided the maintenance of Hart's submarine force in the days that followed.

commander in the Philippines until December 28 and in turn that commander did not inform his subordinate units until December 31.[15]

What probably provoked the Japanese attack against the dock area -- *open city* status notwithstanding -- was the existence of seven merchant ships anchored in close proximity to each other just above the Jones Bridge near the entrance to the Pasig River.[16] On the morning of December 27, the Collector of Customs ordered all shipping out of the inner harbor and the dock areas. Concern over the presence of shipping at the piers heightened during the noon hour when the Japanese launched an unusually heavy raid -- this time directly against the docks. Two hours later, they again struck. Nearby buildings were destroyed including a church and part of the Santa Rosa College complex. By the following morning, all of the ships -- including the seven at anchor near the Jones Bridge -- were without their crews, the raids having caused panic among them. In a last ditch effort to get the inner harbor and the Pasig River emptied of shipping, the tug *La Florecita* was commandeered by naval officers -- its Filipino skipper subsequently volunteering to do whatever he could to move those ships still afloat out into the outer harbor anchorage. The crew of *La Florecita,* joined by a number of American officers from the adjacent naval headquarters and some Filipino employees from the Customs office, managed to move the seven ships that were near the Jones Bridge along with two others laying alongside a pier. Once out of the inner harbor, most of the ships were cast adrift because of difficulties encountered in releasing their anchor windless brakes. Six more ships, located in the Pasig River and unable to be moved due to bomb damage or because of their difficult locations, were scuttled in place, their superstructures dynamited so that from the air they would resemble wrecks -- this having been done in the hope that further air raids could be avoided.[17]

---

[15] It seems probable, though, that the Japanese commanders in the Philippines would have received notification via the Tokyo Radio announcement of December 26.

[16] Under International Law, the term *open city* applies to a population area within which all defensive activity has ceased and where no opposition is to be offered against entry by an enemy. Conversely, and upon receipt of such a declaration, an attacker must stop all offensive action pending his entry to such a place. Japanese Army aircraft flying bombing missions against the Manila metropolitan area ceased on December 27; but bombing raids conducted by Japanese naval aircraft against the harbor's shipping lasted until December 31. There is nothing which discloses when the Japanese Navy was made aware of the open city status. The naval aircraft raids were concentrated against the port area, but the bombing also damaged and destroyed a number of buildings within the adjacent business district. At the same time, American military personnel who remained in Manila through the nighttime hours of December 31 were occupied in demolition and with moving supplies from the city over to Corregidor and Bataan. Therefore, the inescapable facts hold that both the Americans and the Japanese were in technical violation of the *open city* doctrine -- the Japanese Navy by its bombing and the Americans by transshipping from the city materiel to be later used in military operations. For further discussion of Japanese reaction to the open city declaration, see Alvin P. Stauffer, *The Quartermaster Corps: Operations in the War Against Japan,* (Washington, DC: Office of Chief of Military History, 1956), pp 12, 13.

[17] Memorandum No. 4 dated Ft. Mills, January 14, 1942. (Report made by Lt. F. L. Worcester, USNR.) Source: RG-407, PAC, Box 1566, Folder Marine Statistics Branch. Also see RG-407, PAC, Box 1570. What of those ships removed from the inner harbor at Manila by *La Florecita*? The *Magallanes* and *Dos Hermanos,* having been cast loose by the tug *La Florecita,* were later reported sunk in the outer bay area. According to one account, *Dos Hermanos* was refloated by the Japanese and renamed *Himeno Maru*. The *Palawan* was scuttled on December 29, to be later salvaged by the Japanese and renamed *Pran Maru*. The freighter *Bohol II* was to become one of three ships engaged in a later effort to supply beleaguered Bataan with foodstuffs from the southern islands. Two of the ships which received heavy bomb damage making them incapable of being moved from the Pasig River were *Bicol* and *Anakan*. The U.S. Army Harbor Boat *General Miley,* which had also

On December 28, the Navy ordered all remaining merchant shipping which was not being utilized by either the Army or the Navy to evacuate Manila Bay. American and British masters were advised to head south to Australia or to the southern Dutch East Indies for further routing instructions. Filipino coasters not already requisitioned by the ATS were to proceed to one of the southern Philippine islands. All small craft, inclusive of tugs, launches, and barges, were to remain at Manila awaiting the ATS's determination as to how they might best be put to use.

~

As the ships departed, they left behind a bay littered with wrecks and rising smoke from fires at the bomb-damaged dock area and from burning fuel tanks adjacent to the harbor. Manila, once the jewel of the Philippines and a monument to the benevolence of an American occupation which had lasted 43 years, was never to be the same again.[18]

~

One of the strange things about that last week prior to the entrance of Manila by the Japanese were attitudes held by the majority of the American and European civilians residing at Manila. The general belief at the time seems to have been that a Japanese occupation, although unpleasant, would not be catastrophic, nor would it be long lasting. This optimism was to an extent fostered by governmental authorities such as when Francis B. Sayre, the United States High Commissioner to the Philippines, assured the city's population on December 16 that early-on military assistance from the United States was a certainty. Remembering those last days before the Japanese occupation, A. V. H. Hartendorp, who was then the Editor of *Philippine Magazine,* recalls that an almost holiday spirit seemed to exist. Morton relates that night clubs, hotels, and cabarets remained open on New Year's Eve and that a dance was even held at the Manila Hotel, *to which ladies attended -- many dressed in evening gowns.* Although it was general knowledge that the Japanese had been guilty of unspeakable atrocities, including massive rape when occupying Chinese cities, few

---

received heavy bomb damage while in the Pasig River was towed clear. Later, the *La Florecita* was sent to Corregidor where she grounded, her crew abandoning her. She was repaired by the ATS, but was later either scuttled on ATS orders or sunk by enemy action at the time of the Japanese occupation of the port of Mariveles on Bataan.

[18] By December 29, at least twenty large ships were already on the bottom, either at the Manila docks or within the anchorage areas. Across the bay off Corregidor, there were other ships that had been sunk or damaged beyond capability of further movement. Some of the wrecks of those ships lost at Manila Bay in December 1941, as well as Japanese ships sunk or scuttled during the recapture of the Philippines by American forces three years later, still litter the bottom and are considered a present danger to navigation as stipulated within *Sailing Directions, Philippine Islands,* (Washington, DC: U.S. Defense Mapping Agency, 1996). The journey to safety for those ships which escaped from Manila would not prove easy. To give but two examples: The *USAT Liberty,* an Army freighter that had left Manila in late November after discharging ordnance and other military cargo, had gone to Borneo and then Java to take on rubber for her return voyage to San Francisco. After leaving Java, she was transiting the Badung Straits when she was torpedoed by a Japanese submarine. Japanese air attack claimed other victims, as in the case of *Ruth Alexander* which left Manila December 28; she was sunk by bombing in the proximity of Balikpapan, Borneo. Once ships were clear of the Southwest Pacific area, the route across the Pacific had its own hazards created by the presence of Japanese submarines operating south of the Hawaiian Islands and along the west coast of the United States.

westerners residing in the Philippines believed that the Japanese would dare perpetrate such outrages against American or European citizens.[19]

Onto Bataan

According to *War Plan Orange 3*, supplies to last 43,000 troops for a 6-month defense were to be moved on to Bataan and Corregidor. As of the first week of January 1942, that planned-for number of troops would be exceeded by another 63,000 persons -- a number which included Filipino refugees who had fled to Bataan to escape the Japanese. A failure of *War Plan Orange 3* was that its planners had envisioned having ample time to move in supplies before the Bataan peninsula was cut off from the rest of Luzon. But as things developed, the reality was that only a single week would be available. Not only had the time been shortened, but there had been a severe lack of ground transportation.[20] The withdrawal was carried out with such haste that a considerable part of the supplies stockpiled in depots at Wainwright's rear during his retreat had to be abandoned or else were overlooked.[21] There seemed to be little possibility of holding out beyond the coming spring -- well short of the six months envisioned under *War Plan Orange 3*. As early as January 6, the food shortages would be recognized as being critical, and troop rations were then ordered cut by half. The future promised only slow starvation, a situation which was to create a fertile environment for demoralization and disease.

One bright spot within the logistical chaos had been that immediately following the opening of hostilities, Brig. Gen. Charles C. Drake, MacArthur's Chief Quartermaster, had instructed the commander of the Quartermaster depot in the Manila area to impound anything that was stacked on the Manila docks or in covered storage that could be considered as having military value. That materiel was therefore available on December 23 when the order came to move supplies over to Bataan.

During the time frame between December 12 and December 26, a certain amount of military materiel had been shipped from Manila to the military's depots in the southern islands, but how much was sent south is unclear. One known shipment consisted of balanced rations and artillery weapons consigned to the Quartermaster and Ordnance depots at the port of Cebu, island of Cebu, which were

---

[19]   Concerning the subject of rape against American and other Occidental women, the confidence exhibited by those in Manila in December 1941 proved to be well placed. As can best be determined from accounts on the Japanese occupation of the Philippines, there was a near total absence of assaults against American or European women either prior to or following their interments. Neither were atrocities committed against the Army and Navy nurses who were captured at Corregidor.

[20]   An additional difficulty encountered in getting foodstuffs onto Bataan was a hindrance displayed by civil officials in the rural provinces who were fearful of depriving the Filipino populations in their districts. There were even cases where foodstuffs, earlier purchased by the Army Quartermaster for the Army's own use, were denied the Army by some civil administrators. This was partially the Army's own undoing as some of the quartermaster officers serving with Wainwright -- long conditioned to acceptance of requests made of them by the civilian government arm -- respected the administrators' refusals.

[21]   The supply situation on Bataan is well covered in Brig. Gen. Charles C. Drake's *Operations of the Quartermaster Corps, Philippine Islands, July 27, 1941, to May 6, 1942*, Part I, p 21, to be found in Records of the Adjutant General, Report of Operations, Quartermaster Corps, WW II, National Archives.

loaded aboard the Filipino cargo-passenger ship *Corregidor*.[22]   Colonel Ward had arranged with the *Corregidor's* owners to take aboard the Army cargo at the standard tariff freight rate, leaving the owners the right, if they wished, to also book commercial passengers.   The latter arrangement turned out to have tragic consequences for the nearly one thousand Filipinos who bought tickets.   The *Corregidor* left Manila on December 16 and had supposedly cleared the defensive minefield when she struck a mine, sinking almost immediately and taking with her all but 283 of her more than one thousand passengers and crew.[23]

When the movement of supplies to the Bataan peninsula began, they initially went by overland route; but the roadways were so heavily congested with refugees that movement was at a snail's pace.   Complicating matters, enemy air raids had destroyed most of the railroad bridges leading north from Manila, making movement by rail almost impossible.   The only means thus available was to send everything which went to Bataan from Manila across the bay by boat.   Interisland coasters together with tugs and steam launches towing barges made up the bulk of the vessels utilized for the evacuation.[24]   Because of the constant danger of enemy air attack, this movement had to be done under cover of darkness.

Once boats arrived off Bataan, discharging of cargo would prove slow and difficult.   What there was by way of pier facilities at Mariveles and at the other selected navigation points along Bataan's eastern coast was primitive and proved totally insufficient to handle the volume of traffic being sent.   Over-the-beach discharge off the communities of Limay, Lamao, and Cabcaben was contemplated, but that proved impractical due to onshore winds which produced overly rough conditions.

A critical need had arisen for labor, both for vessel crews and for stevedores, much of the regular labor force having deserted Manila's waterfront area

---

[22]   *Corregidor* had begun her career prior to World War I under the British flag as a cross-channel passenger vessel.   During 1915, she became *HMS Engadine,* being converted by the Royal Navy to a seaplane carrier.   As *HMS Engadine,* she participated with Rear Adm. David Beatty's cruisers at the Battle of Jutland. Although her pilots did not succeed in locating the German battle fleet, *HMS Engadine* later took the disabled *HMS Warrior* in tow; and when that cruiser foundered, rescued most of its crew.   *Engadine* was sold out from the British flag after that war.

[23]   A postwar compensation claim was filed on behalf of the *Corregidor's* owners, Compania Maritima. The claim's basis was that the loss of the ship was the responsibility of the U.S. Army.   That claim was disallowed.   Heirs of the lost crewmembers filed their own claims under the Missing Persons Act, arguing that the crew had been made Army employees on the questionable basis that the Army had offered them a danger bonus.   Those claims were also denied.   Information on the *Corregidor* claims cases -- both regarding the shipping company and the heirs -- is contained within RG-407, PAC, Box 1568, Folder - "*Corregidor*".

Corregidor was not the first vessel to go down as a result of striking a mine at the entrance to Manila Bay.   On November 19 the sail vessel *Del Pido* went down from the same cause with the loss of half her 12-man crew.   Information on *Del Pido* is from *Lloyd's War Losses.*

[24]   Towing launches were the most common craft available at Manila where they were normally employed for moving barges and scows.   Most were fairly seaworthy with a capability of making interisland passages in fair weather.   These launches were described by Hale L. Hutchins in an article titled "We Were There, Too" which appeared in the July 1947 issue of *Mast Magazine* (initially a War Shipping Administration publication continued by the Maritime Commission following the dissolution of the WSA in 1946).   Hutchins's description: *...old fashioned steam launches approximately 40' long and powered by compound* [steam] *engines.*   Prior to 1938, the annual publication *U.S. Merchant Vessels,* listed vessels of the Philippine Island merchant marine, inclusive of many of these launches.   From that source we can conclude that on average, they were between 25 and 50 gross tons and so between 35 and 75 feet length overall.   Most, but not all, were coal burning.

because of the bombings.[25] To supplement the manpower shortage, the ATS called for volunteers from the city's American and European business community, a call that was responded to even though the majority of those who volunteered were businessmen totally unused to the hard physical labor which would be entailed. Once on the job, most of them stuck it out, working extremely long shifts under the constant threat of air attack.

The greatest shortage was for skilled seamen to handle the tugs and launches. There were a number of American and European merchant seamen then located in the city who had no direct ties to ships. Among these were Americans -- at least 130 in number. The willingness among that group to volunteer was not high, judging from what occurred on December 31 near the conclusion of the evacuation of supplies from Manila.[26] Army officers asked for seamen to accompany the Army to Bataan and Corregidor, but the spirit of volunteerism on the part of American and European merchant seamen was low. Only fifteen of the American seamen volunteered -- the majority choosing instead to remain in demilitarized Manila despite the fact that the city would soon be occupied by the Japanese.[27]

~

---

[25] The affidavit of Alfredo de Leon, Insular Collector of Customs at Manila, states that following the initial bombing of ships in the outer harbor on December 10, Japanese attacks against ships at anchor outside the breakwater did not resume until December 14 after which the bombing attacks became heavy and frequent. He confirms the statement of others who were there that the bombings directed at the inner harbor shipping did not begin until December 24. RG-407, PAC, Box 1566, Folder Marine Statistics Branch.

[26] Hale L. Hutchins, a participant in the evacuation of supplies from Manila, and when writing of it in *Mast,* stated that only about twenty Americans responded to the Army's request for volunteers. The estimated 130 American seamen ashore in Manila, as of December 24, included 69 crewmembers from the U.S. flagship *Ruth Alexander* and *President Grant* who had been left behind when their ships departed for sea. The *President Grant* had left Manila precipitously, leaving behind crewmembers who were ashore on authorized shore leave. Those left behind from the *Ruth Alexander* had disobeyed the master's orders, being absent from their ship outside of the prescribed hours designated by the master for shore leave. They were later listed by the master as deserters. (The desertion charges were dropped following the war.) Another thirty seamen consisted of those crewmen from *Capillo* who had not been injured when that ship had been set afire and was abandoned as a result of the December 10 bombings. Additionally, there were around three dozen others who possessed American merchant seamen's documents but who had no known ship affiliation, being either between ships or living in Manila when they were engaged in shoreside employment. Indications are that most, if not all of these men were contacted by the ATS through shipping company agents and were asked to volunteer their services.

[27] The absence of motivation to volunteer for hazardous duty, as was exhibited by the majority of the beached American merchant seamen at Manila, was not a universal characteristic of the American merchant mariner. Many acts of courage would be exhibited on the part of merchant ship crews -- both in the Pacific and in the Atlantic during the months to come. One early example took place in Honolulu during March of 1942 where plans were taking form to send the merchant ship *Thomas Jefferson* to the Philippines with relief foodstuffs. William A. Parta, then the ATS Marine Superintendent at Honolulu, was asked to approach the officers and crew of the *Thomas Jefferson* and offer them whatever was necessary in bonuses, explaining that the mission they were to be asked to perform involved extreme danger which could very well mean capture and imprisonment by the enemy, and that the ship would be rigged with demolition charges since to surrender it would be out of the question. According to Parta, to a man the crew agreed to go, even turning down the bonus offer, asking only for extra insurance payable to their beneficiaries. Prior to sailing, the merchant crew of the *Thomas Jefferson* was replaced by naval personnel, it having been decided that it was too dangerous a mission on which to send civilians. It was soon determined, however, that the risk would be so great as to be judged prohibitive, regardless of what crew was used. The relief mission was accordingly scratched. Source: Article -- part of a series -- appearing in *Amerikan Uutiset* March 20, 1986: "The Story of a New American and an Old Mariner," by William A. Parta.

Following the entry of the enemy, those who chose to remain in Manila, together with other American and allied civilians, were to find themselves incarcerated at civilian internment centers for what became a far longer period of time than many of them had probably envisioned.[28] For those men who had volunteered to serve with the ATS at Bataan and Corregidor, it was to be a much more difficult future -- three months of almost daily exposure to aerial bombing and at the end, artillery fire. Those who survived that were to face three years as prisoners of war under unimaginably harsh conditions. A number of them died in captivity. [29]

---

[28] For a detailed discussion of the detention of merchant marine personnel by the Japanese in the Philippines and elsewhere, see Charles D. Gibson, "Prisoners of War vs Internees: The Merchant Mariner Experience of World War II," *American Neptune,* Summer 1994, pp 187-193.

[29] Appendix I of this volume contains the names and fates, if known, of those Americans, together with citizens of Britain, Canada, and Norway who are named within the archival records as having chosen to volunteer for the ATS following the evacuation from Manila.

CHAPTER XII

THE SIEGE BEGINS

Prior to the outbreak of the war, the Office of the Superintendent, Army Transport Service (ATS), Philippines, reported directly to the Army's Quartermaster General, being in that respect organizationally autonomous from the rest of Quartermaster Corps operations in the Philippines. In 1941, the ATS Superintendent for the islands was Col. Frederick A. Ward. His responsibilities entailed the handling of all Army-related shipping and cargoes coming to or leaving from the Philippines. Colonel Ward's authority did not, however, include the management of the vessels or personnel of the Quartermaster Corps's Harbor Boat Service (HBS) -- that being an organization operated directly by the Chief Quartermaster, Philippines.

As previously mentioned, on July 29, 1941, the War Department had announced the pending creation of a new command to be known as U.S. Army Forces, Far East (USAFFE) at the head of which was placed Douglas MacArthur.[1] Under USAFFE fell all U.S. Army units in the Philippines as well as those units of the Philippine Army then under schedule for mobilization. Prior to that organizational change, Colonel Ward had been a member of MacArthur's staff coordinating ATS movements with the supply functions of Brig. Gen. Charles C. Drake, Chief Quartermaster of the U.S. Army's Philippine Department. Under the USAFFE arrangement which was scheduled to take effect on January 1, 1942, Colonel Ward's ATS operation was to be made a direct part of Drake's Quartermaster Corps command. With the advent of the Japanese invasion in early December, that time table was advanced, and the USAFFE command entity went into immediate effect. As of

---

[1]   Shortly after the creation of USAFFE, Douglas MacArthur was elevated in rank to 4-star general. During 1944, he would receive his fifth star.

that point, the vessels and personnel of the Harbor Boat Service and the activities of the ATS were amalgamated, with Colonel Ward assigned to head up both of those activities.

When the U.S. Army's overall reorganizations of March 1942 went into effect, the ATS was removed as a function of the Quartermaster Corps and placed under the newly formed Service of Supply; but this was not made to apply to the Philippines. There, the ATS function would stay part of the USAFFE Quartermaster function, remaining so until the time of the surrender of the Philippines in May 1942.

Theoretically, all movement by water in the Philippines dealing with troops and military supply was to be orchestrated under the direction of Colonel Ward. However, as a practical matter, Ward's direct supervision applied only to that part of the archipelago where there was an ATS presence.

Beginning with the evacuation from Manila, ATS headquarters was established in company with other Quartermaster functions at Fort Mills on Corregidor. ATS sub-offices would be established at Cabcaben on Bataan; and later at Cebu City on the island of Cebu as well as at Iloilo on the island of Panay.[2] Wherever an ATS officer was not present at a port (a circumstance which encompassed the majority of the islands to the south of Luzon) but where there developed a military need for vessels, their requisitioning was carried out under the authority of the senior Army officer on the scene. Covering the period December 24, 1941, to May 6, 1942, the archival evidence indicates that close to 80% of those Filipino vessels in excess of 5 tons were taken under USAFFE --later U.S. Forces in the Philiippines (USFIP) -- control, either by direct authority of the ATS or by officers representing the Visayan-Mindanao force.[3] As far as can be ascertained, all formally executed charter parties were made under the signature of an ATS representative or of his designee -- none having been executed by the Visayan- Mindanao force.

Boat Lift From Manila

Considering the handicaps involved, the supply lift from Manila to Corregidor and Bataan had gone surprisingly well. Approximately three hundred vessels -- the majority manned by Filipino crews -- were employed at the height of that movement. These included coastal freighters, tugs, launches, barges, and scows. In terms of materiel evacuated, the boat lift from Manila translated into nearly 30,000 tons of dry cargo.[4] The movement of supply of all type made available at Bataan and Corregidor had been further increased on December 28 when the Navy's Port Director at Manila ordered merchant shipping then laying off that city to move to anchorages

---

[2]   Prior to the outbreak of the war, Cebu City was the location of a Quartermaster Depot; but there was no ATS presence until an office was established there in February 1942 under the command of Maj. Cornelius Z. Byrd.

[3]   In March 1942, the Visayan- Mindanao force was separated into two separate commands, the Visayan Force under Brig. Gen. Bradford G. Chynoweth and the Mindanao Force under Brig. Gen. William F. Sharp. However, probably for reasons of simplification, ATS reports, even after that command change, usually referred to these commands collectively by continuing to reference *the Visayan- MindanaoForce.*

[4]   "Report of Army Transport Service Activities in the Philippine Islands from 8 December 1941 to 6 May 1942" as compiled by Col. Frederick A. Ward, as annexed to *Report of Quartermaster Activities* by Brig. Gen. Charles C. Drake. Office of Chief of Military History, Historical Manuscript File, Call Number 8-5.10.

either off Corregidor or along the east coast of Bataan. A number of those ships incapable of movement under their own power, either because of bomb damage or the desertion of their crews, were taken across Manila Bay under tow. Although the evacuation of shipping from Manila was mainly carried out by night, the shift in shipping concentration soon became apparent to Japanese reconnaissance planes, and heavy air attacks occurred on January 4 and 5 against the anchorage off Bataan as well as that off Corregidor.

On January 2, the ATS formally took over the movement of all marine transportation, including several small craft previously employed under naval direction (the exception being the handful of naval craft left in the Philippines which were designated by USAFFE for combatant operations).[5] During the first week of January when navigation points on Bataan had been established by the ATS at Cabcaben, Lamao, and Mariveles, those places became scenes of hectic activity where stevedore gangs labored to unload the newly arrived ships, barges, and scows. To thwart enemy observation from the air, most of that unloading was done at night without lights with the vessels being dispersed come daylight to offlying anchorages. The major problem, Japanese air attacks aside, was difficulty encountered with the Filipino stevedores. To gather the needed gangs, Quartermaster officers had to make daily trips into the barrios and the surrounding countryside looking for willing workers.

Because of a shortage of large tugs, launches were the major means by which the barges and scows were brought to and from the anchorage areas for unloading. Launches were also used in assistance to the lighters employed in the unloading of merchant ships at anchor off the coast. The fleet of tugs and launches initially used in the evacuation from Manila had originally been adequate in number, but those numbers had dwindled when during the hours of darkness, and without authorization, a sizable number were taken by their crews back to Japanese-occupied Manila.[6]

Before the war, the Quartermaster Corps in the Philippines had come to rely less and less upon the vessels of its own Harbor Boat Service (HBS), instead calling upon local contractors to supply whatever marine transportation services the Army required. What vessels the HBS was still directly operating by 1941 were concentrated at Corregidor, being used there for the direct support of that installation and its satellite facilities. At the time of the Japanese attack, the HBS possessed only three small cargo/passenger vessels and seven launches. The HBS inventory suffered badly during the first week of the attack when two of its cargo / passenger vessels were

---

[5]   When Adm. Thomas C. Hart left from Manila with those naval ships which were to be joined with the British and the Dutch defending the Malay Barrier. His orders from the Navy Department were to turn over to General MacArthur the command of any naval vessels as well as all naval and Marine Corps personnel remaining in the Philippines.

[6]   It is doubtful that the tugs and launches in which their crews absconded were scuttled by those crews upon arrival in Manila. Chances are that most were eventually utilized by the Japanese. Many Filipino craft which found employment under the Japanese were tugs, launches, and barges whose owners (some of Japanese heritage) had secreted them out of sight of U.S. requisitioning teams at the time of the evacuation from the city. Such small craft types were used in quantity by the Japanese during operations against American forces on Bataan. Source: Certificate of Col. Rosco Bonham, C.E., as given by way of his written testimony, October 30, 1945. RG-407, PAC, Box 1565 - Claims File.

either sunk or badly damaged.[7]   Despite those losses and the overnight disappearances of so many civilian-owned tugs and launches -- a blow to ATS capabilities -- enough small craft remained, together with their crews, to accomplish the tasks ahead, albeit at a lowered rate of speed and efficiency than would have otherwise been the case.

Prior to the outbreak of the war, the ATS had employed around two hundred fifty civilians, almost all of whom were Filipinos.   A report by Colonel Ward, submitted in 1945 following his release from POW camp, stated that a total of five hundred forty civilians had been directly employed by the ATS after the evacuation to Bataan and Corregidor.   It would therefore follow, assuming that close to the entirety of the prewar HBS work force had chosen to remain in the Army's service, that at least three hundred civilian volunteers augmented the HBS force during the siege.[8]

Navigation Points - Bataan

Following the withdrawal from Manila, all movement of troops and supplies by water was administered by Colonel Ward who, as already stated, directed operations from his ATS headquarters on Corregidor.   A satellite ATS office was established on Bataan's southeast coast at the town of Cabcaben, four miles directly across the North Channel from Corregidor.

The distribution of supplies on Bataan was over a surfaced road running through Cabcaben which connected with Mariveles to the west; thence paralleling Bataan's South China Sea coastline northward to the town of Mauban where the initial USAFFE defensive positions were anchored as of January 8.   The defensive line from Mauban then stretched eastward across the Bataan peninsula to the town of Mabatang fronting on Manila Bay.   From Mabatang, another surfaced road ran southward along the Manila Bay coastline, touching on the towns of Pilar, Orion, Limay, and Lamao,

---

[7]   The cargo / passenger vessels which the HBS had been operating prior to hostilities were its own *USHB General Miley* and *USHB General John McE. Hyde* as well as the time-chartered *Mambukal*.   The launches were: *Adams, Forby, Tilley, Geary, Mitchell, J. M. Jewell,* and *Maxwell*.   There were also two self-propelled lighters, ten motorized lorchas, and fourteen cargo scows.   In October 1941, the Quartermaster General's Office had requested of the Chief Quartermaster, Philippines, an updated list of the names of all HBS employees in the Philippines.   On November 19, this request was responded to and from that response the pre-hostility composition of the HBS, Philippines, can be ascertained, both as to the vessels in service and employees to the number of 249 men.   Judging by the rosters listing these employees, practically all of them possessed Hispanic names, indicating in all probability that they were Filipinos.   Source: RG-407, PAC, Box 1565, correspondence dated October 13, 1941, from Otto Totman, Captain, QMC, to QM Philippines and response to same by Lt. Col. Frank Brozina, QMC.

[8]   Col. Frederick A. Ward stated in a post-war report submitted after his release from captivity that immediately prior to the surrender of Corregidor (which occurred on May 6, 1942), the payrolls for those civilians employed by the Army Transport Service had been sent from Corregidor aboard a submarine and that those payrolls were later received by the War Department's Finance Office in Washington.   He stated that all ATS civilian employees were included on those payrolls.   (Accordingly, the Federal Civilian Employment Records which are now [2001] held at the Civilian Personnel Center at St. Louis, MO, should include the names with pay status and dates of service for each of those employees.)   Source: Ward's report, p 6, as annexed to the Drake Report, cite File 563-22 900 QM 563.3 T-N-4 Philippines, originally located (early post-war) at the Office, Chief of Transportation, War Department.   The Ward report is also held by the Office of Military History, Washington: Call No. 8-5.10.   Ward's report additionally references a list of photographs of vessels, shore facilities, and some personnel.   This list was forwarded [apparently from Corregidor on the same submarine] to the Quartermaster General.   The cite given for this was War Department File 563-22 900, which was at one time located within QM 413-3-TW.

connecting finally to the point of beginning at Cabcaben. Rations and munitions which were unloaded at the navigation points and which traveled this road system were moved to troop units along satellite dirt tracks.

Food and munitions were not the only commodities needed for the defense. Petroleum was vital to the mobility of the vehicles which moved on the roads. (The petroleum that was consumed during the siege of Bataan came mostly from three tankers brought over from Manila in late December and which were safely discharged at the navigation points.)[9] Coal was also an essential since it powered not only a number of electrical generating plants, but it also fueled the fire boxes of Colonel Ward's tugs and launches. Coal was available in sufficient quantity aboard the collier *Kaiping* which had been anchored at Sisiman Bay before being abandoned by her crew following a bombing attack. (Sisiman Bay was a small indentation off Mariveles Bay, located about a mile east of the town of Mariveles.) Working at night without lights and often standing waist-deep in water in the partially flooded cargo holds, Filipino laborers discharged from the *Kaiping* up to 20 tons of coal per night, transferring it onto barges laying alongside.[10]

During the first weeks of the siege, the Japanese, through an oversight on their part over the potential importance of the docking facilities at Cabcaben, Mariveles, and Lamao, neglected to bomb any of those three installations. Instead, they concentrated their air attacks on the scattered shipping offlying the Bataan coast. In early January, Ward's staff instituted a survey of that shipping and whatever it might contain to be considered useful. That survey included all ships, tugs, launches, and barges -- whether at anchor, sunk, or aground. Together, the tally came to slightly over 200 separate floating units. Not only were most of the vessel's cargoes deemed vital to the defense, but any ship equipage not considered immediately necessary for the operations of vessels was removed and stored ashore for later use when and wherever it might be required. Vessels aground were pulled clear and towed to designated anchorage areas where their cargoes were lightered ashore on the basis of the priority that the particular commodity or items of equipment might represent. Some ships and small craft proved too damaged to be moved, and those were left where they were, their cargoes to be unloaded to barges when time became available. By the end of January, practically everything considered useful had gone ashore and had either been moved by truck to forward depots or had been stashed away at the rear echelon supply dumps located at Cabcaben and Mariveles. The Japanese had failed to attack this salvage effort which was another error on their part, especially since the majority of the salvage was conducted during daylight hours, it being impossible to undertake such work in the dark. It would have been easy picking for aircraft and the resultant losses a serious blow to American forces. Such luck, however, was to be temporary. In early February, the pier at Lamao would be shelled from Manila Bay by Japanese warships; and on February 13, the navigation point at Cabcaben would be heavily bombed with

---

[9]   The amount of petroleum cargo taken to Bataan / Corregidor aboard three tank vessels is not stated within the Drake Report.

[10]   During March, attempts were made to relocate the partially foundered *Kaiping* from Sisiman Bay and bring the ship with its remaining coal cargo over to Corregidor. According to a participant in that effort: On the fourth attempt by the tug *Henry Keswick*, *Kaiping* was towed across the North Channel and anchored off Corregidor where part of her remaining cargo was barged ashore. Source: Hutchins, *Mast Magazine*.

the pier there set afire.[11] Mariveles was also bombed about that time; but its pier remained undamaged. Ward intended at one point to develop Sisiman Bay for bringing in supplies by employing an ingenious scheme of using two lighters, lashed together. These were to be pulled off the beach by a tug each evening at sunset and positioned to act as a pier for coasters and barges brought alongside for unloading. Shortly before daylight, the lighters were to be pushed back up onto the beach and quickly offloaded -- the coasters, or barges, being moved back to their anchorages. If performed as planned, it was hoped that the activity would escape detection by the enemy. At Ward's request, the Army Engineers constructed a roadway leading from the selected beach location connecting to the surfaced road described earlier. Ward's idea had been to construct the connector road in such a fashion that it would be concealed from the air, but in that the engineers either misunderstood or otherwise failed in the attempt as the road ended up as a naked gash through the jungle. This open invitation to observation from the air canceled out Sisiman as an offloading site.[12]

During January, in their quest to keep Wainwright's army fed, the Quartermasters established a fishery center at Lamao from which place Filipino fishermen sallied forth to produce catches which on one particular day reached as high as 12,000 pounds. The fishermen faced hazards not only from Japanese planes but from friendly troops as well who, in one instance, upon sighting the fishing boats working near the beaches, opened fire, apparently believing the fishermen to be Japanese infiltrators. That was enough for the fishermen who thereafter refused to leave port, eliminating what could have been a valuable source of protein. The rice-producing areas on Bataan, at least early in the siege, were mostly within USAFFE lines; however, the husking mills to process that rice were between the lines. This presented what at first seemed to be a dilemma -- and a very serious one since unhusked rice was virtually unusable. The problem was rectified through the heroic efforts of seven civil engineers -- Czech-Slovak civilians -- who had volunteered their services while in Manila, later accompanying the Army to Bataan. Crossing out between the lines, the Czech-Slovaks disassembled the rice mills -- a 36-hour job -- at times working under enemy fire. After they were brought back into the USAFFE perimeter lines and reassembled, the mills provided the means to process a rice crop that would not otherwise have been made part of the troop ration.[13] The temporary infusion of fish into the limited ration, and of course the rice which otherwise would have largely gone to waste helped out immeasurably. However, if MacArthur was to

---

[11]   The ATS instituted a nightly passenger and freight service from Corregidor, leaving there at 1900 hours for Cabcaben, returning from Cabcaben at 2000 hours. Lamao, which was initially used to receive some of the cargoes evacuated from Manila, was abandoned as a navigation point around mid-February. When blockade running started from the southern islands, the few ships which made it through unloaded at either Cabcaben or at Corregidor. This effort is discussed at length in Chapter XIII and XVII. Chapter XVII contains a list of vessels known to have participated as blockade runners. Following Chapter XVII are annotated listings of all vessels which participated in the internal defense of the Philippine Islands while under the aegis of USAFFE.

[12]   *History of ATS Activities in Manila and Cebu*, December 1941 to May 1942, RG-407, PAC, Box 1568.

[13]   According to an official military history, the reassembled mills, *in four weeks of operation turned out every day about 30,000 pounds of dehusked rice.* A letter written by Col. M. A. Quinn, QMC, following his release from Japanese prison describing the rescue of the rice mills has been reproduced as our Appendix H. We could not locate within the record anything to indicate that the Czech-Slovaks ever received the recognition that Colonel Quinn had sought for them.

maintain resistance for any length of time, foodstuffs of a more balanced nature and in far greater quantity, along with medicines and munitions, would have to be obtained either by way of the southern islands or directly from Australia or the United States. This would mean running the Japanese naval blockade, a most difficult undertaking since the approaches to Manila Bay were already being monitored by the Japanese Navy.

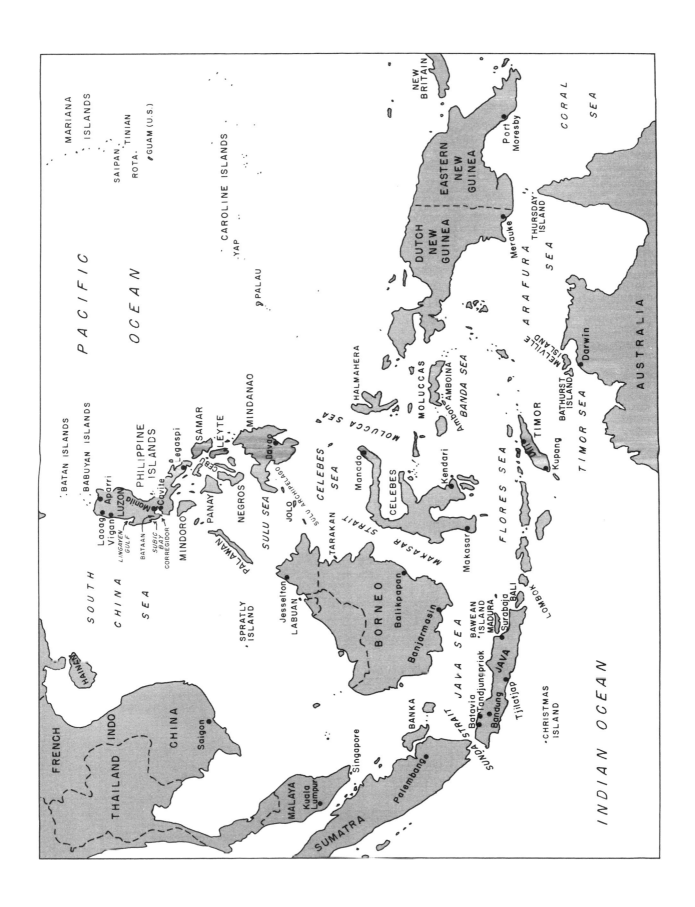

CHAPTER XIII

ATTEMPTS TO SUPPLY BATAAN AND CORREGIDOR FROM EASTERN AUSTRALIA: December 1941 - March 1942

On December 12, 1941, newly promoted Brig. Gen. Dwight D. Eisenhower was stationed at Fort Sam Houston, Texas, when he received orders to report to Washington. The Army's Chief of Staff, Gen. George Catlett Marshall had requested Eisenhower's presence because of his proven value as a staff planner and partly because of his experience during the mid-1930s as then Maj. Gen. Douglas MacArthur's deputy in the Philippines. Upon arrival in Washington the following day, Eisenhower was briefed by Marshall on the deteriorating situation in the Philippines. The Chief of Staff described the near total air and sea superiority held by the Japanese and the probability that Manila would fall with MacArthur being forced onto Bataan in a holdout operation. Supply-wise, it was believed that food and munitions would be sufficient for a limited time after which the survival of the Bataan force would be dependent on help from the outside. Marshall gave Eisenhower the task of recommending what the War Department's policy should be toward the support of MacArthur as well as the role of United States military presence in the Southwest Pacific. [1]

Returning to Marshall's office a few hours later, Eisenhower outlined his recommendations: Foremost, Australia must be held with a strong line of communication running to it from San Francisco as well as from the Panama Canal Zone. This line of communication would touch at the Hawaiian Islands and from there stretch southward to Tahiti, westward to Samoa (inclusive of the islands of New Caledonia and New Zealand) and terminate on Australia's east coast at the ports of Sydney, Melbourne, and Brisbane. Looking at the

---

[1] General Marshall was himself no stranger to the Philippines, having served two tours of duty there, the first in 1908 and the second in 1915.

long-term, Eisenhower felt Australia should become the launching pad for offensive actions against the Japanese. In the short term, his view was that the outlook for holding the Dutch East Indies was not much better than that for the Philippines. Eisenhower's opinion was that to send troop reinforcements to the Philippines would be overly risky given Japan's probable domination of the approaches by sea; however, a holding action, even though of a temporary nature, could be affected for the Dutch East Indies, provided those islands were immediately infused with American air power. With that in place, they could become a base point from which fighter support could be sent to MacArthur. They could also provide ports of departure for supply ships attempting to reach the Philippines. Airlifts of supplies directly to the Philippines as well as supply runs by ship from Australia might prove perfectly feasible, provided fighter air support and naval escort could be provided. His recommendations concluded with the statement that to do nothing would be viewed as an abandonment by the United States which would cause it to lose credibility, not only with the Filipinos but also with the peoples of China and the Dutch East Indies as well. Marshall immediately agreed which gives the distinct impression that as one familiar with the geopolitical factors inherent to the situation, this had also been his own feelings.[2]

Outbound from Hawaii at the time of the Japanese attack on Pearl Harbor was a convoy slated for Manila. Under the escort of the cruiser *USS Pensacola* and the sub-chaser *USS Niagara*, the convoy included the troop and supply ships *USAT Willard A. Holbrook, USAT Meigs, USS Republic, USS Chaumont,* and the chartered merchant ships *Admiral Halstead, Coast Farmer, and Bloemfontein.*[3] When news of the Japanese attack on Pearl Harbor was received in Washington, the convoy commander on *USS Pensacola* was contacted and ordered to bring the convoy into Suva in the Fiji Islands -- there to await further orders. Considerable discussion then followed between the War Department and the Navy Department as to whether the Pensacola Convoy should proceed to Manila or Australia, or whether it should return to Hawaii. The debate reached as high as the White House where President Roosevelt joined with those who advocated Australia as the destination. The question of whether the ships would continue on to the Philippines once they reached Australia was tabled, to be decided later.

On December 22, the day of the arrival of the Pensacola Convoy in Brisbane, a wireless message was received in Washington from the U.S. Embassy in Australia informing Washington that Australian naval authorities were of the opinion

---

2   Dwight D. Eisenhower, *Crusade in Europe,* (New York: Doubleday and Co., 1948), pp 13-22. Also Morton, who states (p 146) that upon first receiving news of the Japanese attack on the Philippines, Marshall had wired MacArthur that he had the complete confidence of the War Department and that MacArthur could expect *every possible assistance within our power.* This wireless was sent well before Eisenhower's summons to Washington.

3   The Pensacola Convoy carried War Department passengers and cargoes consisting of a field artillery brigade and a separate artillery regiment; ground crews for the Army Air Corps, 7th Bombardment Group; 18 P-40 fighters; 52 A-24 dive bombers; 500,000 rounds of 50-caliber ammunition, and 9600 rounds of 37 mm anti-aircraft ammunition; together with an assortment of vehicles and miscellaneous items. Also a number of casual officers, along with assorted Army service personnel as well as naval personnel, together with civilian construction workers, the latter aboard *USS Chaumont* and *USS Republic.*

that it might be practicable to send the ships of the convoy to a port in the Philippines, that being conditional on whether the U.S. Navy was in a position to provide adequate escort. The message went on to state, however, that a British Admiralty communication earlier received at Australian naval headquarters reported that the U.S. Navy Department had stated to the British that the troops and equipment of the Pensacola Convoy *May be very important to the defense of Port Darwin.* [4] The Australians had been taken by surprise over this since they were aware of a marked contradiction contained within directions recently sent by wireless from General Marshall to Brig. Gen. Julian F. Barnes, the senior Army officer accompanying the Pensacola Convoy. This informed Barnes that the Philippines were to receive the convoy's cargoes.[5] These contradictions were typical of the confusion which effected the U.S. Army command in Australia at that juncture and which were no doubt a factor which delayed sending supplies to the Philippines. On December 13, MacArthur, having been told by Marshall that help was on the way, spoke with Adm. Thomas C. Hart, commander of the Asiatic Fleet. A number of Hart's ships as well as the admiral himself were still in Manila.[6] MacArthur urged Hart to provide escorts to bring supply ships north from Australia; but Hart's response had been decidedly negative, beginning with the argument that before the Pensacola Convoy would be ready to leave Australia, the Japanese would have established a complete blockade of the southern approaches to the Philippines. MacArthur's impression was that Hart believed the Philippines already doomed and that the admiral's primary concern was that if he delayed in sending his ships to join the British and Dutch fleets, the Japanese might block his departure by mining the exits from Manila Bay. Besides that, the Office of the Chief of Naval Operations had not given Hart any instructions to depart from *War Plan Rainbow 5* which called for the Asiatic Fleet to reinforce the British and Dutch navies in efforts to hold the Malay Barrier. In fact, the Chief of Naval Operations had recently reinforced that concept, urging that the faster the remainder of the Asiatic Fleet left Manila to join the British and Dutch, the better. It appears that the only thing even bordering on encouragement which Hart gave MacArthur was assurance that the Asiatic Fleet's submarines would contest Japanese attempts to reinforce its invasion force; but even with that, he expressed the reservation that the submarines could do little to prevent more landings, nor could they noticeably disrupt a Japanese blockade once put into place.[7] MacArthur's appeals had, however, garnered the support of

---

[4] Port Darwin is on the northern coast of Australia.

[5] From wireless message received at "IB" at 1945 hours on December 18, 1941, and paraphrased for transmittal to War Department by Lt. Col. M. W. Pettigrew, designated IB No. 11, 12-18-41; wireless signed by "Merle Smith". To be found in files of U.S. Army, Chief of Transportation, Modern Military Records, National Archives.

[6] Morton, p 147, cites wireless, MacArthur to Marshall, 13 December 1941, OPD, Exec. O. Following the long-standing plan of the Navy Department, Admiral Hart had already begun a withdrawal of his command to aid the British and Dutch on the Malay Barrier. On December 10, he had ordered the gunboats *USS Tulsa* and *USS Ashville* and the minelayers *USS Lark* and *USS Whippoorwill* south to Borneo from where they would go to Java. Hart would himself leave for Java on December 26 aboard the submarine *USS Shark.*

[7] Morton, p 150, citing radio message CINCAF to OPNAV, 101330 and 131026, 10 and 13 Dec 41, War Diary, 16th Naval District, Office of Naval Records. As it would turn out, Hart's statement regarding his submarines was more prophetic than he realized at the time. Design problems with the U.S. Navy's torpedoes had reduced effectiveness from what it otherwise could have been. This torpedo problem would not be corrected until later in the war.

President Roosevelt who ordered the Navy to cooperate with MacArthur -- an instruction that the Navy Department seems to have temporized, as no orders were issued to provide escorts for any supply ships which were to later depart either from Australia or from the Dutch East Indies.[8]

~

Maj. Gen. George H. Brett, who on January 5 was designated the commander of U.S. Army Forces in Australia (USAFIA), had orders stipulating that Australia was to be considered the Army's advance base of communications in the Pacific. Despite his designation as USAFIA commander, Brett was to consider himself subordinate to MacArthur's USAFFE, a command arrangement which clearly spoke to the War Department's newly developed policy to do whatever was possible to supply the Philippines, short of troop reinforcement.[9]

Following their arrival at Brisbane, the *USAT Willard A. Holbrook* and the chartered merchantman *Bloemfontein* were to be sent north toward the Philippines with field artillery troops (147th Field Artillery and the 148th Field Artillery, less one battalion) together with the majority of their guns and other organizational equipage. The rest of their unit equipment was scheduled to follow on the American merchant ship *Portmar* which had sailed from the west coast on the heels of the Pensacola Convoy.[10]

By January 3, the Japanese had established a beachhead on northern Borneo while simultaneously launching air attacks against military installations in the Bismarck archipelago. By January 8, they had supremacy of the skies over Borneo; and during the following week, Australian and Dutch installations on New Guinea began receiving heavy bombing raids.

On January 16 word was received at USAFIA headquarters that the Japanese had completed their occupation of northern Borneo, a situation which heightened the probability of interception of ships passing through the Makassar Strait. In consequence of that, *USAT Willard A. Holbrook* and *Bloemfontein* (then underway for the Philippines) and in their wake the *Portmar,* were instructed via radio to reroute

---

[8]   Following Roosevelt's declaration, the Chief of Naval Operations' immediate instructions to Admiral Hart were that he was only to assure MacArthur of the assistance of some Navy PDYs to be used to fly supplies to the Philippines from Australia. Those same instructions ordered that upon his departure from Manila (which would occur on December 26), Hart was to turn over all Navy Department property and personnel left in the Philippines to USAFFE control. None of the naval vessels chosen to remain with USAFFE were of a type suitable for ocean escort. See Morton, p 151, citing OPNAV to CINCAF, 170105, 17 Dec 41, War Diary, 16th Naval District, Office of Naval Records.

[9]   Prior to Maj. Gen. George H. Brett's arrival in Australia, the temporary command of USAFIA had been vested in Brig. Gen. Henry B. Claggett who on December 22 had flown to Brisbane from the Philippines. Brett arrived nine days later, relieving Claggett. The command arrangement in the Southwest Pacific area was constantly changing during the first six months of the war. To aid the reader in that respect, we have provided a short synopsis of those arrangements within Appendix L.

[10]   According to the records of the U.S. Maritime Commission (USMC), File #901-3512-A, Part 2, *Portmar* was requisitioned by the USAFIA at either Sydney or Brisbane under the format of a time charter to the Army *to be executed.* Prior to that, she had been under time charter to USMC. The record shows that the time charter to USMC was not canceled until the late fall of 1942 when title was passed from her owners, the Calmar SS Co., to USMC's successor agency, the War Shipping Administration (WSA) which immediately transferred title over to the War Department.

to Darwin on Australia's north coast.[11] The remainder of the Pensacola Convoy -- *Admiral Halstead, Coast Farmer,* and *USAT Meigs* -- was held over at Brisbane awaiting further developments. Later, *Admiral Halstead* and *USAT Meigs* would also be sent to Darwin as would the Navy's *USS Chaumont* and *USS Republic.* Of the shipping which had composed the Pensacola Convoy, only *Coast Farmer* would then remain on Australia's east coast.

The importance the War Department had placed on supplying the Philippines did not end with the ship diversions to Darwin. It was merely postponed until a strategy could be developed as to how the Philippines were to be supplied. That planning would be centered with the assignment to Australia of Brig. Gen. Patrick J. Hurley.[12] Hurley was en route by air to Australia from Washington with orders to report to Maj. General Brett's headquarters when a wireless message was received by Brett from Brig. Gen. Charles C. Drake, MacArthur's Chief Quartermaster. In that message, Drake described a critically short supply situation and requested balanced field rations in 1000-ton lots to be shipped without delay. This was followed up by Drake's personal letter sent from Corregidor by submarine, again urging haste and requesting immediate shipment of a 60-day ration for fifty thousand men together with ammunition. The ratio requested was six tons of rations to one ton of ammunition. Meanwhile, on January 18, Chief of Staff Marshall wired Brett that the forwarding of rations to MacArthur was imperative,...*and that money 'be spent without stint'...'Bold and resourceful men' well supplied with dollars to fly to islands not yet in Japanese hands and there to buy food, charter ships and offer cash bonuses to their crews for the actual deliveries of cargoes.* [13] The planning for how this was to be accomplished was being focused around a group to be designated as the Joint Administrative Planning Committee, operating within the staffing confines of USAFIA, and to which Hurley on his arrival became the key party. The major problem as then envisioned was going to be the gathering of ships with crews willing to undertake what was clearly going to be a highly dangerous undertaking. The fact that money was to be of no consequence was exemplified by the dispatch from Washington of Col. Stephen J. Chamberlin and Lt. Col. Lester J. Whitlock, together carrying letters of credit in the amount of $10 million.

On January 23, the Japanese were in possession of Rabaul and Kavieng in the Bismarcks as well as Balikpapan, a port midway on the Makassar Strait. Around the same time, they occupied the port of Kendari which fronts on the western side of the Molucca Passage separating Celebes from western New Guinea. With every passing day, and with the increasing enemy dominance of the approaches by sea, getting supplies to MacArthur was growing less promising.

---

[11]   At Darwin, *Portmar's* cargo was distributed to those artillery units to which it belonged.

[12]   Eisenhower, *Crusade in Europe, p* 25. In civil life, Hurley had been the Secretary of War during the Hoover Administration.

[13]   Stauffer, pp 21, 22, fn 63. This wireless message was the impetus for what became the "Robenson Mission" which is covered in detail within Chapter XV of this volume.

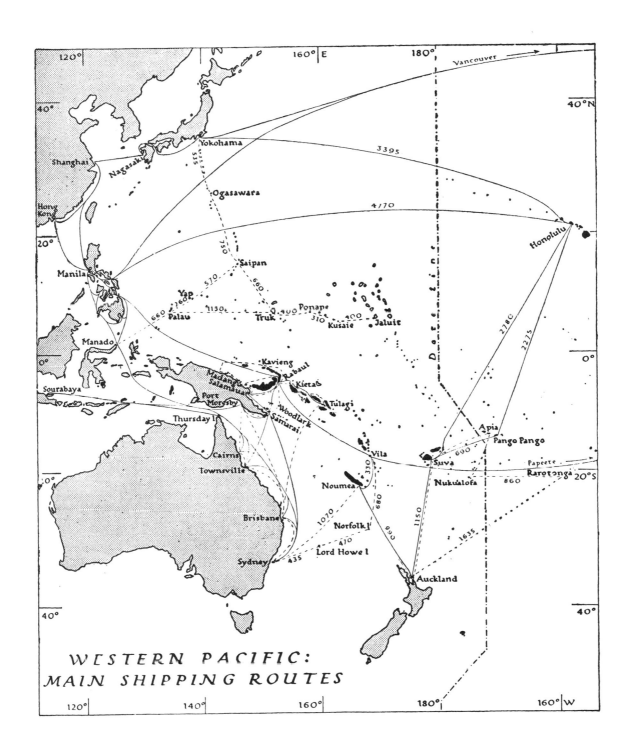

120°   160° E   180°

40°   Vancouver   40°N

Shanghai   Yokohama

Nagasaki   3395

Ogasawara

Hong Kong   4170   Honolulu

20°   750

Saipan

Manila   570   660

Yap   260

Palau   660   1150   Ponape   2780   2215

Manado   Truk   510   200   Jaluit

0°   Kusaie   0°

Kavieng   Rabaul

Sourabaya   Madang   Kieta   Date line

Salamaua

Port Moresby   Tulagi   Apia

Woodlark   Pango Pango

Thursday I.   Samarai

Cairns   Vila   690   Papeete

Townsville   310   Suva   Rarotonga   20°S

Noumea   Nukualofa   860

Brisbane   1070   680   1150   1635

Norfolk I.   990

Lord Howe I.

Sydney   435   470

Auckland

40°   40°

WESTERN PACIFIC:
MAIN SHIPPING ROUTES

120°   140°   160°   180°   160° W

Following the aborted supply attempts by *USAT Willard A. Holbrook, Bloemfontein,* and *Portmar* which had been diverted to Darwin, five other ships would be selected to attempt to run the blockade from eastern Australia. Of those five, only three would deliver their cargo, the remaining two being diverted from the mission when their crews refused to continue. Of the three ships which successfully reached the Philippines, one would discharge its cargo on Mindanao and the other two at Cebu City on the island of Cebu. At those destinations, the cargo was to be reloaded onto interisland freighters for the final and even more dangerous run north to Bataan / Corregidor. The stories of those ships follow:

The first of the successful blockade runners was the American freighter *Coast Farmer,* 3290 gross tons, which had arrived in Australia as part of the Pensacola Convoy. Since that time, she had been held over at Brisbane on orders of USAFIA. On January 10, her master, John A. Mattson, was informed that the ship's owner, Coastwise (Pacific Far East) Lines, had chartered her to the U.S. Maritime Commission (USMC), and that upon the Army's request, USMC had immediately redelivered her over for the use of USAFIA.[14] The terms gave the Army unrestricted usage with no limitations as to operating areas. Mattson, informed of *Coast Farmer's* status, was told that the ship had been selected to run supplies to a forward base. The following day, Mattson was visited by Maj. John Dietz, a member of the USAFIA staff. The purpose of that visit was to contract Mattson, his officers, and crew for a special mission (destination still undisclosed) which, if successfully undertaken, would result in a bonus for every member of the ship's company amounting to the equivalent of 9-months' pay, or, if captured, the continuation of each man's monthly pay until the date of liberation.[15] To this the entirety of the ship's company apparently agreed.

Coast Farmer was next unloaded of the cargo it had carried transpacific, and the reloading of a new cargo consisting of cased ammunition and bagged flour began. With the reloading almost complete, the ship was visited by another Army officer. After being informed by Mattson of the *Coast Farmer's* limitation in speed (it was normally only 10 knots), the officer announced that the ship

---

[14] The paperwork for the chartering of *Coast Farmer* has not been found by us either among the records of USMC or USAFIA; however, the arrangement seems to have been a modified form of time charter with the ship falling under Army control. The master, officers, and crew were retained in the employment of the owner. At that stage of the war (January 1942) the War Shipping Administration (WSA) had not yet been organized. Even when that organization came into being on February 7, 1942, it would be some weeks before charter and subcharter arrangements undertaken between USMC and the War Department were put into proper format under WSA. This was especially the case for those American merchant ships located at that time in Australia. Once the WSA organization was set up and running, time charter arrangements with USMC through which the Army had gained the use of merchant ships were phased out and replaced -- starting with the summer of 1942 -- by either sub-bareboat charters from WSA to Army or, as in the majority of cases, by WSA's allocation of shipping to the Army. Under the allocation system, WSA retained control of the crew, its victualing, and the internal management of the ship while the Army was given the ship's use for a specific voyage or for a period of time. There is little material within either Army or USMC (or WSA) files which deals specifically with arrangements for the acquisition methods used in obtaining U.S. merchant shipping in Australia during the early period of December 1941 through March of 1942.

[15] Although compensation was to be paid for services rendered *to the Army* by the *Coast Farmer's* officers and crew, the contract was merely a bonus arrangement and not one which would remove the officers and crew from the status of being the employees of the ship's owners.

would never make it and ordered the cargo offloaded -- the ammunition and flour to be placed aboard the Moore - McCormack Line's *Mormacsun,* a much faster ship. However, as soon as *Mormacsun's* master was made aware of the of the destination of the cargo, he refused to sail his ship, continuing that posture despite the urgings of the USAFIA staff. Considerable discussion had been taking place between the War Department and USMC over the future use of *Mormacsun,* USMC being reluctant to risk the ship in undertakings of severe risk. It is not clear as to whether *Mormacsun's* master was aware of those discussions and if so, whether that was the reason for his refusal. In the end, the War Department gave way to USMC as indicated within a memorandum transmitted to the Secretary of the General Staff by Lt. Gen. Brehon B. Somervell, Assistant Chief of Staff. Dated January 22, 1942, Washington, DC, it read:

> Mormacsun *should not be used beyond Dutch Archipelago as no unloading facilities available in Philippines for large ships.* Mormacsun *particularly fitted for transpacific plane carrier* [16]

While the controversy over *Mormacsun* was ensuing, the question of sending *Coast Farmer* north was revisited, the decision being made that she was to be sent after all. Since the cargo for the Philippines was by then aboard *Mormacsun* and unloading it would be time-consuming, *Coast Farmer* was now loaded with 7000 tons of rations together with ordnance (mostly ammunition) and a quantity of medical supplies. Mattson's orders were to first stop at Thursday Island (located off the western side of Australia's York Peninsula) where final routing instructions would be issued.

Coast Farmer entered the Thursday Island anchorage on February 18. Her routing instructions given there were for the final destination, Gingoog Bay, located on Mindanao's north coast. She was to transit the western coast of New Guinea; thence to the eastward of Halmahera Island and the Djailolo Passage. From there the route was to take her well to seaward of Mindanao's east coast until reaching the latitude of the Surigao Straits. Once through those straits, Mattson was to head for the anchorage at Gingoog Bay. The voyage north took a full week.[17] That she was not spotted by either Japanese aircraft or a patrolling warship was mainly luck; but a lot was probably also due to *Coast Farmer's* engineers who had coaxed their power plant

---

[16]   The refusal of *Mormacsun's* master to undertake the supply mission as well as related matters of loading, unloading, and subsequent reloading of the Philippines-bound cargo is derived from Robert L. Underbrink, *Destination Corregidor,* (Annapolis, MD: U. S. Naval Institute, 1971). Underbrink obtained his information of this and other events surrounding the February - March 1942 voyage of *Coast Farmer* directly from Col. Ben Hur Chastaine (the quartermaster officer who received the *Coast Farmer's* cargo on Mindanao) and from John A. Mattson (*Coast Farmer's* master). Other sources we have used pertaining to *Coast Farmer's* cargo and the ship's arrival on Mindanao were RG-407, *History of ATS Activities in Manila and Cebu,* Archive File 500-21, December 1941 - May 1942 as well as RG-407 PAC, Box 25, Folder "*Elcano,*" (*Elcano* had loaded from *Coast Farmer* at Mindanao). In the final analysis, it was decided not to send *Mormacson* to the Dutch East Indies. Instead, she took on a cargo of Australian hides and other bulk items for the United States.

[17]   *Coast Farmer's* dates of sailings and arrivals are contained within *Merchant Ship Movement Report Cards,* a system the U.S. Navy maintained during World War II. These card records are now held by Modern Military Records, Archive II, National Archives, College Park, MD. The described routing of *Coast Farmer* from Brisbane north to Gingoog Bay was, however, not given in the Movement Report Cards but rather is from the Underbrink interviews with Capt. John A. Mattson conducted during the 1960s.

to deliver a previously unattained 15 knots during those parts of the passage which Mattson viewed as being vulnerable for detection.

The evening following *Coast Farmer's* arrival at the Gingoog Bay anchorage, two Filipino coasters, *Lepus* and *Elcano,* pulled alongside and the offloading of *Coast Farmer's* cargo began. The transfer from *Coast Farmer* to the smaller ships took place at night, being accomplished by native stevedores who man-handled the bags of flour and ammunition cases from ship to ship. During hours of daylight, all cargo work ceased while *Lepus* and *Elcano* sought inshore anchorages so as to lessen the chances of Japanese aircraft or surface patrols spotting the inviting target of the three ships rafted together. Once *Coast Farmer's* holds were emptied, other coasters moored alongside her for the transfer to *Coast Farmer* of a return cargo consisting of tin and baled rubber.[18] This was highly strategic materiel which by then was in critically short supply due to the Japanese occupation of the major production areas located on the Malay Peninsula and within the Dutch East Indies. The tin and rubber which went aboard *Coast Farmer* had been taken off the American freighter *Admiral Y. S. Williams* which had run aground on a reef in the Celebes Sea during September 1941. The cargo had since been held in storage at Cebu City.[19]

---

[18]   In interviews conducted in the 1960s was told by John A. Mattson, that upon *Coast Farmer's* arrival at Gingoog Bay, its cargo was offloaded to *Lepus* and *Elcano.* Those two ships are also mentioned within RG-407 as being involved in the unloading activity. Both ships were of adequate size to accommodate the entirety of *Coast Farmer's* cargo, so there is no reason to question Mattson's remembrance. Nevertheless, other Army records found within RG-407 speak in somewhat vague terms to the activities of three other Filipino vessels, *Agustina, Cegostina,* and *Emilia* -- inferring, but not definitely stating, that each of those three also were loaded with *Coast Farmer's* incoming cargo. Taking all the evidence into account, the more probable scenario was that *Agustina, Cegostina,* and *Emilia* were involved only with offloading to *Coast Farmer* the tin and rubber that had been brought south from Cebu City, island of Cebu. The timing element reinforces this belief in that *Coast Farmer* left Gingoog Bay directly for Australia either February 28 or March 1, but certainly not later than March 2. Otherwise, she could not possibly have arrived at Thursday Island on March 6 which is the officially recorded date of that arrival. According to the Army's records, *Agustina, Cegostina,* and *Emilia* were in port at Bugo, island of Mindanao, within the time frame of February 28 to March 3 -- two of three Army accounts giving the date as March 3. Within that period, and while at Bugo, they were shelled and subsequently sunk by a Japanese destroyer. Quite obviously, the Army's quartermaster authority at Gingoog Bay, Col. Ben Hur Chastaine, would never have allowed three ships loaded with needed supplies for the defenders of Bataan / Corregidor to divert to Bugo or to do anything less than head directly north. The only logical conclusion that fits the cases of *Agustina, Cegostina,* and *Emilia* is that they departed from Cebu City with the tin and rubber which was loaded onto *Coast Farmer;* and that these three were subsequently ordered to proceed to the port of Bugo to take aboard foodstuffs indigenous to that island which were to be delivered to Bataan / Corregidor. While loading or waiting to load at Bugo, they met their end at the hand of the Japanese destroyer.

[19]   Following the grounding of *Admiral Y. S. Williams,* that ship had been lightened by means of removing her cargo which was taken to Cebu City. Advised of *Coast Farmer's* scheduled arrival at Gingoog Bay, the tin and rubber from *Admiral Y. S. Williams* was then shipped by Filipino coasters to Cagayan de Oro on Mindanao. From there it was taken to Gingoog Bay to await its February - March 1942 transfer to *Coast Farmer.* Upon being floated off the reef, *Admiral Y. S. Williams* was towed to Kowloon, China, and placed in dry-dock. The ship was still in the dry dock when the war started. The British dynamited the dry dock gates in advance of the Japanese occupation of that port, the *Admiral Y. S. Williams* being damaged in that dynamiting. She was later repaired by the Japanese and entered into their service as the *Tasutama Maru.* Source: *War Casualty Shipping Research, 1941 - 45,* Record Group 26, National Archives, as we have quoted it from "Notes on *Admiral Y. S. Williams"* from Robert M. Browning, Jr.'s *U.S. Merchant Vessel War Casualties of World War II,* (Annapolis, MD: Naval Institute Press, 1996).

On March 13, *Coast Farmer* was back at Brisbane, having made the return trip without intervention.[20] [21] It had been a very lucky voyage for *Coast Farmer;* but of the cargo offloaded to *Lepus* and *Elcano,* only that transshipped on *Elcano* arrived at its intended destination. The *Lepus* was intercepted on its way north by a Japanese destroyer -- ship and crew taken captive. Although only part of the tonnage of what *Coast Farmer* had brought from Australia arrived at Bataan / Corregidor, the trip had been of value, made so by the delivery back to Australia of the tin and rubber which otherwise could have ended up in the enemy's hands.

⚓

The next ship to leave Australia for the Philippines was *Dona Nati,* a freighter of 5500 gross tons owned by the De la Rama Steamship Company of Manila. *Dona Nati* was requisitioned during January 1942 by Col. Alexander Johnson representing USAFIA. Negotiations with the agents of De la Rama (or possibly with the master acting as the company's agent) led to an agreement giving USAFIA full operational control without restrictions as to geographic limits.[22] The War Department at Washington was notified of the negotiations, and coordination was instituted between the War Department and USMC, the latter being the agency involved in bringing under centralized control all Philippine-registered shipping located outside of the home islands.

Colonel Johnson had approached Ramon Pons, *Dona Nati's* master, with an even sweeter package than that which had been negotiated with the crew of *Coast Farmer.* Pons seems to have been told at the onset that the destination was to be the Philippines and that as a reward for merely making the attempt there would be 4-months' salary for all hands. If the voyage was successful, they would receive the

---

[20]   The officers and crew of *Coast Farmer* received their promised bonus, and a grateful USAFIA awarded the Army's Distinguished Service Medal (DSM) to Captain Mattson. The memorandum dated 8 April 1942 and signed by Brig. Gen. James E. Whorton, relating to the award of the DSM to John A. Mattson can be located in RG-407, Adj. General's Classified Decimal File 220.5, 1940-42, Box 109, Folder 200.5, 1942. Within that correspondence, the person indicated as the master of *Coast Farmer* is incorrectly identified as a *Captain Moffit.* In addition to the Army's DSM, John A. Mattson was also awarded the U.S. Maritime Commission's Merchant Marine Distinguished Service Medal, being the only person to have been so doubly honored. The officers and crewmembers of *Coast Farmer* were promised the Legion of Merit, provided a bill then pending before the Congress authorized it for award to civilians. That bill was not passed, and whether any alternative decoration was awarded to the others on *Coast Farmer* is not of record within the files. For a more complete discussion of the U.S. Army's policy for the award of decorations to merchant marine personnel, as well as to other civilians, the reader is referred to Appendix K of this volume.

[21]   Luck eventually ran out for *Coast Farmer.* While transiting the Australian coast in July 1942 and still on time charter to the Army, she was torpedoed and sunk by a Japanese submarine. Captain Mattson and all but one of his ship's company survived the attack and were safely landed at Jarvis Bay, Australia. Source: Arthur Moore, *A Careless Word...A Needless Sinking,* (Kings Point, NY: U.S. Merchant Marine Academy, 1986).

[22]   Radio message dated Jan 30, 1942, from Commanding General USAFIA as referenced by letter signed by Brehon B. Somervell, Asst. Chief of Staff, dated Feb 3, 1942, as found within the records of the Chief of Transportation, Modern Military Records, National Archives. The exact date of the agreement regarding *Dona Nati* is not known, but it almost certainly would have been before the ship left Australia for the Philippines. Later, and while the *Dona Nati* was on her way to the Philippines, the ship went under a formally executed time charter (with indefinite term) between the vessel's owners and the War Shipping Administration, with the War Department being annexed, giving it full operational control as to the use of the ship *without restrictions to geographic limits.* James R. Masterson, *U.S. Army Transportation in the Southwest Pacific Area, 1941 - 1947,* (Washington, DC: Office of the Chief of Military History), p 329. This document is within Historical Manuscript File, Call No. 2-3.7 AZ C1.

equivalent in bonus of 9-months' salary payable on arrival back in Australia. Life insurance was to be provided with a pay-out to beneficiaries worth 6-months' salary. The officers and crew agreed to the terms, and *Dona Nati* was ordered first to Sydney to take on part of her cargo with another stop at Melbourne to take on more. It was then back to Brisbane to finish loading. Before leaving for the Philippines on February 18, a small deck gun and two 50-caliber machine guns were mounted -- these manned by six U.S. Army enlisted men. *Dona Nati's* cargo consisted of foodstuffs; 4000 rounds of mortar shells; 100,000 rounds of 50-caliber ammunition; over 1,000,000 rounds of 30-caliber ammunition; and 5000 rifle grenades for a total laden amounting to nearly 1,000 tons.

From Brisbane, Pons's orders were to sail directly to Cebu City. Splitting up incoming shipments at Cebu City and reloading them onto small Filipino coasters increased the odds of at least some of the incoming cargoes arriving at Bataan / Corregidor.[23]

Dona Nati's routing instructions would take the ship on a wide diversion, planned not only for the avoidance of the Japanese but also to keep her clear of areas assigned to patrolling U.S. submarines which might have a difficult time deciding the difference between a friendly freighter and one of the enemy. Clearing Brisbane, the course was to be east into the open Pacific. When south of New Caledonia it would change to a northerly heading designed to pass east of the New Hebrides and Solomon Islands. Upon reaching the latitude of the equator, *Dona Nati's* route was to take her west - north - west, until off southern Mindanao. Then when still out of sight of that island's coastline, Pons was to proceed through the Surigao Straits and thence northward up the inland sea to the Canigao Channel before crossing over to Cebu City located on the east coast of the island of Cebu.

On March 6, the *Dona Nati* tied alongside the wharf at Cebu City, and her unloading commenced. The holds were emptied within three days and not any too soon as a radio alert was received the morning of the 9th, warning that a Japanese destroyer was heading north up the coast of the island of Cebu on a course that would take it close to Cebu City. Without waiting for re-routing instructions, Pons got *Dona Nati* underway and departed the harbor by way of the north channel which separates the large island of Cebu from the small offlying island of Mactan. Mactan's elevation is only around ten feet, but on the island at that time were extensive coconut plantations, the trees at most points shielding from view those vessels leaving the port by the north channel from those approaching the port from the south. By taking the north channel, *Dona Nati* was not sighted by the destroyer which was approaching from the south.[24]

---

[23]   Cebu City was designated as an ATS subport on February 10, 1942. It was also established as a staging area for military supplies routed to the islands of Leyte, Bohol, and northern Mindoro. Piers 1, 2, and 3 there had been reserved solely for the reception of Army cargoes. A major advantage of the port was that it possessed both adequate wharves and roofed warehousing. Maj. Cornelius Z. Byrd was assigned there as ATS Port Superintendent. Source: RG-407, PAC, Box 1568, Archive File 500-21, *History of ATS Activities in Manila and Cebu, Dec 1941 to May 1942.*

[24]   Cebu City's port facilities were bombarded by the Japanese destroyer. A coaster, *Kanlaon II,* which was in dry-dock there, became an easy target of opportunity being hit by at least two rounds from the destroyer's deck guns. *Kanlaon II* was repaired after the March 9 attack and was to be made ready to leave Cebu City with cargo for Bataan / Corregidor. However, she was still there on April 10, the day the Japanese occupied Cebu City, *Kanlaon II* being earlier scuttled to avoid her use by the enemy. Underbrink (p 128) states that his sources

His ship having escaped loss or capture by a thin margin, Pons must have thought his luck had run out for certain when later that afternoon, having rounded Bohol Island's north coast and about to proceed south through the Canigao Channel, the ship's lookouts spotted a ship in camouflaged colors located in or near to that channel at a position which would have brought *Dona Nati* close abeam if she continued on her present course. Stopping all headway, Pons and his officers studied the other ship, reaching the conclusion that she was out of the channel and probably aground. As the day was late with darkness approaching, Pons swung north to give the impression that he was heading toward Luzon via the San Bernardino Channel. When darkness and distance had separated him from the other ship, Pons anchored off the hamlet of Inopacan and sent one of his officers ashore to make inquiries as to the suspect ship's identity. The officer returned later that evening with the news that it was the *Anhui,* flying the British flag. Pons had seen *Anhui* while both ships were back at Brisbane and knew her to be British; yet for some unexplained reason, he kept *Dona Nati* at anchor for almost two days before again getting underway, proceeding south into the Canigao Channel. When nearly abeam of *Anhui,* a launch came alongside to request assistance in pulling *Anhui* off. Pons agreed to assist, and the operation was scheduled for the higher tide due the following morning. With daylight the next day, a tug and barge from Cebu City appeared, bringing the news that at least one coaster together with one or two sail vessels were also en route, the plan being to first lighten the grounded *Anhui* of most of her cargo which should allow her to float off with minimal assist. Aboard the tug was a naval officer who had with him routing instructions for *Dona Nati's* return to Australia, a route closely identical to that on which the ship had come north. Pons's assistance being no longer needed, an immediate departure was advised.

On the return trip to Australia, a scare resulted when three vessels were sighted. At a distance, they had the appearance of a tender and two submarines rafted together. To evade, Pons ordered full speed and a course change. What presumably was the enemy appeared to give chase; but distance and speed were on *Dona Nati's* side, and on March 30, she arrived back at Brisbane.[25]

⚓

The next ship scheduled to depart eastern Australia for a successful run to the Philippines was the previously-mentioned British freighter *Anhui* of 3500 gross tons. Registered out of Hong Kong, her master and officers (except for one engineer) were British; the rest of the crew were Chinese. At the outbreak of the war, *Anhui,* like other British ships then in the vicinity of the northern Philippines, had been ordered by the British Admiralty to seek safe harbor at Manila where she arrived on December 9. The first Japanese air raid on shipping in Manila's outer harbor occurred

---

told of the coaster *Luzon* being sunk in the March 9 shelling of Cebu City, but Army records kept by the ATS state otherwise, claiming that *Luzon* had been earlier sunk in January during a bombing attack on Cebu City and that it had been declared a total loss at that time.

[25]   Following *Dona Nati's* arrival in Australia, her services were continued under the Army's control. In that employment, she became one of the nucleus ships which made up the U.S. Army Transportation Corps, Southwest Pacific Area Command *Permanent Local Fleet. Dona Nati* was withdrawn from Army service in or around March of 1943, being returned at that time to full WSA control. See Masterson, pp 320, 324, 326, 338, 383.

the next day, and as a result, the British Consul advised *Anhui's* master, Louis Evans, that the ship's passengers, numbering around six hundred British women and children -- all having been evacuated from China, should seek hotel accommodations in the city.

On either December 12 or the 14th, while the *Anhui* was lying at anchor (all her passengers by then safely ashore), Evans was handed orders to immediately depart and take his ship south to Australia. The passengers remained at Manila, apparently on instruction of the British Consul, seemingly in the belief that they were safer there than they would be at sea, the approaches to Manila Bay being thought at the time as being infested with Japanese naval units. As it turned out, the passage south, at least for the *Anhui,* was free of hazard, and she arrived safely at Sydney on December 24.

No sooner was *Anhui* moored at Sydney than her Chinese engine room gang went on strike, a walkout which lasted well into the first week of February. While in a state of operational limbo, an officer from USAFIA headquarters approached Captain Evans with a proposal that his ship go under charter to the U.S. Army, a decision that Evans no doubt fielded to the nearest British Consulate.[26] Shortly after this, the Chinese crewmen decided to return to work. It is unclear as to what motivated their change of heart. It may have been a planned coercion directed against the Chinese in which the Australian police authorities cooperated with USAFIA, or it may have been the offer of fiscal rewards promised by USAFIA -- the same pay and bonus arrangements that were offered to the officers and crew of the *Dona Nati.* With its labor problems settled, *Anhui* was loaded with a partial cargo at Sydney before heading for Brisbane where she took on the remainder. All told, her laden came to nearly 450 tons of foodstuffs in addition to 6000 rounds of 81-mm mortar shells; 2,500,000 rounds of 30-caliber ammunition; assorted medical and engineer supplies. As deck cargo, she carried three P-40 fighter planes boxed in crates well lashed down on the hatch tops. For protection, guns were mounted, these to be served by a U.S. Army gun crew.

Anhui sailed on February 22 with routing instructions similar to those given *Coast Farmer,* except that in *Anhui's* case, once through the Surigao Straits, she was to swing north toward the Canigao Channel and then cross over to Cebu City, the assigned destination. The trip went well until Evans reached the northern end of the Canigao Channel where shortly before a course change was due for the rounding of the north end of the island of Bohol, the ship went hard aground. Despite all the steam her engineers could muster, she would not come off. (It was now March 9, and unknown to Evans, this was the night before the *Dona Nati* would depart Cebu City in barely enough time to avoid the Japanese destroyer attack.) With the coming of dawn, Evans

---

[26] As far as we have determined, the proposal to charter *Anhui* to the USAFIA was referred to the British Ministry of War Transport (BMWT). This was an agency which controlled British merchant shipping during World War II in much the same manner as the U.S. Maritime Commission (succeeded by WSA) did for U.S. merchant shipping. Although the British when approached do not appear to have resisted the chartering of *Anhui*, a formal charter was not executed between BMWT and the U.S. Army until March 4 by which time *Anhui* had departed for the Philippines. The terms of the March 4 charter were that the ship, having been taken over by BMWT on a bareboat basis, was then sub-time chartered to the U.S. Army under a format giving the Army full and unrestricted usage and which gave the Army the option -- if it so desired to execute it -- of crewing the ship as it wished. Source: Masterson, pp 332, 338.

sent one of his deck officers and the third engineer off in the ship's launch to Cebu City for help. Cebu City was approximately fifty miles by water, and under normal circumstances that is not an undue distance for a ship's launch; but for the one being used, powered as it was by a 1930s vintage outboard motor, it was an awesome distance -- but arrive they did. When informed of *Anhui's* plight, Maj. Cornelius Z. Byrd, the senior ATS officer present at Cebu City, put things into motion. Within the hour, 1st Lt. Thomas W. Juricka, riding aboard a tug with a barge in tow, was sent to the scene of *Anhui's* grounding. Byrd had also made arrangements with the Filipino master of the coaster *Princesa* to proceed to the scene as soon as he had gathered together his crew.[27] At the same time, Byrd dispatched two auxiliary sail vessels to assist the coaster in the lightering of *Anhui's* cargo.

Early the following morning, the tug put its barge alongside *Anhui* and by using *Anhui's* booms, the crated planes were swung onto the barge thus allowing access to the ship's cargo hatches. Time being of the essence, the crated planes were taken into a mangrove creek on Bohol and camouflaged with vegetative cover until later when they could be safely moved. Following the arrival of *Princesa* and the sail lighters and after sending *Dona Nati* on its way, enough cargo was taken off *Anhui* so that the ship, through the use of its own power with the assist of the tug and a rising tide, came off the reef. She was then piloted into Cebu City where the remainder of the cargo was to be unloaded. On the following day, operations came to a halt when word was received over Cebu Radio that a Japanese warship (another destroyer) was coming up the coast. That news emptied out the dock area with everyone literally taking to the hills. From that observation point, the destroyer was seen to swing around the harbor; and seemingly finding everything to its commander's liking, left without firing a shot. Fortunately the Japanese had not seen any sign of *Anhui's* cargo, since that which had been offloaded had been quickly moved out of sight into the adjoining warehouses.

On March 16, with her holds empty and with a number of American naval personnel aboard for evacuation, *Anhui* left for Australia. The way south was not to be free of enemy detection as off Bougainville, the ship was attacked by a single plane, its bombs narrowly missing. There still remained a long way to go before reaching the safety of Australian waters, and all aboard anticipated a return of the bomber, probably in company with others. Luckily, that threat never materialized, and Sydney was reached on April 3. *Anhui* was the last surface ship to breach the Japanese blockade from outside of the Philippines.[28]

---

[27] In *Destination Corregidor*, Underbrink mentions the *Zambales* as participating in the attempt to get the grounded *Anhui* off the reef. However, Army files do not contain any information on *Zambales* as having been chartered or hired by the Army. Apparently her participation, if in fact it occurred, was of an informal nature.

[28] The voyage of the *Anhui* as related here is in part taken from Underbrink's *Destination Corregidor* and in part from *History of ATS Activities in Manila and Cebu*, Archive File 500-21, RG-407, PAC, Box 1568.

Following *Anhui's* return to Australia, the ship remained on charter to the Army. In October of 1942, it was assigned as part of the Transportation Corps, Southwest Pacific Area Command *Permanent Local Fleet*, serving in that capacity as a troopship operating between Australia and New Guinea. She is known to have still been in the Army's service as late as 1944. Source: Masterson, pp 347, 388.

CHAPTER XIV

EARLY DEFENSE OF JAVA AND THE RAID ON DARWIN
January - February 1942

The Dutch East Indies were also to play a part -- albeit a futile one -- in the attempts to supply the American and Filipino forces in the Philippines. Java was the selected point from where those attempts would be made.

The defense of Java rested with an allied military coalition consisting of American-British-Dutch-Australian (ABDA) naval, ground, and air units. As a command entity, ABDA-COM was activated on January 2, 1942, with headquarters initially established at Soerabaja on Java. Maj. Gen. George H. Brett, then Commander of U.S. Army Forces in Australia (USAFIA), was ordered on January 3 to take up the role of ABDA Deputy Commander, under ABDA's Supreme Commander, British Gen. Archibald P. Wavell. Shortly after Brett's arrival at ABDA-COM, he wired Washington his assessment of the staff performance he had encountered there.

> *Tenacious adherence to age-old custom of procedure is of primary importance here. Aggressive initiative is of secondary consideration, and committees are the rule. If the war is to be won, it is most evident that a different attitude of aggressive action be taken.*

As inefficient as ABDA-COM seems to have been, the military situation which it faced as of the day of its creation could best be described as chaotic. Enemy progress on the Malay Peninsula had been relentless ever since December 8, the day the Japanese landed on the peninsula's east coast near Kota Bharu. Reports coming to ABDA-COM on what was transpiring were limited and often proved unreliable, no doubt adding to much of the staff ineptitude to which Brett was a worried witness. Events -- especially as they related to land warfare -- were occurring so rapidly that by the time ABDA-COM produced reactionary plans, another crisis had developed -- throwing things once again out of kilter.

January 1942 would be a time of continuous allied reversals along the Malay Barrier. Gen. Arthur E. Percival, commander of land forces on the Malay Peninsula, possessed a hastily put together army of British, Australian and Indian troops -- most poorly trained and none with jungle fighting experience. Percival's troops were badly coordinated and proved no match for the battle-hardened and well led Japanese. The airfields on Singapore Island had come under heavy air attack by early January. Unable to make an adequate response, the Royal Air Force began evacuating its surviving planes and personnel south to airfields on Sumatra and Java.

The national commanders of the air and land elements of ABDA seemed intent upon their own agendas. The British were primarily preoccupied with the deteriorating situation in Burma and on the Malay Peninsula -- the Dutch with holding on to Java. The Americans were focused on the pressing need to support the Philippines, an effort which was now to use the East Indies as a staging point for that relief. The goal of the Americans meshed with that of the Dutch insofar as their intent to hold Java. Accordingly, the United States contribution made by land and air units, although by circumstances limited, was concentrated toward Java. Defense responsibility on that island was divided into three sectors: the British had the western end of the island nearest to Sumatra; the Dutch the center; the Americans the eastern end nearest Australia.

Ground forces committed by the United States to the defense of Java consisted of the 131st Field Artillery and the Headquarters Battery of the 26th Field Artillery Brigade. The artillerymen and their guns which had come from the United States on the Pensacola Convoy were initially scheduled for reinforcement of the Philippines. Instead, the ships had been rerouted to Darwin. From there, the artillerymen were sent to Java aboard the *Bloemfontein*, arriving (probably at Tjilatjap) on January 13. Except for one element of the 131st which was assigned to the defense of the air strips being utilized by Maj. Gen. Lewis H. Brereton's air groups, they were immediately deployed in fire support of Dutch infantry units.

At the start, the air defense of the island was divided proportionately; but with the arrival of increasing numbers of American bombers and pursuit aircraft, ABDA's air arm became largely a United States function and in recognition of that, Brereton was appointed ABDA-COM (for air).[1]

The first American planes to reach Java from Darwin consisted of those B-17 bombers which during mid-December had left the Philippines. As originally planned, they were to use the Dutch island as a base from which Japanese installations in the Philippines were to be attacked. However, by the time the B-17s arrived on Java, the original plan was canceled, and the B-17s were integrated as part of the ABDA air arm operating largely against enemy shipping. The original group of B-17s

---

[1]   Brereton had been MacArthur's air commander in the Philippines. With Japanese air supremacy taking form over Luzon, Brereton was ordered to evacuate his B-17s to Mindanao. On December 15, 1941, the B-17s were sent south from there to Australia at about the same time that Brereton was himself ordered to leave. Brereton first touched down at Darwin and from there went to Brisbane where he was given brief command of USAFIA before receiving orders to take up the ABDA-COM post for air which was then headquartered on Java.

was soon joined by other bombers (B-17s, B-24s, Liberators, and LB-30s) the bulk of the planes flown in from the United States via the African transatlantic route. Pursuit planes not flown in from Java arrived by sea on the following vessels:

President Polk, with fifty-five pursuit planes and four C-53 cargo planes, arrived at Brisbane, leaving there for Soerabaja, presumably with the same cargo, less the C-53s. (Soerabaja is at the eastern end of Java near the west side of Madura Strait.) *President Polk* also carried the pilots of the 14th, 20th, 35th, and 51st Pursuit Groups plus assorted ground crew personnel.

Sea Witch left Freemantle with twenty-seven crated P-40s, arriving Tjilatjap on Java's southwest coast. *Sea Witch's* cargo which was landed on the night of February 27-28 never got into the fight as within a matter of hours, the still-crated planes had to be destroyed in advance of the Japanese occupation of that port.[2] [3]

What success the American air units enjoyed proved short-lived. Plane losses and personnel casualties mounted rapidly. From the beginning, there were never enough ground crews to repair damaged aircraft or even to perform routine maintenance, the result being that flight crews had to pitch in to maintain their own aircraft which added to the fatigue factor of the crews which in turn contributed to even more combat losses. Almost all of the pursuit pilots were routed through Darwin where they were to receive advanced P-40 flight training to prepare them for combat. The P-40 was not an easy plane on which to train, and by mid-January the instructor staff at Darwin -- alarmed by a high accident rate -- begged to be provided with the slower A-24 which was better suited for the instruction being given. Getting nowhere with that request which had been made through the normal chain of command, they tried another tack, appealing directly to Washington.

> *Seventy so-called pursuit pilots assigned to us for training, average total pursuit time approximately fifteen hours.*
>
> *Have had eight accidents and one death due to pilot inexperience. Estimate three months and fifteen wrecked planes to fully train these pilots for combat operations.*
>
> *Request we be allowed two transport airplanes, type C-53 for purpose of bringing Colonel George and two squadrons of experienced pilots from Bataan.*
>
> *If request cannot be granted, request we [the instructors] be allowed to proceed north with squadron of fully qualified pilots taken partially from light bombardment group.* [4]

---

[2] Description of *President Polk's* cargo is from a transcript of telephone messages "Gen. Gilbreath to Lt. Col. Soule," San Francisco, Dec 18-19, 1941, as held in the Records of the Chief of Transportation, Modern Military Records, National Archives. Both *President Polk* and *Sea Witch* escaped enemy intervention after leaving Java, each returning safely to the United States. The Navy's aircraft carrier *USS Langley*, with a load of thirty-two P-40s, departed Freemantle on February 22, bound for Tjilatjap, but she never made it, being sunk by Japanese bombers on February 27 near Christmas Island, to the south of Java.

[3] Another ship providing logistical support was the Navy oiler *USS Pecos.* However, whether the *USS Pecos* brought high octane aviation gasoline to Tjilatjap for Army Air Corps use, as is claimed within Craven and Cate's history; or was sent to refuel naval vessels, as the *Dictionary of American Naval Fighting Ships* states, is a question. The *USS Pecos* was lost to air attack in late February.

[4] From the Walter D. Edmonds Manuscript Collection held within the Archives Branch, Headquarters, AFHRA/ISR, Maxwell Air Force Base, Alabama.

The instructors were denied on both counts, instead receiving orders to shorten the training period. By February 12, the outlook for Java had become so desperate that the training was done away with completely, and incoming pursuit pilots were forwarded directly to squadrons on Java. Soon the supply of replacement and other air crews dried up completely.

After the war, Brereton would write of the concluding days of the air defense, quoting from his diary entry dated February 17:

> *...combat replacements did not exist. Reinforcing aircraft contained only skeleton crews. Fatigue and combat weariness had worn men to their last ounce of resistance. Pilots returned from attacks crying with rage and frustration when a crewmember was killed or when weather or mechanical failure prevented successful completion of the mission. A flight commander, a fine leader, committed suicide. Boys were on the verge of mental and physical collapse.*

On January 27, Percival received permission from Wavell to withdraw his ground forces onto the island of Singapore. For the next two weeks, there was enough ABDA naval presence within the waters immediately south of Singapore to allow the evacuation of key military personnel and a number of British and Australian civilians to the Dutch islands. That evacuation route was closed on February 14 when Percival surrendered Singapore along with his army of 64,000 British, Australian, and Indian troops. Communications with Australia to or from Java would now be limited to the southern sea approaches via the narrow opening of the Sunda Strait which separates western Java and southern Sumatra and through the even narrower Bali Straits between eastern Java and the island of Bali.

~

The ABDA naval force, as it operated during January and well into February, although performing with more cohesiveness than the ground and air arms of ABDA, had its own measure of inherent confusion. Naval historian Samuel Eliot Morison made the observation,

> *Rapid and sometimes over-lapping changes in command relations were confusing indeed; even the admirals themselves hardly knew what their status really was.* [5]

The slot for ABDA-COM (Navy) had been given to Adm. Thomas C. Hart upon his arrival from the Philippines in early January. While assuming that position, he had also retained command of the U.S. Asiatic Fleet, a job which lasted until the beginning of February when Rear Adm. W. A. Glassford took over the fleet responsibility. With the arrival of the American ships, the combined ABDA fleet consisted of one American and one British heavy cruiser; two American, two British, and three Dutch light cruisers; and twenty-three destroyers of which thirteen were American, seven were Dutch, and three British.[6] The ABDA under-sea force consisted of twenty-five American and sixteen Dutch submarines. Naval support vessels were American and Australian, most of them based out of Darwin. These included two

---

[5]   Morison, Vol. III, *Rising Sun in the Pacific*, p 179.

[6]   The British naval force with ABDA included ships of the Australian Navy which served ABDA under Royal Navy command.

supply transports, two fleet oilers; a chartered Panamanian flag commercial tanker; a destroyer tender, three seaplane tenders, and the aircraft transport *USS Langley*.[7] The naval campaign of ABDA was to be costly with the allied command losing five cruisers, fifteen destroyers, seven submarines, an aircraft transport, and two support ships. The combined fleet fought with great tenacity; but the odds, when measured in terms of fire power alone, were clearly in favor of the Japanese. Additionally, the Japanese had a carrier force which ABDA did not, and that added immeasurably to the enemy's striking power as well as its well-coordinated scouting ability which ABDA sorely lacked. There were, though, a few bright spots for the allies, one occurring in January when a task group of United States destroyers attacked Japanese troop transports at Balikpapan Bay on the southeast coast of Borneo. Although it did little to blunt the landings then underway, four of the enemy's transports were sunk. The downside of that attack was that it alerted the Japanese to the need to provide sufficient surface and air protection for future landing operations. With the large number of ships and aircraft available to the Japanese, this was not a difficult goal to attain. As the ABDA naval commanders soon found out, it then became difficult if not impossible to approach a Japanese task group or any assemblage of Japanese transports without taking crippling losses. As allied ship casualties increased, it was found that even moderate damage was as good as taking a ship out of the war as available repair facilities were poor at best. Once Singapore was surrendered, it left only Soerabaja and Tjilatjap on Java with dry docks. When the destroyer *USS Stewart* was damaged through enemy action in the Badung Straits, she was taken to Soerabaja where the dry dock had already been damaged and where air raids were becoming familiar events. Haste was the order of the day for getting *USS Stewart* into the dock. In the hurry, shoring used to brace the destroyer's bilge keels was improperly placed as were bracing timbers to keep her off the dry dock walls. When the ship came against the bracing as water was being pumped out of the dry dock, the destroyer rolled over on her side, putting both ship and dry dock permanently out of action.[8] That left only Tjilatjap with a dry dock, and the one there was usable for only the smallest of naval craft.

The Japanese naval strategy in their 1942 offensive in the East Indies was one of avoiding contest with any major ABDA force, the rationale being that the Japanese task groups had become widely scattered in order to protect their many landing operations which were taking place. Offensive operations directed against ABDA naval units were concentrated on small groups of ships, a strategy easy to employ with the scouting aircraft which the Japanese operated both from their aircraft

---

[7]   The Panamanian merchant ship which served the Asiatic Fleet as an oiler (with civilian crew) was the *George G. Henry* owned by Standard Oil Co.. For an account of her service with ABDA, see *Ships of the Esso Fleet in World War II*, (Standard Oil Co. [New Jersey], 1946. The *USS Langley* was the Navy's first combatant aircraft carrier; however, by 1941, she was no longer used for that purpose, being instead relegated to service as a transport for the carriage of aircraft.

[8]   Although heavy demolition charges were used to destroy *USS Stewart's* usefulness prior to the Japanese occupation of Soerabaja, the enemy was able to repair her. She was commissioned by them during 1943 as *Patrol Boat No. 102*. While at Mokpo, Korea, in 1945, she was hit by American bombs which damaged her to the extent that she was moved to Kure, Japan, for lay-up. After Japan was occupied by the United States later that year, the shopworn old destroyer was repaired and commissioned into the U.S. Navy (without name) as *DD-224*. She was decommissioned in May 1946, ending her days as a floating target off San Francisco. Source: *Dictionary of American Naval Fighting Ships*.

carriers and from the airfields which came into their possession as the islands of the East Indies rapidly fell to conquest. As described by one historian of those events:

> *The manner of the Japanese advance resembled the insidious yet irresistible clutching of multiple tentacles. Like some vast octopus, it relied on strangling many small points rather than concentrating on a vital organ. No one arm attempted to meet the entire strength of the ABDA fleet. Each fastened on a small portion of the enemy, and by crippling him locally, finished by killing the entire animal.* [9]

As of January 24, Japanese task groups had supported, among other occupations, the taking of Balikpapan on the coast of eastern Borneo and of Kendari on the southeast coast of Celebes, thereby effectively closing off prospective routings through those straits for any blockade running attempts aimed toward the Philippines.

On February 4, U.S. Army Air Corps planes then based at air strips on Java sighted a group of twenty Japanese transports escorted by three cruisers and a bevy of destroyers apparently approaching the Makassar Straits. An ABDA force headed by Dutch Rear Admiral Doorman rushed to intercept. The force consisted of four cruisers, two of which, *USS Marblehead* and *USS Houston,* were American, and eight destroyers, four of them American. The air superiority of the Japanese was strongly brought into focus when Doorman's force, at a position north of Bali, was attacked by waves of enemy aircraft and forced to retire with both *USS Marblehead* and *USS Houston* in damaged condition, *USS Marblehead* seriously enough to eliminate her from further use.[10]

Strike At Darwin

To keep communications open between Darwin and Java, it was vitally necessary to keep Timor in allied hands. For their own reasons, the value of Timor was also appreciated by the Japanese. Both adversaries were now to act, practically simultaneously, to occupy that strategic island.

On February 15, an American - Australian convoy formed at Darwin's harbor mouth. It consisted of the *USAT Meigs,* the Australian merchantman *Tulagi,* and the American merchantmen *Mauna Loa* and *Portmar.* [11] The escort force was headed

---

9 Morison, *The Rising Sun in the Pacific,* p 292.

10 *USS Marblehead* went into Tjilatjap where her bow was raised by tilting it precariously on the forward edge of the small dry dock located there. That was just enough, though, so that a temporary patch could be applied to the damaged bow plates. She then went on to Ceylon where further temporary repairs were made and from there left for Simonstown, South Africa, for more extensive work which enabled her to reach the Brooklyn (New York) Navy Yard in May. A number of her wounded, as well as other wounded from *USS Houston* were evacuated from Java to Australia aboard a Dutch merchant ship through the heroic efforts of Lt. Cmr. Corydon M. Wassell, Medical Corps, USNR. In 1944, Wassell's effort was the subject of a movie titled *The Story of Doctor Wassell,* starring actor Gary Cooper as Wassell.

11 According to the WSA files, the *Mauna Loa* had been intended for use as a blockade runner to the Philippines, but with the ABDA-COM order to occupy Timor, she was unloaded at Darwin in order to take aboard troops for the Timor mission.

by the cruiser *USS Houston*.[12] Other escorts were the destroyer *USS Peary* and the Australian Navy sloops *HMAS Swan* and *HMAS Warrego*. The convoy's destination -- Timor. Aboard the *Tulagi* were the men and guns of the U.S. 148th Field Artillery. *USAT Meigs* and the *Mauna Loa* carried the troops of an Australian infantry battalion along with some support elements.

The allied move to occupy Timor had been anticipated by the Japanese, and it was one they intended to discourage by an air strike at the probable departure point for such an allied movement, namely Darwin. By the same strike, they hoped to eliminate Darwin as a danger to Japanese forces in the East Indies. Volume of the strike was to be of a level equal to that which had hit Pearl Harbor on December 7 -- the Japanese commander, Adm. Chuichi Nagumo, and the air leader, Cdr. Mitsuo Fuchida, both having played the same roles in that attack. The concept for the raid on Darwin was to bring about complete destruction made possible only by an overwhelming force. Nevertheless, the use of four aircraft carriers, four heavy cruisers, nine destroyers, and an air fleet totaling 242 aircraft which included land-based planes from enemy-held airfields in the East Indies seems to have been overkill, or so thought one senior Japanese admiral who later remarked, *If ever a sledge hammer was used to crack an egg, it was then.* [13]

Within hours of the Houston Convoy having gotten underway and well before it reached Timor, it was attacked by enemy aircraft. Although none of the transports were lost, hull leaks of varying severity were started in most of them by the concussion of near-bomb misses. The attack had been sustained, and *USS Houston* as well as the other escorts found their anti-aircraft ammunition dangerously depleted. Because of those shortages and the fact that any surprise element had evaporated, the convoy was ordered to return to Darwin where it arrived to re-anchor on February 18.

The Australian government as well as USAFIA had anticipated possible Japanese landings at or near Darwin. Accordingly, Australia's Northern Territory had been on a war footing since mid-December and by late January most of the women and children in the territory had been evacuated to the south.[14] Neither the Northern Territory nor even the town of Darwin had been placed under martial law. Had that been done, it would have put into being a centralized military authority, and Darwin

---

[12]   During the Japanese air attack on Doorman's task group north of Bali, *USS Houston* had been damaged but not enough to cancel her usefulness, thereafter being considered adequate for escort duty. In that capacity, she had been sent south to Darwin as an escort for the Timor-bound convoy.

[13]   Douglas Lockwood, *Australia's Pearl Harbor,* (Sydney: Cassell Australia Ltd, 1966), p 5, quoting Adm. Isoroku Yamamoto.

[14]   The Japanese plans for conquest included the totality of the East Indies. From the beginning, they had viewed Darwin as a restraint to that goal. Adm. Isoroku Yamamoto, the Commander-in-Chief of the Japanese Combined Fleet, had voiced a solution to the problem advocating an amphibious invasion of northern Australia with landings at or near Darwin; but the idea was rebuffed at the time by both the Japanese Army and Navy General Staffs. An invasion of northern Australia, although never seriously contemplated by the Japanese during the war, would certainly not have served them well for any follow-up expansion into that continent. Darwin and the territory of which it was a part were isolated from the rest of Australia, having no all-weather road connections and but one rail line running to a terminal connection at Alice Springs some one thousand miles to the south. The territory's only means of supply in the 1940s was by sea and by air. The surrounding country for hundreds of miles was barren and arid, incapable of producing foodstuffs, thus all consumables had to be imported from elsewhere. For the same reasons, an American - Australian force would have found it difficult to dislodge a Japanese presence at Darwin once it became established, at least by overland means.

and its environs would probably have been in a much better state of preparedness than circumstances were to find them when the Japanese launched their attack. As it was, authority was divided between the Territorial Civil Administrator and an admixture of Australian and American military commanders. Encamped outside the town were five thousand American troops representing the ground force defense. Air defenses included both American and Australian units.[15] To support the defenders logistically, everything was coming in by ship, the result being a harbor overcrowded from an unprecedented number of ship arrivals. The place had only one wharf facility, a long *L* dock at which only two ships could berth for unloading, and even then, only the dock's outer face was able to accommodate a ship of any size. Adding to the difficulties was a 22-foot tidal range which made it impossible at periods of low tide for ship's cargo handling gear to reach the elevated wharf platform. At such tidal periods, all unloading was, out of necessity, halted. The returning Houston Convoy only added to the congested state of the harbor.[16] As of the early morning of February 19, *USAT Meigs* and the *Mauna Loa* had discharged their troop passengers; but those aboard *Portmar* were still waiting to go ashore.[17]

The first observers of approaching Japanese planes were the occupants of a mission station on nearby Bathurst Island. There, at 0930, large numbers of planes were seen coming in from the northwest. Before any definite identification could be made, the mission's air strip came under strafing attack. One of the missionaries managed to get off a radio warning to Darwin; but the system in place for air raid warnings was in such absolute disarray that by the time the sirens went off the bombs had started falling.[18] Nine American P-40 fighter planes which were stationed as air guard at a nearby airfield were destroyed in the air with minimal impact on the attackers. Two remaining P-40s and seven bombers were destroyed before they could get off the ground.[19] The thrust of the attack, though, was against the shipping in the harbor. Of the American ships there: The destroyer *USS Peary* took bomb hits setting her afire before she finally sank with eight of her crew killed, including her commanding officer; *USS William B. Preston*, a seaplane tender was damaged; *USAT Meigs* and the merchant ship *Mauna Loa* were sunk; and *Portmar* was beached to prevent her from sinking. The *Admiral Halstead* was damaged to such an extent as to require extensive repairs before she could be put back into service. The American personnel casualties, with the exception of those on the *USS Peary*, were light which was a miracle considering the heavy damage to their ships.[20] A British merchant ship, the *Motorist*,

---

[15] The American contingents at Darwin, both ground and air, were commanded by Col. John A. Robenson. He had been in the Pensacola Convoy on his way to join Maj. Gen. Jonathan M. Wainwright as his Chief of Staff in the Philippines. Diverted to Darwin instead, and as senior American officer there, he was assigned as the American commander with orders to coordinate defenses with the Australian authorities in the area.

[16] The *USS Houston* after refueling (and presumably taking on more anti-aircraft ammunition) departed Darwin for Java on February 18. The remainder of the convoy, including its other escorts, remained at Darwin.

[17] Source: Marine Extended Protest, American Consular Service, initially filed at Melbourne, March 25, 1942. This document is now incorporated within U.S. Maritime Commission File No. 901-3512-A, *Portmar*.

[18] Lockwood, pp 22-29.

[19] Craven and Cate, Vol. I, p 393.

[20] Although declared at the time a total loss, *Portmar* was salvaged and repaired to the account of USAFIA. On November 17, 1942, title to the ship passed to the War Shipping Administration, immediately transferring from that agency over to the U.S. Army. The Army subsequently employed her on cargo shuttles along the Australian coast with a makeshift crewing arrangement consisting of a civilian British master,

was also sunk. The Australians fared the worst with a hospital ship, the *Manunda,* badly damaged with heavy casualties and the naval escort vessel *HMAS Mavie* sunk. In addition, *HMAS Platypus, HMAS Kara Kara, HMAS Kookaburra, HMAS Kangaroo,* and *HMAS Coongoola* were all damaged to varying degrees. Of Australia's merchant ships present that day, the heaviest loss was *Neptuna,* an ammunition ship which exploded with a heavy personnel toll. The Australians also lost the freighters *Zealandia* and *Kelat.* Their merchant ships *Baroosa,* and *Tulagi* were sunk but later salvaged. Also damaged in the attack was a Norwegian tanker, the *Benjamin Franklin.*[21]

The raid on Darwin turned out fortuitously in that it was not a prelude to a Japanese landing which, as feared at the time, might follow. However, the damage suffered in the attack and the subsequent occupation of Timor by the Japanese placed a damper on plans to use Darwin as a departure point for shipping bound northward for Java or for relief shipping to the Philippines.[22]

Australian civilian deck and engineering officers, and a crew of U.S. Army enlisted men. On June 16, 1943, while part of a convoy off the east coast of Australia, the ship was torpedoed and sunk. Sources: Records on *Portmar,* now held by U.S. Maritime Administration, Washington, DC; and Statement of Survivors, taken by Lt. E. K. Pegg, USNR, from Records of U.S. Army Chief of Transportation, Modern Military Records, National Archives.

[21] Information on the ship casualties suffered at Darwin during the raid of February 19, 1942, was in large part taken from *Summary of Statements by Survivors,* files of the Chief of Naval Operations (regarding Japanese attack on the Port of Darwin, Australia, February 19, 1942). That report was accompanied by supplemental statements on *Admiral Halstead, Portmar,* and *USAT Meigs* -- those depositions having been taken by Lt. H. A. Burch, USNR, who was at Darwin at the time of the raid. These reports are now held by Modern Military Records, National Archives.

[22] Before the war was over, Darwin would be bombed a total of fifty-nine times, the last raid occurring during November of 1943.

CHAPTER XV

THE ROBENSON MISSION AND DEFEAT AT JAVA

On January 11, 1942, *Don Isidro,* a Philippine-registered cargo/ passenger ship of 3,263 tons, (Rafael J. Cisneros, master) had been delivered at Brisbane to the Army by instruction of her owners. The method by which she was received by Maj. George A. Dietz acting for USAFIA on behalf of the United States government is but one example of how early in the war the Army obtained the services of Philippine-registered vessels and their crews that were then located outside of the Philippines. The case of *Don Isidro* seems, though, to have been unique. A charter rate of $1200 a day had been agreed on via radio communications conducted between USAFIA at Brisbane and the owner's representatives acting through the conduit of the Maritime Commission (USMC) at Washington.[1] As the records available on *Don Isidro* seem to imply, all concerned parties were of the impression that the ship would, after leaving Australia, touch at Java for final instructions. From there, it would sail for the Philippines. One thing that made the arrangements between the crew of *Don Isidro* and the USAFIA different from those entered into by crews of the other blockade runners which had left Australia for the Philippines was that the crew of *Don Isidro* had collectively turned down the Army's offer of risk bonuses. They had asked only that pensions be awarded to their next of kin should they be killed during the period of the charter, a proposal which was accepted by Col. Alexander Johnson acting for USAFIA headquarters. Leaving Brisbane with 700 tons of rations and munitions, the ship then went around Australia's southern coast, stopping briefly at Freemantle before departing for Batavia, Java (renamed Djakarta after the war).

---

[1] See Appendix N this volume for further discussion on the status of this particular ship.

Don Isidro was but one part of an ambitious program orchestrated by USAFIA headquarters at Brisbane to supply MacArthur via the East Indies.[2] The program, which had three objectives, was to be put into action by Col. John A. Robenson.[3]

First Objective: To supply sixty days of rations for a force estimated at fifty thousand men. A part of the cargoes were to be drawn from U.S. Army supplies thought to be on Java, being held there for the mission's purpose. More was to arrive on *Don Isidro* which, at the time of Robenson's receipt of instructions, was being loaded at Brisbane. Another source would be cargoes coming to Australia from the United States. Some of this was to be loaded on *Coast Farmer* -- provided that ship returned safely to Australia from her projected run to Mindanao. Another ship to take part was *Mauna Loa*, due to arrive at Brisbane from San Francisco. When ready, *Coast Farmer* and *Mauna Loa* were to take rations and munitions from Brisbane to Macassar, a port town located on the south coast of Celebes.[4][5] At Macassar, the cargoes from both ships were to be transshipped to local vessels hired at whatever price their owners asked for the final run to the Philippines.

Second Objective: To send from Australia's east coast ports to Butung Island (located off the southeast coast of Celebes) an additional sixty days of rations for fifty thousand men. At Butung Island, the cargoes were to be transshipped to vessels procured there locally for the final run to the Philippines.

Third Objective: The dispatch of another sixty days of rations for fifty thousand men, provided it could be sent with relative safety directly from Australia to the Philippines; however, if that should turn out not to be possible, the rations were to be purchased from local markets on Java and sent directly from there to the Philippines aboard locally procured shipping.

---

[2]   The possibility of supplying MacArthur's army in the Philippines from ports on Australia's east coast had been viewed as a limited proposition from the very onset. Ships of the type which could be risked on such a blockade running mission were in short supply. Most of those ships arriving in Australia from the United States were of a tonnage and class which could be ill-spared for the risks involved in making an attempt to reach the Philippines. However, this was not to prevent such ships from making intermediate runs to points in the East Indies with cargoes that could then be transshipped to smaller vessels for the final leg of the trip.

[3]   Unless otherwise noted, our primary source for the account of the Robenson mission to Java has been Col. John A. Robenson's personal manuscript (never published) as it was taken from his diary entries made during the mission. During 1995, the senior author interviewed John E. Lundberg who had been Robenson's typist and clerk on the Java mission, an interview that provided a particularly valuable insight into what occurred on Java. The Robenson diary -- or the resultant manuscript -- seems to have been consulted by Walter D. Edmonds as the Edmonds's Manuscript Collection located in the Maxwell Air Force Base Archives contains verbatim reference to the mission as described by Robenson.

[4]   At the time the order was transmitted from USAFIA headquarters at Brisbane to Colonel Robenson at Darwin, *Coast Farmer* had not yet left Brisbane for Mindanao. According to USAFIA plans, once *Mauna Loa* had arrived from the west coast, she was to be routed first to Darwin before leaving there under naval escort to Macassar.

[5]   The port town of Macassar is spelled on some Atlases, circa WW II, as Makassar. Following World War II, the place was renamed Ujung Pandang.

Col. John A. Robenson, the officer who had been selected to put these objectives into being, had arrived in Australia with the Pensacola Convoy. When circumstances had canceled his being sent on to the Philippines, he was assigned to Darwin to take charge of the American troops recently sent there for the defense of Australia's Northern Territory. The most probable reason that Robenson had been chosen by USAFIA to head up the Philippine supply effort was his track record for getting things accomplished under difficult circumstances, the Darwin assignment having been a recent example of that attribute. The most pressing problem Robenson encountered at Darwin upon his arrival had been the unloading of shipping which had brought in men and materiel necessary for the Territory's defense. Hampered by the attitude of the Australian longshoremen who seemed indifferent to the fact that the Japanese were practically on their doorstep, operations on the docks were proceeding at a snail's pace. To speed things up, Robenson put his soldiers to work alongside the longshoremen who protested loudly, threatening work stoppages. The threat was quieted when armed guards with fixed bayonets were brought on to the docks. After that, efficiency improved dramatically.[6]

For assistance on his mission, Robenson was authorized to pick six officers and whatever he required by way of enlisted men. He selected Capt. S. J. Randall and five lieutenants -- J. C. Boudoin, R. E. Stensland, Albert B. Cook, Paul M. Nestler, and Franklin H. Andrews -- as well as one enlisted man, Pvt. John E. Lundberg whose skills as a typist and office manager were to prove invaluable as the mission took form.

Robenson would first send Lieutenant Andrews to Butung Island and Lieutenant Stensland to Macassar. Once at their respective locations, each was to await the supplies scheduled to arrive by ship from Australia and which were to be transshipped to local vessels procured for the purpose. Each officer held a letter of credit -- Andrews's worth 600,000 guilders, equaling about $300,000; and Stensland's worth 800,000 guilders, equaling about $400,000. While awaiting the incoming cargoes from Australia, Andrews and Stensland were to gather together whatever local shipping that would be needed, offering whatever was required in the way of bonuses to their owners and the crews.

Robenson, with Randall, Boudoin, Cook, Nestler, and Lundberg, left Darwin on January 24, flying first to Koepang on Portuguese Timor. At Koepang, frantic activity was underway by the Australians who were preparing the local airport for the arrival of B-17 bombers being sent there to back up defenses which, it was thought, would soon bear the brunt of Japanese attention.[7] Leaving Koepang the next

---

[6] A commentary note found within the Edmonds Manuscript Collection offers speculation that Colonel Robenson's selection to head the Philippine supply mission may have been the colonel's lack of finesse in handling Australian labor elements. Historically, the Darwin longshoremen were the most difficult of the labor groups with which the Australian government had to deal. In light of the delicacy over establishing a good working relationship between the American military and Australian officials, it may have been decided by USAFIA that the opportune place for Robenson was the Dutch East Indies where toughness might be necessary.

[7] The day that the Robenson party departed Koepang, the airfield there suffered the first of the many Japanese air raids which were to follow. That day also marked the departure from Darwin of fourteen P-40 pursuit planes destined for ABDA air defense on Java. Only half of those fourteen P-40s reached their destination, the rest all suffering mechanical problems en route, forcing their diversions to air strips on Bali or a return to Timor.

day, Robenson and his party continued by plane to Soerabaja, Java, where they arrived during the late afternoon.[8] Checking into the Oranje Hotel, the first order of business was to assign Lieutenants Cook and Nestler to the task of gathering ships and the needed supplies to go aboard them. Cook was instructed to contact a ship's broker whose identity had been given to Robenson before he left Australia. Cook was to have the broker obtain the use of five small ships of between 200 and 1000 gross tons, each to have a cargo capacity of at least 30 tons. Charter rates were to be negotiated on a one-trip basis with Cook to proceed on the basis of *damn the price, just get the ships.* For the time being, the Philippine destination was to be kept from the broker as well as from the ship owners and crews. In fact, only the master was to be told the actual destination and then only upon his departure. Considering the events then unfolding in the East Indies, of which even a dullard must have been cognizant, such a withholding of information, when viewed in retrospect, seems to have been unrealistic. Nevertheless, Robenson felt that security was paramount, and he also believed at that juncture that to offer high rewards would circumvent any concern over the danger implied. In this, Robenson was soon to be disillusioned. Once a ship's owner agreed to a charter and its related terms, an advance of the daily rate was to be made with the balance due once radio communication was received informing of the delivery of the cargo at its destination. In the negotiations Cook was to conduct with the crews, he was given wide latitude. Robenson suggested a bonus of 200% of base pay to be payable on delivery of the cargo -- Cook being allowed to go higher if forced into it.

For his part, the cargoes to be gathered by Lieutenant Nestler were to be in the form of balanced rations which were believed to be soon arriving on the *President Polk,* and of which, according to instructions that had been issued in Australia, Robenson had full access. Additionally, Nestler was to purchase canned and dry foodstuffs locally.

Cook was soon to find out that regardless of whether or not ship owners or their crews were willing to undertake the voyage, no ship would be allowed to leave before first receiving a series of clearances from ABDA-COM as well as from the Dutch naval and port authorities. This was not going to be easy. In the case of British and Norwegian ships, the British Consul's permission would also be needed.[9]

After issuing his orders to Cook and Nestler, but prior to discovering the difficulties that had to be overcome, Robenson left Soerabaja for Bandoeng, a town located in Java's central highlands to where ABDA-COM had recently moved. Reporting there to the senior American officer, Lt. Gen. George H. Brett, Robenson was briefed on the overall military and naval situations, neither of which were encouraging. While at Bandoeng, he was introduced to a civilian named Henry *Hank* Q. Quade who represented General Motors Corporation as that company's Managing Director for Java. Clued in by Robenson as to the needs of the mission, Quade volunteered to do whatever he could, an assistance which was to prove invaluable as

---

[8]   For what he was to accomplish at Java, Robenson carried letters of credit worth 5,000,000 guilders, equaling about $2.5 million in U.S. currency.

[9]   As far as can be surmised, the British on Java were acting for the Norwegian government insofar as Norwegian shipping affairs were concerned.

Quade's long experience in the East Indies gave him an insight into the local way of doing things. Quade also knew who was to be contacted and for what purposes. Robenson would later write of that assistance:

> *Hank knew everyone that one should know in this part of the world, and if it had not been for him, I would never have made the contacts I did. We lived together, ate together, and slept together for about two weeks and traveled the country. Whatever success the mission attained was a direct result of his efforts. [10]*

Upon returning to Soerabaja, Robenson determined that there was not enough work to justify retaining the services of Captain Randall or of Lieutenant Boudoin, both of whom were told to report to ABDA-COM at Bandoeng for reassignment. Lieutenants Andrews and Stensland were by then both at Macassar. Butung Island had been rendered untenable by the pending arrival of the Japanese, an event which was occurring even as Andrews was en route there by plane to take up his assignment on that island. During the flight, the pilot, upon hearing of the approaching Japanese, reversed course, returning to Macassar where he deposited Andrews who joined Stensland. It was not long before the situation at Macassar became as dangerous as it was on Butung and since little hope remained of getting ships either in or out of Macassar, much less from there to the Philippines, the two lieutenants had themselves evacuated by plane to Java where they both reported to Robenson on February 8.[11]

When a convoy consisting of *President Polk, Hawaiian Planter* and *USS Pecos* arrived at Java, Robenson's worry over obtaining ammunition and other ordnance was notably lessened. Enough ammunition was aboard the two merchant ships to allow a sizable allotment for Philippine shipment. The food stores aboard *President Polk* were also to be Robenson's for the asking.

Cook reported that a Philippine-registered ship, *Florence D* of 2638 tons (C. L. Manzano, master), was at anchor in Soerabaja harbor. She was thought to be available; however, a glitch developed when it was discovered that the ship was under the control of the U.S. Navy which had chartered her during January. Cook was then told that the Navy had no intention of giving her up. The Navy's position, as it would be voiced personally to Robenson by Rear Adm. W. A. Glassford, was that the ship was too valuable to send on a mission which had scant hope for success.[12] When

---

[10]   Robenson's manuscript, p 35.
[11]   The *Mauna Loa* originally intended for Macassar where she was to offload her cargo to native vessels, was not sent due to the encroaching Japanese advance. Instead, she was routed to Darwin. Her loss there has been described within the preceding chapter. Upon his arrival at Soerabaja, Lt. R. E. Stensland, being a field artillery officer, was detached by Colonel Robenson for duty with the 131st Field Artillery. According to sources cited by Gavin Daws within his *Prisoners of the Japanese,* (New York: William Morrow and Co., Inc. 1994), Stensland was distinguished by his heroism with the 131st Field Artillery during later actions on Java against the Japanese. With the surrender of that island in March, he became a POW during which time he exhibited extraordinary courage. Rumored by other prisoners as possessing large sums of money, Stensland was instrumental in obtaining extra foodstuffs for his fellow prisoners, both officers and enlisted men. He survived his captivity and was twice voted president of the Prisoners of War Association.
[12]   *Florence D* had arrived at Soerabaja after escaping the December 10 Japanese bombing of Manila Bay. Poorly stocked with provisions as of her arrival at Java, and with her master not having the money to pay the crew, the crew had deserted the ship and gone ashore. On January 16, the Navy chartered the ship, her master

Robenson left Glassford after receiving the admiral's refusal, he announced that he would return the next day, and the next -- whatever proved necessary -- until *Florence D* was turned over to him. Probably impressed by the colonel's optimism if not his determination, the admiral released the ship the following day and the loading of what had become available from the *President Polk* and *Hawaiian Planter* was begun. In the meantime, Robenson was informed that the *Don Isidro* had arrived from Australia and was then up the coast at Batavia. Carrying the rations and munitions which had been loaded at Brisbane, her master said the ship was ready to leave for the Philippines as soon as Robenson gave the order.

Don Isidro left Soerabaja on February 12. The route she was to take, one selected by the Dutch naval authorities, was south through the Sunda Strait, then farther south for 150 miles before heading eastward toward the Timor Sea to pass between the island of Timor and the north coast of Australia. Once the offing of Darwin had been reached, the route was to change so as to pass east of Celebes with her final destination Gingoog Bay, Mindanao.[13] The *Florence D* would leave Soerabaja the following day (February 13), routing through the Bali Straits and then south for 150 miles before she, too, headed for the Timor Sea and thence north to the Philippines.[14]

During the loading of *Florence D,* her master was handed a plaque prepared by the Dutch authorities for delivery to the troop commander on Bataan:

> *General Jonathan M. Wainwright, this is a small token of the esteem with which we soldiers of Dutch East Indies hold you and your brave men. It is an honor to present this.*
>
> *Capt. W. J. L. DeLange*

Wainwright was a close friend of Robenson, the two having ridden together (in Robenson's words) *over many a long dusty trail.* Appreciative of

---

probably having acted in that regard on behalf of the owners. Apparently the original crew returned to the vessel since later, at the time of the ship's loss, the entirety of the crew listed was Filipino.

[13] The route as here described is from a postwar affidavit filed by Capt. Rafael S. Acosta of the U.S. Army Transportation Corps. Acosta had been the 3rd Officer on *Don Isidro* on the trip from Java toward the Philippines in February 1942. After *Don Isidro* was lost to enemy action while en route, Acosta, probably already a reserve officer in the Philippine Commonwealth Army, entered the Army of the United States, being commissioned in Australia. His affidavit, which was filed at Manila after the retaking of the Philippines in 1945, is now located within RG-407, Philippine Archive Collection, Box 1566, Folder Marine Statistics Branch, *Don Isidro*. Acosta stated in his affidavit that the *Don Isidro* carried a 16-man gun crew of U.S. Army personnel commanded by *2nd Lieutenant Kane* -- the gun crew having been assigned to the ship at Brisbane. Acosta also stated in his affidavit that the final destination of *Don Isidro* was to be Corregidor; but that destination is not in agreement with instructions sent by wireless to Colonel Robenson, signed MacArthur, and which are paraphrased within Robenson's manuscript, p 58. According to that wireless, the assigned destination for the voyages of both *Florence D* and *Don Isidro* was to be Gingoog, Mindanao, where transfer of both of their cargoes was to be made to coasters for carriage north to Corregidor.

[14] According to Robenson, *Florence D* had a cargo of *the best balanced rations that any ship ever carried to troops...including canned fruit, jams, jellies, candies, cigarettes, beer, molasses...and included large amounts of quinine.* Whether this had been the original contents of the *Florence D* cargo holds at the time of her release by the Navy is not made clear by Robenson's account. It is probable that at least a part of the luxuries and almost certainly most if not all of the 3" AA ammunition which Robenson would mention in his note to Wainwright had come from *President Polk* and *Hawaiian Planter*. Other foodstuffs were probably purchased in Java through the efforts of Lieutenant Nestler.

Wainwright's fondness for beer, Robenson bought a case and packed it together with the plaque, enclosing his own note:

Soerabaja, Java
February 11, 1942

Major General J. M. Wainwright
Dear Skinny:
 This token, I hope by all my faith in God, gets to you. I am doing the best that I can with the aid of the United States Treasury to get supplies to you. This ship contains a well balanced ration for several days and quite considerable ammunition. You've got practically all the 3" A.A. ammunition that there is in the Far East. I have full faith in the Captain of the ship and anything that you can do to help him on a return trip will be so much the better. You're doing a great job and everybody in the whole United States and the Far East knows it.
 My best love and good wishes,

John A. Robenson, Colonel, Cavalry [15]

  Except for the 16-man U.S. Army gun crew which had been placed aboard *Don Isidro* at Brisbane, the officers and crew of that ship and as well as the *Florence D* were totally Filipino. On the strength of their expressed desire to assist in the defense of their homeland, Robenson had confidence that they would do their utmost to see the job through. However, the spirit of *can-do* which pervaded the Filipino ships was not again to be encountered by Robenson with other allied merchant crews at Java with which the mission would soon have to deal.

  While arranging for the departure of *Don Isidro,* Quade, who was still in company with Colonel Robenson, had bumped into a Dutch civilian, A. C. Bodeker who, as Quade told Robenson, *knew more about the local shipping business than anyone in the Far East.* On that recommendation, Robenson hired Bodeker on the spot to make a survey and report on those ships between 200 and 5000 tons which were then available at Java or at Bali. Bodeker came up with thirteen which were flying either the British or Norwegian flags. He told Robenson that all thirteen had been placed under a hold-in-port order issued by ABDA-COM and that if any of them were to be obtained for the mission, a release would be needed, to be followed by a restraint order reserving the ships for Robenson's purpose. Any release would apply only to the ships themselves. Getting willing crews to sail the ships would be an entirely separate undertaking. Probably alerted over what might take place, the British Vice Consul at Soerabaja, not an enthusiast for risking his national shipping in the enterprise Robenson had in mind, cleared six of the British ships which immediately left port for safer climes. As for the seven remaining ships, Robenson was now to become all too familiar with the numerous layers of naval and civil bureaucracy from which permission would be needed before any of them could be obtained. This included both the Dutch and the British fleet commanders at ABDA-COM and even the Chinese Consul since the non-officer elements of many of the crews then at Soerabaja were Chinese nationals. Even the Dutch attorney general on Java and the Office of Commerce had to be queried. Some of the red tape was avoided when the Dutch bureaucracy was overridden by the personal intervention of the senior Dutch naval

---

[15] Robenson manuscript, pp 58, 59.

officer on Java, Vice Adm. C. E. L. Helfrich, who, expressing his personal enthusiasm for the mission, wistfully said that he would like to take one of the ships through himself. Technically all commercial shipping within the Dutch East Indies had come under Dutch control. Robenson was to discover from Helfrich that the key to obtaining releases for the ships would be for Helfrich to requisition them. The stumbling block on that, though, was that the Dutch would not requisition British-owned shipping and, presumably British-controlled Norwegian shipping, unless the British acquiesced. Despite the best efforts of Hank Quade, who had volunteered to act as Robenson's personal envoy at ABDA-COM, Quade got nowhere since neither the British nor the Americans in command positions thought that shipping could get through the Japanese blockade and reach the Philippines. To waste valuable tonnage in such a hopeless endeavor was, in their opinions, unwarranted.[16] In retrospect, such a viewpoint was militarily valid; yet to Robenson, the response must have appeared heartless.

Soerabaja was coming under increased air attack. By Robenson's count, one such raid consisted of fifty-four enemy aircraft. Damage to personnel had been comparatively light; but destruction to the wharves and to the naval and merchant shipping in the harbor was mounting. After the heaviest of the raids, Robenson counted seven ships on fire, making it appear that if the Philippine mission was not given the use of the ships it needed, the enemy bombers would soon make the whole matter a mute issue.

Despite the lack of cooperation from ABDA-COM, Robenson -- who had by now decided that four ships would serve his needs adequately -- was not one to give up, and his pleas continued. In line with the possibility that there might be a change in ABDA-COM thinking, he and his officers went ahead gathering and warehousing foodstuffs. A Dutch army captain made the suggestion that pigs on the hoof could be purchased on Bali and then slaughtered, dried, and salted on Java. The captain even volunteered to find the pigs. In company with the Dutch officer, Nestler contracted for three thousand pigs from their owners, and arrangements were made to have them brought to Java in open boats. About 1500 pigs had reached Java and had been processed before the Japanese occupied Bali. The last boatload leaving Bali while carrying a cargo of 150 pigs was strafed by a Japanese plane, killing most of the native crew and all but a half dozen of the pigs.

---

[16]   When discussing his mission's plans for evacuation from Java, Colonel Robenson had offered to see that Henry Q. Quade would go out with him no matter the means. Reportedly, Quade received a similar offer from the American naval staff at ABDA-COM. In both instances, Quade refused, saying that his office staff -- both British and Dutch -- had stayed with him, and he could not now desert them. Following the Japanese occupation of Java, Quade was imprisoned by the Japanese in a civilian penal prison under conditions of solitary confinement during which time, and on a number of occasions, he was beaten by his captors with *the bamboo*. He was taken out of that prison after twenty-two months and placed in a military prisoner of war camp where he remained for eight months before being transferred to a civilian internment camp where he remained until his release on September 1, 1945. Following the war, Quade stayed on with General Motors, finally retiring in 1965 as a Regional Manager of the company's Overseas Operations Division in northern Europe. In 1948, Quade was decorated by the Dutch government with *The Royal Order of Orange Nassau* for his contributions during World War II. Source: General Motors Corporation, Business Research Library, Detroit, Michigan.

Robenson was awakened at the Oranje Hotel at about that time by an American Army officer who announced that he was a special courier from Australia with orders to hand deliver a large package wrapped in dirty canvas and secured with rope. The instructions were that the package was only to be opened by Robenson and in the courier's presence. Out rolled a huge pile of United States paper currency. The package had with it no accompanying memorandum nor did the courier know from whence it originated or its purpose -- only that he required a receipt for the exact amount of money. This meant that the two officers had to painstakingly count the contents which was no mean task considering that most of the money was in small bills and that the total amounted to $250,000.[17]

The day the *Florence D* sailed from Soerabaja, events took a turn for the better when ABDA-COM at last released the four needed ships. One, the *Taiyuan,* was of British (Hong Kong) registry; the other three were the Norwegian-flagged *Proteus, Tunni,* and *Bordvik.* The following day, Robenson received written clearance for all of the ships, to become effective once they were ready to leave port on Robenson's orders. Loading was begun, beginning with the *Taiyuan;* but one more difficulty had yet to be surmounted, namely the gathering of crews.

~

Before Robenson left Australia, and before he experienced the realities of the situation in Java, he had held a belief *that anything or anybody could be had for sufficient money... and that , men would be willing to sacrifice life if it was for love or patriotism.* His rude awakening would come from *...the old sea captains of the China coast which proved that their only interest was themselves, and then very much so -- their own comforts, as they saw them, their shore pleasures and scotch.* [18] It was fortunate that the colonel also had a taste and tolerance for scotch as he was soon to discover that whenever negotiating with the salty fraternity of the Far East, it was customary to preface discussions with at least two if not three drinks. Only then could business be discussed. When Robenson finally got a captain to the point where he could be asked whether he would take one of the ships on *a dangerous mission* (destination was never stated but probably was assumed by the captain to be the Philippines), the masters would agree. However, in each and every instance, the acquiescence was recanted the following day, usually accompanied by a variety of excuses. When told that the particular concerns could be rectified, the captain then usually voiced an outright refusal. The one exception, at least at first, was the master of *Taiyuan*, a Captain Fraser, who after three *well-watered* conferences, agreed to sail; but even then, his willingness was only given halfheartedly.

---

[17]   During the process of counting the currency, the courier remarked that he had heard someone in Australia say that two more such packages were on their way; but if that was so, Robenson never received them. Having already more cash on hand than he needed, Robenson took all but $9,000 of it to a Soerabaja bank for deposit where it was to stay until he later left for Australia. Although Robenson later wrote that he was never told the origin of the $250,000, the Edmonds's manuscript contains a comment that it was sent as a result of concern on the part of Brig Gen. Julian F. Barnes in Australia who believed that the eroding situation in the Dutch East Indies could render the Dutch guilder worthless in the minds of those persons with whom Robenson was to deal. If such happened, U.S. currency would serve the mission with much greater effectiveness.

[18]   Robenson manuscript, p 62.

Before the loading of *Taiyuan* could begin, a problem with her sailors and engine room gang -- all of them Chinese -- had to be rectified. The entire bunch was under indictment for mutiny and was confined under guard aboard the ship. Calling on the British Vice Consul who had ordered the arrests, Robenson was told that there was no room for the mutineers in the local jail. They were therefore to remain on *Taiyuan* until provisions for a trial could be arranged. This appeared to be an unlikely event, at least on Java, as the closest British Admiralty Court was in India. Seeking some remedy, Robenson called on Soerabaja's chief of police who, *after the third drink agreed to take the Chinese off the ship...,* provided Robenson could have a barbed wire enclosure erected somewhere ashore to contain them. Returning to the British Consulate, he received approval to move the prisoners off the ship, but only after agreeing to pay the Chinese their daily wage since under British maritime law, wages were to be paid up until the time mutineers were actually convicted.[19]

With the prisoners ashore and within the barbed wire enclosure under tight guard, the ship was inspected and found to be the *vilest ship anyone ever saw; a description would be repulsive.* [20] A thorough cleaning was necessary to make her ready to receive the foodstuffs to be loaded. The supervision of the cleaning proved *too colossal for Captain Fraser to tackle, so he went to his cabin and stayed drunk for three days,* during which time Robenson attempted to get a firm commitment both from him and from his British officers that they would sail.[21] The *old lush,* as Robenson described him, hemmed and hawed before finally giving his outright refusal, joined in by all of the ship's engineers but one. Out of the ship's entire officer complement, only the chief officer, one of the mates, and one engineer would agree to sail. The ship's radio operators who were Chinese had also refused. To get the master and the others who had refused away from the ship where their presence had become a disquieting influence, Lieutenants Cook and Nestler *poured* them on to a train for Batavia where they were to be put aboard a ship leaving for Calcutta.

The selection of a new master (with agreement of the British Vice Consul) was *Taiyuan's* former chief officer, John W. E. Warrior. That gentleman proved to be the one exception of what Robenson must have settled on as the stereotype of British mariners who worked the Far East trade. Warrior was sober! He was, however, possessed more of self-interest than any patriotic desire to support the war effort. That self-interest led to demands for fiscal remuneration which were beyond imagination -- demands which Robenson had little choice but to meet. The job of recruiting other ship's officers as well as sailors and firemen became the task of Lieutenant Andrews who Robenson had empowered to pay whatever was necessary by way of wages and bonuses. Canvassing other merchant ships, both at Soerabaja and at Batavia, Andrews started to gather together what he hoped would be the kind of individuals who, regardless of motivation, might see the voyage through. The lieutenant's biggest break came when the American freighter *Collingsworth* put in at

---

[19]   The trial of the Chinese never took place since within days Soerabaja would be occupied by the Japanese, and the U.S. Army was never billed for their wages. Robenson later surmised that the mutineers would have ended up as prisoners of the Japanese which may have tamed them down as in the colonel's opinion, they *were as ferocious as wolves.*

[20]   Robenson manuscript, pp 63, 64.

[21]   Robenson manuscript, p 64.

Soerabaja. After considerable discussion with its master, five of her crew who volunteered were allowed to sign off the *Collingsworth's* Articles for service on the *Taiyuan*.[22] Andrews finally managed to put together enough crew for the voyage.[23] The one crewing slot still left to be filled was that of a radio operator, an essential element as the ship would have to be able to make contact with army authorities in the Philippines some hours prior to its arrival there. A radio operator (probably off one of the Norwegian ships) had been recruited, but he backed out at the last minute. The only avenue remaining from which a radio operator might come was the Army Air Corps based at Malang. Roberson finally obtained a promise from the commanding officer of that base that a radio operator would be provided -- but only on a voluntary basis. To counter any reluctance to volunteer, a sum as high as $5,000 was to be offered to any qualified radio operator, payable upon his reporting for duty on the ship.[24]

~

While *Taiyuan* was still in the process of being loaded, General Brett's office reached Robenson's office at Soerabaja on February 25 with the message, *Tell the Colonel to get back to Australia for a conference as soon as possible. Either go direct or via Bandoeng.* How Robenson and his party were to get to Australia was left unsaid, but that was partially cleared up by a second message stating that they were to

---

[22] The *Collingsworth* had departed from Seattle, Washington, on October 30, 1941, bound for Manila via Pearl Harbor. Stopping over at Port Moresby, New Guinea, she was diverted to Darwin when the war broke out. After a short stay at Darwin, orders came to leave for Batavia, where she arrived on December 30. While there, the master attempted to sell the ship's cargo consisting of flour and general merchandise which had been the consignment for Manila, but there were no buyers. The ship remained at Batavia for a month. It is presumed that she must have finally unloaded at least some part of the cargo either at Batavia or at Singapore as at the end of January, she loaded rubber as well as eighty-seven American civilians for evacuation. Returning to Batavia, the passengers were landed, and, according to what the crew of *Collingsworth* were told, they were flown south to Australia. From Batavia, the ship moved down the coast to Soerabaja (presumably for bunkers). It was there that the five volunteers who were to go to *Taiyuan* were signed off Articles. Under escort of the destroyer *USS Isabel,* the *Collingsworth* left Soerabaja reaching safety at Ceylon and from there sailed for New York via Capetown. Source on the *Collingsworth* has been: Remembrances of a *Collingsworth* crewmember Everett Johnson which were published during 1995 in *The Newsletter*, a quarterly publication of the American Merchant Marine Veterans Association. Although five *Collingsworth* crewmembers had volunteered their services for *Taiyuan*, two of them changed their minds, one escaping to Australia and the other remaining on Java to be eventually imprisoned and beheaded by the Japanese. See Appendix O for a listing of the *Collingsworth* volunteers as well as a true copy of the contract entered into between Colonel Robenson and John W. E. Warrior, master of the *Taiyuan.*

[23] Officers and other crewmen recruited by Lieutenant Andrews for the *Taiyuan* were to receive four times their normal salary plus a bonus for delivery and life insurance. The payments promised each officer and crewman for serving on *Taiyuan* are stated within the contract executed between Robenson and Warrior which is reproduced within Appendix O.

[24] An Air Corps sergeant, Wyatt Warrenfeltz, volunteered. Colonel Robenson and his party was to leave Soerabaja for Australia before the *Taiyuan* was ready to sail and therefore before Warrenfeltz appeared. Robenson had left instructions that Warrenfeltz was to report to a Dutch officer at the port *Captain* [W. J. L.] *DeLange* where the $5,000 enticement would be paid to Warrenfeltz who was then to immediately board the *Taiyuan.* U.S. Army files (Adjutant Generals Office, 1946) contain a number of pieces of correspondence including the contract between *Taiyuan's* master and Colonel Robenson, executed on February 26, 1942. The AGO files deal with a claim following the war by the three former crewmembers of the *Collingsworth* who had signed on the *Taiyuan.* The claim was for inclusion under the Missing Persons Act. It was denied on the grounds that the claimants were not employees of the War Department but rather were contractual personages mentioned in the contract made between Robenson and the *Taiyuan's* master. Additionally, shipping articles were reportedly never signed, nor was the voyage commenced.

go to Tjilatjap, to arrive there not later than the next day. Before Robenson and his party could leave, much had to be done, not the least of which was to pay promised advances to the *Taiyuan's* crew. If requested by the individual crewmember, sums were to be forwarded from the local bank to addresses the individuals might designate. Bills also had to be settled, and the remaining moneys, including the U.S. currency previously deposited by Robenson in the local bank, had to be withdrawn. A Dutch Army officer, Captain DeLange agreed to act as Robenson's agent in settling whatever accounts came due once the final loading of *Taiyuan* had been completed.[25] Early the following morning, Robenson, Cook, Nestler, Andrews, and Lundberg left for Tjilatjap by road. After a hectic drive across the island during which time they managed to get lost on two occasions, they reached Tjilatjap by mid afternoon. Still unknowing as to how he and his men were to get to Australia, Robenson located an office occupied by the U.S. Navy port command where after much hunting through piles of transmitted messages, travel orders originating from ABDA-COM, were located. They disclosed that Robenson was himself to leave by commercial seaplane for Australia while the three lieutenants and Private Lundberg were to go by sea aboard the Dutch freighter *Albukirk*. Despite the conditions on Java, the telephone system was still operating, and Robenson was able to get through to DeLange who reported that *Taiyuan* was to sail on the tide the following day and that the Air Corps radio operator had appeared and was already aboard. Robenson then saw his lieutenants and Lundberg to the dock where *Albukirk* was taking on passengers. The scene there was a mass of uniformed humanity, almost 50% of whom were drunk but who still retained a certain semblance of discipline. Everyone was waiting his turn to board with no signs of fighting or panic. Bidding good-bye to his officers and Private Lundberg, Robenson left for the airdrome from where he was to fly. Early the next morning, lugging a leather suitcase within which was the quarter of a million dollars in U.S. currency, Robenson, in company with other senior officers, boarded a plane and flew to Broome on Australia's northwest coast. From there, after a stopover of a day, Robenson was flown on to Brisbane.[26] [27]

~

The Robenson mission, despite the great effort that had been expended to pull it off, was not to succeed -- its sad finality being the failure of *Taiyuan* to sail. In the mid-afternoon of February 27, while the ship's hatches were being closed preparatory for leaving Soerabaja, an allied fleet under the command of Dutch Rear Adm. K. W. F. M. Doorman was about to enter the port. Doorman received a radio report from Admiral Helfrich at ABDA-COM stating that an enemy force had been sighted from the air in the area of Bawean, an island located to the north of Soerabaja. Unknown to ABDA-COM at the time was that the enemy force was but one part of a huge invasion armada taking aim on Java. It was divided into three separate attack

---

[25] Once bills were approved for payment by DeLange, the bank at Soerabaja was to make disbursement with an amount which Robenson left on deposit. Any balance remaining was to be refunded by wire transfer to the USAFIA Finance Office in Australia -- that is if time allowed before the Japanese occupied.

[26] Lieutenants Cook, Nestler, Andrews, and Private Lundberg reached safety at Freemantle, Australia, after a harrowing voyage on *Albukirk* which suffered strafing attacks on two separate occasions during the voyage. Robenson's departure from Broome by air had been timely as the next day Broome and its airdrome facility were the recipients of a devastating air raid.

[27] For his work on the mission to Java, Colonel Robenson was awarded the Distinguished Service Medal.

divisions. Coming from the south was a surface and carrier group consisting of six aircraft carriers, one battleship, five heavy cruisers, one light cruiser, and thirteen destroyers; approaching from the east were forty-one troop transports escorted by four heavy cruisers, two light cruisers, nineteen destroyers, six patrol craft, and three mine warfare craft; approaching from the west were fifty-six troop transports and cargo ships escorted by one aircraft carrier, four heavy cruisers, two light cruisers, and twenty-five destroyers. D-Day for the Japanese landings was to be February 28.

The enemy expedition committed for the invasion of Java was the largest single amphibious force that the Japanese had so far employed in the Southwest Pacific. Unbeknown to the Japanese such strength would hardly be necessary since ABDA (air and ground) was already evaporating. On February 20, General Wavell had requested and had received London's permission to evacuate all British (inclusive of Australian and New Zealand) ground and air forces. On February 19, Maj. General Brereton, ABDA-COM (for air) had decided to evacuate all American air personnel and bombers to India.[28] Receiving agreement from Wavell's deputy, Lt. General Brett, and from Washington, Brereton flew his bombers out on February 24. On February 25, both Wavell and Brereton flew to India. Brett had left for Australia the day before. In what can only be viewed as an act of callous indifference, neither Wavell nor any other British or American officer at ABDA-COM had informed the Dutch ground commander, Maj. Gen. Hein Ter Poorten, of the pullout. When the news leaked out, Ter Poorten was understandably shocked. Concerned that the expected Japanese invasion was not going to be opposed by the American and British naval forces under ABDA command, Ter Poorten inquired of U.S. Navy Rear Admiral Glassford as to the intentions of the Americans. Glassford replied that his orders were to stay and fight if ordered to do so by the Dutch naval commander, a decision which must have been joined at the time by the British naval commander, Rear Adm. A. F. E. Pallister, who still had a substantial number of his ships operating with Dutch Rear Admiral Doorman in the waters north of Java.[29]

Following the receipt of the report that an enemy naval force had been sighted north of Soerabaja, Doorman had led his fleet consisting of Dutch, British, and American cruisers -- screened by destroyers -- to intercept. At 1600 hours on February 27, *USS Houston* and *HMS Exeter* came under heavy enemy surface fire. This marked the opening of what has become known as the Battle of the Java Sea, a struggle which would take place over a wide expanse of the narrow sea bordered to the south by Java and north by Borneo. The battle lasted for over seven exhausting hours during which time Doorman was killed, going down with his flagship *HNMS De Ruyter*. Also sunk, all with heavy personnel losses, were the cruiser *HNMS Java* and the

---

[28]   As previously related, a shipment of crated P-40s had been scheduled to arrive by ship at Tjilatjap on February 26. They were unloaded, only to be burned in their crates the following day to avoid having the planes fall into the possession of the enemy. By that time, few P-40s were left on Java -- most having been lost in combat. Of the remainder, few were in a condition to be flown anywhere.

[29]   U.S. Army Air Corps ground crews as well as many of the American troops and those P-40 pilots still alive and able to travel, would leave Tjilatjap on February 27, all of them crammed aboard the Dutch merchantmen *Abeekerk* and *Kota Gede*. The *Abbekerk* would reach safety at Freemantle and the *Kota Gede* at India. The only American left behind on Java where they were to provide direct artillery support for the Dutch Army was one battalion of the American 131st Field Artillery.

destroyers *HMS Electra, HMS Jupiter,* and *HNMS Kortenaer.* Java now lay open for the Japanese landings which would take place on the following day.

Java's north coast was no longer tenable for the remnants of the ABDA fleet. Of the northern ports on Java, only Soerabaja still had intact bunkering facilities, but the place was under almost constant air attack. So far, Tjilatjap on the south coast had been spared the heavy air raids which had by now knocked out the port facilities at Batavia and were about to do the same thing for Soerabaja. Four American destroyers, *USS John D. Ford, USS John D. Edwards, USS Paul Jones,* and *USS Alden* were compelled to enter Soerabaja for bunkers as they did not have enough fuel to reach Tjilatjap. The *USS Houston* and *HMAS Perth*, both with battle damage, had sheltered up the coast from Soerabaja at Tanjong Priok. From there, on the night of February 28, in company with one destroyer, the two cruisers sortied on a westerly heading toward the Sunda Straits. Nearing the northwestern tip of Java, they ran headlong into the enemy's western invasion group whose troopships were preparing to send landing craft into the beach. Closing, the Americans and Australians chose to attack, *USS Houston* sinking one transport and forcing three others to beach in foundering condition. The enemy's escorts then rushed in for the kill. At close to midnight, *HMAS Perth* went down, followed shortly by *USS Houston* -- both ships having been perforated by the enemy's shell fire.

Also separated following the battle of the 27th was *HMS Exeter* with its two screening destroyers, *USS Pope* and *HMS Encounter.* This group was trying to reach the Sunda Straits from Soerabaja where the two destroyers had refueled when it ran afoul of four enemy cruisers covering landings being conducted at Karanganjan about 100 miles to the west of Soerabaja. The *HMS Exeter* and the two destroyers were sunk.

The four American destroyers which had been the first to enter Soerabaja were luckier. Once fueled, they had headed east to the Bali Straits from where, on receiving wireless instructions to evacuate to Australia, they made their way south.

On the morning of March 1, Rear Admiral Pallister and Rear Admiral Glassford again called on Vice Admiral Helfrich. Pallister announced that he had received British Admiralty instructions to withdraw the remaining British ships to India. Helfrich strenuously objected, pointing to the fact that the Dutch had devoted their full resources in the support of the British fleet in the defense of Malaya and that the least he now expected from the British was time so the Dutch Governor General could be consulted as to whether or not the fight was to continue in Java's waters. Pallister stated that there was no time to spare and that he was ordering the immediate departure of all British ships for India. Turning to Glassford, Helfrich asked what the American's orders were. Glassford replied that he was under Dutch command and that whatever order Helfrich gave would be obeyed -- Washington having told him that he was to retire to Australia only if Java was to be abandoned. In resignation of the fact that without the British ships any further defense of the island was hopeless, Helfrich told Glassford to order his American ships to Australia.[30] Within hours of that unhappy conference, the Dutch Governor General ordered that ABDA be dissolved.

~

On February 27, when the news arrived at Soerabaja of the naval battle being fought only a few miles to the north, the Dutch harbor authorities advised that sailings be delayed until the way was considered clear for a breakout. Before the day was over, Japanese fortunes had progressed to the point that departure from the harbor by any vessel was an impossibility. As the appearance of the enemy as expected at any moment, the Dutch authorities ordered that all ships in the harbor were to be immediately scuttled.[31]

The defense of Java was now about to enter its final hour in which only the Dutch Army and a small contingent of American artillerymen were left to face the Japanese. It was a defense which would be short-lived, the defenders overwhelmed.

The last radio message to be transmitted from an American officer on Java was sent out on or about March 7 under the sign-off of Col. Albert C. Searle. *Sending aircraft from now on unsafe.* [32] The final Dutch message was sent out on March 9: *We are shutting down now. Good-bye till better times. Long live the Queen.* [33]

The voyages of *Florence D* and *Don Isidro* might best be described as excursions to the wrong places at the wrong times. As earlier related, the Dutch authorities had assigned to each ship a route which would take it through the Timor

---

[30]   This release of the American ships by Helfrich is the reason why the four American destroyers which had left Soerabaja for Tjilatjap, instead changed course for Australia following receipt of those radioed instructions. Working possibly on the theory that at least a semblance of allied unity had to be preserved and that in numbers there was strength, Pallister would order his remaining British ships south to the Exmouth Gulf of West Central Australia instead of India. Glassford's orders for the evacuation of the American ships to Australia would be successful only for the four mentioned destroyers. In the waters south of Java, the destroyer *USS Pillsbury* and the gunboat *USS Nashville* were lost, both with no survivors.

[31]   *Taiyuan* was one of those scuttled as were *Bordvik, Proteus,* and *Tunni. Taiyuan's* chief officer, acting for the master who had for some unexplained reason gone ashore, scuttled the ship. Warrior and the two British officers who had chosen to remain with the ship under the contract of agreement made with Colonel Robenson, were taken by the Japanese as prisoners of war as were the three Americans from the *Collingsworth* and one other American. The fates of five Scandinavians, one Panamanian, one other Caucasian of unknown origin, and two Filipinos was not revealed from our research. We are also unaware of the fate of the radio operator, Sgt. Wyatt Warrenfeltz, or of the remainder twenty of the crew who were Javanese natives. See Appendix O for the fates of those for whom information was available.

[32]   Of the many examples of heroism and self-sacrifice exhibited by United States military personnel during the defense of Java, one seems to stand out above the rest. It involved Col. Albert C. Searle, the senior officer of the American field artillery troops which had been sent to Java. Even though Searles was under direct orders to leave for Australia, he refused to go, giving as his reason that the battalion of the 131st Field Artillery, which was under orders to remain, was a Texas National Guard outfit. Searle took the position that it would be morally wrong for him, the senior American ground force officer on Java and a career Army officer at that, to leave for safety while National Guard troops had been ordered to remain behind. According to a broadcast received in Australia a year later, Searle was then alive, being held as a prisoner of war by the Japanese.

[33]   Unless otherwise footnoted, our summarization of the air and ground defense of Java was derived from the Walter D. Edmonds Manuscript Collection held within the Archives Branch, Headquarters, AFIIRA/ISR, Maxwell Air Force Base, Alabama. The microfilm call numbers for that part of the Edmonds Manuscript Collection which we utilized are: 168.7022-7; 168.7022-33; 168.7022-1; 168.7022-6, these call numbers covering the year 1941-42.

Sea before heading north toward a delivery destination on Mindanao. Neither ship made it as both were to cross the paths of the Japanese air groups which on February 19 raided Darwin.

On February 18, an enemy plane, then scouting the westward entrance to the Timor Sea, spotted *Don Isidro* and over-flew her for an identification check after which the plane made two bombing runs, dropping a single bomb each time which missed. With the plane's departure, *Don Isidro's* master assembled his officers, stating to them that since the Japanese now knew of the ship's location, they would be back and that it was his intention to alter course either for Darwin or Thursday Island for new naval routing instructions. The collective vote of the officers was for Darwin, it being closer and the most provident choice under the circumstances. The following morning at the approaches to Darwin, *Don Isidro's* radio operator announced that the town was under attack, *by about 100 planes.* Within minutes, four fighters commenced strafing runs on *Don Isidro,* followed within a quarter of an hour by dive bombers which scored between four and six hits, wrecking the ship's engines and setting fires throughout the ship. With the fear that ammunition in the cargo was about to explode at any moment, the order was given to abandon ship. With the aid of two rafts, the survivors were able to reach nearby Bathhurst Island within a few hours. Once on the beach there, a count was made which disclosed that eleven of the crew were missing and that two others were wounded. (They were to later die.) After a night and day without food or water, the survivors were rescued by an Australian gunboat and brought to Darwin from where they were flown to Brisbane. At least some of those men were inducted at Brisbane into the American Army, either in a commissioned or enlisted status.[34]

Another loss that February 19 was a U.S. Navy PBY patrol plane whose arc of reconnaissance had directly crossed the flight path of Japanese carrier-based bombers heading toward Darwin. Attacked by fighters in escort to those bombers, the PBY was shot down in flames, its crew barely managing to crowd aboard one of two of the plane's life rafts, the other raft having been perforated by machine gun fire.[35] Seeing the flames on the horizon and probably also having received the plane's distress call, the master of *Florence D* diverted and at around the noon hour rescued the plane's crew. About an hour after that rescue, a single Japanese plane flew over *Florence D*, dropping bombs which missed. At 1400, the enemy reappeared. This time it was a group of seventeen dive bombers which took the ship under heavy attack, several of the bombs setting fires and putting the ship down by the head, stopping all

---

[34] The account of *Don Isidro's* loss is taken from an affidavit of Rafael S. Acosta. At the time of the loss of *Don Isidro,* Acosta was serving on the ship as its 3rd Officer. After the ship's loss and Acosta's arrival at Brisbane, he was inducted as a commissioned officer into the Army of the United States. Acosta's affidavit is to be found within RG- 407, Philippine Archive Collection, Box 1566, Folder Marine Statistics Branch, *Don Isidro.* Following Col. John A. Robenson's return to Australia from Java, he would again meet the masters of both *Don Isidro* and *Florence D .* Following their reunion, Robenson would write in his diary that both had received commissions in the U.S. Army prior to their meeting. It can be presumed that their assignments were with USAFIA, Service of Supply, for duty in relationship to Australian-based supply ship function. It is of interest that the table of organization for SOS in Australia for the year 1942 includes a Filipino-manned ship section.

[35] The senior pilot of the PBY shot down that day was a young lieutenant, Thomas H. Moorer. Many years later, Moorer would become a 4-star admiral and the Chief of Naval Operations during the Johnson and Nixon administrations.

headway. Because of the fire and risk of explosion, those who still could jumped overboard. Following the departure of the Japanese planes, a number of the crew cut away two of the lifeboats with which they picked up those still in the water -- many of whom were badly burned. The lifeboats having separated during the night, the following morning, each boat landed at separate locations on Bathhurst Island from where the survivors were rescued. All the *Florence D* survivors were taken to Darwin from where they were flown to Brisbane. Despite the burns received in the attack and the later strafing of the lifeboats which resulted in more wounded, there were few fatal casualties, only three crewmen being lost in the sinking, including one of the PBY's crew; of the wounded, all eventually recovered.[36]

---

[36] The account of the sinking of the *Florence D* is taken from Browning, *U.S. Merchant Vessel War Casualties of World War II,* p 29.

SS Portmar. Bomb-damaged during air attack on Darwin; then beached to prevent sinking. Later was salvaged by the U.S. Army, becoming the *USAT Portmar.* Lost by submarine attack off the east coast of Australia in 1943. Grover Collection (National Maritime Museum).

USAT Don Esteban. Taken under bareboat charter by the Army Transport Service at Manila on October 30, 1941. While attempting to run supplies from Panay to Corregidor was attacked by enemy bombers on March 1, 1942, becoming a total loss. Grover Collection.

SS Dona Nati. She was one of the three vessels which successfully ran the Japanese blockade from Australia to Philippines during early 1942. Her Philippine destination was Cebu City, island of Cebu. Grover Collection (Mariners Museum).

SS Coast Farmer. One of only three ships which succeeded in running the Japanese blockade from Australia to the Philippines during early 1942. Her Philippine destination was Mindanao. Grover Collection (National Maritime Museum).

SS Elcano. Filipino ship chartered by the Army Transport Service during the defense of the Philippines, 1941–42. Arrived at Corregidor with supplies offloaded from *Coast Farmer* at Mindanao. Sunk by Japanese shellfire off Corregidor either April or May of 1942. Grover Collection.

SS Legazpi. Filipino ship chartered by the Army Transport Service to run the Japanese blockade from Corregidor to Capiz on Panay, and return. She was lost on her third trip from Capiz by Japanese naval attack on March 1, 1942. Grover Collection.

SS Taiyuan. British merchant ship taken under contract by the U.S. Army (Robenson mission) at Java to attempt to run the Japanese blockade of the Philippines. Was loaded for departure but was trapped at Soerabaja by Japanese naval forces. She was scuttled by her crew. Arthur R. Moore Collection.

USAT Teapa, ex *SS Teapa*, ex *USS Putnam*. Former destroyer converted to a fast banana carrier. One of three such vessels bareboat chartered by the Army Service of Supply to run the Japanese blockade of the Philippines during early 1942. While en route, the mission was canceled and the ship was reassigned to Alaskan duty. Grover Collection (Mariners Museum).

CHAPTER XVI

FAST SHIPS AND SUBMARINES

On March 4, with the defense of Java having entered its final hour, Lt. Gen. George H. Brett and Brig. Gen. Patrick J. Hurley were back in Australia. On that day, Hurley informed the War Department that supplying the Philippines from Australia was no longer feasible. This also seems to have been the opinion of MacArthur who had earlier (on February 22) radioed Chief of Staff Gen. George C. Marshall stating that the most expedient route for getting supplies to the Philippines would be from Hawaii. Hurley emphasized to Marshall that in order to reach the Philippines from Australia with any chance of success, ships would have to divert so far to the east that their track would be almost equal to the distance undertaken by ships routing from Hawaii.[1]

The idea of sending ships from the United States via the Hawaiian Islands had its origins with Washington, the plan having been conceived over a month prior to Marshall's receipt of the radio message from MacArthur. As early as January 12, the War Department had radioed MacArthur that seven converted World War I destroyers were to be loaded with food and medical supplies at New Orleans and sent to the Philippines via Honolulu. That was, however, the last word on the subject reaching MacArthur, a disturbing silence on a matter which no doubt MacArthur thought needed revitalizing.[2] The identification of those *seven destroyers* remains somewhat of a mystery as in fact only three such ships were actually obtained by the Army for that use. Those three, which were sub-bareboat chartered by the Army from

---

[1]   Stauffer, p 25.

[2]   Files of Chief of Transportation, memorandum titled *Blockade Running from Z/I,* noted as being "Report of OPNE, QMC, USA, in Philippine Campaign, 1941-42."

the War Shipping Administration on February 5, were: *Teapa* (ex *USS Putnam);* *Matagalpa* (ex *USS Osbourne);* and *Masaya* (ex *USS Dale).* [3] [4]

MacArthur's radioed message of February 22 had been copied to the White House which immediately inquired of the War Department as to what measures, if any, were being taken to comply with MacArthur's request. On February 24, General Marshall informed President Roosevelt by memorandum that *three naval destroyers were having diesel engines installed and cargo holds rearranged.* Marshall went on to state that the first of the three would be ready to sail from New Orleans in a few days and the other two by the first week in March. He also said there were three more ships *of the same type being operated commercially in the Caribbean...Arrangements are being made to take them over and add them to the three boats referred to above...A radio has been sent to General MacArthur notifying him accordingly of this, we hope, cheering possibility.* [5]

As it applied to the overall subject of the ships, Marshall's understanding was in error, the result of what appears to have been considerable confusion over what was taking place at the Service of Supply level in New Orleans. This particularly applied to the three other ships *of the same type.* Those three -- *USAT Texada* (ex *El Cicuta; ex Lake Dunmore); Alencon* (ex *Brookings; ex Cowiche*) *; Vannes* (ex *West Planter; ex Texas Planter; ex Lake Flatonia*) --were not former destroyers, nor by any stretch of the imagination could they have been considered as fast express carriers.[6] Each had been built on the Great Lakes as cargo ships under a contract of the U.S. Shipping Board executed shortly after the end of World War I.[7] None was capable of exceeding 10 knots, therefore being totally unsuitable for running the Japanese blockade.

---

[3]   Declared surplus to the Navy's use, the three destroyers had been sold by the Navy to commercial buyers in the early 1930s and converted into express banana carriers operating between Central American and New Orleans.

[4]   In tracing these ex-destroyers, we utilized *Merchant Vessels of the United States* for the years 1931-1941*; Lloyd's Registry of Steam and Motor Vessels*, 1941-42*; Record of the American Bureau of Shipping,* 1938, 1940*;* and the *Dictionary of American Naval Fighting Ships.*

[5]   From Files of Chief of Transportation, Memorandum for the President, from G. C. Marshall, Chief of Staff, February 24, 1942.

[6]   The *Texada* (U.S. flag) went under bareboat charter to the War Shipping Administration (WSA) on March 20, being sub-bareboat chartered to the Army the same day. *Alencon* (French flag) was taken over by the WSA on February 7 but was not bareboat chartered to the Army until March 19. *Vannes* (French flag) was taken over by WSA on March 25 but did not go under bareboat charter to the Army until July 13. The charter dates on all three of these vessels were derived from *Vessel Status Cards* maintained by the War Shipping Administration and now part of the records of the U.S. Maritime Administration. From that source, it became clear that the Army's control over all three did not begin until well after February 24, the date of the Marshall memorandum to Roosevelt.

[7]   Source: Files of Chief of Transportation, Memorandum for General Syter. Subject: Freighters for Special Mission, signed by Col. Frank S. Ross, Chief, Port and Water Section, Transportation Division, dated [no day] March 1942, Chief of Transportation File 000-900 Philippines. In the Ross memorandum of March, *SS Vannes* is incorrectly spelled as *Vaunes.* In tracing the three Lake-class freighters we utilized *Merchant Vessels of the U.S.* and *Lloyds Register of Shipping.* It appears that another ship, *USAT Nevada,* may have been considered for the Philippine mission as she is referenced in related correspondence: Marshall to USAFIA, Melbourne, Record File 400 Philippines, dated April 22, 1942. The inclusion of *USAT Nevada* might possibly have accounted for the *seven* as referenced in the "Memorandum Report of OPNS, QMC in Philippine Campaign 1941 - 42," previously cited.

The first of the converted destroyers to sail was *USAT Masaya* which departed New Orleans on March 2, stopping at Los Angeles, and arriving Honolulu on May 5. *USAT Matagalpa* sailed on March 11, stopped at Los Angeles, and arrived at Honolulu on May 8. *USAT Teapa* sailed on March 18, stopping at Los Angeles, and arriving at Honolulu May 25.

On April 13, the War Department issued instructions that all further efforts to supply the Philippines were to be canceled. Apparently this order also applied to vessels in transit. Leaving Honolulu *USAT Masaya* and *USAT Matagalpa* sailed for Australia; *USAT Teapa* returned to the west coast and was later assigned to Alaskan duty.[8] [9]

Another ship -- this one unrelated to those discussed by Marshall in his February 24 memorandum to the President -- was the merchantman *Thomas Jefferson*. The original plan for this ship seems to have been to have her placed under ATS time or voyage charter utilizing her regular merchant crew which reportedly had all volunteered for the mission. However, the trip was considered so hazardous that it was decided to replace the civilian merchant crew with uniformed naval personnel. That switch-over delayed her sailing until around April 4 when under temporary bareboat charter to the Navy, *Thomas Jefferson* left Honolulu for the Philippines. En route, the mission was aborted on the advice of Lt. Gen. Brehon B. Somervell, the ship being ordered to New Caledonia instead.[10]

Blockade Breaking by Submarine

By mid-January of 1942, the Navy Department's attitude on running the blockade to the Philippines had softened, at least in regard to the use of its submarines. This was not a sentiment shared by the British commander of ABDA, Gen. Archibald P. Wavell. Even though Wavell's ABDA jurisdiction did not extend as far east as the Philippines, he expressed reservations concerning the dissipation of any naval strength -- inclusive of submarines -- from the main business of defending the Malay Barrier, and he had so informed Washington. In response, Adm. Ernest J. King, Commander in Chief, U.S. Fleet, forwarded to General Marshall at the War Department the Navy Department's disagreement with Wavell's policy.[11]

---

[8]   Instructions for the cancellation of supply missions to the Philippines are to be found within RG-407, PAC. The cancellation order was attributed to be from Chief of Transportation, Service of Supply, as stated within an instructional memorandum signed by Maj. Richard D. Meyer, General Staff, Allocations and Scheduling Section.

[9]   *USAT Masaya* was lost to enemy action off New Guinea during 1943. *USAT Matagalpa* was judged a total loss while at Australia after accidental flooding caused her to capsize at dockside.

[10]   Source: Chief of Transportation files, File 400 - Philippines, dated April 11, 1942. The chartered merchant ship *Thomas Jefferson* which left Honolulu for the Philippines in April 1942 should not be confused with the *USS Thomas Jefferson* (AP-60), ex *President Garfield*, which was acquired by the Navy in May 1942 at Newport News, VA, where she entered shipyard for conversion into an attack transport.

[11]   Memorandum, U.S. Fleet, Office of the Commander in Chief, Navy Department, Washington, DC., January 29, 1942, as found in correspondence File WPD 4560-9, Modern Military Records Center, National Archives.

> *General Wavell's dispatch is entirely too restrictive as to use of submarines for getting supplies into the Philippines.*
> *I agree -- fully -- with the points made in your memo to me of this date with emphasis on the morale factor as well as the containing factor.*
>
> */s/ E. J. King*

Before the capitulation of Corregidor to the Japanese in May, eight U.S. submarines were to successfully run the blockade. The first to reach the Philippines was *USS Seawolf* which sailed from Darwin carrying as cargo between 30 and 40 tons of 50-caliber machine gun ammunition. Leaving Darwin on January 16, *USS Seawolf* delivered that cargo eleven days later at the Corregidor dock and after discharge took aboard twenty-five Army Air Corps pilots who were landed at Soerabaja, Java, on February 7.

The second submarine to run the blockade was *USS Seatrout*. Following a 21-day passage from Pearl Harbor, she unloaded at Corregidor 2750 rounds of 3" anti-aircraft ammunition. The return cargo was much more impressive, comprised of 583 gold ingots together with a number of canvas sacks holding silver coins as well as negotiable securities from the Philippine Treasury. (The shipment was at the time worth over $12 million.) *USS Seatrout* returned to Pearl Harbor on March 3 where the valuables were offloaded to a Navy cruiser which delivered them to the Federal Reserve Bank in San Francisco.

The next to run the blockade was *USS Sargo* which left Soerabaja, Java, on February 5. She delivered at Polloc Harbor, island of Mindanao, around one million rounds of 30-caliber ammunition and then took aboard for the return passage twenty-four ground crew personnel belonging to an Army Air Corps bomber squadron, whose planes had earlier been sent to Java.

On February 19, the skipper of *USS Swordfish*, then on patrol in the South China Sea, received orders to proceed to Corregidor to pick up key personnel scheduled for evacuation. The evacuees included the President of the Philippines, Manuel Quezon, and his family. Upon delivering these passengers to San Jose de Buenavista, Antique, island of Panay, *USS Swordfish* was ordered back to Corregidor -- this time to evacuate Francis B. Sayre, High Commissioner of the Philippines, together with his family and fourteen other civilians and five enlisted men. *USS Swordfish* arrived at Freemantle, Australia, with the evacuees on March 9.[12]

Recalled from combat patrol, *USS Permit* was ordered to proceed to the Philippines to evacuate key military personnel to Australia. At Corregidor, the submarine contributed her own 3" deck gun's ammunition to the island's defenses and then took aboard forty Army personnel for evacuation to Freemantle where she arrived safely on April 7.[13]

---

[12]   From Antique, President Quezon boarded *Princess of Negros* and departed for Iloilo and then on to the Negros islands for a tour of those provinces. From there he was taken by U.S. Navy PT boat to Mindanao from where he left for Australia. Source: Col. Carlos P. Romulo, *I Saw the Fall of the Philippines,* (New York: Doubleday, Doran, and co., 1943).

[13]   The Navy's usually authoritative *Dictionary of American Naval Fighting Ships,* Vol. V, states that *USS Permit* rendezvoused off Corregidor and unloaded her ammunition to *the carrier* Ranger (CV-4) *on the night of 15-16 March.* The *Dictionary* is incorrect on that point. The vessel to which *Permit* offloaded was actually the coastal tug *Ranger* of 512 gross tons, owned by the Luzon Stevedoring Co.. In December, the tug had been

USS Seadragon made two trips to the Philippines. The first was to Corregidor (arriving on February 4) where she took aboard submarine spare parts for evacuation, together with a number of passengers. After leaving Corregidor, *USS Seadragon* put into Java from where she was ordered to Freemantle.[14] In March, *USS Seadragon,* then on patrol off Indochina, was again diverted to the Philippines, this time to Cebu City, island of Cebu. From there, she was to ferry supplies north to Bataan as by that point in time the food situation had reached an acute stage for the men on Bataan, and efforts to bring in replenishment supplies by surface ship had come to a standstill. On April 3, *USS Seadragon* reached Cebu City and was immediately sent to Mactan, a small island off Cebu's east coast where, after unloading her torpedoes to make room for cargo, she took on a full load of rice and flour. Because of the deteriorating situation on Bataan, *USS Seadragon* was ordered on April 6 to take the cargo to Corregidor. Upon arrival an enemy air attack was in progress forcing her to leave for sea before being fully unloaded. There was time, though, to load twenty-one passengers who were crowded into whatever space remained. One of those passengers was an Army colonel, three were naval officers, and nineteen were naval enlisted men. The remaining person, a stowaway, was not discovered until *USS Seadragon* was at sea.[15]

On April 6, the Commander of Submarine Force in Australia received a coded message from Commander, U.S. Fleet, Western Pacific (COMWESPAC):

> *Plenty of food available on Mindanao. Instructing maximum practical number of submarines to be diverted from patrol to Mindanao to load food for Bataan.*

USS Snapper -- already en route to Cebu when COMWESPAC sent out its April 6 instructions -- arrived at Corregidor April 9 with rice and flour loaded at Mactan. She was met a mile off Corregidor by the salvage and repair ship *USS Pigeon.*

---

taken over by the ATS and in turn assigned a Navy crew. According to a correct entry under *USS Ranger* within the *Dictionary*, Vol. VI, in March (1942), the carrier *USS Ranger (CV-4)* was thousands of miles away on operations in the South Atlantic and would continue to be so employed until March 22, 1942, when she *entered the Norfolk Navy Yard for repairs*. In early 1942, the only U.S. aircraft carrier in the western Pacific was the *USS Langley* which was sunk during February off the coast of Java.

[14]   Whether her passengers went ashore on Java or traveled all the way to Freemantle is not clear.

[15]   Although unnamed, in all probability, the stowaway was a civilian named Chester Judah. Formerly in the shipping business in Manila, Judah had volunteered to accompany the Army to Corregidor and in a civilian capacity was made part of Colonel Ward's ATS staff. Robert J. M. Wilson, an Army officer who served with the Small Ships Division of Service of Supply in Australia and later on New Guinea, was interviewed by the senior author in November 1996. Wilson remembered a Chester Judah who told him that in 1942 he had been working for the ATS on Corregidor. Grasping the opportunity to escape, Judah had stowed away on a submarine shortly before Corregidor was surrendered. Volunteering to the Army in Australia, Judah was commissioned and assigned to the staff of the Small Ships Division, Service of Supply, USAFIA. The document *History of the ATS Activities in Manila and Cebu,* page 8, File No. 500-21, RG-407, PAC, Box 1568 names a number of American civilians *who rendered excellent service from the start of the war until Corregidor fell*. Chester Judah was one of those so named. The confusion of those last days before the capitulation was such that Judah's departure would probably have gone unnoticed; but if it had been witnessed -- being rather insignificant in light of those chaotic events -- the memory of Judah's disappearance would have been forgotten by those who compiled the notes which went into the ATS historical document. Another escapee from the Philippines to Australia who was also connected to the ATS was 1st Lt. Thomas W. Juricka who had been assigned to Cebu City as ATS Operations Officer. There is no information in the files to indicate how Juricka escaped to Australia. Juricka is referenced in an early post-war report as a *major*, having apparently been promoted during the war.

After unloading the foodstuffs to *USS Pigeon,* twenty-seven passengers were taken aboard for evacuation. *USS Snapper* returned safely to Freemantle with her passengers despite an unscheduled detour to take in tow another U.S. submarine which had suffered a disabling engine room fire off the Borneo coast.

The last submarine to run the blockade was *USS Spearfish* which picked up twenty-five passengers from Corregidor on May 3, three days before that place was surrendered. In early May, *USS Swordfish* had been scheduled for a second try through the blockade, but that was canceled as a result of Corregidor's capitulation as was a similar mission which had been scheduled for *USS Sailfish* (ex *USS Squalis*).

~

Louis Morton claims that altogether 53 tons of foodstuffs, 3500 rounds of 3" anti-aircraft shells, 37 tons of 50-caliber ammunition, 1,000,000 rounds of 30-caliber ammunition and 30,000 gallons of diesel oil were carried to the Philippines by submarine prior to the surrender of Corregidor. In the total scheme of things, these cargoes may have had little effect in delaying the capitulation, yet from the viewpoint of morale, the value was significant. Beyond that, the 185 known men and women who were evacuated aboard the submarines were in the main indispensable to the eventual defeat of Japan.[16] [17] [18]

---

[16] Sources we have used in this account of the blockade running submarine effort were the eight volumes of *Dictionary of American Naval Fighting Ships*. Washington, DC: Naval History Division, 1959-1981 as well as Morton, *The Fall of the Philippines*. It is not known from either source as to how many passengers were evacuated by *USS Seadragon* on her first trip from Corregidor during February 1942.

[17] According to Morton, among the passengers carried to Australia on *USS Spearfish,* were *Col. Constant Irwin who carried* [with him] *a roster of all Army, Navy, and Marine personnel still alive; Col. Royal G. Jenk, a finance officer with accounts; Col. Milton A. Hill, the inspector general; three other Army and six Navy officers; and about thirteen nurses.* Included as cargo on *USS Spearfish* was mail and USAFFE and USFIP operational records. On his page 548, fn 46, Morton states that all of these records eventually reached the Adjutant General's Office and were (at the time of Morton's writing) at the Historical Records Center, Department Records Branch, Adjutant Generals Office files. In a later footnote, however, Morton contradicts this by stating that some of the Finance records may have been misplaced in Australia. On that subject, also see Morton's "Sources" (p 586).

[18] Besides that carried to the Philippines by the submarine blockade breakers, ten separate shipments of cargo were sent to the Philippines from Australia by aircraft. The aircraft, in like manner to the submarines, did yeoman service in evacuating key military and civilian personnel, including General Douglas MacArthur who, with his family and key staff members, were flown to Australia from the island of Mindanao after PT boat evacuation from Corregidor. According to the historian Morton, the majority of the incoming aircraft from Australia landed their cargoes on Mindanao where it accumulated with little if any of it being forwarded on to Bataan / Corregidor. Exceptions were two Navy PBYs which flew directly to Corregidor with their cargoes.

CHAPTER XVII

THE FINAL WEEKS

Since early January, the USAFFE army on the Bataan Peninsula had been on half rations. Combat casualties had been high, and many units were seriously under strength from the scourges of dysentery and malaria. If there was good news to be had, it was that the enemy was not faring much better. Their casualties had also been heavy -- over 7,000 killed and wounded so far, and many more were out of the lines, down with the same diseases which were inflicting the Americans and Filipinos.

The USAFFE main line of resistance (MLR) had remained generally the same as that to which Maj. Gen. Jonathan Wainwright and his North Luzon Defense Force and Maj. Gen. Alfred M. Jones and his South Luzon Defense Force had deployed on January 8. That line ran from the town of Mauban on the South China Sea eastward to the town of Mabatang on Manila Bay. The Japanese had made many attempts to penetrate the MLR since January 8, their heavy artillery fire being the cause of most of the USAFFE casualties. Apprehensive that the Mauban/ Mabatang line would not hold -- especially if the Japanese were reinforced -- on January 20, MacArthur ordered a gradual withdrawal to pre-planned secondary positions. The retrograde movement was completed by the 26th, most of it carried out with minimal enemy interference.

The new MLR ran from Bagac on the South China Sea eastward through the Mt. Samat region of central Bataan reaching Manila Bay a mile or so to the south of the town of Orion. The new MLR was considerably shorter than the Mauban/ Mabatang line had been, a definite advantage considering the reductions in USAFFE strength. It also had the merit of shortening access to the main supply depots located near the ports of Cabcaben and Mariveles. There was, however, an inherent problem in that by shrinking in the space between the MLR and Bataan's southern shoreline, little flexibility was left for tactical readjustment -- a handicap which could, and would, seriously interrupt the flow of reinforcements once combat resumed. Another problem was with transportation as the Bagac/ Orion line lacked the east-west road network which had been extant along the old Mauban/ Mabatang line, thus resupply to the new positions was to prove more difficult.

In large part, due to the high casualties which they had suffered to date, the Japanese would limit their scope of action throughout February and March. During that hiatus, the enemy's commander, Lt. Gen. Masaharu Homma, received much-needed reinforcements -- most of which were tough, battle-hardened veterans from the China Theater.

On the American/ Filipino side of the wire, nutritional deprivation, dysentery, and malaria took an increasing toll during this hiatus. The will to resist still remained, yet the sad realization had begun to sink in that on Bataan, there was *no Mama, no Papa, and no Uncle Sam.* Only the most optimistic continued to believe that help might be on the way.

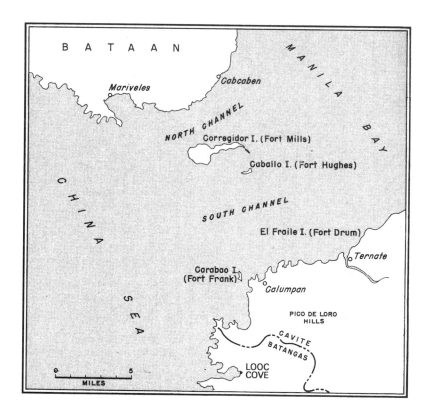

Blockade Running Within the Philippines

In November (1941), Brig. General Drake, the Chief Quartermaster for the islands, had ordered a Quartermaster depot established at Cebu City, Col. John D. Cook as commander. As originally planned, the Cebu Depot was to act as the distribution point from where supplies received from the Quartermaster depots at Manila were to be transferred to garrisons then in the process of establishment within the command area known as the Visayan group (the islands of Panay, Mindoro, Cebu, Leyte, Samar, Bohol, Negros Occidental, and Negros Oriental). The first shipment sent to the Cebu Depot left Manila on December 16 aboard *Corregidor*, but the shipment never arrived, the *Corregidor* having been lost to a mine explosion at the entrance to Manila Bay. Immediately after, Cook received instructions from Drake that the mission for the Cebu Depot had been changed. The new mission was to establish gathering points on the various islands of the Visayan group from where food would be forwarded to those garrisons for which the Cebu Depot held responsibility.[1][2] Starting in February, the Cebu Depot would be designated as the transshipment point from where foodstuffs and other materiel arriving from outside the Philippines was to be sent on to Bataan / Corregidor. Shipment of all Cebu Depot USAFFE cargoes, whether going to Bataan / Corregidor or to other islands, was to be by interisland cargo vessels placed under charter to the Army.[3]

After the *Coast Farmer*, which at Mindanao had unloaded its cargo onto Filipino coasters for transshipment to Corregidor, only two other ships with relief cargoes originating from outside of the Philippines arrived in the islands. These were *Dona Nati* and *Anhui* which discharged at Cebu City, their stories having been covered within Chapter XIII.[4]

Nineteen interisland Filipino cargo ships were chosen for running the blockade to Bataan / Corregidor from within the Philippine archipelago. All were placed under ATS charter for those missions. Their departures were to be either from

---

[1] According to *Report of the Cebu Advance Quartermaster Depot, Cebu,* which was incorporated to the *Drake Report:* As of January 1942 there were about 50,000 troops, mainly Philippine Commonwealth Army divisions (either mobilized or due to be mobilized) within the Visayan - Mindanao jurisdiction. The gathering points for foodstuffs within the Visayan Islands were designated as: Cebu City for Cebu; Dumaquete for Negros Oriental; Bacolod for Negros Occidental; Iloilo for Panay; Tagbilaran for Bohol; Tacloban for Leyte and Samar.

[2] The gathering and distribution system operated by the Cebu Depot worked well. As of April 10, 1942, the date on which the Japanese were to occupy Cebu City, there was a 12-month supply of rice and other dry foodstuffs in stockpile for the garrisons stationed on the islands of Cebu and Panay, and a 6-month supply of foodstuffs for the other garrisons within the Visayan group.

[3] During February, a sub-office of the Fort Mills ATS headquarters was established at Cebu City with Lt. Col. Cornelius Z. Byrd placed in charge as ATS Superintendent for the Visayan District. This relieved Colonel Cook of the direct responsibility for managing the shipping previously chartered by the Cebu Depot, such chartering having begun during December. Along with their other responsibilities, Cook and Byrd were respectively given charge of supply and shipment to the leper colony on Culion Island. Previous to the war, the leper colony on Culion Island had been operated by the Commonwealth government. As far as can be determined, once the war broke out, no supply shipments ever reached the leper colony. All attempts to do so resulted in ship losses, despite the fact that for those humanitarian missions, the supply ships (chartered by the ATS at Cebu City) had all prominently displayed the Red Cross insignia.

[4] One other ship from outside the Philippines came into Cebu City during the 1941-42 defense. This was the merchant ship *James Lykes* which had arrived in early December, having been diverted by news of the Japanese attack while on a voyage from the United States to Shanghai. Whether any of her cargo was unloaded when she arrived at Cebu City is not known. By error, the Ward Report gives this ship's name as *John Lykes*.

Mindanao or from the islands of the Visayan group. Of the nineteen which were selected, only two ever reached Bataan / Corregidor. The first success was *Princesa* which arrived at Corregidor on February 20 carrying indigenous foodstuffs loaded at Cebu City. The second and only other successful trip was made by *Elcano* with ammunition and foodstuffs loaded from *Coast Farmer*. Of the remaining seventeen, all were either sunk by enemy action, captured, or scuttled to avoid capture.[5] The majority of the blockade running attempts were made during the last part of February. Prior to that, a window of opportunity had existed within which the chances of getting past the Japanese blockade would have been reasonably good. This changed, however, on February 27 when an enemy amphibious force landed on the northeast coast of Mindoro for the purpose of occupying a small airstrip. From that airstrip, a tight aerial surveillance of the approaches to Manila Bay was inaugurated which had the effect of shortening the odds for running surface ships through the blockade to a virtual zero.

Of the cargo from *Coast Farmer* which reached Corregidor aboard *Elcano,* that part comprising rations turned out to be a rank disappointment. Canned goods were so poorly packed that the cardboard cartons containing them broke open. In the damp environment of the ship's hold, most of the cans had lost their labels rendering the contents a mystery. A large number of the sacks containing flour and sugar had burst, scattering the contents throughout the ship's hold, and the onions and potatoes stacked on the *Elcano's* deck had rotted.[6] In contrast, the *Princesa's* cargo which consisted of 700 tons of foodstuffs that had been gathered from within the Visayas arrived in good condition.

⚓

In early January, a program was instituted by Quartermaster Headquarters at Fort Mills to employ fast Filipino coasters of not more than 1000 tons cargo capacity to operate directly from Corregidor. The ships that were to be used were located at the south anchorage off that island, having been anchored at that location since the evacuations from Manila in late December. With these ships, cargoes of balanced rations were to be picked up at Capiz on the north coast of Panay. (A second loading destination would later be selected -- Looc Cove in Batangas Province.)

Chief Quartermaster Drake launched the idea in the form of a proposal made to Brig. Gen. Manuel Roxas, aide de camp to MacArthur. Roxas, who possessed first hand knowledge of the situation on Panay, confirmed that livestock, fish, fruits, rice, coffee, and root vegetables were readily available and that cooperation could be expected from both the Commonwealth officials as well as from the business community there. With authorization from MacArthur's Chief of Staff, Maj. Gen. Richard K. Sutherland, preparations began with a radio message sent to Brig. Gen. Bradford G. Chynoweth who was then on Panay. Chynoweth was given the types of balanced rations needed and instructions for their assembly at the port of Capiz into

---

[5]   Further information on each of the interisland Filipino ships that had been picked to run the blockade to Bataan / Corregidor is contained within a table within this chapter. Following this chapter is a group of five detailed ship lists under the overall heading *Lists of Vessels and Particulars When Known, Defense of the Philippines, December 1941 - May 1942.* List 4 of that group gives full details, when known, of all vessels of Filipino ownership which were chartered by the Army within the Philippines, 1941-42. Such entries have the dates of charter as well as the final disposition for each of the vessels.

[6]   Morton, 396.

lots of 50-tons pre-packed for shipment. Of the three ships which would be used, the first to leave was *Legazpi*, 1179 gross tons (Lino T. Conajero, master). *Legazpi* departed for Capiz on January 17 and returned with a full cargo.[7] During the first week in February, *Legazpi* made a second successful run. Upon its return, MacArthur personally awarded Conajero and *Legazpi's* pilot, Jose A. Amoyo, the U.S. Army's Distinguished Service Cross, announcing that the rest of the *Legazpi's* ship's company was to receive the U.S. Army's Silver Star.[8] On February 19, *Legazpi* left Corregidor for her third trip, this time carrying wounded and a number of Army Air Corps and Navy personnel selected for evacuation. The trip to Capiz went well; but on the return, *Legazpi* was intercepted by enemy destroyers at a position off the coast of Mindoro near Porto Galera. Under heavy shelling which started fires throughout the ship, Conajero ordered the seacocks smashed while he headed for the nearby beach where *Legazpi* was grounded, becoming a total loss. Only one crewman was killed during the attack. The remainder of the ship's complement (including a number of military gunners) reached shore on Mindoro, most managing to evade capture by blending in with the local population.[9]

⚓

On January 20, *Kolumbugan,* 691 gross tons, was sent to Looc Cove, a destination picked because of its proximity to Corregidor.[10] USAFFE agents in the Batangas region had been earlier contacted with instructions to arrange for foodstuffs to be made ready for loading upon the ship's arrival at Looc Cove. *Kolumbugan* made two round trips to Looc Cove, picking up full cargoes each time. The first run was on January 20 and the second on February 6. Later, after having been warned off at least twice by light signals sent from agents on shore, the Looc Cove operation was canceled -- *Kolumbugan* then being assigned to the Capiz run. On her first try, she was overhauled by an enemy cruiser and captured intact, the crew apparently having made no attempt to scuttle.

⚓

A third ship to run round trips from Corregidor was *Bohol II,* 2126 tons (Jose M. Sarte, master). She had been abandoned by her original crew in the Pasig River during the December bombings of Manila and was towed clear of the river under

---

[7]   The trips from Corregidor to Capiz and return were made under cover of darkness with shelter taken during the hours of daylight at secluded coves so as to avoid detection by the enemy's naval patrols.

[8]   Jose A. Amoyo had formerly been the master of *Bohol II.* Because of his knowledge of the Panay coast, he was detached to act as pilot on the *Legazpi.* Appendix P of this volume contains a list of the *Legazpi* officers and crewmen who received the U.S. Army's Silver Star. Although MacArthur announced that the masters and crews of other successful blockade runners were to be similarly decorated, we could find nothing within the Philippine Archive Collection specifying that decorations were ever given to those on either the *Bohol II* or to those on the *Kolumbugan,* the two other ships which operated from Corregidor and which successfully ran the blockade. Nor is there information to indicate that the crews of *Elcano* and *Princesa* ever received decorations.

[9]   The records of *Legazpi's* voyages from Corregidor and of the attack when she was lost are within RG-407, PAC, Box 1569.

[10]   The actual travel distance from Corregidor to Looc Cove (14 miles) was somewhat longer as the U.S. protective mine fields located at the approaches to Corregidor had first to be negotiated before reaching open water. Even with that detour, it was an easy overnight passage. The archival file on *Kolumbugan* does not contain the crew list for the time of her loss on February 27; consequently the name of her master at that time is not known. The *Kolambugan* file is to be found within RG-407, PAC, Box 1569.

Navy orders to be anchored in the outer harbor where she was commandeered by the ATS and towed to Corregidor. Upon her arrival, she received an ATS crew.[11] *Bohol II* left Corregidor on February 6 for Looc Cove and returned with a cargo of rice and cattle. She made a second successful trip to Looc Cove, returning to Corregidor on February 13, having narrowly missed capture by the enemy.[12]

The increased surveillance by the enemy of the waters between Manila Bay and Panay which had resulted in the losses of *Legazpi* and *Kolumbugan* brought to an end further attempts to run ships from Corregidor. The six round trips made from Corregidor by *Legazpi, Kolumbugan,* and *Bohol II* had been significant contributions. In the aggregate, they had brought in 5800 tons of rice and other foodstuffs along with 400 head of livestock (cattle and pigs). While it may not have been enough to stave off defeat, it did help to make the last days of the Bataan campaign more bearable for those who had benefited.[13]

~

The ration shortage became so critical by the end of March that unless some drastic measures were taken, a collapse on Bataan seemed inevitable. What was thought of as a possible solution was worked out between the Philippine command and the Army Air Corps headquarters in Australia. The idea was to send medium and heavy bombers from Australia to Mindanao from where strikes against the Japanese naval presence in the Visayan Islands and at Subic Bay would be conducted. The enemy's airfields on Luzon as well as the one the Japanese had established on northern Mindoro were also to be attacked. In advance of the arrival of the bombers, ships at Cebu City and at Iloilo on Panay were to be loaded with supplies and made ready to leave for Bataan/ Corregidor as soon as the bombers neutralized the enemy's ability to block their passage. Three P-40 fighter planes, then in the process of being assembled on Mindanao, were to provide the further insurance of air cover for the ships while en route.[14] On April 4, Australia informed Corregidor that the bombers would be ready to leave for Mindanao by the following week. Days passed, but no bombers appeared. On April 10, with eight ships loaded and ready to leave from the Visayas, the Japanese landed on Cebu, and enemy destroyers blocked egress from Cebu City and Iloilo, the two ports from which the blockade runners had been staged. On April 11, the bombers from Australia finally landed on Mindanao; but by then it was too late. The ships which had been waiting at Cebu City and at Iloilo had already been scuttled to avoid capture.[15] [16]

---

[11]   The first master assigned to *Bohol II* upon her arrival at Corregidor was Jose A. Amoyo. During early February, Amoyo was reassigned to the *Legazpi* as its pilot and was relieved on *Bohol II* by Sarte. Amoyo served as *Legazpi's* pilot for that ship's second trip to Capiz as well as the third trip upon which the *Legazpi* was lost.

[12]   On April 9, while lying at anchor off Corregidor, *Bohol II* was sunk by artillery fire directed from Bataan's southern shore. The *Bohol II* file is in RG-407, PAC, Box 1569.

[13]   The figure of 5800 tons of rice and the numbers of livestock is taken from the *Drake Report,* p 38.

[14]   The P-40s in the process of being assembled were those which had been offloaded in crates from *Anhui* while she was aground off Bohol. See Chapter XIII. From Bohol they were barged to Mindanao.

[15]   Morton, pp 403,404.

[16]   The identities of seven of the eight ships which had been scheduled to make the run to Corregidor in early April, but which never left is given in the following table, each identified by asterisks.

BLOCKADE RUNNING TO BATAAN / CORREGIDOR FROM WITHIN THE PHILIPPINES

For further details on these vessels consult our List 4 titled: *Merchant Ships and Small Craft Commandeered, Seized, Requisitioned, or Chartered by U.S. Army Forces, Far East: Within the Philippine Islands, 1941 - 1942* as well as our main Vessel Index.

Agustina [†]	Unsuccessful. Shelled and sunk at Bugo, island of Mindanao, either on Feb 28 or Mar 3, 1942, while loading.
Bohol II	Successful. Two trips with around 700 tons of rice and cattle from Looc Cove to Corregidor. Shelled and sunk off Corregidor, Apr 9, 1942.
Bolinao [¥]	Unsuccessful. While en route for Bataan, was captured off Toledo, Cebu, either Mar 14 or 17, 1942.
Cegostina [‡]	Unsuccessful. Shelled and sunk at Bugo, island of Mindanao, on Mar 3, 1942, while loading.
Compania de Filipinas	Unsuccessful. Sunk (or captured) on Feb 21, 1942, while en route Cebu City to Corregidor.
Don Esteban, USAT	Unsuccessful. Attacked by enemy aircraft while sheltering en route to Corregidor at Paluan Bay on Mindoro. Was set afire becoming a total loss on Mar 1, 1942.
Elcano	Successful. One trip with 1100 tons of sustenance offloaded from *Coast Farmer*. Cargo was taken to Corregidor, and what was usable was barged to Bataan.
Emilia	Unsuccessful. Shelled and sunk at Bugo, Mindanao, probably on Mar 3, 1942, while loading.
Governor Smith	Unsuccessful. Scuttled either while loading for or en route to Coron Island.
Governor Taft [¥] [*]	Unsuccessful. Scuttled at Cebu City Apr 10, 1942, to avoid capture.
Hai Kwang [*]	Unsuccessful. Scheduled for run to Corregidor in April 1942 but trip aborted; scuttled at Iloilo, island of Panay.
Kanlaon II [¥] [*]	Unsuccessful. After loading with rations for Corregidor, was scuttled at Cebu on Apr 10, 1942, to avoid capture.
Kolumbugan	Successful. Two trips from Looc Cove to Corregidor with rice and cattle totaling 800 tons. Made other attempts but was warned off. Captured by Japanese cruiser on Mar 1, 1942, while attempting a run to Capiz, island of Panay.

[†]   *Augustina* in some sources.
[¥]   Loaded with some part of the cargoes from *Dona Nati* or of *Anhui*.
[‡]   *Cogostina* in some sources.
[*]   One of the eight vessels which awaited the bombers from Australia.

La Estrella Caltex	Unsuccessful. While en route Cebu City to Bataan, was sunk by air attack off Lubang Island on Feb 24, 1942.
Legazpi	Successful. Two trips from Corregidor to Capiz, island of Panay, with rice and livestock. On third trip was set afire by enemy attack at Porto Galera on Mindoro, Mar 1, 1942.
Lepus	Unsuccessful. Offloaded from *Coast Farmer*. Captured Mar 1, 1942, while en route to Corregidor.
Mayon	Unsuccessful. While loading on Mindanao for Bataan, was bombed and set afire becoming a total loss on Feb 28, 1942.
P. Aboitiz ¥ *	Unsuccessful. After loading with rations for Corregidor, was scuttled. Army records are unclear whether this occurred at Cebu City, or on Mindanao, or at Palawan. Most probably it occurred on Apr 10, 1942, at Cebu City.
Paulino ¥ *	Unsuccessful. After loading with rations at Cebu for Corregidor, was scuttled on Apr 10, 1942, to avoid capture.
Porto Galera Mindoro	Reported en route to Bataan / Corregidor with supplies, but nothing else is known beyond Mar 1, 1942.
Princesa *	Successful on one trip with 700 tons from Cebu for Corregidor. Was being loaded again for Corregidor at Cebu City on Apr 10, 1942, when she was either scuttled or captured.
Regulas	Unsuccessful. While en route Cebu City to Corregidor with gasoline and foodstuffs was captured either Mar 3 or 7, 1942, at San Jose off the southwest coast of Mindoro near Ilin Island.
Surigao	Unsuccessful. While en route Cebu City to Corregidor was either scuttled or captured at Iloilo, island of Panay, probably between April 10-16, 1942.
Venus *	Unsuccessful. After loading for Corregidor was scuttled at Cebu City on Apr 10, 1942.

IN ADDITION: Approximately twelve sail vessels with auxiliary engines were chartered or otherwise hired by the Army for cargo runs to Corregidor. Eight were each loaded with 90 tons of cargo at Iloilo on April 9, 1942, and dispatched toward Corregidor. Four were loaded with foodstuffs at Cebu on April 1 and dispatched toward Corregidor. These last four may possibly have carried some of the cargo which had come into Cebu on *Dona Nati* or *Anhui*. There is nothing in the Drake Report to indicate that any of those cargoes reached Corregidor.

¥   Loaded with some part of the cargoes from *Dona Nati* or of *Anhui*.
*   One of the eight vessels which awaited the bombers from Australia.

MacArthur Departs for Australia

On February 22, with the realization that the loss of the Philippines was probably inevitable, President Roosevelt ordered MacArthur to leave for Australia. At first MacArthur had considered refusing Roosevelt's order; but on advice from his staff, he reconsidered asking Washington for a delay to await the right psychological moment, lest his abrupt departure from the Philippines result in a collapse of troop morale. Washington agreed to this, and MacArthur announced to General Marshall that he would leave on or around March 15. [17] He was first to stop at Mindanao, remaining just long enough to consult with Maj. Gen. William F Sharp on plans for a prolonged defense of that island if Bataan and Corregidor should fall.[18] Once in Australia, MacArthur was to take charge of the American and Australian troop buildup taking form there for what would eventually become a campaign to retake the Southwest Pacific from the Japanese.

In preparation for his departure, MacArthur reorganized the command structure for Bataan and for Corregidor. Focusing directly on a desire to continue a supervision of events for Bataan and Corregidor, he created two entirely independent commands. Corregidor and its satellite defenses were now to become the Harbor Defense Force under Maj. Gen. George F. Moore. The army fighting on Bataan was placed under the command of Maj. Gen. Jonathan Wainwright. Once he reached Australia, liaison between each of these commanders and MacArthur's headquarters was to be carried out through Col. Lewis C. Beebe from Fort Mills on Corregidor. Such an arrangement was clearly unworkable, a conclusion to be reached by the Army's Chief of Staff, Gen. George C. Marshall who would overrule MacArthur once he left for Australia. MacArthur also made a command change for the Visayas where the situation had altered considerably since December. The former Visayan- Mindanao Force was now to be split into two separate commands -- Brig. Gen. Bradford G. Chynoweth given the Visayan group and Maj. Gen. William F. Sharp given Mindanao.[19]

On March 11, MacArthur, his family, and key staff members departed for Mindanao aboard four PT boats. Once notified of MacArthur's departure, Marshall radioed Wainwright that he had been promoted to lieutenant general and placed in command of all USAFFE troops in the Philippines -- that command now to be designated as U.S. Forces in the Philippines (USFIP). Wainwright was to report directly to the Chief of Staff at the War Department with informational copies to be sent by Wainwright to MacArthur's headquarters in Australia.

---

[17] Morton, pp 357, 358.

[18] Sharp had recently been promoted to Major General.

[19] The changeover of the Visayan sector of Sharp's former Visayan- Mindanao command was not a demotion for Sharp but rather was a reorganization made in the belief that Mindanao would be capable of holding out should Bataan / Corregidor fall. Conversely, the prognosis for holding on to the Visayas was not considered promising. Since January, coordination of the Visayas in conjunction with Mindanao had become administratively and tactically impractical, movement by sea and by air between the two areas having become seriously disrupted by Japanese naval patrols. After MacArthur left for Australia and command of the Philippines was turned over to Wainwright, the Visayas and Mindanao were continued as separate command entities -- the Visayas being left under Chynoweth and Mindanao being left under Sharp.

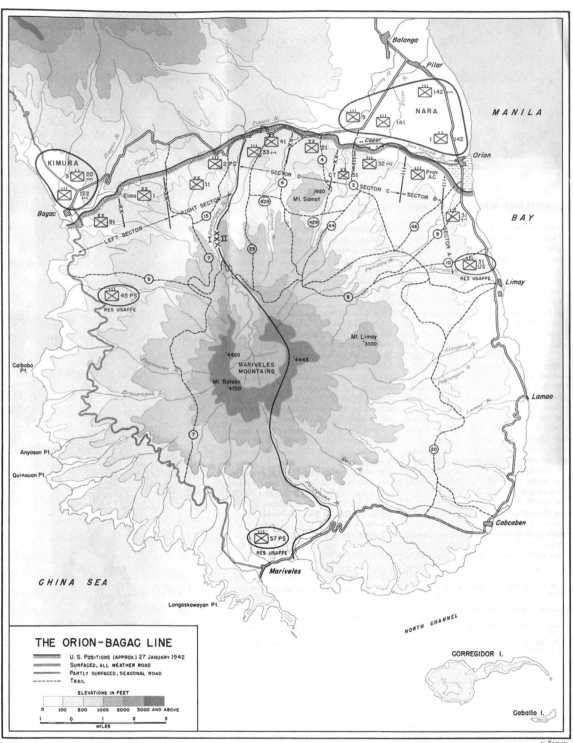

MANILA

Balanga

Pilar

NARA

MANILA

Orion

Cepat

BAY

KIMURA

Bagac

Elms

RIGHT SECTOR

LEFT SECTOR

SECTOR D

Mt. Samat
1920

SECTOR C

SECTOR B

Prov AC

SECTOR A

31
US

RES USAFFE

Limay

45 PS

RES USAFFE

Caibobo Pt.

MARIVELES
MOUNTAINS

Mt. Botoon
4700

4420

4443

Mt. Limay
3100

Lamao

Anyasan Pt.

Quinauan Pt.

Cabcaben

57 PS

RES USAFFE

Mariveles

CHINA SEA

Longoskawayan Pt.

NORTH CHANNEL

CORREGIDOR I.

Caballo I.

THE ORION-BAGAC LINE

▨▨▨▨▨ U. S. Positions (Approx.) 27 January 1942
═══════ Surfaced, All Weather Road
─────── Partly Surfaced, Seasonal Road
- - - - - Trail

ELEVATIONS IN FEET

0   100   500   1000   2000   3000 AND ABOVE

1   0   1   2   3
MILES

H Damon

During the week which followed MacArthur's departure, Wainwright rearranged the command structure on Bataan, turning over that force to Maj. Gen. Edward P. King. Wainwright then left for his new USFIP Headquarters at Fort Mills.

Bataan Falls

By the end of March, the Japanese posture on Bataan had been enhanced with heavy troop reinforcements and extensive resupply which enabled Homma to prepare for what would be called, *The Second Bataan Campaign.* On the morning of April 3, twenty-seven heavy artillery batteries opened a bombardment against USFIP positions. The enemy fired for five straight hours while simultaneously flying one hundred fifty bombing sorties, dropping a total of 60 tons of bombs before the day was out. At 1500 that afternoon, the bombardments ceased, to be followed by heavy infantry attacks (backed by tanks) directed against the right end of the USFIP's main line of resistance (MLR). That sector was quickly breached along a wide front allowing the Japanese to move through in force. Continuity between USFIP units in the eastern sector of the MLR had been lost, the preliminary bombardment having cut most of the field telephone wires. In some areas, smoke caused by brush fires which also started during the bombardment, was so intense that it became difficult for company commanders to see what was taking place within their own sectors, never mind that of the units on their flanks. Some of the Filipino regiments had lost all discipline, their men fleeing toward the rear.

That part of the MLR running from the eastern slope of Mt. Samat westward to the South China Sea was not heavily attacked on the first day, but by the end of that day, its right flank (the Mt. Samat area) lay wide open due to the disintegration of the USFIP units to the east, and it was not long before the Japanese tried to take advantage of this. This time they ran into Filipino regiments which held steadfast causing the Japanese officer in charge of that attack to describe the action as, *The fiercest combat in the second Bataan campaign.* [20] The MLR on the northwest slope of the mountain was not as heavily defended. There, the Japanese penetrated; and by April 5, they had secured the high plateau area of Mt. Samat.

The following day, a counterattack was launched by King with the intent of reestablishing the eastern end of the MLR. For that, King threw in the entirety of his remnant reserves consisting of the U.S. 31st Infantry, one regiment of Philippine Scouts, two battalions of combat engineers, and one part-strength Philippine regiment, supported by a few light tanks. This was King's last ace; but it failed. After that, the situation became one of continuous retrograde. As new positions were reached, relentless enemy pressure forced their abandonment even before the defending troops could dig in.

King reached the decision on the morning of April 8 that further resistance was useless. Already, the main base hospital on Bataan which was overflowing had come within the enemy's artillery range, and a slaughter of the

---

[20]   Statement of Colonel Oishi from *Statements of Japanese Officials on World War II* as quoted by Morton, p 430.

wounded would become inevitable if the fighting was allowed to continue. Steps were started to contact all unit commanders, ordering the demolition of equipment and supplies preparatory to the surrender.[21] King handed one of his staff officers who had been given the unpleasant charge of contacting the Japanese, a list of requests to be made of the Japanese, one being that because of the weakened condition of most of the USFIP troops, it would be difficult to move the men any distance by foot to POW enclosures. If a march had to be made, King's request was that it be carried out under the supervision of American and Filipino officers.[22] By the morning of April 9, the entire right half of the USFIP line had shrunken to a number of small perimeters. The day before, an evacuation to Corregidor had begun, and it would continue through most of April 9. Under orders, about two thousand persons, including Army nurses, were evacuated to Corregidor. The evacuation was conducted in part by the ATS and in part by the Navy's small craft from Mariveles, although some men utilizing row boats made their way to Corregidor unofficially as did a handful of swimmers.

When King was escorted to meet with the Japanese, he got nowhere over his request for terms, the Japanese insisting only on unconditional surrender to which King had no choice but to acquiesce. Over 70,000 Americans and Filipinos were to be marched into a captivity from which many would not return.[23]

Surrender of Corregidor

As early as 1908, the defense of the Philippines was focused on Manila Bay with the concentration to be on the fortress of Corregidor (Fort Mills) and satellite installations to be located at Fort Drum on El Fraile Island, Fort Hughes on Caballo Island, and Fort Frank on Carabao Island. Prior to the First World War, the Corregidor defense complex was thought of as being nearly impregnable; however,

---

[21] King did not inform Wainwright of what he was about to do. When Wainwright finally received word that King was about to surrender, he ordered that King be contacted and given orders to continue the fight; but by then it was too late. As events were to prove, King's decision had been a correct one to which later no blame was to be attached.

[22] Memo, King to Williams dated April 8, 1942. According to Morton, p 459, a copy of this memo was at the Office of the Chief of Military History (circa 1950). King's request was ignored by the Japanese, and it was the Japanese who would later supervise the march to the POW enclosures. Under Japanese management, that march has gone down in history as *The Death March,* a monument to Japanese brutality and mismanagement.

[23] The breakdown of organization within the USFIP which started on April 3 on Bataan, as well as the loss there of most unit returns which were either abandoned or destroyed, prevents making anything close to an accurate assessment of casualties for the American/ Filipino army on Bataan. John W. Whitman in his excellent work, *Bataan Our Last Ditch,* (New York: Hippocrene Books, 1990), p 605, claims, *...returns for April 3 carried 78,100 Filipinos and Americans still on the rolls.* The Army's historian, Morton, infers that around 2,000 personnel were evacuated from Bataan to Corregidor about the time of the surrender -- that figure generally agreeing with other accounts. Whitman's research came up with 45,000 Filipinos and 9,300 Americans located at the prisoner of war compound to which they were marched -- that figure being tallied within the statistical period April 10 to June 4, 1942 and representing those who had survived the *Bataan Death March.* From Whitman's figures, it can then be determined that between the opening of the Japanese offensive on April 3 until June 4, nearly 22,000 of the USFIP troops which had been on Bataan had simply disappeared. That figure may not, however, include those wounded who had been admitted to the base hospitals located on Bataan prior to April 3. The fate of those wounded has not been accurately determined, but it is probable that many either soon died or were killed by the Japanese. After some months, most of the Filipino troops taken prisoner were released by the Japanese; however, the Americans continued to be held as prisoners for the duration of the war. Whitman does not give the number of Bataan veterans who died in Japanese POW camps following June 4, 1942.

technologies coming out of that war indicated that improvements were needed to bring the fortifications up to date, but the disarmament treaties of the 1920s limited what could be accomplished. Treaties aside, tunneling was developed on a grandiose scale. Corregidor's extensive system of tunnels protected its inventories of vital supply as well as its command center and its wartime hospital facilities. The vulnerability of Corregidor was that its abundance of above-ground installations, such as the rail distribution system as well as the water supply reservoir and wells which supplied that reservoir, were totally dependent on electrical power -- the bulk of which came from an above-ground (Topside) power house. The water supply, although more than adequate for a normal garrison, proved inadequate for an increase of over 9,000 military and civilian personnel who arrived following the evacuation from Manila, and of the additional 2,000 or more who arrived after Bataan's surrender.

Air raids conducted against Corregidor (or *The Rock* as its inhabitants called it) started as early as December 29, continuing through to January 6 at which time the Japanese shifted their focus to Bataan. During the raids against Corregidor, damage to many of the installations above ground had been heavy; yet the coastal defense batteries remained intact as did the power house, the water system, and a majority of the 3" anti-aircraft installations located Topsides. Anti-aircraft fire during those eight days of raids had utilized an inordinate amount of 3" ammunition which was vital to Corregidor's air defense since the Japanese commonly made their bombing runs from 20,000 feet -- a height which made 50-caliber machine gun fire useless.

The population on Corregidor did not suffer the nutritional deprivation that was experienced on Bataan; nevertheless, rations had been cut in half as on Bataan, and the ration was not well balanced, resulting in symptoms of nutritional deficiencies which began to appear as early as February. Fortunately, malarial cases were rare, at least until the surrender of Bataan at which time it arrived with the evacuees.

On March 24, air attacks resumed. Heavy raids continued to April 1 when they slackened off -- not to start again until April 9. The power plant had suffered a number of bomb hits during the latest raids but was still functioning, and most of the beach defenses had survived serious damage. Should the power plant be knocked out, enough portable diesel generators were arranged on line to provide most of the essential services, including power for the blowers which made the tunnel complex habitable. There was sufficient fuel on hand to keep those generators running until early June. Wainwright's immediate worry was the water supply as a shortage was already being felt. If the above-ground reservoir was destroyed (it only held about 300,000 gallons) the situation could become critical.

With the surrender on Bataan, the Japanese began moving artillery batteries on to the shoreline near Mariveles from where they now threatened Corregidor.[24] Their fire soon became uncomfortably accurate, the result of observers spotting from balloons flown from the Mariveles hills. On April 9, the air raids were resumed. Between that date and the end of the month, there were 108 raids totaling

---

[24]   As early as the beginning of February, the satellite installations at Fort Frank and at Fort Drum began receiving incoming artillery rounds from Cavite Province. Occasionally rounds were also directed during that time at Corregidor. By mid March, the enemy's artillery fire against the satellite forts increased in intensity destroying two of Fort Frank's heavy guns and damaging others.

eighty hours of actual air attack.[25] The worst air raid came on April 29, the Emperor's birthday -- a date which also marked the arrival of two U.S. Navy PBY float planes which brought in a quantity of medicine and 740 proximity fuses for 3" anti-aircraft shells. Tragically, the fuses were largely wasted since the supply of 3" shells was almost depleted.[26] [27]

On May 1, the Japanese intention to make a landing was announced by their bombardment of the island's beach defenses. Although a substantial portion of the guns protecting the beaches were destroyed in that bombardment, enough remained so that when the landings began, they were not made without heavy cost to the enemy. There was considerable confusion on the part of the assault barge coxswains -- in one instance an entire group of barges grounding on an offlying reef, opening their passengers to devastating machine gun fire from the beach. However, once the Japanese got ashore, their progress was relentless.

By May 6, Wainwright had become certain that further resistance would be useless. Fearing for the over one thousand wounded who lay hospitalized in the tunnels, he issued the order to make preparations for surrender.[28] He followed with a radio message sent for the attention of President Roosevelt:

> *With broken heart and head bowed in sadness but not in shame, I report...that today I must arrange terms for the surrender of the fortified islands of Manila Bay....Please say to the nation that my troops and I have accomplished all that is humanly possible and that we have upheld the best traditions of the United States and its Army....With profound regret and with continued pride in my gallant troops, I go to meet the Japanese commander.*[29]

---

[25]   Morton, p 539.

[26]   Morton, p 540. Four days later, on May 3, the submarine *USS Spearfish* arrived at Corregidor to take out the last evacuees totaling twenty-five military personnel including twelve nurses. Going out on *USS Spearfish* were personnel records, lists of casualties, and Army Finance Corps records. The reader is again referred to Morton's "Sources" (p 586) for disposition of those records.

[27]   Despite the heavy and constant bombardment from artillery and air, a medical officer on Corregidor made an interesting observation that *...only six to eight mental cases were encountered. Here the war was always with us and once the adjustment was made, there were no other new adjustments to be made.* It is doubtful that this is an indication that the personnel trapped on Corregidor were somehow extraordinarily strong but is more likely a reflection of the fact that there was no alternative but to tough it out. From Morton, p 545, fn 24, citing Cooper, Med. Dept. Activities, pp 18, 84. Copy now held by the Office, Chief of Military History, Washington.

[28]   The number of persons on Corregidor on the day of its surrender could not be located by our research. There is, however, some evidence to go by. In the book *General Wainwright's Story* (as quoted on Morton's p 570) Lt. General Wainwright stated that as of the surrender of Corregidor, there were 11,000 USFIP military and naval personnel, not counting Army and Navy nurses. That figure did not, however, include civilians of which there were many. Unlike those taken captive on Bataan, those who were surrendered on Corregidor were spared a march to prison compounds. The horrors they suffered while as POWs were, however, no less then that of the Bataan POWs. The Japanese, in a rare observance of international law, did not incarcerate the nurses as POWs but instead, recognizing them as medical personnel, sent them to the Civilian Internment facility located at Santo Tomas in Manila. See Appendix J "note" as to the estimate of total U.S. Army losses -- dead and captured -- in defense of the Philippines, December 1941 to June 1942.

[29]   Radio, Wainwright to Roosevelt, 6 May 1942. Morton, p 561, citing Jonathan M. Wainwright, *General Wainwright's Story...The Account of Four Years of Humiliating Defeat, Surrender, and Captivity,* (Garden City, NY: Doubleday, 1946), pp 122, 123. It is to be noted that Wainwright's message of May 6 only announced the surrender of, *the fortified islands of Manila Bay.*

The Final Surrender -- The Southern Islands

Outside of the landings made at Davao on Mindanao and on the island of Jolo back in December, no further operations were conducted against the Southern Islands until March when a small Japanese force occupied Zamboangao, also on Mindanao. The Japanese were to reserve their conquest of the southern islands until such time that they had secured Bataan.[30]

In December, MacArthur had ordered Maj. General Sharp, then commander of the Visayan- Mindanao Force, to transfer some units then garrisoning the islands of the Visayan group for the reinforcement of Mindanao. After those transfers, the troop strength which remained within the Visayas was: 7,000 on Panay; 6500 on Cebu; 2500 on the combined Negros; 2500 on Samar; and about 1000 on Bohol. Except for field grade officers, the majority of whom were American, the Visayan garrisons, as well as the forces on Mindanao, consisted of Philippine Commonwealth Army divisions, most of which had been recently mobilized with few of their enlisted men having received even a modicum of training. In fact, many had never fired their rifles due to a shortage of ammunition.[31] In contrast, the fresh troops which the Japanese were to employ for their central and southern Philippine campaigns were veterans of the Malayan campaign and of those who had participated in the conquest of Borneo.

On April 9, the Japanese offensive against the central and southern islands was opened with a landing on Cebu. The following day, Cebu City was occupied. By April 19, the enemy had secured most of Cebu leaving only the central mountains in USFIP hands.[32] With Chynoweth no longer able to maintain communication throughout his command area, Wainwright ordered Sharp to reinstate the Visayan- Mindanao Force and take over via radio the direction of operations on those islands of the Visayas not yet under Japanese control.

On Panay, it had long been decided that without adequate artillery support which the garrison lacked, it would be impossible to defend that island's coastal population centers. A plan was set into place whereby if the Japanese landed in strength, the garrisons at those locations would retreat into the central mountains from where they would conduct guerrilla operations. Panay was invaded on April 16. By the end of that day, the enemy was in possession of Capiz and Iloilo; and by April 18, San Jose de Buenavista and Lambuneo had fallen. The pre-planned withdrawal into the mountains was implemented beginning on the 16th.

The Japanese landing at Davao in December had as its purpose the establishment of a beachhead from which the enemy's conquest of Mindanao would later be launched. Despite a number of attempts which had been made throughout January and continuing into March, the Japanese were never able to penetrate more

---

[30]   As earlier related, the Japanese also made a landing on northern Mindoro on February 27, but it was conducted solely for the purpose of establishing an air base there to be used for surveillance of the seaward approaches to Manila Bay.

[31]   During February, the supply of 30-caliber rifle ammunition improved with the delivery to Mindanao of one million rounds carried in aboard the submarine *USS Sargo*.

[32]   A small force of two hundred men under Chynoweth withdrew into Cebu's central mountains from where Chynoweth planned to conduct a guerrilla campaign. On Wainwright's direct order, Chynoweth would surrender on May 15.

than a few miles beyond Davao's city limits. Even holding Davao had proved difficult -- its continued occupation only made possible by the superior firepower of the Japanese. The Japanese had also failed to penetrate the interior following their landing at Zamboanga in March.

MacArthur's strategy for the final defense of the Philippines had been to have Sharp hold Mindanao until such time that the United States was in a position to undertake an offensive from Australia. Since such an offensive could not begin at its earliest for some months into the future, to have expected a long-term delaying action by Sharp was a tall order.

On April 29, the Japanese heavily reinforced their presence on Mindanao with a number of landings made at diverse locations. Sharp's defenders fought with what they had, but it was to be a losing battle from its start.

Wainwright's surrender of the Philippines had not only been made on unconditional terms but the Japanese had further humiliated him by having him broadcast a surrender order to his subordinate commanders located throughout the central and southern islands. On May 8, Wainwright sent under duress a second radio message addressed to all commands throughout the archipelago stating that in order to prevent serious Japanese repercussions, the surrender of the entirety of U.S. Forces in the Philippines was now mandated.

There were objections on the part of many commanders to that order -- a sentiment also shared by many of the troops -- which was only overcome by the dispatch of American officers to convince them that to continue hostilities would result in fatal consequences for those Americans already being held as prisoners of the Japanese. On that basis, and on direct orders issued by Sharp who had surrendered his own Mindanao Force on May 10, the Visayan garrisons surrendered: May 20, Col. Albert F. Christie on Panay; May 26, Col. Therodore M. Cornell on Samar and Leyte; June 3, Col. Roger B. Hilsman on the Negros Islands.[33] [34]

~

The defense of the Philippines had not been in vain. The nearly six months that the struggle lasted had exhausted the original Japanese invasion force which could have been profitably used elsewhere. Most importantly, the defense had bought time for the buildup in Australia of an allied army which, beginning with the New Guinea Campaign, would fight its way to the liberation of the Philippines. On September 2, 1945, the armed forces of Japan were themselves humbled by that nation's unconditional surrender signed on the deck of the *USS Missouri*.

---

[33] The date of Hilsman's surrender had been caused by the difficulty he and his staff had in trying to gather enough troops together to convince the Japanese that his surrender would be meaningful. Because the Filipinos under his command were terrified of becoming captives of the Japanese, there were only a small handful of officers and men with Hilsman on the day he surrendered.

[34] The formal ending of hostilities did not conclude operations against the Japanese. Isolated military units were to fight on as guerrillas as would quasi-military groupings which were formed following the surrenders. Guerrilla operations continued throughout the Japanese occupation, escalating with the American invasion of the Philippines during October of 1944 and continuing until July 15, 1945, with the linkup on Mindanao of a guerrilla force with elements of the 24th Infantry Division. Source: *U.S. Army in World War II, Chronology 1941-1945,* compiled by Mary H. Williams. (Washington, DC: Office Chief of Military History, 1960.)

LISTS OF VESSELS AND PARTICULARS, WHEN KNOWN
DEFENSE OF THE PHILIPPINES: DECEMBER 1941 - MAY 1942

List 1: Vessels of the U. S. Army Transport Service and U.S. Army Harbor Boat Service: Defense of the Philippines, 1941 - 1942

List 2: Vessels Belonging To or Otherwise in the Employment of the U.S. Navy But Assigned to U.S. Army Forces, Far East: Defense of the Philippines, 1941 - 1942

List 3: Vessels of the Offshore Patrol - Philippine Army, Inducted into U.S. Army Forces, Far East, December 19, 1941

List 4: Merchant Ships and Small Craft Commandeered, Seized, Requisitioned, or Chartered Within the Philippine Islands, 1941 - 1942, by U.S. Army Forces, Far East:

List 5: Merchant Vessels Not Known to Have Been in Service of U.S. Army Forces, Far East But Which Were Sunk, Damaged, Scuttled, or Taken Over by the Japanese Within the Philippine Islands, 1941-42.

Note: Three ships *Dona Nati, Don Isidro,* and *Florence* D -- all owned by Filipino companies -- were chartered while outside of the Philippines by the Army to run the Japanese blockade of the Philippine Islands. The story of *Dona Nati* is covered within Chapter XIII and that of *Don Isidro* and *Florence D* within Chapter XV.

Primary Source Bibliography for Vessel Lists

AF 500-21: Refers to *History of ATS Activities in Manila and Cebu,* Archive File No. 500-21, Dec 1941 to May 1942, within Record Group 407 (RG-407), Philippine Archive Collection (PAC), Box 1568. *History of ATS Activities in Manila and Cebu City* is a lengthy and largely illegible document which appears to have been microfilmed from either an onion skin copy or from a 2-sided mimeographed copy since on some of its pages *bleeding* of type occurred from the back side onto the front. In August of 2000, we had that document digitally enhanced enabling a transcription of 95% of the first part of the report and 45%-50% of the remainder. The probability is that it was prepared by ATS participates who composed it from notes preserved during their captivity as POWs of the Japanese.

ATS File: List titled *ATS Vessels Manila, Corregidor, Bataan* as found in RG-407, Philippine Archive Collection (PAC), Box 1570, Miscellaneous File. This is a list of vessels and their missions for the Army Transport Service as well as some final ship disposition information, e.g., bombed, sunk, captured, scuttled, etc.

ATS: Refers in the general sense to Army Transport Service records.

BR 1337, *British and Foreign Merchant Vessel Losses, World War II:* Naval Staff (Trade Division), British Admiralty, 1945.

Charter Party: Indicates that within RG-407 there is a charter specific to the particular vessel as executed between the owner or his representative and an officer representing ATS. These charters were the standardized format utilized by the ATS in the Philippines following Dec 24, 1941, through to the surrender of Corregidor in May 1942. Prior to Dec 24, 1941, most charter parties drawn by the ATS in the Philippines seem to have been of a time charter format, an exception being the *USAT Don Esteban* which was employed under bareboat charter. Following Dec 24, charter policy was changed in that the charter's Paragraph 7 gave the ATS, as the charterer, the option of retaining or replacing crewmembers and the full control of the vessel. At the military's option, the ship's employment term covered up to the duration of the war unless sooner canceled. Under the format, the master was enjoined to obey all instructions of the Army officer placed in charge of the mission. Payment to the owner was to be at the conclusion of the war. (From a practical viewpoint, the only factor which varied from traditional bareboat language seems to be the somewhat ambiguous Paragraph 4 which pertains to the party held responsible for victualing the vessel.) Payment of crew's wages was the ATS's responsibility although at the very beginning of the period, the ATS at times asked an owner to pay the crew on the basis that the Army would make reimbursement. This was but a temporary accommodation as it appears that by early Feb of 1942, Army finance officers were paying all the crews directly, the wage rate being based on prewar Filipino shipping industry rates plus 100% applied for war risks. A copy of the standard charter form employed following Dec 24, 1941, has been reproduced as Appendix G of this volume. Various vessel folders within RG-407, PAC, contain such charters, all of which are identical in their composition.

Cook: This reference pertains to a letter of Cook's dated Jan 6, 1942, addressed to La Naviera Filipina, Inc., which is to be found in RG-407, PAC, and which lists seven vessels requisitioned from that company by the U.S. Army: five were taken over on Dec 15, 1941, and two on Jan 5, 1942. In November 1941, a Quartermaster Depot was established at Cebu City, island of Cebu. Cook was named its commander. In that capacity, he was to supervise ATS activities until Feb at which point Lt. Col. Cornelius Z. Byrd was assigned there as Superintendent, ATS, for the port of Cebu City and for the Visayan group.

Cook '47 Survey: Pertains to a list compiled by Col. John D. Cook, QMC, on his revisit to the Philippines following the war (1947) during which time Cook (who had commanded the port at Cebu City, island of Cebu, during the defense of 1942) made inquiries as to the final disposition of vessels which had operated from there and from other southern islands of the Philippines during 1942. Cook's results from his inquiries were then forwarded to Col. Frederick A. Ward. The Cook report, together with a supplemental report from Ward were later transmitted to Brig. Gen. Charles C. Drake. These reports are all located within RG-407, PAC, Box 1570.

Crew, Mar 42: This pertains to crew listings of chartered interisland vessels. The lists were transmitted to Adj. Gen., War Department, under the date Mar 26, 1942, and signed by Carl H. Seals, Brig. Gen., HQ, USFIP, Fort Mills, Philippines. These lists can be found within RG-407, PAC, Boxes 1565 and 1568, Folders *Army Transport Service.* A number of other crew lists not within Seals's submissions are to be found scattered in various folders within RG-407, PAC, and where that applies have been so noted in our listing of the particular vessel.

Dean: References an affidavit of Alfred P. Dean attested before Robert G. Smith, 1ˢᵗ Lt., Inf. HQ, U.S. Army Forces Western Pacific, dated 18 Feb 1946. Dean attests to charter parties that were drawn between ATS *on the following vessels* (he lists 22 vessels) -- all charters having been executed by *Major* C. Z. Byrd, QMC, during 1942 -- and includes the dates of those charters. This is to be found within RG-407, PAC, Box 1570, File *Miscellaneous*. This notation additionally pertains to another list found in the same file, dated Apr 1, 1942, which was in Dean's possession and which was signed by *Col.* [probably Lt. Col.] C. Z. Byrd. Because many of the reports we examined were prepared *after the fact* by memory, some refer to Byrd as Major and others refer to him as Lt. Col. or Colonel. It is unclear as to when Byrd received his promotion to lieutenant colonel; however, it seems that this probably occurred during the siege and that for the period of the lists herein he retained that title; thus, we have opted to refer to Byrd as *Lt. Col.* in all cases. For the same reasons, we refer to William F. Sharp of the Visayan- Mindanao Force as *Major General*.

Drake: Pertains to report filed by Brig. Gen. Charles C. Drake titled *Report of Operations, Quartermaster Corps; U.S. Army in the Philippine Campaign, 1941 -42,* as originally filed within Records of the Adjutant General, WW II, and now to be found within RG-407, PAC, Box 1570.

Edmonds Collection: A manuscript collection dealing with the war in the Southwest Pacific, 1941-42, taken from mainly official sources. Now held by Archives Branch, AFHRA/ISR, Maxwell Air Force Base, Alabama.

Giagonia: *The Philippine Navy, 1898 - 1996 by* Regino Dodds Giagonia. Giagonia's history contains an excellent summary of the organization and operation (up to May 1942) of the Offshore Patrol, Philippine Army, as incorporated on December 19, 1941, to USAFFE.

Hartendorp: References A. V H. Hartendorp who was the editor during 1941 of the *Philippine Magazine.* Hartendorp was interned by the Japanese at Santo Tomas Civilian Interment Camp, Manila, where he became the camp historian during the three years of his confinement there. After the liberation of the Philippines, Hartendorp became one of the few historians who wrote first hand of the experiences suffered by the Philippines during the Japanese occupation. After the war, he became the editor of the American *Chamber of Commerce Journal*, published at Manila. He authored a 2-volume work published in 1967 in Manila titled *The Japanese Occupation of the Philippines*. In his Volume I, pp 186-189, he relates an interview he conducted with Federico Narruhn, a Spanish-born harbor boat captain (American citizen) who had been at Corregidor at the time of its surrender. For some unexplained reason—perhaps he had told the Japanese that he was a Spanish citizen—he was not made a prisoner of war but instead was taken to Manila and interned at Santo Tomas. While at Santo Tomas, Narruhn told Hartendorp his recollections as to the fate of certain ships known to him. When applicable, those remembrances have been cited. We have found them to be accurate when compared against other supportive evidence.

Lloyd's Register of Shipping, 1941 - 42: An annual publication listing particulars on the world's shipping, inclusive of American and foreign vessels.

Lloyd's War Losses: *Lloyd's War Losses, The Second World War,* Volume I: *British, Allied and Neutral Merchant Vessels Sunk or Destroyed by War Causes.* Readers are cautioned when using this *Lloyd's* in that the dates and places of sinkings in the Philippines were usually taken from information given by vessel owners and shipping agents not directly involved in the ship's activities at the time of its loss. Such post facto reports accordingly proved questionable when compared against U.S. Army records, many of which were either prepared at the time or were derived from notes made by Army officers during the war which were put into report form following the release of those officers from POW camp. Misinformation seems to be inherent within *Lloyd's War Losses* regarding *flag* identification for vessels owned and documented in the Philippines. *Lloyd's* lists some of those vessels as *U.S. flag* and some as *Philippine Islands*. The Philippines, circa 1941-42, was still a commonwealth of the United States as its full independence had not yet been granted. All vessels therefore holding documentation in the Philippine Islands (circa 1941-42), whether employed in foreign trade or in interisland service, would have flown the U.S. flag.

Merchant Vessels of the United States for the year 1937: Through 1937, the United States Department of Commerce recorded the documentation of all Philippine Island vessels. The Philippines were due to be granted independence in 1946, and perhaps in accordance with that, following 1937, vessels registered in the Philippines were no longer reported within the Department of Commerce's annual publication *Merchant Vessels of the United States*. The exact reason is unclear, but it was probably because the Philippine Commonwealth Government rather than the U.S. Commerce Department began performing the actual registration at that time. The fact remains, though, that throughout World War II, all Philippine vessels were U.S. flag vessels, and they remained as such up until the Philippines became an independent nation. For further discussion regarding the status of Philippine-registered vessels, pre-1941, a researcher is referred to a letter dated October 26, 1938, from the Assistant Secretary of Commerce, J. M. Johnson, to The Honorable, The Secretary of State, filed at the Division of Communications and Records, Division of Far Eastern Affairs, Department of State, November 4, 1938, with copies received at the Office of Philippine Affairs, Department of State, as filed on October 28, 1938.

PAC: Refers to Philippine Archive Collection held within Record Group 407 (RG-407) at the National Archives, Washington, DC

Provost Marshal's Listing of Civilian Internees: CFN-127, for the period: 7 Dec 1941 to 14 August 1945. (Records of the Adj. General's Office), Modern Military Records, National Archives, Washington, DC.

RG-407: This citation references material found on a particular vessel within Record Group-407, Philippine Archive Collection, at the National Archives, Washington, DC. Cites include the particular box number within that collection and, when known, the file folder identification.

Spec Crew List: This citation refers to the existence within RG-407, PAC, of a crew list on the particular vessel. Crew lists are to be found scattered throughout the various boxes of the Record Group and are accordingly identified in our ship listings.

Stauffer: Alvin P. Stauffer, *The Quartermaster Corps: Operations in the War Against Japan.*

SWPA: Refers to an historical monograph titled *U.S. Army Transportation in the Southwest Pacific Area, 1941 - 1947* by James R. Masterson, of the Office of the Chief of Military History. Masterson's monograph, which is of considerable length, covers the entire period of World War II and concerns itself only in small part with the resupply of the beleaguered Philippines from the United States via Australia and the Dutch East Indies. There is very little within it dealing with those Filipino vessels chartered within the Philippines by the ATS or by the Visayan- Mindanao Force between Dec 1941 and May 1942. SWPA has therefore had little utilization by us for those operations, but where it does make reference, it is cited accordingly. Page 383 of the Monograph lists a few of the Filipino ships known to have been chartered by ATS, Philippines.

Vessel Name File: This pertains to files maintained within the Records of the Chief of Transportation, Record Group 336, Modern Military Records, National Archives.

Ward Report: Lt. Col. Frederick A. Ward, QMC, was Superintendent of the Army Transport Service in the Philippines, 1941-42. Following Ward's liberation from a Japanese POW camp, he prepared a narrative report derived from wartime notes and memory as well as from interviews he conducted with other officers while in the POW camps. The Ward Report pertains to the activities of the ATS during the defense of 1941 - 42. It was written by Ward at the request of Brig. Gen. Charles C. Drake who had been Chief Quartermaster, Philippines, during the defense. Colonel Ward names vessels taken over by the ATS during the defense, and when known, their fate. The Ward Report was incorporated as part of Drake's Report.

Ward, Apr 42: This pertains to a wireless message sent to QM General, Washington, dated Apr 1, 1942, signed by Lt. Col. Frederick A. Ward, listing vessel charters and their dates as executed under the jurisdiction of ATS headquarters at Fort Mills, Corregidor. It covers the period Feb 20, 1942, to Mar 28, 1942. Action copies were sent to Service of Supply, QMD, G2, AG. This message is now to be found in RG-407, PAC, Box 1565, Folder "Army Transport Service, Maritime Matters." This list was duplicated by memorandum of Maj. C. Z. Bird, and dated the same day. There are slight differences between dates of charter by Ward and within the Dean list earlier referenced, probably because Dean gives charter dates as being the requisition dates while Ward's dates are based upon the later signature of owners or owners' representatives who may not have been available to sign the charters on the day when each ship was actually taken over.

Willoughby: Maj. Gen. Charles A. Willoughby was Gen. Douglas MacArthur's Chief of Intelligence during World War II. Following the war, Willoughby published *The Guerrilla Resistance Movement in the Philippines, 1941 - 1945,* (New York, Washington: Vantage Press, 1972), a compilation of photo reproductions of intelligence reports and summarization from Volumes I and II of the official Army publication *The Intelligence Services.* On pages 254 and 255 of Willoughby's book is a list of the status of forty-nine Filipino vessels, stating their operational or lack of operational status during the time frame 15 Jan 1943 to 20 October 1943. That information was derived from American and/or Filipino intelligence agents operating within the Philippines. According to Willoughby, such reports were later checked and were found accurate. In all but the case of one vessel, our own cross-checking against other sources substantiates Willoughby's evaluations.

List 1:

Vessels Of The U. S. Army Transport Service And U.S. Army Harbor Boat Service: Defense Of The Philippines, 1941 - 1942

Colonel George F. E. Harrison. 1.172'; 704 GT; Blt 1919, Milwaukee, WI.

Mine Planter. Prewar function was to service the mine fields which protected the approaches to Manila Bay. After outbreak of hostilities, she was utilized for general transportation purposes by the ATS. On May 2, 1942, was hit by bombs near Corregidor and reported sunk on May 5. According to Hartendorp's informant, she was afloat on or around the time of Corregidor's surrender and was scuttled then by American forces. At that time, her crew consisted of U.S. Army personnel. According to one affidavit, the U.S. Army enlisted men were from the Philippine Scouts. According to post war affidavits located in RG-407, she was later salvaged by the Japanese and employed by them within the Manila area. At one point when the Japanese had her, she was crewed by Filipino merchant seamen from the *Lepus* following that crew's delivery of *Lepus* to Japan and the crew's repatriation to the Philippines. (See *Lepus.*) [ATS file; Ward Rpt; RG-407, PAC, Box 25, Folder *Lepus* and Box 1569, Folder *Colonel George F. E. Harrison*; Hartendorp.]

Derrick Barge

Harbor Boat. Sunk by bombing Jan 5, 1942, at North Harbor, Corregidor. [ATS file]

Don Esteban. 1.267'; 1616 GT; Blt 1936, Kiel, Germany.

Cargo and troopship. Owned by De la Rama SS Co. but taken under bareboat charter by ATS Manila on Oct 30, 1941. Unlike the many Philippine vessels which the ATS chartered following the outbreak of hostilities, *USAT Don Esteban*—having been bareboat chartered prior to that time—was organized along the same crewing and staffing lines as were the Army Transport Service's regular transports, although crew wages, at least initially, were below stateside ATS standards. Following her charter, *USAT Don Esteban* departed Manila for Port Moresby, New Guinea; thence to Australia (Darwin and Cairns) before returning to Manila where she arrived on Dec 10, 1941. Between then and Dec 15 she transferred supplies from Manila to Corregidor which included the towing of cargo lighters to Corregidor. On Dec 16, she departed Manila for the island of Negros, thence to Cebu City, island of Cebu, and on to Bugo, island of Mindanao, for discharge before returning to Manila on Dec 23. On Dec 24, she took General MacArthur and his family and staff to Corregidor from Manila. Until Dec 31, *USAT Don Esteban* was engaged in evacuating personnel and supplies to Corregidor. On Feb 22, 1942, she departed Corregidor with a *special party* (all officials of the Philippine Government) for Iloilo, island of Panay, where they were disembarked to *Princess of Negros.* She then left for Antique, island of Panay, to take on foodstuffs for Corregidor. While sheltering en route at Paluan Bay, island of Mindoro, on Mar 1, she was bombed and strafed, the attack setting her afire, becoming a total loss. That afternoon, enemy warships were sighted outside the bay. Following the bombing, the officers and crew escaped under the command of the military transport commander. Traveling overland across the island, they chartered a sail vessel for Cebu City, island of Cebu, arriving there Mar 12 where the crew was paid off. Lloyd's lists a different date and place of loss, but that is almost certainly not correct in light of the clear Army evidence to the contrary. [ATS file; Spec Crew List; RG-407, PAC, Box 1569; Lloyd's]

Geary. 54 GT; Blt 1908, Hong Kong

Harbor Boat. Reported as actively employed in evacuation of personnel and vital materiel from Bataan to Corregidor in advance of Japanese occupation of Mariveles. Reported missing from Corregidor as of May 6, 1942. The possibility exists that her disappearance may have been at the hands of persons attempting to escape on the day of the surrender of Corregidor. [ATS Files; AF 500-21]

General John McE. Hyde. l. 150'; 900 GT; Blt 1921, Charleston, West Virginia

Originally a river steamer refitted by ATS for limited ocean service. On September 15, 1930, she sailed from New York to Manila via Panama. On arrival in the Philippines, she was designated as the interisland flagship of the Quartermaster Corps, being assigned to the Harbor Boat Service for transportation of Army inspection parties throughout the archipelago. According to an Army nurse quoted in *We Band of Angels,* the *McHyde* was bombed and observed as having sunk off Bataan during Christmas week of 1941. That is not, however, correct. ATS records have her as being bombed at Cavite after which she was towed to Corregidor for repairs and was put back into service. According to two ATS records as well as Hartendorp's informant, she was lost off Corregidor on Apr 9, 1942, a victim of shellfire from by then enemy-held southern Bataan. A third Army report has the loss, also at Corregidor, as occurring on Apr 13. [ATS File; Vessel Name File, Chief of Transportation; Elizabeth M. Norman, *We Band of Angels,* (New York: Random House, 1999); AF 500-21; Hartendorp.]

General Miley. 364 GT; Blt 1911, Hong Kong

Harbor Boat. Passenger - freight vessel. Suffered bomb damage Dec 24, 1941, and again three days later in Manila's inner harbor. Towed to Corregidor on Dec 30. Shelled by Japanese Apr 23, 1942, at Corregidor, being set afire. Sank on Apr 25. [ATS File; Spec. Crew List; RG-407, PAC, Box 1569, Folder *Miley*; Hartendorp.]

Henry Keswick. l.165'; 671 GT; Blt 1921, Hong Kong. British flag

Considered as one of the largest oceangoing tugs in the world during the 1940s. Requisitioned by U.S. Navy for evacuation of Manila with British officers and her Chinese crewmen being retained. Abandoned by that crew at Manila on Dec 29. (Her British master and his officers had refused to volunteer their service to the U.S. Army, preferring civilian internment by the Japanese.) The abandoned tug was then seized by ATS and towed to Corregidor where *Henry Keswick* was crewed by ATS personnel. She served continuously until Apr 10, 1942, when she was hit by enemy shellfire from Bataan while off Corregidor. Was beached as a total loss. *Keswick's* last master under ATS was Lt.(jg) Trose E. Donaldson, USNR; he was posthumously awarded the Distinguished Service Cross. For more on Donaldson, see *Trabajador* under List 2 which follows. Most of her ATS crew consisted of American and Norwegian merchant seamen volunteers who, with one exception, were awarded the Merchant Marine Meritorious Service Medal. (The exception was a Norwegian who refused duty and was court-martialed.) Lloyd's states *Henry Keswick* was refloated by the Japanese on 6 Sept 1942 and renamed *Keishu Maru,* being sent to Shanghai either in 1942 or 1943 to be utilized by the Japanese Navy. Was abandoned by the Japanese during Jan 1945. [ATS File; RG-407, PAC, Box 25, Folder "ATS—Awards Records", MARAD; Lloyd's; AF 500-21; Hale Hutchins, "We Were There, Too," *Mast Magazine,* 1947.]

J 54

Harbor Boat. Tender to *USAT Don Esteban* from which *J 54* was reported as having gone adrift on Feb 15, 1942. At that time, *USAT Don Esteban* was at anchor off Corregidor. [ATS file]

J 161

Harbor Boat. Reported as active in moving supplies and priority troops from Bataan to Corregidor immediately before surrender of Bataan. Thought to have been sunk in South Harbor, Corregidor, May 6, 1942. [ATS File; AF 500-21]

J 162	Harbor Boat. Sunk Jan 4, 1942, at Corregidor. [ATS file]
J 163	Harbor Boat. Sunk Jan 4, 1942, at Corregidor. [ATS file]
J 230	Harbor Boat. Reported as active in moving supplies and priority troops from Bataan to Corregidor immediately before surrender of Bataan. Carried Lt. General Wainwright and staff to Cabcaben for surrender meeting with the Japanese. On return to Corregidor, she grounded and sank. [ATS file; AF 500-21; RG-407, PAC, Box 1565]
J. M. Jewell. 55 GT; Blt 1908 Hong Kong.	Harbor Boat. Reported sunk about May 4, 1942, off Corregidor. [ATS file]
Jet.	Harbor Boat. Disposition unknown. [RG-407, PAC, Box 1565]
Ledyard. 70 GT; Blt 1910, Shanghai.	Harbor Boat. Tug assigned to Fort Wint, which was located at entrance to Subic Bay. Sunk by U.S. shellfire at Olongapo, west side of Subic Bay, when it was discovered that the Coast Artillery had by accident laid a minefield around her. [ATS File]
Maintenance Barge 181	Harbor Boat. Sunk by Japanese aircraft off Corregidor on Dec 29, 1941. [ATS file; AF 500-21]
Maxwell.	Harbor Boat. Sunk Jan 5, 1942, at Corregidor, a result of bombing. [ATS file]
McConville. 70 GT; Blt 1910, Shanghai.	Harbor Boat assigned to Fort Mills, Corregidor. Reported missing May 6, 1942, from Corregidor, *possibly lying aground at Naig* on the Luzon shoreline on the south side of Manila Bay. [ATS file]
Milly	Harbor Boat. Disposition unknown. [RG-407, PAC, Box 1565]
Mitchell. 53 GT; Blt 1900, Hong Kong	Harbor Boat. Was active in moving supplies and personnel from Bataan to Corregidor in advance of enemy occupation of Mariveles. Reported missing from Corregidor as of May 6, 1942. Later was reported as aground and abandoned at Naig. This probably was the result of an escape attempt from Corregidor immediately prior to surrender of that place. [Ward Rpt]
Wahoo.	Harbor Boat. Disposition unknown. [RG-407, PAC, Box 1565]
WB 89.	Harbor Boat. Water boat captured Apr 9, 1942, on Bataan. [ATS file]
WB 145.	Harbor Boat. Water boat damaged in bombing or by shellfire May 2, 1942. Reported as sunk the next day. [ATS file]
Yu Sang, ex *Hai Yuan.* 1.328'; 3357 GT; Blt 1934, Newcastle, England. British flag	Freighter. Owned by the Indo-China Steam Navigation Co. After merchant ships were ordered to evacuate the Manila anchorage, she was moved to an anchorage offlying Bataan. In Feb 1942, she was commandeered by ATS and her cargo of *oint and pepper* unloaded. Reloaded with aerial bombs that had been stored on Corregidor, she was remanned with an ATS crew, most of her non-officer ratings (all Chinese) having

ed around the end of December. Scheduled for departure to Mindanao, she was attacked by Japanese aircraft in Mariveles harbor, Bataan, on Apr 8 and sunk. Her ATS crew consisted in largest part of U.S. merchant seamen and other U.S. citizen volunteers with the remainder being Filipinos. Despite her dangerous cargo, the ship did not explode, and the entire crew escaped injury. [ATS file; Lloyd's; Ward Rpt; SWPA; RG-407, PAC, Box 1568, Folder *Yu Sang;* Spec. Crew List; AF 500-21.]

List 2:

Vessels Belonging To Or
Otherwise In The Employment Of The U.S. Navy
But Assigned To U.S. Army Forces, Far East:
Defense Of The Philippines, 1941-42

Additional Sources Specific to this List: *Dictionary of American Naval Fighting Ships*; *Naval Chronology, World War II.*

Vessel	Dsp Tons	Remarks
Arionte (or Apiontes)		Used to evacuate dead and wounded from Cavite to Manila. Then taken to Corregidor by the ATS whereupon she was turned over to the Navy.
Bittern, USS	840	Minesweeper. Heavily damaged at Cavite on Dec 16, 1941. Subsequently scuttled in Manila Bay to avoid capture.
Canopus, USS	5975	Submarine tender, built 1919. Scuttled at Bataan.
Finch, USS	840	Minesweeper, built 1917. Sunk by bombs at Corregidor.
Genessee, USS		Tug. Scuttled May 5, 1942, to avoid capture.
Jem	23 GT	Taken over by ATS requisition at the Manila Yacht Club from owner J. W. Hausserman on Dec 26, 1941. Utilized by Navy in evacuation from Manila and then abandoned after being damaged from air attack. May have been captured as Hartendorp claims that attempts to scuttle her proved unsuccessful.
Luzon, USS	560	Gunboat built 1927. Severely damaged by bombers. Sunk May 6, 1942, by gunfire from U.S. forces when capture of Corregidor appeared imminent. Salvaged by Japanese and renamed *Karatsu*. Torpedoed by *USS Narwhal* on March 3, 1944.
Maria Delores		Yacht taken over by Navy. Attempt was made to scuttle but apparently this was unsuccessful as she was captured by Japanese at Corregidor.
Marianne		Taken over by ATS at Manila from J. Marsman and turned over to the Navy on Jan 5, 1942. Disposition after that unknown.
Mindanao, USS	560	Gunboat bombed and sunk, probably May 6, 1942, in the vicinity of Corregidor.
Napa, USS	735	Tug built 1919. Scuttled at Bataan to prevent its use by the enemy.
Oahu, USS	450	Gunboat built 1927. Previous to Corregidor surrender was sunk either by enemy gunfire from Bataan or by scuttling.
Pigeon, USS	950	Minesweeper. On May 4, 1942, was sunk by enemy aircraft off Corregidor. Her valiant service during the defense earned her the first Presidential Unit Citation ever awarded by the Navy.
PT-31, USS		Went aground and then scuttled to avoid capture.
PT-32, USS		Scuttled March 13, 1942, at Cuyo Island after abandonment in leaking condition on Cuyo Island. Was serving as escort to MacArthur's evacuation from Corregidor at time of abandonment.

PT-33, USS		Went aground and then scuttled to avoid capture.
PT-34, USS		Was engaged in evacuation of MacArthur's key staff personnel from Corregidor in March. On Apr 9, went aground during operations against the enemy and was subsequently scuttled at Cebu.
PT-35, USS		Carried members of MacArthur's staff on their evacuation from Corregidor in March. Scuttled at Cebu on Apr 12, 1942.
PT-41, USS		Evacuated MacArthur, his wife, and child from Corregidor in March. Scuttled at 07° 53' N; 24° 15' E on Apr 15, 1942.
Quail, USS	840	Minesweeper. Scuttled May 5, 1942, at Corregidor to avoid capture.
Ranger	512 GT	Coastal tug, built 1940. RG-407, PAC, has her as being taken over at Manila from the Luzon Stevedoring Co. by the Navy in Dec 1941. *Lloyds War Losses* states she was lost during the defense of the Philippines but gives no particulars. It is known that this tug was still operational in mid-Mar 1942 so her loss followed that date. Hartendorp's informant claims she was scuttled in May at Corregidor.
San Felipe		Ferryboat in employment of Navy. Hartendorp's informant said she was scuttled at Corregidor. She may have been salvaged by the Japanese.
Sealion, USS	1475	Submarine built in 1939. Damaged by bombs and subsequently destroyed at Cavite, Manila Bay, to avoid falling into enemy hands.
Tanager, USS	840	Minesweeper built in 1918. Sunk near Corregidor by enemy gunfire from Bataan before the surrender of Corregidor.
Trabajador	248 GT	Coastal tug, built 1931. Taken over by Navy from Visayan Stevedore Transportation Co. on Dec 13 at Manila and placed under the command of Lt.(jg) Trose E. Donaldson, USNR, a former merchant marine master recently called to active duty. Served as the tender to PT Boat Squadron 3 until the withdrawal of U.S. forces from Bataan. Was sunk at Corregidor. Army reports for Apr 1942 indicate that the Army was manning *Trabajador* at that time. Donaldson then took command of the ATS tug *Henry Keswick* which shortly afterward was itself lost to enemy shellfire off Corregidor. During that action, Donaldson was killed. A 1943 intelligence report stated that *Trabajador* had been salvaged and was being used by the Japanese in their Philippine coastwise service.
Vaga, USS	529	Coastal tug built 1910. One Army report seems to indicate that the Army may have manned this tug in Apr of 1942. However, *Dictionary of American Naval Fighting Ships* and the *Naval Chronology of World War II* lists her as being scuttled by the Navy at Corregidor to avoid capture. This is further confirmed by Hartendorp's informant. Affidavits in RG-407, PAC, Box 1569, Folder - *Miley:* attest that the Japanese, beginning the day following the surrender of Corregidor, placed captured Filipino employees of the Army Transport Service aboard *USS Vaga* as prisoners to serve as its crew and that the tug served the Japanese at Manila and later in Borneo waters until she was lost to Allied bombing on or about Jan 15, 1944.

List 3:

Vessels of the Offshore Patrol - Philippine Army, Incorporated into U.S. Army Forces, Far East December 19, 1941

Information for this list is taken primarily from:
Lloyd's War Losses; Giagonia's *The Philippine Navy, 1898 - 1996*; *Merchant Vessels of the United States* for the year 1937; Willoughby's *Guerrilla Resistance Movement in the Philippines*.

Abra (Q-112). l. 55'	Torpedo boat. British built; delivered to OSP in March 1939. Used in ferrying MacArthur to Bataan from Corregidor for inspection of front-line troops—the only such inspection MacArthur conducted on Bataan during the siege. Unable to complete a successful escape from Bataan in April, *Abra* was scuttled at Poambong.
Agusan (Q-113). l. 65'	Torpedo boat. Built in the Philippines on a government contract. Delivered to OSP in 1941. Destroyed at Corregidor prior to the surrender.
Arayat. 904 GT	Bureau of Customs Revenue Service cutter inducted with crew into the OSP, USAFFE on Dec 19, 1941. Shortly after was bombed and severely damaged at Manila. Set on fire, becoming total loss.
Baler	Tender to the Presidential yacht *Casiana*. On Jan 11, 1942, this tender was converted into an armed launch. Captured in Apr while attempting escape from Bataan.
Banahaw. 667 GT	Either Lighthouse Service tender or a Bureau of Customs Revenue Service cutter. Inducted with her crew into OSP, USAFFE, on Dec 19, 1941. Set on fire and sunk by bombing attack near end of month. Intelligence report of 1943 stated she was refloated by Japanese.
Canlaon. 667 GT	Lighthouse Service tender, inducted with crew into the OSP, USAFFE on Dec 19, 1941. Bombed and reported sunk at Manila shortly after. However, Hartendorp claims she was scuttled. An intelligence report received by the Intelligence Section, Southwest Pacific Area Command, at Australia during 1943 states that she had probably been salvaged by the Japanese for their use.
Casiana. l. 260'	Presidential yacht. Ordered to OSP service on or around Dec 10, 1941, and with her crew was activated into USAFFE on Dec 19, 1941. On Dec 29, while off Corregidor, was hit by a bomb and sunk. Another source gives that loss as Jan 6, 1942. An intelligence report stated that during 1943, she was thought to have been salvaged by the Japanese.
Danday (Q-114), ex Carmen	Motor launch taken over by OSP at Lamao, Bataan, in early Jan 1942, following evacuation from Manila. Burned at Lamao either by enemy attack or scuttling before surrender of Bataan.

Fathometer.† 550 tons displacement

Survey vessel owned by Philippine Government and assigned to U.S. Coast and Geodetic Survey operation. Inducted with her crew into OSP, USAFFE, at Manila on Dec 19, 1941. Bombed on Jan 17 at Sisiman Cove, Bataan and then beached. According to a 1956 issue of *Shipping Gazette,* Manila, she was salvaged following the war, probably for scrap.

Fisheries I

Philippine Government fishery research vessel. Inducted with her crew into OSP, USAFFE, on Dec 19, 1941. Final disposition unknown.

Luzon (Q-111) l. 65'

Torpedo boat. British built. Delivered to OSP in June 1939. Attacked by aircraft and destroyer while attempting escape from Bataan in Apr 1942; rendered into sinking condition, was scuttled by her crew.

Mindoro. 341 GT

Bureau of Customs Revenue Service cutter. On Dec 19, 1941, inducted with her crew into OSP, USAFFE. Not known as to whether she was actually operated by OSP. Set afire by bombing attack, probably at Manila, on or before Dec 28.

Research †, ex *USCGS Pathfinder.* 875 GT

Survey vessel owned by Philippine Commonwealth Government but assigned to U.S. Coast and Geodetic Survey. Inducted with her crew into OSP, USAFFE on Dec 19, 1941, but not known as to whether she was made operational by OSP. Bombed and badly damaged at Engineer Island on Dec 28. Was again bombed on Dec 29 and 30, being then damaged so badly that she was beached on the western side of Manila Bay. A 1943 intelligence report stated she had been salvaged and was being used by the Japanese in Philippine coastal service.

Note: The reader is referred to Appendix M of this volume for a summarization of the history of the Offshore Patrol - Philippine Army and of its inclusion within the United States Army Forces, Far East and later within the United States Army's Southwest Pacific Area Command.

---

†   *Fathometer* and *Research* had American masters and Filipino officers and crew. When they were inducted on Dec 19, 1941, into OSP, USAFFE, this included the Filipinos but not the American master.

List 4:

Merchant Ships And Small Craft
Commandeered, Seized, Requisitioned, Or Chartered
Within The Philippine Islands, 1941 - 1942
By U.S. Army Forces, Far East:

Length; gross tonnage; year of building, and place as given in this list are taken from a large variety of sources as described within the Primary Source bibliography for Vessel Lists.

Within this list, there are certain references to the *Visayan- Mindanao Force* as those references comments have been derived from archival files. That force was dissolved into two separate commands as of mid-March 1942 -- one command thereafter known as the Visayan Force; the other as the Mindanao Force or *Sharp's Command*. Despite that command change, the term *Visayan-Mindanao Force* was still being used within reports filed after mid-March in reference to shipping controlled by other than the Army Transport Service.

Few of these vessels survived the military's employment, most having been lost to enemy action. Their losses were of considerable consequence to the Philippine economy. Fortunately, following the war, the majority of the losses were made good through a process of claims adjustments paid out by the United States.

Aboitoz	Thought to be the same vessel as *P. Aboitiz*.
Active. 1.61'; 36 GT; Blt 1924, Manila	Probably a tug. Chartered or requisitioned from Luzon Stevedoring Co. by ATS and then assigned to Army Engineers. Sunk in South Harbor, Corregidor on May 5, 1942. [ATS file]
Adams. 27 GT; Blt Shanghai	Launch. Mentioned as doing outstanding work during evacuation from Manila. While under ATS employment was lost to air attack on Dec 29, 1941, while at anchor off Corregidor. [AF 500-21]
Adonis	Probably a tug. Sunk Jan 4, 1942, off Corregidor by bombing.
Agrigao	This name was found on a nearly illegible list of vessels within "History of ATS Activities in Manila and Cebu, Dec 41 to May 42." Nothing more could be discerned as to the vessel's service or final disposition. The list contains the names of twenty-seven vessels plus others with completely illegible names. Of the twenty-seven legible names there are only five on which we do not have other records tying them directly to ATS employment. Therefore, it is probable that this vessel was employed in some fashion by the Army between Dec 7, 1941 and May of 1942. [AF 500-21]
Agustina. 1.134'; 296 GT; Blt 1929, Hong Kong	Owned by La Naviera Filipina, Inc. Requisitioned by ATS at Cebu City, island of Cebu, Dec 15, 1941. According to one Army account was shelled and sunk at Bugo, island of Mindanao, on Feb 28, 1942. One Army account claims sinking was on Mar 3 which Colonels *Killen and Morse* were stated to

have witnessed. According to Cook '47 Survey, a cargo that was being handled at that time had come from Australia, having been brought in by *Coast Farmer*. The actual circumstances were something quite different in that *Agustina* had apparently brought from Cebu City tin and rubber that was offloaded onto *Coast Farmer* for that ship's return voyage to Australia from Mindanao. See Vessel Index for further discussion on this vessel's activity. [Cook; Ward Report; Cook '47 Survey; SWPA; Statement of Claims in RG-407, PAC, Box 1566; AF 500-21; Drake]

Alert. 1.61; 35 GT; Blt 1929, Philippine Islands

Launch owned by Luzon Stevedoring Co. First taken over by Navy at Manila in Dec 1941; then went to ATS. Assigned by ATS to Army Engineers. Reported as being returned without authorization by its civilian crews to Manila after Japanese occupied the city. [ATS file; Ward Rpt]

Amelia

Interisland freighter. Used by Visayan- Mindanao Force. Disposition unknown. [AF 500-21]

Antonio. 1.87'; 73 GT; Blt 1897, Hong Kong

Owner given as Aboitiz - Elcano Fleet. According to Army Claims File was commandeered at Manila on Dec 24, 1941, remaining in ATS service until Dec 28, being used for troop evacuation to Bataan. Was scuttled on either Dec 28 or 29 by order of Manila's Harbor Police. [Army Claims File, RG-407, PAC, Box 1566, 1568, 1570; Folder *Antonio*]

Augustina, see Agustina

Aviador. 1.87'; 86 GT; Blt 1930, Sorsogon, Philippine Islands

Tug. Charter beginning Mar 1, 1942, registered by ATS HQ at Fort Mills, Corregidor, on Mar 5. Prior to date of charter, was employed by ATS under some form of daily hire. She towed barges interisland before entering dry dock at which time she was placed under charter. There is no employment stated for vessel after she went under charter. No record of her loss or other disposition can be found. [Ward, Apr 42; Dean; Charter Party; RG-407, PAC, Box 1568, Folder *Aviador.*]

Bacolod I. 1.65; 55 GT; Blt 1936, Philippine Islands

Tug owned by Visayan Stevedore Transportation Co. Requisitioned by the Army at Iloilo, island of Panay, during Feb of 1942 and taken to Cebu City, island of Cebu, for operations with the ATS. Was later chartered on Mar 4 by Lt. Col. C. Z. Byrd. While at Cebu City, was used under the supervision of 1st Lt. Thomas W. Juricka in salvaging a Navy PT boat stranded off the coast of Negros as well as for assistance in loading food and fuel aboard two Navy submarines scheduled to be sent to Corregidor for discharge. *Talisay* also participated in these activities. (See text for discussion regarding submarine blockade runners.) On Apr 10 while at Cebu City, and on orders of the Army, was blown up and set afire to prevent falling into the hands of the Japanese. [Charter Party; illegible crew list; RG-407, PAC, Boxes 1565 and 1568; SWPA]

Basilan, ex *Gouverneur General Roume,* ex *Victoria.* 1.335'; 2969 GT; Blt 1902, Dundee, Scotland

Owned by Compania Maritima. Ward Report states she was used either by the Visayan- Mindanao Force or by the ATS at Cebu City, island of Cebu. According to ATS file, was sunk at Cebu City, in Dec 1941. Cook '47 Survey disagrees, stating she was scuttled Apr 10, 1942, at Cebu City, to avoid capture, Cook '47 Survey probably being correct. [ATS File; Ward Report; Cook '47 Survey.]

Bataan, see Danao

Batabiya. 1.130'; 14 GT; Blt 1932, Philippine Islands

Motor launch. Charter (Contract No. 15) recorded as of Mar 10, 1942, by ATS HQ at Fort Mills. [Ward Apr '42 lists this launch incorrectly as *Databiya*; Dean]

Bertha

Launch owned by Manila Yacht Club. Taken over by ATS. Reported as probably sunk at Corregidor May 6, 1942. [ATS file]

Bohol, ex *Sirius,* ex *Suva.* 1.300'; 2126 GT; Blt 1906, Belfast, Ireland

Owned by Compania Maritima. According to Lloyd's was in the *Philippine area* when lost Apr 16, 1942; cause unknown. Hartendorp's informant claims she was sunk while inside the breakwater of Manila Harbor on either Dec 27 or 28, 1941. Lloyd's states *believed was chartered to U.S. Army;* however, we found no Army record for her, and it is doubtful that Lloyd's information was correct. Probably Lloyd's had her confused with *Bohol II.* [Lloyd's; Hartendorp]

Bohol II. 1.134'; 249 GT; Blt 1930, Hong Kong

Owned by Cebu - Bohol Ferry Co., Inc. Abandoned by crew in Pasig River, Manila, and towed to outer harbor by Navy. Was then commandeered by ATS. Made trip from Corregidor to Looc Cove, lying to the south of Corregidor on the shore of Batangas Province, for rice and cattle on Feb 6, 1942. Made a second trip from there, arriving Corregidor Feb 13. Sunk on Apr 9 by Japanese shelling while at Corregidor. By all accounts, the vessel was definitely assigned to the ATS for its operations although a charter party is not of record. [ATS file; Spec. Crew List; RG-407, PAC, Boxes 1565, 1566, and 1568; SWPA; Stauffer; Willoughby; Hartendorp.]

Bolinao. 1.134'; 247 GT; Blt 1884, Paisley, Scotland

Owned by Ramon Aboitiz. Bombed but not sunk either on Mar 14 or 17, 1942, at Toledo, island of Cebu. Captured on Mar 17 by Japanese naval vessels. At time of capture was loaded with food supplies for relief of Bataan. [ATS file; Ward Rpt; Cook '47 Survey; Drake]

Bronzewing. 1.103'; 99 GT; Blt 1908, Philippine Islands

This name was found on a nearly illegible list of vessels within "History of ATS Activities in Manila and Cebu, Dec 41 to May 42." Nothing more could be discerned as to the vessel's service or final disposition. The list contains the names of twenty-seven vessels plus others with completely illegible names. Of the twenty-seven legible names there are only five on which we do not have other records tying them directly to ATS employment. Therefore, it is probable that this vessel was employed in some fashion by the Army between Dec 7, 1941 and May of 1942. [AF 500-21]

Candioa	Spelling uncertain on this vessel. Ward comments that she was in ferry service before the war, running between the southern islands. ATS sent her from Iloilo, island of Panay, to Mindanao. Ward believed she was captured at Boliol [sic]. [Ward]
Cargo Scows	Thirteen unpowered cargo scows were taken over by the ATS at Manila and elsewhere on Luzon. Eleven of them were either sunk or captured at various locations on Bataan. One was known to have been captured by the Japanese at Corregidor following the surrender; another was known to have been scuttled at Subic Bay, island of Luzon. [ATS file]
Carmen 1.68'; 37 GT; Blt 1900 Hong Kong	Reported as part of Aboitiz - Elcano Fleet. Commandeered at Manila on Dec 24, 1941. The following day while loaded with Quartermaster stores for transport to Bataan, she was bombed and holed, her engine rendered useless. After emergency repairs were made to plug holes at the waterline, she was towed to Bataan by the tug *Henry Keswick* where her cargo was discharged. ATS removed some of the ship's equipment for use at the navigation point at Lamao (on Bataan). Was sunk by bombing attack off that port while at anchor during Mar 1942. Intelligence report of 1943 states she was probably salvaged as of that date. [RG-407, PAC, Boxes 1566, 1568, 1570; Willoughby]
Cebu, ex Nuen Tung. 1.250'; 1408 GT; Blt 1900, Bremerhaven, Germany	Requisitioned by Capt. Judson B. Crow, Commander, 3rd Battalion, 92nd Infantry, on either Dec 8 or 10, 1941, at Malitbog, island of Leyte. Sailed for Manila with troops but was diverted to the Lubang Islands, arriving there Dec 14. Ordered to leave in ballast for Porto Galera, island of Mindoro; thence ordered to Calapan, Mindoro, where on Jan 1, 1942, was sunk by Japanese bombers. [RG-407, PAC, Box 1569, Folder *Cebu*; Lloyd's]
Cegostina	Shelled and sunk at Bugo, island of Mindanao, on or around Mar 3, 1942, possibly Feb 28 while engaged in loading supplies destined for Corregidor or Bataan. According to ATS file, sinking was witnessed by Colonels *Morse and Killian* [probably *Killen*]. She is believed to have brought to Gingoog Bay, island of Mindanao, a cargo of tin and rubber which was loaded onto *Coast Farmer* for that vessel's return trip to Australia. *Cegostina* then moved down the Mindanao coast to Bugo to load cargo for Bataan or Corregidor. See Vessel Index for further discussion of the activities of this vessel prior to her loss. [ATS File]
Cia de Filipinas, see Compania de Filipinas	
Compania de Filipinas. 1.180'; 784 GT; Blt 1890, Renfrew, Scotland	Owned by Compania Gen. de Tabacos de Filipinas. Allegedly bombed and sunk while en route to Corregidor with cargo of corn and rice loaded at Cebu City, island of Cebu. According to Cook, sinking occurred on Feb 21, 1942, off the island of Mindoro, the result of Japanese naval gunfire. That report is

contradicted by Lloyd's which states she was captured off Fortune Island by a Japanese destroyer. Intelligence report of 1943 states she was salvaged by the Japanese, this indicating she would have been sunk at some point. One report states she was removed from Philippine waters. Lloyd's further states that she was renamed by Japanese as the *Hoei Maru* and was later sunk by striking a mine on July 3, 1945. [ATS File; Lloyd's; Ward Rpt; SWPA; Cook '47 Survey; Willoughby]

Condesa

Ferry, normally operating Iloilo, island of Panay, to Bacolod, island of Negros. Charter recorded as of Mar 26, 1942, by ATS HQ at Fort Mills. Dean, who at one time had in his possession a copy of the charter party, states that charter was executed by Lt. Col. C. Z. Byrd on Jan 24, 1942. Reported sunk on supply run, Iloilo, island of Panay, to Mindanao, but according to another Army report, may have been captured at town of Bohol, island of Palawan. [Ward Apr 42; Crew Mar 42'; Dean; ATS File; Spec. Crew List; RG-407, PAC, Box 1565; SWPA]

Cordova

Motor launch. Charter registered on Feb 23, 1942, by ATS section HQ at Fort Mills. Charter had taken place south of Luzon, probably at Cebu City, island of Cebu, under authority of either Col. John D. Cook or Lt. Col. C. Z. Byrd. [Ward, Apr 42; Dean]

Corregidor. 1.316'; 1881 GT; Blt 1911, Dumbarton, Scotland

Although carrying Army cargo at the time of its total loss, *Corregidor* was not under U.S. Army control. See List 5 as well as the Vessel Index for the *Corregidor* story.

Crown

Probably a tug or towing launch. Chartered by ATS from B and J Baldwin. Damaged by bombing off Cabcaben, on east coast of Bataan, subsequently sinking on or around Apr 1, 1942. [ATS file]

Customs IV

Owned by the Philippine Government. Taken over by ATS and assigned to Army Engineers. Sunk, probably by Japanese artillery fire, while lying at Engineer Dock, Corregidor, May 4, 1942. [ATS file]

Damaquete, see Dumaquete

Danao

Towing launch. At some point in her Army service was renamed *Bataan*. According to an affidavit by the former operator, this launch was requisitioned (or hired) by the Army at the outbreak of war, continuing until Mar 5, 1942, at which time, he attested, the Army ordered him to abandon her at Iloilo, island of Panay. According to that affidavit, she had been engaged in towing lighters with ammunition between Iloilo, island of Panay, and Bacolod, island of Negros. He claimed that the reason for her abandonment was the lack of fuel at Iloilo. He further states that the crew was paid by the owner and not the Army; therefore, the launch must not have been commandeered or chartered but must have been on a daily hire basis. [RG-407, PAC, Box 1568, Folder *Danao;* Spec. Crew list.]

Databiya, see Batabiya

Del Monte. 1.82'; 83 GT; Blt 1927, United States

Towing launch or tug. Owned by Luzon Stevedoring Co. During Dec 1941 taken over by Navy at Manila. Then went to ATS. Assigned by ATS to Army Engineers. Final disposition unknown. Ward's report states that without Army authorization, crew returned her to Manila after Japanese had occupied the city. That information could not, however, be further substantiated. [Ward Rpt]

Dominga (or Domingo). 20 GT

Towing launch. The sole evidence that she was requisitioned by the Army is contained within three affidavits by former crewmembers. They attested to the vessel having towed barges with war materiel and military personnel to Iloilo, island of Panay, from other islands. Conflict in dates on the affidavits casts doubt as to the authenticity of that source. Lloyd's lists her under losses but gives no other information. Affidavits made no claim that the crew worked directly for the Army. [RG-407, PAC, Box 1569, Folder *Dominga;* Lloyd's]

Don Esteban

See *USAT Don Esteban* within List 1 titled *Vessels of the U.S. Army Transport Service and U.S. Army Harbor Boat Service: Defense of the Philippines, 1941 - 1942.*

Dos Hermanos. 1.200'; 838 GT; Blt 1882, Glasgow, Scotland

One report mentions this vessel as used to evacuate troops (Air Corps) from *Lamao* [a navigation point on Bataan] to Manila *on 27 December.* Whether she was formally hired for that service is unknown. Scuttled December 31 in outer harbor. Refloated by Japanese, renamed *Himeno Maru,* and sunk by Allied submarine Dec 5, 1943, in 9° 10' N; 124° 30' E. [ATS File; Willoughby]

Dumaquete

Uncertainty exists as to whether this vessel was used initially by ATS or by the Visayan- Mindanao Force. Charter was recorded as of Mar 26, 1942, by ATS HQ at Fort Mills, Corregidor. Dean, who at one point possessed the charter document, claims charter actually began Dec 13, 1941. No further information in ATS records as to final disposition of vessel. SWPA lists her as one of the Filipino vessels in service to Army that was lost during 1941-42 but gives no particulars. [Ward, Apr 42; Crew Mar 42; Dean; Spec. Crew List; RG-407, PAC, Box 1565, 1566, Folder "Marine Statistics Branch"; SWPA; AF 500-21]

Elcano. 1.214'; 1435 GT; Blt 1938, Hong Kong

Owned by Philippine Steam Navigation Co. Commandeered Jan 1, 1942, at Cebu City, island of Cebu. According to Ward, Apr 42 list, charter was registered as of Mar 26, 1942, by ATS HQ at Fort Mills with charter party dated Jan 1, 1942. Known to have been used on supply runs to and from Mindanao. Arrived Corregidor or Bataan with 1100 tons of supplies originating from Australia which had been transferred to *Elcano* at Mindanao on either 26 or 27 Feb from *Coast Farmer. Elcano* was the only ship that successfully brought supplies to Corregidor from *Coast Farmer. Elcano* was then held over at Corregidor. In early Apr when select troops and supplies were being evacuated from Bataan to Corregidor in advance of the surrender of Bataan, *Elcano* was employed in that effort. Charter party was canceled on Apr 19. According to Army records, she was shelled and sunk May 6 between Corregidor and Fort Hughes; however according to Hartendorp's informant, that occurred on Apr 21. Lloyd's states that the owner's claim it was Apr 20. [Ward Apr 42; Crew Mar 42; Dean; ATS File; RG-407, PAC, Box 25, Folder *Elcano;* also Boxes 1566 and 1570; Charter party; Cook '47 Survey; Ward Report; Spec. Crew List; Lloyd's; SWPA; AF 500-21]

Emilia. 1.142'; 278 GT; Blt 1931, Cebu

Owned by La Naviera Filipina, Inc. Requisitioned by ATS, on Dec 15, 1941, at Cebu City, island of Cebu. Reported in ATS documents that while loading supplies near Bugo, island of Mindanao, either Feb 28 or Mar 3, 1942, vessel was *bombed or shelled* resulting in her sinking. According to ATS File, sinking was witnessed by Colonels *Morse and Killen.* Supplies involved were reported to be for Corregidor, having come from *Coast Farmer.* This was probably an assumption by those reporting the vessel's activity at the time of its loss as it is most probable that *Emilia* had instead come south from Cebu City with a cargo of tin and rubber which she had offloaded to *Coast Farmer* for that ship's return voyage to Australia. Cook's 1942 report has loss of *Emilia* occurring on Feb 28 which agrees with 1942 correspondence of Lt. Col. C. Z. Byrd. Drake report states sinking was on Mar 3. For a complete discussion on *Emilia's* activities prior to her loss, refer to the Vessel Index. [Cook, Jan 6, 1942; ATS File; Ward Rpt; Cook '47 Survey; Spec. Crew List; RG-407, PAC, Boxes 1565 and 1566; SWPA; Drake]

Engeno

No dated record of ATS takeover of this launch; however, it is reported in ATS file as being utilized by Army Engineers. No information on final disposition. [ATS File]

Escalante R. 1.110'; 95 GT; Blt 1925, Philippine Islands

No record of charter or requisition; however, according to Army correspondence (Colonel Dalton to Colonel Roper), this vessel was used by the Army in the *Zamboanga - Sulu* sector during Dec 1941. Around Jan 1, 1942, her crew having deserted, vessel was dockside at Zamboanga, island of Mindanao, when she was damaged beyond repair by enemy air attack. Lloyd's states she was later scuttled on Army orders in early April. Affidavit from an alleged crewmember seeking claim lists other crewmembers, but this can be considered questionable. That affidavit says the scuttling took place on Army orders on Jan 3. [RG-407, PAC, Box 1569; Lloyd's]

Escano, see F. Escano

Evelyn

Chartered by ATS and assigned to Corregidor. Sunk Jan 4, 1942, at Corregidor. [ATS File]

Explorador. 1.88'; 78 GT; Blt 1933, Philippine Islands

Tug. According to claims' affidavits filed by Filipino crewmembers and dated 1945, this tug was employed as a patrol vessel for the Philippine Constabulary, USAFFE, in waters off the island of Panay between Jan 9, 1942, to the date of the vessel's alleged scuttling on Apr 16, 1942. The affidavits include a crew list. There is, however, no Army record on this vessel. [RG-407, PAC, Box 1569, Folder *Explorador*]

F. Escano, ex *Panglima*. 1.180'; 452 GT; Blt 1914, Sandakan, British North Borneo

Owned by La Naviera Filipina, Inc. Requisitioned by ATS, at Cebu City, island of Cebu, Jan 5, 1942. According to Cook '47 Survey, was scuttled on Apr 10 at Cebu City to avoid capture. [Cook; Ward Rpt; Cook '47 Survey; RG-407, PAC, Box 25, Folder *Escano*.]

Flora D. 1.60'; 14 GT; Blt 1930, Philippine Islands

Launch. Charter registered as of Mar 10, 1942, by ATS HQ at Fort Mills; Contract No. 13. No further information. [Ward, Apr 42; Dean]

Floricita, see La Florecita

Forby. 27 tons; Blt 1910, Shanghai

Tug. Formerly part of the U.S. Army Mine Planter Service. Sold to private interests before the war. Commandeered at Manila by ATS in Dec 1941 for use in the evacuation from that city. Damaged at some point prior to surrender of Corregidor. Reported missing at time of surrender which could suggest her possible use for escape attempt. [Ward; ATS File]

Fortuna. 1.148'; 528 GT; Blt 1928, Kiel, Germany

Owned by Rio Y Olbarrieta. Requisitioned by Lt. Col. Carter R. McLennan on Dec 23, 1941, at Iloilo, island of Panay. Remained at Iloilo until Feb 28, 1942, when on Army orders sailed with supplies for the leper colony at Culion Island (Calamian Group). On Mar 6 was attacked by Japanese aircraft whose strafing set cargo of gasoline drums on fire. Ship totally destroyed, sinking in three fathoms about one-quarter mile from shore, probably off Culion Island but exact location uncertain from records. [ATS File; Lloyd's; RG-407, PAC, Box 25, Folder *Fortuna*; Ward Report; Spec. Crew List]

Gold Dug

Diesel tug, owned by East Mindanao Co. Commandeered by Mindanao- Visayan Force. Final disposition unknown. [RG-407, PAC, Box 1565; AF 500-21]

Governor Smith. approx. 400 GT

Part of Aboitiz - Elcano Fleet. Taken over by ATS at Cebu City, island of Cebu. AF 500-21 states that while en route from Cebu City to Culion with rice for the lepers, was overtaken by Japanese cruiser and then scuttled by her crew off Coron Island on Mar 7, 1942. Another Army report states that she was scuttled at Cebu City on Apr 10 to avoid capture while loaded for Corregidor. This last was probably the case and is in agreement with the Drake report. [Ward Rpt; Cook '47 Survey; SWPA; RG-407, PAC, Box 1566; AF 500-21; Drake]

Governor Taft. 1.140'; 249 GT; Blt 1930, Hong Kong

Owned by Visayan Transportation Co. Charter recorded as of Mar 26, 1942, by ATS HQ at Fort Mills. Charter was executed by Lt. Col. C. Z. Byrd at Cebu on Mar 26, 1942. (See Appendix G of this volume.) Evidence points to her use by ATS prior to that time. According to one Army report was scuttled to prevent capture near the island of Culion in March; however, Cook '47 Survey states she was scuttled at Cebu City, island of Cebu, on Apr 10 when the Japanese occupied that place. AF 500-21 also states scuttling was at Cebu City after being loaded with rations for Corregidor, but this may have been a case of confusing this vessel with *Governor Smith*. [Ward, Apr 42; Crew Mar 42' Charter Party; ATS File; Spec. Crew List; Cook '47 Survey; RG-407, PAC, Boxes 1565 and 1566; SWPA; AF 500-21.]

Governor Wood

Mentioned by Ward, but he makes no definite statement that she was employed either by the ATS at Cebu City, island of Cebu, or by the Visayan- Mindanao Force. Ward states vessel was sunk near Culion Island in Mar 1942. Cook '47 Survey agrees, claiming she sank on Mar 17 near Culion while en route to the leper colony there with Red Cross supplies. Cook was of the opinion that at time of loss, she was under charter to the ATS. [Ward Rpt; Cook '47 Survey]

Hai Kwang. 1.190'; 905 GT; Blt 1926, Shanghai. British flag

Tanker owned by Asiatic Petroleum Co. Requisitioned by ATS at Corregidor on Feb 28, 1942, and sent to Cebu City, island of Cebu, where following a dry-docking, was loaded with diesel fuel and gasoline before proceeding to Iloilo, island of Panay, to await promised air escort to Corregidor. The air escort never materialized. She was destroyed by U.S. forces before Japanese entered Iloilo. Lloyd's claims her loss was at Manila Bay, but that is certainly incorrect. Cook '47 Survey confirms that she was scuttled in Iloilo harbor on Apr 10 to prevent capture. [Ward Rpt; Spec. Crew List; Cook '47 Survey; Lloyd's; RG-407, PAC, Box 1565; SWPA]

Hope Wing

Schooner yacht owned by Gene Wing and loaned by Wing to the ATS. Employed for unknown period of time with volunteer yachtsmen as crew while at Corregidor and later at Mariveles on Bataan. Departed (date unknown) for south in what was apparently an escape attempt. Aboard her at the time *Wing, H. Miller, and T. Atkins.* According to ATS records, she was last heard from through rumor as being at the island of Negros. The escape of Wing, Miller, and Atkins from the Philippines may have been successful, this based upon the fact that neither a T. Atkins or a Gene Wing or Eugene Wing are listed as being interned by the Japanese. A person named Herbert Miller was an internee, but this may or may not have been the H. Miller of *Hope Wing.* [ATS File; Provost Marshal's Listing of Civilian Internees.]

Idoto

Small tug belonging to Cebu Stevedoring Co. Used by ATS at Cebu City, island of Cebu, probably on daily hire basis. [AF 500-21]

Jockchiu. 1.41'; 5 GT; Blt 1926, Philippine Islands

Diesel river launch. Owned by Agusan Commercial Co. Taken over by military (probably on Mindanao) with wages of crew *guaranteed by Army.* Final disposition unknown. [RG-407, PAC, Box 1565; AF 500-21]]

Kalawan, see *Miss Kalawan*

Kanlaon II. 1.181'; 477 GT; Blt 1931, Philippine Islands

Not to be confused with *Canlaon,* a lighthouse tender of the Philippine Government. Owned by the Iloilo Shipping Co., Inc. Commandeered by Lt. Col. Carter R. McLennan on Jan 7, 1942, at Iloilo, island of Panay. Charter executed on Mar 5 at Iloilo by Lt. Col. C. Z. Byrd for ATS. According to Filipino master's affidavit: Ship was taken over by Army early on Dec 22, 1941, sailing that night to Bugo, island of Mindanao, after which she was returned to Iloilo. During Jan 1942, she made two trips to the island of Negros. In February, she left Iloilo for Cebu City, island of Cebu, with rice and was dry-docked on her arrival there. She was shelled and damaged while at Cebu City by a Japanese light cruiser on Mar 9. On Apr 3, following repairs, was ordered to Tagbilaran, island of Bohol, where she took aboard 700 troops for Cebu City. According to AF 500-21, was loaded with rations for Corregidor when on Apr 10, Army ordered her scuttled at Cebu City to avoid capture. [Ward Apr 42; Crew Mar 42; Dean; ATS File; Ward Report; Cook '47 Survey; Charter Party; RG-407, PAC, Box 1569, Folder *Kanlaon II;* Spec. Crew List; SWPA; AF 500-21]

Katipunan, ex *Tayabas,* ex *Gifford Jones.* 1.136'; 208 GT; Blt 1875, Newcastle, England

Spelled *Katapunan* in some records. Requisitioned by Lt. Col. J. D. Cook at Cebu City, island of Cebu, on Jan 6, 1942. Charter recorded as of Mar 26, 1942, by ATS HQ at Fort Mills, Corregidor. Dean, who at one time had a copy of charter party, states that charter was executed by Lt. Col. C. Z. Byrd on Jan 3, 1942. According to AF 500-21, she was in continuous service between Bugo and Butuan, both on the island of Mindanao. *Katipunan* was scuttled on Cagayan River, Mindanao, to prevent capture on May 3, 1942; however Cook '47 Survey claims she was sunk by Japanese naval gunfire. [Ward Apr 42; Crew Mar 42; Dean; ATS File; Cook '47 Survey; RG-407, PAC, Box 1576; SWPA; AF 500-21]

Kentucky. 1.45'; 14 GT; Blt 1913, Philippine Islands

Tug or launch owned by the Ohta Development Co. Operated by Quartermaster Corps Construction Service on Corregidor. Sunk Dec 29, 1941, at Corregidor. [ATS File]

Kolumbugan. 1.188'; 691 GT; Blt 1929, Hong Kong

Owned by La Naviera Filipina, Inc. Commandeered by ATS at Manila on Dec 24, 1941. Initially used in evacuation of supplies from Manila. Made two successful supply trips from Corregidor on Jan 20, 1942 and Feb 6, each trip being to Looc Cove lying to the south of Corregidor on the shore of Batangas Province for cattle and unhusked rice. On Feb 27, en route on her third trip, this time to Capiz on Panay to load more supplies, was overhauled by a Japanese cruiser off Varadero, island of Mindoro. Her master was taken to Manila for interrogation in company with the masters of the captured ships *Lepus* and *Compania de Filipinas.* Intelligence reports state she was being used in Philippine coastwise service by the Japanese during 1943. [ATS File; RG-407, PAC, Boxes 25, 1566, 1569, 1570; SWPA; Stauffer; Willoughby]

La Estrella Caltex, ex *La Estrella Texaco.* 1.145'; 495 GT; Blt 1931, Hong Kong

Tanker. Taken over by ATS on Dec 29, 1941, after merchant ships were ordered from Manila. ATS sent her to Cebu City, island of Cebu, from where she sailed en route to Mariveles on Bataan with cargo of assorted petroleum products. Sunk by Japanese air attack off Lubang Island. Date of loss Feb 24, 1942. [Cook '47 Survey; Ward Report; ATS File; RG-407, Box 25, Folder 15 *La Estrella Caltex;* also Box 1565 which contains a largely illegible crew list; Lloyd's; SWPA; Drake.]

La Florecita (or Florecita). 1.141'; 330 GT

Tug owned by Dee C. Chuan and Co. Was initially taken over by Navy on Dec 27, 1941. While manned by Filipino crew under U.S. Navy direction, this tug performed excellent service in towing unmanned ships from the inner harbor at Manila during the December air raids which targeted the docks there. After the evacuation from Manila, she was sent to Corregidor where she grounded, her crew then abandoning her. Was later towed to Mariveles on Bataan and repaired there by ATS. Sunk at Mariveles either by enemy gunfire or by scuttling on Apr 9, 1942. Must have been salvaged by the Japanese as 1943 intelligence report states that in that year she was in service with the Japanese. [ATS file; Ward Rpt; Willoughby]

La Paz

Motor boat chartered at Fort Mills, Corregidor, on Jan 10, 1942. Released from charter Feb 15, 1942. What happened to her after that date is unknown. [Dean]

La Paz

Interisland freighter. Requisitioned by ATS or other QM officers at Iloilo, island of Panay for carriage of rice to Culion. Sunk en route. [AF 500-21]

Legazpi. 1.213'; 1179 GT; Blt 1937, Hong Kong

Throughout many Army records, the name of this vessel is incorrectly spelled *Legaspi.* Owned by Philippine Steam Navigation Co. Commandeered at Manila by Lt. Col. Richard G. Rogers, QMC, on Dec 24, 1941. Was used in evacuation of military supplies from Manila to Corregidor and Bataan. On Jan 17, 1942, made a trip from Corregidor to Capiz, island of Panay, thence back to Corregidor with foodstuffs. On either Feb 3 or 4 made a second round trip to Capiz from Corregidor. On Feb 19, departed Corregidor with wounded and Navy and Army Air Corps personnel to Capiz. On return trip to Corregidor with supplies was overhauled and shelled by two Japanese destroyers off Porto Galera, island of Mindoro on Mar 1, 1942. Set on fire, the master grounded her. Crew (minus one wounded man) escaped by swimming ashore. On direct orders of General MacArthur, Lino T. Conajero, the master and Jose A. Amoyo, the pilot, were each awarded the Army's Distinguished Service Cross, and 36 of her crew the Silver Star. See Appendix K this volume for discussion of military awards made to Army Transport Service crews. [ATS File; RG-407, PAC, Box 1569, Folder "Maritime Matters" and Box 1566; RG-338, USA, Pacific, Gen. Corr. 200.6, Box T-3338; Spec. Crew List; Ward Rpt; Lloyd's; SWPA; RG-407, Adj. Gen. Decimal File 700.6, Box 350, Folder 7/29/46; Drake.]

Lepus, ex *Ming Sang,* ex *Kwong Eng.* 1.265'; 1936 GT; Blt 1906, Lubeck, Germany

Owned by Madrigal and Co. Commandeered by order of Maj. General Sharp, Visayan- Mindanao Force, probably in mid-Dec 1941 at Cebu City, island of Cebu, shortly thereafter being placed in the service of the ATS. According to her Filipino master, ship began making trips for ATS in early Jan 1942 when she sailed from Cebu City to Bais, island of Negros, with 800 troops. In the middle of January, after returning to Cebu City, left there for Dumaquete, island of Negros, to take aboard 1000 troops for return to Cebu City. At end of Jan, sailed from Cebu City to Bugo, island of Mindanao, with cargo of 5000 barrels of gasoline (in drums). During Feb made a number of short trips to Dumaquete and Iloilo, island of Panay for rice for Cebu City. Then, according to Army records (report of Thomas W. Juricka, 1st Lt., QMC), she departed for the island of Mindanao to take on a cargo of foodstuffs and medicine from *Coast Farmer* which had arrived from Australia. That cargo was consigned for

Corregidor. According to affidavits of the master and other crewmen while en route to Corregidor, *Lepus* was overhauled on Mar 1 by Japanese destroyers. There was no attempt by the crew to scuttle. Under Japanese escort, *Lepus* proceeded to Subic Bay for unloading of foodstuffs whereupon the master and a Filipino Army officer were taken ashore. Rest of crew was placed under a Japanese master who took *Lepus* to Lingayen on the island of Luzon for bunkers and then on to Hainan Island to load iron ore for Japan. At Japan ship was renamed *Rein Maru*. Her remnant Filipino crew was then returned to the Philippines after being commended by the Japanese for their service. (See List 1, Mine Planter *Colonel George F. E. Harrison* for the subsequent employment of the *Lepus* crew after their repatriation to the Philippines.) According to Army reports, the former master, Jesus L. Medina, collaborated with the Japanese during the occupation as of course did the crewmembers who sailed on *Lepus* to Japan. According to Lloyd's, *Lepus* was sunk May 11, 1943, at 33° 58' N; 130° 53' E (cause of sinking unknown). Intelligence report of 1943 states that she had been salvaged and then removed from Philippine waters, but one suspects that the report was not accurate in light of all other pertinent information on this vessel. [ATS File per *Nippon Times* May 31, 1943; Ward Rpt; Cook '47 Survey; Spec. Crew List; RG-407, PAC, Boxes 25, 1565, and 1569 Folder *Lepus*; Lloyd's; SWPA; Willoughby]

Little Guanaco	This name was found on a nearly illegible list of vessels within "History of ATS Activities in Manila and Cebu, Dec 41 to May 42." Nothing more could be discerned as to the vessel's service or final disposition. The list contains the names of twenty-seven vessels plus others with completely illegible names. Of the twenty-seven legible names there are only five on which we do not have other records tying them directly to ATS employment. Therefore, it is probable that this vessel was employed in some fashion by the Army between Dec 7, 1941 and May of 1942. [AF 500-21]
Louisville, ex *Yun Choi*. 43 GT; Blt 1899, Hong Kong	Launch. Taken over by Quartermaster Corps's Construction Service. Lost Jan 4, 1942, from grounding off Bataan. [ATS File; AF 500-21]
Luzon, ex *Yazoo*, ex *Marudu*. 1.257'; 1679 GT; Blt 1905, Lubeck, Germany	Owned by Compania Maritima. Requisitioned by Lt. Col. John D. Cook by order of commander, Visayan- Mindanao Force on Dec 18, 1941, at Dumaquete, island of Negros. Taken to Cebu City, island of Cebu, where ship was bombed and machine-gunned on Jan 18, 1942, while at the dock. In a sinking condition, she was beached, subsequently being judged a total loss. According to Lloyd's, she was salved by Japanese and renamed *Ruson Maru*. Intelligence report of 1943 agrees that she was salvaged. Was ultimately lost Mar 1, 1945. [RG-407, PAC, Box 1569, File *Luzon*; Spec. Crew list; Cook '47 Survey; Lloyd's; SWPA]
Maayo. 1.147'; 249 GT; Blt 1902, Shanghai	Owned by Filomene Cimafianca. Placed under charter by ATS at Cebu City, island of Cebu, (date unspecified) by Lt. Col. John D. Cook or Lt. Col. C. Z. Byrd. Scuttled at Cebu City to avoid capture. [Cook '47 Survey]

Mactan, ex *Hai Kong,* ex *Moura,* ex *North Lyall.* l.300'; 2090 GT; Blt 1899, Newcastle, England

Owned by Compania Maritima. Beginning Dec 10, 1941, was utilized by Army on a daily rental arrangement for the transfer of supplies from Manila to Mariveles on Bataan. On Dec 28, was released from Army service to be converted into a hospital ship under the auspices of the Philippine Red Cross. *Mactan* then evacuated American and Philippine Army wounded to Australia, arriving there on Jan 17, 1942. (See William L. Noyer, *Mactan: Ship of Destiny,* (Fresno, CA: Rainbow Press, nd.) Later, while in Australia, *Mactan* was placed under charter to the Service of Supply, USAFIA, and assigned as a barracks ship and later for troop carrying functions during the New Guinea Campaign. Remained in Army service until 1945. [RG-407, PAC, Box 1569, Folder *Mactan*]

Mambukal (Mambukel in some reports*).* l.134'; 190 GT; Blt 1925, Hong Kong

Tug owned by De la Rama SS Co., Inc. Prior to outbreak of war was placed under time charter to the Harbor Boat Service at Manila and assigned to Fort Mills, Corregidor. Was in collision with *USHB Neptune* on Dec 24, 1942, during evacuation of supplies from Manila to Corregidor. Sank shortly following the collision. [ATS file; Ward Rpt; RG-407, PAC, Box 25, Folder *Mambukal,* and Box 1569]

Maria A. l.40'; 9 GT; Blt 1928, Philippine Islands

Diesel coastal tug owned by Anakan Lumber Co. Army records contain a letter signed by Capt. Elden L. McKown stating that vessel was requisitioned by the Visayan- Mindanao Force on May 6, 1942. There is no record of her final disposition. [RG-407, PAC, Box 25 in folder with *Tito*; Box 1565; AF 500-21]

Masayon. l.106'; 98 GT; Blt 1936, Philippine Islands

Owned by Central Shipping Co. of Cebu City. Army records show that the adjutant of the U.S. Army contingent at Bohol, island of Palawan, acting under orders received from the commander Visayan- Mindanao Force, commandeered this vessel on May 2, 1942, and ordered *Masayon's* master to proceed to island of Mindanao for further instructions. No other information as to vessel's service or her final disposition. [RG-407, PAC, Box 1569, Folder *Masayon* Wage Data; Spec. Crew List]

Mayapay

Diesel powered coastal tug. Seized by the Philippine Constabulary at Mindanao for its use. [AF 500-21]

Mayon, ex *Iroquois,* ex *Gutierrez II.* l.347'; 3371 GT; Blt 1930, Barrow, England

Owned by the Manila SS Co. Evacuated President Quezon from Manila to Corregidor, Dec 24, 1941. Time chartered by Chief Quartermaster, USAFFE, to undertake voyage from Mariveles, Bataan, to Del Monte, island of Mindanao. Left Mariveles Dec 27 with 800 Army Air Corps personnel and 31 tons of cargo. Bombed en route while at anchor behind reef at Mindoro Island by Japanese aircraft but did not suffer serious damage. Left Mindoro that evening with a reduction in crew size as approximately one-third of crew had deserted. Anchored next day at Campomanes Bay, island of Negros, and there picked up survivors of *Panay* which had recently been sunk, the result of enemy air attack. On Dec 30, arrived Cebu City, island of Cebu, where vessel was requisitioned and subsequently bareboat chartered by the ATS. From Cebu City, she sailed for Misamis, island of Mindanao, where presumably the troops were disembarked. Vessel remained at Misamis until Feb 20, 1942, when she left for Cebu City. On Feb 22, sailed for Butuan, island of Mindanao, to take on supplies consigned to Bataan. On Feb 28, while loading, she was attacked by Japanese bombers, four bombs hitting vessel causing heavy casualties, including her master, and setting fires which burned for three days. Crew forced to abandon vessel. Lloyd's has vessel's loss, but date given is incorrect. Witness to bombing and loss was *Colonel Killen.* Stated within 1943 intelligence report as probably salvaged by the Japanese. [ATS File; Ward Rpt; Spec. Crew List; RG-407, PAC, Boxes 25 and 1565; SWPA; AF 500-21; Thesis by M. I. Tibayan presented to Lyceum of the Philippines; Willoughby]

Milad

Launch owned by Manila Yacht Club. Taken over by ATS. Sunk at Corregidor May 4, 1942. [ATS files]

Miss Kalawan

Owned by Mateo Cruz. Either a tug or launch requisitioned by ATS on Dec 25, 1941. Used during evacuation from Manila for towing lighters to Cabcaben on Bataan, making in all three round trips. Following this, she made a series of runs between Bataan and Corregidor, presumably towing barges. According to one crewman's affidavit, crew was told to leave vessel on Jan 17, 1942. Another crewman's affidavit states that an Army officer instructed crew to leave tug at Cabcaben and return to their homes if possible, but there is no Army version from which to confirm that. There is also no information as to final disposition. [RG-407, PAC, Box 25, Folder *Kalawan*]

Miss Priscilla

This name was found on a nearly illegible list of vessels within "History of ATS Activities in Manila and Cebu, Dec 41 to May 42." Nothing more could be discerned as to the vessel's service or final disposition. The list contains the names of twenty-seven vessels plus others with completely illegible names. Of the twenty-seven legible names there are only five on which we do not have other records tying them directly to ATS employment. Therefore, it is probable that this vessel was employed in some fashion by the Army between Dec 7, 1941 and May of 1942. [AF 500-21]

Moago

Nothing explicit on this vessel exists in the Army files except that she was utilized either at Cebu City, island of Cebu, under orders the ATS or by the Visayan-Mindanao Force at one of the more southern islands. [Ward Rpt]

Neptune. 1.75'; 162 GT; Blt 1930, Hong Kong

Owned by the Luzon Stevedoring Co., Manila. Apparently was an interisland freighter. Assigned to Fort Mills on Corregidor as an auxiliary minesweeper. Shelled and burned at Fort Frank (a satellite defense installation of Corregidor) on Feb 20, 1942. [ATS file; AF 500-21.]

Nighthawk, see Customs IV

North

Claimant file for vessel *Pathfinder* contains an American investigator's comment that a vessel named *North* was commandeered by Army and lost in that service from scuttling. A filing error was probably the reason that the *North* file is presently contained within *Pathfinder's* file. [RG-407, PAC, Box 25, Folder *Pathfinder]*

Opon I. l.80'; 46 GT; Blt 1931, Philippine Islands

Owned by the Opon Ferry Co., Cebu City, island of Cebu. Ward report is unclear as to whether this vessel was requisitioned by ATS at Cebu City or by the Visayan-Mindanao Force. Reported as being sunk at Cebu City. [Ward Report; Cook '47 Survey]

P. Aboitiz. l.134'; 321 GT; Blt 1928, Hong Kong

Owned by La Naviera Filipina, Inc. Requisitioned by ATS, at Cebu City, island of Cebu, on Dec 15, 1941. Charter was recorded by ATS, HQ, Fort Mills, as of Mar 26, 1942. According to AF 500-21, she was loaded with rations at Cebu City, to go to Corregidor but was scuttled to prevent capture before leaving. Conversely, Cook '47 Survey states scuttling was either at Bugo, island of Palawan, or somewhere on the island of Mindanao, by means of scuttling to prevent capture. A crewmember claims report agrees with AF 500-21 stating that this occurred on Apr 10. [Cook; Dean; ATS File; Ward Rpt; Cook '47 Survey; RG-407, PAC, Box 1566; AF 500-21]

Pacita. 152 GT

Owned by Insular Navigation Co. Requisitioned by Col. John D. Cook or Lt. Col. C. Z. Byrd effective Jan 7, 1942. Was used by Army until Jan 25 when she was returned to her owners due to leakage of hull. According to one Army report was later rumored to have been captured by the Japanese while either at Cebu City, island of Cebu, or at Bohol, island of Palawan. [Cook '47 Survey; RG-407, PAC, Boxes 1566 and 1576]

Panay. l.276'; 1871 GT; Blt 1912, Newcastle, England

Owned by Compania Maritima. Placed under a one-trip time charter by Traffic Control Officer, QMC, at Manila on Dec 22, 1941, and ordered to Pier 1, Manila, for loading of arms and ammunition and then ordered to outer anchorage. On Dec 25, sent to Corregidor from where she sailed on Dec 28 for island of Mindanao. Whether she was then carrying cargo is not known. Put in at Campomanes Bay, island of Negros, on Dec 30 and was attacked there by Japanese bombers, suffering severe damage. Her crew was evacuated by the *Mayon* while an Army officer on Negros made arrangements for salvage of *Panay's* cargo. The ship was reported as then having been scuttled. [Spec. Crew List; ATS File; Ward Rpt; RG-407, PAC, Box 1568, Folder *Panay;* Lloyd's]

Pathfinder Estate. l.40'; 14 GT; Blt 1929, Philippine Islands

Launch owned by Goodyear Rubber Plants Co. Requisitioned at Zamboanga, island of Mindanao, by order of Col. A. E. Wilson, commanding USAFFE sector Zamboanga. [RG-407, PAC, Box 25, Folder *Pathfinder*]

Paulino. l.120'; 200 GT; Blt 1937, Philippine Islands

Launch. Commandeered by Visayan-Mindanao Force on Dec 15, 1941, and released on Jan 6, 1942. Chartered by Lt. Col. C. Z. Byrd, ATS, Apr 6, 1942 at Cebu City, island of Cebu. Reported as loaded at Cebu City with rations for Corregidor but before leaving was scuttled to avoid capture on Apr 10. [Dean; Cook '47 Survey; RG-407, PAC, Box 1566; AF 500-21]

Pelicon

Although mentioned in Army reports, it was not definitively stated whether she was under Army control when sunk or captured off Zamboanga, island of Mindanao. [ATS file; F 500-21]

Perla Del Oriente

Launch. Charter recorded by ATS HQ at Fort Mills on Feb 20, 1942, charter having taken place earlier at Cebu City, island of Cebu. [Ward, Apr 42; Dean]

Picket II. 1.105'; 139 GT; Blt 1924, Pilar, Philippine Islands

Ferry boat taken over by Maj. General Sharp of the Visayan-Mindanao Force. Disposition not known. [Ward Rpt; AF 500-21]

Porto Galera Mindoro

Reported en route to Bataan or Corregidor with supplies as of Mar 1, 1942, but that is somewhat uncertain. Nothing else is known. [ATS File]

Princesa. 1.161'; 409 GT; Blt 1930, Hong Kong

Owned by Insular Navigation Co. of Cebu City. Requisitioned by the Visayan- Mindanao Force on Jan 1, 1942. Assisted in getting *Anhui* off a reef between the islands of Bohol and Leyte in mid-Mar 1942. Record of her formal charter by ATS at Cebu City, island of Cebu, she left for Corregidor, arriving there Feb. 20. At that point, the Army's files regarding her differ widely. AF 500-21 has her at some point transporting supplies to Mindanao. According to Claims files in RG-407 as well as information alluded to by Ward, she was captured at Cebu City on Mar 10, 1942, but that is almost certainly an error, off by one month since the Japanese did not enter Cebu City until Apr 10. The Cook '47 Survey has her as having been sunk by gunfire from a Japanese gunboat while trying to escape Cebu City on Apr 10. Still another Army account has as scuttled by explosives at Cebu City on Apr 10. According to Hartendorp's informant, she was captured by the Japanese. [Ward Apr 42; Crew Mar 42; Dean; RG-407, PAC, Box 25, Folder *Princesa;* and Box 1565; Cook '47 Survey; Spec. Crew List; SWPA; AF 500-21; Hartendorp; Drake]

Princess of Cebu, ex *Marapara.* 1.154'; 415 GT; Blt 1930, Hong Kong

Owned by La Naviera Filipina, Inc. Charter recorded as of Mar 26, 1942, by ATS at Fort Mills. Dean, who had possession of charter party claims charter was executed by Lt. Col. C. Z. Byrd as of Jan 5, 1942. For a time she ran supplies between Cebu City, island of Cebu, and Mindanao. Crewmember claims file indicates her loss occurred on Apr 10, probable place of loss being Cebu City through scuttling. Intelligence report of 1943 states that she was salvaged and taken out of Philippine waters by the Japanese as of that year. [Ward Apr 42; Crew Mar 42; Cook; Dean; SWPA; Cook '47 Survey; RG-407, PAC, Box 1566; AF 500-21; Willoughby]

Princess of Negros. 1.184'; 522 GT; Blt 1933, Hong Kong

Owned by Negros Navigation Co., Inc. Commandeered at Iloilo, island of Panay, on Dec 15, 1941, by Lt. Col. Carter R. McLennan. Made a number of short trips to neighboring islands with troops and civilians. On Dec 24, loaded flour for Surigao, island of Mindanao, where upon arrival, she loaded dynamite for Iloilo. On arrival at Iloilo, was placed by ATS on standby status. On Jan 2, 1942, sailed to the island of Romblon to pick up stranded Philippine Constabulary personnel. In Feb she was turned over to Philippine President Quezon for his interisland tour within the southern island groups which was conducted prior to Quezon's departure from the Philippines. On Mar 1, an ATS charter party was executed at Iloilo, signed by Lt. Col. C. Z. Byrd. On Mar 7, she left Iloilo for the island of Negros near to which she was captured by Japanese naval vessels on Mar 19. In contradiction, Cook '47 Survey has her being bombed and sunk on Apr 10 at Cebu City, but that information is probably a result of confusion between this vessel and another named *Princess of Cebu* since other records substantiate the capture of *Princess of Negros* on Mar 19 *at or near Negros*. According to Lloyd's, following her capture, the Japanese renamed her *Toyohime Maru*. Intelligence report of 1943 states she was operating in Philippine waters for Japanese forces in that year. [Ward Apr 42; Dean; ATS File; Ward Rpt; Cook '47 Survey; Charter Party; Spec. Crew List; RG-407, Box 1568, Folder *Princess of Negros* and Box 25, Folder *Princess of Negros*; Lloyd's; AF 500-21; Willoughby]

Regulas. 1.227'; 1173 GT; Blt 1911, Hoboken, Belgium

Owners Madrigal and Co. Requisitioned by Lt. Col. Carter R. McLennan at Iloilo, island of Panay, on Dec 25, 1941. Made several local voyages from Iloilo. On or about Feb 15, 1942, vessel was ordered to Cebu City, island of Cebu. Around Mar 1, she was loaded with 2,000 tons of gasoline in drums and foodstuffs for Corregidor, along with a guard detail of Philippine Army personnel. Her master's orders were to sail only at night, taking shelter in harbors during daylight hours. Following the first night's passage, she anchored at San Jose off the southwest coast of Mindoro near Ilin Island. An Army Air Corps officer stationed there flew to Bataan to seek routing instructions before *Regulas* proceeded to Corregidor. In the interim, the ship was spotted by Japanese observation plane whereupon the master and crew left the ship to take shelter ashore. The following morning, according to the master, the military guard upon sighting an enemy warship approaching, attempted to scuttle but was driven off by shell fire from the warship which had entered the harbor. Lloyd's states that after her capture by the Japanese she was renamed *Syotai Maru* and was sunk or damaged on Aug 3, 1945. [RG-407, PAC, Box 25; Box 1568, Folder *Regulas*; and Box 1570; ATS File; Ward Rpt; Cook '47 Survey; Spec. Crew List; Lloyd's; SWPA; Drake]

Reliance. 1.60'; 39 GT; Blt 1930, Philippine Islands

Either a launch or a tug. Owned by Luzon Stevedoring Co. According to correspondence between Brig. Gen. Charles C. Drake and Col. Frederick A. Ward written some years following the war, *Reliance* was commandeered at Manila on Dec 28, 1941, and sent to Corregidor. After the retreat from Bataan to Corregidor in early May 1942, this vessel disappeared, her Filipino crew believed to have deserted with her—taking her to some point along the shores of Cavite Province. [ATS File; AF 500-21]

Rizal. 1.171'; 576 GT; Blt 1930, Hong Kong

Owned by La Naviera Filipina, Inc. Requisitioned by ATS at Cebu City, island of Cebu, Dec 15, 1941. Crewmember claims file states vessel was released on Jan 18, 1942. According to Cook '47 Survey, she was scuttled at Cebu City, to avoid capture in Apr 1942. [Cook; Cook '47 Survey; RG-407, PAC, Box 1566]

Romblon. 1.149'; 385 GT; Blt 1889, Liverpool, England

Owned by Compania Maritima. There is only one page of information on this vessel in the PAC records, this being an undated crew list signed by *E. V. Buness, Records and Fiscal Division.* It gives no other indication as to whether *Romblon* was actually taken under Army employment. Lloyd's states her loss *during Japanese invasion of the Philippines.* This is verified by a 1943 intelligence report listing her as *lost.* [RG-407, PAC, Box 1570; Lloyd's; Willoughbyl]

SAILING VESSELS (unnamed); approximately 12 in number

Eight (names unknown) sailing vessels, some with auxiliary power, some not, are known to have been taken over by ATS at Iloilo, island of Panay. These were subsequently loaded with rations under orders of Capt. M. E. McClelland and sent north to Corregidor or Bataan. None of them were heard of again. Four more sailing vessels were chartered on Apr 9, 1942, from the Visayan Shipping Co. at Cebu City, island of Cebu, under direction of Lt. Col. C. Z. Byrd, also to carry relief supplies to Corregidor. None of them were reported as arriving. Taking the dates into consideration for the four which were chartered at Cebu City, they may possibly have been carrying some of the cargo which had been brought in by *Dona Nati* or *Anhui.* [ATS file]

Samal, ex *Pompey.* 1.237'; 1303 GT; Blt 1897, Sunderland, England

Owned by Compania Maritima. On Dec 22, 1941, the Quartermaster at Manila ordered this vessel to dock at Pier No. 1 where she was to be loaded with military cargo. On Dec 23 or 24, a Japanese bombing attack damaged the ship causing serious leaks which resulted in her master being ordered to leave the dock area and proceed outside the breakwater where *Samal* was beached. The Army supervised emergency repairs and on Dec 26, the vessel was returned to Pier No. 1 where loading was resumed. On Dec 29 she was moved to pier No. 7 for more cargo and was again bombed, this time being sunk. To this, Hartendorp's informant agrees except he stated that the date was either Dec. 27 or 28. A time charter with the Army had been agreed to on Dec 23 but apparently had not been formalized by the time of the loss. (It was not until Dec 24 that the Army began taking over Filipino vessels under the standard charter form.) Lloyd's lists her loss but with no date or other details. RG-407 indicates that the crew had left vessel at time of her final bombing and that at the time, the ship was under the command of *Army or Navy officers.* A 1943 intelligence report states that at that time she was sunk in Manila Bay, probably scheduled for salvage. [RG-407, PAC, Boxes 1568, 1570; Spcc (partial) crew list; Lloyd's; Hartendorp; Willoughby]

Santo Domingo. 1.153; 420 GT; Blt 1928, Hong Kong

Affidavit of chief purser of Aboitiz and Co., Inc., states that on Dec 24, 1941, this vessel was at Manila and was requisitioned or commandeered by the ATS at that time. It appears that shortly afterward she left Manila for the southern islands. Ward states that some uncertainty exists as to whether she was later used by the ATS at Cebu City, island of Cebu, or within the islands of Mindanao; and if the latter was the case, whether her employment was with the ATS or the Visayan- Mindanao Force. Disposition is unknown. [RG-407, PAC, Box 1565, Folder "Maritime Matters"; Ward Rpt]

Silvestre

Owned by Agusan Commercial Co. Taken over by military (probably on Mindanao) with wages of crew guaranteed. Final disposition unknown. [RG-407, PAC, Box 1565]

Simmis. 1.67'; 55 GT; Blt 1927, Philippine Islands

Launch owned by Luzon Stevedoring Co. In Dec 1941 was taken over by Navy at Manila. Then went to ATS and was assigned by ATS to Army Engineers. Ward states that without authorization the crew returned her to Manila after Japanese had occupied the city. [Ward Rpt]

Sta Rose (or Santa Rosa)

Launch. Charter recorded by ATS section at Fort Mills as of Feb 21, 1942; however, her use by Army probably began well before that time. [Ward, Apr 42; Dean]

Suntay III, IV, VIII, and *IX.* Blt 1930s, Philippine Islands

Launches. John O. Zimmerman, who was a lieutenant on the ATS staff at Fort Mills, Corregidor, certified after the war that all of the *Suntays* were motor launches which had been equipped as tugs. They were hired or requisitioned by ATS on or around Dec 15, 1941, being used to tow barges and scows from Manila to Bataan and later between Bataan and Corregidor. Zimmerman believed they were all in good condition at the time of the surrender of Bataan, probably being captured there by the Japanese on or about Apr 9, 1942. [ATS file; RG-407, PAC, Box 1570]

Surigao

In some Army records, the name *Surigao I* is used. A vessel of that name registered in the Philippines was of 129 GT, owned by Agusan Coconut Co. Another of the same name, also registered in the Philippines, was of 797 GT; Blt 1938, Hong Kong, owned by La Naviera Filipina, Inc. Which one the Army employed is unknown. Considering the valuation the Army placed on the vessel relevant to the value assigned to it in a later claims case and the use to which the Army put her, the larger one of 797 GT was without much doubt the one the Army employed. That *Surigao* was requisitioned by the Army either at Cebu City, island of Cebu, or at Iloilo, island of Panay, on Dec 15, 1941. The employment is given as being continuous through to Apr 16, 1942. Much of that service may have been for the Visayan-Mindanao Force. She was taken under formal charter at some point between Dec 15, 1941, and Mar 3, 1942, that charter being recorded at Fort Mills, Corregidor. The Filipino master's affidavit claims she sailed from Cebu City on Feb 22, loaded with rations and ammunition for Bataan. According to one Army report, she was at Iloilo, loaded with rations and ammunition slated for Bataan, when she was scuttled to avoid capture. Another Army report gives her as having been captured by the Japanese. Lloyd's has a *Surigao* of 797 tons lost in the *East Indies,* the date given as Feb 1942, but the entirety of the Army's evidence points to Lloyd's as being incorrect. As of May 1952, Lloyd's reported a *Surigao* as lying stranded at 14° 35' N; 120° 57' E, which is a position located in Manila Bay, thus reinforcing the premise that she was captured in 1942 and was subsequently employed by the Japanese. [Ward Apr 42; Crew Mar 42; Cook; Dean; Spec. Crew List; RG-407, PAC, Box 25, Folder *Surigao,* and Boxes 1565 and 1566; Lloyd's; Cook '47 Survey; Ward Rpt; SWPA; AF 500-21]

Tagbilaran. 1.50'; 13 GT; Blt 1917, Philippine Islands

Launch. Ward's report indicates the Army requisitioned this launch but is unclear as to whether it was taken by the ATS at Cebu City, island of Cebu, or by the Visayan- Mindanao Force at a more southern location. Cook '47 Survey claims she was chartered either by Col. John D. Cook or Lt. Col. C. Z. Byrd which would indicate the ATS, but no dates are given. There is no information on her final disposition. [Ward Rpt; Cook '47 Survey]

Talisay. 49 GT

Tug or launch. Owned by Visayan Stevedore Transportation Co. Requisitioned by the Army at Iloilo, island of Panay, during Feb 1942. Then taken to Cebu City, island of Cebu, for ATS operation where she was formally chartered on Mar 4 by Lt. Col. C. Z. Byrd. The ATS used her at Cebu City in conjunction with another launch, *Bacolod,* in attempting the salvage of a Navy PT boat off the coast of the island of Negros. Was also utilized in assisting in the loading of two Navy submarines with food and fuel for Corregidor. (See text for discussion regarding submarine blockade runners.) On Apr 10 after the Japanese landings on Cebu, *Talisay* was scuttled to prevent capture. [Charter Party; Spec Crew List (illegible); RG-407, PAC, Box 1565 and Box 1568, Folder *Talisay*; Dean; Crew Mar 42; Ward; SWPA]

Teako

Probably a launch. Known to have been chartered by the Army at Cebu City, island of Cebu, as her charter party (no copy exists in the file) was reported as transmitted by Lt. Col. C. Z. Byrd to the Quartermaster General's office through the Army Quartermaster at Fort Mills as dated Apr 1, 1942. The formal date of charter was given as Mar 10, 1942, executed at Cebu, Contract No. 14. [ATS File; Ward; Dean]

Three Sisters, ex *Cubu/Negros*

A ferry reported *taken over by Sharp.* (Then Maj. Gen. William F. Sharp of the Visayan- Mindanao Force.) [Ward Rpt.]

Three Sisters

Probably a tug or launch. Ward Report is uncertain as to whether this vessel was used by ATS at Cebu City, island of Cebu, or by the Visayan- Mindanao Force. No information as to disposition. [Ward Rpt]

Tilley. 27 GT

Army records circa 1911-1919 list this vessel as an Army tug/artillery steamer. There is no record of her being retained under Army ownership beyond 1919. Accordingly, it is believed that she was sold to private interests on or around that time. The means or authority by which the Army employed her during 1941-42 is not stated. Destroyed by air attack Dec 29, 1941. [ATS file; AF 500-21]

Tito. l.89'; 127 GT; Blt 1911, Hong Kong

Tug. Misspelled in one piece of Army correspondence as *Tite*. Owned by Anakan Lumber Co. Army records contain a letter of requisition for this vessel dated May 6, 1942, at Butuan, Agusan, island of Mindanao, signed by Capt. Elden L. McKown. Indications are that she may have been employed by Army Air Corps units attached to the Visayan-Mindanao Force. [RG-407, PAC, Box 25, Folder *Tito*]

Trovador. l.75'; 79 GT; Blt 1940, Hong Kong

Tug or small coaster. According to Army information supplied by *Col. McLennan* (Lt. Col. Carter R. McLennan) *Trovador* was chartered by ATS at Iloilo, island of Panay. According to crew affidavits, the vessel was employed by the ATS beginning in Jan 1942, running between Iloilo and the island of Negros and the island of Romblon hauling gasoline and other supplies. One report has her as having been scuttled on orders of Army at Iloilo in April, but there is no corroboration of this. A crew list of sort exists, having been prepared in 1945 by alleged former crewmembers seeking back wages from the Army. Lloyd's gives her loss but no particulars. [ATS file; Lloyd's; RG-407, PAC, Box 1568, Folder *Trovador*]

Tubigon

Launch chartered at Fort Mills, Corregidor, on Jan 10, 1942. Released from charter Feb 15, 1942. [Dean]

Varga

Vessel referenced in AF 500-21 as being utilized by *Major Hughes* during the evacuation from Bataan to Corregidor. [AF 500-21]

Venus. l.210'; 1050 GT; Blt 1880, Dundee, Scotland

Probably a freighter. Owned by Manila SS Co. According to Drake, this vessel was scuttled at Cebu City on Apr 10, 1942, to prevent her capture. [Drake Report: *Operations of the QM Corps, PI, July 27, 1941 - May 6, 1942*; AF 500-21]

Vigilant. l.61'; 40 GT; Blt 1929, Philippine Islands

Launch owned by Luzon Stevedoring Co. During Dec 1941, she was taken over by Navy at Manila. Then went to ATS, being assigned to Army Engineers. Disposition unknown, but it was reported that without Army authorization, her crew returned the launch to Manila after Japanese had occupied that city. [ATS File; Ward Rpt]

Viscaro

This name was found on a nearly illegible list of vessels within "History of ATS Activities in Manila and Cebu, Dec 41 to May 42." Nothing more could be discerned as to the vessel's service or final disposition. The list contains the names of twenty-seven vessels plus others with completely illegible names. Of the twenty-seven legible names there are only five on which we do not have other records tying them directly to ATS employment. Therefore, it is probable that this vessel was employed in some fashion by the Army between Dec 7, 1941 and May of 1942. [AF 500-21]

List 5:

Merchant Vessels Not Known To Have Been In Service Of U.S. Army Forces, Far East But Which Were Sunk, Damaged, Scuttled, Or Taken Over by the Japanese Within the Philippine Islands, 1941-42

Information for this list is taken primarily from *Lloyd War Losses, The Second World War,* Volume I; *BR-1337, British and Foreign Merchant Vessel Losses, WW II;* U. S. Army reports within Record Group 407, Philippine Archive Collection; Intelligence Reports within Willoughby's *The Intelligence Services, SWPA Command.*

Vessel	Flag ‡	GrTons	Remarks
Aloha	US	239	Motor vessel scuttled in Manila Bay.
Anakan	US	837	Motor vessel. Abandoned by crew. Scuttled in Manila harbor. Raised by Japanese and renamed *Anan Maru.* 1943 intelligence report states she was then taken out of the Philippines. Subsequently lost.
APO	US	1075	Cable vessel shelled and destroyed by U.S. Army artillery fire on south coast of Bataan after Bataan was taken by Japanese, Apr 1942. Reported by 1943 intelligence agent as probably salvaged off Corregidor.
Arayat	US	904	Philippine Bureau of Customs Revenue Service cutter. Broadcast *from Friesland* on Dec 28 reported vessel set on fire at Pier 5, Manila, by Japanese aircraft. A 1943 intelligence report stated that at that time, she was undergoing repairs *at Ernshaw's.*
Baga, ex *General Weeks*	US		Tug. Reported by intelligence agent during 1943 that she had been salvaged and was being used by the Japanese in Philippine coastwise service.
Bessie Ann	US	226	Reported by intelligence agent during 1943 that she had been salvaged and was being used by the Japanese in Philippine coastwise service.
Bicol	US	369	Abandoned by her crew on Dec 28, 1941, in the Pasig River, Manila. Scuttled there by Army Engineers. Reported in 1943 intelligence report as *lost.*
Bisayas	US	2833	Was scuttled on Pasig River but salvaged by Japanese and renamed *Hisigata Maru.* Sunk by Allied aircraft Jan 2, 1945 in 16° 37' N; 120° 19' E. *Under repairs at Ernshaw's,* in 1943, according to intelligence report.
Boxwood	US		According to records in the Edmonds Collection, was sunk Jan 21, 1942, at Cebu City.

---

‡   Vessels documented in the Philippines during this period flew the U.S. flag since the Philippines in 1941-42 was a Commonwealth of the United States. Some photographs of Philippine-registered ships taken circa 1930 - 1941 within Philippine waters show at the jack staff the Commonwealth flag being flown beneath the U.S. flag. Other photographs show only the U.S. flag.

Capillo	US	5135	Abandoned at Manila on Dec 10, 1941, owing to fire which was the result of Japanese air attack. Fire was later taken under control, and she was towed to Corregidor and then over to Bataan coast. According to Army, was sunk there in bombing attack on Dec 29. Hartendorp agrees.
Cepo	US		Anchored off the coast of Bataan when captured by the Japanese on Apr 9, 1942. She was subsequently shelled by U.S. forces on Corregidor to prevent her use by the Japanese.
Cetus	US	943	Sunk -- possibly by U.S. B-17s -- at Aparri, Cagayan River Dec 10, 1941. Believed salvaged and renamed *Hokuhi Maru* which was sunk by aircraft March 2, 1945 in 23° 35' N; 119° 35' E. A 1943 intelligence report agrees with her having been salvaged at Aparri.
Conquistador	US	15	Motor tug; no information as to her disposition
Corregidor	US	1881	Sunk by defensive mine in Manila Bay; heavy losses. Was carrying Army freight and personnel but was not under Army requisition or charter.
Don Jose	US	10893	Sought shelter at Manila after outbreak of war while on voyage Vancouver to Hong Kong with cargo for British forces at that place. Commandeered at Manila, then ordered to Corregidor after partial discharge of cargo at Manila. Set on fire by Japanese aircraft and beached. While afire, ATS pumped 2500 tons of fuel oil from her. Taken to Hong Kong by Japanese. Further damaged by Allied bombing. Was slated to be scrapped. However, a 1943 intelligence report states that at that time she was damaged but afloat in the Philippines.
Don Juan O	US	498	According to Hartendorp informant, was captured at Manila by Japanese. Reported by intelligence agent during 1943 as being used by them in Philippine coastal service.
Dredge Manila	US	817	Suction dredge. Lost in Manila Bay.
Dredger	US		Reported by intelligence agent in 1943 that she was being employed in dredging work in Manila Bay.
Escalante	US		According to Hartendorp informant, was captured at Manila by Japanese. Reported by intelligence agent during 1943 as being used by them in Philippine coastal service.
Esteban Riu	US	123	According to 1943 intelligence report, this vessel was being used in the service of the Japanese in Philippine coastwise service.
Ethel Edwards	US	395	Motor vessel. Set on fire by Japanese aircraft at Manila
Forafric	Br	3475	On voyage for Hong Kong; diverted to Iloilo. Arrived there Dec 8, 1941; arrived Cebu Dec 19; sailed Dec 22. Carrying coal; 2395 tons firewood; 1490 bags charcoal. Sunk off PI at 3 40 N; 121 E by aircraft.
Fundador	US	50	Motor tug; no other information
Governor Wright	US	496	Hit by aircraft 12° 55' N; 123° 55' E. Reported refloated (presumably for scrap) sometime previous to Aug 25, 1956. (*Shipping Gazette, Manila* 8/56)
Hareldawins	Br	1523	In at least one report is incorrectly spelled *Hareldswine.* On voyage Hong Kong to Singapore. Sunk by Japanese aircraft off Barigayos Point, island of Luzon. Survivors were machine-gunned in lifeboats, but without casualties.

Himulat	US	70	Motor tug; destroyed by an explosion
Hydra II	Nor	1375	On a voyage from Bangkok for Hong Kong, carrying 2000 tons rice and salt, deviated to Manila. Sunk 30 miles from Manila. Survivor reported that torpedo came from the direction of the shore. No Japanese submarine was reported in the vicinity at the time.
Iona	US	99	Claimant stated vessel was commandeered by Army, but there is no collaborating evidence of that. No further information as to final disposition.
Isla de Mindoro	US	322	Lost at *Ceba* (probably Cebu); no details.
Isla Filipinas	US	1014	Lost during Japanese invasion of Philippines
Jolo	US	167	Lost during Japanese invasion of Philippines
Kaiping	Br	2563	Owned by Chinese Engineering and Mining Co. Either towed or taken by crew in bomb-damaged state from Manila to Sisiman Bay, Bataan, where part of her coal cargo was salvaged. Was later towed to Corregidor by *USAT Henry Keswick* and beached where much of her remnant cargo was offloaded. Subsequently was sunk either by air attack or scuttling. According to Lloyd's was later salvaged by the Japanese and renamed *Kaiho Maru*. Lost by striking mine in Apr 1945 at 34° N, 130° 50' W. [ATS File; Ward Report; AF 500-21; Hale L. Hutchins, *Mast Magazine,* July 1947.]
Lanao	US	2104	According to Hartendorp, she was anchored off Malabon at time of loss on either Dec 27 or 28, 1941.
Latouche	US	2156	Captured at Manila; renamed *Azuchi Maru*. Intelligence report of 1943 states she was salvaged thus indicating she must have either been sunk or badly damaged at a point prior to 1943. Subsequent fate unknown.
Leyte	US	893	According to Hartendorp was bombed and lost on Dec. 27 or 28, 1941, in Manila Bay.
Liluang	French	?	Bombed and sunk of Marivelles, Bataan on Dec 24, 1941.
Magallanes	US	1376	Abandoned by crew in Pasig River, Manila. Removed by Navy and scuttled in outer harbor. Reported as later salvaged by Japanese and put into service. Intelligence report of 1943 states that in that year, she underwent repairs at Cavite.
Majang	Dutch	536	Sunk in Moiesi River, PI, by Japanese cruiser. Motor vessel which may have been the *Majang* was raised by the Japanese but then grounded (presumed lost) in the Philippines in Dec 1944.
Makasser	Dutch	537	Sunk in Moesi River, PI, by Japanese cruiser.
Manatawny	US	5030	Tanker. While on voyage Los Angeles and Seattle to Honolulu, Guam, and Hong Kong carrying dynamite, diverted to Philippine waters. Sunk by Japanese aircraft off Paracale on Jan 13, 1942.
Mauban	US	1253	Scuttled in Pasig River on Dec 28, 1941. Raised and renamed *Manbo Maru*. Sunk by mine off Kobe, Japan, on May 12, 1945.
Mindanao	US	5236	While undergoing repair at Cavite, was bombed and badly damaged by Japanese aircraft Dec 10, 1941 at 14 35' N; 120 55' E. Captured by Japanese and renamed *Palembang Maru*. Sunk by Allied submarine March 4, 1945 in 12° 52' N; 109° 30' E.

Montanes	US	1236	According to Hartendorp's informant, was beached and then scuttled on Dec 30, 1941, at Manila. Intelligence report of 1943 verifies that vessel was lost.
Nuestra Senora de la Paz	US	248	According to Hartendorp, was scuttled in Manila Harbor. Later salvaged by Japanese and put into their service. 1943 intelligence report states that in 1943 she was being used by Japanese in Philippine coastal service.
Nuestra Senora del Guia	US		A 1943 intelligence report states she had been salvaged by the Japanese and placed into their service.
Nuestra Senora del Rosario	US	430	According to Hartendorp, was scuttled in Manila Harbor and later salvaged by Japanese. 1943 intelligence report states merely that she had been lost.
Palawan	US	562	Motor vessel. Abandoned by crew in Pasig River. Scuttled Manila Bay about December 29, 1941. According to Hartendorp's informant was recovered by Japanese and renamed *Paran Maru*. 1943 intelligence report claims vessel was taken out of Philippine waters. Thought sunk by aircraft and surface craft on Jan 30, 1944, in 8° 42' N; 167° 44' E.
Paz	US	4260	Had cargo of coal when bombed at Manila and set on fire December 26, 1941. A 1943 intelligence report confirms that vessel was salved by Japanese and renamed *Hatsu Maru*. Sunk by Allied aircraft off Manila on November 20, 1944.
Pelagi	US		Cause of loss not known; however was reported by intelligence agent during 1943 as having been salvaged and was being used by the Japanese in Philippine coastwise service.
Pelayo	US	149	Reported by intelligence agent during 1943 that she had been salvaged and was being used by the Japanese in Philippine coastwise service.
Perla	US	346	Scuttled Jan 1942 at Lamit Bay on the east coast of Luzon.
Ravanaas	Nor	4019	Motor vessel. When off Surigao was sunk December 8, 1941. Salved by Japanese and renamed *Ikutagawa Maru*. Sunk by Allied aircraft Jan 12, 1945 at 10° 45' N; 106° 43 29' E.
Sagoland	US	5334	Hit by Japanese aircraft at Manila on Dec 10, 1941, with seven casualties. Sank the 11th. A 1943 intelligence report claims she was sunk at Manila but was probably scheduled for salvage.
Santa Teresita	US	222	Report in 1943 intelligence report as being in the service of the Japanese at that time in their Philippine coastwise service.
Sarangani	US	2691	Tank vessel captured in the Philippines and renamed *Sanraku Maru*. Sunk by Allied submarine June 15, 1943 at 5° 9' N; 119° 3' E.
Seistan	Br	2455	Sunk by Japanese aircraft, of Bataan coast on Dec 26, 1941.
Si Kiang	US	7014	Hit by Japanese aircraft, Bay of Marse, Manila. Vessel was set on fire and fire lasted at least two days. Obvious total loss. Vessel had been slated for requisitioning by American military and had a military guard on board but had not yet been placed into Army service.
Sintang			With cargo of gasoline and oil as well as flour was taken to Marivelles on Bataan and unloaded by ATS. On Dec 26, 1941, while there was bombed and sunk.

Stevedore	US	9	Motor launch; no other information
Tamarao I	US	31	Motor vessel. Lost during Japanese invasion of Philippines
Tamaun	US		Property of Philippine Government. Sunk by bombing in December at Pier 5, Pasig River.
Tangog	US		May possibly be *Tangob,* 156 GT, homeport of Cebu. Cause of loss unknown; however, it as reported by intelligence agent during 1943 that she had been salvaged and was being used by the Japanese in Philippine coastwise service.
Tanon	US	234	Reported by intelligence agent during 1943 that she had been salvaged and was being used by the Japanese in Philippine coastwise service.
Tantalus	Br	7724	Sunk by Japanese aircraft attack at anchorage off Bataan on Dec 26, 1941.
Taurus	US	1251	Scuttled in the Pasig River. At some point was salvaged and taken over by the Japanese for their service.
Ventura	US	130	Cause of loss unknown; however, it was reported by an intelligence agent during 1943 that she had been salvaged and was being used by the Japanese in Philippine coastwise service.
Vizcaya	US	1249	Scuttled at Manila Bay in mid December. 1943 intelligence report has her stranded *off Tondo* in the province of Manila which would indicate that she must have been salvaged by the Japanese following her scuttling in December 1941.
Volador	US	25	Motor vessel; no other information as to cause of loss
Zamboanga	US	215	Report in 1943 intelligence report as being in the service of the Japanese at that time in coastwise service.

Notes Regarding Filipino Shipping during the Japanese Occupation

Agents' report from the Philippines transmitted to the Headquarters, Intelligence Section (G-2), Southwest Pacific Area Command in Australia, covering the period January to September 1943, included the following information regarding Japanese salvage and subsequent repair of Filipino small craft.

Approximately 90% of harbor launches have been salvaged and [now] *in use. About 50% of lighters, barges, bancas, cascos, etc., have been refloated and in use. Lost materials are rapidly being replaced from new shipways. In Manila for instance, on 15 August 1943, four wooden ships (about 200 tons) were put to service although under sail only as no motors were available. About 18 launches (approximately 50') are also awaiting motors.* [*]

According to a master's thesis prepared in June 1965 for the Faculty of the Claro M. Recto Academy, Lyceum of the Philippines, presented by Manuel I. Tibayan: The Japanese at Manila ordered the salvaging of interisland vessels sunk by Japanese bombs during the December 1941 to May 1942 attacks as well as those which were scuttled during the defense on USAFFE orders. The salvage operation was undertaken by the Sirake Salvage Company (a Japanese firm). The vessels salvaged (unnamed by Tibayan) were used exclusively by the Japanese during their occupation of the Philippines.

---

[*] See "Willoughby" under "Primary Bibliography for Philippine Vessel Lists" for full citation regarding this 1943 Intelligence Report.

APPENDICES

APPENDIX A

THE WORCESTER OBSERVATIONS ON THE PEOPLES OF THE PHILIPPINE ISLANDS

Source: The Writings of Dean C. Worcester:

- *The Philippines, Past and Present,* (New York: The MacMillan Company, 1921).
- "The Non-Christian People of the Philippine Islands," *National Geographic,* Vol XXIV, No. 11, November 1913.
- "Head-hunters of Luzon" *National Geographic,* Vol XXIII, No. 9, September 1912.

Dean C. Worcester was the Secretary of the Interior of the Philippine Islands from 1901 to 1913. Within various papers he wrote on the Islands' peoples, he made detailed observations regarding those population groupings which still retained their native cultures. Worcester termed such groupings as *The Wild People* or *Wild Tribes* as differentiated from that part of the Philippine population which over the years had come under the cultural and religious influence of the Spanish and which lived in civilized communities governed by the Spanish occupation. These civilized groups which were apart from the *Wild Tribes* were commonly termed Filipinos. The civilized Filipinos were scattered throughout the archipelago, living mainly in urban areas such as Manila as well as coastal communities and areas adjacent to major inland waterways. In 1898, those considered as Filipinos numbered around seven million. In general, the civilized Filipinos were of four ethnic sub-groupings: Ilacanos, Tagalogs, Pampangans, and Visayans. Racially, these sub-groupings were of Malayan and Indonesian population stocks which had reached the Philippines probably centuries before the start of the Spanish occupation. Of the sub-groupings, the Ilacano were generally deemed (opinion circa late 1800s) to have been the more progressive, although by the time the

American occupation was underway, it had become difficult to differentiate ethnic traits because of frequent interbreeding with other sub-groupings as well as with more recent Chinese and Spanish emigrants to the islands. The better educated Filipinos spoke Spanish, but the majority spoke various native dialects which had become bastardized with Spanish words. Once the American occupation took hold during the first decades of the 1900s, English was taught to many of the children of school age. The first teachers were American soldiers detailed to the task; later civilian contract teachers were sent out from the United States. Contact with Americans and the teaching of English did not reach into the remote areas of the islands until well into the latter part of Worcester's tenure.

General Observations

When Worcester traveled throughout the Philippine Islands, the *Wild People* were living apart from the Filipino population either by choice or from geographic necessity. Over the years, many of the wild tribes had various degrees of contact with both Filipino traders and with the Spanish Jesuit priests; however, some of the tribes lived so remotely that few of their members had ever seen a Spaniard or even a civilized Filipino.

Between 1901 and 1907, the U.S. civil authorities conducted widespread explorations throughout the archipelago. The information they gathered was augmented by the reports of the American military. When viewed from a scientific basis, Worcester's observations are the most thorough. Although Worcester traveled in the Philippine Islands over a period of 18 years, only once during that time was he attacked by native tribesmen. That exception occurred during an ambush arranged by the Moro on Palawan Island in which the U.S. provincial governor was specifically targeted. Fortunately for the governor and for Worcester who accompanied him, the Moro were driven off. Worcester stated that he had been threatened on a number of other occasions by members of *wild tribes;* but by *exhibiting friendliness,* he managed to avert attacks.

Roads, or even paths suitable for use by the small Filipino ponies, were lacking at the beginning of the American occupation. Therefore, trips into the interior had to be made by river using launches or more primitive craft. Worcester believed that the best aid toward civilizing the tribes of the interiors would be good roads. Road construction was accomplished at first under the supervision of the American military and later under the American structured civil government within which Worcester served. These started out as cut trails and were improved over time. Both the trail construction and the follow-up road construction was accomplished through a law requiring each male native to supply ten days of his labor annually or pay a tax equivalent to $1.00. Exemptions to taxation were allowed if the tribe affected did not appear advanced enough to appreciate the needs and advantages of good transportation access; however, most of them realized the benefits that would accrue to their localized economies by the opening of trade with neighboring tribes and with the Filipinos. From the American perspective, an adequate transportation network allowed mobility for the civilian appointed Constabulary as well as the Army-run Philippine Scouts. Worcester believed that when dealing with the wild tribes, Constabulary recruited from local tribes were much more effective than were Filipinos since prior exploitation by Filipino traders had created bitterness and suspicions on the part of the tribesmen which was not conducive to a cooperative attitude between them and the Filipinos.

The work the American civil government performed with most of the *wild peoples* proved to be successful within a relatively short period of time. The Negritos and the Moro were another matter. In the case of the Negritos grouping, Worcester came to believe that they were unteachable and therefore hopeless to work with. He found that the religious beliefs of the Moro were intensely anti-Christian therefore negating the prospects of success with that group as well.

Alcoholism was never considered a serious problem with the civilized Filipinos; but with some of the wild tribes, it was epidemic. It became the American policy to prohibit all importation of alcohol; however, some of the tribes made their own. That manufacture through distillation, which was native to their culture, was not interfered with by the administration. Narcotic use by most of the wild tribes or by the Filipinos had never been serious during the Spanish reign, and it never became one under the American administration. The Moro were the exception, being users of hard drugs. By 1911, American authorities had begun to see an increased importation of drugs into areas inhabited by the Moro, and the matter was considered a dangerous hindrance to the pacification of the Moro population.

There was never any push by the American authorities to *Mother Hubbard* the wild tribes, especially the women, as had been done by the American missionaries to Hawaii during the early part of the nineteenth century. Worcester believed that *morality was not influenced by being fully clothed.* His opinion was that *to make a loin-clothed person cover himself might well produce ill health effects in hot climates.* In time, the natives on their own came to adopt European clothing, a practice which by 1911, was becoming widespread. In Worcester's enlightened opinion, this was an unfortunate trend leading toward the disappearance of the nature cultures.

Trading practices which had been carried on by Filipinos under the Spanish had been generally exploitative against the tribes. To discourage this old style of trade, the civil administration established government-operated exchanges where the tribal peoples could trade their native goods for manufactured *necessities.* Weapons of native manufacture (spears, knives, etc.) were key items of that exchange system. The American managers would purchase these items and then wholesale the weapons as well as native art objects into the tourist market places at Manila and in the United States where they soon became popular curios. The establishment of the exchanges proved of considerable value toward developing a trusting relationship with the tribes' peoples.

THE NEGRITOS PEOPLES OF THE ARCHIPELAGO

The Negritos were thought by Worcester to have been the original aboriginal population of the Philippines. He was of the opinion that at one time they inhabited most, if not all the islands within the archipelago. By the late part of the nineteenth century at the time when the Americans entered upon the scene, the Negritos were to be found only in northeastern Mindanao; the island of Samar; central Negros; central Panay and north central Palawan; and on Luzon in that island's northern and central sections as well as within the mountain region of the Bataan Peninsula. The Negritos found on Luzon were the only Negrito group which practiced head-hunting. Those Negritos habitually made raids against Filipino villages located on the coasts, and they were greatly feared as a result. Their head-hunting practice was carried on because of their belief that one head taken annually by each male of a family group guaranteed against misfortune for that particular family for that year.

Physically, the Negritos were diminutive, *dwarfish in stature, had flattened noses, skins dark brown to black, woolly hair, and limbs covered by peppercorn hair.* Unlike some of the wild people of Chinese, Indonesian, or Malayan origins who adorned their bodies with tattoos, the Negritos decorated their bodies with scar patterns. They were skilled hunters, and Worcester's photographs indicate that they hunted with well-crafted bows and arrows. Worcester believed that almost without exception the Negritos practiced little social discipline within their village groups. As an example, he noted that they would plant garden patches and then for no apparent reason immediately move to a new location before the crops were ready for harvest, thereby abandoning their work to the ravages of nature. Unless they were able to conveniently purchase cotton goods from Filipino traders, they commonly clothed themselves with the bark from trees. Worcester believed that they were on a par both mentally and in skill levels with the aborigines of Australia which he believes they resembled in general appearance.[*] The northern Luzon Negritos had pointed front teeth which they created by chipping the corners of their teeth giving them a somewhat alarming look. On all of the islands which they inhabited, their death rates exceeded their birth rates, and by 1912, the Negritos were thought to be dying out in most of the areas they inhabited. With the apparent exception of the head-hunting group of Negritos who were found in northern Luzon and who the Filipinos feared, the Negritos had been badly oppressed by the Filipinos over the past. Worcester recommended that this oppression would have to be stopped if the Negritos were to have any chance of racial survival. Despite the empathy which Worcester had for their plight, he believed that they were *absolutely incapable of being civilized.*

THE WILD PEOPLE OF THE ISLAND OF LUZON

The Ifugaos

The Ifugao tribe, numbering about 125,000, inhabited the rugged mountainous terrain of the north central part of Luzon. They were warlike and were thought to have practiced head-hunting in the immediate past. Advanced in the skills of agriculture, they were growers of rice, beans, onions, and other vegetable crops planted on superbly designed irrigated terraces. Photographs taken in the early 1900s show these terraces as being walled with well laid up stone which most trained observers believed had been constructed over a span of hundreds of years. By 1905,

---

[*] The Australian aborigines and the original natives of New Guinea are now thought to have been derived from the same racial stock.

the head-hunting practice of most of the Ifugaos had been effectively curtailed under the supervisory control of the Army. Although Ifugao relations with the Spanish were never good, they became especially friendly toward Americans, and this tribe would become a fertile source for Scout and Constabulary recruitment by the U.S. Army.

The Igorots

Another tribe on Luzon was the Igorot of the provinces of Benquet, Lepanto, and Bontoc as well as in the areas of Kalinga and Amburayan. The tribe numbered around 160,000. Although of a single ethnic identity, the Igorots were so geographically scattered that not all of them spoke the same dialect. They did, though, practice the same spirit religion. The Igorots raised rice on terraces, but their terrace construction was not of the same sophistication as that of the Ifugaos.

Standing out as being quite different in habit and custom from the rest of the Igorot peoples to which Worcester believed them to be a part, were the Bontoc Igorots. Numbering about 76,000, they comprised almost half of the total Igorot peoples. The Bontoc area subtribe was known for its extreme filthiness, both in personal hygiene and its habitations. The American military had great difficulty in suppressing head-hunting among this subtribe of the Igorot since the men practiced the taking of heads as a means for obtaining admiration and favors from the female sex.

The Kalingas

The Kalinga was a tribe located on the open plains region of the northern part of Luzon. They were estimated at around 70,000 in number. Historically known as head-hunters, they were a clean people with neat houses being a special trait. The American military at first considered them dangerous because of their long-held antagonism toward the coastal Filipinos. Worcester reported that as late as 1913, the dangers to Filipinos traveling in Kalinga country was great. This hostility was never exhibited against the Americans, either military or civil; instead, they soon became regarded as a friendly and pleasant people despite a continued reputation as head-hunters against neighboring tribes. That predatory practice included the removal of the victim's brains which were then mixed with a sort of home brew to form a gruel which was passed around for anyone wishing to partake of the mixture. Worcester reported that he had personally witnessed this.

The Tingians (civilized pagan segments)

This subgroup was thought by Worcester to be the *most attractive of the non-Christian tribes.* The civilized Tingians numbered around 14,000. They mainly inhabited the area of Abra in northern Luzon but were scattered within the adjoining provinces as well. The one criticism of this grouping as made by Worcester concerned the women's bracelets which were placed on the arms of a girl in early childhood. As the child grew, the bracelets would constrict the arms' growth causing a deformity. He found the cleanliness and the social order of these people especially pleasing. Worcester felt that they were largely superior to *their Filipino Christian neighbors,* particularly in the construction and upkeep of housing. He further commented that their sexual customs exhibited a level of high morality when compared against other tribes within the archipelago.

The Tingians (wild segments)

Worcester believed this grouping was of the same ethnic background as the civilized Tingians. He was told by the Jesuits that this wild group had become isolated from the rest of the tribal grouping sometime during the late seventeenth or early eighteenth century and that they had withdrawn from Spanish influences, retreating into the mountainous regions of the northern part of the island. As of 1912, they were thought to number around 53,000. Remarking on the women, Worcester wrote that they were well dressed and cleanly except during periods of mourning when they followed the custom of going naked from the waist up and remaining unwashed for as long as six months. Like the civilized segment of the tribe, the Tingians constructed strong dwellings but in a more primitive style. They were believed to practice head-hunting up to at least the end of the first decade of the 1900s. Their head-hunting practices appeared to be centered around their mourning rituals which could only be ended when a male family member of the female mourner presented her with the head of some unfortunate victim. This group was never regarded as a danger to Americans.

The Irongots

On the shores of Laguna de Bay east of Manila there resided an outcast group of uncertain ethnic strain known as the Irongots (not to be confused with the Igorots.) The Irongots were thought to have emerged as a result of intermixing between members of various *Wild Peoples* and the Negritos. Dwarfish in appearance like the Negritos, they were infamous for their lack of personal hygiene and sanitation. As a result, they suffered from all sorts of skin diseases. Recent to the start of the American occupation, they had been known for their aggressive habit of ambushing any Filipinos who ventured their way. Hated for this, in 1900, Aguinaldo's insurgents had driven them away from the Laguna de Bay area, scattering them to the northward in small family groupings.

The Ilongots

This was another hybrid tribal group showing evidence of extensive interbreeding with the Negritos. Residing in scattered villages, they were considered treacherous in nature. Worcester wrote of an ethnologist named William Jones who had lived with them in apparent harmony for over a year but who was suddenly murdered by them, apparently without warning. As late as 1911, Worcester still considered them as very dangerous. They were head-hunters, but the practice seemed to have little ritual purpose as once the victim was killed, the head would be tossed aside as so much garbage.

The Macabebes

Not covered in Worcester's writings but recorded by a number of others was a population grouping which resided within and near to Macabebes which was a village located in Pampanga Province on Luzon. The Macabebes were solidly hated by the Filipinos as well as by their neighboring *wild people.* The Macabebes in turn hated the Filipinos and showed an equal hostility toward any tribal peoples who were unfortunate enough to cross their path. The Macabebes had a long history of soldiering under the Spanish for which they had served as Constabulary troops. They would later perform the same service for the Americans. At that time, they were believed by both the Spanish and by the Americans to have descended from Mexican Indians brought to the Philippines by the Spanish during the late sixteenth century or the early seventeenth century. The Macabebes were by no means the only natives enlisted by the Americans into the Constabulary and the Philippine Scouts; but of all those who were enlisted during the early 1900s, they were considered the most reliable and the best fighters.

THE WILD PEOPLE OF THE ISLAND OF MINDANAO

The Subanos

The Subanos inhabited the near coastal fringe of western and northern Mindanao. They were a peaceful agricultural people, partly Islamic and partly Christian in their faiths. They had been heavily preyed upon by the Moro who habitually had enslaved them. Unlike the Moro, those of the Subanos who practiced Islam were not known to be militant against Christians.

The Tirurayes

The Tirurayes was another tribe which had been heavily raided by the Moro. They were believed to be rapidly dying out as a result of those attacks as well as from interbreeding with outsiders. The raids by the Moro prevented them from building villages as they were kept constantly on the move to escape the raids. The Jesuit priests believed that in the past the Tirurayes had numbered close to 10,000; but by 1911, their numbers were far less.

The Mandayas

This tribe, numbering around 30,000, inhabited the upper reaches of the Agusan River in the central part of the island and the area around the town of Mati on the east coast. They were skilled in various art forms such as weaving and metal working. On the negative side, they had the unsavory reputation of being slave owners raiding for that purpose neighboring tribes. As late as 1913, the slave raiding had not been eradicated despite the best efforts of the American military.

The Manguan

The Manguan tribe resided in the island's interior. Its numbers were uncertain but had been estimated by the Jesuits as between 5,000 and 20,000. Primitive and nomadic in habit, Worcester considered them of low average intelligence. Observers had been amazed to witness their eating habits which included the consumption of *rotten animal flesh crawling with maggots,* an indulgence which apparently caused them no harm. Despite their dietary backwardness and nomadic nature, they had the ability to build substantial and well designed houses. Worcester believed that some of them had the skin coloring and features to indicate inbreeding with the Negritos.

The Manobos

The Manobos had a population of around 60,000 and were found scattered in villages at various locations around Mindanao. They varied widely in their general appearance from the other tribal populations on the island. Social habits and native skills also differed from those of the other tribes. They lived in tree houses, and their agricultural practices were *haphazard*. They kept slaves captured from adjoining tribes and were especially infamous for their cruelty to the captives. For instance, they were known to tie up a slave and then let a young boy practice his skills with a spear by repeatedly stabbing the slave until the slave was dead. Given time, Worcester believed that they could be *civilized*, surmising that to a degree their savage nature was the result of long exploitation by Filipino traders who had debauched them with rot-gut liquor. They occasionally performed rites of human sacrifice which Worcester described as being part of their spirit belief. When under one of their religious spells, they could be *dangerous to those in the immediate surroundings*.

Miscellaneous Tribal Groups

Another tribe found on Mindanao was the Atas, numbering around 8,000. Despite their geographic proximity to the Moro, they had managed to retain their independence.

Additionally, there were five or six other small tribes on Mindanao, each exhibiting distinctive ethnic diversity from other tribes. Most of these small tribal units had their own distinct dialects which were scarcely discernible even to their close neighbors. Most of these groupings were suspected of practicing human sacrifice on occasion.

The pagan tribes of Mindanao (other than of course the Moros which are later discussed) were generally considered by the Spanish Jesuits as inoffensive to Europeans. In fact, the Jesuits had lived and worked with most of them for years. Although these tribes had conducted intertribal warfare in the past, by the end of the nineteenth century such outbreaks had become rare.

THE MONTESES OF THE ISLANDS OF PANAY AND NEGROS

Inhabiting the interior of these islands was a population referred to by the Filipinos as Monteses, a term taken from the Spanish meaning *mountain people*. The Jesuits referred to some of them as the Bukidnon, but Worcester lumped them under one tribal identity as Monteses. Their common religious beliefs encompassed the theory that once a man died, he had to be accompanied by a companion. This resulted in a somewhat chaotic society since obviously that heavenly arrangement had to come about through acts of murder. There was continuous quarreling taking place between the various village groups, most of the disagreements ending up with mayhem. When Worcester was staying in one of their villages, he discovered through a Filipino guide that, *They sought an opportunity to kill my companion and myself.* The reason, as he later found out, was that they suspected that Worcester and his companion were there to poison the village's water.

THE TAGBANUAS OF THE ISLAND OF PALAWAN

A tribe called the Tagbanuas inhabited central and northern Palawan, numbering perhaps 5,000 people. Physically well developed, they were relatively dark skinned indicating the probability of some past interbreeding with the Negrito. Where Tagbanuas settlements were in close contact with the Moro, they had adopted the dress of the Moro except for their hair style. They were not thought by Worcester to be Islamic. Agriculturally oriented, part of their crops went toward satisfying annual tribute demands imposed on them by the Moro. Hunting was supplemental to their agriculture. The tribe's skills in hunting were of an especially high attainment level.

<u>Worcester's Observations on the Moro</u> [†]

The Moro people were widespread, being found on the islands of Palawan, Balabac, Cagayan de Job, Tawi-Tawi, Siassi, Lapac, Jolo, and Basilan as well as within various enclaves in the coastal regions of western and southern Mindanao and that island's interior Lake Lanao region. The first thing which immediately distinguished the Moros from the other people of the Philippine Islands was their form of dress. Their headgear consisted of either a turban or a fez. Their dialects and customs were widely different from other population groups. Although there were certain variations in the dialects of the Moro on the different islands, what they all had in common was their Islam religion. This was the fundamental social factor that set them so completely apart from all the other peoples of the Philippine Islands.

With the exception of the Lake Lanao population on Mindanao and those Moro living in the interior of Basilan, the Moro were a maritime people. Many of them lived on boats while others lived in houses built on stilts hanging over the water. Many were outright pirates, that practice being the mainstay of much of their economic welfare. Some Moro were migratory. For uncountable years, Moro men from Jolo were employed as divers in the pearl fisheries, some as far afield as Ceylon. In general, they were fanatical fighters under the cloak of the Islam banner. There were certain branch cults whose members had taken the oath to die while in the act of killing Christians. These fanatics were infamous for carrying concealed weapons into public places where Christians were known to be. Then, without warning, they would set upon everyone in reach until they themselves were finally cut down. A death under such circumstance was thought by the Moro to provide them an entrance into heaven. The Spanish had never been able to subjugate them, relying instead upon keeping them relatively contained and clear of areas of particular concern to Spanish interests. [‡]

[†] Modern anthropologists are of the opinion that the Moro of the Philippine archipelago were descended from the peoples of Borneo.

[‡] The last grouping of Moros to be brought under American military control were those living in the Lake Lanao region on Mindanao. This subjugation did not occur until 1913.

APPENDIX B

THE HISTORY OF U.S. LAW AND JURIDICAL RULINGS THAT DIFFERENTIATED "PUBLIC VESSEL SEAMEN" OF THE ARMY TRANSPORT SERVICE FROM SEAMEN OF THE MERCHANT MARINE

In a somewhat abbreviated form, the contents of this Appendix were published within an article by Charles Dana Gibson; *American Neptune,* LX, No. 2 (2000).

Two categories of character change can take place which remove a merchant ship from the peaceful identification normally applicable to the pursuits of a ship engaged in the nation's commerce. The first category is when a merchant ship, either private or government owned, operates in behalf of its government during a period of hostilities. The second and most altering is attained when a merchant ship operates (especially if armed) in conformity with the warlike purpose of the nation and is under authority to do so. An extenuating criteria to that condition would be that the ship's gunners have been authorized to initiate fire against the enemy -- that is, without waiting to be attacked before opening hostile action of their own. Such a ship, by that last circumstance, effectively becomes *a ship of war.*

Having become a *ship of war* does not necessarily mean that such a ship loses her identity as a *merchant vessel* nor does it necessarily mean that crewmembers lose their status as *merchant seamen.* World War II gives the best example of this. During the early part of World War II, following the beginning of nationalization of the United States merchant marine in April of 1942, the seagoing personnel were, therefore, considered as having become *employees of the United States* since in the majority of cases the ships they sailed were operated by agents under the contractual employ of the government's War Shipping Administration. The federalized condition did not alter the seaman's basic identity as a merchant mariner, for the ships remained under the laws and regulations governing merchant vessels of the United States. It did initially evoke a quasi-status where, in addition to merchant seamen's rights and privileges, the mariner was also encompassed under federal benefits normally granted only to seamen serving on *public vessels.* Temporary legislation would be drafted to change that multiplicity; that would not occur until March of 1943 through an Act of Congress, a subject which will be discussed later in this paper.

For a ship's crew to part company from the status of being merchant seamen, it must first undergo a transformation which under law removes it from being subject to the statutes governing the merchant marine.

Under United States law, there is a clear distinction between those statutes governing merchant seamen and merchant ships as opposed to those statutes governing public vessels and their crews when such ships are being operated by the military. The body of law developed over time which makes up this distinction was reviewed and thoroughly discussed in a U.S. Supreme Court certiorari delivered on May 26, 1952. The Supreme Court had before it two separate cases, namely Case 401, *Johansen v. United States,* and Case 414, *Mandel v. United States.* Case 401 involved Konrad G. Johansen, an Army civilian seaman injured aboard ship in 1949. He had attempted to sue the government under the rights enjoyed by merchant seamen. A Court of Appeals (Second Circuit) had upheld the government in denying Johansen the right to sue. Case 414 involved the death in 1944 of Assistant Engineer Robert W. Dillehay whose ship, the U.S. Army tug *LT-221,* struck a mine on October 15 of that year while attempting to enter the harbor of Cagliari, Sardinia.[1] Following the war, the heir of Dillehay (Mandel) made claim against the government on the basis that the deceased was a merchant seaman entitled to the fiscal rights inherent to that occupational calling. (Under U.S. law, the rights of merchant seamen include the avenue to sue and recover from the vessel's owner.) A lower District Court had overruled the government's motion to dismiss petitioner Mandel's suit for damages; however, as in the case of the Johansen suit, a Court of Appeals (Third Circuit) reversed that lower court's decision.

In its determinations leading to the certiorari of Cases 401 and 414, the Supreme Court determined that neither Johansen nor Dillehay were serving on merchant ships at the time of their respective injuries or deaths, and that they therefore were not merchant seamen, being instead *public vessel seamen.* In making the joint certiorari, the Supreme Court cited a series of U.S. laws and juridical rulings dating back to the late nineteenth century. A review of those statutes as well as those past juridical rulings, all of which preceded cases 401 and 414 can be helpful in understanding how the difference in identification between the two groups of seamen had become established.

In 1890, and later in 1917, the federal courts indicated their understanding of the difference between merchant marine ships and their crews as against *public vessels* and their crews. No body of law to that time had clearly spelled out the distinction.

---

[1] In 1998 Italian divers found the wreck of a large tug off the harbor of Cagliari, Sardinia. According to correspondence from the diver to the H. Lee White Maritime Museum in Oswego, NY, artifacts recovered from the wreck identified it as the *USAT LT-221.*

Merchant Seamen *in this title* [Title 46, U.S.C., Ed.] *simply means seamen in private vessels as distinguished from seamen in the Navy or public vessels, and seamen employed on private vessels of all nations are* 'merchant seamen' *and literally included in this phrase.* [2]

Prior to World War I, it had been generally recognized in the United States that ships belonging to the U.S. Government were all *public ships* and were therefore held exempt from the laws and regulations governing *merchant ships*. On June 17, 1917, this understanding was partially reversed, albeit temporarily, by Presidential Order applicable to merchant ships requisitioned under the authority of the *Shipping Act of 1916*. The Presidential Order was, however, explicit in continuing exemptions to those vessels in the service of the Army or Navy. It appears that the Presidential Order of 1917, as issued under the authority of the then extant War Powers Acts, was the first distinction made during World War I which separated publicly owned and/or publicly operated merchant ships and their crews from those ships of the civilian-manned military and naval auxiliary services. The 1917 order stated that requisitioned merchant ships:

> *...shall not have the status of a public ship and shall be subject to all laws and regulations governing merchant vessels. When, however, the requisitioned vessel is engaged in the service of the War or Navy Departments, the vessel shall have the status of a public ship and the masters, officers, and crew should become the immediate employees and agents of the United States with all the rights and duties of such, the vessel passing completely into the possession of the masters, officers, and crew absolutely under the control of the United States.* [3]

On October 25, 1919, the Congress made permanent the spirit of the Presidential Order of 1917 by legislating that all *public vessels,* other than those owned or under the demise (bareboat charter) control of the Army or Navy, were to come within the purview of the *U.S. Navigation and Inspection Laws.* [4] These are the laws presently encompassed within Title 46 of the U.S. Code. It is Title 46 that sets the governing authority under which the ships of the United States merchant marine and their officers and crews are regulated, and under which non-judicial punishment is applied by the master toward the maintaining of shipboard discipline. [5]

---

[2]   *U.S. v. Sullivan*, C.C. Or. 1890, 43 F602. See also *Scharrenberg v. Dollar SS Company*, Cal 1917, 38 S.Ct.28, 245 US 122, 62 L.Ed. 189.

[3]   *International Law Situations,* (Newport, RI: The Naval War College, 1930), p 49

[4]   Laws of 1919, *c. 82*, 41 Stat. 35. This statute was continued under recodification by the Acts of June 10, 1933, and June 29, 1936. Under the 1950 reorganization plan No. 21 § 305 and § 306, 15 F. R. 3178, 64 Stat. 1277, the language then and now within Title 46 § 363 states:

> *All steam vessels owned or operated by the Department of Commerce, or any corporation organized or controlled by it should be subject to all the provisions of Title 52 of the Revised Statutes for the regulation of steam vessels and acts amendatory thereof or supplemental thereto.*

The National Oceanic and Atmospheric Administration (NOAA), which maintains a fleet of survey and research vessels, is a subagency to the Department of Commerce; therefore, the vessels of NOAA (and its predecessor U.S. Coast and Geodetic Survey) operated under the same Inspection and Licensing laws (Title 46) which are applicable to the ships and seamen of the merchant marine.

[5]   During World War II, beginning in early 1943, merchant seamen serving on both private ships and WSA ships in war zones were placed -- at least technically -- under a limited scope of military and naval justice;

Following Congress's Act of October 25, 1919, the only vessels which were not governed by *Title 46, U.S.C.*, were those ships commissioned as naval vessels, those ships of the Army Mine Planter Service, and those ships operated as auxiliaries of the Army or Navy.[6] On auxiliary ships of the Army, the law that applied to the discipline of their civilian crews could be imposed under the Articles of War. However, this was a method rarely invoked in peacetime as the master's non-judicial authority and the criminal statutes were considered adequate toward enforcing discipline.[7]

Part of the legislated authority which governed merchant seamen -- but not *public vessel seamen* of the Army or Navy -- was Consular Authority which is applicable within terrestrial areas outside of U.S. jurisdiction. An opinion rendered in 1919 by the Judge Advocate General of the Army and quoted within a digest of Army legal policies published in 1942 makes a distinction in that particular regard between merchant seamen and *public vessel seamen*:

> *A consular officer of the United States has no jurisdiction whatsoever over the members of the crew of Army chartered transports or tugs, either when a member is under arrest or under confinement by direction of the master, or when in service on board vessel; and the master of an Army chartered transport or tug is not required in a foreign port to discharge or ship its crew before a consular officer.* [8]

The *Treaty of Berlin* as entered into by the warring powers following the surrender of Germany in 1918 outlined, among other things, the obligation under which Germany became obligated to compensate for Allied civilian property if lost or damaged by a German act of war. After the *Treaty of Berlin* had been ratified by the United States Senate in 1921, basic rules were put into place for establishing the grounds for claims against Germany.

1. Damage to persons or property caused by Germany during the active period of World War I.

2. The damaged person or company was civilian in character.[9]

---

however, this did not preclude or alter the civil authority of a master to impose non-judicial punishment under the authority allowed him by Title 46, U.S.C..

[6] As a practice, the Army Transport Service availed itself, through inter-agency agreement, of the services of the Steamboat Inspection Service, Department of Commerce, by asking that agency to conduct the same annual safety inspections of Army ships as were mandated under law (Title 46) for merchant ships. The Army -- at least for its large tonnage vessels -- also made a general practice of employing and upgrading its officers on the basis of licenses issued by the Steamboat Inspection Service. Thus the Army was able to run its fleet without its own separate inspection service but at the same time run it in conformity with various international safety-at-sea standards to which the United States was signatory.

[7] The crews of the Army Transport Service were civilians. Shipboard disciplinary measures as exercised by the ship masters generally followed the format as set by Title 46, U.S.C.; however, this discipline was not imposed under the authority of that Title. Instead, it was applied under the authority of stated Army Regulations drafted specific to the Army Transport Service.

[8] *Opinion of the Judge Advocate General of the Army,* 230.821, *Feb. 28, 1919.* As found within *Digest of Opinions of the Judge Advocate General of the Army, 1912-1940,* § 359 (11), (Washington, DC: Government Printing Office, 1942).

[9] *Report of the Mixed Claims Commission -- United States and Germany,* Administrative Decisions and Opinions of a General Nature, pp 75-201.

When addressing claims regarding shipping, the Germany and American members of the Mixed Claims Commission placed their major reliance on the exact employment of a ship and of its crew at the time of loss or damage. Was it civilian or military in character? A part of that answer lay with the charter terms under which a ship operated. These would have to be examined to determine the ship's relationship with the entity which employed it and of the status of the crews. United States Shipping Board (*USSB*) charters drafted during 1917-18 as they were entered into with private ship owners had stipulated under their standard formats that in pending emergencies, the subject ship could on immediate order be used for the support of the Army or the Navy; however, if the ship remained during that employment under the management of the *USSB* or of its agent, then the ship shall not have the status of a public ship but rather would remain subject to all the laws and regulations governing merchant vessels. By way of further explanation regarding the terms applicable to vessels taken under requisition by the military, the *USSB* charters stated that when a vessel is engaged in the service of the War or Navy Department and its physical operation is then undertaken by either one of those departments, then the vessel would take on the status of a *public ship, the master, officers, and crew shall become the immediate employees and agents of the United States with all the rights and duties thereof.*

With a foundation set in place, the Mixed Claims Commission subsequently drafted more definitive guidelines to be used in evaluating the maritime cases brought before it:

"I. *In order to bring a ship within the excepted class [military or naval character] she must have been operated by the United States at the time of her destruction for purposes directly in furtherance of a military operation against Germany or her allies.*

"II. *It is immaterial whether the ship was or was not owned by the United States; her possession, either actual or constructive, and her use by the United States in direct furtherance of a military operation against its then enemies constitutes the controlling test.*

"III. *So long as a ship is privately operated for private profit, she cannot be impressed with a military character, for only the Government can lawfully engage in warlike activities.*

"IV. *The fact that a ship was either owned or requisitioned by the Shipping Board, or the Fleet Corporation, and operated by one of them, either directly or through an agent, does not create even a rebuttable presumption that she was impressed with a military character.*

"V. *When, however, a ship either owned by or requisitioned by the United States during the period of belligerency passed into the possession and under the operation of either the War Department or the Navy Department of the United States, thereby becoming a public ship, her master, officers, and crew all being employed and paid by and subject to the orders of the United States, it is to be presumed that such possession, control, and operation by a military arm of the government focusing all of its powers and energies on actively waging war, were directly in furtherance of a military operation. Such control and operation of a ship will be treated by the Commission as prima facie, but not conclusive, evidence of her military character.*

"VI. *Neither (a) the arming for defensive purposes of a merchantman, nor (b) the manning of such armament by a naval gun crew, nor (c) her routing by the Navy Department of the United States for the purposes of avoiding the enemy, nor (d) the following by the civilian master of such merchantman of instructions given by the Navy Department for the defense of the ship when attacked by or when in danger of attack by the enemy, nor, (e) her seeking the protection of a convoy and submitting herself to naval instruction as to route and operation for the purpose of avoiding the enemy, or all these combined, will not suffice to impress such merchantmen with a military character.*

"VII. The facts in each case will be carefully examined and weighed and the Commission will determine whether or not the particular ship at the time of her destruction was operated by the United States directly in furtherance of a military operation against Germany or her allies. If she was so operated, she will fall within the excepted class, otherwise she will not.

The Commission next selected from its pending files twelve test cases involving claims for awards -- the claimants having stated that the ships involved were civilian in characteristics.

A. A. Raven	Lost March 14, 1918; requisitioned by U.S. and chartered to War Department; military cargo; armed; civil service crew
Almance	Lost Feb 5, 1918; requisitioned by U.S., under agency management for U.S.; commercial cargo; armed; merchant crew
John G. McCullough	Lost May 18, 1918; requisitioned by U.S. and chartered to War Department; military cargo; armed; civil service crew
Joseph Cudahy (Tanker)	Lost Aug. 17 1918; requisitioned by U.S. and chartered to War Department; military cargo; armed; civil service crew
Merak	Lost Aug 6, 1918; requisitioned by U.S., under agency management for U.S.; commercial cargo; unarmed; merchant crew
Montano (Tanker)	Lost July 31, 1917; privately owned and operated; military cargo; armed; merchant crew
Moreni (Tanker)	Lost June 12, 1917; privately owned and operated; commercial cargo; armed; merchant crew
Pinar De Rio	Lost June 8, 1918; requisitioned by U.S.; time chartered to shipping company operation; Commercial cargo; unarmed; merchant crew
Rochester	Lost Nov 2, 1917; privately owned and operated; commercial cargo; armed; merchant crew
Santa Maria	Lost Feb 25, 1918; requisitioned by U.S., under agency management for U.S.; commercial cargo; armed; merchant crew
Texel	Lost June 2, 1918; requisitioned by U.S., under agency management for U.S.; commercial cargo; unarmed; merchant crew
Tyler	Lost April 13, 1918; requisitioned by U.S., under agency management for U.S.; commercial cargo; armed; merchant crew

Of the above twelve ships which it had selected, the Commission deemed nine of them as having civilian character thus allowing the ship owners and the crews reparations awards. The three Army transports, *John G. McCullough, Joseph Cudahy,* and *A. A. Raven* were denied since in the Commission's opinion, each possessed military character.[10]

The judgments of the Mixed Claims Commission as made during the 1920s carry one step further the understanding of the separation of merchant shipping and that of public vessels in the employ of the armed forces. Further, those judgments help lay out a basis by which a ship should be considered a *ship of war* in the light of international law.

---

[10]   For those with further interest in the rationales as they were developed by the Mixed Claims Commission, refer to: *Mixed Claims Commission, U.S. and Germany, Administrative Decisions and Opinions of a General Nature to June 30, 1925.* Cases of specific interest relating to civilian employment categories as they were established by the Commission's work, consult the above for Christian Damsen, *United States v Germany,* Docket 4529, Decisions and Opinions 1925-26, 242, 259-263; Arthur Elliot Hungerford, ante, pp 173, 174.

During the year which followed the United States's entry into World War II, an issue arose over merchant seamen's status as that status was applied to those seamen employed on government owned vessels which were operated either directly by a civilian agency of the government or under management contract agreements on behalf of a civilian arm of the government. In the 1930s, a number of U.S. merchant seamen became employed upon ships belonging to and operated by the U.S. Maritime Commission, the crews being classed as civil service personnel. Starting in early 1942, the Maritime Commission's offshoot agency, the War Shipping Administration (WSA) took over the Maritime Commission's former ship operations. Seamen employed by the Maritime Commission then became hirees of WSA, either directly or indirectly through private agents designated by WSA and which operated under various forms of management contracts undertaken between those agents and WSA. In either case, the seamen so engaged would have been acknowledged as *employees of the United States*. As such, they came under the Federal Employees Compensation Act (FECA) and the Civil Service Retirement Act. In April of 1942, the War Shipping Administration, under authority of a Presidential proclamation, began the wholesale nationalization of the merchant marine. By mid-summer of 1942, WSA ship requisitions had been so widely applied that the overwhelming majority of U.S. merchant ships had been placed under federal operation -- their crews therefore having become employees of the United States. The Congress, apparently anticipating a huge post-war FECA disability pension debt, the result of the mounting dead and disabled seamen caused by enemy action and industrial accidents, drafted a remedial law to become known as the *Clarification Act.* This law was Public Law 17 of March 24, 1943. The *Clarification Act* removed officers and seamen directly employed through the War Shipping Administration program from the status of being *employees of the United States,* thus effectively eliminating such persons from the benefits of FECA as well as from the ability to earn civil service retirement credits. The *Clarification Act* remained in force for the period of the war, but it was automatically revoked following the war with the termination of other War Powers Acts. The Senate Report which had accompanied the introduction of the 1943 *Clarification Act* [Report No. 62, 78th Congress, 1st Session, Senate] gave, as one justification for the law, that *Present day operating conditions often make uncertain in some cases whether a vessel is a merchant or 'public vessel.'* With passage of the *Clarification Act* in March of 1943, that uncertainty was removed as henceforth all seamen who were employed either directly by WSA or through agency operating agreements, were to be considered in the same category as if they were, *employed on a privately owned and operated American vessel.* A purported benefit of the 1943 *Clarification Act* was that seamen on civilian ships would once again attain the right to sue and recover for personal damages, a benefit not granted to employees on *public vessels.* This looked good to the minds of Union lobbyists who had also feared the *employees of the United States* status of their members as being potentially destructive to the Unions' post-war role in the shipping industry. In reality, though, the merchant mariner's privilege to sue and recover damages was soon negated through the government's War Risk Insurance. The Maritime War Emergency Board, which administered War Risk Insurance, began ruling in almost every case that the cause of injury or death to seamen was considered war risk.[11] Collision, for instance, usually occurring either in blackout conditions or in a crowded harbor, was an event deemed by the Maritime War Emergency Board as being attributable to war conditions. The same reasoning began to apply to what in peacetime would be ordinary industrial accidents. The rules of negligence and unseaworthy conditions were no longer being applied. For the wartime seaman or his heirs, the only realistic option was acceptance of the Maritime War Emergency Board's award of the War Risk Insurance. For death, that award was limited to $5,000.

Civilian seamen employed upon vessels of the United States Army or Navy[12] as *public vessel seamen* were not addressed by the 1943 *Clarification Act* nor (according to the study of the matter made in 1952 by the Supreme Court concerning Case No. 401, *Johansen v. United States)* was it considered applicable in any way to civilians employed upon military operated vessels. The 1943 *Clarification Act* had applied solely to those seamen employed by the government on ships owned by or requisitioned by the War Shipping Administration, or by other government civilian agencies, or by private companies. Its language is clear in that all crewmembers on privately owned ships, as well as on WSA owned and/or operated ships, or those private ships operated under WSA agency agreements, were in the *merchant marine* and therefore were *merchant seamen.* Left out of the descriptive term *merchant marine* were those ships owned by the Army and/or operated under demise (bareboat) charter by the Army. These continued to be considered *public vessels,* and their crews *public vessel seamen.* The Supreme Court in *Johansen v. United States* used this difference in status as one of the primary arguments for its certiorari in both Case 401 and Case 414.

As said earlier, the Court had concluded that the right to sue and recover was never made applicable to *public vessel seamen.* In writing up the *Johansen v. United States* case, the Court further stated this when discussing the *Public Vessel Act of 1925.* It cited the two cases of *American Stevedores, Inc. v. Porello* 330, U.S. 446 (and) *Canadian Aviator Ltd. v. United States*, 324, U.S. 215. These were cases where non civil service crews were employed. The Courts had held that suits for damages were allowable; however, if crewmembers were held to be *employees of the United States,* then bringing suit would not be allowed. Under the *Public Vessel Act of 1925*, the Court's argument emphasized that *public vessel* employees had never legislatively been granted the right to sue and recover.

The Supreme Court also argued in its certiorari for *Johansen v. United States* that the *Suit in Admiralty Act of 1920*[13] gave a broad remedy to seamen on United States merchant vessels but that it did not extend the benefits of that coverage to *public vessel seamen.* The Court commented that an extension of such coverage to *public vessel seamen* had been proposed in the Congress but that had been defeated.

---

[11] The Maritime War Emergency Board was a joint agency of the War Shipping Administration and the Department of Labor. This agency, in addition to administering War Risk Insurance, established merchant marine base pay rates, war zone bonuses, attack bonuses, and related agenda.

[12] During the early part of World War II, there were probably around a dozen vessels (cargo ships and at least one salvage tug) operated by the Navy's Naval Transport Service (NTS) with civilian crews. These were, of course, classed as *public vessels* in the same sense as were Army transports.

[13] 41 Stat. 525, 46 U.S.C. § 742

The Supreme Court made the point, on page 440 of its Opinion, that the government had established a uniform compensation for *injuries or death for those in armed services*. It later explained that *duties and obligations of civilian and military members of a crew of a* public vessel *are much the same*. This same rationale had been emphatically stated within the opinion of the Court of Appeals in *Mandel v. United States*. The Court of Appeals was quoted by the Solicitor General to have reasoned:

> *The typical makeup of the personnel of public vessels is a crew of employees some of whom are in the Armed Forces, some of whom are civilians. They are all said to be subject to the same discipline while engaged in the particular voyage.*

Having said this, the Court of Appeals had then further reinforced its position:

> *The Second Circuit has twice concluded that the military components of the crews of public vessels cannot sue....*

In like manner the Court of Appeals had denied to the civilian crewman plaintiff [*Mandel v. United States*] the right to sue. In the hearing for that case as it was argued before the Supreme Court, the Solicitor General had put it quite simply:

> *...military authorities have absolute power of control, enforced by rigorous sanctions over the civil service crewmembers no less than those of the military component.* [14]

The history of U.S. law and government policy shows a clear distinction between *public vessel seamen* and *merchant seamen*. This began with the Presidential order of 1917 and was made legislative in its nature by Congress in 1919. It was carried through in the *Admiralty Act of 1920* and again with the *Clarification Act of March 24, 1943* [Public Law 17]. A juridical understanding of the identification of the two seamen groups, as being separate and apart from each other, was comprehensively endorsed by the certiorari of the United States Supreme Court in the cases of *Johansen v. United States* and *Mandel v. United States* as decided on May 26, 1952.

~

From the diplomatic viewpoint, although not directly germane to the decisions arrived at in the cases of *Johansen v. United States* or *Mandel v. United States,* it is interesting to look at the subject of *public ships* as it was viewed under international law during the first decade of the twentieth century.

The legal status of U.S. Army transports became a subject of controversy during 1900 when the matter arose at a number of foreign locations. One such place was Nagasaki, Japan, where a coaling depot had been established by the U.S. Army Quartermaster Department. Army transports routing to the Philippines following the Spanish surrender at Manila were stopping at Japan for coal. Nagasaki was also used as a recoaling stop for those transports in support of the American participation with the *International Column* engaged in the relief of Peking. Japanese port officials claimed that the Army transports stopping there were subject to the same

---

[14]   Brief for the United States, Cases 401 and 414, in the Supreme Court of the United States, October term 1951, p 39. Within 191 *Federal Reporter,* 2nd Series, *Mandel v. United States* No. 10385, pp 167, 168.

duties normally made applicable to merchant ships. The Army officer who had been detailed as the resident Depot Quartermaster protested, but with little success. During one replenishment, a crewmember aboard the *USAT Thomas* assaulted a Japanese national who was aboard that transport engaged in stowing coal. The Japanese police wanted to arrest the seaman, but the attempt was resisted by the Depot Quartermaster backed by the American Consul. The Consul took the case before the Japanese Imperial Government and obtained a ruling that Army transports had the full status of public vessels, being entitled to the same immunities and privileges of vessels of war belonging to nations in amity as that status is recognized under international law.[15] The Japanese ruling not only exempted the seaman from local justice but it settled the question of port duties as well.

The issue over the status of military transports had also arisen in Hong Kong. In that situation, acting under U.S. Army instructions, the master of *SS Ohio*, time chartered to the Army, refused to pay British harbor dues and other levies normally imposed against merchant ships but not against vessels of war. He argued that his ship was a public vessel and was therefore immune from such charges. The British Governor's office informed American authorities that the ship would not be billed if it was determined that United States law entitled the ship with the status of a public vessel. The Army forwarded the question to the U.S. State Department which passed it along to the Treasury Department for review. The ruling given was that time-chartered merchant ships were not entitled in the United States to public vessel status in the same manner as were ships belonging to or being directly operated by the Army or the Navy. The British authorities at Hong Kong accepted that ruling. Thereafter, the Army's own ships or those under its demise charter were held free of Hong Kong's port charges; however, those transports under time charter and which were being operated by shipping companies were charged.[16]

Another country was heard from on the issue when the Khedive of Egypt granted immunity as a public vessel to any ship (apparently whether directly operated by the military or under time charter to the military) provided its cargo consisted entirely of military materiel not intended to be channeled into commercial markets.[17]

---

[15]   Depot QM, Nagasaki, Letter to Chief QM Div. Philippines, August 16, 1900, from QMG file 156930; American Consul Nagasaki, Letter to Depot QM, Nagasaki, August 15, 1900, from QMG file 156930.

[16]   American Consul General, Hong Kong, Cable 149, to the Hon David J. Hill, December 2, 1899, QMG file 146801; Secretary of the Treasury Letter to Secretary of State, January 22, 1900, QMG file 146801.

[17]   Secretary of State Letter to Secretary of War, December 7, 1900, from Secretary of War file 4500. At this time, ships time chartered by the Army on the United States east coast were being routed to Pacific service via the Mediterranean and the Suez Canal.

APPENDIX C

FIRST TO LAND
1st TRANSPORT WORKERS BATTALION: AEF

As of the entry of the United States into World War I and prior to U.S. east coast port operations being taken over by the U.S. Army's Embarkation Service, the shipment of troops fell under the aegis of the Army Quartermaster Corps -- specifically the Army Transport Service (ATS). During the preparation for the departure to France of the first troop convoy in June of 1917, members of a French advisory commission then in Washington warned of difficulty to be expected in unloading transports once they arrived at the French port of St. Nazaire, explaining that the only available stevedore labor consisted of women and children together with a few prisoners of war. The French suggested that the Americans send over stevedores from the United States. The ATS at New York was given only five days to assemble such a labor force if it was to leave as part of the convoy. The requirement called for five hundred civilian dock laborers to be hired under a one-year contract. At the time, a stevedore strike was taking place in the ports of Boston and New York. Although it was thought possible for some recruiting to take place from that labor pool, it was considered unwise since stevedores at Boston and New York were largely of Irish extraction then considered of questionable loyalty. In 1916, part of the population of southern Ireland had broken out into open rebellion against the British, and most Irish were generally thought to be sympathetic to the German cause. This sentiment -- as it was believed at the time -- pervaded much of the Irish-American population, including even those second and third generation Irish.

Ports from Baltimore southward to New Orleans were therefore chosen as the best places to recruit. In those ports, blacks were predominant in the stevedore labor force. Recruiting efforts done on practically an overnight basis proved highly successful; and as the men were gathered, they were sent by train to New York -- all arriving within the stipulated 5-day period. When a delay developed in convoy departure creating a hiatus of a day or two before the troopships could be boarded, the blacks were taken to Governors Island in outer New York Harbor where temporary housing was assigned for them. While there, the men, despite their civilian status, were uniformed and ordered onto the parade ground where they were taught the rudiments of close-order drill. They were then organized into stevedore companies of fifty men each and placed under the command of a white Army officer. From the scant accounts dealing with their employment, apparently none of the men entertained second thoughts as to what they were about to undertake or expressed resentment over the regimentation they were experiencing.

Once the convoy arrived in France, the black stevedores were among the first Americans to go ashore where they were immediately put to work handling the convoy's cargo. Gen. John J. Pershing was quoted as making favorable comment as to the professional way the blacks handled ships' gear as well as their deportment and amenability to discipline. Pershing wired Washington requesting an additional eight hundred stevedores, stating that the ones on hand ... *look like and behave like soldiers, therefore make them as such.*

The record is silent as to whether the original five hundred blacks were militarized or if they finished out their obligated year as civilians under contract. However, all stevedores subsequently sent from the United States were military personnel. By the war's end, four full regiments of stevedores (probably blacks) were working in the French ports.

Major source: *Report of Chief of the Transportation Service for 1919,* pp 129, 130. During the invasion of Cuba in 1898, Pershing served as an officer commanding black troops. That service is said to have influenced him in a positive way as to the value of blacks as soldiers.

APPENDIX D

THE POLISH AMERICANS
1914 - 1920

The events which had led to the foreign enlistment of Americans of Polish descent is rarely mentioned within the literature surrounding the First World War; nevertheless, that involvement was distinctly germane to the peace which followed. The story begins in the eighteenth century when, between 1772 and 1795, the Monarchy of Poland underwent a series of partitions by Austria and by Prussia. The last of those partitions eliminated Poland as a sovereign state for the next 123 years; however, as a people, the Poles were never willingly submissive toward either their Prussian or Austrian rulers. When war broke out in 1914, thousands of Poles made their way to France to fight in the trenches on the Western Front under the banner of the French Foreign Legion, their goal being a free Poland, if and when the Central Powers were defeated. Some estimates have it that almost half of the Poles who made up the Polish contingents within the French Foreign Legion of 1914-1918 were American citizens who had left the United States between 1914 and 1917 for the purpose of joining the Polish contingents fighting with the French.

During 1918, the major Allies -- France, Britain, and the United States -- decided that the terms of peace with the Central Powers should assure that Poland would again become a nation. From the Allied viewpoint, the cease-fire agreement between the Bolsheviks and Germany entered into on March 13, 1918, on the Eastern Front gave particular importance to the re-establishment of Poland. Once the Allies had defeated the Central Powers, a reborn Poland would serve as a buffer between the Bolsheviks and Europe.

In Paris on June 22, 1918, Poland was formally declared a sovereign nation, and it became part of the alliance of the Western Powers. With that declaration came the establishment of a Polish Army formed in large part from those Polish contingents which had fought within the French Foreign Legion.

Following the German surrender in November, the new Polish Army was shipped to Poland where it provided a stabilizing presence while the rebuilding nation underwent the formulation of civic government. By 1920, Poland -- once again a part of the map of Europe -- partially demobilized which allowed the release from military service of those American citizens who had helped restore the country. Those men were then returned to the United States as passengers aboard U.S. Army transports.

Source: *Report of Chief of Transportation Service, 1920,* p 10. Also Francis W. Halsey, *History of the World War*, Volume V, (New York and London: Funk and Wagnalls Company, 1919), pp 192-195. In his work, Halsey seems to infer that following the Armistice of November 1918 when the Polish National Army left for Poland, additional Polish-Americans enlisted in its ranks. Whether that actually happened and if so, whether men were released from the American Army in France to undertake such enlistment, could not be uncovered through our own research efforts.

APPENDIX E

THE STORY OF ONE ARMY TRANSPORT SERVICE MASTER

Unfortunately, little has come down to us by way of written accounts from those who chose a career path as an officer aboard Army ships. An exception is the memoir of William A. Parta, who was born in 1888 and as a young child immigrated with his parents from northern Sweden (now known as Lapland) to settle in Minnesota. Educational opportunities were then sparse in that part of the country, and young Parta's attendance at school was limited to the first three grades. At the age of 15, he left home, eventually reaching the Pacific coast where he suffered through an assortment of adventures. In 1906 at the age of 17, he enlisted in the Navy at San Francisco. This was the year of the great San Francisco earthquake, and while undergoing training, Parta's recruit class was sent into the city as part of a Provost guard, albeit, as he relates, with unloaded rifles.

Following boot training, Parta was assigned to the Asiatic Fleet. He and his fellow recruits were transported to Manila aboard the *USS Lawton*, then being used to supply that fleet. Although steam propelled, this ship was rigged as a topsail schooner for purposes of training outbound recruits in the use of sail. Parta recalled that each morning while crossing the Pacific, the recruits were ordered up the ratlines on one side of the ship to the top of the mainmast and down again via the ratlines on the other side -- the last man down receiving an unauthorized kick on the rear end for his tardiness.

On arrival in Manila, Parta was ordered to the light cruiser *USS Baltimore*, being shortly transferred to the heavy gunboat *USS Helena* which became part of the Yangtze River Patrol. Parta returned to San Francisco after his enlistment was up but soon missed Navy life and reenlisted -- a move which brought promotion to a quartermaster rating.

Following the end of his second enlistment, Parta worked ashore for a time and then entered the merchant marine, signing on a sail vessel outbound from Texas with cargo for Italy. Attacked by a German submarine, the vessel went down west of Gibraltar. After his repatriation to the United States in 1917, he reenlisted in the Navy and was assigned to the minesweeping force working the approaches to the French ports. There Parta experienced the confusion and ineptness of crews hastily thrown together in a wartime melange where professional skills and the old Navy way of doing things were in short supply. After his discharge in 1919, Parta sat for examination before the Steamboat Inspection Service as a 2nd Mate and received that license. The early 1920s was a period during which growing labor militancy had destroyed much of the ordered structure surrounding shipboard life. As a ship's officer having to deal with the problems which ensued, Parta witnessed some of the worst of those manifestations.

By 1931, Parta had upgraded his license to Chief Mate. Many shipping firms were folding at the time, and jobs were harder and harder to come by. Attracted by the job security and benefits offered under civil service, he applied and was accepted as a 3rd Officer in the Army Transport Service (ATS). In 1932, that security was threatened when yet another attempt was made by the shipping companies to abolish the ATS through Congressional action. The attempt failed, thanks in large part to the leadership of Captain Bror E. Torning, master of the *USAT Chateau Thierry*. Torning solicited the lobby efforts of firms which were suppliers of goods and services to the Army fleet. Fearful of losing the substantial business that such shipping provided, these firms launched a deluge of mail and telegrams to the Congress citing the disastrous effects that an ATS closure would have on their businesses. Torning even enjoined New York's dynamic mayor, Fiorello H. LaGuardia, who, as Parta relates, added substantial political muscle to the campaign's success. Parta's assistance to Torning in that effort, together with a demonstrated competence as a ship's officer, were to soon win him a promotion to master with assignment to the Philippines where he took over command of the 900-ton interisland passenger vessel *USAT General John McE. Hyde*. A good part of the *Hyde's* function involved the transporting of senior officers of the Philippine command on inspection trips throughout the archipelago. This was a demanding and difficult task for a master since in those years, the southern islands were largely devoid of navigational aids and the only charts had been made from Spanish surveys of the mid-nineteenth century which were of dubious accuracy.[1] Parta's competence in navigating those dangerous waters and his untiring diligence in performing his job were witnessed by those Army officers who had been engaged on the inspection trips. Those contacts resulted in his next assignment as Marine Superintendent for ATS operations in the Hawaiian Islands. Transferred to Honolulu in 1939, he served there throughout World War II.

In 1946, Captain Parta was asked to accept sea duty, an invitation he happily accepted. His first assignment came as master of the hospital ship *USAHS Mercy,* followed by a succession of troopship and transport commands including *USAT Cardinal O'Connell* and *USAT Major General Charles Gould Morton*. When the

---

[1]   During the early 1930s, the U.S. Coast and Geodetic Survey began surveying Philippine waters; but charts from that effort were still well into the future.

Army's oceangoing fleet was transferred to the Military Sea Transport Service in 1950, Parta made the transition over to Navy employment. His last command before retirement was USNS *General Nelson M. Walker*.

By the time of his retirement in the mid 1950s, William A. Parta had served over 40 years in the profession of mariner, 33 of those years having been in government service -- a good part of that as ship's master.[2]

---

[2]   The memoirs of Captain William A. Parta were published in a series of articles in the Finnish-American weekly *Amerikan Uutiset* between 1984 and 1986. Parta appropriately titled his memoirs *SAGA -- The Story of a New American and an Old Mariner*.

APPENDIX F

THE CRYSTAL PROJECT, 1941 - 43

Starting in 1941, a critical need arose for transporting bomber aircraft to Britain. In response to that need, the planes were flown from the United States and Canada, utilizing landing fields in Greenland and Iceland which had been constructed specifically for that purpose. That air route could not, however, accommodate fighter aircraft due to the long distances between stopovers. Fighters were being sent over by ship, requiring that they be broken down into component units and boxed, a process involving an inordinate amount of time and labor for reassembling once at the overseas destinations. Besides that, there was the menace of the German submarine force which by 1941 was beginning to extract a heavy toll of ships. Getting assembled fighters to Britain in relative safety and in the numbers needed required an air route with shorter flight legs so as to accommodate the lesser endurance of that type of aircraft. As envisioned, such a route would have its start in northern Montana with the first layover to be the port town of Churchill located on Hudson Bay's western shore. The flight path would then take an easterly course line across the Canadian subarctic territories with stopovers to be developed on the Labrador coast or perhaps more to the north -- possibly as far north as Baffin Island. The flight course would then be direct to Greenland, then to Iceland, and on to the British Isles. The endeavor to create the planned route was to be given the code name *Crystal Project.*

The three subarctic bases (Crystals I, II, and III) which were constructed owed their conception, and in large part their development, to five men: Elliot Roosevelt (FDR's son) was one of the scheme's originators following his reconnoitering of the Labrador coast on an over-flight in 1940 in company with the

Arctic aviator Burnt Balchen. As the President's son, Elliot would lend the project a certainty and a priority which it might not otherwise have had. Another major player was Alexander Forbes, by profession a psychiatrist, but by avocation a self-taught topographer who had visited and surveyed the Labrador coast as a yachtsman and later by air in the 1930s.[1] John T. Crowell, a master mariner with extensive experience within subarctic and Arctic waters, would be brought in during the planning stage, having been commissioned into the Army Air Corps specifically for the project. The fourth prime mover was Paul Grening, a master mariner and a civilian employee of the Army Transport Service. Grening would hold primary responsibility for gathering together the shipping which would ferry north the men and construction materials for the bases. Since the purpose of Crystal was aeronautic in nature, it came under the overall purview of the Army Air Corps with Lt. Col. Robert W. C. Wimsatt, an Air Corps officer, appointed as project commander.

Besides the U.S. Army Air Corps, a number of other service branches were also involved: Topographical surveying of the sites and their later construction fell to the U.S. Army Corps of Engineers. (The actual construction was performed by civilian contractors employed by the Corps.) All hydrographic surveying and chart preparation was conducted by Alexander Forbes who, in the capacity of a naval reserve officer, was placed on that assignment by the Hydrographic Office of the U.S. Navy. The U.S. Coast Guard provided aerial reconnaissance; laid out buoyage; and at one point, assigned its commissioned trawlers to assist the Army Transport Service in the movement north of men and materiel. The Crystal Project would employ not only American vessels but also those flying the Norwegian flag and in one case, the flag of Free France. Despite the assortment of participating entities, the project, wrought as it was with difficulty, went surprisingly well with little friction arising between the services or nationalities. One is led to surmise that much of the inter-service harmony may have existed because few of those involved had belonged to the military establishment before the war, and they therefore placed minimal emphasis on the encroachment of service turf by another. Another contributing to the relatively smooth operation was that the project's commander, Lt. Colonel Wimsatt, although a career officer, had the wisdom to leave most of the decision making to the experienced Arctic hands.

Alexander Forbes was called to Washington in the spring of 1941 and after being briefed, was asked for advice as to the suitability of northern Labrador for the construction of air strips. He hedged his answer, explaining that more survey flights as well as on-the-ground inspection would be needed before a concrete judgment could be offered. He was thereupon entered as a civil service employee of the War Department and flown to Gander, Newfoundland, where he reported to Elliot Roosevelt who had been placed in charge of an aerial reconnaissance initially to be

---

[1]   Forbes would later publish a participant's account of the World War II Crystal Project, the only such account giving more than a superficial description of the project. Alexander Forbes, *The Quest for a Northern Air Route,* Cambridge, MA: Harvard University Press, 1953. In 1932, following his visit to Labrador, Forbes published a paper titled "Surveying in Northern Labrador," *Geographical Review,* Volume XXII; and in 1938 an article, *Northern Labrador from the Air,* American Geographical Society.

confined to the Labrador coast.[2] The sites to be surveyed were the ones photographed by Forbes in the 1930s and more recently by the Roosevelt-Balchen over-flight of 1940. One location in particular which was to be looked at was the elevated terrace along the south shore of Goose Bay. But after reflying the area at low level, Roosevelt and Forbes agreed that neither it nor a number of other locations which earlier had seemed feasible appeared acceptable. Upon their return to Gander, Roosevelt secured Washington's authorization to over-fly the Ungava Bay region of northern Quebec, concentrating on an area near Fort Chimo. Fort Chimo had long been one of the major northern trading posts of the Hudson Bay Company with a history going back as far as the early nineteenth century. It was served by the Koksoak River, a water course over a mile in width which presented itself from the air as being extremely shallow. According to the Canadians, coastal steamers of medium draft were able to reach Fort Chimo which was considered to be the head of navigation for larger vessels.[3] Roosevelt was informed by the Canadian authorities that during the summer months a hundred or more Eskimos used Fort Chimo as a supply base. From there, several auxiliary sloops of 30 feet or so in length were known to navigate the river above Fort Chimo transporting Eskimo families to their seasonal hunting and fishing grounds.

Making the flight to Fort Chimo by float plane, Roosevelt and Forbes sighted a large flat area about four miles upriver from the post. They landed across the river from the post and from there hiked upstream to confirm what they had seen from the air. By pacing off the area, they estimated that two or more runways of up to 5,000 feet in length could be constructed without any undue amount of earth moving. They then returned to Gander from where Roosevelt continued on to Washington to recommend the site. The War Department approved the recommendation, and Crystal I now became a new place on the map to which considerable funds and much human energy would be expended over the next two years.

The Crystal Project called for two additional landing locations north of the Hudson Straits. One, to be code-named Crystal II, was to be somewhere in the area of Frobisher Bay on Baffin Island.[4] The other, Crystal III, was to also be on Baffin Island, but farther north and east by around 150 miles at a location on or near Cumberland Sound. Since both locations were too distant from Gander to be reconnoitered by float plane and since ground inspection would be necessary, transportation by ship was required. Due to the lateness of the season, once the sites had been selected, base camps would have to be established for over-wintering so that work could begin in the spring well before ice breakup allowed ships to reach that far north again. These requirements meant immediately pulling together enough vessels to

---

[2]   Although Alexander Forbes's first contact with the Crystal Project was as a civilian employee of the War Department, he would later be called to active duty as a naval officer. That activation occurred later when he was assigned the task of hydrographic survey team leader in charge of mapping the approaches to both Crystal I and Crystal II.

[3]   At Fort Chimo, the range of tide is almost 30 feet, and it was only at the state of high tide that the river was considered navigable by ships of any real size. The coastal steamers which normally plied the Koksoak from Ungava Bay to Fort Chimo would start up the river only after the flood tide was well underway. Even then, most ship masters using the route employed a local pilot.

[4]   Frobisher Bay is a deep inlet, *thrice the area of Long Island Sound. It penetrates Baffin Island for 170 miles in a northwesterly direction. Forty-five miles wide at the mouth, the bay tapers to fifteen miles near the head where it receives the waters of two rivers.* Forbes, p 51.

carry north the needed men and construction materials -- the assemblage of shipping becoming the responsibility of Paul Grening. From the New England fishing fleets, Grening chartered five diesel powered trawlers (complete with their regular crews) which were then sent on to Halifax. They were: *Fabia, Flow, Cambridge, Lark,* and *Cormorant.*[5] Two other trawlers, *Polarbjorn* and *Quest,* of Norwegian registry, located at the time in Nova Scotia, were also chartered. At Halifax, the American and Norwegian trawlers were to load base camp personnel, radio equipment, pre-prefab housing, and enough fuel and other supplies to subsist the base camps over the coming winter. All of this was to be brought to Halifax from Boston on the Army freighter *USAT Sicilien.* At Halifax, the freighter's cargo would go aboard the trawlers to the extent of whatever could be stowed in their holds. Three of the trawlers would be selected, each to tow a barge. A medium-sized bulldozer was lashed down on one barge. It was to be delivered on site at Fort Chimo to be used in leveling the landing strip there. The trawlers would then follow *USAT Sicilien* to a final departure point on the northern Labrador coast. There each of them would take on a deck load of lumber from *USAT Sicilien.* The trawlers would then split into three groups, the first group to go to Fort Chimo (Crystal I). The second group was to proceed to Frobisher Bay (Crystal II) and the third to a point at the northeast end of the Cumberland Peninsula near where it was thought a site for Crystal III could be found.

Grening had tentatively selected the harbor of Hebron on the coast of Labrador as the place where the trawlers were to take on their deck loads from *USAT Sicilien.* Lt. Cdr. Charles J. Hubbard, USNR, who had been chosen to accompany the expedition was a long-time acquaintance of Forbes and a man with considerable experience in the Arctic. He argued that Hebron was a poor choice as there were deadly tide rips along that section of the coast in addition to uncharted ledges. He recommended Port Burwell on the southern side of the Hudson Straits as a substitute location, a recommendation approved by Wimsatt.

Once the loading of the trawlers had started at Halifax, it was discovered that their holds did not have the capacity to handle all the cargo that had come north aboard *USAT Sicilien.* Hurriedly, the *Selis,* a Norwegian Navy anti-submarine trawler which Grening located at Lunenberg, Nova Scotia, was time chartered from the Norwegian government and sent to join the expedition at Halifax. Even with *Selis* added, a good part of the supplies still remained aboard *USAT Sicilien,* necessitating that the freighter continue beyond Port Burwell to the selected Crystal II and III locations. Prior to leaving for Port Burwell, the command arrangements for each of the base camps was decided upon as was the allotment of the trawlers which would be in support of each base group.

- *Crystal I,* Fort Chimo: Lt. Commander Schlossbach, USNR. Schlossbach's polar experience had included over-wintering in the Arctic when he had been associated with the British explorer Sir Hubert Wilkins. Trawler support: *Fabia, Flow, Cambridge.*

---

[5]   Within the trawler fleets then operating out of New England ports, there were two vessels named *Lark.* The *Lark* Grening chartered was of 237 tons, owned by Cape Cod Trawling Corp. of Boston. Following her civilian service with the Crystal Project, she was taken over by the Coast Guard (31 July 1942) and renamed *USCGC Amarok.*

- *Crystal II,* Frobisher Bay: Major John T. Crowell, U.S. Army Air Corps. Crowell had sailed as master of the schooner *Thebaud* during Donald MacMillan's Arctic explorations, and like Schlossbach, he had over-wintered north of the Arctic circle. Trawler support: *Lark, Polarbjorn.*[6]

- *Crystal III,* the most northern base to be located on or adjacent to the Cumberland Peninsula, Baffin Island. Lt. Cdr. Charles J. Hubbard was to be in command until a base location was selected. The over-wintering party was then to be commanded by a Captain Dyer, Army Air Corps. Trawler support: *Cormorant, Quest.*[7]

Upon arrival at Port Burwell, the expedition found the place deserted except for two aged Eskimo women living in an old hut. The Hudson Bay Company's post which had once existed there stood abandoned, most of its buildings either demolished or in ruins. There were no usable docks, so the offloading from *USAT Sicilien* to the trawlers was done at anchor. The trawler group scheduled for Crystal I was the first to take on its deck loads; on October 9, it left for Fort Chimo on the Koksoak River. As soon as the Crystal II and Crystal III trawlers received their loads, they sailed north for Baffin Island.

Crystal I

The three trawlers assigned to Crystal I left Port Burwell on a course which would take them on a southerly routing across Ungava Bay toward the mouth of the Koksoak River. Aboard one of them was Forbes who had been assigned the responsibility for preparing sketch charts of the approaches to that river and its channel up to Fort Chimo. The Forbes party's arrival at the mouth of the river coincided with maximum ebb tide. Since the current was raging, upstream passage was precluded until the tide slacked. Schlossbach ordered the trawlers anchored, but this proved a difficult task as the skipper of *Cambridge* soon discovered. With its anchor bouncing along the rocky bottom, *Cambridge* went hard aground in a matter of a few short minutes. Meanwhile, the *Fabia* had anchored at what later proved to be the position of maximum current. Her anchor cable paid out at such a rapid rate that the man on the anchor winch could not brake off the drum. Barely in time, *Fabia's* skipper throttled his engine, and while the vessel was headed in an upstream direction, the winchman was able to gain enough slack in the anchor cable to lock down the dogs on the winch drum. The trawler came up hard on the cable, and that time, the anchor held. The not-so-lucky *Cambridge,* hard aground with its hull pressed against an underwater boulder, was heeling to the point where she began taking on water through her engine room ventilators. Fortunately, the crew was able to seal things off, and around midnight, the rising tide floated her off without any serious damage. Early the next morning, all three trawlers headed upriver on the flood tide toward Fort Chimo. By October 18,

---

[6] Although it is fairly certain that the *Selis* accompanied the expedition past Port Burwell, Forbes does not tell us to which group she was assigned. However by his definitive statements as to the composition of the trawler groups assigned to Crystal I and Crystal III, it is probable that *Selis* was with the Crystal II group.

[7] The first names of Lt. Commander Schlossbach or Captain Dyer were not given within any of the sources we used.

Cambridge and *Flow* had been offloaded and were headed downriver on the ebb tide, but without a pilot. This was a mistake which soon became apparent as they neared the river's mouth. A ledge which had escaped everyone's attention when going upriver on the flood tide now showed itself standing well out of the water, necessitating that the trawlers double back to successfully find a safe channel. When later joined by *Fabia* at the river's mouth, the group cleared Ungava Bay, and by October 22 the trawlers were passing through the Straits of Belle Isle on their way back to Boston.

Crystal II and III

By early October, the subarctic waters of northern Canada were normally vacated by shipping; but by the second week of October, the job of locating sites for Crystal II and III was just getting started. Navigating the waters off Baffin Island so late in the year was not going to be an easy matter. No one on the mission had any first-hand knowledge of the area. Hubbard, in charge of the Crystal III group, had at least over-flown the region, and he hoped that he could find his way into the Tangnirtung, a deep fjord far up into Cumberland Sound where one of the few settlements that far north was located. There he hoped to find someone who would be willing to guide him in his search for a site. When his group arrived at the settlement, an epidemic of influenza was underway which had impacted most of the population (primarily Eskimo). The one Eskimo who knew the coast well enough to assist them was sick abed on the verge of pneumonia. When told of the urgency of Crystal III to the war effort, the settlement's doctor filled his patient with sulfa drugs and had him carried aboard the *Cormorant* where it was hoped the man would recover. In three days, the Eskimo was well enough to stand upright on the bridge, thus enabling Hubbard to move south to the mouth of Frobisher Bay where he was scheduled to meet *USAT Sicilien.*

Meanwhile, Crowell and his Crystal II group, badly pressed for time, established a base camp despite the fact that the area adjacent to it seemed of questionable merit for an airstrip. He and eight companions would spend the winter there. Exploration for a suitable site could resume in the spring. The needed over-wintering materials and supplies were ferried ashore from the *USAT Sicilien* and the trawlers. The freighter then left to meet with Hubbard while the trawlers departed for their home ports.

After the *USAT Sicilien* joined up with Hubbard, he continued his search under the guidance of the Eskimo. A likely spot was located on Padloping Island which is off Baffin Island. Construction material for winter quarters along with supplies for Dyer and his party were quickly moved ashore. It was none too soon as the *USAT Sicilien* and the two trawlers barely cleared in time to avoid being closed in by ice.[8]

~

---

[8] As it would turn out, the following year, the Padloping Island area was clear of ice during the summer for a lesser period of time than was the Crystal II site. For that reason, Crystal III (Padloping Island) would not be given the same importance as the Crystal II (Frobisher Bay) site.

When Forbes reported at Washington after his return from Ungava Bay, he discovered that he had been called to active duty in the Navy. With the rank of commander, he was to be occupied at the Navy's Hydrographic Office during the winter, plotting the soundings that he had recorded both of Ungava Bay and of the Koksoak River. From those observations, a number of adjustments would be made to the British Admiralty charts drawn from surveys made during the nineteenth century. Although Forbes's work was superior to the old British charts, his own survey had been a hasty one, and as he himself cautioned, it should not be relied upon. His recommendation to the Hydrographic Office was that a survey ship, accompanied by a tender equipped for wire dragging, should leave for the Ungava area as soon as ice broke up in the late spring. Priority emphasis should be placed on mapping the mouth of the Koksoak River and the upriver channel to Fort Chimo, a task which should be accomplished before the arrival of the supply ships carrying materials for the construction of the air field above Fort Chimo. Their appearance was scheduled beginning in July 1942. Following a survey of the Koksoak, Forbes recommended that approaches to the Crystal II and Crystal III sites should also be surveyed. To Forbes's own surprise -- his hydrographic skills having been gained only as an amateur pursuit -- he was selected by the Navy to lead these efforts using as his survey headquarters the chartered schooner *Effie M. Morrissey*, owned and skippered by Robert A. Bartlett.[9] Forbes was to join Bartlett's schooner at St. Johns, Newfoundland, early in the coming summer.

~

Arriving in Newfoundland in July 1942, Forbes would discover that the Norwegian trawlers *Polarbjorn* and *Polaris* which were chartered for that summer by Paul Grening, had just departed for Fort Chimo with an engineer from the Al Johnson Construction Company, the firm that the Army Corps of Engineers had selected to build the Crystal bases.

Forbes's initial instructions from the Hydrographic Office were that once he and his team had completed the survey of the Koksoak River, they were to go to Frobisher Bay where Crowell had established his base camp the previous October.[10] However, since it was subsequently felt that enough was known about the Koksoak River to allow it to be navigated -- at least for the time being -- Forbes's orders were changed. Now, instead of first going to the Koksoak, he and his survey team were to

---

[9]   Robert A. Bartlett, 67 years of age, was a veteran Arctic explorer who had brought Cdr. Robert E. Peary to the edge of the north polar ice in 1909. Despite his age, he was still considered one of the best of the Arctic navigators and ship masters. But age, it seems, had taken a toll on Bartlett's disposition. Although well respected and liked by those who were on the Crystal Project, those who worked directly with him commented that he was at times unreasonable. Unlike the other chartered vessels utilized on the Crystal Project, the *Effie M. Morrissey* was not chartered in 1942 by the Army Transport Service but rather by the North Atlantic Division of the Army Corps of Engineers. During the following 1943 season when *Effie M. Morrissey* would again support Crystal, that year's charter was with the Army Transportation Corps - Water Division. Although under charter to entities of the War Department during both years, *Effie M. Morrissey's* assignment was to perform naval hydrographic survey under the command of a naval officer, Cdr. Alexander Forbes, USNR.

[10]   Despite Forbes's recommendation of the previous fall that a wire-drag survey be made of the Koksoak and its approaches, Forbes had not been provided with the types of vessels necessary for properly conducting that type of survey. Wire drag surveys employ two vessels towing a cable between them; this type of survey has the capability of discovering underwater hazards otherwise not detectable by one survey vessel employing parallel lines of soundings.

go to Port Burwell aboard *Effie M. Morrissey* and meet the trawler *Polaris* on which they would go to Frobisher Bay. Bartlett's schooner, being slower than the trawler, was to follow. The site for the Crystal II air strip had yet to be established, and Forbes was urgently needed to assist both in that endeavor and to conduct a survey of the approaches to the site by sea once the location had been selected. With the advent of spring, Crowell, who had wintered over at Frobisher Bay, visited a location farther up the bay that had been suggested by Elliot Roosevelt who had earlier viewed it from the air. Upon checking it, Crowell deemed it unsuitable since it had no protected anchorage from which supplies and building materials could be offloaded.

When the *Effie M. Morrissey* arrived at Port Burwell, *Polaris* was no where to be seen. Rather than wait for her, Forbes instructed Bartlett to continue on to Frobisher Bay. On entering that bay, they encountered an extensive ice pack around which Bartlett had to maneuver, at times even ramming the ice to get through. Once through the ice pack, Forbes's first task was to find Crowell's base camp -- not an easy undertaking since Crowell's radio had been inoperative for some time. Bartlett anchored the schooner to the south of Fletcher Island while Forbes took the whale boat and began to search. On the second day, Forbes, went ashore on an island higher than most, climbed to its summit, and saw in the distance what appeared to be buildings and a flag. Reboarding the whale boat, he headed toward it, being shortly met by Crowell and one of his men with their rifles at-the-ready, not sure whether Forbes and his party were friend or foe.[11] Crowell then returned with Forbes to the *Effie M. Morrissey* and piloted the schooner to an anchorage off the camp. Forbes agreed that the terrain near where Crowell's party had over-wintered was not suitable for an airstrip, and continued the search. Later in the week, they found a suitable location about 30 miles from where the over-wintering camp had been. The site abutted on Koojesse Inlet east of the Sylvia Grenell River where the alluvial plain formed by that river provided an excellent platform for an air strip.

In that summer of 1942, the Russian front stood in danger of collapse. If that were to happen, the need to fly fighters to the United Kingdom would take on added urgency. Washington wanted the Crystal Projects quickly brought to fruition. On August 16, word came by radio that the chartered transport *Fairfax,* carrying construction workers and their equipment, was to leave Halifax earlier than had been initially scheduled, a change that pressed Forbes toward immediately finding a safe entrance channel into the Crystal II site. The immediate need was to fix geographic coordinates at the entrance to a channel which Forbes and his survey team had tentatively selected. There was one major fault with that selection in that the channel could only be used by deep draft ships at times of high tide; but due to the exigency of the moment, it would have to do. At the entrance point to that channel the arriving ships were to pick up a pilot (in this case Crowell). Providentially, a Coast Guard cutter carrying a seaplane as part of its regular equipage put in its appearance. Going

---

[11]   At this point in the war, it was not that clear as to what intentions the Germans had for landing raiding parties in the Canadian subarctic. Crowell would probably have known that German weather detachments had been discovered on Greenland the summer before. That knowledge, when taken in context that the Crystal II base camp had had no outside communication for some weeks, would account for Crowell's apprehension as to who was in the approaching whaleboat.

USAT Lt. Col. Lawrence O. Matthews. Employed during the Crystal Project during 1942. She stranded while on the Koksoak River, Northern Quebec. Total loss with heavy crew casualties. Grover Collection.

Effie W. Morrissey. Owned by the Arctic explorer Bob Bartlett; time chartered for the years 1942 and 1943 for the Crystal Project, Canadian Arctic. Her 1942 charter was to the Corps of Engineers; her 1943 charter was to the Transportation Corps, Water Division. Grover Collection.

aboard, Forbes arranged for a flight to take him over the channel at low tide. It was a lucky move, as Forbes spotted a rock pinnacle practically on the range that he had marked out for Crowell to use when bringing in the ships.[12] The range was adjusted in time for the arrival of *Fairfax*, followed closely by the freighter *Eleanor*. On their heels came the Army tug *USAT Lt. Col. Lawrence O. Matthews* accompanied by a smaller tug which was to be used to assist in barging in cargoes from the *Fairfax* and *Eleanor*.

As the construction work was being carried out, *Fairfax* anchored off, serving as a barracks ship for the workers. The small tug with a barge on the hip was kept busy offloading trucks, earth movers, and building materials from arriving ships.[13] A major setback was experienced in August when the freighter *Arlyn*, which had aboard much-needed equipment, was torpedoed and sunk in the Straits of Belle Isle. According to the official history of the Army Air Corps in World War II, much of what was needed to bring the Crystal Project to completion was lost on the *Arlyn*.[14]

The last cargo ship to leave Crystal II in the fall of 1942 had to break her way out through five inches of ice in order to reach open water. Throughout the winter of 1942-43, work continued on the Crystal II base complex. Bartlett, who stopped there on *Effie M. Morrissey* during the following summer (August of 1943), wrote that by then, the Crystal II base housed around fifteen hundred construction workers, together with a garrison of one hundred soldiers.[15]

In April 1943, Forbes was placed in charge of another Navy hydrographic team, this one first tasked with making a detailed survey of the Koksoak River before proceeding to Frobisher Bay to refine the work accomplished there during the previous summer.[16] *Effie M. Morrissey* was again chartered to serve the survey party.

Forbes's description of the Koksoak River as he viewed it in 1943 illustrates the danger it then posed to shipping:

> *Though limited in extent, it was a passage of unusual danger to ships, for though the river is a mile wide, the navigable channel is less than half of that and is bounded by enormous boulder trains concealed at high tide by the muddy water which rushes past them on the ebb tide at an 8-knot speed. The dangers of this river were brought home with a tragic emphasis in the late fall of 1942 when a tugboat with a barge in tow entered the river on a flood tide. The tugboat skipper, unable to summon a guard ship from the base in time to pilot him up the river before dark, [and] fearing the*

---

12   In those waters, rock pinnacles are very small in area, often precipitously dropping away to depths as great as 100 fathoms (600 feet). Only wire dragging could have provided the certainty of discovering such hazards, and as mentioned, Forbes did not have the vessels and equipment to do that. Outside of that one discovered pinnacle, the remainder of the channel would prove to be safe.

13   In addition to the *Fairfax*, the freighters *Denny, Norluna, Eagle,* and *Maltran* are mentioned by Forbes and others as arriving at Crystal II during the 1942 construction phase for Crystal II.

14   Wesley F. Craven and James Lea Cate, Editors, *The Army Air Forces in World War II,* Vol. VII, *Services Around the World,* Volume VII, (Chicago: University of Chicago Press, 1958), p 94. Correspondence between the senior author and John M. LeCato who was a participant in Crystal tells of severe problems that year in locating essential items within cargoes arriving on other ships. When not found, the common refrain was, *It must have been on the* Arlyn.

15   Robert A. Bartlett, "Servicing Arctic Air Bases," *National Geographic,* Vol LXXXIX, May 1946, pp 602-616.

16   The Koksoak River was selected as the location for the first survey that summer as it became ice free earlier than did Frobisher Bay.

stormy weather outside in Ungava Bay, attempted to find his way up the river unaided. Guessing at the channel, he guessed wrong. Strong flood tides swept tug and barge broadside against the boulder train. The tug was wrecked, and the skipper and most of his crew was lost. A few survivors reached the shore, swimming in the icy water and shivering through the wintry night, barely missed dying of exposure. [17]

When Forbes and his party reached Fort Chimo in 1943, they witnessed the system that had been set in place for supplying the Crystal I base. Ships as well as tugs with barges were proceeding as far as Fort Chimo where everything was offloaded onto small barges which were towed upriver to the airstrip by shoal draft gasoline-powered motor launches. Even then, that towage was performed only during the tidal periods of half flood to full flood. The Crystal I base had developed into an impressive facility with all the comforts including a movie theater as well as an assortment of other amenities including at one point that summer a visit by a United Service Organization (USO) troupe. It was a far cry from the uninhabited, barren scene that Forbes and Elliot Roosevelt had viewed back in 1941.

While on the Koksoak, Forbes visited the wreck of *Norluna* which had run afoul of the rocks during the previous summer, and he related the circumstances of that disaster:

At dusk, a sudden gale from the north started the ships dragging their anchors; the Norluna *had no steam up, and her anchors dragged until she was driven hard aground on the north point of Little Elbow Island. There she stood bolt upright, her starboard side nearly touching the precipitous cliffs and the rocks on which she rested fitting into her battered hull as nearly as the dentist's inlay fits the remnants of a tooth. Her valuable cargo of oil in barrels was buried deep under a solid mass of ice, for the river water flowed freely through the gaps rent in her plating. Warmths of summer had hardly begun to melt it. One day, we went aboard and explored the abandoned ship; we found chaos and order alternately prevailing in different parts of the vessel. A number of cans of tin pemmican were temptingly displayed. We sampled one and found it excellent. Later, we used the ship's rudder post as a tide gauge, writing a calibrated rod to it so the tide level could easily be read from the shore with binoculars. Late in the summer of 1943, much of her oil cargo was salvaged.*[18]

Following the survey of the Koksoak River, Forbes and his survey party went north to Frobisher Bay to complete that work.

~

By the end of 1943, the Crystal Project had been completed, but the endeavor would not serve the purpose for which it was intended. By the fall of 1943, the submarine menace in the Atlantic had largely abated, and practical methods had been developed for shipping fully assembled light aircraft on tanker well decks. Thus it was no longer necessary to fly planes over the Arctic wastes. Following completion, Crystal I functioned in part as a support base for the two more northerly facilities,

---

[17]   Forbes's description of the Koksoak as quoted here is from *Quest for a Northern Air Route, p* 100. The tug referred to by Forbes was the *USAT Lt. Col. Lawrence O. Matthews.* According to Army records, sixteen men were lost.
[18]   Forbes, *Quest for a Northern Air Route, p* 104. During the summer of 1986, the authors visited Fort Chimo by air and from a distance viewed the rusty remains of *Norluna* still lying just as Forbes had described in his book.

Crystal II and III, which would serve as weather reporting stations until the conclusion of the war in Europe.[19]

Forbes related in his book that following the project's completion, *Not one plane had been ferried to Britain by this northern most route.* He tells of his feeling of *dejection and futility* that his contribution in Crystal did not serve toward the winning of the war, *but,* he related,

> *I found consolation of sorts when I saw the gunners standing by their anti-aircraft guns on the banks of the Potomac, waiting patiently for the German bombing planes that were to have bombed Washington but never came. Comparing my lot with that of the gun crews, I realized that although my job had been almost as barren of military achievement as theirs, at least it had been a whole lot more fun.* [20]

Although Forbes's interpretation of the use of the Crystal bases for ferrying aircraft overseas was generally accurate, the bases were used to a substantial degree by military aircraft for other war-related missions. The U.S. Army historian Stanley W. Dziuban, in his work *Military Relations Between the United States and Canada, 1939 - 1945,* states:

> *During 1943 and 1944, a total of eighty-five and eighty-seven aircraft landings, respectively took place at Crystal I [Fort Chimo] and about two-thirds of these landings were the result of Coast Guard PBY (Catalina) ice patrol operations. Crystal II [upper Frobisher Bay] recorded 323 aircraft arrivals in 1943....An insignificant number of ferry aircraft passed through these bases, and air supply, aerial photography, and other miscellaneous operations accounted for most of the aircraft arrivals.* [21]

---

19   According to expenditure statistics factored on the 1944 dollar, the facility at Crystal I (Fort Chimo) cost $9,756,500. Crystal II (Frobisher Bay) cost $8,065,700. Source: Stanley W. Dziuban, *Special Studies...Military Relations Between United States and Canada, 1939 - 1945,* (Washington: Center of Military History, 1959), 324.

20   Forbes, *Quest for a Northern Air Route,* pp 121, 135.

21   Dziuban, pp 192, 193.

VESSELS EMPLOYED BY THE ARMY ON
THE CRYSTAL PROJECT, 1941 - 1943

Army Transport Service Vessels

USAT Belle Isle. 1960 GT; Blt 1932 at Newcastle, England. Freight vessel. Purchased by U.S. Maritime Commission and bareboat chartered to War Department 3 September 1942.

USAT Lt. Col. Lawrence O. Matthews. Tug. Lost, marine casualty. Stranded in Koksoak River, northern Quebec, in 1942.

USAT Sicilien. 1654 GT; Blt 1938. Danish flag. Freight vessel. Delivered to U.S. Maritime Commission under Executive Order on 12 July 1941. Bareboat chartered to War Department 23 July 1941.

A number of MTL class 40' motor launches along with other Army small craft were employed at the Crystal bases. The MTL was the type of launch used in towage of barges between Fort Chimo and the Crystal I air base.

Coast Guard Vessels

USCGC *Aklak.* (Trawler), ex *Weymouth*

USCGC *Amarok.* (Trawler), ex *Lark* (see U.S. flag fishing trawler *Lark* below)

USCGC *Arluk.* (Trawler), ex *Atlantic*

USCGC *Bear.* (Cutter) Forbes mentioned a *USCGC Bear* at Crystal II; but this may have been the *USCGC Northland.* U.S. Coast Guard records show *Bear* as having become a U.S. Navy vessel by 1941.

USCGC *Laurel.* (Buoy tender)

U.S. flag fishing trawlers chartered by the Army Transport Service

Cambridge.

Cormorant.

Fabia.

Flow.

Lark. Following her time charter in the summer of 1942, *Lark* was taken over by the Coast Guard and renamed *USCGC Amarok* and in that capacity continued to serve the Crystal Projects during part of 1943.

Norwegian Trawlers

Polarbjorn. Wooden fishing trawler. Time chartered from Norwegian owner in 1941 by U.S. Maritime Commission and later allocated by the War Shipping Administration to the War Department 30 June 1942.

Polaris. Trawler. Not known whether she was a time-chartered fishing vessel or if obtained by charter or loan from the Norwegian Navy.

Quest. Sealer, ex *Foca I.* Time chartered to War Department by owner. She was once owned by Sir Ernest Shackleton who made his fourth Antarctic expedition aboard her. He died aboard *Quest* on January 5, 1922.

Selis. Norwegian Navy anti-submarine trawler utilized either under time charter or direct loan of vessel with its crew.

Free French Fishing Vessel

Izarra. Schooner. Probably time chartered by the Army Transport Service.

Merchant Ships on Time Charter or Allocation to Army for the Crystal Project

Arlyn. U.S. flag. 3304 GT; Blt 1919, Gloucester City, NJ. Time chartered to WSA on 9 April 1942 and on same day placed on time charter agreement with A. H. Bull and Co. While en route to Crystal II with construction materials was torpedoed and sunk in Belle Isle Straits on 27 August 1942.

Atlantic Trader, ex *Frank J. Peterson.* U.S. flag. 2241 GT; Blt 1918, Ashtabula, OH; U.S. flag

Denny. 1255 GT; Blt 1915, Fredrikstad, Norway. Title to vessel passed to WSA from Lithuanian Government on 5 June 1942 and vessel placed under the Panamanian flag. Delivered to Agwilines under General Agency Agreement same day. Was at Crystal II in 1942.

Eagle. This ship may have been ex-*Peerless,* a Socony-Vacuum tanker of 6,003 GT; Blt 1917, San Francisco. Time charted to WSA by Socony-Vacuum. On 20 April 1942 WSA time chartered vessel back to Socony-Vacuum.

Effie M. Morrissey. U.S. flag. Schooner. 119 GT; Blt 1894, Essex, MA. Documented as a yacht

Eleanor. Flag and other particulars unknown; mentioned by Forbes as being at Crystal I

Fairfax. U.S. flag. 5649 GT; Blt 1926, Newport News, VA. Bareboat chartered to U.S. Maritime Commission 22 January 1942 and operated by Agwilines throughout war under a General Agency Agreement

Maltran. U.S. flag. 3513 GT; Blt Jacksonville, FL. Cargo vessel. Time chartered to War Shipping Administration on 12 April 1942 and sub-time chartered to Marine Transport Lines same day.

Norluna. U.S. flag. 2637 GT; Blt 1919, Chicago, IL. Lost; marine casualty on Koksoak River, northern Quebec, 25 October 1942.

Bibliography for Appendix F

Bartlett, Robert A. "Servicing Arctic Air Bases," *National Geographic,* Vol. LXXXIX, May 1946.

Bykofsky, Joseph and Harold Larson. *The Transportation Corps: Operations Overseas.* Washington: Center of Military History, 1957.

Craven, Wesley Frank and James Lea Cate. *The Army Air Forces in World War II.* Volume I and VII. Chicago: University of Chicago Press, 1950 and 1958.

Dziuban, Stanley W. *Special Studies...Military Relations Between United States and Canada, 1939 - 1945.* Washington: Center of Military History, 1959.

Forbes, Alexander, "Surveying in Northern Labrador," *Geographical Review,* Volume XXII, 1932.

Forbes, Alexander, *Northern Labrador from the Air,* American Geographical Society, 1938.

Forbes, Alexander. *Quest for a Northern Air Route,* Cambridge: Harvard University Press, 1953

Sailing Directions for Hudson Bay Route, From Atlantic to Churchill Harbor, 2nd edition. Ottawa: Hydrographic and Map Service, Department of Mines and Resources, 1940.

Correspondence between the senior author and Bertram G. Snow of Rockland, ME, during 2000.

Correspondence between the senior author and Captain John M. LeCato of Charleston, SC, during 1987.

Interview by the authors with John T. Crowell, formerly Major, U.S. Army Air Corps, at Crowell's home on Kimball's Island, Maine, in the summer of 1985.

APPENDIX G

Sample of Standard Charter Party as entered into between the Army Transport Service (Philippines) 1941-42 and owners of vessels taken into service under requisition during the Defense of the Philippines, December 1941 - May 1942

Contract No. ___6___
Office Identifying No. _____

CONTRACT FOR THE CHARTER
of the
M/S *GOVERNOR TAFT*

This CHARTER PARTY entered into this ____26th____ day of March, 1942, in the City of Cebu, Philippines, by and between -

VISAYAN TRANSPORTATION CO., INC., a corporation duly organized and existing under and by virtue of the laws of the Philippines with principal office in the City of Cebu, owner of the M/S *GOVERNOR TAFT*, represented herein by its duly authorized President, JOSE COROMINOS, per Resolution of its Board of Directors approved March 4, 1942 (hereinafter designated as THE OWNER)
and

C. Z. BYRD, Major, QMC, Assistant Superintendent of ARMY TRANSPORT SERVICE, Cebu Station, for and on behalf of the Government of the United States (hereinafter designated as THE CHARTERER)

WITNESSETH;

That for and in consideration of the terms, conditions and stipulations herein stated, THE OWNER and THE CHARTERER do hereby mutually agree with each other as follows:

1. That THE OWNER does hereby grant and let, and THE CHARTERER does hereby take the M/S *GOVERNOR TAFT*, subject-matter of this contract, more particularly described as follows:

Length	134' 0"
Breadth	27' 0"
Depth	11' 2"
B.H.P.	330
Year built	1930
Engine	DEUTZ Diesel
Gross tonnage	269.83
Net tonnage	173.48
REPLACEMENT COST	$100,000.00

registered at the Port of Cebu with Certificate of Ownership No.   and Certificate of Philippine Register No. 961 issued by the Collector of Customs of   on February 27, 1934;

2. That THE OWNER hereby guarantees that the motor ship above described is in first-class condition, and the Government of the United States has satisfied itself that its interests are fully protected; that a survey of the hull and other equipment required under Par. 8, AR 30-1315 has been waived, and THE OWNER consents to accept the motor ship when it is returned at the conclusion of this Charter Party without any further examination of hull or machinery, and that the said motor ship will be accepted as is, fair wear and tear excepted;

3. That the motor ship hired under the terms of this contract will be used at such time as she may be required in the military service of the United States for the duration of the war;

4. That the motor ship now is, and while in the service of the United States Government shall be, kept and maintained tight, staunch, strong, victualed, tackled, appareled and ballasted;

5. That an inventory shall be taken of the accessories and personal effects on said motor ship,, which inventory is hereby incorporated by reference and made an integral part of this Charter Party. All supplies on board shall go with the motor ship;

6. That THE CHARTERER shall, upon termination of the period for which the said motor ship was hired, return to THE OWNER at Cebu City, or to its duly authorized representative, said motor ship in the same order as when received, ordinary wear and tear, damage by the elements, collision at sea and in port, groundings, fires, bursting of boilers, and breakage of machinery excepted;

7. That THE CHARTERER shall be free to use and employ any officer, engineer or member of the crew and shall likewise have the power to dismiss or make changes in the appointment for the good of the service; and that THE CHARTERER, at its election, may engage the present complement of said motor ship and compensation paid to said complement as per pay schedule of the ARMY TRANSPORT SERVICE for this class of vessel;

8. That every member of the crew shall be a citizen of the Philippines or of the United States, native-born, or completely naturalized;

9. That the war risks shall be borne by THE CHARTERER or the Government of the United States; the marine risks by THE OWNER;

10. That the master of the vessel shall obey all orders or instructions which he may receive from the Army Officer in charge of the operations;

11. That for and in consideration of the faithful performance of the stipulation of this agreement, THE OWNER shall be paid by THE CHARTERER for each month of actual service of its motor ship above-mentioned a monthly rental of FOUR THOUSAND ONE HUNDRED SIXTY-SIX DOLLARS AND SIXTY-SIX CENTS ($4,166.66), U.S. Currency;

12. That payment shall be made at the end of the war by the Finance Officer at Cebu City, Philippines out of funds furnished for the purpose by the Government of the United States, upon presenting bills duly certified by the Quartermaster that the said motor ship *GOVERNOR TAFT* has faithfully performed its part of this contract;

13. That neither this contract nor any interest therein shall be transferred by THE OWNER to any other party, and any such transfer, when made, shall cause the annulment of this contract in so far as THE CHARTERER or the Government of the United States is concerned. All rights of action, however, to recover for any breach of this contract by THE OWNER are reserved to THE CHARTER;

14. That no member or delegate of Congress or Resident Commissioner, nor any person belonging to or employed in the military service of the united States is or shall be admitted to any share or part of this contract or to any benefit which may arise herefrom, but under the provisions of Sec. 116 of the Act of Congress approved March 4, 1909 (35 Stat. 1088), this stipulation so far as it relates to members or delegates of Congress or Resident Commissioner shall extend or be construed to extend to any contract made with an incorporated company or its general benefit;

15. That in the event of the loss of time from deficiency of men, stores, fire, breakdown, or damage to hull, machinery or equipment, caused by direct negligence of the employees of THE OWNER drydocking for the purpose of examination or painting bottom, the payment of the hire shall cease for the time thereby lost; and if upon the voyage the speed of the motor ship be reduced by defect in or breakdown of any part of her hull, machinery or equipment, the time so lost and the cost of any extra fuel consumed in consequence thereof, and all extra expense shall be deducted from the hire;

16. That should any dispute arise between THE OWNER and THE CHARTERER, the matter in dispute shall be referred to the arbitration of three persons - one appointed by THE OWNER; one by THE CHARTERER; and the third by the two members chosen. They may proceed in any manner determined by themselves and their decision or that of any two of them shall be final, and for the purpose of enforcing any award hereunder, the agreement may be made a rule of court. Such arbitration shall be a condition precedent to the commencement of any action;

17. The penalty for non-performance of this contract shall be proved damages; and in the event of any statement by THE OWNER contained in this contract being found by THE CHARTERER to be incorrect as to the tonnage of the motor ship herein involved, a penalty of one-fourth (¼) of the total charter cost to the Government of the United States shall be imposed to THE OWNER;   and

18. That this Charter Party shall go into effect on the 20th of December 1941, retroactive as of the date the M/S/ *GOVERNOR TAFT* was taken over by THE CHARTERER.

IN WITNESS WHEREOF, the parties hereto have signed this contract on the date and place first hereinabove stated.

VISAYAN TRANSPORTATION CO., INC.
By

President	C. Z. BYRD
OWNER	Major, QMC
	Assistant Superintendent
	ARMY TRANSPORT SERVICE
	CHARTERER

Signed in the Presence of:

_____/s/_____   _____/s/_____

UNITED STATES OF AMERICA)
COMMONWEALTH OF THE PHILIPPINES (
CITY OF CEBU)

Before me, the undersigned Notary Public in and for the City/Province of Cebu, personally appeared Mr. JOSE COROMINOS who exhibited to me his Resident Certificate No. A____1325841____ issued at Cebu City, Cebu, on February 24, 1942, President of the VISAYAN TRANSPORTATION CO., INC., charterer, and Major C. Z. BYRD, QMC (exempt from resident certificate per Par. (b), Sec. 4, of Com. Act No. 485), Assistant Superintendent of ARMY TRANSPORT SERVICE, charterer, both known to me and by me known to be the persons who executed the foregoing Charter Party on the M/S *GOVERNOR TAFT*, and they acknowledged before me that they executed said contract as their free and voluntary act and deed, and as the free and voluntary act and deed of their respective principals.

IN WITNESS THEREOF, I have hereunto set my hand and affixed my notarial seal on this 26th day of March 1942.

/s/
Notary Public
Commission expires December 31, 1942

Rec. No. 114
Page No. 20
Book No. XXII
Series of 1942

Source: National Archives: Record Group 407, Philippine Archive Collection, Box 1568, Folder - Status of ATS Employees.

APPENDIX H

RESCUE OF THE RICE MILLS - BATAAN

The following letter by M. A. Quinn, Colonel, QMC, was made part of Appendix C of Brig. General Charles C. Drake's *Operations of the Quartermaster Corps, Philippine Islands, July 27, 1941 to May 6, 1942.*

ARMY SERVICE FORCES
Sixth Service Command
Mayo General Hospital
Galesburg, Illinois

9 January 1946

Lieut. Gen. E. B. Gregory
The Quartermaster General
Washington 25, D. C.

My Dear General Gregory:

On December 30, 1941 I was called to the office of Department Quartermaster at San Bedas College, Manila, P.I., and there introduced to a delegation of Czech-Slovaks, headed by the Czech Consul. These Czechs volunteered for service by and for themselves and other members of the Czech colony. Altogether fourteen were involved. Despite the fact that these men were business executives or consul agents of their own government, they volunteered to serve the United States. They made arrangements to take care of their families, giving what food and money was available, to them. Attention is here invited to the fact they were not subject to internment due to German occupation of their native land.

Their work and devotion to duty were outstanding. Had they been citizens of the United States they would call for commendations and awards of very high order. They did so many things for us in Bataan that it is impossible to enumerate all of them. However, I would like to invite attention to the following --- On or about February 7, 1942, the American-Philippine Force had been evacuated to Bataan. In the occupied area there were no rice mills. However, there were rice mills in the town of Orani, Bataan, and the following named Czechs volunteered to go forward to Orani, which was at that time between the lines, dismantle the rice mills, and bring them back to Bataan, and set them up. This they did, remaining under fire for 36 hours. That we were able to supply rice to the troops in Bataan after the middle of February was due greatly to the devotion of these volunteers.

1. Dr. Paul Fuchs (Died in Camp O'Donnel)
2. John Bzoch (Dead. Left Bilibid December 13, 1944 for Japan)
3. Leo Herman
4. Fred Hermann
5. Fred Lenk
6. Otto Hirach
7. Ernest Moravek

It is my belief that such outstanding service and quiet heroism deserve some mention from higher authority than a mere Colonel of Quartermaster, and I respectfully request that the men whose names are mentioned be given whatever recognition through the State Department that our Government can give.

A more complete account of the general work of these volunteers will be furnished in another letter to you.

/s/ M. A. Quinn

M. A. QUINN
Colonel, QMC

Exhibit C

APPENDIX I

CIVILIANS (EXCLUSIVE OF FILIPINOS) WHO VOLUNTEERED TO SERVE IN THE PHILIPPINES WITH THE ARMY TRANSPORT SERVICE DECEMBER 31, 1941, TO MAY 6, 1942

Sources for this Appendix:
- U.S. Army Provost Marshall List *CFN-127*
- Crew Lists of *USAT Henry Keswick* and *USAT YuSang* located in RG-407, Philippine Archive Collection, National Archives
- WSA files and correspondence, including USCG report of 15 February 1953 to WSA Division of Insurance from P. G. Prins, Commander, USCG. Of the seven seamen known to have died and who are within this Appendix, only one man, Harry L. Briggs, is listed on insurance records indicating that his heir received the life insurance benefit from the government that was applicable for seamen employees of the War Department during World War II.

AMERICAN, BRITISH, AUSTRALIAN, NORWEGIAN, AND CANADIAN CIVILIAN PERSONNEL KNOWN TO HAVE SERVED WITH THE ARMY TRANSPORT SERVICE DURING THE DEFENSE OF BATAAN / CORREGIDOR

Abbot, J. H. (U.S.)	Either killed in action or if made POW fate unknown
Albie, D. (U.S.)	Either killed in action or if made POW fate unknown
Andresen, Earl C. (U.S.)*	Repatriated after war from POW camp
Bailet, ?? (U.S.)	Either killed in action or if made POW fate unknown
Bailey, R. G. (U.S.)	Either killed in action or if made POW fate unknown
Berger, M. (U.S.)	Either killed in action or if made POW fate unknown
Berkowitz, Morris (U.S.) *	Died on POW ship *Arisun Maru* en route to Japan
Briggs, Harry L. (U.S.)	Died as a POW
Chung, Alfred (U.S.) *	Repatriated after war from POW camp
Crook, T. N. (British)	Either killed in action or if made POW fate unknown
Edwards, E. (U.S.)	Either killed in action or made POW; fate unknown
Fouts, Ray H. (U.S.)	Either killed in action or if made POW fate unknown
Godfrey, Raleigh G., (U.S.) *	Repatriated after war from POW camp
Gomm, A. B. (Canadian)	Either killed in action or if made POW fate unknown
Hanna, William (U.S.)	Either killed in action or if made POW fate unknown
Harrington, James C., (U.S.) *	Died in POW camp or en route to Japan aboard prison ship
Harris, H. G. (British)	Made POW but fate unknown
Hatton, Ival H. (U.S.)*	Died on POW ship *Arisun Maru* en route to Japan
Holton, Patrick M. (U.S.) *	Repatriated after war from POW camp
Hutchins, Hale L., (U.S.) *	Repatriated after war from POW camp
Ing, Alvin K., (U.S.) *	Repatriated after war from POW camp
Juel, Audun (Norwegian)	Either killed in action or if made POW fate unknown
Kipagard, Thorvald (Norwegian)	Either killed in action or if made POW fate unknown
McWilliams, Leslie (British)	Made POW but fate unknown
Olferieff, Sergei (U.S.)*	Died on POW ship *Arisun Maru,* en route to Japan
Owens, Arthur, (U.S.) *	Died on POW ship en route to Japan
Rogers, Harold V. (U.S.)	Repatriated after war from POW camp
Rose, Edwin (British)	Either killed in action or if made POW fate unknown
Rounds, Allen (U.S.)	Repatriated after war from POW camp
Sevenoaks, H. A. (U.S.)	Either killed in action or if made POW fate unknown
Seymour, Charles (U.S.) *	Made POW but fate unknown
Verhey, Dick (or Dirk?) (U.S.) *	Repatriated after war from POW camp
Weber, Herman, (U.S.)*	Repatriated after war from POW camp
Weisman, Joseph (U.S.)*	Either repatriated from POW camp or died on prison ship
Whittle, Harold A. (Aust.)	Killed in action on Corregidor

* Received the Merchant Marine Meritorious Service Medal

AMERICANS KNOWN TO HAVE BEEN EMPLOYED BY THE ARMY'S HARBOR BOAT SERVICE PRIOR TO DECEMBER 8, 1941, AND WHO SUBSEQUENTLY SERVED WITH THE ARMY TRANSPORT SERVICE IN THE DEFENSE OF BATAAN / CORREGIDOR, DECEMBER 31, 1941 - MAY 6, 1942

Green, Joseph M.	Repatriated from POW camp after the war
Keaton, Thomas J.	No record in CFN-127 to indicate he was a civilian internee or POW as of the date of the first prisoner inventory in 1943. The probability is that he was either killed in the defense or died as a POW prior to 1943
Williams, Harry	Repatriated from POW camp after the war

APPENDIX J

DATES OF CAPITULATION OF AREAS WITHIN THE PHILIPPINE ISLANDS TO JAPANESE FORCES

Source: Report located within RG-407, Philippine Archive Collection, Box 1568, consisting of correspondence of Major General T. B. Larkin, Quartermaster General.

To our best knowledge, there is no published data enumerating the exact numbers of U.S. Army personnel killed or taken captive by the Japanese within the Philippines during the defense of those islands, 1941-42. According to Morton, as of the autumn of 1941 and prior to the mobilization of the Philippine Commonwealth Army into the USAFFE, there was a total of 31,095 U.S. Army personnel present within the Philippines (inclusive of the Philippines Scouts, an integral part of the U.S. Army).[†] Presumably most if not all of those persons would have been present on December 8, 1941, the date of the Japanese attack. Assuming that at most 600 officers, nurses, and men were evacuated prior to the surrenders, the number of those killed and/or surrendered during the period December 1941 through May 1942 would have been approximately 30,500. Of those who surrendered, the accepted figure for deaths of American personnel while in the captivity of the Japanese is one third.

[†]   According to Morton, of that number, all but four hundred Americans were stationed on the island of Luzon. The figure 31,095 does not include the personnel of the 4th Marine Regiment and those naval personnel who were incorporated to the USAFFE by order of Admiral Hart prior to his leaving the Philippines in December 1941.

<u>LUZON</u>
Asparri	10 Dec 41
Conzaga	10 Dec 41
Vigan	10 Dec 41
Tugurgarao	16 Dec 41
San Fernando (Lingayen Gulf)	22 Dec 41
Mauban-Antimonan Area	23 and 24 Dec 41
Manila	1 Jan 42
Olongapo - Subic Bay	16 Jan 42
Bataan	9 Apr 42
Corregidor	6 May 42

<u>MINDANAO</u>
Davao	20 Dec 41
Zamboanga	3 Mar 42
Parang	29 Apr 42
Colabato	1 May 42
All Mindanao	10 May 42

<u>CEBU</u>
Cebu City	10 Apr 42
Toledo	10 Apr 42
Avagao	10 Apr 42
Pinamungajan	10 Apr 42
Naga	10 Apr 42
Talisay	10 Apr 42

<u>PANAY</u> *
Iloilo	16 Apr 42
Capiz	16 Apr 42
San Jose de Buenavista	18 Apr 42
Lambuneo	18 Apr 42

<u>MINDORO</u>
Calapan	7 Mar 42

<u>PALAWAN</u>
Puerto Princesa	17 May 42

<u>LUBANG</u>	9 Dec 41
<u>JOLO</u>	2 Jan 42
<u>MASBATE</u>	10 Feb 42
<u>ROMBLON</u>	27 Mar 42
<u>BUSUANGA</u>	17 May 42
<u>BOHOL</u>	23 May 42
<u>BASILAN</u>	25 May 42
<u>NEGROS</u> **	26 May 42

<u>PLACE NAMES IN SOLID CAPITALS AND UNDERLINED REPRESENT ISLANDS</u>

* According to Morton, the formal surrender of Panay did not occur until May 20.

** According to Morton, the formal surrender of the Negros did not occur until June 3.

APPENDIX K

MILITARY DECORATIONS TO CIVILIANS
WORLD WAR II

U.S. Army Regulation (600-45) of September 22, 1943, sheds light on the U.S. Army's policy regarding military decorations to which civilians -- including merchant marine personnel -- were made eligible during World War II.[1]

- *The Purple Heart may be awarded by Army field commanders, or hospital commanders, to accredited civilians who are citizens of the United States and to the officers and members of the crew of ships of the U.S. Merchant Marine serving within [Army] commands.* (This also included personnel of the Army Transport Service as they were accredited to the Army. Ed.)

- *The Distinguished Service Cross and the Silver Star [§10] may be awarded to civilians by a theater commander or by any commander of the rank of major general or higher to officers and crews of ships of the U.S. merchant marine or to those serving, 'in any capacity with the Army.'* (Serving with the Army would pertain to civilian employees of the Army, inclusive of Army Transport Service personnel. Ed.)

- *Distinguished Service Medal [§11] may be awarded to persons 'while serving in any capacity with the Army.'* (This would include all civilian employees, inclusive of Army Transport Service personnel; and probably would also include persons under contractual obligation to the Army. Ed.)[2]

---

[1] Explicitly stated [§8-d] *The Medal of Honor, the Legion of Merit, the Distinguished Flying Cross, and the Soldiers Medal will not be awarded to civilians.*

[2] There exists one case wherein the Army's Distinguished Service Medal and the Merchant Marine Distinguished Service Medal were awarded to the same person for the same act. The recipient was John A. Mattson, the master of *Coast Farmer.* AR 600-45 dated 19 May 1947 states that in the future, the Distinguished Service Medal could only be awarded to members of the armed forces, thus rescinding the earlier authority

As interpreted from AR 600-45 of September 22, 1943, both U.S. citizens and foreign nationals are eligible for all of the above decorations except for the Purple Heart which was restricted to U.S. citizens.

- Under AR 600-45 of September 22, 1943 [§ 28] there is a description and requirement for the award of the *Medal for Merit* which was to be awarded only to civilians and is to include only those prosecuting the war under *the joint declaration of the United Nations and of other friendly foreign nations as have since 8 September 1939 distinguished themselves by exceptional meritorious conduct in the performance of outstanding service.* The President of the United States has the sole authority to make that award. (Presumably, eligibility for the Medal of Merit would have included merchant marine personnel of all the Allied nations as well as the free civilian elements of those nations which were under Axis occupation. Presumably it would also have included civilians serving with, or in accompaniment to, the armed forces of any of the Allied nations. Ed.)

- According to AR 600-45 of 25 April 1944, civilian eligibility for the *Bronze Star* had been stipulated by the AR 600-45 of 9 March 1944. This new regulation would have allowed the Bronze Star to be awarded *to any person who, while serving in any capacity in or with the Army of the United States...* (This allowed eligibility to both military and civilian personnel as long as they were attached to units of the Army in the field. Ed.)

~

The Army awarded its decorations according to set criteria to both merchant marine and Army Transport Service personnel. That is confirmed by the record. In doing so, the Army followed a rather strict interpretation as to the recipient's direct relationship with a military command and/or military operation, although some liberalness was exercised in the case of the crews of merchant ship blockade runners -- Australia to the Philippines, 1942 -- who were in fact contractual personnel specially rewarded financially for that undertaking. As the war progressed, it became the general policy for some Army commands to make decoration recommendations to the War Shipping Administration (WSA) for merchant marine personnel, as a result of which that civilian agency awarded its own decorations to such recommended personnel. Starting in 1943, under an interagency agreement between the Army and the WSA, WSA awards and decorations were (upon the Army's recommendation) also dispensed to the civil service seamen employees of the Army Transportation Corps - Water Division).[3] Intermittently, and on occasion up through 1945, the Army continued to bestow its military decorations to its civil service seamen employees, and in a few isolated instances to merchant marine personnel as well. This was illustrated by the award of the Bronze Star to the masters of both Army and WSA tugs which were employed during the invasion of Normandy.

---

allowing the award to civilians. However, §1130 of Title 10, USC, would appear to make this inapplicable in cases where an award to an individual was overlooked by reason of untimely submission in the past.

[3]   During 1942, the vessels of the Army Transport Service and its civil service seamen employees were absorbed into the Transportation Corps - Water Division. Certain employees of the old Army Transport Service (U.S. citizens) who performed meritorious service in the Philippines, 1941 - 42, were retroactively awarded WSA decorations for that Army service, e.g., *USAT Henry Keswick* crewmembers who served during the defense of Bataan/ Corregidor. See Appendix I.

APPENDIX L

U.S. COMMAND OVERVIEW, SOUTHWEST PACIFIC
DECEMBER 1941 THROUGH MAY 1942

Sources U.S. Army in World War II, Special Studies *Chronology 1941 - 1945,* compiled by Mary H. Williams, (Washington: Office of the Chief of Military History, 1960); *The Harmon Memorial Lectures in Military History, 1959 - 1987,* Washington: Office of Air Force History, 1988.

December 8-9:   Within hours of the December 8 Japanese attack against the Philippines, a command entity known as U.S. Army Forces, Far East (USAFFE) is activated under Lt. Gen. Douglas MacArthur giving MacArthur supreme command over all U.S. Army forces in the Philippines, to be inclusive of any U.S. naval force which might in the future be incorporated under his command. MacArthur will soon be promoted to 4-star general.

December 22, 1941: Pensacola Convoy arrives at Brisbane, Australia. The troop commander with the convoy is Brig. Gen. Julian F. Barnes who for a brief time holds command of all U.S. military in Australia.

December 24: Maj. Gen. George H. Brett is flown to Australia from Europe via Chungking, China.   On arrival in Australia, by orders emanating from MacArthur, Brett is given command of U.S. Army Forces in Australia (USAFIA). Brig. Gen. Henry B. Claggett, having held temporary command of USAFIA pending Brett's arrival, is made deputy commander.

January 2, 1942: The Allied command known as American-British-Dutch-Australian (ABDA) is formally established but is not activated at this time. Its commander becomes British General Archibald P. Wavell. Brett is named Wavell's deputy commander. On January 4, Brett is promoted to Lieutenant General to give him rank appropriate to the ABDA position. The post of ABDA (for air) was offered to Maj. Gen. Lewis H. Brereton; however, shifting around within the American command structure makes that impossible, and that post is handed to Brett who now has two jobs to perform within ABDA, that of command of ABDA (for air) as well as deputy (executive officer) to Wavell.

January 5: Australia is designated by the War Department as the base of supply for all U.S. Army forces operating in the Southwest Pacific. That supply responsibility is accordingly vested to USAFIA of which at the time Brett is still commander; however, within the next day or two, Brett will leave for Java, turning USAFIA interim command over to Barnes.

January 15: ABDA-COM is activated at Batavia (later called Djakarta), Java. Shortly after the activation, ABDA-COM will transfer its location and all headquarters personnel to the interior of Java at Bandoeng.

January 18: Brereton, who had been ordered to evacuate his B-17 bomber force from the Philippines on December 15, and who had later flown to Darwin, had gone to Java with Brett in early January. He now returns to Australia from Java to take over command of USAFIA -- albeit briefly -- from its interim commander, Barnes.

January 26: Brereton receives new orders that he has been appointed as Deputy Commander of ABDA (for air). (This was done in order to relieve Brett of his dual responsibilities.) Brereton leaves Melbourne for Java after turning over USAFIA interim command to Barnes.

February 23: Brett evacuates from Java to Australia, taking over as commander of USAFIA from Barnes.

February 25: Brereton evacuates Java, flying with his staff to India, having been assigned to other duties unrelated to Southwest Pacific operations. ABDA is now close to dissolution due to the Japanese conquest of the entirety of the Dutch East Indies.

March 9: Java falls to the Japanese.

March 11: MacArthur evacuates from the Philippines (on direct presidential orders). The direct command of the U.S. Army and its integrated Filipino force on Bataan goes to Maj. Gen. Jonathan M. Wainwright, and that force as well as other forces in the Philippines are made subordinate by MacArthur to his new headquarters to be established in Australia. The War Department takes the position that such a remote command structure -- as it will effect the Philippines -- is unworkable.

March 20: The command of all forces in the Philippines -- to be designated U.S. Forces in the Philippines (USFIP) -- goes to Wainwright who is promoted to lieutenant general.

March 21: Brett becomes the commander of Combined U.S.-Australian Air Forces, while still retaining his command function over USAFIA.

April 18: MacArthur assumes the newly created position of commander of the Southwest Pacific Area (SWPA) as approved by President Roosevelt on March 30, and USAFFE is deactivated at this time. Wainwright remains head of U.S. Forces in the Philippines (USFIP). Brett is retained as the commander of Combined U.S.-Australian Air Forces based in Australia but relinquishes his command function over USAFIA -- that function being turned over to Barnes. As of that organizational change, Barne's command becomes mainly concerned with administrative and supply functions directly pertinent to the Australian base of operations.

May 10: With the surrender of the U.S. Army command on Mindanao (Wainwright had surrendered Corregidor on May 6), USFIP becomes a non-existent force and as a command is deactivated. Future guerrilla operations in the Philippines will be directed by MacArthur's SWPA Headquarters from Australia.

APPENDIX M

THE OFFSHORE PATROL – PHILIPPINE COMMONWEALTH ARMY

Published Source: Regino Dodds Giagonia, *The Philippine Navy, 1898 - 1996.* (Manila: Philippine Navy), 1997.

Unpublished Sources, all of which are documents located within Modern Military Records, National Archives:

- Records of the Small Ship Section, Service of Supply, USAFIA
- General Orders 71, HQ., USAFIA, Office of Commanding General, Chief of Staff, WESPAC, RG-338, General Correspondence File found under *Orders*
- MacArthur to Marshall, letter dated October 28, 1941, Chief of Transportation Files, SWPA, i.e., Philippine Shipping

During 1935, the Philippine Commonwealth government enacted Act No. 1, the Philippine National Defense Act. On January 11, 1936, the Philippine Commonwealth Army was organized under Executive Order 11. Article 26 created the Offshore Patrol (OSP) which was integrated as part of the Philippine Commonwealth Army. The purpose of the OSP was to act as the maritime arm for the defense of the Philippines under the following guidelines:

> *The Offshore Patrol shall comprise all marine equipment and personnel acquired by the Philippine Government and assigned either in peace or war to the control of the Chief of Staff (Philippine Commonwealth Army). It shall have such duties and powers as may be described by the Chief of Staff.*

The regulations for uniforms for OSP commissioned officers were identical to those of other officers of the Philippine Commonwealth Army, except for an anchor insignia which was to be worn on the lapels of blouses (or shirt collars) designating the branch.

~

Lt. Gen. Douglas MacArthur, the architect of the Philippine Commonwealth Army, had developed the concept that in lieu of a battle fleet, a naval defense of the islands would be best served by *flotillas of fast torpedo boats supported by an air force.* Although evidence is scanty on the origins of the OSP idea and the development of a torpedo boat fleet, it appears to have started with Sidney L. Huff, a retired American naval officer. Huff, who had joined MacArthur's staff in 1936 as his civilian naval advisor, had never seen a torpedo boat; but in order to rectify that inadequacy, he instituted an investigation into developments made in their design since the end of World War I. The conclusion he reached was that the type being used by the British was the most suitable for use in the Philippines.[1] The original planning for the OSP called for construction of a fleet of fifty-five torpedo boats which were to be later designated as *Q* boats.[2] Five million dollars was budgeted for that purpose; however, at that juncture, there was no definite schedule for implementation.

On April 15, 1938, the OSP was activated with the Philippine Commonwealth Army's Maj. Rafael Ramos named as its chief. A follow-up directive instructed that all U.S. Naval Academy graduates then within the officer corps of the Philippine Commonwealth Army were to be assigned to the patrol. Ramos was also handed a list of graduates of the Philippine Nautical School (the Commonwealth's Merchant Marine Officers Academy) who were presently officers of the Army either in an active or a reserve status. From such personnel, selections were to be made to fill out OSP commissioned ranks.

Shortly after being given the command of OSP, Ramos received orders to attend a Quartermaster training course in the United States. In his absence, Lt. Jose V. Andrada (U.S. Naval Academy, Class of 1930) was designated acting OSP chief. One of Andrada's first moves was to increase the OSP officer allotment by accepting civilians as officer candidates -- requirements being that the candidate was either a graduate of the Philippine Nautical School or holder of a Philippine merchant marine license (provided the licensee was a high school graduate). Andrada established a school for officer candidate training which was a year-long course. Nine officer candidates were graduated and commissioned the first year.

In December 1939, the officer candidate program was enlarged to accommodate undergraduates of the Philippine Military Academy who were given a 3-month course in maritime subjects. If completed successfully, the graduates qualified as third lieutenants assigned to the OSP Reserve. Seven of those who completed that

---

[1]   William Manchester, *American Caesar,* (Boston: Little Brown and Co., 1967), pp 167, 168.

[2]   According to Filipino naval historian Giagonia, the designation "Q" for the torpedo boats had been picked in honor of Philippine Commonwealth President Manuel L. Quezon.

3-month course and were commissioned were then picked for the regular OSP officer's year-long course.[3]

Having been ordered from a British yard, the first torpedo boat arrived fully equipped from England via the port of Antwerp on March 2, 1939. It was christened *Abra* and was designated as Q-112. It measured 55' LOA, 11' beam, and at flank speed produced 50 knots. The concept at that time for the size of the fleet was decreased from fifty-five to a goal of thirty boats by 1946, with a minimum of three being scheduled for delivery each year. Under MacArthur's concept for Philippine self-reliance in military procurement, the British boats were to be augmented by locally built ones. The yard which received that local building order was the Marine Railway and Repair Shop on Engineer Island which was owned and operated by the Commonwealth's Department of Public Works and Communication.[4]

The second British-built Q-boat, also fully equipped by the British, was of slightly different design measuring 65' LOA. It arrived that June and was christened *Luzon* (Q-111).[5] When tested in heavy sea conditions, Q-111 performed at 41 knots, slightly less than Q-112. At this point, when the outbreak of the war in Europe canceled out further deliveries from British yards, MacArthur's plan for the construction of the boats in the Philippines paid off. However, since armaments, especially torpedoes, were not manufactured in the Philippines, this created a problem but one which was solved when in early January 1941, the U.S. Congress introduced a bill authorizing the U.S. Navy to transfer naval equipment to the Philippine Commonwealth. In either late 1939 or during 1940, the OSP ranks were opened for reserve enlisted personnel to serve under what was by then a roster of 184 OSP reserve officers on inactive status.

During 1941, the first, and as it was to turn out, the only Philippine-built Q-boat was launched. Constructed on the specifications of the Q-111, it was named *Agusan* and designated Q-113. On trial it proved faster than either the Q-111 or the Q-112 -- that being the result of a lighter weight wood used for the hulls. The Q-113 trial was so satisfying that MacArthur called for production of ten more identical boats to be completed by March 1942 by which time another fourteen were to be well into production. During October of 1941, MacArthur wrote the U.S. Army's Chief of Staff of the progress being made:

---

[3]   There were three grades of lieutenant in the Philippine Commonwealth Army. As far as can be determined, forty officers were trained at the regular officers' course. All forty regular officers were probably on active duty when on December 19, 1941, OSP was inducted as part of U.S. Army Forces in the Far East (USAFFE). Under Andrada's leadership, a school had been established for enlisted men either in 1938 or 1939; but the number of enlisted personnel assigned to OSP as of the induction of December 19, 1941, is not known.

[4]   On December 8, 1941, twenty-four future Q-boats were on the stocks at Engineer Island, all of them destroyed that month during the Japanese bombing raids.

[5]   Why the numerical designation of the second boat to arrive was of a lessor number than that of the first was probably the result of contractual sequence.

HEADQUARTERS
United States Army Forces in the Far East
Office of the Commanding General
Manila, P. I.

October 28, 1941

My dear Marshall:

..... The naval component of the Philippine Commonwealth Army has reached a milestone in its development, having recently placed in service the first locally built torpedo boat, and having laid down ten new ones that are expected to be in the water by the end of March. My original plans in 1935 included a project for a fleet of fast motor torpedo boats. The protected waters of this archipelago provide an ideal theatre for effective operations. The U.S. Navy at that time could not be stirred to interest itself in the development, and I was forced to turn to British builders to get what I wanted. Two boats were delivered and found satisfactory; three more were built, but were diverted to Finland; five additional were finished, but the British Admiralty commandeered those. I closed out the contract, securing delivery of ten sets of engines in return for the payments already made on boats, purchased the right to build from the British design and constructed a boat here. It was successful and we are now going into, comparatively speaking, quantity production. Meanwhile the successful use of this type in the war led the Navy into belated experimental development, followed by a production schedule. At my suggestion, Admiral [Thomas C.] Hart asked the Navy Department to send some of their craft here, resulting in the allocation of twelve, of which six have arrived. They naturally provide a welcome addition to defense potentialities, and should give an impetus to the development of the Philippine Commonwealth Army element. The naval component has not yet been called into U.S. service, but its development is continuing as originally planned. I informed Hart that I would insure the order whenever he wanted the unit, but it will be called only in case of war. I am satisfied.

I wish to reiterate my appreciation of the splendid support you and the War Department are giving me. No field commander could ask more. Your attitude has been a marked factor in the building of morale here.

Faithfully yours,

/s/ Douglas MacArthur

General George C. Marshall
War Department
Washington, D.C.

During the fall of 1941, the six U.S. Navy PT boats to which MacArthur's letter to Marshall had referenced arrived under the command of Lt. John D. Bulkeley, USN. Bulkeley's squadron soon became engaged in combined maneuvers with the Q-boats during which time a reasonable but not perfect working coordination was reported to MacArthur as having been achieved.

On December 4, 1941, four days before the Japanese were to strike, the overall administrative command of OSP went from Major Andrada to another Philippine Commonwealth Army officer, Capt. Enrique Jurado (U.S. Naval Academy, Class of 1934). Prior to that change of command, Jurado had held the afloat leadership of the Q-boat squadron which was now given to Lt. Albert Navarrete.[6]

---

[6]   As surmised by the Philippine naval historian Regino Dodds Giagonia, the relief of Andrada may have come about because of a conflict between him and Bulkeley over the methods the American officer had advocated for combined operations. Giagonia also wrote that Andrada had run afoul of MacArthur's temper due to the

The outbreak of hostilities on December 8, 1941, put a hiatus on whatever plans were scheduled for combined operations between Bulkeley's PT-boats and the Filipino commanded Q-boat squadron -- Bulkeley having been handed the direct responsibility for defending Manila Bay on orders of Adm. Thomas C. Hart.

On December 19, 1941, the OSP was mobilized as part of U.S. Army Forces, Far East (USAFFE).[7]   At that time, the Chief of Staff of the Philippine Commonwealth Army issued orders calling OSP reserve officers into active duty.   The same order called for the commissioning and/or enlisting of the officers and crews of the vessels of the Philippine Bureau of Customs Revenue Service as well as personnel employed by the Marine Port Terminal Authority at Manila.   In compliance with that mobilization order, the cutters of the Bureau of Customs Revenue Service were ordered to be placed under OSP jurisdiction.   These vessels were: *Arayat, Mindoro, Banahaw,* and *Canlaon* -- the last two being lighthouse tenders.   The *Research* and the *Fathometer,* which were both Philippine government survey vessels, were also taken as was the presidential yacht *Casiana* and with it her large tender, the *Baler.*[8]   A government research vessel, the *Fisheries I,* with its crew was also taken over at that time.

Near the end of December, MacArthur declared Manila to be an open city.   Under international law, once a city is so designated, all military personnel are to be removed and all military operations within the confines of the city are to be ended. In the case of Manila, the city's boundaries included Manila harbor.   According to historian Giagonia, following the open city declaration and the military's evacuation from the city, MacArthur's headquarters then on Corregidor ordered a demolition team back to the Manila harbor area to scuttle any ships which were lying at anchor or which still remained afloat.   On a volunteer basis, OSP personnel were selected for the task. Those picked were personally told by MacArthur that the mission was *unofficial,* and that if they were caught they were to deny that the Army's high command had any knowledge of the mission.   The scuttling party left from Corregidor for Manila aboard *Abra* (Q-112) during the early morning of January 1.   Upon return, they reported their mission a success, declaring that within the time frame of 0930 in the morning to 1900 that evening, they were able to complete the scuttling of all shipping which had been still afloat within an area lying between the Manila Yacht Club and the mouth of the Pasig River.[9]

Filipino officer's earlier recommendation that the service of foreign consultants (British) who had been engaged by MacArthur to supervise the building going on at Engineer's Island should be dispensed with as unnecessary and superfluous.

[7]   Mobilization of the Philippine Commonwealth Army was begun on September 1, 1941. By December 8, it had reached an active duty strength of 75,000 officers and men. The mobilization was in stages, a process carried beyond December 8, the Offshore Patrol being one example of later call-up.

[8]   Although they were the property of the Commonwealth Government, the survey vessels *Research* and *Fathometer* had been operated by the U.S. Coast and Geodetic Survey prior to their mobilization into OSP. Their masters were Americans while the remainder of the officers and crew were Filipinos. The American masters, USCGS employees, were not inducted into USAFFE.

[9]   Although Lieutenants Alcarax and Gomez, the two OSP officers conducting the scuttling, reported a complete success, at least one ship, *Palawan*, was later reported as being left afloat and subsequently taken over by the Japanese for their use.

As of January 1, the OSP was placed under the direct operational control of USAFFE Headquarters at Fort Mills on Corregidor. Those OSP personnel not assigned to vessels for related maritime functions were detached with orders to report for duty as infantrymen with the 2nd Regular Division of the Philippine Commonwealth Army.

During the defense of Bataan, OSP vessels were used for patrol and for ferrying intelligence agents between Corregidor and the Cavite and Pampanga-Bulacan areas. During the months of January and February, the *Abra* (Q-112) and the *Luzon* (Q-111) escorted the blockade runner *Kolumbugan* on two runs to Looc Cove where rice and cattle were loaded to be brought back to Corregidor.

As of the surrender of the American and Filipino elements of USAFFE -- which after MacArthur's evacuation to Australia had been designated U.S. Forces in the Philippines (USFIP) -- all the vessels of the OSP had either been lost through enemy action or had been scuttled to avoid their capture.[10]

~

The Offshore Patrol continued as an organizational entity well past the May 1942 surrender of the Philippines. Although the evidence is scant and vague as to the activities of the Patrol and its personnel during that time, this much is known:

⇒ During July 1942, U.S. Army Forces in Australia activated a command known as *Ship and Gun Crew Command No. 1* to which was an attachment, *Detachment, Offshore Patrol, Philippine Commonwealth Army.*

⇒ The Philippine registered merchant ships *Don Isidro* and the *Florence D* which sailed from Java in February 1942 with supplies for the Philippines, but which were both sunk en route, had aboard as ships' officers those holding commissions in the Offshore Patrol. (It is probable that these officers were in an inactive reserve status, when they left the Philippines as December 19 marked the date when the OSP was mobilized.[11])

⇒ The Filipino hospital ship *Mactan,* which left Manila for Australia in mid-December 1941, had among its ship's officers five reserve officers of the Offshore Patrol.

⇒ A number of Filipinos who were at Australian ports during 1942 appear to have been inducted into the Army of the United States, probably with the same ranks they had held within the Philippine Commonwealth Army. The exact circumstances of such persons and how many were so affected is, however, not known; nor, for that matter, is it known as to how many of them had a prior affiliation with the OSP.

~

During the defense of the Philippines, December 1941 - May 1942, how many Filipino merchant ships had as part of their complements either commissioned or enlisted members of the Offshore Patrol reserve will probably never be ascertained.

---

[10] See List 3 of *List of Vessels and Particular, When Known, Defense of the Philippines, December 1941 to May 1942.* That list gives details, inclusive of reasons for the losses of each of the OSP vessels. Maj. Enrique Jurado, the commander of OSP who survived the enemy sinking of *Luzon* (Q-111), later became a prominent guerrilla operative. It has been alleged that at the close of the war, Jurado was murdered by members of a rival guerrilla band.

[11] Rafael J. Cisneros, master of the *Don Isidro,* is definitely known to have held a commission in the Offshore Patrol at the time that the ship made its attempt to reach the Philippines. For that service, he was awarded the Philippine Commonwealth's Gold Cross Medal.

Record Group-407, the Philippine Archive Collection, which in part deals with civilian shipping employed by the U.S. Army Transport Service within the Philippine archipelago is silent on that subject. Although only conjecture, it is probable that a number of OSP members were so employed, serving while on military orders as part of those respective ship's crewing complements. Such seems to have been the case with at least some of the officers and perhaps others in the crews of the blockade runners *Legazpi, Bohol II,* and *Kolumbugan.* These three ships operated directly from Corregidor on runs to Looc Cove, lying to the south of Corregidor on the shore of Batanaga Province, and to the island of Panay, returning to Corregidor with foodstuffs.[12]

---

[12] The Corregidor based runs of the *Legazpi, Bohol II,* and *Kolumbugan* were conducted during the months of January and February 1942 after which the Japanese blockade tightened at the entrance to Manila Bay making such runs prohibitive. The *Legazpi* was lost to enemy action off Mindoro on March 1. *Kolumbugan* was captured on February 27 off Mindoro. *Bohol II* which made its last trip in mid-February was shelled and sunk at Corregidor on April 9. The master of *Bohol II*, Jose A. Amoyo, and the master of *Legazpi,* Lino T. Conajero, were each awarded the Distinguished Service Cross by General MacArthur. It is known that Conajero was an officer in the OSP and that he had been detailed for duty with the Army Transport Service.

APPENDIX N

LEGAL STATUS OF *DON ISIDRO*
LOST TO ENEMY ACTION, FEBRUARY 1942

U.S. Maritime Commission files now held within the Maritime Administration's Records, National Archives, Washington, on *Don Isidro,* a vessel owned by the De la Rama Steamship Company of Manila, include a letter dated April 10, 1943, addressed to E. A. McLaughlin of the War Shipping Administration (WSA) from James L. Adams, Asst. General Counsel, WSA, sent in reply to earlier correspondence of February 12, 1943, Adams from McLaughlin. This correspondence discloses that *Don Isidro's* owners or representatives entered into negotiations with the U.S. Maritime Commission on January 11, 1942, at Brisbane, Australia. A charter document had been drawn for *Don Isidro* using the standard time charter format being employed at that time by USMC; however, for some unexplained reason, it was not executed by the involved parties until almost two years later, by which time the ship had long been considered a constructive total loss. According to the master, the Shipping Articles signed between the ship's master and his crew at the time of the negotiations at Brisbane had listed the Army as the charterer. Those Articles went down with the ship. Whether the arrangement for the *Don Isidro's* employment by the Army was of a strict bareboat agreement is not at all clear; nevertheless, the crew, as later stated by the master, was under the impression that they had become employees of the Army. That impression is corroborated by War Shipping Administration insurance records which lists those later killed on *Don Isidro* as direct employees of the War Department.[1] While the negotiations were transpiring at Brisbane, the crew of the vessel, as represented by the master, entered into a contractual agreement with

---

[1] Letter to senior author from C. R. Hart, Jr., Chief Insurance Branch, MARAD, dated July 9, 1971, with enclosures.

representatives of U.S. Army Forces in Australia (USAFIA). That agreement did not, however, bring the officers and crew of *Don Isidro* into the status of being civil service employees of the War Department such as would have normally been the case with the crew of a ship bareboat chartered by the War Department. When the ship left Brisbane for Java via Freemantle, her legal status consisted of an agreement made between the U.S. government, as represented by Maj. George A. Dietz of USAFIA, and either the owner or his agent, as then represented by the ship's master, in that the ship was under requisition by the Army to carry out the voyage upon which she was embarked.[2][3]

The protection of Filipino ship crews under U.S. government employment while outside of their home islands (other than those aboard ships on bareboat charter) during early 1942 seems to have been limited, at least up to the point that ships' owners became signatory to the provisions of the U.S. Maritime War Emergency Board. The De la Rama Steamship Company did not become a signatory to those Board agreements until on or after August 1942. In the case of the *Don Isidro* crew, it was recognized that she had been employed at the time of her loss as a transport of the U.S. Army -- that being a determination finally arrived at through the joint acquiescence of the War Shipping Administration and the War Department.

The status surrounding the situation of the vessel itself was such that it was not until on or about February 1944 that the previously unexecuted charter agreement negotiated at Brisbane in January 1941 was finally executed, thus allowing the *Don Isidro's* owner to file a claim against the U.S. Government for the loss of the ship. Payment for the loss was made possible through the authority of General Order No. 53 of the U.S. Maritime Commission which by amendment, General Order No. 20 dated September 7, 1942, allowed U.S. Government subsidized War Risk Insurance to include vessels defined as:

> *U.S. flag vessels and foreign flag vessels owned by a national of the United States. Philippine corporations, although not citizens of the United States, are nationals.* [4]

---

[2]   According to an affidavit executed toward the end of the war by Rafael S. Acosta, Captain, U.S. Army Transportation Corps, *arrangements were conducted between Rafael J. Cisneros, the ship's master, and the Army* before the ship left Brisbane. Acosta had been the 3rd Officer of the ship at that time. The Acosta affidavit is contained within RG-407, PAC, Box 1566, Folder "Marine Statistics Branch - *Don Isidro.*"

[3]   Remaining in question is the possible military status of the officers and perhaps others of the crew of *Don Isidro*. It is known, for instance, that the ship's master, Rafael J. Cisneros, held a commission in the Offshore Patrol, Philippine Commonwealth Army. On December 19, 1942, the OSP was mobilized as part of U.S. Army Forces in the Far East, and shortly following that mobilization, reserve officers belonging to the Offshore Patrol were called to active duty status.

[4]   Quotation is taken from Memorandum dated February 13, 1946, attention of L. W. Higgeman, Acting Director, Division of Marine Insurance from F. B Goertner, Special Council, now held in MARAD record files (WSA) under *Don Isidro*. The language of the Goertner memorandum should not be misunderstood as suggesting that a Philippine-registered vessel during the period of World War II was not an American flag vessel. Up to the date of Philippine independence in 1946, all Philippine-registered vessels were considered U.S. flag vessels and as such, they flew the U.S. flag.

APPENDIX O

VOLUNTEERS TO THE *TAIYUAN*

Sources: Award file of War Shipping Administration, now held by U.S. Maritime Administration; as well as U.S. Army, Files of the Adjutant Generals Office, January 1946, regarding claims made under the "Missing Persons Act" by Godfrey, Horn, Young

   Listed below are the names of five American merchant seamen who during February of 1942 volunteered their services at Soerabaja, Java, to help crew the British merchant ship *Taiyuan* (John W. E. Warrior, master) recently obtained by Col. John A. Robenson, acting for the U.S. Army under the authority of the American-British-Dutch-Australian (ABDA) high command then headquartered on Java. These men were reportedly informed that the mission the ship was to undertake was of a highly dangerous nature, presumed correctly by those involved as a run through the Japanese blockade with supplies for the defenders of Bataan/ Corregidor. On the eve of the *Taiyuan's* scheduled departure, Japanese naval forces occupied Soerabaja. In advance of that occupation, *Taiyuan* was scuttled. The names of the five *Collingsworth* crewmen are listed below along with their fates.

C. L. Godfrey	Made a POW; repatriated after the war
C. O. Young	Made a POW; repatriated after the war
W. B. Barr	Escaped to Australia
R. A. Horn	Made a POW; repatriated after the war
R. E. Woodruff	Reported as beheaded by the Japanese while a POW

Each of the above individuals was either personally or posthumously awarded the Merchant Marine Meritorious Service Medal. Apparently little investigative work was undertaken by the WSA Awards Committee Board as the board was apparently not cognizant that the volunteers had been promised an extraordinary fiscal bonus for the risk to be undertaken -- half of which was to be paid prior to the *Taiyuan's* departure. Nor could it have been aware that W. B. Barr and R. E Woodruff had a change of heart since according to the Contract concerning crewing of the vessel as drawn between Robenson and Warrior, neither of those men were engaged as part of the crew of *Taiyuan.*

Following is the Contract regarding the crewing of *Taiyuan,* as executed on February 26, 1942, between Colonel Robenson and John W. Warrior, master of *Taiyuan:*

CONTRACT

Soerabaja, Java
February 26, 1942

Contract of the United States Government with Captain J. W. E. Warrior of the British Merchant Ship *Taiyuan,* now under control of the Allied Governments (American, British, Dutch and Australian), having been requisitioned by the High Command and released to Colonel JOHN A. ROBENSON, United States Army, under authority as given in attached copy of telegram and marked Inclosure Number 1 and requested by Colonel ROBENSON on the British Vice consul, Soerabaja, Java, as indicated in Inclosure Number 2.[†]

The following agreements and stipulations are entered into on this date between Colonel JOHN A. ROBENSON, U.S. Cavalry, in charge of Special Mission and representing the United States Army, and Captain J. W. E. Warrior, Captain of the *Taiyuan,* which vessel belongs to the China Navigation Company, London, England, and now under the control of the Allied Forces.

That: For the attempted accomplishment of this Special Mission, Captain Warrior will receive 20,000 Guilders ($10,554.09), his chief engineer 10,000 Guilders ($5,277.05) and that the other officers listed below will be paid 5,000 Guilders ($2,638.52) each. One-half of this bonus will be paid the officers prior to their departure from Soerabaja, the remainder will be paid to the individual on his return or by claim of his beneficiary on the Chief Finance Officer, United States Army, Washington, D.C.:

NAME	CAPACITY	MONTHLY SALARY	CLOTHING ALLOWANCE	BENEFICIARY	AMOUNT OF INSURANCE
John W. E. Warrior	Master	$450.00	$250.00	Mrs. E. Picton, 10 Cavan Road, Maesteg, England.	$5000.00
John Reid	Mate	315.00	200.00	Mrs. K. Coughlin, 28 Main St., Ayr, Scotland	2500.00
T. G. Terjersen	2nd Mate	285.00	200.00	Mrs. Terjersen, Dramneuseveien 37, Oslo, Norway	2500.00
Carl O. Young	Chief Eng.	450.00	200.00	Mrs. L. M. Young, Bellingham, Wash., Rte 2, Box 171	5000.00
E. G. Morris	2nd Eng.	285.00	200.00	Miss A. C. Smith, Aberhondda Road, Porth South Wales, Great Britain.	2500.00
T. A. Fox	3rd Eng.	275.00	200.00	Barnet Weinstein, 1239 Ave. S., Brooklyn, N.Y.	2500.00

[†]   Note: The telegram was not found within the AGO file.

That: Members of the crew listed below will receive four (4) times their normal salaries which are set after their respective names. This bonus is to be effective from the 15th of February, 1942, and to continue only during the actual time necessary to deliver the cargo, and if a return passage is made, to be effective from the date of departure of the *Taiyuan* until its arrival at the port of the Headquarters of this Special Mission. Members of the crew will be paid their regular salaries from the 15th of February, 1942, until the 1st of March, 1942, prior to their departure from Soerabaja. The Captain of the *Taiyuan* will be given sufficient money prior to the departure to pay the crew on March 31, 1942, wherever the ship may be. The additional money which constitutes the bonus will be held in trust by the Chief Finance Officer, United States Army, Washington, D.C. (out of funds set aside for this Special Mission) subject to the claim of the individual or his beneficiary as designated by him and given below:

NAME	CAPACITY	MONTHLY SALARY	CLOTHING ALLOWANCE	BENEFICIARY	AMOUNT OF INSURANCE
Rock A. Horn	Bosun	$102.50	$100.00	Mrs. R. R. Horn, Cheney, Washington	$2500.00
C. L. Godfrey	Steward	125.00	150.00	Mrs. E. S. Godfrey, 32/23 West 60th St., Seattle, Washington	5000.00
Joseph Cvic	2nd Steward	87.50	100.00	Mrs. Michael Cvic, c/o U.S. Army Finance Officer	2500.00
Frank Foster	4th Engineer	62.50	100.00	Mrs. R. Foster, 633 Merced, Paeo, Manila, c/o U.S. Army Finance Officer	500.00
K. A. Olafssan	Chief Cook	75.00	100.00	Mrs. Elin Olsen, Odsbey, Munkedal, Sweden	500.00
Ahar Nilsson	2nd Cook	50.00	75.00	Mrs. Gus Nilsson, Lanvinkilsgatan, Halsingborg, Sweden	500.00
Vinc Foster	Oiler	55.00	100.00	Mrs. R. Foster, 633 Merced Paeo, Manila, c/o U.S. Army Finance Officer	500.00
G. A. Benjiman	Fireman	45.00	50.00	Mrs. Benjiman, c/o P.O. Cristobel, Panama	500.00
Gus Arne Fallgren	Sailor	87.50	50.00	Mrs. Anna Fallgren, Box 204, Hallefors, Sweden	500.00
Sven Larrsson	Sailor	87.50	50.00	In trust, U.S. Finance Officer	500.00

CREW (Native)

NAME	CAPACITY	MONTHLY SALARY	CLOTHING ALLOWANCE	AMOUNT OF INSURANCE
Aboeadelan	Cook	20 Builders	10.00	500.00
Kidjan	Cook	20 Guilders	$10.00	$500.00
Aboe	Fireman	20 Guilders	10.00	500.00
Boesi	Fireman	20 Guilders	10.00	500.00
Djais	Fireman	20 Guilders	10.00	500.00
Embran, aliaes Pak Tiham	Fireman	20 Guilders	10.00	500.00
Kasan	Fireman	20 Guilders	10.00	500.00
Mardjoeki	Fireman	20 Guilders	10.00	500.00
Pakih	Fireman	20 Guilders	10.00	500.00
Soekri	Fireman	20 Guilders	10.00	500.00
Soeparman	Fireman	20 Guilders	10.00	500.00
Taman	Fireman	20 Guilders	10.00	500.00
Doel	Sailor	20 Guilders	10.00	500.00
Kasbola	Sailor	20 Guilders	10.00	500.00
Pak Aspin alias Moenasrip	Sailor	20 Guilders	10.00	500.00
Ekran	Boy	20 Guilders	10.00	500.00
Oesin	Boy	20 Guilders	10.00	500.00
Saloewi	Boy	20 Guilders	10.00	500.00
Sanoesi	Boy	20 Guilders	10.00	500.00
Soelkan	Boy	20 Guilders	10.00	500.00

That: In view of the fact that no Life Insurance Company in this locality will accept Insurance on individuals for this mission, and that the urgent need for rapidity of action precludes any correspondence with Life Insurance companies in other countries, it is necessary that the United States Army, through the Chief Finance Officer, assume the role of an insurance company. It is therefore agreed that the Finance Officer, United States Army, Washington, D.C. assume the Life Insurance liability of the above named officers and crew to the amount set opposite their respective names (out of funds set aside for this Special Mission), for only such time as it takes to accomplish the mission on which they are about to undertake. Such period of liability will extend to 60 Days from the date that the Steamship *Taiyuan* leaves this port on this Mission, presumably on or about February 26, 1942. *In case of death during this period as a result of injury or accident incident to this mission, the above named sum or sums will be paid by the Finance Officer, United States Army (out of funds set aside for this Special Mission), to the beneficiaries listed above.* - The native crew listed above have been paid four (4) times their regular salary per month for two (2) months, which is deemed ample for the Mission in question unless a second mission is undertaken in which event they shall receive like compensation. The insurance for $500.00 to be paid in the case of each member of the native crew will be paid upon claim on the Finance Officer, United States Army, Washington, D.C. by the Wedono of Grissee through F. De Haas, Soerabaja, Java.

That: Such supplies (sea stores) as deemed advisable by Captain Warrior will be purchased by him and paid for by funds allotted for this Mission.

That: In case officers and members of the crew are left stranded without wearing apparel in a neutral or friendly port they will be supplied by their respective consuls with sufficient clothing as is deemed necessary by said consul but not to exceed that amount listed in the column of officers and members of the crew.

That: It is deemed advisable that Captain Warrior have with him upon sailing, five hundred dollars ($500.00) in cash for incidental expenses, and one (1) months salary in dollars for payment of salaries to officers and crew when due, salaries amounting to (exclusive of native crew) a total of 2837.50 Dollars.

That: In event of the loss of the Steamship *Taiyuan* as a result of hostile fire or bombing or capture by hostile forces, the owners thereof, China Navigation Company, London, England, will have just claim against the United States Government for fair price on such vessel. The compensation for the use or rental of this ship for this Mission, will be $3.95 per dead weight ton per month, effective February 15, 1942. When this vessel is no longer required on this Special Mission, Captain Warrior will report by cable to his company and to the United States Maritime Commission, Washington, D.C. the date upon which this contract is terminated.

That: In event of the loss of the Steamship *Taiyuan* and that the members of the crew report to a neutral or friendly port, the officers and members of the crew will be repatriated, that is sent to their respective homeland at the expense of the United States Government. In event that the Steamship *Taiyuan* after completing its mission, puts in at a friendly or neutral port such officers and members of the crew who were not originally employed by the China Navigation Company, London, England, will be repatriated that is sent to their respective homeland at the expense of the United States Government, if so desired. Those who were employed by the China Navigation Company, London, England will report to their company headquarters for instructions.

That: It is agreed by Captain Warrior that in case of evident capture by hostile forces, his ship will be scuttled and will not be surrendered to the enemy in serviceable condition.

The above stipulations are agreed to by both parties concerned as indicated by their respective signatures as witness below:

signed/ John W. E. Warrior

signed/ John A. Robenson

JOHN W. E. WARRIOR
Captain, *Taiyuan*

WITNESSES:

JOHN A. ROBENSON
Colonel, Cavalry
United States Army
WITNESSES:

Signed / Franklin H. Andrews
1st Lt., Inf.

Signed / Albert B. Cook
1st Lt., F.A.

I certify that the above is a true copy.

/S/ John A Robenson,
JOHN A. ROBENSON,
Colonel, Cavalry.

APPENDIX P

Legazpi Crewmembers Awarded the Silver Star For Supply Missions: Corregidor to Capiz, Panay, 1942

Source: Memorandum from Brig. Gen. Carl H. Seals (by command of General MacArthur) to Juan Echevarria, February 16, 1942. RG-407, PAC, File No. 220.5, Misc - AG-v

Abellana, Celso	Libre, Ricardo
Alfonso, Tarciano	Macalindol, Quintin
Antechamara, Nicannor	Malait, Ponciano
Balbirona, Ciriaco	Matranas, Segundo
Balbirona, Juan	Moreno, Fernando
Barasona, Cerilo	Quisay, Agripino
Barasona, Deoscoro	Romero, Felix
Betiarente, Agaton	Rosal, Donato
Caluya, Juanito	Rosalijos, Cerilo
Cavan, Guillermo	Roselijos, Julian
deVera, Lorenzo	Solis, Sol Vil
Echevarria, Juan	Solon, Benito
Emia, Marciano	Suarez, Flaviano S.
Fernandez, Diego	Tancinco, Jose
Fernandez, Sabino	Tirol, Fabian
Flores, Pelagio	Ursal, Leoncio
Fornis, Pedro	Ursal, Terino
Labores, Antonio	Young, Maxime

Note: The master of the *Legazpi,* Rafael J. Cisneros, an officer in the Offshore Patrol, Philippine Commonwealth Army, on detached duty with the Army Transport Service at Fort Mills, Corregidor, was awarded the Distinguished Service Cross. The pilot assigned to the *Legazpi,* Jose A. Amoyo, was also awarded the Distinguished Service Cross. It is not known whether Amoyo was a member of the Offshore Patrol on detached duty to the ATS.

APPENDIX Q

General Policies Involving
Vessels of the War Department - World War II

The Introduction to Part II of this volume is concerned primarily with the vessels and crews that were part of the Army Transport Service which was reorganized during early 1942 as the sea transportation arm of the Service of Supply. Later in 1942, another reorganization placed them within the Water Division of the Transportation Corps, part of the Army Service Forces. In addition to the Transportation Corps, other service branches as well as combat arms of the War Department also utilized floating equipment in the performance of their wartime missions. To provide a comprehensive picture of manning policies for all vessels operated by the War Department, we have here duplicated in its entirety a report issued during 1943 by the Office of the Chief of Transportation now under Files of the Chief of Transportation, RG-336, Modern Military Records, National Archives.

THE CREWING, MAINTENANCE, AND REPAIR OF WAR DEPARTMENT VESSELS

1.   *The crewing and the maintenance and repair of War Department vessels vary with the area of employment and the service involved. Vessels may be employed either in the zone of the interior or in the overseas theaters. The majority of the War Department vessels are attached to the Transportation Corps, Army Service Forces. However, War Department vessels are also operated by the Army Air Forces, by the Corps of Engineers, Army Service Forces, and by the Coast Artillery Corps, Army Ground Forces. In the discussion below, vessels are classified first by area of employment and thereunder by the operating service.*

2.   *WAR DEPARTMENT VESSELS IN THE ZONE OF THE INTERIOR.*

  a.   <u>*Army Air Forces.*</u>

  These vessels are crewed by AAF military personnel, who are also responsible for repairs in the first, second, and the minor third echelons. The Transportation Corps is responsible for repairs in the balance of the third, as well as the fourth and fifth echelons, in addition to furnishing marine supplies and spare parts.

  b.   <u>*Coast Artillery Corps.*</u>

  Crews are composed of military personnel of the Coast Artillery Corps, who are also responsible for maintenance repairs in the first and second echelons. The Transportation Corps is responsible for maintenance and repairs in the third, fourth and fifth echelons, as well as for marine supplies and spare parts.

  c.   <u>*Corps of Engineers.*</u>

  The Corps of Engineers utilizes only civilian crews, and is responsible for all maintenance, repairs, marine supplies, and spare parts.

3.   *WAR DEPARTMENT VESSELS IN OVERSEAS THEATERS.*

  a.   <u>*Army Air Forces.*</u>

  So far as is known, vessels sent overseas are manned by military personnel. First and second and minor third echelon maintenance are provided by the boat crews. Major third and all fourth echelon maintenance are the responsibility of Transportation Corps units. Fifth echelon maintenance is provided at available base shops by the Transportation Corps. The Transportation Corps also furnishes all spare parts and various supplies for these vessels. (See A. G. Memorandum No. W55-28-43, 25 June 1943, titled 'Maintenance of Army Air Forces Floating Equipment.')

  b.   <u>*Coast Artillery Corps.*</u>

  So far as is known, this Corps has no vessels overseas. [That statement is qualified in that vessels of the Mine Planter Service stationed in the Philippines during 1941-42 had been manned by military personnel. Ed.]

  c.   <u>*Corps of Engineers*</u>

  Crews are made up of military personnel. Spare parts, supplies, maintenance and repairs are all provided by the Corps of Engineers. [This category was also inclusive of vessels assigned to the Army's Amphibious Engineer Brigades. Ed.]

d.   *Transportation Corps.*

Except for the owned and chartered transports, all of which are operated by civilian crews, the vessels of the Transportation Corps utilize both civilian and military personnel. Civilian crews, however, are in the majority. A special situation obtains [sic] in the Southwest Pacific, where the Coast Guard has agreed to provide personnel for a limited number of vessels to be operated from advanced bases. Overseas the Transportation Corps has two types of military units for handling small boats. The first is the so-called Harbor Craft Company which is organized to ferry cargo ashore from freighters and transports arriving in the theaters of operation. The second type is the Small Boat Company which is organized to haul cargo and passengers to bases along the coast or on neighboring islands within the theaters of operation. In addition, Port Marine Maintenance Companies engage in ship repair and maintenance. All maintenance, repairs, and marine supplies for these vessels are the responsibility of the Transportation Corps.

4.   *As employed above, included in first, second, and minor third echelon maintenance are those repairs which normally the crew can perform with available tools, spare parts, and equipment. More extensive repairs requiring special skills and facilities fall within the higher echelons.*

5.   *In general, on all larger armed War Department vessels, including the troop and cargo transports of the Transportation Corps and the port repair ships of the Corps of Engineers, gun crews of varying sizes are furnished by the Navy Department.* [During 1942, gun crews on many of the Army's large vessels were Army personnel. Army personnel continued to serve as gun crews on many of the Army's civilian-manned small vessels within the Pacific through to the end of the war. Ed.]

[initialed by] *H. L.*

APPENDIX R

Army and Naval Officers Assigned to the Army Transport Service, Bataan / Corregidor: January 1941 - May 1942

Taken from *The Ward Report* which was incorporated as part of Drake's Report titled *Operations of the Quartermaster Corps, Philippine Islands, July 27, 1941 to May 6, 1942*. These documents were originally filed as "No. 83" within Records of the Army Adjutant General, WW II but are now to be found within RG-407, PAC, Box 1570.

The following officers were assigned to the Army Transport Service. Those known to be dead are so indicated.

Ward, Frederick A., Col., 0-7566, QMC, Superintendent ATS

Kramer, Joseph A., Col., QMC, Executive Officer, ATS, Corregidor

Kerr, Edwin V., Lt. Col., 0-12304, FA, Commanding Officer of Troops, *USAT Don Esteban,* transferred to II Corps Luzon. Died on board Japanese prison ship *Oryoko Maru,* en route to Japan.

Byrd, Cornelius Z., Lt. Col., 0-17760, Inf (QMC) Executive Officer ATS, Manila and Corregido, and Assistant Superintendent ATS, Cebu. Died at Camp 3, Moji, Japan.

Hughes, Joseph J., Maj. 0-288858, QMC, Assistant Superintendent ATS, Bataan, died December 1944, on board Japanese prison ship en route to Japan.

White, Walter A., Maj., 0-278768, QMC, Administrative Officer, ATS, Corregidor.

Ennis, Robert H., Maj., QMC, Maintenance and Repair Officer, ATS, Corregidor. Transferred to Motor Transport Service. Died at Cabanatuan Prison Camp, 2 September 1942.

Strang, Arthur E., Maj. QMC, Officer-in-charge, ATS activities at Mareveles, Bataan.

Juricka, Thomas W., Maj.,* QMC, Operations Officer, ATS, Cebu; escaped to Australia

Baldwin, James H., Capt., 0-384778, QMC, Operations Officer, ATS, Corregidor

Zimmerman, John O., Capt., QMC, Assistant Operations Officer, ATS, Corregidor

Wilson, William J., Capt., QMC, QM *USAT Don Esteban*

Hinck, John, Capt., QMC, QM *USAT Don Esteban;* died in Australia about 1 December 1941.·

Fossum, Orville J., Capt, Inf, QM, *USAT Elcano;* reported dead in Japanese prison camp at Davao, Mindanao

Cleland, M. E., Jr., Capt., QMC. Maintenance and Repair Officer, ATS, Cebu. No information as to present status.

Holton, William E., 1st Lt., CAC, Assistant Operations Officer, ATS Corregidor. Reported dead on Japanese prison ship, en route to Japan.

Burson, ??, 1st Lt., QMC, Assistant to the Assistant Superintendent, ATS Cabcaben, Bataan. Transferred to Infantry. Reported as missing on surrender of Bataan.

Mallet, Graham S., 1st Lt., 0-1385061, Assistant to the Assistant Superintendent, ATS, Cabcaben, Bataan. Died in prison camp at Tanagawa, Japan, 1943.

Baldwin, Barry, 2nd Lt., 0-890029, QMC, Asssistant Operations and Supply Officer, ATS, Corregidor. Died 3 February 1943, at Tanagawa, Japan.

Harris, Richard E., 2nd Lt., QMC, Assistant to the Assistant Superintendent, ATS, Cabcaben, Bataan. Reported dead in Cabanatuan Prison Camp.

Grainger, ?, 2nd Lt., QMC, Assistant to the Assistant Superintendent, ATS, Cebu, reported 29th Replacement Depot, Philippines, en route to U.S. about the 1st of October 1945.

Claussen, ?, 2nd Lt., QMC, Assistant to the Assistant Superintendent, ATS, Cebu. No data as to present status.

Holmes, George, 2nd Lt., QMC. Former Staff Sgt., QM on *USAT Don Esteban,* appointed 2nd Lt. by Commanding General Cebu Forces; temporary duty with Cebu QM Depot. Died on Japanese Prison Ship, *Oryoku Maru,* en route to Japan.

Audet, Charles W., Warrant Officer, ?-901831, AMPS, Assistant Operations Officer, ATS, Corregidor. Last known to have been in Cabanatuan Prison Camp.

Donaldson, [Trose E.], Lt. (jg), USNR, Commanding Officer, *USAT Henry Keswick.* Killed in action April 9, 1942.

Glatt, Robert L., Ensign (CC) USNR, Maintenance and Repair Officer, ATS, Corregidor. Died on Japanese prison ship *Oryoku Maru,* en route to Japan December 1944.

Whitman, Ensign H. C. (CC), USNR, Assistant Maintenance and Repair Officer, ATS, Corregidor. Died on Japanese prison ship en route to Japan, December 1944

McGrath, James M., Ensign, USNR, 1st Assistant Engineer, *USAT YuSang.*

Dobbler, H, Machinist, USN, 2nd Assistant Engineer, *USAT YuSang.* No data as to present status.

[On page 6, Ward mentions a naval engineer N. M. Nilson who, operating under Ensign Glatt, supervised the repair of vessels assigned to the ATS on Bataan and Corregidor. Ed.]

---

* Within a February 1942 report concerning operations at Cebu City, Juricka's rank was given as 1st Lieutenant. Presumably the rank on the Ward list was what he held at the end of the war.

APPENDIX S

The Army's Mine Planter Service

Sources:
- Captain Werner W. Moore, "Harbor Boats," *The Quartermaster Review,* Volume XVIII, September-October 1938, pp 27-31, 63.
- Annual Reports of the Quartermaster General and the Secretary of War, 1908 - 1941
- Capt. H. F. E. Bultman, C.A.C., "The Army Mine Planter Service," *Coast Artillery Journal,* Volume LXX, June 1929, pp 469-472.
- Warrant Office Henry L. Jones, "History of Army Mine Planters," *Coast Artillery Journal,* Volume LXXXII, Sept - Oct, 1939, pp 456-458.
- *Record of the American Bureau of Shipping,* for the years 1938, 1939, 1942.
- *List of Merchant Vessels of the United States* for the years 1909 through 1941. (No volume was issued in 1940.)
- Record Group 336, Transportation Corp correspondence of World War II.

For the American military, the development of the controlled submarine mine came into sharp focus during the American Civil War. The Confederacy employed mines with considerable effect on the western rivers, while both the Confederacy and the Union used them on the eastern seaboard. Following the Civil War, considerable study on defensive mining was undertaken by the Army with that responsibility handed to the Corps of Engineers. That was to change when on February 2, 1901, the Congress established a Corps of Artillery charged with the responsibility for the development, installation, and operation of submarine mines in defense of the nation's harbors. In 1902, the Corps of Artillery organized a School of

Submarine Defense and created a supervisory panel (The Torpedo Board) for developing mining policy.

The first mine planter was a tug, *General Alexander,* which prior to its acquisition by the Corps of Artillery had been operated by the Quartermaster Department within the San Francisco Bay area. A photograph of the *General Alexander* appeared in a 1939 article in the *Coast Artillery Journal* showing her as having an abnormally high pilot house plus a large lifeboat swung from davits on the tug's upper deck. This excessive topside weight produced such a negative stability that only seven mine cases with anchors could be carried at one time; and even then -- when loaded, it was necessary to reduce weight by leaving part of the tug's crew ashore. *General Alexander's* inherent stability problem, together with the fact that there was no deck room for the installation of equipment necessary for training mine planter crews, called for a more suitable vessel. The *Captain Gregory Barrett* replaced *General Alexander* in 1909.[1]

Fully classed senior mine planters constructed during the first decade of the century included *Col. George Armistead, General Henry J. Hunt, General Henry Knox,* and *Major Samuel Ringgold.* All four were delivered during 1904 and 1905. They seem to have been of nearly identical design, each admeasuring at 447 tons. The *Ringgold* and the *Armistead* started their careers on the east coast but left for the west coast in 1910, making the trip by way of the Straits of Magellan. (The Panama Canal would not be completed until 1914.) The *Armistead* and the *Ringgold* were used respectively for service on Puget Sound and at San Francisco. The *Hunt* and the *Knox* were sent to the Philippines by way of the Suez Canal.

In 1909, a group of five senior mine planters measuring between 590 and 622 tons entered service. They were *Joseph Henry, General Royal T. Frank, General John M. Schofield, General E. O. C. Ord,* and *General Samuel M. Mills.* All are known to have served actively as mine planters on either the east or the west coasts -- the *Mills* and the *Frank* each serving for twelve years and the *Ord* and *Schofield* each for thirty-six years. The *Henry* served intermittently as late as 1943.

The next generation of mine planters started with the *General William M. Graham,* 617 tons, built in 1917. By 1919, nine more had been added to the fleet along with five smaller vessels which were classed as junior mine planters. Of those classed as junior mine planters, only two actually ended up in that use -- the rest being employed as freight/passenger vessels under the Quartermaster's Harbor Boat Service.[2]

By 1921, the Mine Planter Service had a total of twenty senior mine planters either actively employed or in reserve lay-up. During that year, in conjunction

---

[1]   The *Captain Gregory Barrett* was classed as a Junior Mine Planter.

[2]   The Quartermaster Department did not become the Quartermaster Corps until 1912. During 1904, the War Department had organized within the Quartermaster Department a Harbor Boat Service (HBS) which was distinct and apart from the oceangoing Army Transport Service. With the establishment of the HBS, mine planters as well as those tugs and freight/passenger vessels which were employed in support of the Corps of Artillery were placed under the custody of the HBS; however, the actual operation of the vessels remained with the Corps of Artillery. Whenever a mine planter or any vessel in support of the Corps of Artillery was no longer being actively used in that capacity, it reverted to the HBS and was either placed in reserve or employed by HBS in some other Army support role.

with a massive reduction of the Army, this number was reduced leaving only eight senior mine planters in commission with one in reserve. In 1938, the fleet slightly increased when *Lt. Col. Ellery W. Niles,* 871 tons, was added.

~

Starting with the establishment of the Mine Planter Service in 1904, the manning of the mine planters was on a part military, part civilian basis. The vessels' commanders were assigned from the Corps of Artillery as were details of enlisted men charged with the actual handling of the mines.[3] The operation of the vessels themselves was carried out by civilians working under a civilian master. While the assigned artillery officer commanded everyone on board, all orders directed to the civilian crew had to be transmitted through the master. It was an awkward way to run any vessel -- large or small -- and from the inception, disciplinary problems developed with the civilian crews. During 1916, the War Department proposed to the Congress that the crews of mine planters be militarized. However the bill failed passage. With the mobilization of 1917, and a subsequent increase in job opportunities for maritime workers, disciplinary difficulties increased. Finally in 1918, the Chief of the Coast Artillery succeeded with a request to militarize the crews.[4] To fill officer slots on the mine planters, a special authorization allowed for one hundred warrant officers to be divided into five grades depending on the positions to be filled.[5] The warrant openings were offered to qualified civilians who were already employed on the mine planters as well as to applicants from the merchant marine, and eventually to enlisted personnel who passed examinations that were established for each deck and engineering position. Later, when the Army's Nautical School was established at Fort Monroe, Virginia, it became another source for warrant officers. During 1921, with the reduction of the number of mine planters from twenty to nine, warrant officer positions were reduced by over half, the surplus warrant officers being forced into early retirement.

* * * * * *

The Coast Artillery's Mine Planter Service continued in being throughout World War II. In 1947, the Army began a phase out of its mine planting responsibilities, much of it passing to the Navy. During 1949, with the reorganization of the armed services, the Army transferred the remainder of its mine planting functions to the Navy.

---

[3]   Prior to the First World War, the Corps of Artillery had been divided into the Coast Artillery and the Field Artillery.

[4]   Complete militarization was not achieved until 1922.

[5]   Non-officer crewing positions were filled by enlisted personnel of the Coast Artillery.

U.S. Army Mine Planter Service Vessels

and

Artillery Support Vessels of the U.S. Army Harbor Boat Service

1904 through 1941

LIST GLOSSARY

ATS: Army Transport Service

CA: Coast Artillery Corps, previously known as the Corps of Artillery, as established in 1901

HBS: Harbor Boat Service

MVUS: *Merchant Vessels of the United States,* an annual government publication

USCG: United States Coast Guard

JUNIOR MINE PLANTERS WHICH ENTERED SERVICE BETWEEN 1909 and 1919

‡ Indicates confusion within MVUS regarding the year of building and tonnage of a vessel.

Dates of Mine Planter Service		Remarks
1919-35	*Captain Fred L. Perry.* 177 GT; Blt 1919‡, Rocky River, Ohio; under contract	Junior Mine Planter.
1909-31	*Captain Gregory Barrett.* 159 GT; Blt 1909‡, Portland, Oreg; under contract	Replaced the *General Alexander* for training mine planter crews at San Francisco.
1909-41	*Captain James Fornance.* 153 GT; Blt 1909‡, Portland, Oreg; under contract.	Originally slated as a Junior Mine Planter but placed with HBS as a freight/passenger vessel. In 1924-33 MVUS, incorrectly carried as *Captain Joseph Fornance.* Starting in 1934, *MVUS* carried as *James Joseph Fornance.*
1909-36	*General G. W. Getty.* 153 GT; Blt 1909‡, Quincy, MA; under contract	Originally slated as a Junior Mine Planter, but placed with HBS as a freight/passenger vessel.
1909-41	*General Richard Arnold.* 159 GT; Blt 1908, Quincy, MA; under contract	Originally slated as a Junior Mine Planter, but placed with HBS as a freight/passenger vessel.
1909-41	*General Robert Anderson.* 153 GT; Blt 1908, Quincy, MA; under contract	Originally slated as a Junior Mine Planter, but placed with HBS as a freight/passenger vessel.
1919-41	*Lt. Col. Herman C. Schumm.* 170 GT; Blt 1919, Bay City, MI; under contract	Junior Mine Planter.
1919-41	*Major Albert G. Jenkins.* 170 GT; Blt 1919‡, Bay City, MI	Originally slated as a Junior Mine Planter, but placed with HBS as a freight/passenger vessel. Damaged at Fort Barrancas, FL, during hurricane in 1927; during 1932 underwent extensive repairs.
1919-41	*Major Clarence M. Condon.* 170 GT; Blt 1919‡, Bay City, MI.	Originally slated as a Junior Mine Planter under the designation JMP 7; redesignated *Major Clarence M. Condon.* Was placed with HBS as freight/passenger vessel. Beginning in 1934, MVUS carried her as *Captain C. M. Condon.*
1919-33	*Major William P. Pence.* 170 GT; Blt 1919‡, Bay City, Mich; under contract.	Junior Mine Planter. Transferred to USCG in 1933.

ARTILLERY SUPPORT VESSELS OVER 50 GROSS TONS
WHICH ENTERED SERVICE BETWEEN 1907 and 1941

In addition to the vessels here listed, the Mine Planter Service utilized a large number of vessels less than 50 gross tons for servicing defensive mines. They ranged from the "L" or "DB" class of Distribution Box Boats to the smaller Mine Yawls and personnel launches.

‡ Indicates confusion within MVUS regarding the year of building and tonnage of a vessel.

Years of Utilization			
1919-21	*ATS Tug No. 1*, ex *John G. Stewart*	tug/artil stmr	Blt 1911; Port Richmond, NY. See also *John G. Stewart*
1919-22	*ATS Tug No. 2*, ex *Hamburg-American No. 2*	tug/artil stmr	52 GT; Blt 1903; Tottenville, NY
1919-22	*ATS Tug No. 3*, ex *Hamburg-American No. 3*	tug/artil stmr	284 GT; Blt 1913; Port Richmond, NY
1919-21	*ATS Tug No. 5*, ex *American*	tug/artil stmr	88 GT; Blt 1914; Ferrysburg, MD
1919-21	*ATS Tug No. 6*, ex *William J. McCarthy*	tug/artil stmr	98 GT; Blt 1912; Ferrysburg, MD
1919-21	*ATS Tug No. 7*, ex *Harvey D. Goulder*	tug/artil stmr	156 GT; Blt 1898; Buffalo, NY
1918-21	*Baltimore No. 1*	tug/artil stmr	Blt 1918; Baltimore, MD
1918-20	*Boswell*	tug/artil stmr	311 GT; Blt 1890; Camden, NJ. Sent to France during 1918.
1941	*Brig. Gen. Arthur W. Yates*, ex *St. Ignace*	Pass/artil/frt	528 GT
1938-41	*Brig. Gen. Patrick W. Guiney*, ex *General R. B. Ayers;* ex *H.R. Carter.*	Pass/artil/frt	159 GT; Blt 1908; Quincy, MA; under contract. See also *General R. B. Ayers.*
1941	*Brig. Gen. William E. Horton*, ex *Macinaw City*	Pass/artil/frt	528 GT
1918	*Britannia*, ex *Britannia*	tug/artil stmr	146 GT; Blt 1914; Noank, Conn.
1907-21	*Captain A. M. Wetherill*	tug/artil stmr	128 GT; Blt 1907; Newburg, NY; under contract
1907-22	*Captain Charles W. Rowell*	tug/artil stmr	128 GT; Blt 1907; Wilmington, Del; under contract
1904-22	*Captain Drum*	tug/artil stmr	62 GT; Blt 1875; New York, NY; under contract
1919-30	*Captain Edward P. Nones*	Pass/freight; tug/artil stmr	177 GT; Blt 1919‡; Rocky River, Ohio; under contract
1919-21	*Captain Edwin C. Long*	tug/artil stmr	177 GT; Blt 1919‡; Rocky River, Ohio; under contract
1919-22	*Captain Samuel C. Cardwell*	tug/artil stmr	177 GT; Blt 1919‡; Rocky River, Ohio; under contract
1907-23	*Captain T. W. Morrison*	tug/artil stmr	128 GT; Blt 1907; Wilmington, Del; under contract

1919	*Captain Theodore W. Gaines*	tug/artil stmr	Blt 1919; North Tonawanda, NY; under contract
1919-21	*Captain W. McKie*	tug/artil stmr	170 GT; Blt 1919; Bay City, MI; under contract
1919-22	*Chester*	tug/artil stmr	98 GT; Blt 1918; Delanco, NJ
1919-31	*Col. Clayton, ex Maren Lee*	tug/artil stmr	132 GT; Blt 1916; Tottenville, NY
1919-22	*Columbia*	tug/artil stmr	96 GT; Blt 1892; Grand Haven, MI
1918-21	*Diplomatic, ex Diplomatic*	tug/artil stmr	76 GT; Blt 1912; Grassy Point, NY
1941	*Egeria*	Pass/artil/frt	291 GT; Blt 1918; Kearny, NJ.
1922	*Engineer*	tug/artil stmr	298 GT; Blt 1907; Hong Kong, China
1920-21	*Fred E. Richards, ex Fred E. Richards*	tug/artil stmr	357 GT; Blt ; Philadelphia, PA
1909-41	*General A.M. Randol*	Pass/freight; tug/artil stmr	153 GT; Blt 1909; Quincy, MA; under contract
1920-41	*General Charles R. Krauthoff, ex Cuba*	tug/artil stmr	594 GT; Blt 1901; Bath, ME
1909-22	*General Harvey Brown*	tug/artil stmr	163 GT; Blt 1909; Quincy, MA; under contract
1909-21	*General J. M. Brannan*	tug/artil stmr	160 GT; Blt 1908; Quincy, MA; under contract
1938-41	*General John T. Knight, ex Bolivar*	Pass/artil/frt	234 GT
1909-22	*General R. H. Jackson*	tug/artil stmr	162 GT; Blt 1909; Quincy, MA; under contract
1909-21	*General R. B. Ayers*	tug/artil stmr	163 GT; Blt 1908; Quincy, MA; under contract. See also *Brig. Gen. Patrick W. Guiney.*
1911-30	*General Weeks*	tug/artil stmr	338 GT; Blt 1910; Shanghai, China
1917-21	*Gibbon, ex USQMD Sumner; ex Major McKinley.*	tug/artil stmr	59 GT; Blt Tompkins Cove, NY. MVUS, *List of Army Vessels*, gives the date of building as 1897; Army records give her date of building as 1887. Cost to Army $13,000. Served in Atlantic ATS Fleet, 1899. Circa 1910 was at Havana; served with ATS and HBS to 1915; 1915-16 was on loan to Corps of Engineers. Then went to Mine Planter Service.
1918-21	*Gosnold, ex Gosnold*	Hospital ship; tug/artil stmr; pass/freight	181 GT; Blt 1906; Noank, Conn. MVUS for 1918 gives incorrect place and date of building, an error that was subsequently corrected in later editions.
1918-20	*Grover Cleveland, ex Grover Cleveland*	tug/artil stmr	59 GT; Blt 1908; Buffalo, NY
1918-22	*Gwalia, ex Gwalia*	Tug/formerly artil steamer	415 GT; Blt 1907; Philadelphia, PA. Sent to France during 1918.
1918-22	*Gypsum Prince*	Formerly tug/ artil steamer	299 GT; Blt 1917; Baltimore, MD. Sent to France as AEF shiphandling tug during 1918.
1919-21	*H. C. Cadmus, ex John Scully; ex Echo*	tug/artil stmr	413 GT; Blt 1899; Camden, NJ
1918-21	*Howell*	tug/artil stmr	73 GT; Blt 1873; Philadelphia, PA. MVUS lists of Quartermaster vessels give former names as ex *Ionian; ex Columbia*. That is not correct. *Columbia* is the former name of the tug/artil stmr *Ionian.*
1919	*Huckey*	tug/artil stmr	418 GT; Blt 1919; Superior, WI
1919	*Hulver*	tug/artil stmr	418 GT; Blt 1918; Superior, WI

1920-21	*Ionian*, ex *Columbia*	tug/artil stmr	212 GT; Blt 1904; Camden, NJ MVUS lists of Quartermaster vessels gives former name as *Howell*; but that is incorrect.
1911-41	*J. M. Jewell*	Launch, steam; tug/artil stmr	55 GT; Blt 1908; Hong Kong, China. Utilized in PI in operations against the Moro, island of Jolo before becoming an artil. auxiliary. Sunk off Corregidor, May 4, 1942.
1919-21	*Jennie S. Wade*	tug/artil stmr	67 GT; Blt 1918; New Baltimore, NY
1918	*John G. Stewart*	tug/artil stmr	Blt 1911; Port Richmond, NY. Also in records as *J. C. Stewart, John C. Stuart, J. C. Stuart.* See also *ATS Tug No. 1.*
1919-21	*Kentucky*, ex *Kentucky*; ex *Alpha*	tug/artil stmr	86 GT; Blt 1881; Chicago, IL
1911-41	*Ledyard*	tug/artil stmr; launch	70 GT; Blt 1910; Shanghai, China. Assigned to Subic Bay in the Philippines. Either just before the Japanese attack of Dec 8, 1941, or soon after, she was accidentally placed within a U.S. minefield. Was subsequently scuttled by friendly artillery fire.
1919-21	*Leopold Adler*, ex *John H. Estill*	tug/artil stmr	243 GT; Blt 1894 \n Newport News, VA
1904-22	*Lt. Alonzo H. Cushing*	tug/artil stmr	114 GT; Blt 1899; Baltimore, MD; under contract.
1919	*Lt. Cochrane*	tug/artil stmr	Blt 1919; Crisfield, MD; under contract
1919-22	*Lt. Col. Robert C. Gildart*	tug/artil stmr	170 GT; Blt 1919; Bay City, MI; under contract. Incorrectly listed as *Col. Robert C. Gildert* in 1919 and 1920 *MVUS.*
1919	*Lt. Franz F. Schilling*	tug/artil stmr	Blt 1919; Crisfield, MD; under contract
1919	*Lt. Frederick K. Hirth*	tug/artil stmr	Blt 1919; Crisfield, MD; under contract
1906-22	*Lt. George M. Harris*	tug/artil stmr	134 GT; Blt 1905; Seattle, WA; under contract
1919; 1923-28†	*Lt. Harold B. Douglas*	Pass/freight; tug/artil stmr	177 GT; Blt 1919; Rocky River, Ohio
1919	*Lt. Harry E. Crosby*	tug/artil stmr	Blt 1919; North Tonawanda, NY; under contract
1919	*Lt. Howard T. Baker*	tug/artil stmr	Blt 1919; North Tonawanda, NY; under contract
1919	*Lt. Lawrence Dwight*	tug/artil stmr	Blt 1919; North Tonawanda, NY; under contract
1919	*Lt. Leonard C. Hoskins*	tug/artil stmr	Blt 1919; Crisfield, MD; under contract
1909-22	*Major Albert G. Forse*	tug/artil stmr	128 GT; Blt 1907; Wilmington, Del; under contract
1919-22	*Major Carl A. Lohr*	tug/artil stmr	170 GT; Blt 1919‡; Bay City, Mich; under contract
1918-19	*Major Harry L. Pettus*	tug/artil stmr	Blt 1917; Havana, Cuba
1919-22	*Major John W. McKie*	tug/artil stmr	170 GT; Blt 1919; Bay City, Mich; under contract. Carried incorrectly in 1919-21 MVUS as *Captain W. McKie.*
1919-22	*Major Lester E. Moreton*	tug/artil stmr	170 GT; Blt 1919; Bay City, Mich; under contract
1919-21	*New Rochelle*	tug/artil stmr	54 GT; Blt 1907; Tottenville, NY
1919-20	*Perseverance*, ex *Bradley*	tug/artil stmr	112 GT; Blt 1910; Perth Amboy, NY

1903-22	*Petersen*, ex *Flosie*	tug/artil stmr	104 GT; Blt 1898; Tacoma, WA. Purchased in 1903 for Alaskan service.
1918-21	*Printer*, ex *Printer*	Tug/formerly artil steamer	110 GT; Blt 1889; Hoquiam, WA. Sent to France during 1918.
1918-22	*Progresso*, ex *Progresso, Br*	tug/artil stmr	90 GT; Blt 1915; Montreal, Canada
1918-22	*Protector*, ex *Protector*	tug/artil stmr	98 GT; Blt 1882; Camden, NJ
1902-41	*Reno*, ex *Britannia*	tug/artil stmr	135 GT; Blt 1889; Philadelphia, PA. Cost to Army in 1898 was $40,000. MVUS editions 1927-41 incorrectly give ex-name of this vessel as *Gypsum King*. *Gypsum King* became the *USAT Slocum*.
1915-41	*San Pedro*	tug/artil stmr	113 GT; Blt 1890; England
1911-13	*St. Louis*, ex *Amanda*	tug/artil stmr	56 GT; Blt 1899; Hong Kong
1918-21	*Tascony*	Tug/formerly artil steamer	353 GT; Blt 1899; Philadelphia, PA. Sent to France during 1918.
1918	*Underwriter*, ex *Charles Pearson*	tug/artil stmr	327 GT; Blt 1863; Philadelphia, PA
1920-22	*V 1*, ex *USN sub chaser 414*	tug/artil stmr	77 dsp; Blt 1918; College Point, NY
1920-24	*V 2*, ex *USN sub chaser 234*	tug/artil stmr	77 dsp; Blt 1918; Morris Heights, NY
1920-22	*V 3*, ex *USN sub chaser 233*	tug/artil stmr	77 dsp; Blt 1918; College Point, NY
1920-22	*V 4*, ex *USN sub chaser 108*	tug/artil stmr	77 dsp; Blt 1918; College Point, NY
1920-22	*V 5*, ex *USN sub chaser 267*	tug/artil stmr	77 dsp; Blt 1918; College Point, NY
1920-23	*V 6*, ex *USN sub chaser 18*	tug/artil stmr	77 dsp; Blt 1918; College Point, NY
1920-22	*V 7*, ex *USN sub chaser 20*	tug/artil stmr	77 dsp; Blt 1918; College Point, NY
1920-22	*V 8*, ex *USN sub chaser 279*	tug/artil stmr	77 dsp; Blt 1918; College Point, NY
1920-22	*V 9*, ex *USN sub chaser 281*	tug/artil stmr	77 dsp; Blt 1918; College Point, NY
1920-22	*V 10*, ex *USN sub chaser 275*	tug/artil stmr	77 dsp; Blt 1918; College Point, NY
1920-22	*V 11*, ex *USN sub chaser 276*	tug/artil stmr	77 dsp; Blt 1918; College Point, NY
1920-22	*V 12*, ex *USN sub chaser 280*	tug/artil stmr	77 dsp; Blt 1918; College Point, NY
1919-21	*Vigilant*	tug/artil stmr	98 GT; Blt 1902; Long Island City, NY
1902-18	*West Point*, ex *Lee Fat*	Launch, steam; tug/artil stmr	70 GT. Purchased at Manila in 1898.

APPENDIX T

Identification of Dust Jacket Illustrations

Descriptions which follow are taken from John E. Standberg and Roger J. Bender, *The Call of Duty*, (San Jose, CA: R. James Bender Publishing Company, 1994.)

The campaign and operations medals here described reflect the operations in which the ships of the Army Transport Service participated with their logistical support.

1. <u>Spanish Campaign Medal, Army</u>. Established 1905 for service ashore or en route to Cuba: 11 May - 17 July 1898; Porto Rico (as it was then known), 24 July - 13 August 1898; Philippine Islands: 30 June - 16 August 1898. Original ribbon was red and yellow but since these were the national colors of Spain, the ribbon was changed in 1913 to yellow and blue as shown upon the dust jacket. The Army issued about 18,400 of these medals.

2. <u>Army of Occupation, Porto Rico</u>. Established in 1919. For service in Porto Rico (as it was then known) between 14 August and 10 December 1898.

3. <u>Philippine Campaign, Army</u>. Established in 1905. For service ashore in the Philippines between February 1899 and July 1902; as well as for various expeditions within the islands which occurred between 1899 and 1913. About 44,000 of these medals were issued.

4. <u>Army of Cuban Occupation</u>. Established in 1915. For military government service in Cuba between 15 July 1898 and 20 May 1902.

5. <u>Philippine Congressional</u>. Established 1906. Issued to those who entered the Army between 21 April and 26 October 1898 and who served in the Philippines beyond the date of their discharge eligibility - or - were ashore in the Philippine Islands between February 1899 and July 1902. Approximately 6,200 of these medals were issued.

6. <u>Boxer Rebellion (China Campaign), Army</u>. Established 1905. For service ashore in China with the Peking Relief Expedition between 20 June 1900 and 27 May 1901. Approximately 2,300 of these medals were issued.

7. <u>Mexican Service, Army</u>. Established 1917. For service in any one of ten different operations which occurred between 1911 and 1917. About 15,000 of these medals were issued.

8. <u>World War I Victory</u>. Established 1918. For active duty in the Armed Services, 1917 - 1919.

9. <u>American Defense Service, Army</u>. Established 1942. For service between 8 September 1939 and 7 December 1941, for 12 months' honorable service during that stated time of limited emergency.

10. <u>Philippine Defense</u>. Established by the Government of the Philippines following World War II for issue to members of the Philippine and United States armed forces who fought with USAFFE and USFIP in the defense of Bataan and Corregidor, 1941-42.

11. <u>American Campaign</u>. Established 1942. For service within the American theater between 7 December 1941 and 2 March 1946 for thirty consecutive days or sixty non-consecutive days outside of Continental U.S. Waters, or for service within the United States for an aggregate period of one year.

12. <u>Asiatic - Pacific Campaign</u>. Established 1942. For service between 7 December 1941 and March 1946 within the theater of operations for thirty consecutive days or sixty non-consecutive days.

Note regarding the absence of a medal for <u>Army of Cuban Pacification</u>: This medal was established in 1909 for service between October 1906 and April 1909 in Cuba. Unfortunately, we were not able to obtain this medal for inclusion within the dust jacket illustration. The medallion portrays two soldiers, each standing at ground arms, one on each side of the shield of the Cuban Republic. The ribbon has a broad vertical dark gray band at center with narrow bands of red, white, and blue on each side.

GLOSSARY

ACRONYMS FREQUENTLY UTILIZED WITHIN OVER SEAS

ABDA	American-British-Dutch-Australian (Command)
AEF	American Expeditionary Force to Europe (1917 - 1919)
ATS	Army Transport Service
BB	Bareboat Charter.
CTF	Navy's Cruiser and Transport Force
IRF	International Relief Force
MARAD	Maritime Administration
NOTS	Naval Overseas Transportation Service
NTS	Naval Transport Service
OSP	Offshore Patrol, Philippine Army
PI	Philippine Islands
QM	Army Quartermaster Department (after 1912, Army Quartermaster Corps)
SWPA	Southwest Pacific Area (Command)
TC	Army Transportation Corps (formed in 1942, absorbing the ATS)
USAFFE	United States Army Forces in the Far East
USAFIA	United States Army Forces in Australia
USAT	United States Army Transport
USCG	United States Coast Guard
USCGC	United States Coast Guard Cutter
USCGS	United States Coast and Geodetic Survey
USFIP	United States Forces in Philippines
USHB	United States Harbor Boat
USMC	United States Maritime Commission
USSB	United States Shipping Board
WSA	War Shipping Administration

CHARTER TERMS FREQUENTLY USED WITHIN OVER SEAS

TIME CHARTER: A form of charter party issued when the vessel is chartered for an agreed period of time. It places the vessel in the possession of the charterer. It may, however, provide that the owner shall man and provision the vessel. In ocean traffic, the usual practice is for the charterer to pay to the owner for the hire of the ship an agreed rate per deadweight ton per month and to furnish the fuel and pay all expenses at the ports except crew and provision expenses. [*International Maritime Dictionary*]

GROSS CHARTER: A somewhat ambiguous and often misused term but is often accepted to mean the same as a VOYAGE CHARTER under which the ship's owner pays for all regular expenses incident to the voyage from the time the ship is berthed until the cargo is discharged. [*International Maritime Dictionary*]

SUB CHARTER: An agreement made by the charterer of a vessel to sublet in part or totally, the said vessel to other persons. [*International Maritime Dictionary*]

BAREBOAT CHARTER: 1. "Same as demise charter." [*International Maritime Dictionary*, by Rene de Kerchove, Second Edition, (New York: Van Nostrand Reinhold Company, 1961.) 2. "Lease of a ship without equipment or crew." [*Naval Terms Dictionary,* Fourth Edition, Noel and Beach, (Annapolis: Naval Institute Press, 1978).] 3. "Charterers obtain the complete control of the vessel which they are operating as if she belonged to their own fleet. All costs and expense incident to the use and operation of the vessel are for charterer's account. Charterer will keep the vessel in good running order and condition and in substantially the same condition as when delivered by her owners. They will have her regularly overhauled and repaired as necessary." [*Chartering and Shipping Terms,* by J. Bes, Fourth Edition, (Amsterdam, 1956).]

SUB BAREBOAT CHARTER: As the term is applied to the situation in World War II with War Shipping Administration charters, it would refer to vessels bareboat chartered from owners by WSA and then subsequently sub-bareboated by WSA to another party. This was an arrangement commonly used prior to 1943 by WSA when transferring vessels to Army control wherein the Army crewed and otherwise fully operated the vessel. Starting in 1943, the practice of sub-bareboat chartering was curtailed in favor of the practice of "allocating" WSA vessels to the carriage of military cargoes and personnel. Under under "allocation," WSA remained the vessel's operators.

DEMISE CHARTER: Another term for "bareboat charter." "A charter in which the bare ship is chartered without crew." [*International Maritime Dictionary*]

AFFREIGHTMENT (or Gross Freight): Not a form of charter, but instead is where freight money is paid to the ship owner for the carriage of the cargo without any allowance for navigation charges or dues, cost of fuel, etc. [*International Maritime Dictionary*]

BIBLIOGRAPHY

SOURCES UTILIZED OR CONSULTED DURING THE PREPARATION OF OVER SEAS

GOVERNMENT PUBLICATIONS

Alien and Sedition Act. The Congressional Record, Volume 86, Part 8.

American Ship Casualties of the World War. Compiled by the Historical Section, Navy Department (corrected to April 1, 1923). Washington, DC: Government Printing Office, 1923.

Annual Report, Service of Supply, for the fiscal year ended June 30, 1942.

Annual Reports of the Major General Commanding the Army for the fiscal year ended June 30, 1898. Part 1.

Annual Reports of the Major General Commanding the Army for the fiscal year ended June 30, 1899. Parts 2 and 3 of three parts.

Annual Reports of the Navy Department for the fiscal year ended June 30, 1898, Volume 2: Appendix to the Report of the Bureau of Navigation, "Operations in the North Atlantic Ocean...in Conjunction with the Army: Convoy, Transporting, and Landing of Troops. "

Annual Reports of the Quartermaster General of the Army to the Secretary of War for the fiscal year ended June 30, 1898.

Annual Reports of the Quartermaster General of the Army to the Secretary of War for the fiscal year ended June 30, 1906.

Annual Reports of the Quartermaster General of the Army to the Secretary of War for the fiscal year ended June 30, 1907.

Annual Reports of the Quartermaster General of the Army to the Secretary of War for the fiscal year ended June 30, 1908.

Annual Reports of the Quartermaster General of the Army to the Secretary of War for the fiscal year ended June 30, 1899.

Annual Reports of the Quartermaster General of the Army to the Secretary of War for the fiscal year ended June 30, 1900.

Annual Reports of the Quartermaster General of the Army to the Secretary of War for the fiscal year ended June 30, 1901.

Annual Reports of the Quartermaster General of the Army to the Secretary of War for the fiscal year ended June 30, 1902.

Annual Reports of the Quartermaster General of the Army to the Secretary of War for the fiscal year ended June 30, 1914.

Annual Reports of the Quartermaster General of the Army to the Secretary of War for the fiscal year ended June 30, 1915.

Annual Reports of the Quartermaster General of the Army to the Secretary of War for the fiscal year ended June 30,1916.

Annual Reports of the Quartermaster General of the Army to the Secretary of War for the fiscal year ended June 30, 1917.

Annual Reports of the Quartermaster General of the Army to the Secretary of War for the fiscal year ended June 30, 1918.

Annual Reports of the Quartermaster General of the Army to the Secretary of War for the fiscal year ended June 30, 1919.

Annual Reports of the Quartermaster General of the Army to the Secretary of War for the fiscal year ended June 30 1920.

Annual Reports of the Quartermaster General of the Army to the Secretary of War for the fiscal year ended June 30, 1923.

Annual Reports of the Secretary of War to the President for the fiscal year ended June 30, 1893.

Annual Reports of the Secretary of War to the President for the fiscal year ended June 30, 1894.

Annual Reports of the Secretary of War to the President for the fiscal year ended June 30, 1895.

Annual Reports of the Secretary of War to the President for the fiscal year ended June 30, 1898. Miscellaneous Reports

Annual Reports of the Secretary of War to the President for the fiscal year ended June 30, 1918.

Annual Reports of the Secretary of War to the President for the fiscal year ended June 30, 1919. Volume I, Part 4.

Annual Reports of the Secretary of War to the President for the fiscal year ended June 30, 1919. "Final Report of General John J. Pershing"

Annual Reports of the U.S. Army Chief of Transportation Service to the Quartermaster General, 1919.

Annual Reports of the U.S. Army Chief of Transportation Service to the Quartermaster General, 1920.

Annual Reports of the War Department for the fiscal year ended 30, 1904. "Report of the Philippine Commission." Volume XI, Part 1 and XII, Part 2.

Annual Reports of the War Department for the fiscal year ended June 30, 1900, "Report of the Lieutenant General Commanding the Army". Volume I in seven parts.

Annual Reports of the War Department for the fiscal year ended June 30, 1901, "Report of the Lieutenant General Commanding the Army". Volume I in five parts.

Borowski, Harry R, Editor. *The Harmon Memorial Lectures in Military History, 1959 - 1987.* Washington, DC: Office of Air Force History, U.S. Air Force, 1988.

British and Foreign Merchant Vessel Losses, World War II: "BR 1337". Naval Staff (Trade Division), British Admiralty, 1945.

Bykofsky, Joseph and Harold Larson. *The Transportation Corps: Operations Overseas.* Washington: Office of the Chief of Military History, 1957.

Charles, Roland W. *Troopships of World War II.* Washington: The Army Transportation Association, 1947.

Clary, David A. and Joseph W. A. Whitehorne. *The Inspectors General of the United States Army 1777-1903.* Washington: Office of the Inspector General and Center of Military History, 1987.

Clephane, Lewis P. *History of the Naval Overseas Transport Service in World War I.* Washington, DC: Naval History Division, 1969.

Compendium of Regulations for the Quartermaster's Department. Published by authority of the Secretary of War for use in the Army of the United States. Washington: Government Printing Office, 1898.

Conn, Stetson; Rose C. Engelman; Byron Fairchild. *Guarding the United States and Its Outposts.* Washington, DC: Center of Military History, 1989.

Correspondence Relating to the War with Spain. Volumes I and II. Washington, DC: Center of Military History, 1993, reprint of 1902 edition.

Development of the American Ocean Mail Service and American Commerce. Report presented by Mr. Gallinger. U.S. Senate Document 225, February 6, 1908. Washington: Government Printing Office, 1908.

Dictionary of American Naval Fighting Ships. In eight volumes. Washington, DC: Department of the Navy, 1959-1981.

Digest of Opinions of the Judge Advocate General of the Army, 1912-1940. Washington, DC: Government Printing Office, 1942

Dodge Commission, see *Report of the U.S. Commission Appointed by the President to Investigate the Conduct of the War Department in the War with Spain.*

Dziuban, Stanley W. *U.S. Army in World War, Special Studies: Military Relations Between United States and Canada, 1939 - 1945.* Washington: Center of Military History, 1959.

Exterior Views and Deck Plans of Vessels of U.S. Army Transport Service. Published by Army Quartermaster Department, circa 1905 - 1912.

Federal Records of World War II. Volume I, *Civilian Agencies;* Volume II, *Military Agencies.* Washington, DC: General Services Administration, 1951. Republished, Detroit, MI: Gale Research Company, 1982.

Federal Reporter, 191, 2nd Series. Brief for the United States: Cases 401 and 414, in the Supreme Court of the United States, October term 1951.

Hackworth, Green Haywood. *Digest of International Law.* Volume VI. Washington: Government Printing Office, 1961.

Heitman, Francis B. *Historical Register and Dictionary of the United States Army from its Organization, September 29, 1789, to March 2, 1903,* Volumes I and II, 1789 - 1903. Washington, DC: Government Printing Office, 1903.

Huston, James A. *Sinews of War: Army Logistics, 1775 - 1953.* Washington, DC: Office of the Chief of Military History, 1966.

Inquiry of the House in Relation to the Transport Service Between San Francisco and the Philippine Island. Letter from the Secretary of War to the House of Representatives, Document 537, Part 1 and 2, April 8, 1902. Washington: Government Printing Office, 1902.

International Law Situations. Newport, RI: The Naval War College, 1930.

Jacobsen, Commander ——. *Sketches From the Spanish-American War.* Translated from the German. Office of Naval Intelligence, War Notes No. III, Information From Abroad. Washington: Government Printing Office, 1899.

Leighton, Richard M. and Robert W. Coakley. *Global Logistics and Strategy, 1940-1943.* Washington: Office, Chief of Military History, 1955.

List of Merchant Vessels of the United States, an annual U.S. Government publication, which we utilized for the years 1898 through 1942.

Manual for the Quartermaster Corps, U.S. Army, 1916. Washington: Government Printing Office, 1917.

Millett, John D. *The Army Service Forces: The Organization and Role of the Army Service Forces.* Washington, DC: Office, Chief of Military History, 1954.

Mixed Claims Commission, United States and Germany, Administrative Decisions and Opinions of a General Nature to June 30, 1925. Washington: Government Printing Office, 1925.

Morton, Louis. *The Fall of the Philippines.* Washington: Office, Chief of Military History, 1953.

Núñez, Severo Gómez, Captain of Artillery. *The Spanish-American War. Blockades and Coast Defense.* Translated from the Spanish. Office of Naval Intelligence: War Notes No. VII, Information From Abroad. Washington: Government Printing Office, 1899.

Order of Battle of the United States Land Forces in the World War. American Expeditionary Forces, Volumes I and II. Washington, DC: Center of Military History, 1988.

Order of Battle of the United States Land Forces in the World War. Zone of the Interior. Volume III, part 1 of 3 parts. Washington, DC: Center of Military History, 1988.

Plüddlemann, Rear-Adm. M., (German Navy). *Comments on the Main Features of the War With Spain.* Translated from the German. Office of Naval Intelligence: War Notes No. II, Information From Abroad. Washington: Government Printing Office, 1899.

Register of Ships Owned by United States Shipping Board. Third Edition. Washington, DC: United States Shipping Board, Emergency Fleet Corporation, 1919.

Regulations for the Army of the United States, 1889.

Regulations for the Army of the United States, 1910.

Regulations for the Harbor Boat Service, Quartermaster's Department, U.S. Army, October 1, 1904.

Regulations for the U.S. Army Transport Service 1908.

Regulations for the U.S. Army Transport Service, 1898.

Regulations of the Quartermaster's Department, 1898.

Regulations Prescribing Flags, Signals, Funnel Marks, etc., as well as regulations for uniforms of the U.S. Army Transport Service. Washington: Secretary of War, 1899. Military History Institute Call No. UC323 A5

Report of Introduction of Domestic Reindeer into Alaska. 55th Congress, Senate, 3rd Session, Document No. 34, 1898.

Report of the Philippine Commission to the President, Volumes I, II, III, IV. Washington, DC: Government Printing Office, 1900 and 1901.

Report of the U.S. Commission Appointed by the President to Investigate the Conduct of the War Department in the War with Spain. 56th Congress, U.S. Senate Document No. 221 in eight volumes. Washington: Government Printing Office, 1900. (The Commission was informally known as "The Dodge Commission.")

Risch, Erna. *Quartermaster Support of the Army: A History of the Corps, 1775-1939.* Washington, DC: Quartermaster's Historian Office, 1962.

Sailing Directions for the Hudson Bay Route, From Atlantic to Churchill Harbor, 2nd edition. Ottawa: Hydrographic and Map Service, Department of Mines and Resources, 1940.

Sailing Directions, Philippine Islands. Washington, DC: Defense Mapping Agency, 1996.

Sailing Directions: Labrador and Hudson Bay. Fifth edition. Ottawa: Department of Fisheries and Oceans, 1983.

Smith, R. Elberton. *United States Army in World War II: The War Department. The Army and Economic Mobilization.* Washington: Office of the Chief of Military History, 1959.

Stauffer, Alvin P. *The Quartermaster Corps: Operations in the War Against Japan.* Washington: Office of Chief of Military History, 1956, reprinted in 1978.

Technical Manual 10-380. *Water Transportation*. War Department, February 14, 1941.

Technical Manual 20-205. *Dictionary of United States Army Terms*. War Department, 18 January 1944.

The Spanish-American War. A Collection of Documents Relative to the Squadron Operations in the West Indies. Office of Naval Intelligence: War Notes No. VII, Information From Abroad. Washington: Government Printing Office, 1899.

Transportation of Military Property Under Contract by Rails, Water, and Wagon. A Report of the Quartermaster General of the Army. Washington: Government Printing Office, 1884.

U.S. House Documents Volume 109, Appendix QR. War Department, Quartermaster General's Office, Washington, June 5, 1900.

United States Army in the World War, 1917 - 1919: Reports of the Commander in Chief, AEF, Staff Sections and Services. Washington, DC: Department of the Army, 1948.

United States Naval Chronology, World War II. Washington: Government Printing Office, 1955.

Wardlow, Chester C. *The Transportation Corps: Responsibilities, Organization, and Operations*. Washington, DC: Office, Chief of Military History, 1951.

Williams, Mary H., compiler. *U.S. Army in World War II*, Special Studies *Chronology, 1941 - 45*. Washington: Office of the Chief of Military History, 1960.

Y Topete, Rear Adm. Pascual Cervera. *The Spanish American War: A Collection of Documents Relative to the Squadron Operations in the West Indies*. Department of Navy, Office of Naval Intelligence: War Notes No. VII. Washington, Government Printing Office, 1899..

GOVERNMENT MONOGRAPHS

Drake, Charles C. *Report of Operations of the Quartermaster Corps in the Philippine Campaign, 1941-42*. In two parts. This report is located within the National Archives, Records of the Adjutant General, Report of Operations, Quartermaster Corps, WW II, as well as within the Office of Chief of Military History, Historical Manuscript File, Call No. 8-5.10.

Dunham, H. H. *Transportation and the Greenland Basis*. Historical Unit of the Office of the Chief of Transportation, Army Service Forces, February 1945.

Dunham, H. H. *Transportation of the U.S. Forces in the Occupation of Iceland, 1941-1944*. Historical Unit of the Office of the Chief of Transportation, Army Service Forces, April, 1945.

Kaufman, Lt. J. L. Comments contained within Kaufman's draft portfolio for an unpublished monograph on the Naval Armed Guard of WW I. Naval Records Collection of Office of Naval Records and Library, File "ZSA", 11W4-Box 984.

Larson, Harold. *Role of the Transportation Corps in Overseas Supply*. Office of the Chief of Transportation, Army Service Forces, May, 1946.

Larson, Harold. *The Army's Cargo Fleet in World War II*. Office of the Chief of Transportation, Army Service Forces, May, 1945.

Larson, Harold. *Troop Transports in World War II*. Office of the Chief of Transportation, Army Service Forces, March, 1945.

Larson, Harold. *Water Transportation for the United States Army, 1939-1942*. Washington, DC: Office, Chief of Transportation, Army Service Forces, August 1944.

Masterson, Dr. James R. *U.S. Army Transportation in the Southwest Pacific Area, 1941-1947*. Prepared by the Transportation Unit, Historical Division Special Staff, U.S. Army, October 1949. Historical Manuscript File Call No. 2-3.7 AZ C1.

Operations of the Quartermaster Corps, U.S. Army During the World War. A series of monographs put together by the Quartermaster Corps School at Schuylkill Arsenal, Philadelphia. Held within the archives of the Military History Institute, Carlisle Barracks.

Some Establishments of the Services of Supply, American Expeditionary Forces. Prepared under the direction of James G. Harbord, Commanding General, Services of Supply. Held at Military History Institute.

Wardlow, Chester C. *Supervision of Transportation By the Supply Division of the General Staff, War Department 1940-42*. Washington: Office of the Chief of Transportation, Army Service Forces, June 1944.

Wardlow, Chester C. *The Administration of Transportation in the United States Army, April 1917 - March 1942*. Washington, DC: Office of the Chief of Transportation, Army Service Forces, July 1944.

Wardlow, Chester C. *The Transportation Advisory Group, Office of Quartermaster General, 1941-1942*. Historical unit, Office of the Chief of Transportation, Army Service Forces, 1946.

Wardlow, Chester C. *Organization and Activities of the Traffic Control Branch, Office of Quartermaster General 1941-1942*. Historical unit, Office of the Chief of Transportation, Army Service Forces, 1946.

Webb, William Joe. *The Administration of United States Ocean Cargo Shipping During World War I*. Unpublished paper prepared in 1977.

GOVERNMENT MICROFILM FILES

Edmonds, Walter D. Edmonds Collection. Microfilm call numbers 168.7022-1, 168.7022-6, 168.7022-7, 168.7022-33. Held at Archives Branch, Headquarters, AFHRA/ISR, Maxwell Air Force Base.

Record Group 92, Microfilm F-119. Records of Army Vessels, Miscellaneous.

Record Group 92. Microfilm records of the Quartermaster General, National Archives Film Series 1794, 1808, 1829, 1870, 1874, 1882, 1886. These cover some of the records of the Army Transport Service for the years 1898 through 1910 with some information leading through to 1916.

Record Group 395, M 917, Roll No. 11, Z1-46, American Expeditionary Forces, Siberia. Office of Chief Quartermaster, Vladivostok, January 30, 1919.

GOVERNMENT FILES

Adjutant General's Office. Files and correspondence dated January 1946 regarding claims of Raleigh G. Godfrey, R. A. Horn, and C. O. Young under the Missing Persons Act.

Annual Reports of the Depots at Savannah, Tampa, and Charleston for the fiscal year ended June 30, 1899, submitted to the Quartermaster General by Major J. B. Bellinger, Depot Quartermaster, Savannah, GA. Military History Institute, Carlisle Barracks, Call No. UC323.3 1899 A5.

Annual Reports of the U.S. Army Chief of Transportation Service to the Secretary of War for the Fiscal Year 1919 as contained within *Annual Reports, War Department, Fiscal year Ended June 30, 1919.*

Applications made to the government under the provisions of Public Law 95-202 on behalf of:

> *Civil Service Seamen Who Served as Crewmembers on Army Transports During the Period December 7, 1941 to August 15, 1945.* Application was approved by the Acting Assistant Secretary of the Air Force on 19 January 1988.

> *Quartermaster Corps* [tug USAT Henry] *Keswick Crew on Corregidor, WW II.* The application was approved by the Acting Assistant Secretary of the Air Force on 7 February 1984.

> *U.S. Civilian Volunteers Who Actively Participated in the Defense of Bataan.* Application was approved by the Acting Assistant Secretary of the Air Force on 7 February 1984.

> PL 95-202 is administered by the Civilian/Military Defense Review Board under the Department of the Air Force. The service of those civilians whose group application is approved under PL 95-202 is thence *"considered active military service in the Armed Forces of the United States for purposes of all laws administered by the Veterans' Administration."*

Army Regulation AR 55-305, October 10, 1942, paragraph 5

Army Regulation AR 55-455, November 18, 1942, Paragraph 10.

Changes and Laws Affecting Army Regulations and Articles of War to June 25, 1863, (as affecting troops on transports) Article XXXVII

General Order 122 of the War Department, dated August 18, 1898. (This order created the Army Transport Service.)

General Order 276, August 8, 1863, as reproduced within Appendix H, Gibson and Gibson, *Assault and Logistics.*

Hearing Record on HR-5348, 67th Congress, 1st Session, May 1921. Hearing before the Committee on the Merchant Marine and Fisheries.

Humphrey, Lt. Col. Charles F. *Report of The Expedition to Santiago de Cuba Under the Command of Major General William R. Shafter, USV.* Washington, DC: War Department, October 20, 1898. Report is held at Military History Institute, Carlisle Barracks, Call No. UC323.3 1898 A3.

Manning Report, 30 June 1944, signed by Nathan Pool. U.S Coast Guard, Office of the Historian.

Marine Extended Protest, American Consular Service, initially filed at Melbourne, March 25, 1942. This document is now incorporated within U.S. Maritime Commission File No. 901-3512-A, *Portmar.*

Mason, Lt. Col. C. H. *Catalogue of Documents Pertaining to the Subject of Transportation AEF.* Prepared under the direction of Col. W. D. Smith, Chief, Historical Section Army War College. Part III of Volume 10 of Records of the World War, 1934.

Merchant Ship Movement Report Cards. Modern Military Records Center, Archive II, National Archives, College Park, MD

Miller, O. D. *History of the Army Transport Service, AEF.* (Miller was the Executive Officer with the ATS, AEF. The report was prepared at the request of the Chief of Staff, American Expeditionary Forces.)

Naval Armed Guard files: Letter from Chief of Naval Operations to shipping company executives, April 10, 1917. Center for Naval History, Washington, DC.

Provost Marshal's Listing of Civilian Internees: CFN-127, for the period: 7 Dec 1941 to 14 August 1945. Records of the Adj. General's Office, Modern Military Records, National Archives, Washington, DC.

Record Group 92. *Preliminary Inventory of the Textual Records of the Office of the Quartermaster General,* File Nos. NM-81 and NM-85. National Archives.

Record Group 165, Entry 310. War College and War Plans Division: Records of Historical Section, 1900-1941, Box 145, Folder *History of the American Expedition to Siberia.*

Record Group 336, Files of the U.S. Army, Chief of Transportation regarding the Southwest Pacific Area Command, specifically Philippine Shipping, and Letter, Mac Arthur to Marshall, dated October 28, 1941.

Record Group 336, Files of the U.S. Army, Chief of Transportation, which contains records of the Water Transport Branch of the Quartermaster General's Office.

Record Group 336, General Vessel Files of the U.S. Army Quartermaster Corps and Transportation Corps.

Record Group 338, General Orders 71, HQ., USAFIA, Office of Commanding General, Chief of Staff, WESPAC. National Archives, Modern Military Records.

Record Group 407, Philippine Archive Collection, Boxes 12, 25, 109, 1565, 1566, 1568, 1570. Modern Military Records, National Archives.

Records of the U.S. Maritime Commission, File 901-3512-A.

Report of the U.S. Army Transport Service Office, Philippines, the Officer in Charge, Water Transportation as addressed to Chief Quartermaster, Division of the Philippines, dated June 30, 1902. Held at Military History Institute: Records, Office of the QM General - AN4.

Reports of Quartermaster's Depot at Tampa and Port Tampa as well as the Ocean Transportation Service at Port Tampa, May 18 to August 31, 1898. Submitted by Lt. Col. J. B. Bellinger, Depot Quartermaster. Report is undated. On file at Military History Institute, Call No. UC323.3 1898 A4.

Slavens, Maj. Thomas H. *Report of the Embarkation of the Expedition for Cuban Intervention from Newport News, VA, Between the Dates of September 29, 1906, and October 19, 1906.* Report prepared under the orders of J. Franklin Bell is now held at the Military History Institute, Carlisle Barracks, Call No. UC323.3 1906 A3.

State Department files, 212.11/293a/288a/304/306d/446 containing: Letter, Secretary of State to the Secretary of War, Washington, April 25, 1912; Telegram, Secretary of State to the American Ambassador, April 26, 1912; as well as other related letters and communications regarding Mexico.

Summary of Statements of Survivors. Files of the Chief of Naval Operations. Naval Historical Center, Washington.

War Shipping Administration Insurance Claims Files for U.S. Army Transport personnel losses as paid by WSA for the account of the War Department. Records are now held by the Division of Insurance, Maritime Administration, Washington, DC.

Ward, Frederick A. "Report of Army Transport Service Activities in the Philippine Islands from 8 December 1941 to 6 May 1942." Ward's report was annexed to the overall report of Brig. Gen. Charles C. Drake which is located within the National Archives, Records of the Adjutant General, Report of Operations, Quartermaster Corps, WW II: Office of Chief of Military History, Historical Manuscript File, Call No. 8-5.10.

WSA files and correspondence, including USCG report of 15 Feb 1953 to WSA Division of Insurance from P. G. Prins, Commander, USCG. Now held by the Maritime Administration's Records Section.

Zimmerman, John O. *My Report of the History of the War.* Record Group 407, Philippine Archive Collection, Box 12. Zimmerman was Asst. Operations Officer, Army Transport Service, Corregidor.

BOOKS

Ackerman, Carl W. *Trailing the Bolsheviki, Twelve Thousand Miles With the Allies in Siberia.* New York: Charles Scribner's Sons, 1919.

Astor, Gerald. *Crisis in the Pacific: The Battles for the Philippine Islands by the Men Who Fought Them.* New York: Donald I. Fine Books, 1996.

Bain, David Howard. *Sitting in Darkness: Americans in the Philippines.* Boston: Houghton, Mifflin Company, 1984.

Baker, Chauncey B., Major. *Transportation of Troops and Materiel.* Kansas City, MO: Franklin Hudson Publishing co., 1905.

Baptiste, Fitzroy Andre. *War, Cooperation, and Conflict. The European Possessions in the Caribbean, 1939-1945.* New York, Westport, CT: Greenwood Press, 1988.

Bartlett, Colonel Merrill L., Editor. *Assault From the Sea.* Annapolis, Naval Institute Press, 1985.

Blue Book of American Shipping for the years 1910, 1911, 1912, 1913. Annual Marine Naval Directory of the United States. The Penton Publishing Co.

Bradford, James C. Editor. *Crucible of Empire, The Spanish-American War and Its Aftermath.* Annapolis, MD: Naval Institute Press, 1993.

Brands, H. W. *Bound to Empire: The United States and the Philippines.* New York: Oxford University Press, 1992.

Browning, Robert M., Jr. *U.S. Merchant Vessel War Casualties of World War II.* Annapolis, MD: Naval Institute Press, 1996.

Churchill, Winston S. *Their Finest Hour.* Boston: Houghton Mifflin Company, 1949.

Cooley, Henry B. *Chartering and Charter Parties.* Cambridge, MD: Cornell Maritime Press, Inc., 1974.

Cosmas, Graham A. An *Army for Empire: The United States Army in the Spanish American War.* Columbia, MO: University of Missouri Press, 1971.

Craven, Wesley Frank and James Lea Cate, editors. *The Army Air Force in World War II.* Volumes I and VII. Chicago: University of Chicago Press, 1950 and 1958.

Crowell, Benedict and Capt. Robert F. Wilson. *How America Went to War, The Road to France.* New Haven, CT: Yale University Press, 1921.

Davis, Richard Harding. *The Cuban and Porto Rican Campaigns.* New York: Charles Scribner Sons, 1898.

Dawes, Charles G. *A Journal of the Great War.* Volume II. Boston and New York: Houghton Mifflin Company, 1917.

Daws, Gavin. *Prisoners of the Japanese.* New York: William Morrow and Co., Inc. 1994.

de Kerchove, Rene. *International Maritime Dictionary.* Second edition. New York: Van Nostrand Reinhold Company, 1973.

de Olivares, Jose, editor. *Our Islands and Their People.* Volumes I and II. New York, Chicago: N. D. Thompson Publishing Co., 1899.

Dear, I. C. B. and M. R. D. Foot, Editors. *The Oxford Companion to World War II.* New York and Oxford: Oxford University Press, 1995.

Dierks Jack Cameron. *A Leap to Arms: The Cuban Campaign of 1898.* Philadelphia: J. B. Lippincott Company, 1970

Eisenhower, Dwight D. *Crusade in Europe* New York: Doubleday and Company, 1948.

Eisenhower, John S. D. *Intervention! The United States and the Mexican Revolution 1913-1917.* New York: W. W. Norton and Company 1993.

Emerson, William K. *Chevrons...Catalog of U.S. Army Insignia.* Washington: Smithsonian Institution Press, 1983.

Feuer, A. B. *Combat Diary: Episodes From the History of the 22nd Regiment, 1866-1905.* New York: Praeger, 1991.

Forbes, Alexander. *Quest for a Northern Air Route.* Cambridge: Harvard University Press, 1953.

Ganoe, Colonel William Addleman. *The History of the United States Army.* New York and London: D. Appleton Century Company, 1942.

Giagonia, Regino Dodds. *The Philippine Navy, 1898-1996.* Manila: Publication of the Philippine Navy, 1997.

Gibson, Charles Dana *Merchantman? or Ship of War.* Camden, ME: Ensign Press, 1986.

Gibson, Charles Dana and E. Kay Gibson. *Dictionary of Transports and Combatant Vessels, Steam and Sail, Employed by the Union Army, 1861 - 1868.* The Army's Navy Series. Camden, ME: Ensign Press, 1996.

Gibson, Charles Dana with E. Kay Gibson. *Assault and Logistics.* The Army's Navy Series, Volume II. Camden, ME: Ensign Press, 1995.

Gibson, Charles Dana. *Boca Grande, A Series of Historical Essays.* St. Petersburg, FL: Great Outdoors Publishing Co., 1982.

Gleaves, Albert. *History of the Transport Service.* New York: George H. Doran Co., 1921.

Grover, David H. *U.S. Army Ships and Watercraft of World War II.* Annapolis, MD: Naval Institute Press, 1987.

Grunawalt, Richard J., editor. *International Law Studies, 1993, Targeting Enemy Merchant Shipping.* Newport, RI: Naval War College, 1993.

Hagood, Johnson. *The Services of Supply: A Memoir of the Great War.* Boston and New York: Houghton Mifflin Company, 1927.

Halsey, Francis W. *Literary Digest History of the World War.* Volumes IV and V. New York and London: Funk and Wagnalls Company, 1919

Halstead, Murat. *Full Official History of the War With Spain.* Philadelphia, PA: Elliott Publishing Co., 1899.

Hard, Curtis V. *Banners in the Air: The Eighth Ohio Volunteers and the Spanish-American War.* Kent, OH: Kent State University Press, 1988.

Harper's Pictorial History of the War With Spain, with text. Introduction by Maj. Gen. Nelson A. Miles. New York and London: Harper and Bros., 1899.

Hartendorp, A. V. H. *The Japanese Occupation of the Philippines,* Volumes 1 and 2. Manila: Bookmark, 1967.

Hemment, John C. *Cannon and Camera Sea and Land Battles of the Spanish-American War in Cuba, Camp Life, and the Return of the Soldiers.* New York: D. Appleton and Company, 1898.

Hinckley, Ted C. *The Americanization of Alaska, 1867-1897.* Palo Alto, CA: Pacific Books, 1972.

Holt, Daniel D., editor. *Eisenhower: The Prewar Diaries and Selected Papers 1905-1941.* Baltimore: The Johns Hopkins University Press.

Hoyt, Edwin P. *The Lonely Ships: The Life and Death of the U.S. Asiatic Fleet.* New York: David McKay Company, Inc., 1976.

Hurley, Edward N. *The Bridge to France.* Philadelphia: Lippincott, 1927.

Karnow, Stanley. *In Our Image: America's Empire in the Philippines.* New York: Random House, 1989.

Kieffer, Chester L. *Maligned General, Biography of Thomas S. Jesup.* San Rafael, CA: Presidio Press, 1979.

Langley, Lester D. *The Banana Wars: United States Intervention in the Caribbean, 1898-1934.* Lexington, KY: University Press of Kentucky in cooperation with Wadsworth Publishing Co. 1988.

Linn, Brian McAllister. *Guardians of Empire: The U.S. Army and the Pacific, 1902 - 1940.* Chapel Hill, NC and London: University of North Carolina Press, 1997.

Linn, Brian McAllister. *The U.S. Army and Counterinsurgency in the Philippine War, 1899-1902.* Chapel Hill, NC and London: University of North Carolina Press, 1989.

Lloyd's Register of Shipping, 1941 - 42. London: Lloyd's of London, 1941.

Lloyd's War Losses, The Second World War, Volume I: *British, Allied and Neutral Merchant Vessels Sunk or Destroyed by War Causes.* London: Lloyd's of London, 1989.

Lockwood, Douglas. *Australia's Pearl Harbor.* Sydney: Cassell Australia, Ltd., 1966.

Manchester, William. *American Caesar.* Boston: Little Brown and Co., 1967.

McCarthy, Dudley. *Australia in the War of 1939-1945. South-West Pacific Area, First Year, Kokoda to Wau.* Canberra: Australian War Memorial, 1962.

Miller, Darlis A. *Soldiers and Settlers, Military Supply in the Southwest, 1861-1885.* Albuquerque, NM: University of New Mexico Press, 1989.

Miller, Edward S. *War Plan Orange, the U.S. Strategy to Defeat Japan 1897 - 1945.* Annapolis: Naval Institute Press, 1991.

Miller, Stuart Creighton. *Benevolent Assimilation.* New Haven: Yale University Press, 1982.

Millis, Walter. *The Martial Spirit.* Chicago, IL: Ivan R. Dee, 1989, reprinted with permission of Houghton Mifflin.

Moore, Arthur. *A Careless Word...A Needless Sinking.* Kings Point, NY: U.S. Merchant Marine Academy, 1986.

Morison, Samuel Eliot. *History of United States Naval Operations in World War II. The Rising Sun in the Pacific.* Volume III. Boston: Atlantic Little Brown, 1968.

Morison, Samuel Eliot. *History of United States Naval Operations in World War II. The Battle of the Atlantic, 1939-1943.* Volume I. Boston: Atlantic Little Brown, 1970.

Mullins, Wayman C., editor. *1942 -- Issue in Doubt.* From a retrospective symposium presented by the Admiral Nimitz Museum. Austin, Texas: Eakin Press, 1994. Of particular relationship was the article by Adm. Thomas H. Moorer.

Musicant, Ivan. *Empire By Default.* New York: Henry Holt and Company, 1998.

Neely, F. Tennyson. *Fighting in the Philippines: Authentic Original Photographs.* Privately Published: London, Chicago, New York, 1899.

Noble, Dennis L. *The Eagle and the Dragon: The United States Military in China, 1901-1937.* Westport, CT: Greenwood Press, 1990.

Noyer, William L. *Mactan: Ship of Destiny.* Fresno, CA: Rainbow Press, undated. *Mactan* was a Philippine hospital ship which left Manila December 1942.

O'Connor, Richard. *The Spirit Soldiers: A Historical Narrative of the Boxer Rebellion.* New York: G. P. Putnam's Sons, 1973.

O'Toole, G. J. A. *The Spanish American War...An American Epic, 1898.* New York and London: W. W. Norton and Company, 1984.

Ohl, John Kennedy. *Supplying the Troops -- General Somervell and American Logistics in World War II.* DeKalb, IL: Northern Illinois University Press, 1994.

Parker, Brig. Gen. James. *The Old Army, Memories 1872 - 1918.* Philadelphia: Dorrance and Company, 1929.

Pedraja, Rene de la. *An Historical Dictionary of the U.S. Merchant Marine and Shipping Industry Since the Introduction of Steam.* Westport, CT and London: Greenwood Press, 1994.

Perez, Louis A., Jr. *Cuba Under the Platt Amendment, 1902-1934.* Pittsburgh, PA: University of Pittsburgh, Press, 1986.

Post, Charles J. *The Little War of Private Post.* Boston, Little Brown, 1960.

Record of the American Bureau of Shipping. New York: American Bureau of Shipping, for the years 1938, 1939, 1942.

Register of Graduates and Former Cadets, 1802-1985. West Point, NY: Association of Graduates, USMA, 1985.

Rickey, Don, Jr. *Forty Miles a Day on Beans and Hay: The Enlisted Soldier Fighting the Indian Wars.* Norman: University of Oklahoma Press, 1963.

Romulo, Col. Carlos P. *I Saw the Fall of the Philippines.* Garden City, NY: Doubleday, Doran and Company, Inc., 1943.

Rydell, Carl, Captain. *On Pacific Frontiers: A Story of Life at Sea and in Outlying Possessions of the United States.* Part of Pioneer Life Series. Yonkers-on-Hudson: World Book Company 1926. Rydell was Superintendent of the Philippine Nautical School.

Salter, J. A. *Allied Shipping Control: An Experiment in International Administration.* Oxford: The Clarendon Press, 1921.

Sawyer, Frederick, Commander, USN, Retd. *Sons of Gunboats.* Annapolis MD: U.S. Naval Institute, 1946.

Sexton, William T. Sexton. *Soldiers in the Sun, An American Adventure in Imperialism.* Fort Leavenworth, KS: Privately published, 1939 Reprinted Freeport, NY: Books for Libraries Press, nd.

Shanks, Maj. Gen. David C. *As They Passed Through the Port.* Washington, DC: Cary Publishing Company, 1927.

Sharpe, Henry Granville. *The Quartermaster Corps in the Year 1917 in the World War.* New York: The Century Company, 1921.

Ships of the Esso Fleet in World War II. Standard Oil Company of New Jersey, 1946.

Smythe, Donald Smythe. *Guerrilla Warrior, The Early Days of John J. Pershing* Charles Scribner's Sons, New York, 1973.

Sonnichsen, Albert. *Ten Months a Captive Among Filipinos.* New York: Charles Scribner's Sons, 1901.

Standberg, John E. and Roger J. Bender. *The Call of Duty.* San Jose, CA: R. James Bender Publishing Company, 1994.

Stickney, Joseph L. *War in the Philippines and Life and Glorious Deeds of Admiral Dewey.* Boston: The Home Library and Supply Association, nd. Stickney was Dewey's Aide.

Strachan, Hew, editor. *The Oxford Illustrated History of the First World War.* Oxford, New York: Oxford University Press, 1998.

Sturtevant, David R. *Popular Uprisings in the Philippines, 1840-1940.* Ithaca, NY: Cornell University Press, 1976.

Sweetman, Jack. *The Landings at Veracruz.* Annapolis: U.S. Naval Institute Press, 1968.

Tolley, Kemp. *Cruise of the Lanikai.* Annapolis: Naval Institute Press, 1973. Relates to the Southwest Pacific Area, 1941-42.

Underbrink, Robert L. *Destination Corregidor.* Annapolis, MD: U.S. Naval Institute, 1971.

Utley, Robert M. *Cavalier in Buckskin: George Armstrong Custer and the Western Military Frontier.* Norman: University of Oklahoma Press, 1988.

Utley, Robert M. *Frontier Regulars, United States Army and the Indians, 1866-1891.* New York: MacMillan Publishing Co., 1973

Van der Vat, Dan. *The Pacific Campaign, World War II: The Japanese Naval War, 1941-1945.* New York: Simon & Schuster, 1991.

Vanderwood, Paul J. and Frank N. Samponaro. *Border Fury.* Albuquerque: University of New Mexico Press, 1988.

Vandiver, Frank E. *Black Jack: The Life and Times of John J. Pershing.* Vols. I and II. College Station, TX: Texas A & M University Press, 1977.

Venzon, Anne Cipriano. *The Spanish American War: An Annotated Bibliography.* New York: Garland Publishing, Inc., 1990.

Webster's New Geographical Dictionary. Springfield, MA: Merriam-Webster, Inc. 1984.

Welch, R. E. *Response to Materialism.* Chapel Hill: University of North Carolina Press, 1979.

Wheeler, Major General Joseph. *The Santiago Campaign, 1898.* Boston, New York, and London: Lamson, Wolffe, and Company, 1898.

Whitman, John W. *Bataan Our Last Ditch.* New York: Hippocrene Books, 1990.

Willmott, H. P. *Empires in the Balance: Japanese and Allied Pacific Strategies to April 1942.* Annapolis, MD: Naval Institute Press, 1982.

Willmott, H. P. *The Barrier and the Javelin: Japanese and Allied Pacific Strategies, February to June 1942.* Annapolis, MD: Naval Institute Press, 1983.

Willoughby, Amea. *I Was on Corregidor.* New York: Harper and Brothers, 1943.

Willoughby, Maj. Gen. Charles A., compiler. *The Guerrilla Resistance Movement in the Philippines: 1941-1945.* New York, Washington: Vantage Press, 1972. Facsimiles of intelligence reports on the Philippines as found within Southwest Pacific Area command files.

Worcester, Dean C. *The Philippines, Past and Present.* New York: The MacMillan Company, 1921.

Zimmerman, Phyllis A. *The Neck of the Battle: George W. Goethals and the Reorganization of the U.S. Army Supply System, 1917-1918.* College Station, TX: Texas A & M University, 1992.

MANUSCRIPT

Robenson, John A., Colonel. Unpublished manuscript composed from diary entries Robenson made during his mission to forward supplies to the Philippines from Java.

LAWS

Laws of 1896, 225 29 Stat 188.

Laws of 1919, c.82, 41 Stat. 35. Has since been recodified by the Acts of June 10, 1933, and June 29, 1936. Under the 1950 reorganization Plan 2 § 305 and § 306, 15 F.R., 3178, 64 Stat 1277.

Public Law 17 of March 24, 1943, the *Clarification Act.*

United States Code 32, 59 39 Stat. 197

United States Code 38 § 109(c), (1)

United States Code, Title 10

United States Code, Title 46

PUBLISHED ARTICLES

Bartlett, Robert A. "Servicing Arctic Air Bases," *National Geographic.* Volume LXXXIX, May 1946.

Becker, George F. "Are the Philippines Worth Having?" *Scribner's Magazine.* June 1900.

Bultman, Capt. H. F. E. "The Army Mine Planter Service," *Coast Artillery Journal,* Volume LXX, June 1929.

Coast Seamen's Journal, Volume XI, No. 45, p 7, August 10, 1898.

Coffman, Edward M. "The American 15th Infantry Regiment in China 1912-1938: A Vignette in Social History." *The Journal of Military History,* Volume 58, January 1994.

Collar, Dave. "Insignia of the Army Transportation [sic] Service in World War II," *The Trading Post...* Fall, 1994.

Collar, Dave. *Military Collector and Historian...*Journal of the Company of Military Historians. Volume XLV, No. 4, 1993.

Condon-Rall, Mary Ellen. "U.S. Army Medical Preparations and the Outbreak of War: The Philippines 1941-6 May 1942." *The Journal of Military History,* Volume 56, No. 1, January 1992.

Damon, Allan L. "The Great Red Scare." *American Heritage,* XIX, February 1968..

Edwards, Col. Clarence R., Chief, Bureau of Insular Affairs. "Governing The Philippine Islands. " *National Geographic,* Volume XV, No. 6, June 1904.

Edwards, Col. Clarence R., Chief, Bureau of Insular Affairs. "The Work of the Bureau of Insular Affairs." *National Geographic,* Volume XV, No. 6, June 1904.

Emerson, William K. "Tid Bits," regarding Army Transport Service civilian crew uniforms. *The Trading Post,* October-December 1999.

Fogelson, Nancy. "Greenland: Strategic Base on a Northern Defense Line." *The Journal of Military History,* Volume 53, No. 1, January 1989.

Forbes, Alexander. "Surveying in Northern Labrador," *Geographical Review,* Volume XXII, 1932.

Forbes, Alexander. *Northern Labrador from the Air.* American Geographical Society, 1938.

Gary R. Mormino. "Tampa's Splendid Little War: A Photo Essay," *Tampa Bay History,* Volume IV, 2. Article cites George Kennan, *Campaigning in Cuba.* New York: Kennekat, 1899, pp 2-3; and Richard Harding Davis, "The Rocking Chair of the War," *Scribner's Magazine.* IV, August 1898, p 132.

Gibson, Charles Dana "Prisoners of War vs Internees: The Merchant Mariner Experience of World War ." *American Neptune,* Summer 1994

Grover, David. "America's First Coast Guard." *Sea Classics,* Volume 26, Nos. 7 and 8, July - August, 1993.

Hutchins, Hale L. "We Were There, Too," *Mast Magazine,* July 1947. *Mast* was a publication of the War Shipping Administration and its successor, the U.S. Maritime Commission.

Jenkinson, Charles. "Bringing 60,000 Americans Out of Mexico." *The World's Work,* February 1914.

Jones, Henry L. "History of Army Mine Planters." *Coast Artilllery Journal,* Volume LXXXII, September - October 1939.

Kindsvatter, Lt. Col. Peter S. "Santiago Campaign of 1898: Joint and Combined Operations." *Military Review,* Volume LXXIII, January 1993.

Lodge, Henry Cabot. "The Spanish-American War." *Harper's New Monthly Magazine,* Volume XCIX July 1899.

Lowe, Karl H. "American Polar Bears' Defense of Vladivostok." *Military History,* Volume 14 No. 4, October 1997.

Moffett, Samuel E. "Uncle Sam's Seven Navies. *Munsey's Magazine,* April 1905.

Moore, Capt. Werner W. "Harbor Boats," *The Quartermaster Review,* Volume XVIII, September-October 1938.

Morton, Louis. "Military and Naval Preparations for the Defense of the Philippines During the War Scare of 1907". *Military Affairs,* Journal of the American Military Institute, Summer, 1949.

Palmer, Frederick. "With the Peking Relief Column. *Century Magazine,* December 1900.

Parta, William A. "SAGA -- The Story of a New American and an Old Mariner," serialized within *Amerikan Uutiset,* New York Mills, MN, 1984-1986. Memoir of an Army transport master mariner.

Payen, Cecile E. "Besieged in Peking." *Century Magazine,* January 1901.

Pethick, W. N. "The Struggle on the Peking Wall, An Episode of the Siege of the Legations." *Century Magazine,* December 1900.

Potter, Henry C. "The Problem of the Philippines." *Century Magazine,* November 1900 and January 1901.

Taft, William Howard. "American Development of the Philippines." *National Geographic,* May 1903.

Taft, William Howard. "Some Recent Instances of National Altruism: The Efforts of the United States to Aid the Peoples of Cuba, Porto Rico and the Philippines." *National Geographic,* July 1907.

Taft, William Howard. "Ten Years in the Philippines." *National Geographic,* February 1907.

Tornow, Max L. "The Economic Condition of the Philippines." *National Geographic Magazine.* Volume X, No. 2, February 1899.

Webb, William Joe. "The Spanish-American War and United States Army Shipping." *The American Neptune,* Volume XL, No. 3, July 1980.

Worcester, Dean C. "Head-hunters of Luzon." *National Geographic,* Volume XXIII, No. 9, September 1912.

Worcester, Dean C. "The Malay Pirates of the Philippines." Century Magazine, September 1898.

Worcester, Dean C. "The Non-Christian People of the Philippine Islands." *National Geographic,* Volume XXIV, No. 11, November 1913.

NEWSPAPERS

The New York Times, July 29, 1898 and March 3, 1917.
The Tampa Morning Tribune, June 23, 1898.

THESIS

McClellan, Willard Cave. *A History of American Military Sea Transportation.* A doctoral thesis. Washington, DC: American University, 1953.

ATLAS

Lloyd's Maritime Atlas. Compiled and edited by Lloyd's Shipping Publications. London: Lloyd's of London Press, Ltd.

Philip, George, Editor. *New Mercantile Marine Atlas,* 7th edition. New York: C. S. Hammond and Company, 1918.

Atlas de Filipinas - Colección de 30 Mapas. Produced under the direction of P. Jose Algue, S. J., Director del Observatorio de Manila, 1899, reprinted as the *Atlas of the Philippine Islands,* Special Publication No. 3: Washington: Treasury Department, U.S. Coast and Geodetic Survey, 1900.

GOVERNMENT CHARTS

Philippine Islands, Central Part.. U.S. Coast and Geodetic Service, Chart 4706. Date of issue August 29, 1940.

Philippine Islands, South Eastern Part. U.S. Coast and Geodetic Service, Chart 4708. Date of issue August 27, 1940.

Philippine Islands Between St. Bernardino Straits and Mindoro Straits with Adjacent Islands, from Spanish Surveys of 1873. Washington: Department of the Navy, Bureau of Equipment.

MISCELLANEOUS

Braynard, Frank. Records of Braynard consisting of copies of correspondence between shipping company members of the American Steamship Owners Assn., 1925-1933, together with newspaper clippings relative to the association's attempts to have the Army Transport Service abolished and War Department shipping business given to the commercial sector.

Correspondence between Charles Dana Gibson and Bertram G. Snow of Rockland, ME, during 2000 regarding vessels utilized in the Crystal Project.

Correspondence between Charles Dana Gibson and Captain John M. Le Cato of Charleston, SC, during 1987 regarding the Crystal project.

Interviews by authors with John T. Crowell (formerly Major, U.S. Army Air Corps) at Crowell's home on Kimball's Island, Maine, during August of 1985.

GUIDE TO SPECIFIC RECORDS PERTAINING TO THE
ARMY TRANSPORT SERVICE

For those wishing to conduct further research dealing with U.S. Army shipping, we direct your attention to the following sources:

Record Group 92, National Archives: For the period 1898-1935, see the National Archives Guide Pamphlet NM-81, *Preliminary Inventory of the Textual Records of the Office of the Quartermaster General - Record Group 92.*

- Starting with page 167, NM-81 lists micro-films (rolls 1468 - 1474) which pertain to activity for the period 1898 - 1904.

- Starting with page 198, NM-81 lists microfilms (rolls 1781 - 1891) which go through to the year 1935.

- RG-92 contains crew rosters as well as passenger lists for Army transports for many of these years. It also contains a few generalized files on transports; but these are spotty, covering only a small number of ships. NM-81 names those ships on which such files exist.

Caution: One should not count on finding continuity for the Army's shipping within RG-92 as there are large chronological and qualitative gaps. For instance, it lists a collection of ship logs for transports; however, these cover only the 3-year period 1899-1901. For the subsequent years 1902-1916 there are log book abstracts, but these contain only limited information resulting in just broad brush views of particular voyages.

Record Group 407, National Archives: Contains files on Filipino merchant shipping specific to the ships and small craft which served the Army during the defense of the Philippines, 1941-1942. These include crew lists for a number of the vessels. An examination of the bracketed sources following the comment for each vessel within our List 4 (starting on our p 320) brings to light those vessels for which there are crew lists as therein we have indicated the archival box number containing such pertinent information.

Military History Institute at Carlisle Barracks, PA, is a large archival depository holding much information on the Army's sealifts -- especially for the early period.

VESSEL INDEX

Prefixes used within this Vessel Index

OSP	Offshore Patrol Vessel, Philippine Army
USAT	United States Army Transport *
USCGC	United States Coast Guard Cutter
USCGS	United States Coast and Geodetic Survey
USCT	United States Chartered Transport
USHB	United States Army Harbor Boat *
USMP	United States Army Mine Planter **
USQMD	United States Quartermaster Department
USS	United States Ship (United States Navy combatant ship)
USNS	United States Naval Ship (United States Navy supply ship)

* The acronyms "USAT" or "USHB" attached to a vessel's name indicates a vessel either owned by the Army or under bareboat charter or sub-bareboat charter to the Army. Such vessels are operated with crews (either military or civilian) directly employed by the Army. Within the chronological scope of this book, in almost every case, such crews were civilian.

** Prior to 1918, the crews of those Army vessels referred to as "USMPs" were civilian. Starting in 1918, those crews were gradually militarized.

A. A. Raven, USAT: 155, 158, 363
Abeekerk: 275
Aboitoz: 320
Abra (Q-112), OSP: 318, 408, 410, 411
Ace: 208
Ace: see M. G. Zalinski, USAT
Active: 320
Adams: 235, 320
Admiral Halstead: 241, 244, 261, 262
Admiral Y. S. Williams: 248
Adonis: 35, 320
Adonis: see Williams, USAT
Adria: 37
Aeolus : 107
Agrigao: 320
Agusan (Q-113), OSP: 318, 408
Agustina: 248, 299, 312, 320
Aklak, USCGC: 388
Alamo: 20, 37
Albert: 78
Albukirk: 274
Alden, USS: 276
Alencon: 288
Alert: 321
Alfred W. Booth: 41
Alicante: 42, 93
Allegheny: 20, 37
Allen, USS: 139
Almance: 363
Almond Branch: 88
Aloha: 341
Alpha: 435
Alpha: see Kentucky, USHB
Amanda: 436
Amanda: see Saint Louis, USHB

Amarok, USCGC: 379, 388
Amelia: 321
America: 205
America: see Edmund B. Alexander, USAT
American Legion, USAT: 179, 198, 204
American Star, USAT: 204
American: 433
American: see ATS Tug No. 5, USAT
Amerika: 205
Amerika: see Edmund B. Alexander, USAT
Ammen, USS: 139
Amphion, USAT: 155
Anakan: 226, 341
Anan Maru: 341
Anhui: 251-253, 295, 298-300, 335, 337
Anne E. Stevens: 21, 37, 39
Antilles, USAT: 139, 140, 148, 155
Antonio: 321
Aphrodite, USS: 139
APO: 341
Arab: 88
Aransas: 20, 37
Arayat, OSP: 318, 410
Arcadia: 37
Arethusa, USS: 139
Argl: 88
Arionte (or Apiontes): 316
Arizona: 35, 51
Arizona: see Hancock, USAT
Arkadia: see Arcadia
Arluk, USCGC: 388
Arlyn: 385, 389
Arrow: 80
Arthur Murray, USAT: 204
Ashville, USS: 242

GENERAL SUBJECT INDEX